THE SINGLE
FAMILY COURT:
A PRACTITIONER'S
HANDBOOK

THE SINGLE FAMILY COURT: A PRACTITIONER'S HANDBOOK

Gillian Geddes and

Richard Budworth

WS
&H

Wildy, Simmonds & Hill Publishing

© Original contributions, Gillian Geddes and Richard Budworth, 2016

Contains public sector information licensed under the Open Government Licence v3.0

Guidance Note: Disclosure in Financial Order Applications and *Guidance Note: Instructing Experts in Applications for a Financial Order* are reproduced by kind permission of Resolution. These and other guides are available free of charge to Resolution members
www.resolution.org.uk

ISBN: 9780854901838

British Library Cataloguing in Publication Data

A catalogue record for this book is available from the British Library

The right of Gillian Geddes and Richard Budworth to be identified as the authors of this Work has been asserted by them in accordance with the Copyright, Designs and Patents Act 1988.

First published in 2016 by

Wildy, Simmonds & Hill Publishing
58 Carey Street
London WC2A 2JF
England
www.wildy.com

Typeset by Heather Jones, North Petherton, Somerset.
Printed in Great Britain by CPI Antony Rowe, Chippenham, Wiltshire.

For all family law practitioners toiling at the coal face,
and for all visitors to the single Family Court

Foreword

The arrival of the new Family Court has presented us all with many challenges. Not least, for the busy practitioner at the coal face to whom this invaluable book is primarily aimed, the challenge of identifying what is relevant to the case in hand and picking a way through what our authors sternly but fairly call the data avalanche represented by the plethora of Practice Directions, Practice Guidance, Protocols, Circulars, etc, which they have made it their task to distil.

A clearly laid out table of contents aids quick navigation, indicating at a glance what can be found and where. Two introductory chapters summarise practice in children cases (Chapter 1) and financial remedy cases (Chapter 2). The latter, conveniently and appropriately, takes the traditional approach, tracing the typical case through its successive stages. The former, equally conveniently and appropriately, adopts the radical approach of arranging in alphabetical order the many topics which, as the authors discerningly observe, may arise at any hearing. Some of these will be familiar to most practitioners; others, more unusual or more infrequently encountered, will be less familiar and may arise unexpectedly – and there the *Handbook* will be of particular value. The remaining chapters comprise a judiciously chosen compendium of the basic working tools of the Family Court, containing everything essential for daily practice when away from the office or chambers.

As the authors mournfully comment, the tide keeps coming. Inevitably, given the almost ceaseless production of new materials for which, if I am to take at last some of the credit I must also take the blame, some parts of the *Handbook* will require early revision to accommodate yet further changes. That is as it has to be, but it surely points the way to what I hope will be an updated edition in due course of a *Handbook* which deserves and will, I trust, have every success, not just with practitioners but also with the many litigants in person and other users who have to find their way around the Family Court.

The authors have done us proud. They deserve our thanks.

James Munby
President of the Family Division
28 January 2016

Preface

With the advent of the single Family Court, lawyers have had to come to terms with a plethora of Practice Directions, Guidance, circulars and, even, new courts. The speed of it all has been a shock. As family practitioners, we felt that a distillation of this data avalanche would surely assist all those attending the new family courts, and possibly also those thrown into the mix with no or little legal training. Still though, the tide keeps coming as the family practitioner stands, Canute-like, on the flooded beach. It is a real challenge, knowing what to include and what to leave out. What exactly does the hard-pressed family lawyer need to get his/her hands on at the last minute, or when caught by the unexpected at court? We also wanted to provide something portable; there is always far too much to carry to court. This has meant tough decisions about what to leave behind. For example, we have left out the Children Act 1989 (or most of it) and other major legislation in the strong – and hopefully not misguided – belief that most family practitioners will look up the law before attending court. We have included limited information on pensions, but not included information on surrogacy, or the 1980 or 1996 Hague Conventions or BIIR; these areas are too specialist for our handbook and would weigh it down.

Please let us know if there is, in your view, something that you believe should be included in future editions. Like the President, we seek perfection.

Note: References in the text are to the Family Procedure Rules 2010 (FPR 2010) (SI 2010/2955) and the Civil Procedure Rules 1998 (CPR 1998) (SI 1998/3132).

Acknowledgements

Most importantly, we would like to thank Andrew Riddoch, our publisher at Wildy & Sons Ltd, for his enduring patience, encouragement, and on occasions his effective mediation, all of which ensured that this original concept eventually matured into a real book. Without his support, we may have wavered in the face of the deluge.

We would also like to thank our clerks, and in particular our senior clerk, David McDonald, for their understanding and help whilst we completed this book around our respective diaries.

We are grateful also to our previous Head of Chambers, Paul Mallender, along with solicitors Sandra Villani, Sam Martin and Kate Kingham in particular for their assistance, contributions and/or bright ideas along the way, as well as Professor Penny Cooper and everyone at The Advocacy Training Council for allowing us to include some of their material from The Advocate's Gateway in this book, and generally for their hard work and excellent guidance on how we should all be dealing with issues of vulnerability in the family justice system, about which our group knowledge is sadly as yet in its infancy. We also thank Resolution for allowing us use of their excellent materials.

Lastly, our gratitude to Susan Jacklin QC, the immediate past Chairman of the FLBA, for her timely, vital and multifarious FLB Mails which have kept all of the family bar informed about matters of most importance in the family justice system, and without which we may all have felt quite adrift. Keen readers may spot one or two excerpts from these FLB Mails dotted here and there in this book, and we thank Ms Jacklin QC for her tolerant understanding of our poaching.

Contents

Chapter 1

Essential Daily Guidance for Proceedings Concerning Children

Proceedings concerning children take the form either of public law applications issued by local authorities concerned about a child/children, or private law applications issued by individual people concerned about a child/children, the court processes governing each of which are either (respectively) the Public Law Outline (PLO), or the Child Arrangements Programme (CAP), which are both set out in Chapter 3.

It is our experience that in matters concerning children, whilst the PLO/CAP court processes are followed for each case as it progresses through the court system, there are no hearings which can be guaranteed to be 'straight-forward'. Issues can be raised – sometimes unexpectedly – at any hearing. For this reason, in this chapter we decided to set out issues that can arise at any hearing in alphabetical order so that they can be looked up and located, we hope, with relative ease. We provide the most current guidance and legislation that apply to these issues as at the time of writing, but we do not aim to be completely comprehensive on each topic for the purposes of this handbook.

ALCOHOL TESTING AND THE FAMILY DRUG AND ALCOHOL COURT (FDAC)

Alcohol testing – alternative options:

(a) *Breathalyser tests*: cheap, effective, quick, of limited usefulness. Results vary depending on the rate at which the individual metabolises the alcohol, exercise and even mouthwash. Rarely relied upon in court.

(b) *Urine tests*: results up to a maximum of 72 hours. Results not entirely reliable, so of limited usefulness.

(c) *Blood tests*: more widely used. Can detect alcohol 14–28 days after consumption, so snapshot of use during period provided. Results can be abnormal where the individual has liver damage for reasons other than alcohol consumption (e.g. cirrhosis, hepatitis and so on). Most often used to provide evidence to confirm disputed results of hair strand testing. Cannot confirm abstinence.

(d)   *Hair strand tests*: the most common form of testing for alcohol and other drugs. The results can cover a period up to 12 months depending on the available length of hair, though most often requested is 6 months. Scalp hair records monthly usage, body hair records general usage over about 1 year. Note Moylan J's guidance below in relation to the evidential value of hair strand testing for alcohol usage.

(e)   *Transdermal Alcohol Continuous Tests*:[1] available in the United Kingdom since only February 2013, thus not as well established. Uses a base station in the person's home and a water-resistant ankle bracelet (e.g. SCRAM CAM bracelet) on the person, fitted by a trained specialist. The base station transmits data for analysis, tests for alcohol every 30 minutes over long periods, and provides information on specific drinking events and levels. Optional combination with house arrest monitoring. Can be publicly funded by the Legal Aid Agency (at the time of writing).

London Borough of Richmond v B, W, B and CB[2] – considerable caution should be exercised when hair tests for alcohol are being interpreted and relied upon, particularly in isolation. Subject to the proviso that at very high levels (multiples of the agreed cut-off levels) hair tests might form a significant part of the evidential picture, hair tests should not be used to reach evidential conclusions by themselves in isolation from other evidence, but only as part of the evidential picture. In the absence of any peer agreed cut-off level for the line between abstinence and social drinking, the court would need specific justification before accepting any such evidence.

The FDAC was originally set up as a pilot scheme at the Inner London Family Proceedings Court in 2008. Following its success, FDAC models have been set up at other courts around the United Kingdom. On 19 February 2015, an announcement was made that funding is to be provided to nurture the development of further FDACs across the country. To qualify for the FDAC scheme, parents must have access to an FDAC, have a significant drug and/or alcohol problem and be at a stage at which they are willing to tackle their addiction. They will be expected to engage in a highly intensive programme of work and a parenting assessment. FDAC is recognised as being exempt from the 26-week time limit, provided there is evidence to show motivation to change, ability to maintain that change and that this can be achieved within the child's/children's timescales (*Re S (A Child)*[3]).

---

[1]   TACT.

[2]   *London Borough of Richmond v B, W, B and CB* [2010] EWHC 2903 (Fam), [2011] 1 FLR 1345, Moylan J.

[3]   *Re S (A Child)* [2014] EWCC B44 (Fam).

APPEALS

FPR 2010, Part 30, PD30A (see Chapter 7 for both) and Practice Direction on Citation of Authorities (2012).

Family Court (Composition and Distribution of Business) Rules 2014,[4] in force on 22 April 2014. Part 2 – provision for family court when hearing appeals.

CPR 1998, Part 52/PD52.

Note *Piglowska v Piglowski*:[5]

> ... there is the principal of proportionality between the amount at stake and the legal resources of the parties and the community which it is appropriate to spend on resolving the dispute ... the legal system provides for the possibility of three successive appeals from the decision at first instance. The first is as of right and the second and third are subject to screening processes which themselves may involve more than one stage. ...To allow successive appeals in the hope of producing an answer which accords with perfect justice is to kill the parties with kindness ... even if a case does raise an important point of practice or principle, the Court of Appeal should consider carefully whether it is fair to have it decided at the expense of parties with very limited resources or whether it should wait for a more suitable vehicle. (at 1373–1374 per Lord Hoffmann)

Note also PD52C – Respondent's required actions when served with the appellant's notice.

Seeking permission to appeal

CPR 1998, rule 52.3(2), PD52A and *P v P*[6] – it is a matter of good practice to apply first to the judge at first instance for permission to appeal.

CHILDREN AND FAMILY COURT ADVISORY AND SUPPORT SERVICE (CAFCASS)

'The voice of children in the family courts', CAFCASS was set up on 1 April 2001. It is a non-departmental public body accountable to the Minister of State at the Ministry of Justice.[7] Its employees are professionally qualified social work staff, called Family Court Advisers (FCAs), independent of the courts, social services, education and health authorities and all similar agencies.

---

4   SI 2014/840.
5   *Piglowska v Piglowski* [1999] UKHL 27, [1999] 1 WLR 1360.
6   *P v P* [2015] EWCA Civ 447.
7   MoJ.

CAFCASS is asked by the court to become involved in cases once an application has been made to the court, for example:

(a)   When children are subject to an application for care, supervision or adoption proceedings by social services (public law proceedings). In such proceedings, the FCA is called a Children's Guardian, and represents the child so that his/her voice is heard in the proceedings.

(b)   When parents who are separating or divorcing cannot agree on arrangements for their children (private law proceedings). In such proceedings, an FCA will be asked to provide a report on the disputed issue to the court.

(c)   In certain private law proceedings, when the court decides that the child/ children should become a party to the proceedings (FPR 2010, rule 16.4). This may include when a child has been abducted and taken out of the country.

See further www.cafcass.gov.uk.

Note Children Act 1989, section 16A, 'Risk assessments' – in carrying out any function in connection with family proceedings to which this section applies, there is a mandatory duty on 'officers of the Service or Welsh family proceedings officers' to provide a risk assessment if they are given cause to suspect that the child concerned is at risk of harm.

CASE MANAGEMENT IN FAMILY CASES

The new regime for the single Family Court

Re TG (A Child)[8] – strong guidance of Sir James Munby, President of the Family Division, to all court users as to the need for active and robust judicial case management. Obligatory guidance to be read in full to understand the modern flavour and accepted process of court proceedings.

Note also *Re C (Children):*[9]

> ... these are not ordinary civil proceedings, they are family proceedings, where it is fundamental that the judge has an essentially inquisitorial role, his duty being to further the welfare of the children which is, by statute, his paramount consideration ... for this reason a judge exercising the family jurisdiction has a much broader discretion than he would in the civil jurisdiction to determine the way in which an application ... should be pursued. In an appropriate case he can summarily dismiss the application as being, if not groundless, lacking enough merit to justify pursuing the matter. He may determine that the matter is one to be dealt with on the basis of written evidence and oral submissions without the need for oral evidence. He may ... decide to hear the evidence

[8]   *Re TG (A Child)* [2013] EWCA Civ 5.
[9]   *Re C (Children)* [2012] EWCA Civ 1489.

of the applicant and then take stock of where the matter stands at the end of the evidence. (at [14]–[15])

And *Re B (A Child)*:[10]

> ... a judge making case management decisions has a very wide discretion and anyone seeking to appeal against such a decision has an uphill task ... when it comes to making findings of fact, the court's focus should be firmly on an analysis of what evidence is necessary to enable proper findings to be made. Of course, the urgency of the court's decision can sometimes make it imperative that there be limitations on the evidence that is called, however relevant it would be. Similarly, the judge may find himself unable to permit a witness's evidence to be adduced because it has been produced too late in the day or without regard to earlier case management directions or he may determine that it is disproportionate to the issues to permit reliance on it ... Robust case management ... very much has its place in family proceedings but it also has its limits. (Black LJ at [35], [40] and [48])

Note also *London Borough of Bexley v V, W and D*[11] – although social work professionals and lawyers were under enormous strain in the current economic climate, that did not relieve them of the obligation to comply timeously with court orders.

See also *Re T (Children)*[12] – extension of the 26-week time limit; essential reading for public law practitioners. It sets out in detail the procedure if the timetable for the child/children is to be extended beyond 26 weeks. It is also a reminder to all parties (and therefore their representatives) of their duties under FPR 2010, rule 12.24 to:

(a)   monitor compliance with the court's directions; and
(b)   tell the court or court officers about:
    (i)   any failure to comply with a direction of the court; and
    (ii)   any other delay in the proceedings.

Re TM and TJ (Children: Care Orders)[13] – a collaborative approach is required.

Re K and H (Children)[14] – options to consider when an unfunded party must cross-examine:

(a)   the party to be challenged must only give evidence if the unfunded party questions him/her through a legal representative;
(b)   the party to be challenged should be questioned by the judge himself/herself;
(c)   the party to be challenged should be questioned by a justices' clerk;
(d)   a guardian be appointed to conduct proceedings on behalf of the child/children.

---

10   *Re B (A Child)* [2012] EWCA Civ 1742.
11   *London Borough of Bexley v V, W and D* [2014] EWHC 2187 (Fam).
12   *Re T (Children)* [2015] EWCA Civ 606.
13   *Re TM and TJ (Children: Care Orders)* [2015] EWFC B83.
14   *Re K and H (Children)* [2015] EWCA Civ 543.

Special guardianship orders

For procedural guidance about making these orders, see *Re H (A Child) (Analysis of Realistic Options and SGOs)*[15] at [26] to avoid procedural irregularity for lack of notice. Either the proposed special guardian or the local authority should make an application for an order. Then Children Act 1989, section 10(9) should be considered. The court's power to make such an order of its own motion under section 14A(6)(b) should not be the default position.

Court bundles

Practitioners must adhere to PD27A (see Chapter 7), and note also *Re L (Procedure: Bundles: Translation)*,[16] in which the President reduced a total of 591 pages suggested for translation down to a mere 51 pages, plus a 30-page summary from the father's solicitor of the other documents, criticising the failure of professionals to comply with the PD, and warning of naming and shaming of, and other sanctions against, defaulters. Each document in the bundle must be relevant and actually used (read or referred to). All documents must be 'as short and succinct as possible'. In determining what was necessary to be translated in this particular case, it was essential to focus on the forensic context. It was necessary for the father to be able to read in his own language those documents, or parts of documents, which would enable him to understand the central essence of the local authority's case or which relate or refer specifically to him. The remaining documents needed only to be summarised for him in his own language. Essential reading for compiling bundles.

CHANGE OF NAME

Where there is a dispute as to changing a child's surname, a decision of the court must be sought; no change can be made unilaterally.[17] Where there is a child arrangement order specifying with whom the child/children should live, a freestanding application under Children Act 1989, section 13 should be made. Where there is no child arrangement order specifying with whom the child/children should live, either a specific issue order or a prohibited steps order, as appropriate (Children Act 1989, section 8) should be applied for. Note a specific issue order cannot be made for a child in care (Children Act 1989, section 9(1)). The child's/children's welfare will be the court's paramount consideration, and each case decided on its own facts and relevant factors weighed in the balance.[18]

---

[15] *Re H (A Child) (Analysis of Realistic Options and SGOs)* [2015] EWCA Civ 406.

[16] *Re L (Procedure: Bundles: Translation)* [2015] EWFC 15.

[17] *Dawson v Wearmouth* [1997] 2 FLR 629, CA, but note [1999] 1 FLR 1167, HL; *Re C (Change of Surname)* [1998] 2 FLR 656, CA; *Re W, Re A, Re B (Change of Name)* [1999] 2 FLR 930; *Re T (Change of Surname)* [1998] 2 FLR 620.

[18] *Re W, Re A, Re B (Change of Name)* [1999] 2 FLR 930 at 933F.

CHILDREN GIVING EVIDENCE

See *Re W*,[19] and also for guidance and factors to be considered in care proceedings.

See also *Re R (Children)*[20] – a 14-year-old girl was given permission to give oral evidence where she wished to deny allegations of sexual abuse made against her father. The *Re W* guidance is applicable also in private law family proceedings.[21]

See also The Advocacy Training Council Guidelines in *The Advocate's Gateway on Case Management in Young and Other Vulnerable Witness Cases* (Toolkit 1(a)), *Vulnerable Witnesses and Parties in the Family Courts* (Toolkit 13) and other relevant Toolkits (www.theadvocatesgateway.org), and Guidelines for Judges Meeting Children who are subject to Family Proceedings (by the Family Justice Council), April 2010 (see Chapter 4).

Note, in 2010 in criminal proceedings, a conviction for rape was upheld based on the evidence of a child aged 3 at interview (aged 4 at trial) who was describing events which had occurred when she was aged 2.[22] Ruth Marchant, a forensic interviewer and children's intermediary, notes that the court system has developed to rely heavily on spoken testimony, but that very young children are often more able to communicate if they show as well as tell (*Magistrates Association Newsletter*, April–May 2015).

The final *Report of the Vulnerable Witnesses & Children Working Group* (2015) recommended a radical approach to the way in which the wishes and feelings of the child/children should be considered in the decision making process. The Vulnerable Witnesses & Children Working Group (WG) expressed the view that there should be provision for children's evidence to be heard as directly as possible without interpretation by court appointed officers or others: the court should have a more direct and accurate understanding of the child's wishes and feelings. Consideration should be given in each case to the child giving evidence, not necessarily directly in court, but by such means as are appropriate in the particular case. The best practice and procedure already developed in the criminal courts will be used with necessary modifications to form the basis of the new rules and Practice Directions. Similar provisions to those in Youth Justice and Criminal Evidence Act 1999, section 28 may be employed, whereby evidence will be recorded early on in proceedings and possibly, in public law cases, in advance of the issue of proceedings.

The WG pointed out that vulnerable witnesses frequently appear in children cases, particularly in public law cases, and there is a need for intermediaries and representation for litigants in person (LiPs) who would otherwise seek to cross-examine a vulnerable witness. The report stated that at the time of writing, public funding arrangements for

---

[19] *Re W* [2010] UKSC 12, [2010] 1 WLR 701.
[20] *Re R (Children)* [2015] EWCA Civ 167.
[21] *Re B (Child Evidence)* [2014] EWCA Civ 1015.
[22] *R v Barker* [2010] EWCA Crim 4.

intermediaries outside court for the purposes of meetings with professionals, particularly legal advisers, were unsatisfactory and an urgent review was required:

> Failure to provide sufficient and adequate support for vulnerable and intimidated witnesses whether they are children, young people or adults, results in a concomitant failure in their ability to give their best evidence, in turn directly undermining the likelihood of the judge or tribunal reaching a fair decision; it is justice denied. (at para 31)

The report indicated that there will be a new rule inserted after FPR 2010, rule 3, as rule 3B, and the existing rule 3 will become rule 3A. Rule 3B will provide for any witness, including a party, who is identified as vulnerable to be entitled to assistance in order to give evidence coherently, accurately and completely. There will be a duty on representatives and LiPs to identify if any party or witness is vulnerable and to seek directions of the court as soon as practicable regarding appropriate measures to be provided to enable the witness to give their best evidence. The importance of the new rule is to be emphasised by an amendment to the overriding objective in FPR 2010, rule 1.1, by addition to the matters included in 'dealing with a case justly' of, 'make provision for vulnerable parties and witnesses and children to assist them in improving the quality of their evidence and to participate fully in proceedings'. There will be a new PD3C to replace the 2010 Guidelines on judges seeing children, and a new PD3D.

At the time of writing, relevant revised rules and Practice Directions are awaited.

The courts have powers to appoint and fund intermediaries for children or young people in the interests of a fair hearing. If an intermediary is required in family proceedings, Triangle provides skilled intermediaries to enable communication with children and young people from the age of 2 to 25 and can be contacted directly. Triangle also has a strong team of intermediaries skilled at enabling communication with young people with a wide range of needs including learning disability (low IQ), autism, brain injury, attention deficit hyperactivity disorder,[23] mental health difficulties and physical disability (www.triangle.org.uk, tel 01273 305888).

(*Source*: The Advocacy Training Council was the original source of publication for the guidance about the provision of evidence of children and vulnerable witnesses (see Vulnerable Witnesses, pages 46–47).)

CIRCUMCISION

Of males

Circumcision can be lawfully carried out by parents acting jointly. Where there is a dispute, a decision of the court can be sought by applying for a specific issue order

---

[23]   ADHD.

(Children Act 1989, section 8). The court will decide the issue by applying the welfare checklist (section 1(3)).

A specific issue order cannot be made for a child in care (Children Act 1989, section 9(1)).

Options for a child in care are:

(a)   wardship instead of care order;
(b)   to seek agreement of the local authority and the Children's Guardian if the other parent opposes, and raise as an issue for the court to determine.

Examples

A Turkish Muslim father's applications that the child be brought up in the Muslim faith and the child be circumcised were refused. As the father was not a practising Muslim and the child was to live with the mother, it would be wrong to impose the requirements upon her. The father could provide the rudiments of his religion during contact.[24]

A child with a mixed cultural background should be allowed to decide for himself/herself which, if any, religion he/she wished to follow. In *Re S (Specific Issue Order: Religion: Circumcision)*,[25] the court held that a boy should be allowed to decide for himself, once he was *Gillick*-competent, whether to be circumcised for religious reasons.

Of females

In the matter of B and G (Children) (No 2)[26] – the first time female genital mutilation (FGM) was raised in care proceedings and because of the importance of this issue, the judgment was confined to FGM. Sir James Munby, President of the Family Division, adopted the World Health Organization's (WHO's) classification of FGM, which divides FGM into four major types. This case was concerned with type IV FGM, the least physically severe type of FGM, i.e. 'Other: all other harmful procedures to the female genitalia for non-medical purposes, e.g. pricking, piercing, incising, scraping and cauterizing the genital area'.

The President reiterated that 'any form of FGM constitutes "significant harm" within the meaning of sections 31 and 100' (at [68]). At [67] he cited Baroness Hale of Richmond in *Re B (Care Proceedings: Appeal)*,[27] 'that any form of FGM, including FGM WHO Type IV, amounts to "significant harm"'.

---

24   *Re J (Specific Issue Orders: Child's Religious Upbringing and Circumcision)* [2000] 1 FLR 571.
25   *Re S (Specific Issue Order: Religion: Circumcision)* [2004] EWHC 1282 (Fam), [2005] 1 FLR 236.
26   *In the matter of B and G (Children) (No 2)* [2015] EWFC 3.
27   *Re B (Care Proceedings: Appeal)* [2013] UKSC 33, [2013] 2 FLR 1075 at [185].

The President drew parallels between FGM and forced marriage as gross abuses of human rights that dehumanise people (at [57]). He recommended that there should be careful planning for the instruction of an expert to ensure the appropriate level of expertise. Ideally, referrals should be made to FGM specialist clinics. Wherever possible, whoever is conducting the examination should use a colposcope.

The President distinguished FGM from male circumcision for the purposes of Children Act 1989, section 31. Although FGM and male circumcision involve 'significant harm' pursuant to section 31(2)(a), the clear distinction between them is with respect to 'reasonable parenting' in accordance with section 31(2)(b)(i). The President stated that FGM can never be a feature of reasonable parenting, whereas society and the law treat male circumcision as an aspect of reasonable parenting.

COMMITTAL

See FPR 2010, Part 37 (see Chapter 7), PD37A; CPR 1998, Part 81, PD81.

See Practice Direction: Committal for Contempt of Court – Open Court, 26 March 2015 (the Committal PD; see Chapter 7). This applies in all courts in England and Wales, including the Court of Protection, and supersedes Practice Guidance: Committal for Contempt, 3 May 2013;[28] Practice Guidance (Committal Proceedings: Open Court) (No 2), 4 June 2013;[29] and President's Circular: Committals, 2 August 2013.[30]

See also Practice Guidance, 24 June 2015[31] which answers various questions which have arisen on the application and interpretation of the Committal PD.

Unless exceptional, these applications are heard in public. Counsel are robed. Copies of the judgment shall then be provided to the parties and the national media via the CopyDirect service. Copies shall also be supplied to BAILII at feedback@bailii.org and to the Judicial Office at judicialwebupdates@judiciary.gsi.gov.uk for publication on their websites as soon as reasonably practicable.

Note *Hammerton v Hammerton*[32] – 'Required reading for every judge hearing family proceedings where there is an application to commit one of the parties to prison for contempt', per Wall LJ. All defendants to committal proceedings must have legal assistance and are entitled to be represented and if this representation is not available,

---

[28]   Practice Guidance: Committal for Contempt, 3 May 2013, [2013] 1 WLR 1326.
[29]   Practice Guidance (Committal Proceedings: Open Court) (No 2), 4 June 2013, [2013] 1 WLR 1753.
[30]   President's Circular: Committals, 2 August 2013, *The Family Court Practice 2014* (Family Law, 2014), at 2976.
[31]   Practice Guidance: Committal for Contempt – Open Court, 24 June 2015.
[32]   *Hammerton v Hammerton* [2007] EWCA Civ 248.

an adjournment should be granted. Contact and committal proceedings must not be heard at the same time.

Sanchez v Oboz (No 2) (Sentencing for Contempt of Court)[33] – Cobb J sentenced a father to 12 months' imprisonment for breaching court orders requiring the 3-year-old child to be returned from Poland.

COMMUNICATION OF INFORMATION: PROCEEDINGS RELATING TO CHILDREN

See FPR 2010, Chapter VII, rules 12.72–12.75.

See also Practice Guidance Transparency in Family Courts: Publication of Judgments, 16 January 2014 and Transparency in Court of Protection: Publication of Judgments, 16 January 2014 (see Chapter 4).

See also 2013 Protocol & Good Practice Model for disclosure in linked care/criminal proceedings, Protocol on communications between judges of the Family Court and Immigration and Asylum Chambers of the First-Tier Tribunal and Upper Tribunal, 19 July 2013, and Communicating with the Home Office in Family Proceedings, March 2013 (see Chapter 5).

CONTACT AND CONTACT CENTRES

National Association of Child Contact Centres[34] (www.naccc.org.uk, tel 0845 4500 280, contact@naccc.org.uk).

Supported contact

Usually run by volunteers, thus not available daily. Does not provide one-to-one supervision, but volunteers oversee general contact sessions in which various parents have contact at the same time with their children. Suitable when risk is low.

Supervised contact

Run by professionals at dedicated contact centres. One-to-one supervision, and contact reports for each session provided. A referral must be made and if contact can be offered, this must be booked in advance with a fee payable. Suitable when risk is medium to high.

---

[33] *Sanchez v Oboz (No 2) (Sentencing for Contempt of Court)* [2015] EWHC 611 (Fam).
[34] NACCC.

Contact with a child in care

(a)   Children Act 1989, section 8 does not apply to children in care.

(b)   Previous orders made under Children Act 1989, section 8 are discharged (section 91(2)).

(c)   Important/in children's best interests to maintain or create links with children's birth families. See *Re E (A Minor) (Care Order: Contact).*[35]

(d)   Governed by Children Act 1989, section 34, the Contact with Children Regulations 1991,[36] Children Act 1989 Guidance and Regulations, Children Act 1989, Schedule 2, paragraph 15(1).

(e)   The CoramBAAF Adoption and Fostering Academy[37] Guidance.

COURT ETIQUETTE

Modes of address

Lay justices	Sir/Madam/Your Worships
District Judges	Sir/Madam
Circuit Judges (or Recorders)	Your Honour
High Court Judges	My Lord/My Lady; use 'Your Lordship/Your Ladyship' in place of 'you'
Master	Master
Judges of the Court of Appeal/ Supreme Court	My Lord/My Lady

For example, 'My Lady, if I may deal with the points which Your Ladyship has raised ...'.

Use 'His Lordship/Her Ladyship' and 'His Honour/Her Honour' in place of 'him' or 'her', i.e. when referring to the judge in the third person.

If a Circuit judge is sitting also as a deputy judge or judge of the High Court in order to hear a mixed list, i.e. some county court and some High Court cases, then it is the case itself which determines the mode of address. If your case is a county court matter, address the judge as 'Your Honour'. If the case is a High Court matter, address the judge as 'My Lord/My Lady'. Note, however, that if a High Court judge hears a case which is listed as a county court matter, he/she must still be addressed as 'My Lord/ My Lady'.

---

[35]   *Re E (A Minor) (Care Order: Contact)* [1994] 1 FLR 146.
[36]   SI 1991/891.
[37]   Formerly the British Association for Adoption and Fostering (BAAF).

To sit/to stand

Remain seated for lay justices (or their legal advisers) and district judges, otherwise stand.

Robed or not

Robes are worn for committal hearings and for hearings in the Court of Appeal.

DOMESTIC VIOLENCE

New guidance is available on www.gov.uk to help victims of domestic violence or child abuse find out whether they are eligible for legal aid. The guidance also sets out the evidence that individuals need to provide to show that they or their children have been at risk or suffered from domestic violence or abuse, and meet the relevant scope and eligibility criteria. There are useful links to sample letters that a victim of domestic violence or child abuse could use to ask for evidence from the police, courts and other agencies, and templates for professionals to use to give proof about individuals using their service and applying for legal aid in a domestic violence or child abuse case.

See www.gov.uk/government/news/civil-news-resources-and-information-on-domestic-violence-and-child-abuse.

(*Source*: www.gov.uk.)

Women can obtain advice by calling the advice line of Rights of Women (rightsofwomen.org.uk/get-advice/family-law).

EMERGENCY PROTECTION ORDERS (EPOs)

Children Act 1989, section 44.

Children Act 1989, section 44A – the court may include an exclusion requirement in the EPO, and may attach a power of arrest (section 44(5)), or an undertaking (section 44(B)).

Children Act 1989, section 45 – not exceeding 8 days, but extendable once up to 7 days (section 45(5) and (6)).

Children Act 1989, section 45(10) – no route of appeal.

Note Children Act 1989, section 46 – Police Protection Orders, up to 72 hours (section 46(6)).

Guidance from the following authorities is mandatory:

Re X (Emergency Protection Orders)[38] – the 14 key points made by Munby J (as he then was) in *X Council v B (Emergency Protection Orders)* (below) should be copied and made available to the justices hearing an EPO application on each and every occasion such an application is made.

X Council v B (Emergency Protection Orders)[39] (Munby J, as he then was) – key points: 'draconian' order, requiring 'exceptional justification' and 'extraordinarily compelling reasons'. Full, detailed, precise and compelling evidence required. Any order must provide for the least interventionist solution consistent with the preservation of the child's immediate safety. For no longer than is absolutely necessary: the local authority has a continuing duty to keep the case under review day by day so as to ensure that parent and child are separated for no longer than is necessary to secure the child's safety. The court must keep a note of the substance of the oral evidence and must also record in writing not merely its reasons but also any findings of fact.

ENFORCEMENT OF CHILD ARRANGEMENTS ORDERS

Children Act 1989, section 11:

- sections 11A–F – contact activity directions;
- sections 11G–H – monitoring and reporting on contact activity directions (section 11H(6) – not to exceed 12 months);
- section 11I – warning notices must be attached to contact activity directions;
- sections 11J–L – enforcement orders: if satisfied beyond reasonable doubt, but not if the court is satisfied that the person had a reasonable excuse for failing to comply, and/or was under 18 when any failure to comply occurred;
- section 11L(3) – before making an enforcement order as regards a person in breach of a contact order, the court must obtain and consider information about the person and the likely effect of the enforcement order on him;
- section 11M – monitoring of enforcement orders;
- section 11N – warning notices must be attached to enforcement orders;
- section 11O–P – compensation for financial loss occurred due to breach of a contact order.

---

[38]   *Re X (Emergency Protection Orders)* [2006] EWHC 510 (Fam).
[39]   *X Council v B (Emergency Protection Orders)* [2004] EWHC 2015 (Fam), [2005] 1 FLR 341.

Children Act 1989, Schedule A1:

- Part 1 – unpaid work requirement:
  - section 2, Part 1 – references in Criminal Justice Act 2003, Part 12, Chapter 4 to an offender are to be treated as including references to a person subject to an enforcement order;
  - section 3(4)(2) – the work required to be performed under an unpaid work requirement imposed by an enforcement order must be performed during a period of 12 months.
- Part 2 – revocation, amendment or breach of enforcement orders:
  - section 9(9) – the court may increase the number of hours specified in the first order or extend the period of 12 months.

FPR 2010, PD12N – applies where the court is considering an application for an enforcement order under Children Act 1989, section 11J, or for an order following an alleged breach of an enforcement order under Schedule A1, paragraph 9 and asks an officer (CAFCASS) to provide information in accordance with section 11L(5), or to monitor compliance and report in accordance with section 11M. Permission should be given to the officer (CAFCASS) to disclose relevant information to the National Probation Service in relation to the proceedings, to avoid contempt of court.

EXPERTS

Children and Families Act 2014, section 13.

FPR 2010, Part 25 and PD25, and updated PD25B.

Children and Families Act 2014, section 13(1) – a person may not without the permission of the court instruct a person to provide expert evidence for use in children proceedings.

Children and Families Act 2014, section 13(6) – 'the court may give permission [for expert evidence] only if ... the expert evidence is necessary ...'.

In children proceedings, the court's permission is also required for a child to be medically or psychiatrically examined or otherwise assessed for the purposes of the provision of expert evidence in the proceedings (Children and Families Act 2014, section 13(3)). Where the court's permission has not been given, evidence resulting from such instructions or examination or other assessment is inadmissible unless the court rules otherwise.

The court will consider the factors set out at Children and Families Act 2014, section 13(7) when deciding whether to give permission for the instruction of an expert.

In public law proceedings, the court will decide what expert evidence is/is not necessary at the Case Management Hearing.[40]

A Local Authority v DS, DI and DS (By their Children's Guardian)[41] – the question that the court will need to ask is whether the expert report/reports is/are necessary for the resolution of the case.

If all parties agree that expert evidence is necessary, but the court disagrees, it is not a ground for appeal.

Re B-S (Children):[42]

> What the court needs is expert opinion, whether from the social worker or the guardian, which is evidence-based and focused on the factors in play in the particular case, which analyses all the possible options, and which provides clear conclusions and recommendations adequately reasoned through and based on the evidence. (at [48])

Re C (A Child) (Procedural Requirements of a Part 25 Application)[43] – in allowing the father's appeal, Ryder LJ set out the statutory scheme and procedural code for the granting of permission to instruct an expert. He did this 'not least because the frequency with which its aim is frustrated suggests that there is insufficient knowledge of it among practitioners'.

There is an important distinction between treating clinicians and experts.[44] Treating clinicians are not court-appointed experts, and their independence may be questioned. Clinical involvement, however, does not, of itself, affect a doctor's capacity to act as an expert witness (*O-M, GM (and KM) v The Local Authority, LO and EM*[45]). There are numerous different areas of expertise. Each expert should be kept within the bounds of his/her own expertise and work in a collaborative way with the other experts.[46] Not exhaustively:

(a) *Paediatricians* (general and specialist): assessments in relation to development, causation and dating of injuries, and long-term prognoses:
    (i) *Paediatric haematologist*: causation of bleeding.
    (ii) *Paediatric neuroradiologist*: causation of skull fractures and subdural haematomas.
    (iii) *Paediatric neurosurgeon*: causation of subdural haematomas.
    (iv) *Paediatric ophthalmologist*: retinal assessments, causation of retinal haemorrhages.

---

[40] CMH.
[41] *A Local Authority v DS, DI and DS (By their Children's Guardian)* [2012] EWHC 1442 (Fam).
[42] *Re B-S (Children)* [2013] EWCA Civ 1146.
[43] *Re C (A Child) (Procedural Requirements of a Part 25 Application)* [2015] EWCA Civ 539.
[44] *GW and PW v Oldham Metropolitan Borough Council* [2005] EWCA Civ 1247.
[45] *O-M, GM (and KM) v The Local Authority, LO and EM* [2009] EWCA Civ 1405.
[46] *A Local Authority v S* [2009] EWHC 2115 (Fam).

(v)   *Paediatric radiologist*: analysis of skeletal surveys, MRI scans and/or CT scans.

(vi)   *Paediatric metabolic consultant*: testing for metabolic disorders.

(b)   *Consultant psychiatrists* (mental health problems): identification of capacity to give instructions, cognitive capacity, personality disorders, particular mental illnesses, level of substance abuse and addiction, and giving prognoses;

(c)   *Psychologists* (clinical/forensic): assessment and analysis of emotional and relationship problems, parenting ability, attachment, contact issues, general functioning and management of life's responsibilities, and giving prognoses for change.

(d)   *Forensic pathologists*: in relation to death in suspicious circumstances, post-mortems on cause of death.

(e)   *Geneticists*: advice about chromosomal abnormalities, gene deficiencies, and/or rare syndromes.

(f)   *Nephrologists* (kidney specialists): diagnosis and treatment of kidney diseases.

FACT-FINDING HEARINGS

Re S (A Child).[47]

Public law hearings

- 'the use of split hearings must be confined to those cases where there is a stark or discrete issue to be determined and an early conclusion on that issue will enable the substantive determination (i.e. whether a statutory order is necessary) to be made more expeditiously' (Ryder LJ at [27]);
- 'where the threshold for jurisdiction in section 31 CA 1989 would not be satisfied if a finding could not be made thereby concluding the proceedings, [or] for the most complex medical causation cases where death or very serious medical issues had arisen and where an accurate medical diagnosis was integral to the future care of the child concerned' (at [29]);
- 'a split hearing [to enable] a social care assessment to be undertaken is simply poor social work and forensic practice ... In so far as it is necessary to express a risk formulation as a precursor to an analysis or a recommendation to the court, that can be done by basing the same on each of the alternative factual scenarios that the court is being asked to consider' (at [29]–[30]);
- 'a decision to undertake a split hearing is a case management decision to which Part 1 of the Family Procedure Rules 2010 [FPR 2010] and Pilot Practice Direction 12A "Care, Supervision and Other Part 4 Proceedings: Guide to Case Management (the PLO)" apply. A split hearing is only justifiable where the delay occasioned is in furtherance of the overriding objective in rule 1 FPR 2010' (at [31]).

---

[47]   *Re S (A Child)* [2014] EWCA Civ 25.

Note also the President's guidance in *Re A (A Child)*.[48]

Private law hearings

> In private law proceedings it is the court that is defining an aspect of parental responsibility in its determination of the arrangements that are put in place for the child and findings of fact are appropriate, where necessary, to inform that process by reference to the factors in section 1(3) of the 1989 Act and in particular where safety issues have arisen which justify the court's interference with the article 8 ECHR rights of the family members. (Ryder LJ at [28])

See also *In the matter of C (Children)*.[49]

Applications to vary findings

There are three stages:

(a)   consideration of whether the court will permit any reconsideration or review of the earlier finding;

(b)   determination of the extent of the investigations and evidence concerning the review;

(c)   the review.[50]

HEARINGS INCLUDING PARENTS WITH DISABILITIES

New Family Procedure Rules, currently under consideration, will provide for any witness, including a party, who is identified as vulnerable to be entitled to assistance in order to give evidence coherently, accurately and completely. There will be a duty on representatives and LiPs to identify if any party or witness is vulnerable and to seek directions of the court as soon as practicable regarding appropriate measures to be provided to enable the witness to give their best evidence. The importance of the new rules is expected to be emphasised by an amendment to the overriding objective in rule 1.1, by addition to the matters included in 'dealing with a case justly' of: 'make provision for vulnerable parties and witnesses and children to assist them in improving the quality of their evidence and to participate fully in proceedings'. At the time of writing, relevant revised rules and Practice Directions were planned for publication imminently.

---

[48]   *Re A (A Child)* [2015] EWFC 11.

[49]   *In the matter of C (Children)* [2009] EWCA Civ 994 at [17] per Thorpe LJ.

[50]   *Birmingham City Council v H and others* [2006] EWHC 3062 (Fam) (*Birmingham No 2*); *Birmingham City Council v H and others* [2005] EWHC 2885 (Fam) (*Birmingham No 1*); *In Re B (Minors) (Care Proceedings: Issue Estoppel)* [1997] Fam 117; *Re ZZ and Others* [2014] EWFC 9, President.

Cross-examination of a vulnerable witness by an unfunded party

For the options as at the time of writing, see *Re K and H (Children)*[51] which were said to be:

(a)   The party to be challenged must only give evidence if the unfunded party questions him/her through a legal representative.

(b)   The party to be challenged should be questioned by the judge himself/herself.

(c)   The party to be challenged should be questioned by a justices' clerk.

(d)   A guardian be appointed to conduct proceedings on behalf of the child/children.

However, cases involving complex expert evidence or complex and/or confused factual evidence from a vulnerable witness may yet need further consideration.

See in addition *Re A (A Child)*,[52] *Wiltshire Council v N and Ors*[53] and *Re C (A Child)*.[54]

Re C (A Child) provides detailed guidance, particularly where deafness is a feature. McFarlane LJ:

> ... all that I have said is not simply good practice in order to achieve a more informed and focused result for the child. The court as an organ of the state, the local authority and CAFCASS must all function now within the terms of the Equality Act 2010. It is simply not an option to fail to afford the right level of regard to an individual who has these unfortunate disabilities. (at [35])

Principles to be derived from *Re C (A Child)* are:

(a)   It is the duty of those who are acting for a parent who has a hearing disability to identify that as a feature of the case at the earliest opportunity.

(b)   Both those acting for such a party and the local authority should make the issue known to the court at the time that the proceedings are issued. The court should give directions for special measures at the case management hearing.

(c)   The provision of expert advice on the impact of the deaf person's disability in the particular circumstances of the case should be fully addressed at the case management hearing [and/or as soon as possible]. An application for expert involvement for the purpose, if nothing else to advise the court and the professionals how they should approach the individual, should be the subject of a properly constituted application for leave to instruct the expert under Part 25 of the Family Procedure Rules 2010. The legal representatives should normally by the date of the case management hearing identify an agency to assist their client to give evidence through an intermediary [or Deaf Relay Interpreter] or otherwise if the court concludes that such measures are required.

---

[51]   *Re K and H (Children)* [2015] EWCA Civ 543.
[52]   *Re A (A Child)* [2013] EWHC 3502 (Fam).
[53]   *Wiltshire Council v N and Ors* [2013] EWHC 3502 (Fam).
[54]   *Re C (A Child)* [2014] EWCA Civ 128, Rimer, McFarlane and Vos LJJ.

(d)   The issue of funding needs to be grappled with at the earliest stage before the case management hearing and during the case management hearing [i.e. Legal Aid Agency, HM Courts & Tribunals Service (HMCTS), and the local authority].

(e)   There should not be an unrealistic timescale afforded to the assessment process. There may be a reason for extending the timetable for the case by a modest degree.

(f)   It is crucial for professionals and those involved in the court system, in particular judges, to understand the profound difference between the ordinary need in cases where parties to the proceedings may speak a different language for there to be 'translation', and the need for a different character of professional intervention in these cases.

(g)   There are differences between British Sign Language ... and English Supported Sign Language, which is a different and far more structured, in grammatical terms, process. Different people from the population who have a hearing disability will use one or both or neither; they may have their own individual way of communication.

(h)   Deaf Relay Interpretation is a specialist service and process. A relay interpreter is a deaf person who acts as an 'intermediary' between the qualified sign language interpreter and the deaf person. The purpose is for the Deaf Relay Interpreter to approach the communication with the deaf person from a deaf perspective, breaking down issues and providing, what one report we have read refers to as, 'cultural brokerage'.

Funding of intermediaries

Public funding arrangements for intermediaries outside court for the purposes of meetings with professionals, particularly legal advisers, are unsatisfactory and an urgent review is required.

Wiltshire Council v N:[55]

> So far as funding is concerned, there is a distinction between, on the one hand, the cost of obtaining a report from an expert as to capacity and competence and, on the other, the cost of providing services from an intermediary. The former will, subject to the approval of the legal aid agency, fall under the public funding certificate, whereas the latter, as a type of interpretation service, will, as far as I understand the rules, be borne by the Court Service. It is important that those representing the relevant party address these funding issues at the earliest opportunity. They should obtain prior approval from the legal aid agency for the instruction of the expert and, as soon as possible, give notice to Her Majesty's Courts and Tribunal Service that the services of an intermediary are likely to be required. (at [79])

See the President's guidance on the HMCTS funding relevant services in *Re D (A Child) (No 2)*[56] which was not overturned in the later case of *Re K and H (Children)*.[57]

---

[55]   *Wiltshire Council v N* [2013] EWHC 3502 (Fam).
[56]   *Re D (A Child) (No 2)* [2015] EWFC 2.
[57]   *Re K and H (Children)* [2015] EWCA Civ 543 at [40].

Identifying intermediaries

Currently, the internet is a way of identifying private organisations which provide intermediaries (e.g. the Royal College of Speech and Language Therapists, www.rcslt.org, tel 020 7378 1200). There is no standard way of finding suitable intermediaries for family proceedings. In *Re X (A Child)*,[58] the use of an intermediary for a vulnerable teenage witness with Asperger Syndrome was discussed. The judge noted that the absence of an intermediary scheme in family cases led to 'real obstacles' to finding and funding one. The criminal justice system is far more advanced in this respect; a Registered Intermediary (RI) is obtained either by the police or by the Crown Prosecution Service, via the matching service which has been outsourced by the MoJ to the National Crime Agency. The Serious Organised Crime Agency operates and manages the Witness Intermediary Scheme[59] matching service. An RI from criminal proceedings can be provided to family courts only if there is a direct link to a criminal case involving a witness; where one has already been appointed and is available; and where there is no impact on availability of other RIs for witnesses. For assistance in finding a suitable intermediary, contact www.intermediaries-for-justice.org or Communicourt (www.communicourt.co.uk).

Intermediary reports

Once instructed, an intermediary will assess the vulnerable witness/party and report with recommendations for his/her safeguarding and/or communication needs. If obtained in criminal proceedings, intermediary reports may be disclosed to family proceedings. Consent to disclosure of the report beyond its original purpose must be obtained from the relevant police constabulary and from the relevant witness. It is also good practice to consult the RI.

(*Source*: The Advocacy Training Council was the original source of publication for the guidance about the provision of evidence of children and vulnerable witnesses (see Chapter 4). See The Advocates Gateway for relevant Toolkits, www.theadvocatesgateway.org (see Vulnerable Witnesses, pages 46–47).)

HUMAN RIGHTS ACT 1998 – EUROPEAN CONVENTION ON HUMAN RIGHTS, ARTICLES 6 AND 8

Article 6

Right to a fair trial
1 In the determination of his civil rights and obligations or of any criminal charge against him, everyone is entitled to a fair and public hearing within a reasonable time by an independent and impartial tribunal established by law. Judgment shall be

---

[58] *Re X (A Child)* [2011] EWHC 3401 (Fam).
[59] WIS.

pronounced publicly but the press and public may be excluded from all or part of the trial in the interest of morals, public order or national security in a democratic society, where the interests of juveniles or the protection of the private life of the parties so require, or to the extent strictly necessary in the opinion of the court in special circumstances where publicity would prejudice the interests of justice.

2 Everyone charged with a criminal offence shall be presumed innocent until proved guilty according to law.

3 Everyone charged with a criminal offence has the following minimum rights:

(a)   to be informed promptly, in a language which he understands and in detail, of the nature and cause of the accusation against him;

(b)   to have adequate time and facilities for the preparation of his defence;

(c)   to defend himself in person or through legal assistance of his own choosing or, if he has not sufficient means to pay for legal assistance, to be given it free when the interests of justice so require;

(d)   to examine or have examined witnesses against him and to obtain the attendance and examination of witnesses on his behalf under the same conditions as witnesses against him;

(e)   to have the free assistance of an interpreter if he cannot understand or speak the language used in court.

Article 8

Right to respect for private and family life

1 Everyone has the right to respect for his private and family life, his home and his correspondence.

2 There shall be no interference by a public authority with the exercise of this right except such as is in accordance with the law and is necessary in a democratic society in the interests of national security, public safety or the economic well-being of the country, for the prevention of disorder or crime, for the protection of health or morals, or for the protection of the rights and freedoms of others.

INTERMEDIARIES

See 'Hearings including parents with disabilities' (above).

INTERNATIONAL CHILD ABDUCTION

This complex topic is beyond the scope of this handbook, and specialist advice should be sought if necessary. However, in the first instance refer to FPR 2010, PD12F – International Child Abduction (see Chapter 7), for helpful and detailed initial guidance and advice (see pages 44–46). In brief, as follows.

The Child Abduction Act 1984 sets out the circumstances in which the removal of a child from this jurisdiction is a criminal offence. The police provide the following 24-hour service to prevent the unlawful removal of a child:

(a)   they inform ports directly when there is a real and imminent threat that a child is about to be removed unlawfully from the country; and

(b)   they liaise with Immigration Officers at the ports in an attempt to identify children at risk of removal.

Where the child is under 16, it is not necessary to obtain a court order before seeking police assistance. The police do not need an order to act to protect the child. If an order has already been obtained it should, however, be produced to the police. Where the child is aged between 16 and 18, an order must be obtained restricting or restraining removal before seeking police assistance.

Where the child is a ward of court (see FPR 2010, PD12D Inherent Jurisdiction – including Wardship (see Chapter 7)), the court's permission is needed to remove that child from the jurisdiction. When the court has not given that permission and police assistance is sought to prevent the removal of the ward, the applicant must produce evidence that the child is a ward, such as:

(a)   an order confirming wardship;

(b)   an injunction; or

(c)   where the matter is urgent and no order has been made, a certified copy of the wardship application.

The application for police assistance must be made by the applicant or his/her legal representative to the applicant's local police station, except that applications may be made to any police station:

(a)   in urgent cases;

(b)   where the wardship application has just been issued; or

(c)   where the court has just made the order relied on.

The police will, if they consider it appropriate, institute the 'port alert' system (otherwise known as 'an all ports warning') to try to prevent removal from the jurisdiction where the danger of removal is:

(a)   real (i.e. not being sought merely by way of insurance); and

(b)   imminent (i.e. within 24–48 hours).

Where the court makes an order prohibiting or otherwise restricting the removal of a child from the United Kingdom, or from any specified part of it, or from a specified dependent territory, the court may make an order under Family Law Act 1986, section 37 requiring any person to surrender any UK passport which has been issued to, or contains particulars of, the child.

The Identity and Passport Service (IPS) will take action to prevent a UK passport or replacement passport being issued only where the IPS has been served with a court order expressly requiring a UK passport to be surrendered, or expressly prohibiting the issue of any further UK passport facilities to the child without the consent of the court, or the holder of such an order.

If you think a child has already been wrongfully removed from the jurisdiction, contact the International Child Abduction and Contact Unit (ICACU). The ICACU is open Mondays to Fridays from 9.00 am to 5.00 pm. It is located in the Office of the Official Solicitor and Public Trustee and its contact details are as follows:

> International Child Abduction and Contact Unit
> 81 Chancery Lane
> London WC2A 1DD
> DX 0012 London Chancery Lane
> Tel + 44 (0)20 7911 7045/7047
> Fax + 44 (0)20 7911 7248
> Email enquiries@offsol.gsi.gov.uk

In an emergency (including out of normal working hours), contact should be made with the Royal Courts of Justice on one of the following telephone numbers: + 44 (0)20 7947 6000, or + 44 (0)20 7947 6260.

In addition, in an emergency or outside normal working hours, advice on international child abduction can be sought from reunite International Child Abduction Centre, tel + 44 (0)1162 556 234. Outside office hours, you will be directed to the 24-hour emergency service. You can also see information on reunite's website, www.reunite.org.

JOINDER (OF RESPONDENTS)

Any person who is not automatically a respondent to an application may apply to be made a respondent, or may, without application, be made a party by court order (FPR 2010, rule 12.3(3)). To apply, use FPR 2010, Part 18. Where the applicant is a father without parental responsibility, a presumption applies that his application for joinder will be granted unless there is good reason for refusing it.[60] Relevant questions are:

- Does the applicant have a separate point to advance?[61]
- Does the applicant have a positive case to put forward?[62] His/her advocate has a positive duty to set out the reasons justifying the need for representation in the proceedings.

---

[60] *Re B (Care Proceedings: Notification of Father without Parental Responsibility)* [1999] 2 FLR 408, but see *Re P (Care Proceedings: Father's Application to be Joined as Party)* [2001] 1 FLR 781.

[61] *Re M (Minors) (Sexual Abuse: Evidence)* [1993] 1 FLR 822.

[62] *Merton London Borough Council v K; Re K (Care: Representation: Public Funding)* [2005] EWHC 167 (Fam), [2005] 2 FLR 422.

In public law proceedings, the test under Children Act 1989, section 10(9) applies to an application from a prospective intervener. The court shall, in deciding whether or not to grant leave, have particular regard to:

(a) the nature of the proposed application ... ;
(b) the applicant's connection with the child;
(c) any risk there might be of that proposed application disrupting the child's life to such an extent that he would be harmed by it; and
(d) where the child is being looked after by a local authority—
    (i) the authority's plans for the child's future; and
    (ii) the wishes and feelings of the child's parents.

Potential interveners

Local authorities have an obligation to consider at an early stage whether any third party should be joined to the proceedings: *Re H (Children) (Care Proceedings: Sexual Abuse)*.[63]

In *Re B (Paternal Grandmother: Joinder as Party)*,[64] Black LJ reviewed the authorities and stated:

▪ Children Act 1989, section 10(9) does not contain a test, but simply identifies some factors which require particular regard;
▪ having an arguable case may not be sufficient to justify granting permission;
▪ the court has a wide discretion as to the stage at which the application is determined and the amount of evidence required in order to do so; there is no absolute entitlement to an assessment prior to determining the application.

Re H (Leave to Apply for Residence Order)[65] – the 'applicant's connection with the child' may be quite indirect (adopters of the child's half-sibling).

Re A (Section 8 Order: Grandparent Application)[66] and *Re W (Contact: Application by Grandparent)*[67] – the granting of leave to apply for contact does not place the applicant in the same position as a natural parent.

The principle of the paramountcy of the child's welfare does not apply in an application to be joined as a party in proceedings (*G v Kirklees Metropolitan Borough Council*[68]).

---

[63] *Re H (Children) (Care Proceedings: Sexual Abuse)* [2000] 2 FCR 499.
[64] *Re B (Paternal Grandmother: Joinder as Party)* [2012] EWCA Civ 737, [2012] 2 FLR 1358.
[65] *Re H (Leave to Apply for Residence Order)* [2008] EWCA Civ 503, [2008] 2 FLR 848.
[66] *Re A (Section 8 Order: Grandparent Application)* [1995] 2 FLR 153.
[67] *Re W (Contact: Application by Grandparent)* [1997] 1 FLR 793.
[68] *G v Kirklees Metropolitan Borough Council* [1993] 1 FLR 805.

JUDICIAL RECUSAL

A judge may recuse himself/herself from proceedings if he/she decides that it is not appropriate for him/her to hear a case listed to be heard by him/her. A judge may recuse himself/herself when a party applies to him/her to do so. A judge must step down in circumstances where there appears to be bias or 'apparent bias'. Judicial recusal is not a matter of discretion. The test for determining apparent bias is, 'if a fair-minded and informed observer, having considered the facts, would conclude that there was a real possibility that the judge was biased'. If this is so, the judge must recuse himself/herself (see *Porter v Magill*,[69] following Lord Phillips of Worth Matravers MR's comments in *In re Medicaments and Related Classes of Goods (No 2)*[70]). The test is to be applied having regard to all the circumstances of the case.

There are important public policy reasons for this doctrine. The judiciary must ensure that it remains independent and that it is seen to be independent of any influence that might reasonably be perceived as compromising its ability to judge cases fairly and impartially. As was stated in *Mulugeta Guadie Mengiste and Another v Endowment Fund for the Rehabilitation of Tigray and Others*,[71] 'to maintain society's trust and confidence, justice must not only be done but be seen to be done'. Additionally, European Convention on Human Rights, Article 6 rights are clearly at risk: a fair hearing must be seen to take place.

Where questions of possible judicial bias are raised, the decision in *In re Medicaments and Related Classes of Goods (No 2)* applies to family proceedings:[72]

(a)   if a judge is shown to have been influenced by actual bias, his decision must be set aside;

(b)   where actual bias is not established, the personal impartiality of the judge is to be presumed;

(c)   the court then has to decide whether, on an objective appraisal, the material facts give rise to a legitimate fear that the judge might not have been impartial. If they do, the judge's decision must be set aside;

(d)   the material facts are not limited to those which were apparent to the applicant;

(e)   an important consideration in making an objective appraisal of the facts is the desirability that the public should remain confident in the administration of justice.

---

[69]   *Porter v Magill* [2001] UKHL 67, [2002] 2 AC 357 at [102].

[70]   *In re Medicaments and Related Classes of Goods (No 2)* [2000] EWCA Civ 350, [2001] 1 WLR 700.

[71]   *Mulugeta Guadie Mengiste and Another v Endowment Fund for the Rehabilitation of Tigray and Others* [2013] EWCA Civ 1003.

[72]   *M v London Borough of Islington and L* [2001] EWHC 2 (Fam), [2002] 1 FLR 95.

LITIGANTS IN PERSON

See *Litigants in person: guidelines for lawyers*, June 2015 (prepared by the Bar Council, CILEx and the Law Society). Amongst other matters, lawyers should communicate in a manner of which the court would approve, which includes treating litigants in person (LiPs) with courtesy and in a way that any ordinary person would regard as fair and reasonable. This does not mean that practitioners have to tolerate unacceptable behaviour from an LiP, nor does it mean that an LiP has a right to expect practitioners to respond immediately to his/her calls or correspondence.

Some LiPs may be vulnerable adults, and may require additional support from the court or the lawyer. If you believe that an LiP is vulnerable and that their needs in terms of participating in the proceedings have not been recognised, you should bring this to the court's attention.

Re H (A Child)[73] – Ryder J proposed that before any LiP makes any submissions to the court, he/she should be sworn or take an affirmation in order that whatever he/she then says becomes evidence in the case.

MCKENZIE FRIENDS

In the civil and family courts, there is a presumption in favour of permitting an LiP to have reasonable assistance from a lay person, sometimes called a McKenzie Friend (MF). Litigants assisted by MFs remain LiPs. The court's permission for the assistance of an MF must be sought. The fact that a case is straightforward, or that the LiP has chosen to be without representation, or that the proceedings are confidential, are not sufficient reasons for the court to refuse permission.

See Practice Guidance: McKenzie Friends (Civil and Family Courts), 12 July 2010, www.judiciary.gov.uk/publications/mckenzie-friends (see Chapter 4).

See also Guidance from the President's Office – McKenzie Friends, 13 May 2005, www.judiciary.gov.uk/publications/mckenzie-friends.

NATIONAL REFERRAL MECHANISM (NRM)

The NRM is a framework for identifying victims of human trafficking and ensuring they receive the appropriate protection and support. It is also the mechanism through which the UK Human Trafficking Centre (UKHTC) collects data about victims.

---

[73] *Re H (A Child)* [2014] EWCA Civ 271.

The NRM was introduced in 2009 to meet the United Kingdom's obligations under the Council of Europe Convention on Action against Trafficking in Human Beings 2005 (see page 44). It grants a minimum 45-day reflection and recovery period for victims of human trafficking.

The NRM process

Referral to a UK competent authority (first responders)

To be referred to the NRM, potential victims of trafficking must first be referred to one of the United Kingdom's two competent authorities (CAs). This initial referral will generally be handled by an authorised agency such as a police force, the UK Border Force, UK Visas and Immigration (UK VI), social services or certain non-governmental organisations (NGOs). The referring authority is known as the 'first responder'.

The National Crime Agency is a first responder agency, as are the following:

- Police forces.
- UK Border Force.
- UK VI.
- Gangmasters Licensing Authority.
- Local authorities.
- Health and Social Care Trusts (Northern Ireland).
- Salvation Army.
- Eaves' Poppy Project.
- Migrant Help.
- Medaille Trust.
- Kalayaan.
- Barnardo's.
- Unseen.
- TARA Project (Scotland).
- NSPCC (Child Trafficking Advice Centre[74]).
- BAWSO.
- New Pathways.
- Refugee Council.

The first responder will complete a referral form to pass the case to the CA. Referral to a CA is voluntary and can happen only if the potential victim gives his/her permission by signing the referral form. All completed NRM forms are sent to the UKHTC in the first instance (email: communication@nca.x.gsi.gov.uk, telephone: 0370 496 7622 (available 24/7)). The UKHTC will then determine which CA will deal with the case and will forward the papers if needed.

---

[74] CTAC.

Competent authorities

In the United Kingdom the two CAs are:

(a)   the UKHTC, which deals with referrals from the police, local authorities and NGOs;

(b)   the UK VI, which deals with referrals identified as part of the immigration process, for example where trafficking may be an issue as part of an asylum claim.

Once a referral has been made, there are several steps in the process.

Stage one – 'Reasonable grounds'

The NRM team has a target period of 5 working days from receipt of the referral by which to decide whether there are reasonable grounds to believe the individual is a potential victim of human trafficking. This may involve seeking additional information from the first responder or from specialist NGOs or social services. The threshold at the reasonable grounds stage for the case manager is 'From the information available so far I believe but cannot prove' that the individual is a potential victim of trafficking.

If the decision is affirmative then the potential victim will be:

- allocated a place within government-funded safe house accommodation, if required;
- granted a recovery and reflection period of 45 days. This allows the victim to begin to recover from his/her ordeal and to reflect on what he/she wants to do next, for example, co-operate with police enquiries, return home, etc.

The referred person and the first responder are both notified of the decision by letter.

Stage two – 'Conclusive decision'

During the 45-day recovery and reflection period, the CA gathers further information relating to the referral from the first responder and other agencies.

This additional information is used to make a conclusive decision on whether the referred person is a victim of human trafficking. The CA's target for a conclusive decision is within the 45-day recovery and reflection period.

The case manager's threshold for a conclusive decision is that on the balance of probability 'it is more likely than not' that the individual is a victim of human trafficking.

The first responder and the potential victim will both be notified of the decision. If the referred person is conclusively identified as a victim of trafficking, what happens next will depend on his/her wishes.

What happens next?

Co-operating with police enquiries

The victim may be granted discretionary leave to remain in the United Kingdom for 1 year to allow him/her to co-operate fully in any police investigation and subsequent prosecution. The period of discretionary leave can be extended if required.

Other circumstances

If a victim of trafficking is not involved in the criminal justice process, the UK VI may consider a grant of discretionary leave to remain in the United Kingdom, dependent on the victim's personal circumstances.

Returning home

If the victim is from outside the European Economic Area (EEA), he/she can receive help and financial assistance to return home through the UK VI Assisted Voluntary Return of Irregular Migrants[75] process. If the victim is an EEA national, support organisations will put him/her in touch with his/her embassy and any relevant NGOs which may be able to help.

If the referred person is not found to be a victim

If at any stage the referred person is confirmed not to be a victim of trafficking then, dependent on the circumstances, he/she may be referred to the appropriate law enforcement agency – the relevant police force or the Home Office.

If it is decided by the UK VI that the person was not trafficked, and there are no other circumstances that would give him/her a right to live in the United Kingdom, he/she will be offered support to voluntarily return to his/her country of origin. The person can also be offered support to return to his/her country if he/she has been trafficked and does not wish to stay in the United Kingdom.

(See further www.nationalcrimeagency.gov.uk/about-us/what-we-do/specialist-capabilities/uk-human-trafficking-centre/national-referral-mechanism.)

OFFICIAL SOLICITOR

The Official Solicitor's role is to make decisions for people who do not have the mental capacity (as assessed by their/another psychiatrist or general practitioner) to represent themselves or to instruct a solicitor in civil or family court cases.

---

[75]   AVRIM.

Mental Capacity Act 2005

Section 1:

(1) The following principles apply for the purposes of this Act.

(2) A person must be assumed to have capacity unless it is established that he lacks capacity.

(3) A person is not to be treated as unable to make a decision unless all practicable steps to help him to do so have been taken without success.

(4) A person is not to be treated as unable to make a decision merely because he makes an unwise decision.

(5) An act done, or decision made, under this Act for or on behalf of a person who lacks capacity must be done, or made, in his best interests.

(6) Before the act is done, or the decision is made, regard must be had to whether the purpose for which it is needed can be as effectively achieved in a way that is less restrictive of the person's rights and freedom of action.

Section 2:

(1) For the purposes of this Act, a person lacks capacity in relation to a matter if at the material time he is unable to make a decision for himself in relation to the matter because of an impairment of, or a disturbance in the functioning of, the mind or brain.

(2) It does not matter whether the impairment or disturbance is permanent or temporary.

(3) A lack of capacity cannot be established merely by reference to—

    (a) a person's age or appearance, or

    (b) a condition of his, or an aspect of his behaviour, which might lead others to make unjustified assumptions about his capacity.

The Official Solicitor is the litigation friend of last resort. In many cases a protected party will have a relative or close friend who is both suitable and willing to act as litigation friend.

The Official Solicitor will not consent to act until his acceptance criteria are satisfied:

(a) satisfactory evidence that the party lacks capacity to conduct the proceedings, or, in the alternative, a finding by the court that the party lacks capacity to conduct the proceedings and is therefore a protected party within the meaning of FPR 2010, rule 2.3;

(b) confirmation that this is a last resort case, i.e. that there is no other person suitable and willing to act as litigation friend;

(c) confirmation that there is security for the costs of legal representation of the protected party.

Case managers at the Official Solicitor's office (located at 81 Chancery Lane, London WC2A 1DD, www.officialsolicitor.gov.uk) have responsibility for all the cases. The case manager will usually act through a firm of solicitors who will arrange for a solicitor or barrister to attend court to represent the person concerned. The person's first point of contact will be his/her solicitor.

See FPR 2010, Part 15: procedures with regard to appointing a litigation friend for a protected party (see Chapter 7).

See Practice Note, The Official Solicitor to the Senior Courts: Appointment in Family Proceedings and Proceedings under the Inherent Jurisdiction in Relation to Adults, March 2013 (see Chapter 4).[76]

In public law proceedings, a lay advocate specialising in learning difficulties/mental health issues should, if available, be provided to support the parent during meetings such as child protection conferences, Family Group Conferences and consultations with legal representatives. Continuity of lay advocate is important, as are specialist training in child protection issues and access to specialist advice.

The Official Solicitor will also act on behalf of a parent whose children have been abducted from the country, through the ICACU. Contact the website (www.justice.gov.uk) for further details.

OUT OF HOURS HEARINGS

Counsel has a duty to provide a note of the hearing for the respondents.[77]

Note the President's Guidance (see Chapter 4):[78]

(a)   There is always a High Court judge of the Family Division on duty 'out of hours' every day of the year.
(b)   The service is designed for urgent cases and should not be abused. Cases where a court order is required to regulate the position between the moment the order is made and the next available court sitting in conventional hours.
(c)   Any application must be capable of being reduced to one A4 sheet or a short telephone conversation.
(d)   Lawyers who abuse the system may face wasted costs orders or being reported for serious professional misconduct.

---

[76] Practice Note, The Official Solicitor to the Senior Courts: Appointment in Family Proceedings and Proceedings under the Inherent Jurisdiction in Relation to Adults, March 2013 [2013] Fam Law 744,

[77] *C v C (Without Notice Orders)* [2005] EWHC 2741 (Fam), Munby J (as he then was); *Local Authority 1 and Others v AF (Mother) & Others* [2014] EWHC 2042 (Fam), Cobb J.

[78] President's Guidance [2011] 1 FLR 303.

Urgent and out of hours cases in the Family Division of the High Court

FPR 2010, PD12E (see Chapter 7) – Urgent Business (not in relation to adults). Note the strict provisions of the Practice Direction. Whenever possible, make these applications in court hours via the Clerk of the Rules. If not possible, contact the security office at the Royal Courts of Justice (+ 44 (0)20 7947 6000 or + 44 (0)20 7947 6260).

Out of hours applications concerning medical and welfare decisions for adults lacking capacity

See Practice Note, 28 July 2006[79] for the full provisions. The Official Solicitor will act in urgent cases under the inherent jurisdiction concerning medical treatment to, or the welfare of, an adult who lacks capacity to make his/her own decisions. His office should be contacted as soon as possible in urgent cases. An adult patient must be a party and be represented by a litigation friend (CPR 1998, rule 21.3). It may be desirable for a child who is the subject of such proceedings to be made a party. Contact CAFCASS or CAFCASS Cymru.

PARENTAL RESPONSIBILITY

See Children Act 1989, sections 2–5.

All mothers and most fathers have legal rights and responsibilities as a parent – known as 'parental responsibility'. The most important roles are to provide a home for the child and to protect and maintain the child. A parent is also responsible for disciplining the child, choosing and providing for the child's education, agreeing to the child's medical treatment, naming the child and agreeing to any change of name, looking after the child's property, and ensuring that his/her child is supported financially, whether or not he/she has parental responsibility. If a parent has parental responsibility for a child whom he/she does not live with, the parent does not necessarily have a right to contact with the child, but the other parent should keep this parent updated about the child's well-being and progress.

Who has parental responsibility?

A mother automatically has parental responsibility for her child from birth.

A father usually has parental responsibility if he is married to the child's mother or listed on the birth certificate (after a certain date, depending on which part of the United Kingdom the child was born in).

---

[79] Practice Note, 28 July 2006 [2006] 2 FLR 354.

Births registered in England and Wales

If the parents of a child are married when the child is born, or if they have jointly adopted a child, both have parental responsibility. They both keep parental responsibility if they later divorce.

Births registered in Scotland

A father has parental responsibility if he is married to the mother when the child is conceived, or marries her at any point afterwards.

An unmarried father has parental responsibility if he is named on the child's birth certificate (from 4 May 2006).

Births registered in Northern Ireland

A father has parental responsibility if he is married to the mother at the time of the child's birth.

If a father marries the mother after the child's birth, he has parental responsibility if he lives in Northern Ireland at the time of the marriage.

An unmarried father has parental responsibility if he is named, or becomes named, on the child's birth certificate (from 15 April 2002).

Births registered outside the United Kingdom

If a child is born overseas and comes to live in the United Kingdom, parental responsibility depends on the UK country in which they are now living.

Same-sex parents

(a)   *Civil partners*: same-sex partners who were civil partners at the time of the treatment will both have parental responsibility.

(b)   *Non-civil partners*: for same-sex partners who are not civil partners, the second parent can get parental responsibility by either:

  (i)   applying for parental responsibility if a parental agreement was made;
  (ii) becoming a civil partner of the other parent and making a parental responsibility agreement or jointly registering the birth.

Unmarried parents

An unmarried father can only get legal responsibility for his child in one of three ways:

(a)   jointly registering the birth of the child with the mother (from 1 December 2003);
(b)   getting a parental responsibility agreement with the mother (see below);
(c)   getting a parental responsibility order from a court.

Parental responsibility agreement

If a father wants parental responsibility and the mother agrees, they should fill in a parental responsibility agreement (a different agreement form is available for step-parents), and take the agreement to the local county court or family proceedings court, where it can be signed and witnessed, taking also the child's birth certificate and proof of the parents' identity (e.g. a passport or driving licence). Then two copies of the form should be sent to the Central Family Court (Principal Registry of the Family Division, First Avenue House, 42–49 High Holborn, London WC1V 6NP).

Parental responsibility by a court order

(Scotland has its own set of rules, covered under 'ordinary cause procedures'.)

The party can apply to court to get parental responsibility. The requirement is to be connected to the child, for example as their father, step-parent or second female parent. More than two people can have parental responsibility for the same child.

If a surrogate is used to have a child, the parents will need to apply for a parental order.

See also:

- www.gov.uk;
- www.fnf.org.uk/law-and-information/parental-responsibility;
- www.oneplusone.org.uk/content_item/a-short-guide-to-parental-responsibility.

(*Source*: www.gov.uk.)

PUBLIC LAW OUTLINE – EXTENSIONS OF THE 26-WEEK RULE

Time-table of 26 weeks – Children Act 1989, section 32(1).

Revisions to the timetable – Children Act 1989, section 32(4) in relation to:

(a) the impact which any revision would have on the welfare of the child to whom the application relates; and

(b) the impact which any revision would have on the duration and conduct of the proceedings.

Extensions to the timetable – Children Act 1989, section 32(5) – if necessary to enable the court to resolve the proceedings justly, having regard to (section 32(6)):

(a)   the impact which any ensuing timetable revision would have on the welfare of the child to whom the application relates; and

(b)   the impact which any ensuing timetable revision would have on the duration and conduct of the proceedings.

Children Act 1989, section 32(7) – extensions are not to be granted routinely and are to be seen as requiring specific justification.

Children Act 1989, section 32(8) – each separate extension under section 32(5) is to end no more than 8 weeks after the later of:

(a)   the end of the period being extended; and

(b)   the end of the day on which the extension is granted.

Re S (A Child)[80] – three different forensic contexts where an extension of the 26-week time limit in relation to Children Act 1989, section 32(5) may be 'necessary':

(i)   …where the case can be identified from the outset, or at least very early on, as one which it may not be possible to resolve justly within 26 weeks … [for example]:

    (a)   very heavy cases involving the most complex medical evidence where a separate fact finding hearing is directed in accordance with *Re S (Split Hearing)*[81],

    (b)   FDAC type cases … ,

    (c)   cases with an international element where investigations or assessments have to be carried out abroad, and

    (d)   cases where the parent's disabilities require recourse to special assessments or measures (as to which see *Re C*[82]).

(ii)   … where … something unexpectedly emerges to change the nature of the proceedings too late in the day to enable the case to be concluded justly within 26 weeks. [For example]:

    (a)   cases proceeding on allegations of neglect or emotional harm where allegations of sexual abuse subsequently surface,

    (b)   cases which are unexpectedly 'derailed' because of the death, serious illness or imprisonment of the proposed carer, and

    (c)   cases where a realistic alternative family carer emerges late in the day.

(iii)   … where litigation failure on the part of one or more of the parties makes it impossible to complete the case justly within 26 weeks (the type of situation addressed in *In Re B-S*, para 49). (at [33])

Re B-S (Children),[83] Sir James Munby P:

If, despite all, the court does not have the kind of evidence we have identified, and is therefore not properly equipped to decide these issues, then an adjournment must be

---

80   *Re S (A Child)* [2014] EWCC B44 (Fam), Sir James Munby P.
81   *Re S (Split Hearing)* [2014] EWCA Civ 25 at [29].
82   *Re C (A Child)* [2014] EWCA Civ 128 at [34].
83   *Re B-S (Children)* [2013] EWCA Civ 1146.

directed, even if this takes the case over 26 weeks. Where the proposal before the court is for non-consensual adoption, the issues are too grave, the stakes for all are too high, for the outcome to be determined by rigorous adherence to an inflexible timetable and justice thereby potentially denied. (at [49])

... the 26-week [time limit for concluding care cases] is not, and must never be allowed to become, a straitjacket ... rigorous adherence to an inflexible timetable risks putting justice in jeopardy.[84]

See also *Re T (Children)*[85] – essential reading for public law practitioners. It sets out in detail the procedure if the timetable for the child is to be extended beyond 26 weeks. It is also a reminder to all parties (and therefore their representatives) of their duties under FPR, rule 12.24 to:

(a)   monitor compliance with the court's directions; and
(b)   tell the court or court officers about:
   (i)   any failure to comply with a direction of the court; and
   (ii)   any other delay in the proceedings.

PUBLIC LAW OUTLINE – GOOD PRACTICE IN CARE PROCEEDINGS

Applications for care and supervision orders are subject to FPR 2010, Part 12 (see Chapter 7) and PD12A.

Note the important guidance in *Re R (Care: Disclosure: Nature of Proceedings)*[86] and *Re L (Care: Assessment: Fair Trial)*.[87]

See also Basic Guidance to Good Practice in Care Proceedings across London, issued by District Judge Richard Harper (as he then was) and Judge John Altman, which came into effect in October 2010.

Re A (A Child)[88] – imperative reading. The President, Sir James Munby's 'object lesson in, almost a textbook example of, how not to embark upon and pursue a care case' (at [7]). Three fundamentally important points:

(a)   'it is for the local authority to prove, on a balance of probabilities, the facts upon which it seeks to rely' (at [8]):

---

[84]   *Re M-F (Children)* [2014] EWCA Civ 991 at [26] per the President.
[85]   *Re T (Children)* [2015] EWCA Civ 606.
[86]   *Re R (Care: Disclosure: Nature of Proceedings)* [2001] EWHC 8 (Fam), [2002] 1 FLR 755.
[87]   *Re L (Care: Assessment: Fair Trial)* [2002] EWHC 1379 (Fam), [2002] 2 FLR 730.
[88]   *Re A (A Child)* [2015] EWFC 11.

(i)   it must therefore, if challenged, adduce proper (first-hand) evidence to establish what it seeks to prove. 'If the "thing" is put in issue, the local authority must both prove the "thing" and establish that it has the significance attributed to it by the local authority' (at [9]);

(ii)   allegations should never be used in a schedule of findings;

(b)   the facts relied upon by the local authority need to be linked with its case on threshold, to demonstrate why the facts sought justify the conclusion that the child has suffered or is at risk of suffering significant types of harm (at [12]);

(c)   parents are not always perfect, but this does not mean that their children should be removed from their care. Citing various authorities including Hedley J in *Re L (Care: Threshold Criteria)*[89] and Judge Jack in *North East Lincolnshire Council v G & L*:[90]

> ... the courts are not in the business of social engineering. The courts are not in the business of providing children with perfect homes ... we have to have a degree of realism about prospective carers who come before the courts.

PUBLIC LAW OUTLINE – COURT'S ANALYSIS OF THE FINAL CARE PLAN

Children Act 1989, section 31:

(3A)   A court deciding whether to make a care order—

     (a)   is required to consider the permanence provisions of the section 31A plan for the child concerned, but

     (b)   is not required to consider the remainder of the section 31A plan, subject to section 34(11).

(3B)   For the purposes of subsection (3A), the permanence provisions of a section 31A plan are such of the plan's provisions setting out the long-term plan for the upbringing of the child concerned as provide for any of the following—

     (a)   the child to live with any parent of the child's or with any other member of, or any friend of, the child's family;

     (b)   adoption;

     (c)   long-term care not within paragraph (a) or (b).

Contact proposals

Note Children Act 1989, section 34(11).

In relation to long-term placement options, note the following cases.

---

[89]   *Re L (Care: Threshold Criteria)* [2007] 1 FLR 2050.

[90]   *North East Lincolnshire Council v G & L* [2014] EWFC B192.

Re B (Care Proceedings: Appeal):[91]

> a court can only separate a child from her parents if satisfied that it is necessary to do so, that 'nothing else will do... [it is] necessary to explore and attempt alternative solutions.' (Lady Hale at [145] and [198])

Re B-S (Children):[92]

> ... the court's assessment of the parents' ability to discharge their responsibilities towards the child must take into account the assistance and support which the authorities would offer. So before making an adoption order ... the court must be satisfied that there is no practical way of the authorities (or others) providing the requisite assistance and support. (Sir James Munby P at [28])

Re G (A Child)[93] – 'the judicial task is to undertake a global, holistic evaluation of each of the options available for the child's future upbringing' (McFarlane LJ at [50]).

Re R (A Child)[94] – Sir James Munby, President – the court is only required to consider properly the options that are 'realistically possible'.

REMOVAL (OF CHILDREN)

At conclusion of (public law) proceedings

See 'Public law outline – court's analysis of the final care plan' (above).

Before conclusion of (public law) proceedings

See *Re L-A (Children):*[95]

> ... from which can be extracted two propositions, the first that the decision taken by the court on an interim care order application must necessarily be limited to issues that cannot await the fixture and must not extend to issues that are being prepared for determination at that fixture. The second proposition which appears from the final sentence of paragraph 39 is that separation is only to be ordered if the child's safety demands immediate separation. In the subsequent case of *Re M* in paragraph 27 I described that a local authority in seeking to justify the continuing removal of a child from home necessarily must meet a very high standard. In the final authority, *K and H*, the key paragraph is paragraph 16 in which I described the court's approach thus:
>
> > ... at an interim stage the removal of children from their parents is not to be sanctioned unless the child's safety requires interim protection. (Thorpe LJ at [7])

---

[91] *Re B (Care Proceedings: Appeal)* [2013] UKSC 33.
[92] *Re B-S (Children)* [2013] EWCA Civ 1146.
[93] *Re G (A Child)* [2013] EWCA Civ 965.
[94] *Re R (A Child)* [2014] EWCA Civ 1625.
[95] *Re L-A (Children)* [2009] EWCA Civ 822, Thorpe LJ.

This guidance was subsequently applied in *Re GR*,[96] which reiterated the very high standard of proof required. The court also needs to be satisfied that removal is proportionate to the harm the child would be exposed to if he/she was returned to parental care (*Re B (Care Proceedings: Interim Care Order)*[97]).

The court therefore is required to ask itself:

(a)   whether the children's safety (using that term to include both psychological and physical elements) requires removal; and
(b)   whether removal is proportionate in light of the risks posed by leaving the children where they are (*MG & Anor v A Local Authority & Ors*[98]).

REPORTING RESTRICTIONS ORDERS

FPR 2010, PD12I (see Chapter 7) – applications for RRO. Only in the High Court or by urgent application to the Judge of the Family Division (out of hours contact number: +44 (0)20 7947 6000). Without notice applications are exceptional.

Human Rights Act 1998, section 12(2): an injunction restricting the exercise of the right to freedom of expression must not be granted where the person against whom the application is made is neither present nor represented unless the court is satisfied:

(a)   that the applicant has taken all practicable steps to notify the respondent; or
(b)   that there are compelling reasons why the respondent should not be notified.

Practice Note, Applications for Reporting Restriction Orders, 18 March 2005,[99] issued jointly by the Official Solicitor and the Deputy Director of Legal Services, provides valuable guidance and contains links to model forms for both draft orders and explanatory notes.

Note Children Act 1989, section 97, and Administration of Justice Act 1960, section 12.

Avoid drafting excessively wide terms: note the President's guidance.[100]

Note that the Press Association's CopyDirect service only provides notification to those media organisations which subscribe to the Press Association service; not comprehensive notification to all media organisations and particularly not to non-subscribing media organisations. The Injunctions Alerts Service website –

---

[96]   *Re GR* [2010] EWCA Civ 871, Black LJ.
[97]   *Re B (Care Proceedings: Interim Care Order)* [2009] EWCA Civ 1254 at [31].
[98]   *MG & Anor v A Local Authority & Ors* [2011] EWCA Civ 745 at [22].
[99]   Practice Note, Applications for Reporting Restriction Orders, 18 March 2005 [2005] 2 FLR 111.
[100]   *Re J (A Child)* [2013] EWHC 2694 (Fam); *Re P (A Child)* [2013] EWHC 4048 (Fam).

www.medialawyer.press.net/courtapplications/mediaorganisations.jsp – lists the media organisations served, and relevant telephone numbers. Notice must be served on the *Financial Times* and *Sky News* directly. Identify likely relevant local and national media (especially if already interested), or international media organisations, and serve them direct. Injunctions sought against foreign-based bodies such as internet website providers require proper service (see FPR 2010, rules 6.41 and 6.43(3)/FPR 2010, rules 6.1 and 12.1(1)(d)).

Recent cases

- *MXB v East Sussex Hospitals NHS Trust* [2012] EWHC 3279 (QB);
- *Bristol City Council v C & Ors* [2012] EWHC 3748 (Fam);
- *A Council v M & others* [2012] EWHC 2038 (Fam);
- *Z & Ors v News Group Newspapers Ltd & Ors* (Judgment 1) [2013] EWHC 1150 (Fam);
- *Z & Ors v News Group Newspapers Ltd* (Judgment 2) [2013] EWHC 1371 (Fam);
- *Re K (A Child: Wardship: Publicity) (No 2)* [2013] EWHC 3748 (Fam);
- *Swansea v XZ & Anor* [2014] EWHC 212 (Fam);
- *Re E (A Child)* [2014] EWHC 6 (Fam);
- *Haringey LBC v Musa* [2014] EWHC 1200 (Fam).

RE-REGISTRATION OF A BIRTH AND DECLARATION AS TO PARENTAGE

Declarations as to parentage

(a) An application may be made to the High Court, a county court or a family proceedings court for a declaration as to parentage. The application may be made by a parent or the child to be named in the declaration or any other person who can establish sufficient personal interest in the application. The respondents must be the person whose parentage is in issue and any person alleged to be the mother or the father. FPR 2010, rules 8.18–8.22. Form C63.

(b) A court will only have jurisdiction to hear an application for a declaration as to parentage if either of the persons named in the application is domiciled in England and Wales on the date of the application or has been habitually resident in England and Wales for 1 year up to that date, or has died but satisfied either of the above grounds at the date of death. In any event, the court has power to refuse to hear such application if it would not be in the interests of the child to do so. There is a right of appeal to the High Court (from a lower decision of the family court) in relation to the making of, or refusal to make, such a declaration, or any order preventing any further application without leave.

(c) When a declaration of parentage is made, the court notifies the Registrar General of the declaration within 21 days. Under Births and Deaths

Registration Act 1953, section 14A, the Registrar General has a discretion to authorise the re-registration of the birth on the basis of the declaration; neither parent signs the new registration.

(d)   With reference to FPR 2010, rule 8.22(2), the court should not use any discretion that may derive from FPR 2010, rule 4.1(3)(a) (power to extend or shorten the time for compliance with any rule) to extend the period for notification to the Registrar General of a declaration of parentage.

Births and Deaths Registration Act 1953:

10A Re-registration where parents neither married nor civil partners
(1)   Where there has been registered under this Act the birth of a child whose father and mother were not married to each other at the time of the birth, but no person has been registered as the father of the child, ... the registrar shall re-register the birth so as to show a person as the father—
   (a)   at the joint request of the mother and that person; or
   (b)   at the request of the mother on production of—
      (i)   a declaration in the prescribed form made by the mother stating that that person is the father of the child; and
      (ii)   a statutory declaration made by that person stating himself to be the father of the child; or
   (c)   at the request of that person on production of—
      (i)   a declaration in the prescribed form by that person stating himself to be the father of the child; and
      (ii)   a statutory declaration made by the mother stating that that person is the father of the child; or
   (d)   at the request of the mother or that person on production of—
      (i)   a copy of [any agreement made between them under section 4(1)(b) of the Children Act 1989 in relation to the child]; and
      (ii)   a declaration in the prescribed form by the person making the request stating that the agreement was made in compliance with section 4 of [that Act] and has not been brought to an end by an order of a court; or
   (e)   at the request of the mother of that person on production of—
      (i)   a certified copy of an order under section 4 of the Children Act 1989 giving that person parental responsibility for the child; and
      (ii)   a declaration in the prescribed form by the person making the request stating that the order has not been brought to an end by an order of a court; or
   (f)   at the request of the mother or that person on production of—
      (i)   a certified copy of an order under paragraph 1 of Schedule 1 to the Children Act 1989 which requires that person to make any financial provision for the child and which is not an order falling within paragraph 4(3) of that Schedule; and
      (ii)   a declaration in the prescribed form by the person making the request stating that the order has not been discharged by an order of a court; or

(g)   at the request of the mother or that person on production of—

    (i)   a certified copy of any of the orders which are mentioned in subsection (1A) of this section which has been made in relation to the child; and

    (ii)   a declaration in the prescribed form by the person making the request stating that the order has not been brought to an end or discharged by an order of a court,

but no birth shall be re-registered under this section except in the prescribed manner and with the authority of the Registrar General.

(1A) The orders are—

    (a)   an order under section 4 of the Family Law Reform Act 1987 that that person shall have all the parental rights and duties with respect to the child;

    (b)   an order that that person shall have custody or care and control or legal custody of the child made under section 9 of the Guardianship of Minors Act 1971 at a time when such an order could only be made in favour of a parent;

    (c)   an order under section 9 or 11B of that Act which requires that person to make any financial provision in relation to the child;

    (d)   an order under section 4 of the Affiliation Proceedings Act 1957 naming that person as putative father of the child.

(2)   ...

Section 14A – Re–registration after declaration of parentage.

(1)   Where, in the case of a person whose birth has been registered in England and Wales—

    (a)   the Registrar General receives, by virtue of section 55A(7) or 56(4) of the Family Law Act 1986, a notification of the making of a declaration of parentage in respect of that person; and

    (b)   it appears to him that the birth of that person should be re–registered,

he shall authorise the re–registration of that person's birth, and the re–registration shall be effected in such manner and at such place as may be prescribed.

Family Law Act 1986, section 55A(7) or section 56(4):

Section 55A – Declarations of parentage

(1)   Subject to the following provisions of this section, any person may apply to the High Court, a county court or a magistrates' court for a declaration as to whether or not a person named in the application is or was the parent of another person so named.

...

(7)   Where a declaration is made by a court on an application under subsection (1) above, the prescribed officer of the court shall notify the Registrar General, in such a manner and within such period as may be prescribed, of the making of that declaration.

Section 56 – Declarations as to parentage, legitimacy or legitimation

...

(4)   Where a declaration is made by a court on an application under subsection (1) above, the prescribed officer of the court shall notify the Registrar General, in such a manner and within such period as may be prescribed, of the making of that declaration.

TRAFFICKING (HUMAN)

2005 Council of Europe Convention on Action against Trafficking in Human Beings:

> Article 4 – Definitions
>
> …
>
> 'Trafficking in human beings' shall mean the recruitment, transportation, transfer, harbouring or receipt of persons, by means of the threat or use of force or other forms of coercion, of abduction, of fraud, of deception, of the abuse of power or of a position of vulnerability or of the giving or receiving of payments or benefits to achieve the consent of a person having control over another person, for the purpose of exploitation. Exploitation shall include, at a minimum, the exploitation of the prostitution of others or other forms of sexual exploitation, forced labour or services, slavery or practices similar to slavery, servitude or the removal of organs;

European Convention on Human Rights:

> Article 4
> Prohibition of slavery and forced labour
> 1   No one shall be held in slavery or servitude.
> 2   No one shall be required to perform forced or compulsory labour.
> 3   For the purpose of this Article the term 'forced or compulsory labour' shall not include:
>> (a)   any work required to be done in the ordinary course of detention imposed according to the provisions of Article 5 of this Convention or during conditional release from such detention;
>> (b)   any service of a military character or, in case of conscientious objectors in countries where they are recognised, service exacted instead of compulsory military service;
>> (c)   any service exacted in case of an emergency or calamity threatening the life or well-being of the community;
>> (d)   any work or service which forms part of normal civic obligations.

See further, the NRM (see pages 28–30), for guidance as to action to take if you suspect someone is a victim of trafficking.

TRANSFER OUT OF THE JURISDICTION

It is not within the scope of this handbook to deal with matters concerning the abduction of children (Convention on the Civil Aspects of International Child Abduction 1980[101] or Council Regulation No 2201/2003 (BIIR)[102] (see pages 22–24)).

---

[101] 1980 Hague Convention.

[102] Council Regulation (EC) No 2201/2003 of 27 November 2003 concerning jurisdiction and the recognition and enforcement of judgments in matrimonial matters and the matters of parental responsibility, repealing Regulation (EC) No 1347/2000 [2003] OJ L338/1.

However, increasingly, practitioners have to deal with matters which involve a child or parent who originates from another European country. In such cases, the transfer of proceedings from these courts to those of the other European country must be considered.

See BIIR, Article 15:

Article 15 – Transfer to a court better placed to hear the case
1. By way of exception, the courts of a Member State having jurisdiction as to the substance of the matter may, if they consider that a court of another Member State, with which the child has a particular connection, would be better placed to hear the case, or a specific part thereof, and where this is in the best interests of the child:
   (a) stay the case or the part thereof in question and invite the parties to introduce a request before the court of that other Member State in accordance with paragraph 4; or
   (b) request a court of another Member State to assume jurisdiction in accordance with paragraph 5.
2. Paragraph 1 shall apply:
   (a) upon application from a party; or
   (b) of the court's own motion; or
   (c) upon application from a court of another Member State with which the child has a particular connection, in accordance with paragraph 3.

   A transfer made of the court's own motion or by application of a court of another Member State must be accepted by at least one of the parties.
3. The child shall be considered to have a particular connection to a Member State as mentioned in paragraph 1, if that Member State:
   (a) has become the habitual residence of the child after the court referred to in paragraph 1 was seised; or
   (b) is the former habitual residence of the child; or
   (c) is the place of the child's nationality; or
   (d) is the habitual residence of a holder of parental responsibility; or
   (e) is the place where property of the child is located and the case concerns measures for the protection of the child relating to the administration, conservation or disposal of this property.
4. The court of the Member State having jurisdiction as to the substance of the matter shall set a time limit by which the courts of that other Member State shall be seised in accordance with paragraph 1.

   If the courts are not seised by that time, the court which has been seised shall continue to exercise jurisdiction in accordance with Articles 8 to 14.
5. The courts of that other Member State may, where due to the specific circumstances of the case, this is in the best interests of the child, accept jurisdiction within six weeks of their seisure in accordance with paragraph 1(a) or 1(b). In this case, the court first seised shall decline jurisdiction. Otherwise, the court first seised shall continue to exercise jurisdiction in accordance with Articles 8 to 14.
6. The courts shall cooperate for the purposes of this Article, either directly or through the central authorities designated pursuant to Article 53.

AB v JLB (Brussels II Revised: Article 15)[103] (Munby J (as he then was)):

> ... as Article 15(1) makes clear there are three questions to be considered by the court – here The Hague court – in deciding whether to exercise its powers under Article 15(1):
>
> i)   First, it must determine whether the child has, within the meaning of Article 15(3), 'a particular connection' with the relevant other Member State – here, the United Kingdom. Given the various matters set out in Article 15(3) as bearing on this question, this is, in essence, a simple question of fact. For example, is the other Member State the former habitual residence of the child (see Article 15(3)(b)) or the place of the child's nationality (see Article 15(3)(c))?
>
> ii)   Secondly, it must determine whether the court of that other Member State 'would be better placed to hear the case, or a specific part thereof'. This involves an exercise in evaluation, to be undertaken in the light of all the circumstances of the particular case.
>
> iii)   Thirdly, it must determine if a transfer to the other court 'is in the best interests of the child.' This again involves an evaluation undertaken in the light of all the circumstances of the particular child. (at [35])

The court can only consider whether to use its discretion under BIIR, Article 15(1) if all three above questions are answered in the affirmative.

Courts will consider the positive and negative aspects of any potential transfer under BIIR, Article 15. See *London Borough of Barking & Dagenham v C and Others*,[104] and *Nottingham City Council v A Mother & Others*.[105] Delay caused by any such transfer could undermine the use of the Article 15 procedure and this must be taken into account (*Bristol City Council v AA and Another*[106]). The Central Authorities of the respective states have a duty to co-operate and to collect, exchange and provide information (Article 55). See *Leicester City Council v S*[107] for relevant guidance. If evidence rather than information is sought, the procedure under Council Regulation No 1206/2001[108] should be used.

VULNERABLE WITNESSES

In the family justice system there is no definition of a 'vulnerable witness' or a 'vulnerable party'. Vulnerability may not be constant, consistent or continuous within an individual, and/or it may be triggered by a specific factor. Vulnerability may only become apparent or heightened in certain circumstances. It is likely to include witnesses/parties who have mental health problems (including being on the autistic

---

[103] *AB v JLB (Brussels II Revised: Article 15)* [2008] EWHC 2965 (Fam), [2009] 1 FLR 517.
[104] *London Borough of Barking & Dagenham v C and Others* [2014] EWHC 2472 (Fam).
[105] *Nottingham City Council v A Mother & Others* [2014] EWCA Civ 152.
[106] *Bristol City Council v AA and Another* [2014] EWHC 1022 (Fam).
[107] *Leicester City Council v S* [2014] EWHC 1575 (Fam).
[108] Council Regulation (EC) No 1206/2001 of 28 May 2001 on cooperation between the courts of the Member States in the taking of evidence in civil or commercial matters [2001] OJ L174/1.

spectrum), learning difficulties, communication problems, traumatised backgrounds, and/or who might suffer intimidation for reasons of (non-exclusively) domestic violence/honour-based violence/forced marriage. There are potential European Convention on Human Rights, Articles 6 and 8 (see pages 20–21) breaches of the rights of vulnerable parties in family proceedings where an ad hoc approach is taken towards them in proceedings (*Re M (A Child)*,[109] *Wiltshire Council v N*,[110] *Re C (A Child)*[111]). The court must always deal with cases 'justly, having regard to any welfare issues involved' (FPR 2010, rule 1.1(1)). See The Advocacy Training Council guidance on The Advocate's Gateway website (www.advocacytrainingcouncil.org/vulnerable-witnesses/advocates-gateway) and related toolkits.

Vulnerable witnesses frequently appear in children cases, particularly in public law cases, and there is a need for intermediaries for vulnerable witnesses, and representation for LiPs (see Litigants in Person, page 27) who would otherwise seek to cross-examine a vulnerable witness. Public funding arrangements for intermediaries outside court for the purposes of meetings with professionals, particularly legal advisers, are currently unsatisfactory and an urgent review is required:

> Failure to provide sufficient and adequate support for vulnerable and intimidated witnesses whether they are children, young people or adults, results in a concomitant failure in their ability to give their best evidence, in turn directly undermining the likelihood of the judge or tribunal reaching a fair decision; it is justice denied.[112]

The Vulnerable Witnesses & Children Working Group has proposed a new FPR 2010, rule 3B which will provide for any witness, including a party, who is identified as vulnerable to be entitled to assistance in order to give evidence coherently, accurately and completely. There will be a duty on representatives and LiPs to identify whether any party or witness is vulnerable, and to seek directions of the court as soon as practicable regarding appropriate measures to be provided to enable the witness to give his/her best evidence. The importance of the new rule is to be emphasised by an amendment to the overriding objective in rule 1.1, by addition to the matters included in 'dealing with a case justly' of: 'make provision for vulnerable parties and witnesses and children to assist them in improving the quality of their evidence and to participate fully in proceedings'.

(*Source*: The Advocacy Training Council was the original source of publication for the guidance about the provision of evidence of children and vulnerable witnesses.)

See also Chapter 4, 'Children giving evidence' (above) and 'Hearings including parents with disabilities' (above).

---

[109] *Re M (A Child)* [2012] EWCA Civ 1905.
[110] *Wiltshire Council v N* [2013] EWHC 3502 (Fam) at [76] per Baker J.
[111] *Re C (A Child)* [2014] EWCA Civ 128, McFarlane LJ.
[112] *Report of the Vulnerable Witnesses & Children Working Group* (2015).

WARDSHIP

Wardship has been described as the 'parental jurisdiction' of the High Court. After a child has been made a ward of court, it is the court which retains ultimate responsibility for him/her.

Automatic protection

The issue of an application in Form C66 applying for wardship automatically makes the subject child a ward of court (Senior Courts Act 1981, section 41(2); see also *Re R (Minors) (Wardship: Jurisdiction).*[113]

From the moment the originating application for wardship is issued, a ward cannot leave or be removed from England and Wales, without the consent of the court: the court has power to order the surrender of a passport issued with respect to him/her, to prevent removal.

FPR 2010, PD12D – Inherent Jurisdiction (Including Wardship) Proceedings (see Chapter 7):

> 1.1 – It is the duty of the court under its inherent jurisdiction to ensure that a child who is the subject of proceedings is protected and properly taken care of. The court may in exercising its inherent jurisdiction make any order or determine any issue in respect of a child unless limited by case law or statute. Such proceedings should not be commenced unless it is clear that the issues concerning the child cannot be resolved under the Children Act 1989.
>
> 1.2 – The court may under its inherent jurisdiction, in addition to all of the orders which can be made in family proceedings, make a wide range of injunctions for the child's protection of which the following are the most common –
> (a)   orders to restrain publicity;
> (b)   orders to prevent an undesirable association;
> (c)   orders relating to medical treatment;
> (d)   orders to protect abducted children, or children where the case has another substantial foreign element; and
> (e)   orders for the return of children to and from another state.
>
> 1.3 – The court's wardship jurisdiction is part of and not separate from the court's inherent jurisdiction. The distinguishing characteristics of wardship are that –
> (a)   custody of a child who is a ward is vested in the court; and
> (b)   although day to day care and control of the ward is given to an individual or to a local authority, no important step can be taken in the child's life without the court's consent.

FPR 2010, Chapter V – rules 12.36–12.42 (see Chapter 7).

Children Act 1989, section 100 – restrictions on use of wardship jurisdiction.

---

[113] *Re R (Minors) (Wardship: Jurisdiction)* (1981) 2 FLR 416 at 419C.

Children Act 1989, section 91(4) – the making of a care order with respect to a child who is a ward of court brings that wardship to an end.

In *T v S (Wardship)*,[114] wardship jurisdiction was invoked for a 4-year-old child in a high conflict case where there was a likelihood that the court would be required to determine issues relating to the exercise of parental responsibility on an ongoing basis. Despite the court having made a number of section 8 orders, the parents had effectively abrogated parental responsibility because of their incessant conflict and there were many issues on which the parents were unable to agree including issues of medical treatment, travel abroad and residence. Hedley J ordered that each parent should have care and control of the child under the wardship jurisdiction during the time the child spent with them, holding that it was appropriate to make such an order in preference to a residence order because a residence order had assumed 'totemic status' in the parents' minds and was itself creating disputes. In respect of any matter on which the parents agreed, they should exercise parental responsibility and the court would otherwise direct how parental responsibility was to be exercised.

In *Re M (Children)*,[115] the President indicated a range of circumstances in which a child who was a British subject might be made a ward of court, even if the child was outside the jurisdiction, including fears that a forced marriage might take place, or female genital mutilation, or travel to a dangerous war zone.

WELFARE CHECK-LISTS

Children Act 1989:

    1 Welfare of the child.
    (1)   When a court determines any question with respect to—
        (a)   the upbringing of a child; or
        (b)   the administration of a child's property or the application of any income arising from it, the child's welfare shall be the court's paramount consideration.
    (2)   In any proceedings in which any question with respect to the upbringing of a child arises, the court shall have regard to the general principle that any delay in determining the question is likely to prejudice the welfare of the child.
    (3)   In the circumstances mentioned in subsection (4), a court shall have regard in particular to—
        (a)   the ascertainable wishes and feelings of the child concerned (considered in the light of his age and understanding);
        (b)   his physical, emotional and educational needs;
        (c)   the likely effect on him of any change in his circumstances;
        (d)   his age, sex, background and any characteristics of his which the court considers relevant;

---

[114] *T v S (Wardship)* [2011] EWHC 1608 (Fam).
[115] *Re M (Children)* [2015] EWHC 1433 (Fam).

- (e)   any harm which he has suffered or is at risk of suffering;
- (f)   how capable each of his parents, and any other person in relation to whom the court considers the question to be relevant, is of meeting his needs;
- (g)   the range of powers available to the court under this Act in the proceedings in question.

(4)   The circumstances are that—
- (a)   the court is considering whether to make, vary or discharge a section 8 order, and the making, variation or discharge of the order is opposed by any party to the proceedings; or
- (b)   the court is considering whether to make, vary or discharge [a special guardianship order or] an order under Part IV.

(5)   Where a court is considering whether or not to make one or more orders under this Act with respect to a child, it shall not make the order or any of the orders unless it considers that doing so would be better for the child than making no order at all.

Adoption and Children Act 2002:

1 Considerations applying to the exercise of powers

(1)   This section applies whenever a court or adoption agency is coming to a decision relating to the adoption of a child.

(2)   The paramount consideration of the court or adoption agency must be the child's welfare, throughout his life.

(3)   The court or adoption agency must at all times bear in mind that, in general, any delay in coming to the decision is likely to prejudice the child's welfare.

(4)   The court or adoption agency must have regard to the following matters (among others)—
- (a)   the child's ascertainable wishes and feelings regarding the decision (considered in the light of the child's age and understanding),
- (b)   the child's particular needs,
- (c)   the likely effect on the child (throughout his life) of having ceased to be a member of the original family and become an adopted person,
- (d)   the child's age, sex, background and any of the child's characteristics which the court or agency considers relevant,
- (e)   any harm (within the meaning of the Children Act 1989 (c. 41)) which the child has suffered or is at risk of suffering,
- (f)   the relationship which the child has with relatives, and with any other person in relation to whom the court or agency considers the relationship to be relevant, including—
  - (i)   the likelihood of any such relationship continuing and the value to the child of its doing so,
  - (ii)   the ability and willingness of any of the child's relatives, or of any such person, to provide the child with a secure environment in which the child can develop, and otherwise to meet the child's needs,
  - (iii) the wishes and feelings of any of the child's relatives, or of any such person, regarding the child.

(5)   In placing the child for adoption, the adoption agency must give due consideration to the child's religious persuasion, racial origin and cultural and linguistic background.

(6)   The court or adoption agency must always consider the whole range of powers available to it in the child's case (whether under this Act or the Children Act 1989); and the court must not make any order under this Act unless it considers that making the order would be better for the child than not doing so.

(7)   ...

(8)   ...

(9)   ...

Chapter 2

Financial Remedies

As background to this topic, it is worth bearing in mind the recent work and recommendations of the Financial Remedies Working Group (the group).

2.1 THE MONEY ARRANGEMENTS PROGRAMME (MAP)

The group was set up in June 2014 to look into '... ways of further improving good practice in financial remedy cases ... confined to matters of practice and procedure'.[1] The aim was to simplify and streamline the procedure for financial remedy proceedings. The outcome was MAP, which was published in early 2014. It is divided into four sections: Procedure, Litigants in person, Standard forms and Family arbitration.

2.1.1 Procedure

A single procedure for all applications was recommended. Every application should also be deemed to include all applications that a party might have made in relation to any financial issues irrespective of whether they have been made. Financial applications should be separated from divorce/dissolution proceedings.

The first appointment should be used to fix the FDR as soon as possible.

2.1.2 Litigants in person

The group recommended the guide entitled 'Apply for a financial order without the help of a lawyer'.[2] This is a comprehensive step-by-step guide to financial remedy proceedings and has useful links to other sites, including court forms, the substantive law and legal aid. It has a useful guide to the completion of Form E.

---

[1]   See *Report of the Financial Remedies Working Group*, 31 July 2014.
[2]   www.advicenow.org.uk/advicenow-guides/family/applying-for-a-financial-order-without-the-help-of-a-lawyer.

Other recommended websites include 'Money and property when a relationship ends', which has easy-to-use links to the relevant forms,[3] and one which has useful documents including draft documents for the first appointment.[4]

There was approval of the assistance given to litigants-in-person by McKenzie friends, particularly with organising documents and taking notes in court.

2.1.3   Standard forms

The group recommended the adoption of standard form orders for use in financial remedy cases.[5] These will have the status of forms within FPR 2010. It recommended that there should only be one type of Form A and Form E.

2.1.4   Family arbitration

The group supported arbitration and the swift endorsement of arbitration awards by the Family Court of the Family Division.

2.2   NUPTIAL AGREEMENTS

Agreements are one of the 'circumstances' that the court under Matrimonial Causes Act 1973 (MCA 1973), section 25 must take into account. They fall into three categories:

- pre-nuptial;
- post-nuptial; and
- agreements to settle litigation.

2.2.1   Pre- and post-nuptial agreements

In *Radmacher (formerly Granatino) v Granatino*,[6] the Supreme Court stated that when considering the validity of a pre- or post-nuptial agreement, the same principles will be applied. The correct approach to such agreements is governed by the following guidance:

> The court should give effect to a nuptial agreement that is freely entered into by each party with a full appreciation of its implications unless in the circumstances prevailing it would not be fair to hold the parties to their agreement. (at [75])

What then are the factors, which might result in the court ruling that the agreement was not entered into freely? The court will take into account the circumstances of the parties at the time of the agreement, their age and maturity, whether either or both had

---

3   www.gov.uk/money-property-when-relationship-ends/overview.
4   www.nofamilylawyer.co.uk.
5   See *Report of the Financial Remedies Working Group*, 31 July 2014, pp 277ff.
6   *Radmacher (formerly Granatino) v Granatino* [2010] UKSC 42, [2010] 2 FLR 1900.

been married or been in long-term relationships before and whether the marriage would have gone ahead without an agreement or without the terms which had been agreed. Against this background, the Supreme Court analysed the following factors:

- Material lack of disclosure or information and lack of sound legal advice.[7] It is important that each party should have all the information that is material to his/her decision, and that each party should intend that the agreement should govern the financial consequences of the marriage coming to an end.[8] If it can be shown that the party was financially and legally astute enough to appreciate what they were forgoing, the advice or disclosure required may be less onerous.[9] Where the language and purpose of the agreement is plainly intelligible, the level of advice necessary may be lower.[10] Where it is found that the party was indifferent to the absence of advice or disclosure, this could prevent that deficiency being material.[11] Similarly, where a party would not have acted any differently if advice or disclosure had been provided.[12]
- There must have been a genuine intention that the agreement should be effective. The parties need to demonstrate a commonality of intention with regard to the purpose of their agreement. Where there is an agreement to adopt a specific marital property regime, the parties must also demonstrate an intention that the agreement be binding and determinative upon divorce.
- Duress, misrepresentation, illegality or fraud.
- Unconscionable conduct such as undue pressure.
- Exploitation of a dominant position to secure an advantage.

In what circumstances might the court rule that it would not be fair to hold the parties to the agreement? The following circumstances were considered:

- *Children of the family*: a nuptial agreement must not prejudice the reasonable requirements of the children of the family.
- *Where non-matrimonial property is owned by one or both parties at the date of the marriage or at a later date*: there is nothing inherently unfair about making arrangements for this in the event of the marriage dissolving.
- *Future circumstances*: events, unknown or unforeseen at the time of contingency agreements, can lead to unfairness. The parties' circumstances can change in ways, or to an extent, which could not have been envisaged. If

---

7   *Kremen v Agrest* [2012] EWHC 45 (Fam), [2012] 2 FLR 414 at [72].

8   *Radmacher (formerly Granatino) v Granatino* [2010] UKSC 42, [2010] 2 FLR 1900 at [71]–[73].

9   *V v V (Ancillary Relief: Pre-Nuptial Agreement)* [2011] EWHC 3230 (Fam), [2012] 1 FLR 1315 at [48]; *BN v MA* [2013] EWHC 4250 (Fam) at [30]; *AH v PH* [2013] EWHC 3873 (Fam), [2014] 2 FLR 251 at [58].

10 *V v V (Ancillary Relief: Pre-Nuptial Agreement)* [2011] EWHC 3230 (Fam), [2012] 1 FLR 1315 at [50].

11 *V v V (Ancillary Relief: Pre-Nuptial Agreement)* [2011] EWHC 3230 (Fam), [2012] 1 FLR 1315 at [49] and [52].

12 *V v V (Ancillary Relief: Pre-Nuptial Agreement)* [2011] EWHC 3230 (Fam), [2012] 1 FLR 1315 at [49] and [52].

such a change resulted in one party experiencing real need while the other enjoyed excess, it is likely that the agreement would be deemed unfair. A husband, after signing a pre-nuptial agreement that he would make no claim, either during or after marriage, on the wife's separate property or gifts made to her by her wealthy family, was left without a home, income, capital and borrowing capacity; furthermore, he had considerable debts. In these circumstances, he was deemed to be in real need.[13]

2.2.2   *Radmacher (formerly Granatino) v Granatino* in practice

A marriage settlement was not, at first instance, given the weight it should have been, when an award had been made in lieu. The agreement provided a compelling reason for departing from an equal division of assets and was upheld.[14]

On the other hand, where legal advice and full disclosure had been absent, a party could probably not be said to have freely entered into a marital agreement with full appreciation and acceptance of its implications.[15] Similarly, where neither party had a complete understanding of what a post-marriage agreement meant, there was, consequently, no common understanding; the agreement was, in these circumstances, ignored.[16]

Where the wife had signed a post-nuptial agreement, in circumstances where she had been repeatedly and clearly advised as to the likely consequences of such an agreement, she failed in her attempt to vitiate the agreement on the grounds of duress.[17] This case provides a helpful example of the application of *Radmacher (formerly Granatino) v Granatino*.[18]

A pre-nuptial agreement should be applied in the context of an application for an interim remedy, namely, maintenance pending suit. The court should seek to apply the terms of such an agreement as closely and as practically as it can, unless the court can be persuaded that the agreement should not be upheld.[19]

While the court may not hold the parties strictly to their agreement, the pre-nuptial agreement may remain one of the circumstances of the case:[20]

---

13   *Luckwell v Limata* [2014] EWHC 502 (Fam).
14   *V v V (Prenuptial Agreement)* [2011] EWHC 3230 (Fam), [2012] 1 FLR 1315.
15   *Kremen v Agrest (Financial Remedy: Non-Disclosure: Post-Nuptial Agreement)* [2012] EWHC 45 (Fam).
16   *GS v L (Financial Remedies: Pre-acquired Assets: Need)* [2011] EWHC 1759 (Fam).
17   *Hopkins v Hopkins* [2015] EWHC 812 (Fam).
18   *Radmacher (formerly Granatino) v Granatino* [2010] UKSC 42, [2010] 2 FLR 1900.
19   *BN v MA* [2013] EWHC 4250 (Fam).
20   *AH v PH* [2013] EWHC 3873 (Fam); *Y v Y* [2014] EWHC 2920 (Fam) at [110].

- A nuptial agreement does not have to deal with all aspects of the parties' resources so as to be presumptively binding over the assets or resources which it addresses.[21]
- A nuptial agreement that is signed within days of the marriage may be upheld; if the agreement has been subject to some prior negotiation or adequate legal advice has been received, the timing may not matter.[22]

Where a nuptial agreement is not upheld, the terms that are favourable to the successful party should not be singled out and enforced as part of the MCA 1973, section 25 exercise.[23]

2.3 MEDIATION

Dispute resolution is encouraged by FPR 2010, Part 3 (Pre-Application Protocol for Mediation Information and Assessment (annexed to PD3A). Most applicants for financial orders must attend a mediation information and assessment meeting (MIAM) before the issue of any application.[24] The protocol requires a potential applicant to consider with a mediator whether their dispute can be resolved through alternative dispute resolution processes. Subject to the exemptions set out in FPR 2010, PD3A, Annex C, all applicants in relevant family proceedings must comply with the protocol. The Family Mediation Information and Assessment Form[25] must be filed with any application made to the court. Mediation may involve both parties or the mediator may invite the parties to attend separately. Even when the court process is engaged, the possibility of adjourning for further attempts at dispute resolution is encouraged.[26] An unreasonable refusal to engage in mediation may lead to an adverse costs order. Similarly an insistence on an expensive mediator and legal representation could also lead to such an order.[27]

FPR 2010, PD3A, Annex B defines 'relevant family proceedings' as:

1.   Private law proceedings relating to children, except:
     - proceedings for an enforcement order, financial compensation order or order under paragraph 9 or part 2 of Schedule A1 to the Children Act 1989;
     - any other proceedings for enforcement of an order made in private law proceedings; or

---

21   *SA v PA (Premarital Agreement: Compensation)* [2014] EWHC 392 (Fam), [2014] 2 FLR 1028 at [14].
22   *AH v PH* [2013] EWHC 3873 (Fam), [2014] 2 FLR 251 at [12]; *SA v PA (Premarital Agreement: Compensation)* [2014] EWHC 392 (Fam), [2014] 2 FLR 1028 at [63].
23   *AH v PH* [2013] EWHC 3873 (Fam), [2014] 2 FLR 251 at [68].
24   FPR 2010, PD3A.
25   Form FM1.
26   FPR 2010, r 3.3.
27   *H v W (Costs)* [2014] EWHC 2846 (Fam).

- where emergency proceedings have been brought in respect of the same child(ren) and have not been determined.[28]

2. Proceedings for a financial remedy, except:
   - proceedings for an avoidance of disposition order or an order preventing a disposition;
   - proceedings for enforcement of any order made in financial remedy proceedings.

'Financial remedy' is defined by FPR 2010, rule 2.3[29] as:

(a) an avoidance of disposition order;

(b) an order for maintenance pending suit;

(c) an order for maintenance pending outcome of proceedings;

(d) an order for periodical payments or lump sum provision as mentioned in section 21(1) of the 1973 Act, except an order under section 27(6) of that Act;

(e) an order for periodical payments or lump sum provision as mentioned in paragraph 2(1) of Schedule 5 to the 2004 Act, made under Part 1 of Schedule 5 to that Act;

(f) a property adjustment order;

(g) a variation order;

(h) a pension sharing order; or

(i) a pension compensation sharing order.

2.3.1 Exemptions from mediation

Where the mediator is satisfied that mediation is not suitable because:

- another party to the dispute is unwilling to attend a MIAM and consider mediation;
- the case is not suitable for a MIAM; or
- a determination by a mediator within the previous 4 months has been made that the case is not suitable for a MIAM or for mediation.

Where any of the following circumstances apply:

- Any party has, to your client's knowledge, made an allegation of domestic violence against another party and this has resulted in a police investigation or the issuing of civil proceedings for the protection of any party within the last 12 months.
- The dispute concerns financial issues and your client or another party is bankrupt.
- The parties are in agreement and there is no dispute to mediate.
- The whereabouts of the other party are unknown to your client.
- The prospective application is for an order in relevant family proceedings, which are already in existence and are continuing.

---

[28] FPR 2010, r 12.2 defines 'private law proceedings' and 'emergency proceedings'.
[29] FPR 2010, r 2.3(1).

- The prospective application is to be made without notice to the other party.
- The prospective application is urgent, meaning:
  - there is a real risk to the life, liberty or physical safety of your client or his or her family or his or her home;
  - any delay caused by attending a MIAM would cause a risk of significant harm to a child, a significant risk of miscarriage of justice, unreasonable hardship to your client or irretrievable problems in dealing with the dispute, such as an irretrievable loss of significant evidence;
  - there is current social services involvement as a result of child protection concerns in respect of any child, who would be the subject of the prospective application;
  - a child would be party to the prospective application by virtue of FPR 2010, rule 12.3(1);
  - you or your client contact(s) three mediators within 15 miles of your client's home and none is able to conduct a MIAM within 15 working days of the date of contact.

2.3.2   Family mediation funding

From 3 November 2014, financially ineligible parties are exempt from the financial means test in respect of the first mediation session where the other party is financially eligible for legal aid. The Legal Aid Agency (LAA) will pay half a single session mediation fee for the first session only in relation to the ineligible party. For all subsequent mediation sessions following the first session, legal aid will only be available for parties eligible for legal aid.

2.4   PROCEDURE BEFORE FIRST APPOINTMENT

The procedure in the High Court and county courts is governed by FPR 2010, rule 9.14 and is as follows:

- Exchange and filing of Form E not less than 35 days before.[30]
- Form E must be:
  - verified by a statement of truth;
  - supported by financial documents and any other documents necessary to explain or clarify information therein; these include any property valuation obtained within the last 6 months, bank statements, accounts for the last two years to be used to value any business, income from the business, and the three last pay slips and P60;
  - supported by a financial statement with regard to any pension arrangement or valuation.
- Not less than 14 days before, each party must file with the court and serve on the other party the following:[31]

---

[30]   FPR 2010, r 9.14(1).
[31]   FPR 2010, r 9.14(5).

- – a concise statement of the issues between the parties;
- – a chronology;
- – a questionnaire requesting further information and documents with regard to the statement of issues or a statement that no information or documents are required;
- – a notice stating whether that party will be in a position to at the first appointment to proceed to a financial dispute resolution (FDR).[32]
- Not less than 14 days before, the parties should, if possible, with a view to identifying and narrowing any issues between them, exchange and file:
  - – a summary of the case agreed between the parties;
  - – a schedule of assets agreed between the parties;
  - – details of any direction they seek, for example, the appointment of an expert.
- A paginated bundle (using Arabic numbering throughout),[33] arranged chronologically in the usual format – preliminary documents/applications/ orders/statements/expert reports[34] – to be lodged 2 days before the hearing.[35] The preliminary documents must be as short and succinct as possible,[36] cross-referenced against the bundle,[37] and dated on the first page. They must include:
  - – an up-to-date case summary 'confined to matters which are relevant to the hearing' and limited, if practicable, to four A4 pages,[38] to be agreed at a final hearing (and also, if possible, at earlier hearings).[39] Where there is disagreement, the respective positions should be identified on the document;[40]
  - – a statement of issues;
  - – position statements;
  - – where appropriate (not required, if case summary is sufficient) a chronology,[41] skeleton arguments;
  - – a time estimate which should be agreed specifying:
    - time for judicial pre-reading;
    - time required for evidence and submissions;
    - time for preparing and delivering judgment.[42]

It should be noted that the bundle should only include documents relevant for the hearing and should not include bank and credit card statements and other financial records unless specifically directed by the court.[43]

---

[32]   Form G.
[33]   FPR 2010, PD27A, para 4.2.
[34]   FPR 2010, PD27A, para 4.2.
[35]   FPR 2010, PD27A, para 6.3.
[36]   FPR 2010, PD27A, para 4.4.
[37]   FPR 2010, PD27A, para 4.5.
[38]   FPR 2010, PD27A, para 4.3(a).
[39]   FPR 2010, PD27A, para 4.6.
[40]   FPR 2010, PD27A, para 4.6.
[41]   FPR 2010, PD27A, para 4.3(d).
[42]   FPR 2010, PD27A, para 10.1.
[43]   FPR 2010, PD27A, para 4.1(c).

All of the above documents must be copied on one side of paper and printed in a font no smaller than 12 point with 1½ or double spacing.

The applicant must prepare the bundle or, where the applicant is a litigant in person, the respondent, if he/she is legally represented.

Each party must produce at the first appointment a written estimate of the solicitor and client costs hitherto incurred.[44]

The importance of following PD27A has recently been stressed.[45]

2.5   THE FIRST APPOINTMENT

The purpose of the first appointment is to define the issues and save costs. In straightforward cases, however, it may be possible to use the first appointment as an FDR hearing.

With regard to information and documents, the court will determine the following:

- the extent to which questions must be answered. Questions that do not advance the main issues in the case should not be permitted;
- documents, requested, that need to be produced;
- the production of further documents, if necessary.

The court must give directions, where appropriate, about the:

- valuation of assets (including the joint instruction of experts);
- obtaining and exchanging of expert evidence, if required;
- evidence to be adduced by each party;
- further chronologies or schedules to be filed by each party.

The court can also:

- use the first appointment as an FDR having regard to the notices filed by the parties;
- make an interim order, where applied for;
- direct any party with pension rights to file and serve a Pension Inquiry Form;
- direct any party with Pension Protection Fund (PPF) compensation rights to file and serve a PPF Inquiry Form.

---

[44]   FPR 2010, r 9.27(1).
[45]   *Re L (A Child)* [2015] EWFC 15.

Interim orders can include orders for the filing of narrative statements[46] or the inspection or preservation of property.[47]

The court can refer the case for an FDR appointment. If not, the case must be set down for a further directions appointment or an appointment at which an interim order will be made or the case must be fixed for a final hearing.

The court can use the first appointment as an FDR hearing.

Between the first appointment and the FDR appointment, a party is not entitled to the production of any further documents except with the permission of the court.[48] A party may apply for a further directions hearing.[49]

2.6   THE FDR APPOINTMENT

The FDR is held so as discussion and negotiation can take place.[50] The judge hearing the FDR appointment must take no further part in the proceedings apart from sitting on a further FDR appointment or making a consent order or a further directions order.

Not less than 7 days before the FDR appointment, the applicant must file with the court details of all offers and proposals, and responses. This includes those made wholly or partly without prejudice. After the FDR appointment, none of the above documents must be held on the court file.

Parties attending the FDR appointment must use their best endeavours to reach agreement on the issues between them.[51] The court will expect the parties to make offers and proposals, and for these to be given proper consideration.[52] The FDR appointment may be adjourned or, if a settlement is reached, the court will make an appropriate consent order.

In the spirit of trying to achieve a successful resolution, the parties must approach the appointment openly and without reserve. In keeping with this, evidence of anything said or any admission made will not be admissible in evidence except at the trial of a person for an offence committed at the appointment or in very exceptional circumstances.[53]

---

[46] *W v W (Ancillary Relief: Practice)* [2000] Fam Law 473.
[47] FPR 2010, Part 20.
[48] FPR 2010, r 9.16.
[49] FPR 2010, r 9.16(2).
[50] FPR 2010, r 9.17.
[51] FPR 2010, r 9.17(6).
[52] FPR 2010, PD9A, para 6.3.
[53] *Re D (Minors) (Conciliation: Disclosure of Information)* [1993] Fam 231.

If the matter is not concluded at the FDR appointment, the court must give directions for the filing of evidence, including up-to-date information, and fix a final hearing date.

2.7 FINAL HEARING

The district judge who presided over the FDR appointment will not conduct the final hearing.

The applicant must file and serve a concise statement setting out the type of order/orders, which he/she wants the court to make, not less than 14 days before the hearing and the respondent must reply within 7 days thereafter. These are open offers as they do not attract privilege.[54]

2.8 MAINTENANCE

Maintenance or periodical payments orders are usually sought together with property adjustment and lump sum orders.[55] A party to the marriage or a child of the family may apply. No such application can be made by a party who has remarried.[56]

The court will consider the factors set out in MCA 1973, section 25.[57] The court will look, broadly, at the overall position rather than enter upon a detailed investigation of household budgets.[58] Maintenance can be used to compensate for any capital imbalance between the parties.[59] The court is obliged to consider whether the financial obligations of the parties to each other should be terminated or for how long the maintenance should be paid.[60] Attention should focus on the needs of the parties and whether those needs can be met. Such an analysis will include the following factors:

- need;
- earning and potential earning capacity;
- cohabitation and length of the marriage;
- conduct.

---

[54] FPR 2010, r 9.28.
[55] A maintenance order made or registered in the magistrates' court before 22 April 2014 will be treated as if it had been an order of the family court.
[56] MCA 1973, s 28(3).
[57] MCA 1973, s 25(2)(a)–(h).
[58] *Stockford v Stockford* (1982) 3 FLR 58, CA.
[59] *McFarlane v McFarlane* [2006] UKHL 24, [2006] 1 FLR 1186, HL; *Parlour v Parlour* [2004] EWCA Civ 872.
[60] MCA 1973, ss 25(A)(1) and 25(A)(2).

2.8.1   Need

The 'financial needs, obligations and responsibilities' of the applicant is the first of the MCA 1973, section 25 factors to consider.[61] What does the applicant need to maintain a standard of living, which is appropriate given the other section 25 factors such as length of the marriage, standard of living enjoyed by the parties during the marriage and their contributions? The court will subtract from this figure the net income of the applicant, actual or potential, retirement pension, child benefit and any benefits which could be applied for.

The court will then consider how the other party can pay for those needs. Again, the court will look at that party's 'financial needs, obligations and responsibilities', his/her means and all the other MCA 1973, section 25 factors.

It is important to prepare a 'net effect schedule' following each party's proposals and to contrast this with his/her reasonable needs as examined above.

Where there is no need for financial support or it is clear that there are insufficient resources from which such payments could be made, the court is likely to terminate the parties' obligations towards each other and order a clean break.

2.8.2   Earning and potential earning capacity

The court must consider the current and the future financial position of the parties. Is it reasonable to expect a party to improve his/her financial prospects?[62] Is it reasonable or likely that a party could or should become financially independent? The court will consider the parties' financial positions were they to exploit opportunities for increasing their earnings.

2.8.3   Cohabitation and length of marriage

Pre-marriage cohabitation can be added to the length of the marriage, particularly where the relationship has moved seamlessly from cohabitation to marriage; it can be seen as a contribution or conduct under MCA 1973, section 25.[63] The court will consider the date of separation rather than decree absolute as the end of the marriage.[64] While all the section 25 factors should be considered,[65] they may be of less relevance in a short marriage. A child would clearly make the award of maintenance likely.

---

[61]   MCA 1973, s 25(2)(b).
[62]   MCA 1973, s 25(2)(a).
[63]   *Co v Co (Ancillary Relief – Pre-marriage Cohabitation)* [2004] EWHC 287 (Fam), [2004] 1 FLR 1095; *M v M (Financial Relief – Substantial Earning Capacity)* [2004] EWHC 688 (Fam), [2004] 2 FLR 236.
[64]   *GW v RW (Financial Provision – Departure from Equality)* [2003] EWHC 611 (Fam), [2003] 2 FLR 108.
[65]   *Foster v Foster* [2003] EWCA Civ 565, [2003] 2 FLR 299.

What amounts to cohabitation? It is not to be equated with marriage.[66] Elements including cohabiting in the same household, a sexual relationship, a daily life together, joint use of money, and whether there are any children, will help to determine this.[67]

Post-separation cohabitation is one of the circumstances, which the court must consider. It is relevant in so far as it impacts on the financial circumstances of the parties and their disposable income. The court should look behind the label of cohabitation and examine what this means, financially, to the parties.[68] Such an investigation will help determine how much weight should be given to this circumstance in assessing the correct level of spousal maintenance that is fair and just in all the circumstances.[69]

2.8.4 Conduct

If it would be inequitable to disregard the conduct of one of the parties, then the court must take it into consideration.[70] Financial misconduct such as the deliberate dissipation of assets or general dishonesty can amount to such conduct.[71] As can non-financial conduct, such as the sexual abuse by the husband of his grandchildren.[72] In practice, the courts rarely take conduct into account, except in 'the most obvious and gross cases'.[73]

2.8.5 Maintenance pending suit

An order for maintenance before decree absolute, nullity or judicial separation is referred to as maintenance pending suit. Such an order can be made once the divorce petition has been filed for an amount that the court thinks reasonable.[74] There is a corresponding jurisdiction for civil partners.[75]

Where the maintenance payments are to continue after decree absolute, the order should reflect this so that, after the decree absolute, maintenance pending suit would become interim periodical payments.

Maintenance pending suit can be backdated to the date when the petition for divorce, nullity or judicial separation was filed with the court.

---

[66] *Fleming v Fleming* [2003] EWCA Civ 1841, [2004] 1 FLR 667.

[67] *Kimber v Kimber* [2000] 1 FLR 383.

[68] *Atkinson v Atkinson* [1995] 2 FLR 356; *H v H (Financial Provision)* [2009] EWHC 494 (Fam), [2009] 2 FLR 795.

[69] *Fleming v Fleming* [2003] EWCA Civ 1841, [2004] 1 FLR 667.

[70] MCA 1973, s 25(2)(g).

[71] *Martin v Martin* [1976] Fam 335; *H v H (Financial Relief: Conduct)* [1999] 1 FCR 225.

[72] *C v T* [2009] All ER (D) 43.

[73] *Wachtel v Wachtel* [1973] 1 All ER 829.

[74] MCA 1973, s 22. See *TL v ML* [2005] EWHC 2680 (Fam), [2006] 1 FLR 1263; *S v M (Maintenance Pending Suit)* [2012] EWHC 4109 (Fam), [2013] 1 FLR 1173.

[75] Civil Partnership Act 2004, Sch 5, Part 8.

The court will address the factors under MCA 1973, section 25 but from a short-term perspective pending the final determination. This usually means the applicant's immediate needs, which can include legal costs.[76] In determining what is reasonable, account will be taken of the marital standard of living. The parties should prepare a specific maintenance pending suit budget, which excludes capital or long-term expenditure.[77]

A party to the marriage or a child of the family may apply at any stage of the proceedings for:

(a)   an order for maintenance pending suit;
(b)   an order for maintenance pending outcome of proceedings;
(c)   an order for interim periodical payments;
(d)   an interim variation order; or
(e)   any other form of interim order.

2.8.6   Procedure

The FPR 2010, Part 18 procedure applies to an application for an interim order.[78] An application for maintenance pending suit must attach:

(a)   a draft order;[79]
(b)   written evidence in support where the application is made before the Form E has been filed. This evidence must explain why the order is necessary and give up-to-date information about that party's financial circumstances.[80]

Such an application must be served at least 14 days before the court deals with the application.[81] The court has the power to shorten this time frame.[82]

If the respondent has not filed a Form E, he/she must file a statement of his/her means and serve it on the applicant, at least 7 days before the court is to deal with the application.[83]

2.8.7   Key points

- FPR 2010, Part 18 procedure applies.
- In pre-Form E situations, draft order and evidence in support needed.

---

[76] *A v A (Maintenance Pending Suit: Provision for Legal Fees)* [2001] 1 FLR 377; *Currey v Currey* [2006] EWCA Civ 1338, [2007] 1 FLR 946; *Re S (Child: Financial Provision)* [2004] EWCA Civ 1685, [2005] 2 FLR 94; *G v G* [2009] EWHC 494 (Fam).

[77] *TL v ML and Others* [2005] EWHC 2860 (Fam).

[78] FPR 2010, r 9.7(2).

[79] FPR 2010, r 18.7(2).

[80] FPR 2010, r 9.7(3).

[81] FPR 2010, r 18.8(1).

[82] FPR 2010, r 4.1(3).

[83] FPR 2010, r 9.7(4).

- Serve the respondent at least 14 days before the hearing.
- Time for maintenance pending suit hearings often limited to an hour. Core bundle helpful in these circumstances.

2.8.8   Powers to vary, discharge or suspend orders

'Final orders' cannot normally be varied. In general, periodic orders can be varied while capital orders, apart from the detail, cannot. The powers to vary are contained in MCA 1973, section 31.

MCA 1973, section 31(2) provides that the following orders can be varied:

(a)   any order for maintenance pending suit and any interim order for maintenance;
(b)   any periodical payments order;
(c)   any secured periodical payments order;
(d)   any order made by virtue of section 23(3)(c) or 27(7)(b) above (provision for payment of a lump sum by instalments);
(dd) any deferred order made by virtue of section 23(1)(c) (lump sums) which includes provision made by virtue of—
    (i)   section 25B(4), or
    (ii)   section 25C
    (provision in respect of pension rights);
(e)   any order for a settlement of property under section 24(1)(b) or for a variation of settlement under section 24(1)(c) or (d) above, being an order made on or after the grant of a decree of judicial separation;
(f)   any order made under section 24A(1) above for the sale of property;
(g)   a pension sharing order under section 24B above which is made at a time before the decree has been made absolute.

2.8.9   Variation of maintenance orders

This applies to maintenance pending suit and periodical payments. MCA 1973, section 31(7) contains the principles, which govern the court's discretion:

> ... the court shall have regard to all the circumstances of the case, first consideration being given to the welfare while a minor of any child of the family who has not attained the age of eighteen ...

'Child of the family' includes any child who has been treated by both of the parties to the marriage as a child of their family.[84] This would include stepchildren. The child must be under 18 years of age. If the child is over 18, he/she would fall under one of the other factors to be considered, such as financial obligations or as one of the circumstances of the case, but not as the first consideration of the court. First consideration is not the same as paramount consideration.[85]

---

[84]   MCA 1973, s 52(1).
[85]   *Suter v Suter and Jones* [1987] Fam 111, CA; *R v R* [1988] 1 FLR 89, CA.

MCA 1973, section 31(7) continues:

> and the circumstances of the case shall include any change in any of the matters to which the court was required to have regard when making the order to which the application relates.[86]

MCA 1973, section 31(7)(a) provides that:

> ... in the case of a periodical or secured periodical payments order made on or after the grant of a decree of divorce or nullity of marriage, the court shall consider whether in all the circumstances and after having regard to any such change it would be appropriate to vary the order so that payments under the order are required to be made or secured only for such further period as will in the opinion of the court be sufficient ... to enable the party in whose favour the order was made to adjust without undue hardship to the termination of those payments.[87]

2.8.10   Change in circumstances

All relevant matters must be reviewed including any change in circumstances. The court will require some change in circumstances before it varies an order. Where the payer's income has risen, this can justify an upward variation in maintenance for the recipient, 'reasonable requirements' are not a determinative or limiting factor.[88]

MCA 1973, section 31 permits the recipient to apply for a lump sum instead of the maintenance payments. Capitalisation of maintenance can be particularly attractive when the recipient is in a relationship as, on marriage, the maintenance would cease. These were the circumstances in *Dixon v Marchant*,[89] in which, on appeal, it was argued, unsuccessfully, that a remarriage shortly after the capitalisation of maintenance was a *Barder* event.[90]

2.8.11   Maintenance agreements

Maintenance agreement means any agreement in writing made between the parties to a marriage being:

(a)   an agreement containing financial arrangements, whether made during the continuance or after the dissolution or annulment of the marriage; or

(b)   a separation agreement which contains no financial arrangements in a case where no other agreement in writing between the same parties contains such arrangements:

---

[86]   MCA 1973, s 31(7).
[87]   MCA 1973, s 31(7)(a).
[88]   *Hvorostovsky v Hvorostovsky* [2009] EWCA Civ 79.
[89]   *Dixon v Marchant*, 24 January 2008, unreported, CA.
[90]   *Barder v Caluori* [1988] AC 20.

'financial arrangements' means provisions governing the rights and liabilities towards one another when living separately of the parties to a marriage (including a marriage which has been dissolved or annulled) in respect of the making or securing of payments or the disposition or use of any property, including such rights and liabilities with respect to the maintenance or education of any child, whether or not a child of the family.[91]

Provided the parties do not seek to oust the court's jurisdiction, a maintenance agreement may be binding.[92]

2.8.12 Alteration of maintenance agreements

Either party may apply to the family court for their maintenance agreement to be altered. The court must be satisfied either:

(a) that by reason of a change in the circumstances in the light of which any financial arrangements contained in the agreement were made or, as the case may be, financial arrangements were omitted from it (including a change foreseen by the parties when making the agreement), the agreement should be altered so as to make different or, as the case may be so as to contain, financial arrangements, or

(b) that the agreement does not contain proper financial arrangements with respect to the child of the family.[93]

In these circumstances, the court may vary or revoke any financial arrangements contained in the agreement or insert into it such financial arrangements for the benefit of one of the parties to the agreement or of a child of the family as may appear to the court to be just having regard to all the circumstances.[94]

The court would be looking for a change in the circumstances in the light of which the financial arrangements were made, the sort of change which would make those arrangement manifestly unjust, or for a failure to make proper provision for any child of the family. While the court must be alive to the risk of unfair exploitation of superior strength, the mere fact that the agreement is not what a court would have done cannot be enough to have it set aside.[95]

2.8.13 Jurisdiction

From 22 April 2014, neither county courts nor magistrates' courts have any jurisdiction with regard to family proceedings, which includes proceedings for the enforcement of family orders. Proceedings that began in magistrates' courts before 22 April 2014 shall continue on the assumption that they had been issued in the Family

---

[91] MCA 1973, s 34(2)(a) and (b).
[92] MCA 1973, s 34(1)(a) and (b).
[93] MCA 1973, s 35(2)(a) and (b).
[94] MCA 1973, s 35(2)(b)(ii).
[95] *McLeod v McLeod* [2008] UKPC 64, Baroness Hale.

Court.[96] An application to enforce under FPR 2010, rule 33.3(2)(b) will result in an order to attend court, which can be enforced by committal if the debtor does not attend the hearing.

2.8.14 Methods of payment

Whenever a maintenance order is made or, at any time thereafter, the court may specify how the payment is to be made, such as by direct debit.[97] The court can make such an order on its own motion.

Arrears

The leave of the court is required to enforce arrears:

> ... due under an order for maintenance pending suit, an interim order for maintenance or any financial provision order without the leave of that court if those arrears became due more than twelve months before proceedings to enforce the payment of them began.[98]

The court may grant leave with conditions as to the terms and time of payment or it may remit the payment of the arrears or any part of them.[99]

Different methods of enforcement can be found in:

- FPR 2010, Part 33.
- CPR 1998, Parts 70 and 71.

Under FPR 2010, rule 33.3(1), any application to enforce must be made in a notice of application together with a statement, which must set out the amount due under the order and how the sum is arrived at. This must, in turn, be verified by a statement of truth.

The applicant must either consider which is the most appropriate method of enforcement, or leave it for the court to decide.[100] If the latter is chosen, the person served with an order must:[101]

- attend court at a time and place specified;
- produce at court documents as set out in the order;
- answer on oath such questions as the court may require.[102]

---

[96]   Crime and Courts Act 2013 (Family Court: Transitional and Saving Provision) Order 2014 (SI 2014/956).
[97]   Maintenance Enforcement Act 1991, s 1(3), (4) and (5).
[98]   MCA 1973, s 32(1).
[99]   MCA 1973, s 32(2).
[100] FPR 2010, r 33.3(2).
[101] FPR 2010, r 33.3(3).
[102] CPR 1998, r 71.2(6) and (7).

A penal notice will be attached requiring obedience otherwise the debtor may be in contempt and sent to prison as a consequence. In *Hope v Krejci*, a failure to comply with financial remedy orders requiring the husband to transfer cars and a motor cycle to his wife resulted in a contempt finding.[103]

Essentially, the debtor is obliged to produce all the evidence he/she can about his/her financial resources. The court could make one of the following orders:[104]

- judgment summons;
- attachment of earnings order;
- charging order, stop order or stop notice;
- third party debt order;
- writ or warrant of control (seizure or sale of personal property);
- appointment of a receiver.

Judgment summons

The judgment summons must be served on the debtor personally not less than 14 days before hearing. It must be served with a statement setting out:

(a) the amount due under the order;
(b) how that amount was calculated;
(c) all the evidence on which the creditor intends to rely including a copy of the order.[105]

The debtor must be offered reasonable travel expenses.[106]

He/she may not be compelled to give evidence.[107]

Attachment of earnings order

This involves the Family Court ordering that a certain sum be deducted from the debtor's earnings by his/her employer on a weekly or monthly basis. This will leave a protected earnings rate, which the debtor must be allowed to keep. Such an order can be applied to pension payments and can be used to recover an unpaid lump sum.[108]

Charging order

It is usual to obtain an interim charging order by filing a statement in support. Such an order must be served on any joint owner and on such other creditors as the court directs, who can, if they choose, be heard at the on notice final hearing at which the

---

[103] *Hope v Krejci* [2014] EWHC B5 (Fam).
[104] CPR 1998, PD70.
[105] FPR 2010, r 33.11(2).
[106] FPR 2010, r 33.11(3).
[107] FPR 2010, r 33.14(2).
[108] Attachment of Earnings Act 1971 and CCR, Ord 27.

court will determine whether a final charging order is made.[109] A charging order is usually made over real property but can be granted over shares or other forms of property. It is a security for the debt, which can be enforced by applying for an order for sale.

Third party debt order

Where the debtor is owed money by another, the court can order that sum to be paid directly to the creditor. An interim order is made upon the filing of a statement in support of the application. A date is then fixed for a hearing at which a final order could be made.[110]

Writ or warrant of control

This is the seizure and sale of the debtor's goods. In the High Court, a writ of *fieri facias* needs to be issued; in the Family Court, a warrant of control.[111]

Appointment of a receiver

A receiver may be appointed where it is 'just and convenient' to do so. An injunction or order may be made at the same time.[112]

2.8.15 Enforcement of foreign maintenance orders

FPR 2010, rule 33.3.

- The court chooses the most appropriate method for enforcement.
- Enforcement either in the Principal Registry of the Family Division or the Family Court.
- Maintenance Regulation.[113]
- Direct enforcement under Maintenance Regulation, Chapter IV.
- Traditional method of enforcement via the Lord Chancellor and the central authority under Maintenance Regulation, Chapter VII.

The advantage of the first method is that the payments go straight to the applicant.

The attraction of the second method is that it takes the burden of the progress of the application out of the applicant's hands.

---

[109] Charging Orders Act 1979 and CPR 1998, Part 73.
[110] CPR 1998, Part 72.
[111] RSC, Ord 47 and CCR, Ord 26.
[112] Senior Courts Act 1981, s 37(1) and County Courts Act 1984, s 38.
[113] Council Regulation (EC) No 4/2009 of 18 December 2008 on jurisdiction, applicable law, recognition and enforcement of decisions and cooperation in matters relating to maintenance obligations [2009] OJ L7/1 (Maintenance Regulation).

The Maintenance Regulation allows for the recognition and enforcement across Europe of maintenance orders made in any part of the European Union. It includes child support assessments.

Maintenance is given a much wider definition than just periodical payments. It has been interpreted by the European Court of Justice as akin to 'needs'. It could, therefore, include transfers of real property for the accommodation needs of one party and a lump sum constituting capitalised maintenance.

Direct enforcement

- Jurisdiction found in Maintenance Regulation, Article 41.
- Foreign order treated as if it were a domestic order.
- No need for any special or additional procedural steps if the decision to award maintenance was given in a state bound by the 2007 Hague Protocol.[114]
- Maintenance payments made directly to the applicant.

Indirect enforcement

- Will be enforced in the Family Court.
- Same powers as if the order had been made locally.
- Not the same powers as the court making the original order.

For the enforcement of an existing court order for child maintenance in another country, see the Reciprocal Enforcement of Maintenance Orders[115] Unit.[116]

2.9   AGREEMENTS TO SETTLE LITIGATION

The Court of Appeal has stated that an agreement to settle an ancillary relief application was not an agreement that was enforceable in law as ordinary contractual principles did not apply.[117] The court, ultimately, decides on an ancillary relief award. Whether an agreement has been reached is a matter for the court and in every case it must consider the MCA 1973, section 25 factors. The court does not, therefore, automatically 'rubber stamp' agreements.[118]

The Court of Appeal has, however, also stated that an agreement subject to the approval of the court was binding on the parties in so far as neither could resile from it.[119] It is not yet known how these two positions will be reconciled.

---

[114] Hague Protocol of 23 November 2007 on the Law Applicable to Maintenance Obligations. Maintenance Regulation, Article 17.

[115] REMO.

[116] www.gov.uk/remo-unit-helpline.

[117] *Xydhias v Xydhias* [1999] 1 FLR 683, CA.

[118] *Kelley v Corston* [1998] QB 686.

[119] *Soulsbury v Soulsbury* [2007] EWCA 969, [2008] 1 FLR 90, CA.

In the context of a maintenance pending suit application, it has been stated that:

> ... when adjudicating the question of interim maintenance, where there has been a prenuptial agreement, the court should seek to apply the terms of the prenuptial agreement *as closely and practically as it can*, unless the evidence of the wife in support of her application demonstrates, to a convincing standard, that she has a prospect of satisfying a court that the agreement should not be upheld.[120] (emphasis added)

2.10   DISCLOSURE

Applications for financial orders are governed by the FPR 2010, as amended by the Family Procedure (Amendment) Rules 2012,[121] which regulate disclosure in an orderly way and according to a strict timetable. The aim is to identify issues as early as possible while allowing disclosure that is proportionate to the issues in question. Achieving a fair resolution or order depends on there being full disclosure. The importance of being open and honest, where disclosure is concerned, needs to be emphasised to the parties.[122]

The parties must disclose 'facts, information and documents, which are material and sufficiently accurate to enable proper negotiations to take place to settle their differences'.[123] There is a duty to disclose developments on an ongoing basis without being asked.[124]

The duty to disclose extends to any fact within a party's knowledge that might materially affect the exercise of the court's discretion or powers while having regard to proportionality and expense.[125] Adverse inferences can be drawn from a failure to disclose. Orders for costs may be made on an indemnity or standard basis where there has been litigation misconduct.[126] This has a wide ambit and can include failure to comply with the rules, any order of the court or practice direction as well as the manner in which a party has responded to an allegation or issue. In certain circumstances, sanctions may be imposed on legal advisers.

A solicitor has a duty to disclose all relevant information to the client.[127] The duty of disclosure to clients must be reconciled with the duty of confidentiality to clients. Where this is not possible, the protection of confidential information prevails.

---

[120] *BN v MA* [2013] EWHC 4250 (Fam).
[121] SI 2012/679.
[122] *Guidance Notes: Disclosure in Financial Order Applications* (Resolution, 2014).
[123] FPR 2010, PD9A, para 11.
[124] FPR 2010, PD9A; *Livesey v Jenkins* [1985] 1 All ER 586.
[125] FPR 2010, r 1.1.
[126] FPR 2010, r 28.3(6).
[127] Solicitors' Code of Conduct, para 4.2.

A solicitor, as an officer of the court, has a duty not knowingly to permit a client to mislead the court by the provision of inaccurate or misleading information. Information could be imputed to a solicitor, where it has been disclosed to a different department within the same firm. It is essential that there is no conflict of interest within the firm and due consideration is given as to whether the firm can continue to represent the client in matrimonial proceedings.

Where there is voluntary disclosure before the issue of proceedings, the parties should exchange schedules of assets, income, liabilities and other material facts.[128] The Form E can be used as a guide. At the same time, costs should be reasonable and kept in proportion.[129]

Both parties and their legal representatives have a duty to make full and frank disclosure. Such disclosure relates to both facts and documents, and includes:

> ... a duty to provide information that would set the other side on a line of enquiry, or a thought process, on matters to which the court must have regard under s 25 MCA 1973 ... it includes a duty to inform the other side of information that <u>may</u> (a) result in the removal of uncertainty as to the value of assets, or the amount of a party's future income, or (b) inform the assessment of the income or earning capacity of a party to the marriage or the value of his or her assets.[130]

Disclosure should include estimates of discretionary bonuses or awards, negotiations in relation to the sale of a property or shares or to existing or new employment. The Form E requires 'an honest and conscientious estimation of the true net worth of the party' as well as a duty to 'give a presentation that is immediately understandable by a solicitor of average financial sophistication'.[131]

2.10.1 *OS/DS*[132] hearings

Non-disclosure often makes a settlement more unlikely. In such cases, there is often a plethora of allegations by each party concerning their assets, disclosed or otherwise.

2.10.2 Privilege and disclosure

Litigation privilege

In general, communications between parties to a dispute that are written or made with the aim of settling that dispute cannot be admitted in evidence.

---

[128] FPR 2010, PD9A, para 12.
[129] Pre-application protocol annexed to FPR 2010, PD9A, para 11.
[130] *I v I* [2008] EWHC 1167 (Fam) at [114].
[131] *GW v RW (Financial Provision – Departure from Equality)* [2003] EWHC 611 (Fam), [2003] 2 FLR 108; *W v W (Ancillary Relief: Non-disclosure)* [2003] EWHC 2254 (Fam).
[132] *OS v DS (Oral Disclosure: Preliminary Hearing)* [2004] EWHC 2376 (Fam).

'Without prejudice' privilege

Correspondence is often marked 'without prejudice'; this usually relates to an attempt to settle the case. Such correspondence will be privileged. Where, however, the correspondence refers to an admission or a statement of existing facts or refers to the strength of a party's case, it can be referred to in court, despite the 'without prejudice' label.

Privilege against self-incrimination

The FPR 2010 require the disclosure of all relevant information, even if it is incriminatory.[133] This flows logically from the duty imposed on the court by MCA 1973, section 25, as the purpose of this legislation would be frustrated if information or documents could be withheld on the ground that they might incriminate.

Only in very exceptional circumstances will evidence of anything said or of any admission made in the course of an FDR appointment be admissible in evidence.[134] Solicitors should advise their clients:

- to make a full and frank disclosure;
- on the consequences of any failure to do so in terms of both civil and criminal liability.

The position should be confirmed in writing. Clients should be advised to keep their documents safe at all times, particularly where they still share a home with the other party.

2.10.3 Confidential documents

A confidential document will include all documents connected with family or private life, personal and family assets or business dealings. This will cover bank statements, correspondence relating to business or personal finances, and also personal documentation such as diaries.[135] None of this will apply to joint assets, so joint bank account statements can be copied and sent to a solicitor.

'Confidentiality is not dependent upon locks and keys or their electronic equivalent'.[136] The fact that a document is not kept under lock and key or is left lying around the house does not mean that it is not confidential. What matters is how the parties conducted their affairs and what each knew the other would regard as confidential or not.

Where a client obtains privileged client/lawyer documentary information belonging to his/her spouse, the lawyer should make it clear that he/she does not want to know

---

[133] *R v K* [2009] EWCA Crim 1640, [2010] 1 FLR 809.

[134] *Re D (Minors) (Conciliation: Disclosure of Information)* [1993] Fam 231.

[135] *Guidance Notes: Disclosure in Financial Order Applications* (Resolution, 2014). See also *White v Withers LLP & Anor* [2009] EWCA Civ 1122.

[136] *Tchenguiz & ors v Imerman* [2010] EWCA Civ 908, [2010] 2 FLR 814.

about its contents and tell the client to destroy it, unread. Similarly, where a lawyer receives privileged information or documents from his/her client, the lawyer should return the information or document to the client, unread. The client, furthermore, should forward such information or documents directly to the lawyer on the other side. This prevents the lawyer coming into conflict with the client.

Where privileged communications are wrongly sent to the other lawyer, he/she should not read or stop reading the letter or document. In these circumstances, the lawyer is not obliged to disclose the existence of the communication to the client.[137] Where, however, the lawyer has read a material part of the document, he/she has a duty to inform the other side immediately that he/she has received the document by mistake and to discuss any implications, such as the other side obtaining an injunction and/or costs, with the client.[138]

2.10.4 Self-help

Clients should consider the practical and procedural consequences of self-help. These may include:

- the effect on the children, if any;
- an increase in tension and hostility between the parties;
- a tit for tat mentality;
- an increase in costs;
- a reduction of the likelihood of settlement;
- civil/criminal proceedings;
- uncertainty.

At what point does information as between partners become confidential? When is self-help appropriate?

There is a great deal of uncertainty in this area, but the emphasis and analysis would appear now to question whether one party had the implied or actual permission of the other to access the data.[139] If there is no actual or implied permission, it is likely that the document is confidential and could be protected by an action for breach of confidence, trespass to goods, prosecution under the Data Protection Act 1998 and the Computer Misuse Act 1990. Furthermore, such a document will probably be inadmissible as evidence and its acquisition penalised in costs in the ancillary relief proceedings. Following *Tchenguiz & ors v Imerman*,[140] each person in a marriage has a right to privacy and confidentiality. It confirmed *Hildebrand v Hildebrand*[141] to the

---

[137] Solicitors' Code of Conduct, para 4.4(d).
[138] *Ablitt v Mills & Reeve* (1995) *The Times*, 25 October.
[139] *Tchenguiz & ors v Imerman* [2010] EWCA Civ 908, [2010] 2 FLR 814; *White v Withers LLP and Dearle* [2009] EWCA Civ 1122.
[140] *Tchenguiz & ors v Imerman* [2010] EWCA Civ 908, [2010] 2 FLR 814.
[141] *Hildebrand v Hildebrand* [1992] 1 FLR 244; *UL v BK (Freezing Orders: Safeguards: Standard Examples)* [2013] EWHC 1735 (Fam).

extent that if you have a confidential document, it must be disclosed, at the latest, when you serve a questionnaire. *Hildebrand* is no longer authority for a spouse, in otherwise unlawful circumstances, to take, copy and retain copies of confidential documents, even where it is suspected that the other spouse is seeking to hide assets. Informing and providing solicitors with copies before the questionnaire stage of proceedings is no longer a defence. In summary, the right to self-help has been significantly curtailed by *Imerman*. Other forms of self-help are telephone tapping and intercepting mail. The former may be a criminal offence under Regulation of Investigatory Powers Act 2000 (RIPA), section 1 and an actionable breach of confidence and/or privacy under the Human Rights Act 1998. It is not an offence, though, under RIPA to record their private telephone line assuming they have the right to control the operation or use of the system. Intercepting mail may be a criminal offence under Postal Services Act 2000, section 84 and RIPA, section 1.

2.10.5   Post-*Tchenguiz & ors v Imerman*

Where information is exchanged openly, there is no need to resort to litigation and the court process. If, however, there is a reluctance to follow this path, there are two ways forward:

(a)   Use of the court process with its strict disclosure obligations and timetable.

(b)   Where there is still resistance to disclose after the exchange of each party's Form E, the following remedies and their cost need to be considered:

  (i)   production/disclosure appointments to compel third parties to bring documents to court;

  (ii)   search and seizure orders for documents and/or electronic data; such orders now have their statutory base in Civil Procedure Act 1997, section 7.[142] Applications made in a county court must be transferred to the High Court;

  (iii) freezing orders pending the resolution of a settlement. The statutory basis for such orders is Senior Courts Act 1981, section 37 and County Courts Act 1984, section 38.[143]

2.11   PENSIONS

2.11.1   Valuation

- Pensions on Divorce etc. (Provision of Information) Regulations 2000.[144]
- The court will specify a date for valuation of benefits under a pension scheme.
- Cash Equivalent Transfer Value[145] is the most common form of valuation.

---

[142]   FPR 2010, PD20A.
[143]   FPR 2010, PD20A.
[144]   SI 2000/1048.
[145]   CETV.

2.11.2 Pension sharing orders

- Only available where the petition was presented after 1 December 2000.
- Defined by MCA 1973, section 21A.
- Cannot be made with regard to a basic state pension.
- Pension debit/pension credit.
- Valuation of the pension on implementation day is crucial in so far as percentage share ordered will apply to this valuation.[146]
- Internal or external transfer.
- Cannot be made in relation to a pension which is already the subject of a pension sharing order in relation to the marriage.[147]
- Where there has been a pension sharing order in relation to a previous marriage then a pension sharing order may be made in relation to the same pension arrangement.
- Cannot be made where there is already a pension sharing order in relation to shareable state scheme rights.
- Cannot be made where there is already a pension sharing order in relation to the rights of a person under a pension arrangement.[148]

2.11.3 Pension attachment[149]

- Available for petitions filed after 1 July 1996.
- Periodical payments or lump sum orders[150] set against a pension.
- Similar to an attachment of earnings order against a pension fund.
- Cannot be made against a pension which is already the subject of a pension sharing order in relation to the same marriage.
- Payments from the pension in the form of pension attachment periodical payments orders only available from when pension is drawn.
- Pension attachment periodical payments order lapses when the receiving party remarries.
- Prevents a clean break.

2.12 APPEALS

The rules setting out the procedure for appeals in the High Court and county courts are now identical.[151]

---

[146] *H v H (Financial Relief: Pensions)* [2009] EWHC 3739 (Fam), [2010] 2 FLR 173.
[147] MCA 1973, s 24B.
[148] MCA 1973, s 25B or s 25C.
[149] MCA 1973, ss 25B–25D.
[150] MCA 1973, s 23.
[151] FPR 2010, r 30.1.

2.12.1   Permission to appeal

In ancillary relief cases, permission to appeal should be made at the end of the hearing.[152] It has recently been emphasised that an application for permission to appeal must always be made to the judge at first instance.[153] Where this is refused, a further application can be made to the appeal court. Permission may only be given where there is a real prospect of success.[154] This must be a realistic rather than a fanciful prospect of success.[155] It may be conditional on depositing a sum of money or limiting the issues to be heard.[156]

2.12.2   Time for appealing

- 21 days after the decision.[157]
- 7 days (for service of the appellant's notice on each respondent).[158]

The appellant's notice must state the grounds of appeal.

Once served, the appeal notice may not be amended except with permission of the appeal court.[159]

The appeal court can:

- affirm, set aside or vary any order or judgment made or given by the lower court;
- refer an issue for determination by the lower court;
- order a new hearing;
- make an order for costs.[160]

Examples of how the Court of Appeal has exercised its discretion:

- admission of fresh evidence allowed in exceptional circumstances;[161]
- mistake of fact;[162]

---

[152]   FPR 2010, r 30.3.

[153]   *AB v CD* [2014] EWHC 2998 (Fam) and *P v P* [2015] EWCA Civ 447.

[154]   FPR 2010, r 30.7.

[155]   *Tanfield Limited v Cameron-MacDonald & another* [2000] 1 WLR 1311; *NLW v ARC* [2012] EWHC 55 (Fam), [2012] 2 FLR 129.

[156]   FPR 2010, r 30.8. *Radmacher v Granatino* [2008] EWCA Civ 1304; *McHugh v McHugh* [2014] EWCA Civ 1671.

[157]   FPR 2010, r 30.4(2).

[158]   FPR 2010, r 30.4(4).

[159]   FPR 2010, r 30.9.

[160]   FPR 2010, r 30.11(2).

[161]   *Kaur v Matharu* [2010] EWCA Civ 980; *Gohil v Gohil (No 2)* [2014] EWCA Civ 274, [2014] WLR (D) 126.

[162]   *H v H* [2014] EWCA Civ 1523.

- improper procedure;[163]
- error of law.[164]

2.12.3 Setting aside of consent orders

Consent orders can be challenged by appeal via permission to appeal out of time and also by an application to set aside the order for which permission is not required.[165]

Consent orders can be set aside on the following limited grounds:

- fraud or misrepresentation;
- non-disclosure of an essential matter;
- supervening event;
- undue influence.[166]

Fraud or misrepresentation or non-disclosure

Orders will not be set aside if the disclosure does not make a significant difference to the order which would have been made.[167]

Supervening events

Such events have to change the whole factual basis on which the final order was made. The Court of Appeal has recently emphasised that it is rare for a case to fall within the *Barder* principles.[168] In *Barder v Caluori*,[169] the husband had been ordered to transfer his interest in the former matrimonial home to his wife, who subsequently killed herself and the children. The House of Lords set out four conditions that would have to be satisfied before the court would grant permission to appeal out of time:

(a) that the new events that occurred since the making of the order invalidate the basis, or fundamental assumption, on which the order was made, so that, if leave to appeal out of time were to be given, the appeal would be certain, or very likely, to succeed;

(b) that the new events have occurred within a relatively short time of the order having been made;

163 *JP v NP* [2014] EWHC 1101 (Fam).
164 *Piglowska v Piglowski* [1999] UKHL 27.
165 *CS v ACS & Anor* [2015] EWHC 1005 (Fam).
166 *NLW v ARC* [2012] EWHC 55 (Fam), [2012] 2 FLR 129.
167 *Livesey v Jenkins* [1984] AC 424, HL. In this case, an intention to remarry not been disclosed. Such a disclosure was a significant fact, which should have been disclosed. In *I v I (Ancillary Relief: Disclosure)* [2008] EWCA 1167 (Fam), the husband's failure to disclose that he was negotiating a new employment contract was, it was held, unlikely to have made any difference to the final order.
168 *Critchell v Critchell* [2015] EWCA Civ 436.
169 *Barder v Caluori* [1988] AC 20.

(c)   that the application for leave to appeal out of time should be made reasonably promptly in the circumstances of the case;

(d)   that the grant of leave to appeal out of time should not prejudice third parties who have acquired, in good faith and for valuable consideration, interests in property which is the subject matter of the relevant order.

The following three events have been argued to qualify as *Barder* events:

(a)   *change in the valuation of assets*: a final order was not set aside where there had been a change in the value of shares nor was it set aside where shares had been sold at a much greater price than their valuation at the final hearing.[170] In general, it has been held that the natural processes of price fluctuation, whether in houses, shares, or any other property, and however dramatic, do not satisfy the *Barder* test;[171]

(b)   *remarriage or cohabitation*: in *Williams v Lindley*,[172] the wife denied at the final hearing that she was in a relationship with the man she went on to marry soon afterwards. The consent order was set aside;

(c)   *death*: death of one of the parties will not, necessarily, result in the final order being set aside. It would have to undermine the whole basis on which the order had been made.[173] Where the wife died 2 months after the final order, the court held that this was a supervening event and the husband's needs would have to be re-assessed.[174]

The new event must have occurred within a short time after the order was made and the application to set aside must be made promptly. Finally, third parties who have acquired, in good faith and for valuable consideration, interests in property which is the subject matter of the order, should not be prejudiced.

2.13   COSTS

The new costs rules (FPR 2010, rule 9.27) provide as follows:

(1)   Subject to paragraph (2), at every hearing or appointment each party must produce to the court an estimate of the costs incurred by him up to the date of that hearing or appointment;

(2)   Not less than 14 days before the date fixed for the final hearing of an application for ancillary relief, each party must (unless the court directs otherwise) file with the court and serve on each other party a statement giving full particulars of all costs in respect of the proceedings which he has incurred or expects to incur, to

---

[170] *Cornick v Cornick* [1994] 2 FLR 530; *Walkden v Walkden* [2009] EWCA Civ 627, [2010] 1 FLR 174.

[171] *Myerson v Myerson* [2009] EWCA Civ 282.

[172] *Williams v Lindley* [2005] EWCA Civ 103, [2005] 2 FLR 710.

[173] *Amey v Amey* [1992] 2 FLR 89.

[174] *Reid v Reid* [2003] EWHC 2878 (Fam), [2004] 1 FLR 736.

enable the court to take account of the parties' liabilities for costs when deciding what order (if any) to make for such a financial remedy.[175]

The new forms demand far more detail and will enable the court to examine whether an order for costs is justified.[176]

At the first appointment, regard will be had, when considering an order for costs, to the extent to which each party has complied with the requirement to send documents with the financial statement.[177]

A party seeking an order for costs against the other party must comply with paragraph 4 of the President's Practice Direction.[178] Parties must make their intention to seek a costs order 'plain in open correspondence or in skeleton argument before the date of the hearing'.

For a summary assessment of costs, parties are bound to file a statement of costs.[179]

The normal order where one party has been ordered to pay the costs of the other is for those costs to be assessed if not agreed.

2.13.1 Standard basis of assessment

This is the usual basis of assessment, on which the taxing officer must resolve any doubt in favour of the paying party.

2.13.2 Indemnity basis of assessment

The taxing officer must award all costs save where they are held to be unreasonable in amount or where they were unreasonably incurred.[180]

2.13.3 General approach

'The general rule in ancillary relief proceedings is that the court will not make an order requiring one party to pay the costs of another party'.[181]

The idea that the costs of the winning party are paid for by the losing party does not apply to financial remedy proceedings. Each party will, therefore, bear his/her own costs. There are, however, exceptions to this rule, particularly, where 'the conduct of a party in relation to the proceedings (whether before or during them)' is such that it

---

[175] FPR 2010, r 9.27.
[176] See Form H1 and FPR 2010, PD 5A.
[177] FPR 2010, r 9.15(6).
[178] FPR 2010, PD28A, para 4.5.
[179] CPR 1998, Form N260.
[180] CPR 1998, r 44.4(2) and (3).
[181] FPR 2010, r 28.3(5).

is appropriate for that party to pay the costs of the other.[182] This is often referred to as 'litigation misconduct'.

When considering whether to make an order for costs, the court should have regard to the following factors:

- failure by a party to comply with the Rules, any order of the court or any relevant practice direction;
- any open offer to settle made by a party;
- whether it was reasonable for a party to raise, pursue or contest a particular allegation or issue;
- the manner in which a party has pursued or responded to the application or a particular allegation or issue;
- any other aspect of a party's conduct in relation to the proceedings which the court considers relevant;
- the financial effect on the parties of any costs order.

Failure to comply with the Rules and court orders is self-explanatory and would include, for example, failure to adhere to a court timetable.

Only open offers must be considered. 'Without prejudice' offers will not be admissible when considering costs. Where one party has made reasonable offers to settle, which have been ignored, and the final order agrees with those offers, the other party may be ordered to pay the successful party's costs.

The court is likely to make a costs order against a party pursuing unreasonable allegations.[183]

Even where the court decides to make an order for costs, it may decline to do so where the effect would be, for example, harmful to the children of the family or an elderly relative in need of care.

---

[182] FPR 2010, r 28.3(6).
[183] FPR 2010, r 28.3(7)(c).

Chapter 3

The Public Law Outline (PLO) and the Child Arrangements Programme (CAP)

THE PUBLIC LAW OUTLINE 2014 (PD12A)

[FPR 2010, PD12A – Care, supervision and other Part 4 proceedings: guide to case management]

Pre-proceedings

Pre-proceedings Checklist

Annex Documents are the documents specified in the Annex to the Application Form which are to be attached to that form and filed with the court:

- Social Work Chronology
- Social Work Statement and Genogram
- The current assessments relating to the child and/or the family and friends of the child to which the Social Work Statement refers and on which the LA [local authority] relies
- Care Plan
- Index of Checklist Documents

Checklist documents (already existing on the LA's files) are –

(a) Evidential documents including –

- Previous court orders including foreign orders and judgments/reasons
- Any assessment materials relevant to the key issues including capacity to litigate, section 7 and 37 reports
- Single, joint or inter-agency materials (eg health and education/Home Office and Immigration Tribunal documents);

(b) Decision-making records including –

- Records of key discussions with the family
- Key LA minutes and records for the child

- Pre-existing care plans (e.g., child in need plan, looked after child plan and child protection plan)
- Letters Before Proceedings

Only Checklist documents in (a) are to be served with the application form

Checklist Documents in (b) are to be disclosed on request by any party

Checklist documents are not to be–

- filed with the court unless the court directs otherwise; and
- older than 2 years before the date of issue of the proceedings unless reliance is placed on the same in the LA's evidence

Stage 1 Issue and Allocation

Day 1 and Day 2 (see interpretation section)
On Day 1 (Day of issue):

- The LA files the Application Form and Annex Documents and sends copies to Cafcass/CAFCASS CYMRU
- The LA notifies the court of the need for an urgent preliminary case management hearing or an urgent contested ICO [interim care order] hearing where this is known or expected
- Court officer issues application

Within a day of issue (Day 2):

- Court considers jurisdiction in a case with an international element
- Court considers initial allocation to specified level of judge, in accordance with the Allocation Rules and any President's Guidance on the distribution of business
- LA serves the Application Form, Annex Documents and evidential Checklist Documents on the parties together with the notice of date and time of CMH [Case Management Hearing] and any urgent hearing
- Court gives standard directions on Issue and Allocation including:
    - Checking compliance with Pre-Proceedings Checklist including service of any missing Annex Documents
    - Appointing Children's Guardian (to be allocated by Cafcass/CAFCASS CYMRU)
    - Appointing solicitor for the child only if necessary
    - Appointing (if the person to be appointed consents) a litigation friend for any protected party or any non-subject child who is a party, including the OS [Official Solicitor] where appropriate
    - Identifying whether a request has been made or should be made to a Central Authority or other competent authority in a foreign state or a

consular authority in England and Wales in a case with an international element
- Filing and service of a LA Case Summary
- Filing and service of a Case Analysis by the Children's Guardian
- Filing and Serving the Parents' Response
- Sending a request for disclosure to, e.g., the police or health service body
- Filing and serving an application for permission relating to experts under Part 25 on a date prior to the advocates meeting for the CMH
- Directing the solicitor for the child to arrange an advocates' meeting no later than 2 business days before the CMH
- Listing the CMH
- Court considers any request for an urgent preliminary case management hearing or an urgent contested ICO hearing and where necessary lists the hearing and gives additional directions.
- Court officer sends copy Notice of Hearing of the CMH and any urgent hearing by email to Cafcass/CAFCASS CYMRU.

Stage 2 – Case Management Hearing

Advocates' Meeting (including any litigants in person)
No later than 2 business days before CMH (or FCMH [further case management hearing] if it is necessary)

- Consider information on the Application Form and Annex documents, the LA Case Summary, and the Case Analysis
- Identify the parties' positions to be recited in the draft Case Management Order
- Identify the parties' positions about jurisdiction, in particular arising out of any international element
- If necessary, identify proposed experts and draft questions in accordance with Part 25 and the Experts Practice Directions
- Identify any disclosure that in the advocates' views is necessary
- Immediately notify the court of the need for a contested ICO hearing and any issue about allocation
- LA advocate to file a draft Case Management Order in prescribed form with court by 11a.m. on the business day before the CMH and/or FCMH

Case Management Hearing
CMH: Not before day 12 and not later than day 18
A FCMH is to be held only if necessary, it is to be listed as soon as possible and in any event no later than day 25

- Court gives detailed case management directions, including:
  - Considering jurisdiction in a case with an international element;
  - Confirming allocation

- Drawing up the timetable for the child and the timetable for the proceedings and considering if an extension is necessary
- Identifying additional parties, intervenors and representation (including confirming that Cafcass/CAFCASS CYMRU have allocated a Children's Guardian and that a litigation friend is appointed for any protected party or nonsubject child)
- Giving directions for the determination of any disputed issue about litigation capacity
- Identifying the key issues
- Identifying the evidence necessary to enable the court to resolve the key issues
- Deciding whether there is a real issue about threshold to be resolved
- Determining any application made under Part 25 and otherwise ensuring compliance with Part 25 where it is necessary for expert(s) to be instructed
- Identifying any necessary disclosure and if appropriate giving directions
- Giving directions for any concurrent or proposed placement order proceedings
- Ensuring compliance with the court's directions
- If a FCMH is necessary, directing an advocates' meeting and Case Analysis if required
- Directing filing of any threshold agreement, final evidence and Care Plan and responses to those documents for the IRH [Issues Resolution Hearing]
- Directing a Case Analysis for the IRH
- Directing an advocates' meeting for the IRH
- Listing (any FCMH) IRH, Final Hearing (including early Final Hearing) as appropriate
- Giving directions for special measures and/or interpreters and intermediaries
- Issuing the Case Management Order

Stage 3 – Issues Resolution Hearing

Advocates' Meeting (including any litigants in person)
No later than 7 business days before the IRH

- Review evidence and the positions of the parties
- Identify the advocates' views of-
  - the remaining key issues and how the issues may be resolved or narrowed at the IRH including by the making of final orders
  - the further evidence which is required to be heard to enable the key issues to be resolved or narrowed at the IRH
  - the evidence that is relevant and the witnesses that are required at the final hearing
  - the need for a contested hearing and/or time for oral evidence to be given at the IRH
- LA advocate to-
  - notify the court immediately of the outcome of the discussion at the meeting

– file a draft Case Management Order with the court by 11a.m. on the business day before the IRH

IRH
As directed by the court, in accordance with the timetable for the proceedings

- Court identifies the key issue(s) (if any) to be determined and the extent to which those issues can be resolved or narrowed at the IRH
- Court considers whether the IRH can be used as a final hearing
- Court resolves or narrows the issues by hearing evidence
- Court identifies the evidence to be heard on the issues which remain to be resolved at the final hearing
- Court gives final case management directions including:
  – Any extension of the timetable for the proceedings which is necessary
  – Filing of the threshold agreement or a statement of facts/issues remaining to be determined
  – Filing of:
    - Final evidence and Care Plan
    - Case Analysis for Final Hearing (if required)
    - Witness templates
    - Skeleton arguments
  – Judicial reading list/reading time, including time estimate and an estimate for judgment writing time
  – Ensuring Compliance with PD27A (the Bundles Practice Direction)
  – Listing the Final Hearing
- Court issues Case Management Order

Stage 4 (if required) – Final Hearing

2. Flexible powers of the court
(See PD12A for full version)
2.1 Attention is drawn to the flexible powers of the court either following the issue of the application or at any other stage in the proceedings.

2.2 The court may give directions without a hearing ...

2.3 The flexible powers of the court include the ability for the court to cancel or repeat a particular hearing ...

2.4 Where a party has requested an urgent hearing a) to enable the court to give immediate directions or orders to facilitate any case management issue which is to be considered at the CMH, or b) to decide whether an ICO is necessary, the court may list such a hearing at any appropriate time before the CMH and give directions for that hearing ...

2.5 Where it is anticipated that oral evidence may be required at the CMH, FCMH or IRH, the court must be notified in accordance with Stages 2 and 3 of the Public Law Outline well in advance and directions sought for the conduct of the hearing.

2.6 It is expected that full case management will take place at the CMH. It follows that the parties must be prepared to deal with all relevant case management issues, as identified in Stage 2 of the Public Law Outline. A FCMH should only be directed where necessary and must not be regarded as a routine step in proceedings.

3. Compliance with pre-proceedings checklist

3.1 ... The safety and welfare of the child should never be put in jeopardy by delaying issuing proceedings whether because of lack of documentation or otherwise. (Nothing in this Practice Direction affects an application for an emergency protection order under section 44 of the 1989 Act).

3.2 The court recognises that preparation may need to be varied to suit the circumstances of the case ...

4. Allocation

4.1 ... The expectation is that, wherever possible, any question relating to allocation of the proceedings will be considered at the CMH.

5. The timetable for the child and the timetable for proceedings

5.1 The timetable for the proceedings:

(1)   The court will draw up a timetable for the proceedings with a view to disposing of the application—
   (a)   without delay; and
   (b)   in any event within 26 weeks beginning with the day on which the application was issued in accordance with section 32(1)(a)(ii) of the Children Act 1989.
(2)   The court, when drawing up or revising a timetable under paragraph (1), will in particular have regard to—
   (a)   the impact which the timetable or any revised timetable would have on the welfare of the child to whom the application relates; and
   (b)   the impact which the timetable or any revised timetable would have on the duration and conduct of the proceedings.

5.2 ...

5.3 The 'Timetable for the Child' is the timetable set by the court which takes into account dates which are important to the child's welfare and development.

5.4 The timetable for the proceedings is set having particular regard to the Timetable for the Child and the Timetable for the Child needs to be reviewed regularly ...

5.5 Examples of the dates the court will record and take into account when setting the Timetable for the Child are the dates of—

(1)   any formal review by the Local Authority of the case of a looked after child ...
(2)   any significant educational steps, including the child taking up a place at a new school and, where applicable, any review by the Local Authority of a statement of the child's special educational needs;
(3)   any health care steps, including assessment by a paediatrician or other specialist;
(4)   any review of Local Authority plans for the child, including any plans for permanence through adoption, Special Guardianship or placement with parents or relatives;
(5)   any change or proposed change of the child's placement;
(6)   any significant change in the child's social or family circumstances; or
(7)   any timetable for the determination of an issue in a case with an international element.

5.6 To identify the Timetable for the Child, the applicant is required to provide the information needed about the significant steps in the child's life in the Application Form and the Social Work Statement and to update this information regularly ...

5.7 Where more than one child is the subject of the proceedings, the court should consider and will set a Timetable for the Child for each child. The children may not all have the same timetable, and the court will consider the appropriate progress of the proceedings in relation to each child.

5.8 Where there are parallel care proceedings and criminal proceedings against a person connected with the child for a serious offence against the child, linked directions hearings should where practicable take place as the case progresses. The timing of the proceedings in a linked care and criminal case should appear in the Timetable for the Child. The time limit of resolving the proceedings within 26 weeks applies unless a longer timetable has been set by the court in order to resolve the proceedings justly in accordance with section 32(1)(a)(ii) and (5) of the 1989 Act. Early disclosure and listing of hearings is necessary in proceedings in a linked care and criminal case.

6. Extensions to the timetable for proceedings
6.1 ...

6.2 Having regard to the circumstances of the particular case, the court may consider that it is necessary to extend the time by which the proceedings are to be resolved beyond 26 weeks to enable the court to resolve the proceedings justly (see section 32 (5) of the 1989 Act) ... The decision and reason(s) for extending a case should be recorded in writing (in the Case Management Order) and orally stated in court, so that all parties are aware of the reasons for delay in the case (see FPR 12.26C). The Case

Management Order must contain a record of this information, as well as the impact of the court's decision on the welfare of the child.

6.3 The court may extend the period within which proceedings are intended to be resolved on its own initiative or on application. ..Where a date for a hearing has been fixed, a party who wishes to make an application at that hearing but does not have sufficient time to file an application notice should as soon as possible inform the court (if possible in writing) and, if possible, the other parties of the nature of the application and the reason for it. The party should then make the application orally at the hearing.

6.4 If the court agrees an extension is necessary, an initial extension to the time limit may be granted for up to eight weeks (or less if directed) in order to resolve the case justly (see section 32(8) of the 1989 Act). If more time is necessary, in order to resolve the proceedings justly, a further extension of up to eight weeks may be agreed by the court. There is no limit on the number of extensions that may be granted in a particular case.

6.5 If the court considers that the timetable for the proceedings will require an extension beyond the next eight week period in order to resolve the proceedings justly, the Case Management Order should—

(1)   state the reason(s) why it is necessary to have a further extension;
(2)   fix the date of the next effective hearing (which might be in a period shorter than a further eight weeks); and
(3)   indicate whether it is appropriate for the next application for an extension of the timetable to be considered on paper.

6.6 The expectation is that, subject to paragraph 6.5, extensions should be considered at a hearing ...

7. Interpretation

...

CHILD ARRANGEMENTS PROGRAMME (PD12B)

FPR 2010, PD12(B): (CAP 2014) Issued 22 April 2014

1. When does the Child Arrangements Programme Apply?
1.1 The Child Arrangements Programme (the 'CAP') applies where a dispute arises between separated parents and/or families about arrangements concerning children.

1.2 ...

1.3 ...

2. Signposting Services, Parenting Plans, & Public Funding
2.1 ...

2.2 ...

2.3 The following services are recommended:

(1)   For more information about family mediation and to find the nearest mediation service (including those providing a MIAM): www.familymediationcouncil.org.uk;

(2)   For a Guide about children and the family courts for separating parents (including representing yourself in court): the form 'CB7': http://www.cafcass.gov.uk/media/168195/cb7-eng.pdf

(3)   For Cafcass (England): www.cafcass.gov.uk;

(4)   For CAFCASS Cymru (Wales): www.wales.gov.uk/cafcasscymru;

(5)   To find a legal adviser or family mediator: http://find-legal-advice. justice.gov.uk;

(6)   To check whether you can get financial help (legal aid) to pay for non-court dispute resolution, &/or advice and representation at court, and to find a legal aid solicitor or mediator: https://www.gov.uk/check-legal-aid

(7)   For general advice about sorting out arrangements for children, the use of post-separation mediation, &/or going to court: http://www.advicenow. org.uk; http://www.advicenow.org.uk/advicenow-guides/family/sorting-out-arrangements-for-your-children/;

(8)   For general advice on separation services and options for resolving disputes: www.sortingoutseparation.org.uk;

(9)   For general advice about sorting out arrangements for children: http://theparentconnection.org.uk/;

(10)   For advice about Contact Centres, which are neutral places where children of separated families can enjoy contact with their non-resident parents and sometimes other family members, in a comfortable and safe environment; and information about where they are: www.naccc.org.uk;

(11)   For the form to apply for a child arrangements order: https://www.gov.uk/ looking-after-children-divorce/apply-for-court-order;

(12)   For help with taking a case to court without a lawyer, the Personal Support Unit: http://thepsu.org/;

(13)   For guidance on representing yourself at court, including a list of commonly used terms that you may come across: http://www.barcouncil.org.uk/ instructing-a-barrister/representing-yourself-in-court/;

(14)   For advice about finding and using a family law solicitor see: Law Society http://www.lawsociety.org.uk, and Resolution (family law solicitors): http://www.resolution.org.uk;

(15)   For advice about finding and using a family law barrister: see http://www.barcouncil.org.uk/about-the-bar/find-a-barrister/, and for arrangements for using a barrister directly see http://www.barcouncil.org.uk/ instructing-a-barrister/public-access/.

2.4 **Parenting Plan**: A Parenting Plan is widely recognised as being a useful tool for separated parents to identify, agree and set out in writing arrangements for their children; such a plan could appropriately be used as the basis for discussion about a dispute which has arisen. It is likely to be useful in any event for assisting arrangements between separated parents.

2.5 The Parenting Plan should cover all practical aspects of care for the child, and should reflect a shared commitment to the child and his/her future, with particular emphasis on parental communication (learning how to deal with differences), living arrangements, money, religion, education, health care and emotional well-being.

2.6 A Parenting Plan is designed to help separated parents (and their families) to work out the best possible arrangements for the child; the plan should be understood by everyone, including (where the child is of an appropriate age and understanding) the child concerned.

2.7 For help on preparing a Parenting Plan, see:

(1)   Cafcass 'Putting Your Children First: A Guide for Separated Parents' (see also paragraph 4 below);

(2)   A draft of a Parenting Plan for parents or families to complete: http://www.cafcass.gov.uk/media/190788/parenting_plan_final_web.pdf.

2.8 **Publicly funded mediation and/or legal advice**: If parents need access to mediation, and legal advice in support of that mediation, they may be eligible for public funding. The LAA will provide funding for MIAMs and family mediation for all those who are eligible:

(1)   Where at least one party is eligible, the LAA will cover the costs of both parties to attend a MIAM to encourage any non-eligible client to find out about the benefits and suitability of mediation without incurring any costs.

(2)   The LAA will provide public funding for eligible parties to participate in family mediation and they may also receive some independent legal advice connected to the mediation process and where a settlement is reached can receive legal assistance to draft and issue proceedings to obtain a consent order.

(3)   Parties may find out if they are likely to be eligible for legal aid at the following link: https://www.gov.uk/check-legal-aid

(4)   To find the nearest publicly funded mediation service a client can use the search at familymediationcouncil.org.uk. Publicly funded legal advisors can be found at: https://www.gov.uk/check-legalaid

2.9 Public funding for legal advice and/or representation at court is available in limited circumstances. Further information can be found here:

http://www.justice.gov.uk/legal-aid-for-private-family-matters

3. **Explanation of terms**

    …

4. The child in the dispute

4.1 In making any arrangements with respect to a child, the child's welfare must be the highest priority.

4.2 ...

4.3 The child or young person should feel that their needs, wishes and feelings have been considered in the arrangements which are made for them.

4.4 Children should be involved, to the extent which is appropriate given their age and level of understanding, in making the arrangements which affect them. This is just as relevant where

(1)   the parties are making arrangements between themselves (which may be recorded in a Parenting Plan),

as when:

(2)   arrangements are made in the context of dispute resolution outside away from the court,

and/or

(3)   the court is required to make a decision about the arrangements for the child.

4.5 If an application for a court order has been issued, the judge may want to know the child's view. This may be communicated to the judge in one of a number of ways:

(1)   By a Cafcass officer (in Wales, a Welsh Family Proceedings Officer (WFPO)) providing a report to the court which sets out the child's wishes and feelings;

(2)   By the child being encouraged (by the Cafcass officer or WFPO, or a parent or relative) to write a letter to the court;

(3)   In the limited circumstances described in paragraph 18 below, by the child being a party to the proceedings;

and/or:

(4)   By the judge meeting with the child, in accordance with approved Guidance ...

5. Non-court resolution of disputed arrangements for children

5.1 Dispute resolution services, including mediation, are available to provide opportunities for parents and families to work in a positive and constructive way, and should be actively considered and attempted where it is safe and appropriate to do so. ..

5.2 It is not expected that those who are the victims of domestic violence should attempt to mediate or otherwise participate in forms of non-court dispute resolution. It is also recognised that drug and/or alcohol misuse and/or mental illness are likely to prevent couples from making safe use of mediation or similar services; ...

5.3 Attendance at Mediation Information and Assessment Meeting ('MIAM'): Subject to paragraph 5.6 (below), before making a family application to the court (a 'relevant family application' as defined in paragraph 23 below), the person who is considering making such application must attend a family MIAM. A prospective respondent is expected to attend a MIAM – whether this is a separate MIAM or the same MIAM attended by the prospective applicant ... The mediator will also assess whether there has been, or is a risk of,

(1)   domestic violence, and/or
(2)   harm by a prospective party to a child that would be the subject of the application.

5.4 It is the responsibility of the prospective applicant (or that person's legal representative) to contact a family mediator to arrange attendance at a MIAM.

5.5 Only an authorised family mediator can carry out a MIAM. ..

5.6 A prospective applicant is not required to attend a MIAM where one of the circumstances set out in rule 3.8(1) or 3.8(2) FPR applies.

5.7 Information on how to find a family mediator may be obtained from www.familymediationcouncil.org.uk website which hosts the 'find a local family mediator' database (see also 'Signposting Services for Families' – paragraph 2 above).

5.8 The prospective applicant (or the prospective applicant's legal representative) should provide the mediator with contact details for the other party or parties to the dispute ('the prospective respondent(s)'), so that the mediator can contact the prospective respondent(s) to discuss their willingness and availability to attend a MIAM.

5.9 The prospective applicant and, where they agree to do so, the prospective respondent(s), should then attend a MIAM arranged by the mediator. ..

5.10 The Family Mediation Council sets the requirements for mediators who conduct MIAMs ...

5.11 Mediation is a confidential process; none of the parties to the mediation may provide information to the court as to the content of any discussions held in mediation and/or the reasons why agreement was not reached. Similarly, the mediator may not provide such information, unless the mediator considers that a safeguarding issue arises.

5.12 However, it is important that the parties, or either of them, introduce at the MIAM (or any subsequent court application) any other evidence of attempts to resolve a dispute and to focus on the needs of the child.

6. Resolution of disputed arrangements for children through the Court
6.1 The judge is obliged to consider, at every stage of court proceedings, whether non-court dispute resolution is appropriate.

6.2 The parties should also actively consider non-court dispute resolution even if proceedings are issued and are ongoing.

6.3 If the court considers that another form of dispute resolution is appropriate, the court may direct that the proceedings, or a hearing in the proceedings, be adjourned for such specified period as it considers appropriate:

(1)   to enable the parties to obtain information and advice about non-court dispute resolution; and

(2)   where the parties agree, to enable non-court dispute resolution to take place.

6.4 Where the court adjourns proceedings, it shall give directions about the timing and method by which the parties must tell the court if any of the issues in the proceedings have been resolved.

6.5 ..

7. Local Good Practice
...

8. Application to court
8.1 Unless one of the MIAM exemptions applies (see rule 3.8 FPR), an application to court for determination of most issues concerning a child (see the definition of 'relevant family application' in rule 3.6 FPR and paragraphs 11 and 12 of PD3A) can be made only after a MIAM has taken place ... One of the exemptions may be that the case is urgent ... The grounds for urgency are defined in rule 3.8(c) FPR.

8.2 The application for a child arrangements order or other Children Act 1989 private law order shall be made on the relevant prescribed form.

8.3 ...

8.4 ...

8.5 The C100 form may be obtained from the Family Court or from www.gov.uk.

8.6 If the parties have previously prepared a Parenting Plan, this shall be attached to the Form C100.

8.7 ...

8.8 ...

8.9 The court shall send to Cafcass/CAFCASS Cymru a copy of the Form C100 (and the form C1A, if supplied), and the C6 Notice of Hearing no later than 2 working days after the date of issue ...

8.10 The court shall not send to Cafcass/CAFCASS Cymru any other application under the Children Act 1989, or any other private law application, unless the Court has made a specific direction requesting the assistance of Cafcass/CAFCASS Cymru. Therefore, any application which is not in Form C100 or which does not contain a direction to Cafcass/CAFCASS Cymru will be returned to the court at which the application has been issued.

9. Allocation and Gatekeeping
...

10. Judicial continuity
10.1 ...

10.2 Continuity of Judicial involvement in the conduct of proceedings from the FHDRA to the making of a final order should be the objective in all cases.

10.3 Where the case has been allocated to be heard before lay justices, the expectation of judicial continuity should apply where

(1)   There has been a hearing to determine findings of fact,
(2)   A decision yet to be made in the interests of a child by a court depends upon rulings or judicial assessments already made in the proceedings, in which case, wherever possible, the hearing shall be listed before the same lay justices ...

11. Key welfare principles
11.1 Section 1 of the Children Act 1989 applies to all applications for orders concerning the upbringing of children. This means that:

(1)   the child's welfare is the court's paramount consideration;
(2)   delay is likely to be prejudicial to the welfare of the child, and
(3)   a court order shall not be made unless the court considers that making an order would be better for the child than making no order at all.

11.2 Parties, and the court, must also have regard to the FPR in particular the following:

(1)   FPR Rule 1. The 'overriding objective' will apply, so that the court will deal with a case justly, having regard to the welfare issues involved ...

11.3 Where a fact-finding hearing is required, this shall take place in accordance with revised Practice Direction 12J FPR.

11.4 The court shall exercise its powers flexibly. The flexible powers of the court include the ability for the court to cancel or repeat a particular hearing.

12. Urgent and Without Notice Applications

12.1 **Urgent**: Where an order is sought as a matter of urgency, an application may be made to the Court for an emergency order without the requirement for the Applicant to have attended at a MIAM. The categories of urgent application justifying such an exemption are set out in rule 3.8(c) FPR and include cases in which:

(1)   There is a risk to the life, liberty, or the physical safety of the prospective applicant or his or her family, or his or her home;

(2)   Any delay caused by attending a MIAM would cause:
    (1)   A risk of harm to the child;
    (2)   A risk of unlawful removal of a child from the United Kingdom or a risk of unlawful retention of a child who is currently outside England and Wales;
    (3)   A significant risk of a miscarriage of justice;
    (4)   Unreasonable hardship to the prospective applicant;
    (5)   Irretrievable problems in dealing with the dispute (including the irretrievable loss of significant evidence).

(3)   There is a significant risk that in the period necessary to schedule and attend a MIAM, proceedings relating to the dispute will be brought in another state in which a valid claim to jurisdiction may exist, such that a court in that other State would be seised of the dispute before a court in England and Wales.

12.2 **'Without Notice'**: ...

12.3 Without Notice Orders should be made only exceptionally, and where:

(1)   If the applicant were to give notice to the respondent(s) this would enable the respondent(s) to take steps to defeat the purpose of the injunction; cases where the application is brought without notice in order to conceal the step from the respondent(s) are very rare indeed; or

(2)   The case is one of exceptional urgency; that is to say, that there has been literally no time to give notice (either by telephone, text or e-mail or otherwise) before the injunction is required to prevent the threatened wrongful act; or

(3)   If the applicant gives notice to the respondent(s), this would be likely to expose the applicant or relevant child to unnecessary risk of physical or emotional harm.

12.4 Any Order which follows an emergency 'without notice' hearing should specify:

(1)   the reason(s) why the order has been made without notice to the respondent(s),

(2)   the outline facts alleged which have been relied upon by the court in making the order, unless the facts are clearly contained in the statement in support; and

(3)   the right of the respondent(s) to apply to vary or discharge the order.

12.5 ...

13. <u>Safeguarding</u>

13.1 Where an application is made for a child arrangements order (but not necessarily for specific issue or prohibited steps orders), before the FHDRA (see paragraph 14 below) Cafcass/CAFCASS Cymru shall identify any safety issues by the steps outlined below.

13.2 Such steps shall be confined to matters of safety. ..

13.3 In order to inform the court of possible risks of harm to the child Cafcass/CAFCASS Cymru will carry out safeguarding enquiries ...

13.4 Cafcass/CAFCASS Cymru will, if possible, undertake telephone risk identification interviews with the parties and if risks of harm are identified, may invite parties to meet separately with the Cafcass Officer, or WFPO in Wales, before the FHDRA to clarify any safety issue.

13.5 Cafcass/CAFCASS Cymru shall record and outline any safety issues for the court, in the form of a Safeguarding letter (in Wales, this is called a 'Safeguarding report').

13.6 The Cafcass officer, or WFPO, will not initiate contact with the child prior to the FHDRA. If contacted by a child, discussions relating to the issues in the case will be postponed to the day of the hearing or after when the Cafcass officer or WFPO will have more knowledge of the issues.

13.7 Within 17 working days of receipt by Cafcass/CAFCASS Cymru of the application, and at least 3 working days before the hearing, the Cafcass Officer or WFPO shall report to the court, in a Safeguarding letter/report, the outcome of the risk identification work which has been undertaken.

13.8 Further, Cafcass and CAFCASS Cymru are required, under section 16A Children Act 1989, to undertake (and to provide to the court) risk assessments where an officer of the Service ('Cafcass Officer' or WFPO) suspects that a child is at risk of harm.

14. First Hearing Dispute Resolution Appointment (FHDRA)

14.1 The FHDRA may ... take place within 4 weeks, but should ordinarily take place in week 5 ... at the latest ... in week 6 ...

14.2 The respondent(s) shall have at least 10 working days' notice of the hearing where practicable, but the court may abridge this time.

14.3 The respondent(s) should file a response on the Forms C7/C1A no later than 10 working days before the hearing, unless the court has abridged this time.

14.4 Unless the court otherwise directs, any party to proceedings, and any litigation friend of the parties must attend this (and any other) hearing. If a child is a party and represented by a children's guardian, the children's guardian need not attend directions hearings if represented.

14.5 A party may choose to be accompanied at this (or any) hearing by a McKenzie Friend to support them (a McKenzie Friend is someone who can provide moral support at court for the party; take notes; help with case papers; quietly give advice on any aspect of the conduct of the case.) If so, the McKenzie Friend must comply with the relevant Guidance (currently set out in http://www.judiciary.gov.uk/Resources/JCO/Documents/Guidance/mckenzie-friends-practice-guidance-july-2010.pdf).

14.6 A Cafcass Officer or WFPO shall attend this hearing. A mediator may attend where available.

14.7 The Cafcass Officer or WFPO shall, where practicable, speak separately to each party at court before the hearing in particular where it has not been possible to conduct a risk identification interview with either party.

14.8 The FHDRA provides an opportunity for the parties to be helped to an understanding of the issues which divide them, and to reach agreement. If agreement is reached,

(1)   The Court will be able to make an order (which in many cases will be a final order) reflecting that agreement;

(2)   The Court will assist the parties (so far as it is able) in putting into effect the agreement/order in a co-operative way.

14.9 The FHDRA is not privileged. That is to say that what is said at the FHDRA may be referred to at later court hearings.

14.10 ...

14.11 At the FHDRA the judge, working with the Cafcass Officer, or WFPO, will seek to assist the parties in conciliation and in resolution of all or any of the issues between them. Any remaining issues will be identified, the Cafcass Officer or WFPO will advise the court of any recommended means of resolving such issues, and directions will be given for the future resolution of such issues. At all times the decisions of the Court and the work of the Cafcass Officer or WFPO will take account of any risk or safeguarding issues that have been identified.

14.12 ...

14.13 The FHDRA will be conducted in the most appropriate way in the interests of the child. In particular the court shall consider the following matters:

- **Safeguarding**, in this respect:
  (a)   The court shall inform the parties of the content of the safeguarding letter/report provided by Cafcass/CAFCASS Cymru, where it has not already been sent by Cafcass/CAFCASS Cymru to the parties, unless it considers that to do so would create a risk of harm to a party or the child ...
  The court will further consider:
  (b)   Whether a fact finding hearing is needed ...
  (c)   Risk identification followed by active case management including risk assessment, and compliance with the Practice Direction 12J.
  Further:
  (d)   If the safeguarding information is ... not available at the FHDRA, the court should adjourn the application until the safeguarding checks are available. Interim orders (unless to protect the safety of a child) should not be made in the absence of safeguarding checks.
  And further:
  (e)   Where the court so directs, a safeguarding letter/report ought to be attached to any referral to a supported or supervised child contact centre in the event the court directs supported or supervised contact.

- **MIAM**, specifically:
  (a)   Whether, if a MIAM exemption has been claimed, the Applicant has validly claimed the exemption;
  (b)   Whether the Respondent has attended a MIAM;
  (c)   If the court finds that a MIAM exemption has not been validly claimed the court will direct the applicant or direct the parties to attend a MIAM and if necessary adjourn the proceedings to enable a MIAM to take place, unless the court considers that in all the circumstances of the case, the MIAM requirement should not apply to the application in question; when making the decision the court will have particular regard to the matters contained in rule 3.10(3) FPR.

▪ **Mediation, At-Court Mediation assessment, and other Dispute Resolution**: allowing the parties the time and opportunity to engage in non-court dispute resolution.

    (a)   At the FHDRA, the judge will specifically consider whether, and the extent to which, the parties can safely resolve some or all of the issues with the assistance of the Cafcass Officer, WFPO, or a mediator.

    (b)   There will be, at every FHDRA, a period in which the Cafcass Officer, or WFPO, will seek to conciliate and explore with the parties the resolution of all or some of the issues between them if safe to do so ... The court will further consider:

    (c)   What is the result of any such meeting at Court?

    (d)   What other options there are for resolution e.g. may the case be suitable for further intervention by Cafcass/CAFCASS Cymru; Should a referral for mediation be made? Is collaborative law appropriate? Should the parties be advised to complete a Parenting Plan?

    (e)   Would the parties be assisted by attendance at an Activity Separated Parents Information Programme, (or in Wales, Working Together For Children (WT4C)) or other Activity or intervention, whether by formal statutory provision under section 11 Children Act 1989 or otherwise;

    (f)   An at-court assessment of the suitability of the parties for mediation.

▪ **Consent Orders**:

    (a)   Where agreement is reached at any hearing or submitted in writing to the court, no order will be made without scrutiny by the court.

    (b)   Where safeguarding checks or risk assessment work remain outstanding, the making of a final order may be deferred for such work. In such circumstances the court shall adjourn the case for no longer than 28 days to a fixed date ... If satisfactory information is then available, the order may be made at the adjourned hearing in the agreed terms without the need for attendance by the parties. ...

▪ **Reports**:

    (a)   Reports may be ordered where there are welfare issues or other specific considerations which should be addressed in a report by Cafcass/CAFCASS Cymru or the Local Authority ...

    (b)   If a report is ordered in accordance with section 7 of the Children Act 1989, the Court should direct which specific matters relating to the welfare of the child are to be addressed. Welfare reports will generally only be ordered in cases where there is a dispute as to with whom the child should live, spend time, or otherwise have contact with. A report can also be ordered:

        i.   If there is an issue concerning the child's wishes, and/or

        ii.   If there is an alleged risk to the child, and/or

        iii.   Where information and advice is needed which the court considers to be necessary before a decision can be reached in the case.

(c)   ...

(d)   ...

(e)   The court may further consider whether there is a need for an investigation under section 37 Children Act 1989.

(f)   A copy of the Order requesting the report and any relevant court documents are to be sent to Cafcass/CAFCASS Cymru or, in the case of the Local Authority to the Legal Adviser to the Director of the Local Authority Children's Services and, where known, to the allocated social worker by the court forthwith.

(g)   Is any expert evidence required? If so, section 13 Children and Families Act 2014, and Part 25 of the FPR must be complied with. This is the latest point at which consideration should be given to the instruction of an expert in accordance with Rule 25.6(b) of the FPR; the court will need to consider carefully the future conduct of proceedings where the preparation of an expert report is necessary but where the parties are unrepresented and are unable to fund the preparation of such a report.

- **Wishes and feelings of the child**:

(a)   ... children and young people should be at the centre of all proceedings.

(b)   The child or young person should feel that their needs, wishes and feelings have been considered in the court process

(c)   Each decision should be assessed on its impact on the child.

(d)   The court must consider the wishes and feelings of the child, ascertainable so far as is possible in light of the child's age and understanding and circumstances. Specifically, the Court should ask:

    i.   Is the child aware of the proceedings?

    ii.   Are the wishes and feelings of the child available, and/or to be ascertained (if at all)?

    iii.   How is the child to be involved in the proceedings ... ? Should they be encouraged to write to the court, or have their views reported by Cafcass/CAFCASS Cymru or by a local authority?

    iv.   Who will inform the child of the outcome of the case, where appropriate?

- **Case Management**:

(a)   What, if any, issues are agreed and what are the key issues to be determined?

(b)   Should the matter be listed for a fact-finding hearing?

(c)   Are there any interim orders which can usefully be made (eg indirect, supported or supervised contact) pending Dispute Resolution Appointment or final hearing?

(d)   What directions are required to ensure the application is ready for a Dispute Resolution Appointment or final hearing – statements, reports etc?

(e)   Should the application be listed for a Dispute Resolution Appointment (it is envisaged that most cases will be so listed)?

(f)   Should the application be listed straightaway for a final hearing?

(g)   Judicial continuity should be actively considered (especially if there has been or is to be a fact finding hearing or a contested interim hearing).

- **Allocation**:

    ...

- **Order (other than a final order)**: Where no final agreement is reached, and the court is required to give case management directions, the following shall be included on the order [CAP02]:

    (a)   The issues about which the parties are agreed;

    (b)   The issues that remain to be resolved;

    (c)   The steps that are planned to resolve the issues;

    (d)   Any interim arrangements pending such resolution, including arrangements for the involvement of children;

    (e)   The timetable for such steps and, where this involves further hearings, the date of such hearings;

    (f)   A statement as to any facts relating to risk or safety; in so far as they are resolved the result will be stated and, in so far as not resolved, the steps to be taken to resolve them will be stated.

    (g)   Whether the parties are to be assisted by participation in mediation, Separated Parents Information Programme, WT4C, or other types of parenting intervention, and to detail any activity directions or conditions imposed by the court;

    (h)   The date, time and venue of the next hearing;

    (i)   Whether the author of any section 7 report is required to attend the hearing, in order to give oral evidence. A direction for the Cafcass officer or WFPO to attend court will not be made without first considering the reason why attendance is necessary, and upon what issues the Cafcass officer or WFPO will be providing evidence.

    (j)   Where both parties are Litigants in Person, the court may direct HMCTS to produce a Litigant in Person bundle;

    (k)   The judge will, as far as possible, provide a copy of the order to both parties before they leave the courtroom, and will, if necessary, go through and explain the contents of the order to ensure they are clearly understood by both parties. The parties should know the date, time and venue of any further hearing before they leave the court.

15. Timetable for the child

15.1 Court proceedings should be timetabled so that the dispute can be resolved as soon as safe and possible in the interests of the child.

15.2 The judge shall, at all times during the proceedings, have regard to the impact which the court timetable will have on the welfare and development of the child to whom the application relates. The judge and the parties shall pay particular attention to the child's age, and important landmarks in the immediate life of the child, including:

(a)   the child's birthday;
(b)   the start of nursery/schooling;
(c)   the start/end of a school term/year;
(d)   any proposed change of school; and/or
(e)   any significant change in the child's family, or social, circumstances.

15.3 While it is acknowledged that an interim order may be appropriate at an early stage of court proceedings, cases should not be adjourned for a review (or reviews) of contact or other orders/arrangements, &/or for addendum section 7 report, unless such a hearing is necessary and for a clear purpose that is consistent with the timetable for the child and in the child's best interests.

15.4 When preparing a section 7 report, Cafcass/CAFCASS Cymru (or, where appropriate, the local authority) is encouraged to make recommendations for the stepped phasing-in of child arrangements (ie recommendations for the medium and longer term future for the child) insofar as they are able to do so safely in the interests of the child concerned;

15.5 Where active involvement or monitoring is needed, the court may consider making:

(1)   An order under section 11H Children Act 1989 (Monitoring);
(2)   A Family Assistance Order under section 16 Children Act 1989 (in accordance with the Practice Direction 12M FPR, and if all the named adults in the order agree to the making of such an order and if the order is directed to a local authority, the child lives (or will live) within that local authority area or the local authority consents to the making of the order.

16. Capacity of Litigants

16.1 In the event that the judge has concerns about the capacity of a litigant before the court, the judge shall consider

(1)   the Guidance issued by the Family Justice Council in relation to assessing the capacity of litigants;
(2)   Practice Direction 15B (Adults Who May Be Protected Parties and Children Who May Become Protected Parties In Family Proceedings).

17. Evidence

17.1 No evidence shall be filed in relation to an application until after the FHDRA unless:

(1)   It has been filed in support of a without notice application
(2)   It has been directed by the Court by the Directions on Issue (CAP01);
(3)   It has been directed by the Court for the purposes of determining an interim application.

18. Rule 16.4 children's guardians

18.1 The Court should be vigilant to identify the cases where a rule 16.4 children's guardian should be appointed. This should be considered initially at the FHDRA.

18.2 Where the court is considering the appointment of a children's guardian from Cafcass/CAFCASS Cymru, it should first ensure that enquiries have been made of the appropriate Cafcass/CAFCASS Cymru manager ...

18.3 When the court decides to appoint a children's guardian, consideration should first be given to appointing an Officer of the Service or WFPO. If Cafcass/CAFCASS Cymru is unable to provide a children's guardian without delay, or if there is some other reason why the appointment of a Cafcass officer is not appropriate, the court should (further to rule 16.24 of the FPR) appoint a person other than the Official Solicitor, unless the Official Solicitor expressly consents.

18.4 ...

19. Dispute Resolution Appointment (DRA)

19.1 The Court shall list the application for a Dispute Resolution Appointment ('DRA') to follow the preparation of section 7 or other expert report, or Separated Parenting Information Programme (SPIP) (or WT4C in Wales), if this is considered likely to be helpful in the interests of the child.

19.2 The author of the section 7 report will only attend this hearing if directed to do so by the Court.

19.3 At the DRA the Court will:

(1)   Identify the key issue(s) (if any) to be determined and the extent to which those issues can be resolved or narrowed at the DRA;
(2)   Consider whether the DRA can be used as a final hearing;
(3)   Resolve or narrow the issues by hearing evidence;
(4)   Identify the evidence to be heard on the issues which remain to PD 12(B): be resolved at the final hearing;
(5)   Give final case management directions ...
        ...
        (e)   Listing the Final Hearing.

20. Fact-finding hearing

20.1 If the court considers that a fact-finding hearing is necessary it shall conduct that hearing in accordance with revised Practice Direction 12J

21. Enforcement of Child Arrangements

21.1 On any application for enforcement of a child arrangements order, the court shall:

- consider whether the facts relevant to the alleged non-compliance are agreed, or whether it is necessary to conduct a hearing to establish the facts;
- consider the reasons for any non-compliance;
- consider how the wishes and feelings of the child are to be ascertained;
- consider whether advice is required from Cafcass/CAFCASS Cymru on the appropriate way forward;
- assess and manage any risks of making further or other child arrangements order;
- consider whether a SPIP or referral for dispute resolution is appropriate;
- consider whether an enforcement order may be appropriate, and
- consider the welfare checklist.

21.2 ... Enforcement cases should be concluded without delay.

21.3 ...

21.4 ...

21.5 The court has a wide range of powers in the event of a breach of a child arrangements order without reasonable excuse.

21.6 This range of powers includes (but is not limited to):

(a)   referral of the parents to a SPIP, or in Wales a WT4C, or mediation;

(b)   variation of the child arrangements order ... ;

(c)   a contact enforcement order or suspended enforcement order under section 11J Children Act 1989 ... ;

(d)   an order for compensation for financial loss (under section 11O Children Act 1989);

(e)   committal to prison or

(f)   a fine.

21.7 In the event that the court is considering an enforcement order for alleged non-compliance with a court order (under section 11J Children Act 1989) or considering a Compensation order in respect of financial loss (under section 11O Children Act 1989), the court shall (in the absence of agreement between the parties about the relevant facts) determine the facts in order to establish the cause of the alleged failure to comply.

21.8 Section 11L Children Act 1989 provides that if the court finds that a breach has occurred without reasonable excuse it may order the noncompliant party to undertake unpaid work if that is necessary to secure compliance, and if the effect on the non-compliant party is proportionate to the seriousness of the breach. The court must also consider whether unpaid work is available in the locality and the likely effect on the noncompliant party. It is good practice to ask Cafcass/CAFCASS Cymru to report on the suitability of this order. Section 11L(7) also requires the court to take into account the welfare of the child who is the subject of the order for contact.

22. Court timetable
22.1 Working Day 1: ... The application will not be issued unless the form has been completed correctly.

22.2 Working Day 2: ... Case allocated by Gatekeepers ...

22.3 17 working days from the date of its receipt of the application Cafcass/CAFCASS Cymru will provide the safeguarding letter/report to the Court (20 working days in the area of CAFCASS Cymru).

22.4 Week 5 (or latest, week 6): Case listed for FHDRA ...

22.5 Thereafter, case may be listed for fact-finding hearing, DRA &/or final hearing.

23. ...

Annex: Explanation of terms

[Refer to PD12B]

Chapter 4

Essential Practice Guidance

PRESIDENT'S GUIDANCE IN RELATION TO OUT OF HOURS HEARINGS

1. It is perhaps not sufficiently appreciated by the general public that there is always a High Court judge of the Family Division on duty 'out of hours' – that is to say every day of the year including all holiday periods either; (1) between 16.15 on day one and 10.30am on day two of a normal court sitting; or (2) between 16.15 on any given Friday and 10.30 the following Monday. In vacations, when the court is not sitting, a similar service is provided at any time of the day or night.

2. It is of the utmost importance that this service is used for its intended purposes and is not abused. It is designed for urgent cases. In this context 'urgent' has a specific meaning. It means cases in which an order of the court is required to regulate the position between the moment the order is made and the next available sitting of the court in conventional court hours – that is, usually, 10.30 on the following morning.

3. Judges of the Family Division have no complaint, for example, if, in the middle of the night, they are asked to sanction lifesaving medical treatment, or if they have to visit a hospital at such a time in order to decide whether a given individual should undergo urgent and specific treatment.

4. Any application that is 'urgent' within the definition set out in paragraph 2 above must be capable of being reduced to a faxed sheet of A4 (or its email equivalent), or a short telephone conversation. Whether or not a case is 'urgent' will always be a matter for the judge.

5. What is unacceptable is an application which can plainly wait until the normal sitting of the court and/or which involves a substantial amount of documentation. A judge cannot and should not be expected either to receive or to assimilate a substantial volume of documentation in an urgent, out of hours application unless both are absolutely essential to a proper understanding of the order which the judge is being asked to make. Equally, judges who are on duty out of hours should not be expected to make arrangements to sit in court unless such a sitting is strictly necessary to enable

an order to be made. The profession should also remember that the judge on duty, whilst always available on the telephone, will be at home, and that 'home' may not be in London.

6. Lawyers who abuse the system, particularly those who seek to take advantage of an order not made on notice and out of hours with a speedy return date in hours may not only be the subject of orders for wasted costs, but may find themselves reported to their professional bodies for serious professional misconduct. The profession is thus reminded of the definition of 'urgent' set out in paragraph 2 of this note.

7. Nothing in this note supersedes any previous Guidance or Practice Note relating to out of hours applications.

Sir Nicholas Wall
President of the Family Division
18 November 2010

PRESIDENT'S GUIDANCE: FAMILY COURT – DURATION OF EX PARTE (WITHOUT NOTICE) ORDERS

Issued by the President of the Family Division on 13 October 2014

[An order made ex parte or without notice is a one-sided order made without warning]

[Footnotes omitted]

[Essential guidance]

2 … To grant an ex parte (without notice) injunction for an unlimited time is wrong in principle. The practice of granting such orders for an unlimited time must stop.

3 The same principles, as set out below, apply to all ex parte (without notice) injunctive orders made by the Family Court or by the Family Division, irrespective of the subject-matter of the proceedings or the terms of the order.

4 The law is to be found in *Horgan v Horgan* [2002] EWCA Civ 1371, paras 5–6 (Ward LJ), *R (Casey) v Restormel Borough Council* [2007] EWHC 2554 (Admin), paras 37–41 (Munby J), *In re C (A Child) (Family Proceedings: Practice)* [2013] EWCA Civ 1412, [2014] 1 WLR 2182, [2014] 1 FLR 1239, para 15 (Ryder LJ), and *JM v CZ* [2014] EWHC 1125 (Fam), paras 5–13 (Mostyn J).

5 The relevant principles, compliance with which is essential, are as follows:

(i)   An ex parte (without notice) injunctive order must never be made without limit of time. There must be a fixed end date.

(ii)   It is not sufficient merely to specify a return day. The order must specify on its face and in clear terms precisely when it expires (eg, 4.30pm on 19 November 2014).

(iii) The duration of the order should not normally exceed 14 days.

(iv)   The order must also specify the date, time and place of the hearing on the return day. It is usually convenient for this date to coincide with the expiry date of the order (eg, list the return day for 10.30am on 19 November 2014 and specify that the order expires at 4.30pm on 19 November 2014).

(v)   The order (see FPR 18.10(3)) 'must contain a statement of the right to make an application to set aside or vary the order under rule 18.11.' The phrase 'liberty to apply on 24 hours' notice' is not sufficient for this purpose. The order must spell out that the respondent is entitled, without waiting for the return day, to apply on notice (the details of which and the need for which must be set out on the face of the order) to set aside or vary the order.

(vi)   If the respondent does apply to set aside or vary the order the court must list the application as a matter of urgency, within a matter of days at most.

6 Experience suggests that in certain types of case, for example, non-molestation injunctions granted in accordance with Part IV of the Family Law Act 1996, the respondent frequently neither applies to set aside or vary the order nor attends the hearing on the return day. In such cases the court may decide to proceed in the way suggested by Mostyn J in *JM v CZ* [2014] EWHC 1125 (Fam), para 13:

> 'the return date should be listed, say, 14 days after the initial ex parte order had been made but that the respondent ought to confirm in writing, seven days before the return date, both to the applicant and to the court, whether he in fact wished to attend on the return date and to argue for variation or discharge of the order; and that if the respondent failed to write to the court within that period, it would be open to the applicant to notify the court that the return date should be vacated and to invite the court to extend the injunction as a matter of box work.'

7 Courts must remember that, whether or not the respondent attends on the return day, the respondent does not have to demonstrate that the order should not be extended. In every case the burden remains on the applicant to persuade the court that an ex parte (without notice) order should be extended.

8 To ensure compliance with these principles, it is suggested that the following form of order be used:

> '1 Paragraph(s) [*insert*] of this order shall be effective against the respondent [*insert* names] once it is personally served on [him]/[her] [and/or] once [he]/[she] is made aware of the terms of this order whether by personal service or otherwise.
>
> 2 Paragraph(s) [*insert*] of this order shall last until [*insert* date and time] unless it is set aside or varied before then by an order of the court.
>
> 3 The case is listed for a further hearing in the Family Court sitting at [*insert* place] on [*insert* date] ('the return date'), time estimate: [*insert* time]. At the hearing on the return date the court will reconsider the application and decide whether the order should continue. If the respondent does not attend on the date and at the time shown the court may make an order in [his]/[her] absence.
>
> 4 The respondent has the right to apply to the court at any time, and without waiting until the return date, to set aside or vary this order. [*Insert if appropriate*: The respondent must give [*insert* hours/days] [written] notice of the application to the [applicant]/[applicant's solicitors].]
>
> 5 If the respondent intends to rely on any evidence in support of [his]/[her] application to set aside or vary this order, or intends to rely on any evidence to oppose the continuation of the order at the hearing on the return date, the substance of the evidence must be provided in writing to the [applicant]/[applicant's solicitors] in advance.
>
> [Add if appropriate]

6 If the respondent intends to oppose the continuation of the order on the return day [he]/[she] must notify the court [in writing or by email] no later than [*insert* date and time] that [he]/[she] intends to attend the hearing on the return day and to oppose the continuation of the order. If the respondent does not notify the court then the court may, if appropriate, make an order dispensing with the need for any attendance by the [applicant]/[applicant's solicitors] on the return day and may, if appropriate, on the return day make an order extending the injunction.'

Sir James Munby PFD
13 October 2014

PRESIDENT'S GUIDANCE OF 10 NOVEMBER 2014: THE INTERNATIONAL CHILD ABDUCTION AND CONTACT UNIT (ICACU)

[Footnotes omitted]

I am aware that an increasing number of children cases have an international element and that courts often require information from other jurisdictions before being able to proceed. It is not always easy to know how to obtain this information.

While it may not always be possible to obtain the information sufficiently quickly to enable the court to hear these cases within 26 weeks, I am very grateful to the International Child Abduction and Contact Unit (ICACU) for providing the following, which will help practitioners to follow the correct route to obtain information to help the court when necessary. It has been approved by Lady Justice Black and the Senior Master.

Practitioners will also need to be alive to Chapter VI of Part 12 of the Family Procedure Rules 2010 as amended, and to The Parental Responsibility and Measures for the Protection of Children (International Obligations) (England and Wales and Northern Ireland) Regulations 2010.

Sir James Munby
President of the Family Division
10 November 2014

The ICACU

The ICACU is the operational Central Authority for England and Wales for Council Regulation (EC) 2201/2003 ('Brussels IIA' or 'the Revised Brussels II Regulation') and for England only for the 1996 Hague Convention on Jurisdiction, Applicable Law, Recognition, Enforcement and Co-operation in Respect of Parental Responsibility and Measures for the Protection of Children ('the 1996 Hague Convention').

The ICACU provides a standard response/leaflet to enquiries about requests for co-operation from local authorities explaining about other sources of assistance including where to find information and contact details of other bodies which may be able to assist. A copy of that standard response/leaflet is attached as it is a helpful resource.

Can the ICACU help?

The ICACU is a small administrative unit. Its staff are not lawyers or social workers. The ICACU cannot give legal advice.

The ICACU may however be able to help by making a request for co-operation to another country, in particular for the collection and exchange of information if the other country is:

(a)   either a Member State of the European Union (other than Denmark); or

(b)   a State Party to the 1996 Hague Convention;

and

(c)   the request for co-operation is in scope of the Revised Brussels II Regulation or of the 1996 Hague Convention

To decide if the proposed request for co-operation is in scope consider Articles 1, 53–57 of the Revised Brussels II Regulation and Articles 1, 3, 4 , 30–37 of the 1996 Hague Convention.

ICACU can have a role in relation to transfers between courts under Article 15 of the Revised Brussels II Regulation or authorities under Articles 8 and 9 the 1996 Hague Convention; this role is not covered by this 'view'.

Requests for co-operation involving the collection and exchange of information under Article 55 of the Revised Brussels II Regulation or under Article 34 of the 1996 Hague Convention must be distinguished from requests for evidence.

If making a request under the 1996 Hague Convention consideration should be given to Article 37 of the 1996 Hague Convention before deciding to contact the ICACU.

If considering placement of a child in another country:

- for an EU Member State you should consider Article 56 of the Revised Brussels II Regulation and the decision of the Court of Justice of the European Union ('CJEU') on the operation of Article 56 in case C-92/12 PPU;
- for a 1996 Hague Convention country you should consider Article 33 of the Convention.

Whether or not placement of a child in another country is considered to be placement in institutional care or with a foster family, is a question for the requested country not for the requesting country. A placement which from a domestic perspective is a private law placement may be regarded as a public law placement by the requested country. A request for co-operation can be made to establish if, in principle, the consent of the other country would be required for placement even if the care plan for the child is not yet fully informed.

The ICACU may have practical knowledge and experience of the processes and procedures in the other country which it can usefully share in response to an enquiry. However before relying on information formerly provided by the ICACU in another case you should bear in mind that the other country's processes and procedures may have changed since you last contacted the ICACU.

If your request is not in scope of the Revised Brussels II Regulation or of the 1996 Hague Convention, it *may* be in scope of another European Regulation or international Convention and another central authority or body may be able to assist.

For example, in England and Wales:

The **Senior Master** is:

(a)   the transmitting agency under Article 2 of Council Regulation (EC) No 1393/2007 of 13 November 2007 on the service in the Member States of judicial and extrajudicial documents in civil or commercial matters, ('the Service Regulation')

(b)   the central authority under Article 3 of the 1965 Hague Convention on the Service Abroad of Judicial and Extrajudicial Documents in Civil or Commercial Matters ('the 1965 Hague Convention')

(c)   the central body under Article 3 of Council Regulation (EC) No 1206/2001 of 28 May 2001 on cooperation between the courts of the Member States in the taking of evidence in civil or commercial matters ('the Taking of Evidence Regulation')

(d)   the central authority under Article 2 of the 1970 Hague Convention on the Taking of Evidence Abroad in Civil or Commercial Matters ('the 1970 Hague Convention').

The administrative unit which supports the Senior Master is the Foreign Process Section based in the Royal Courts of Justice.

Member States have differing views as to what comes within scope of the Revised Brussels II Regulation and what comes within scope of the Taking of Evidence Regulation. If you are in doubt this may be where the ICACU's practical knowledge and experience of the other country's processes and procedures can be of assistance. In such cases you should make an early enquiry to avoid delay at the point the formal request needs to be made.

The **UKCA-ECR** is the central authority for the exchange of criminal records between Member States of the European Union.

What the ICACU does not do

As the ICACU has no role to play in the operation of:

- the Service Regulation, or of
- the 1965 Hague Convention,
- the ICACU will not serve or arrange service of court documents and nor will its counterpart in the other country.

As the mechanism for the taking of evidence abroad is in the Taking of Evidence Regulation or the 1970 Hague Convention, the ICACU will not assist in acquiring evidence.

Please note that the ICACU does not forward requests for co-operation on to other domestic central authorities or bodies when it receives a request which is outside the scope of the Revised Brussels II Regulation or of the 1996 Hague Convention.

The ICACU does not notify consular authorities about proceedings concerning a child of a foreign nationality either pursuant to *Re E (Brussels II Revised: Vienna Convention: Reporting Restrictions)* [2014] EWHC 6 (Fam), [2014] 2 FLR 151 or at all as that is not a central authority duty or function. Consular authorities, not the ICACU, should also be contacted about passports and other travel documents such as visas.

A request for an opinion on jurisdiction is not a question for central authorities. The ICACU will not offer an opinion on jurisdiction and nor should a question about jurisdiction form part of a request for the collection and exchange of information.

The ICACU will not transmit a request for formal criminal record checks as that is a request properly directed to the UKCA-ECR.

The ICACU does not become directly involved in the court proceedings. Central authorities are not under any obligation to engage in proceedings and do not require a court order before discharging their duties and responsibilities under the Revised Brussels II Regulation or the 1996 Hague Convention.

Contacting the ICACU
The ICACU's general office telephone number is 0203 681 2608 and can be used by parties seeking 'in principle' advice based on the ICACU's experience of the other country. However the ICACU prefers contact to be made by email using the email address:
icacu@offsol.gsi.gov.uk.

Email contact allows the ICACU to manage their busy workload and to collate information about the types of requests and countries. If an enquiry is made by telephone the ICACU will usually ask that the enquiry also be put in writing but understands that if a matter is urgent a telephone enquiry may first be necessary.

Making a request for co-operation
Requests for co-operation need to be **relevant, focussed, timely** and **practical**.

You should specify whether the request is being made under the Revised Brussels II Regulation or under the 1996 Hague Convention. You should identify in your request the Article(s) relied on by you for the purpose of making the request. Remember that the request needs to be in scope of the Revised Brussels II Regulation or the 1996 Hague Convention.

Requests for co-operation should be made as early as practicably possible. There is nothing in the Revised Brussels II Regulation or the 1996 Hague Convention which requires a requested State to respond to a request for co-operation within a particular timescale. The ICACU cannot compel the requested central authority or foreign competent authorities to respond within a specific timetable but their counterparts are more likely to be able to offer assistance if the request is focussed and made on a timely basis. The ICACU therefore asks that any request for co-operation is made as early as practicable in the proceedings and that it is informed about the court timetable including the date of any listed hearing.

When fixing the court timetable the timescale for a response from the other jurisdiction needs to be realistic having regard to the number of steps involved in a request for co-operation. In a public law case those steps may involve:

- the decision to make a request for co-operation by the local authority whether following the court's direction or otherwise;
- request received by the ICACU;
- the ICACU requesting any necessary translations;
- the request being transmitted by the ICACU to the requested central authority;
- the requested central authority making any enquiries directly or of its competent authorities to enable it to respond;
- the requested central authority or the ICACU arranging any necessary translations of the response;
- the ICACU transmitting the response to the local authority here;
- the initial response from the requested central authority may include a request for additional information and documents in order to enable a more detailed response to be provided.

A sealed copy of any relevant court order should be provided to the ICACU promptly (to assist in avoiding delay).

In formulating the request for co-operation you should give consideration to what information practically the requested central authority and their competent authorities may require in order to respond to the request. A clear background case summary will assist. You should always provide the full name and date(s) of birth of the child(ren) and of any relevant adult and an explanation of the family relationship(s). If the case involves a more complex family structure (full, half or step siblings, different generations in the same household etc) then a genogram is likely to be of assistance. Additionally:

- for the benefit of the requested central authority you should explain technical language (for example what is meant by section 20 consent) and acronyms;
- for kinship care assessments it may be useful to explain what the local authority or court would find helpful for the assessment to cover but it is unlikely to be appropriate to ask foreign authorities to complete domestic forms;
- for requests to identify potential kinship carers provide as much information as possible to assist the requested State to trace the individuals concerned; if current contact details are not known, then the last known address in the requested country (or as much information as possible as to where the family

is from in that country), social security details or passport/foreign identity document details may also assist;

- only the documents relevant to the request should be sent; it is not usually necessary for the whole court bundle to be provided;
- if the court's permission is required to disclose information or documents to the ICACU and to the requested central authority the permission application should be made promptly.

The ICACU has a limited budget for translations. It will arrange translation of the request for co-operation but the parties to the court proceedings will need to agree who is to prepare translations of any supporting documents.

If the welfare plan for the child is for placement in the other country you should check if that country's consent to the placement is required under either Article 56 of the Revised Brussels II Regulation or under Article 33 of the 1996 Hague Convention. Whether or not consent is required is a question for the other country. If there is any doubt about whether the consent of the other country will be required a request for co-operation can be made in order to clarify the position.

The ICACU does not require a court order in order to discharge its duties and functions as the operational central authority but it may be helpful if the court directs one party to the proceedings to make the request for co-operation to the ICACU and to do so within a particular time frame. The parties may of course consult with each other as to the content of the request for co-operation.

In public law children cases the ICACU prefers that the local authority (rather than any other party) contact the ICACU about a request for co-operation (or any other request – for example, assistance with an Article 15 transfer request). The ICACU's experience is that a request for co-operation to the other country may be followed by a request from that country about the same child. If the ICACU receives a request from the other country it will transmit it to the local authority and it is administratively more efficient and less likely to give rise to miscommunication if the ICACU is in contact with one party only.

Although the court may request or invite assistance from foreign authorities orders should not be made against foreign authorities including central authorities, consular authorities or other public bodies in another country.

PRACTICE GUIDANCE: MCKENZIE FRIENDS (CIVIL AND FAMILY COURTS)

[Footnotes omitted]

1) This Guidance applies to civil and family proceedings in the Court of Appeal (Civil Division), the High Court of Justice, the County Courts and the Family Proceedings Court in the Magistrates' Courts. It is issued as guidance (**not** as a Practice Direction) by the Master of the Rolls, as Head of Civil Justice, and the President of the Family Division, as Head of Family Justice. It is intended to remind courts and litigants of the principles set out in the authorities and supersedes the guidance contained in *Practice Note (Family Courts: McKenzie Friends) (No 2)* [2008] 1 WLR 2757, which is now withdrawn. It is issued in light of the increase in litigants-in-person (litigants) in all levels of the civil and family courts.

The Right to Reasonable Assistance
2) Litigants have the right to have reasonable assistance from a layperson, sometimes called a McKenzie Friend (MF). Litigants assisted by MFs remain litigants-in-person. MFs have no independent right to provide assistance. They have no right to act as advocates or to carry out the conduct of litigation.

What McKenzie Friends may do
3) MFs may: i) provide moral support for litigants; ii) take notes; iii) help with case papers; iii) quietly give advice on any aspect of the conduct of the case.

What McKenzie Friends may not do
4) MFs may not: i) act as the litigants' agent in relation to the proceedings; ii) manage litigants' cases outside court, for example by signing court documents; or iii) address the court, make oral submissions or examine witnesses.
Exercising the Right to Reasonable Assistance

5) While litigants ordinarily have a right to receive reasonable assistance from MFs the court retains the power to refuse to permit such assistance. The court may do so where it is satisfied that, in that case, the interests of justice and fairness do not require the litigant to receive such assistance.

6) A litigant who wishes to exercise this right should inform the judge as soon as possible indicating who the MF will be. The proposed MF should produce a short curriculum vitae or other statement setting out relevant experience, confirming that he or she has no interest in the case and understands the MF's role and the duty of confidentiality.

7) If the court considers that there might be grounds for circumscribing the right to receive such assistance, or a party objects to the presence of, or assistance given by a MF, it is not for the litigant to justify the exercise of the right. It is for the court or the

objecting party to provide sufficient reasons why the litigant should not receive such assistance.

8) When considering whether to circumscribe the right to assistance or refuse a MF permission to attend the right to a fair trial is engaged. The matter should be considered carefully. The litigant should be given a reasonable opportunity to argue the point. The proposed MF should not be excluded from that hearing and should normally be allowed to help the litigant.

9) Where proceedings are in *closed court*, i.e. the hearing is in chambers, is in private, or the proceedings relate to a child, the litigant is required to justify the MF's presence in court. The presumption in favour of permitting a MF to attend such hearings, and thereby enable litigants to exercise the right to assistance, is a strong one.

10) The court may refuse to allow a litigant to exercise the right to receive assistance at the start of a hearing. The court can also circumscribe the right during the course of a hearing. It may be refused at the start of a hearing or later circumscribed where the court forms the view that a MF may give, has given, or is giving, assistance which impedes the efficient administration of justice. However, the court should also consider whether a firm and unequivocal warning to the litigant and/or MF might suffice in the first instance.

11) A decision by the court not to curtail assistance from a MF should be regarded as final, save on the ground of subsequent misconduct by the MF or on the ground that the MF's continuing presence will impede the efficient administration of justice. In such event the court should give a short judgment setting out the reasons why it has curtailed the right to assistance. Litigants may appeal such decisions. MFs have no standing to do so.

12) The following factors should not be taken to justify the court refusing to permit a litigant receiving such assistance:

(i)   The case or application is simple or straightforward, or is, for instance, a directions or case management hearing;
(ii)   The litigant appears capable of conducting the case without assistance;
(iii)   The litigant is unrepresented through choice;
(iv)   The other party is not represented;
(v)   The proposed MF belongs to an organisation that promotes a particular cause;
(vi)   The proceedings are confidential and the court papers contain sensitive information relating to a family's affairs

13) A litigant may be denied the assistance of a MF because its provision might undermine or has undermined the efficient administration of justice. Examples of circumstances where this might arise are: i) the assistance is being provided for an improper purpose; ii) the assistance is unreasonable in nature or degree; iii) the MF is

subject to a civil proceedings order or a civil restraint order; iv) the MF is using the litigant as a puppet; v) the MF is directly or indirectly conducting the litigation, vi) the court is not satisfied that the MF fully understands the duty of confidentiality.

14) Where a litigant is receiving assistance from a MF in care proceedings, the court should consider the MF's attendance at any advocates' meetings directed by the court, and, with regard to cases commenced after 1.4.08, consider directions in accordance with paragraph 13.2 of the Practice Direction Guide to Case Management in Public Law Proceedings.

15) Litigants are permitted to communicate any information, including filed evidence, relating to the proceedings to MFs for the purpose of obtaining advice or assistance in relation to the proceedings.

16) Legal representatives should ensure that documents are served on litigants in good time to enable them to seek assistance regarding their content from MFs in advance of any hearing or advocates' meeting.

17) The High Court can, under its inherent jurisdiction, impose a civil restraint order on MFs who repeatedly act in ways that undermine the efficient administration of justice.

Rights of audience and rights to conduct litigation

18) MFs do **not** have a right of audience or a right to conduct litigation. It is a criminal offence to exercise rights of audience or to conduct litigation unless properly qualified and authorised to do so by an appropriate regulatory body or, in the case of an otherwise unqualified or unauthorised individual (i.e., a lay individual including a MF), the court grants such rights on a case-by-case basis.

19) Courts should be slow to grant any application from a litigant for a right of audience or a right to conduct litigation to any lay person, including a MF. This is because a person exercising such rights must ordinarily be properly trained, be under professional discipline (including an obligation to insure against liability for negligence) and be subject to an overriding duty to the court. These requirements are necessary for the protection of all parties to litigation and are essential to the proper administration of justice.

20) Any application for a right of audience or a right to conduct litigation to be granted to any lay person should therefore be considered very carefully. The court should only be prepared to grant such rights where there is good reason to do so taking into account all the circumstances of the case, which are likely to vary greatly. Such grants should not be extended to lay persons automatically or without due consideration. They should not be granted for mere convenience.

21) Examples of the type of special circumstances which have been held to justify the grant of a right of audience to a lay person, including a MF, are: i) that person is a close relative of the litigant; ii) health problems preclude the litigant from addressing the court, or conducting litigation, and the litigant cannot afford to pay for a qualified legal representative; iii) the litigant is relatively inarticulate and prompting by that person may unnecessarily prolong the proceedings.

22) It is for the litigant to persuade the court that the circumstances of the case are such that it is in the interests of justice for the court to grant a lay person a right of audience or a right to conduct litigation.

23) The grant of a right of audience or a right to conduct litigation to lay persons who hold themselves out as professional advocates or professional MFs or who seek to exercise such rights on a regular basis, whether for reward or not, will however **only** be granted in exceptional circumstances. To do otherwise would tend to subvert the will of Parliament.

24) If a litigant wants a lay person to be granted a right of audience, an application must be made at the start of the hearing. If a right to conduct litigation is sought such an application must be made at the earliest possible time and must be made, in any event, before the lay person does anything which amounts to the conduct of litigation. It is for litigants to persuade the court, on a case-by-case basis, that the grant of such rights is justified.

25) Rights of audience and the right to conduct litigation are separate rights. The grant of one right to a lay person does not mean that a grant of the other right has been made. If both rights are sought their grant must be applied for individually and justified separately.

26) Having granted either a right of audience or a right to conduct litigation, the court has the power to remove either right. The grant of such rights in one set of proceedings cannot be relied on as a precedent supporting their grant in future proceedings.

Remuneration
27) Litigants can enter into lawful agreements to pay fees to MFs for the provision of reasonable assistance in court or out of court by, for instance, carrying out clerical or mechanical activities, such as photocopying documents, preparing bundles, delivering documents to opposing parties or the court, or the provision of legal advice in connection with court proceedings. Such fees cannot be lawfully recovered from the opposing party.

28) Fees said to be incurred by MFs for carrying out the conduct of litigation, where the court has not granted such a right, cannot lawfully be recovered from either the litigant for whom they carry out such work or the opposing party.

29) Fees said to be incurred by MFs for carrying out the conduct of litigation after the court has granted such a right are in principle recoverable from the litigant for whom the work is carried out. Such fees cannot be lawfully recovered from the opposing party.

30) Fees said to be incurred by MFs for exercising a right of audience following the grant of such a right by the court are in principle recoverable from the litigant on whose behalf the right is exercised. Such fees are also recoverable, in principle, from the opposing party as a recoverable disbursement: CPR 48.6(2) and 48(6)(3)(ii).

Personal Support Unit & Citizen's Advice Bureau
31) Litigants should also be aware of the services provided by local Personal Support Units and Citizens' Advice Bureaux. The PSU at the Royal Courts of Justice in London can be contacted on 020 7947 7701, by email at cbps@bello.co.uk or at the enquiry desk. The CAB at the Royal Courts of Justice in London can be contacted on 020 7947 6564 or at the enquiry desk.

Lord Neuberger of Abbotsbury, Master of the Rolls
Sir Nicholas Wall, President of the Family Division
12 July 2010

ADVOCACY TRAINING COUNCIL GUIDELINES ON VULNERABLE PEOPLE GIVING EVIDENCE

[For full guidance and toolkits, go to www.theadvocatesgateway.org/toolkits]

The Advocacy Training Council toolkits were developed in response to a recommendation of the Advocacy Training Council report *Raising the Bar: the handling of vulnerable witnesses, victims and defendants in court (2011)* that 'all advocates be issued with "toolkits" setting out common problems encountered when examining vulnerable witnesses and defendants, together with suggested solutions ... '.

The toolkits provide advocates with general good practice guidance when preparing for trial in cases involving a witness or a defendant with communication needs. Information should always be sought from the individual witness or defendant or their family/support worker/teachers etc. about their specific communication abilities and needs. Consideration should also be given to the use of an intermediary.

'Advocates should not take it upon themselves to decide what the communications needs are of any of their potentially vulnerable witnesses' (Special Measures Guidance from the Bar Council). Where appropriate, consideration should be given to an assessment by an intermediary.

Each toolkit contains the following statement *'Questioning that contravenes principles for obtaining accurate information from a witness by exploiting his or her developmental limitations is not conducive to a fair trial and would contravene the Codes of Conduct'*.

The toolkits also contain links to source material (checked as of January 2013). Toolkits 3 to 8 contain examples from trial transcript questions, with suggestions about how they might be improved; highlighted examples of **good practice** and **poor practice**; and lists of references, contributors and reviewers.

If you intend to use The Advocate's Gateway materials or toolkits for anything other than personal, non-commercial use to assist with communication, permission must be obtained in advance from the authors.

Toolkits available to download (as at December 2015)

1   Ground rules hearings and the fair treatment of vulnerable people in court
       Ground rules hearing checklist
1a   Case management when a witness or defendant is vulnerable
1b   Case management in young and other vulnerable witness cases – summary
2   General principles from research, policy and guidance: planning to question a vulnerable person or someone with communication needs

3	Planning to question someone with an autism spectrum disorder including Asperger syndrome
4	Planning to question someone with a learning disability
5	Planning to question someone with 'hidden' disabilities: specific language impairment, dyslexia, dyspraxia, dyscalculia and AD(H)
6	Planning to question a child or young person
7	Additional factors concerning children under 7 (or functioning at a very young age)
8	Effective participation of young defendants
9	Planning to question someone using a remote link
10	Identifying vulnerability in witnesses and defendants
11	Planning to question someone who is deaf
12	General principles when questioning witnesses and defendants with mental disorder
13	Vulnerable witnesses and parties in the family courts
14	Using communication aids in the criminal justice system
15	Witnesses and defendants with autism: memory and sensory issues
16	Intermediaries step by step
17	Vulnerable witnesses and parties in the civil courts
18	Working with traumatised witnesses, defendants and parties

(*Source*: The Advocacy Training Council was the original source of publication for the guidance about the provision of evidence of children and vulnerable witnesses.)

PRACTICE NOTE

THE OFFICIAL SOLICITOR TO THE SENIOR COURTS: APPOINTMENT IN FAMILY PROCEEDINGS AND PROCEEDINGS UNDER THE INHERENT JURISDICTION IN RELATION TO ADULTS

[Available in full from www.justice.gov.uk/downloads/about/ospt/ospt-practice-note.pdf]

[Essential guidance:]

3. For the avoidance of doubt, the Children and Family Court Advisory and Support Service (CAFCASS) has responsibilities in relation to a child in family proceedings in which their welfare is or may be in question (Criminal Justice and Court Services Act 2000, section 12). Since 1 April 2001 the Official Solicitor has not represented a child who is the subject of family proceedings (other than in very exceptional circumstances or where a transfer to the Court of Protection is being considered see paragraph 7 below). In cases of doubt or difficulty, staff of the Official Solicitor's office will liaise with staff of CAFCASS Legal Services to avoid duplication and ensure the most suitable arrangements are made.

Children and Protected Parties who require a litigation friend in proceedings
4. <u>Adults</u>: a 'protected party' requires a litigation friend. In family proceedings this requirement appears in Part 15 of the Family Procedure Rules 2010 ('FPR 2010') and in proceedings in the Family Division of the High Court of Justice under the court's inherent jurisdiction it appears in Part 21 of the Civil Procedure Rules 1998 ('CPR 1998'). In family proceedings, a 'protected party' means a party, or an intended party, who lacks capacity (within the meaning of the Mental Capacity Act 2005) to conduct the proceedings: FPR 2010, rule 2.3; and in proceedings under the inherent jurisdiction the expression has the same meaning: CPR 1998, rule 21.2. The following should be noted:

(a) there must be undisputed evidence that the party, or intended party, lacks capacity to conduct the proceedings;

(b) that evidence, and what flows from the party, or intended party, being a protected party, should have been disclosed to, and carefully explained to, the party or intended party;

(c) the party, or intended party, is entitled to dispute an opinion that they lack litigation capacity and there may be cases where the party's, or intended party's, capacity to conduct the proceedings is the subject of dispute between competent experts. In either case a formal finding by the court under FPR 2010, rule 2.3, or CPR 1998, rule 21.2 is required.

5. Non-subject child: a child whose own welfare is not the subject of family proceedings may nevertheless be a party. The most common examples are:

(a)   a child who is also the parent of a child, and who is a respondent to a Children Act 1989 or Adoption and Children Act 2002 application;

(b)   a child who wishes to make an application for a Children Act 1989 order naming another child (typically a contact order naming a sibling);

(c)   a child witness to some disputed factual issue in a children case and who may require intervenor status;

(d)   a child party to an application for a declaration of status under Part III of the Family Law Act 1986;

(e)   a child intervenor in financial remedy proceedings ;

(f)   a child applicant for, or respondent to, an application for an order under Part IV (Family Homes and Domestic Violence) or Part 4A (Forced Marriage) of the Family Law Act 1996.

6. FPR 2010 Part 16 makes provision for the representation of children. Rule 16.6 sets out the circumstances in which a child does not need a children's guardian or litigation friend. Any child party to proceedings under the Children Act 1989, Part 4A Family Law Act 1996, applications in adoption, placement and related proceedings, or proceedings relating to the exercise of the court's inherent jurisdiction with respect to children may rely on the provisions of rule 16.6.

7. Children aged 16–17 years: the Mental Capacity Act 2005 (Transfer of Proceedings) Order 2007 (SI 2007/1899) makes provision for the transfer of proceedings from the Court of Protection to a court having jurisdiction under the Children Act 1989. The Order also makes provision for the transfer of the whole or part of the proceedings from a court having jurisdiction under the Children Act 1989 to the Court of Protection where it considers that in all circumstances, it is just and convenient to transfer the proceedings. Article 3(3) of the Order lists those factors to which the court must have regard when making a determination about transfer either on an application or of its own initiative. Court of Protection proceedings are not family proceedings and therefore transfer of proceedings into the Court of Protection will mean that any involvement by CAFCASS in those proceedings will end.

8. The Court of Protection Rules 2007 apply to proceedings in the Court of Protection. Rule 141 (4)–(6) of those Rules make provision for a child to be permitted to conduct proceedings in the Court of Protection without a litigation friend. However if the child is 'P' within the meaning of rule 6 of the Court of Protection Rules 2007 reference should be made to rule 141(1) and rule 147 of those Rules in relation to the appointment of a litigation friend.

The role of a litigation friend

9. The case law and the Rules provide that a litigation friend must fairly and competently conduct the proceedings in the protected party's or child's best interests,

and must have no interest in the proceedings adverse to that of the protected party or child. The procedure and basis for the appointment of a litigation friend and the duty of a litigation friend are contained in Part 15 (Representation of Protected Parties) FPR 2010 and Part 16 (Representation of Children and Reports in Proceedings Involving Children) FPR 2010 and the associated Practice Directions.

The Official Solicitor's criteria for consenting to act as litigation friend

10. The Official Solicitor is the litigation friend of last resort. No person, including the Official Solicitor, can be appointed to act as litigation friend without their consent. The Official Solicitor will not accept appointment where there is another person who is suitable and willing to act as litigation friend. The Official Solicitor's criteria for consenting to act as litigation friend are:

(a)   in the case of an adult that the party or intended party is a protected party[4];

(b)   there is security for the costs of legal representation of the protected party which the Official Solicitor considers satisfactory. Sources of security may be

    (i)   the Legal Aid Agency where the protected party or child is eligible for public funding;

    (ii)   the protected party's or child's own funds where they have financial capacity or where they do not where the Court of Protection has given him authority to recover the costs from the adult's or child's funds;

    (iii)   an undertaking from another party to pay his costs;

(c)   the case is a last resort case.

[4] The Official Solicitor is able to provide a pro forma certificate of capacity to conduct proceedings and notes for guidance.

Invitations to the Official Solicitor: new cases

11. Solicitors who have been consulted by a child or a protected party (or by someone acting on their behalf, or concerned about their interests) should write to the Official Solicitor setting out the background to the proposed case and explaining the basis on which the Official Solicitor's criteria for acting are met.

Invitations to the Official Solicitor: pending proceedings

12. Where a case is already before the court, an order inviting the Official Solicitor to act should be expressed as being made subject to his consent. The Official Solicitor aims to provide an initial response to any invitation within 10 working days. But he cannot consent to act unless and until he is satisfied both that his criteria are met and that he has a member of his staff to whom the case can be allocated as the case's case manager. So from time to time there will be a waiting list of cases which meet the Official Solicitor's acceptance criteria but in respect of which, because he has no case manager available to take the case, he cannot accept appointment as litigation friend. Save in exceptional circumstances, cases will be accepted in strict chronological order starting with the earliest placed on the waiting list of cases which have met the criteria

for acceptance. What constitutes exceptional circumstances will be fact specific; the decision to expedite acceptance of a case is one for the Official Solicitor.

13. To enable the Official Solicitor to consider the invitation to him to act, he should be provided with the following as soon as possible:

(a)   the sealed court order inviting him to act as litigation friend (with a note of the reasons approved by the Judge if appropriate);

(b)   a copy of the letter of instruction to the expert by which an opinion was sought as to the party's capacity to conduct the proceedings whether in the form of the Official Solicitor's certificate of capacity to conduct the proceedings or otherwise;

(c)   (adult party) the opinion on capacity (the Official Solicitor's pro forma certificate of capacity to conduct proceedings may be requested from his office for the purpose of obtaining an opinion);

(d)   confirmation that there is satisfactory security for the costs of legal representation (including any relevant supporting documents); it is a matter for the Official Solicitor whether the proposed security for costs is satisfactory;

(e)   confirmation that there is no other person suitable and willing to act as litigation friend (including the enquiries made to this end);

(f)   the court file (provision of the court file may not be necessary if the court directs a party to provide a full indexed copy of the bundle to the Official Solicitor on a timely basis).

Litigants in person

14. If one or more parties is or are litigants in person, and there is reason to believe that any litigant in person may lack capacity to conduct the proceedings, the court will need to consider, and if necessary give directions as to:

(a)   who is to arrange for the assessment of capacity to conduct the proceedings;

(b)   how the cost of that assessment is to be funded;

(c)   how any invitation to act as litigation friend is to be made to either any suitable and willing person or the Official Solicitor so as to provide him with the documents and information (including information to enable him to make the enquiries necessary to establish whether or not there is funding available;

(d)   any resulting timetabling and, where the Official Solicitor is being invited to be litigation friend, having regard to the Official Solicitor's need to investigate whether his acceptance criteria are met, the need for him to have a case manager available to deal with the case and the possibility that an application to the Court of Protection (for authority to pay the costs out of the protected party's or child's funds) may be necessary.

15. The Official Solicitor will notify the court in the event he expects a delay in accepting appointment either because it is not evident that his criteria are met or for any other reason. The court may wish to consider:

(a) making enquiries of the parties as to the steps being taken by them to establish that the Official Solicitor's criteria for acting are met in the particular case;

(b) whether directions should be made to ensure that such enquiries are progressed on a timely basis;

(c) fixing a further directions appointment.

16. If, at any time, another litigation friend is appointed before the Official Solicitor is in a position to accept the invitation to him to act, the Official Solicitor should be notified without delay.

Where the Official Solicitor has accepted appointment as litigation friend

17. Once the Official Solicitor is able to accept appointment as litigation friend he will need time to prepare the case on behalf of the protected party or child and may wish to make submissions about any substantive hearing date.

18. To avoid unnecessary delay in progression of the case, he will require from the solicitors he appoints for the protected party or child:

(a) a reading list identifying the material which the solicitors considers will assist by way of introduction to the case in obtaining an overview of the issues from the perspective of the protected party or child;

(b) a summary of the background to the proceedings, of any major steps that have occurred within the proceedings, and identification of the issues in the proceedings;

(c) advice as to the steps the Official Solicitor should now take in the proceedings on behalf of the protected party or child;

(d) copies of <u>all</u> notes of attendance on the protected party or child so that the Official Solicitor is properly informed as to the views and wishes expressed by the protected party or child to date;

(e) confirmation of the protected party's or child's present ascertainable views and wishes in relation to the proceedings.

Advising the court: *Harbin v Masterman* enquiries and Advocate to the Court

19. Where the Official Solicitor is invited, with his consent, to conduct enquiries under *Harbin v Masterman* and it appears to the Official Solicitor that any public body wishes to seek the assistance of the court but is unwilling to carry out the enquiries itself, the Official Solicitor may seek an undertaking from that public body to indemnify him in respect of his costs of carrying out those enquiries.

20. As noted at paragraph 2(c) above, the Official Solicitor may be invited, with his consent, to act or instruct counsel as a friend of the court (advocate to the court) if it appears to the court that such an invitation is more appropriately addressed to him rather than (or in addition to) CAFCASS Legal Services or to the Attorney-General.

Contacting the Official Solicitor

...

Tel. 020 7911 7127 (family litigation) or 020 7911 7233 (divorce litigation)

...

The Official Solicitor's certificate of capacity to conduct proceedings, a sample letter of instruction, other precedent documents and further guidance in relation to the appointment of the Official Solicitor are also available at www.justice.gov.uk (follow the links to the Official Solicitor).

...

E-mail address: enquiries@offsol.gsi.gov.uk

March 2013

Alastair Pitblado
Official Solicitor

GUIDELINES FOR JUDGES MEETING CHILDREN WHO ARE SUBJECT TO FAMILY PROCEEDINGS

APRIL 2010

These Guidelines are produced by the Family Justice Council and approved by the President of the Family Division.

In these Guidelines:

- All references to 'child' or 'children' are intended to include a young person or young people the subject of proceedings under the Children Act 1989.
- 'Family proceedings' includes both public and private law cases.
- 'Judge' includes magistrates.
- Cafcass includes CAFCASS CYMRU.

Purpose

The purpose of these Guidelines is to encourage judges to enable children to feel more involved and connected with proceedings in which important decisions are made in their lives and to give them an opportunity to satisfy themselves that the Judge has understood their wishes and feelings and to understand the nature of the Judge's task.

Preamble

- In England and Wales in most cases a child's needs, wishes and feelings are brought to the court in written form by a Cafcass officer. Nothing in this guidance document is intended to replace or undermine that responsibility.
- It is Cafcass practice to discuss with a child in a manner appropriate to their developmental understanding whether their participation in the process includes a wish to meet the Judge. If the child does not wish to meet the Judge discussions can centre on other ways of enabling the child to feel a part of the process. If the child wishes to meet the Judge, that wish should be conveyed to the Judge where appropriate.
- The primary purpose of the meeting is to benefit the child. However, it may also benefit the Judge and other family members.

Guidelines

1. The judge is entitled to expect the lawyer for the child and/or the Cafcass officer:

(i)   to advise whether the child wishes to meet the Judge;
(ii)   if so, to explain from the child's perspective, the purpose of the meeting;
(iii)   to advise whether it accords with the welfare interests of the child for such a meeting take place; and
(iv)   to identify the purpose of the proposed meeting as perceived by the child's professional representative/s.

2. The other parties shall be entitled to make representations as to any proposed meeting with the Judge before the Judge decides whether or not it shall take place.

3. In deciding whether or not a meeting shall take place and, if so, in what circumstances, the child's chronological age is relevant but not determinative.
Some children of 7 or even younger have a clear understanding of their circumstances and very clear views which they may wish to express.

4. If the child wishes to meet the judge but the judge decides that a meeting would be inappropriate, the judge should consider providing a brief explanation in writing for the child.

5. If a judge decides to meet a child, it is a matter for the discretion of the judge, having considered representations from the parties –

(i)   the purpose and proposed content of the meeting;
(ii)   at what stage during the proceedings, or after they have concluded, the meeting should take place;
(iii)   where the meeting will take place;
(iv)   who will bring the child to the meeting;
(v)   who will prepare the child for the meeting (this should usually be the Cafcass officer);
(vi)   who shall attend during the meeting – although a Judge should never see a child alone;
(vii) by whom a minute of the meeting shall be taken, how that minute is to be approved by the Judge, and how it is to be communicated to the other parties.

It cannot be stressed too often that the child's meeting with the judge is not for the purpose of gathering evidence. That is the responsibility of the Cafcass officer. The purpose is to enable the child to gain some understanding of what is going on, and to be reassured that the judge has understood him/her.

6. If the meeting takes place prior to the conclusion of the proceedings –

(i)   The judge should explain to the child at an early stage that a judge cannot hold secrets. What is said by the child will, other than in exceptional circumstances, be communicated to his/her parents and other parties.
(ii)   The judge should also explain that decisions in the case are the responsibility of the judge, who will have to weigh a number of factors, and that the outcome is never the responsibility of the child.
(iii)   The judge should discuss with the child how his or her decisions will be communicated to the child.
(iv)   The parties or their representatives shall have the opportunity to respond to the content of the meeting, whether by way of oral evidence or submissions.

TRANSPARENCY IN THE FAMILY COURTS

PUBLICATION OF JUDGMENTS

**Practice Guidance issued on 16 January 2014 by
Sir James Munby, President of the Family Division**

[For full guidance, see Practice Guidance: Transparency in the Family Courts – Publication of Judgments [2014] 1 FLR 733]

Effective from 3 February 2014

Essential provisions:

8 As provided in paragraph 14 below, this Guidance applies only to judgments delivered by certain judges. In due course, following the introduction of the Family Court, consideration will be given to extending it to judgments delivered by other judges (including lay justices).

The legal framework
9 The effect of section 12 of the Administration of Justice Act 1960 is that it is a contempt of court to publish a judgment in a family court case involving children unless either the judgment has been delivered in public or, where delivered in private, the judge has authorised publication. In the latter case, the judge normally gives permission for the judgment to be published on condition that the published version protects the anonymity of the children and members of their family.

10 In every case the terms on which publication is permitted are a matter for the judge and will be set out by the judge in a rubric at the start of the judgment.

11 The normal terms as described in paragraph 9 may be appropriate in a case where no-one wishes to discuss the proceedings otherwise than anonymously. But they may be inappropriate, for example, where parents who have been exonerated in care proceedings wish to discuss their experiences in public, identifying themselves and making use of the judgment. Equally, they may be inappropriate in cases where findings have been made against a person and someone else contends and/or the judge concludes that it is in the public interest for that person to be identified in any published version of the judgment.

12 If any party wishes to identify himself or herself, or any other party or person, as being a person referred to in any published version of the judgment, their remedy is to seek an order of the court and a suitable modification of the rubric: Media Access & Reporting, para 82; *Re RB (Adult) (No 4)* [2011] EWHC 3017 (Fam), [2012] 1 FLR 466, paras [17], [19].

13 Nothing in this Guidance affects the exercise by the judge in any particular case of whatever powers would otherwise be available to regulate the publication of material relating to the proceedings. For example, where a judgment is likely to be used in a way that would defeat the purpose of any anonymisation, it is open to the judge to refuse to publish the judgment or to make an order restricting its use.

Guidance

14 This Guidance takes effect from 3 February 2014. It applies

(i)   in the family courts (and in due course in the Family Court), to judgments delivered by Circuit Judges, High Court Judges and persons sitting as judges of the High Court; and

(ii)   to all judgments delivered by High Court Judges (and persons sitting as judges of the High Court) exercising the inherent jurisdiction to make orders in respect of children and incapacitated or vulnerable adults.

15 The following paragraphs of this Guidance distinguish between two classes of judgment:

(i)   those that the judge must ordinarily allow to be published (paragraphs 16 and 17); and

(ii)   those that may be published (paragraph 18).

16 Permission to publish a judgment should always be given whenever the judge concludes that publication would be in the public interest and whether or not a request has been made by a party or the media.

17 Where a judgment relates to matters set out in Schedule 1 or 2 below and a written judgment already exists in a publishable form or the judge has already ordered that the judgment be transcribed, the starting point is that permission should be given for the judgment to be published unless there are compelling reasons why the judgment should not be published.

SCHEDULE 1

In the family courts (and in due course in the Family Court), including in proceedings under the inherent jurisdiction of the High Court relating to children, judgments arising from:

(i)   a substantial contested fact-finding hearing at which serious allegations, for example allegations of significant physical, emotional or sexual harm, have been determined;

(ii)   the making or refusal of a final care order or supervision order under Part 4 of the Children Act 1989, or any order for the discharge of any such order, except where the order is made with the consent of all participating parties;

(iii)   the making or refusal of a placement order or adoption order under the Adoption and Children Act 2002, or any order for the discharge of any such order, except where the order is made with the consent of all participating parties;

(iv)   the making or refusal of any declaration or order authorising a deprivation of liberty, including an order for a secure accommodation order under section 25 of the Children Act 1989;

(v)   any application for an order involving the giving or withholding of serious medical treatment;

(vi)   any application for an order involving a restraint on publication of information relating to the proceedings.

SCHEDULE 2

In proceedings under the inherent jurisdiction of the High Court relating to incapacitated or vulnerable adults, judgments arising from:

(i)   any application for a declaration or order involving a deprivation or possible deprivation of liberty;

(ii)   any application for an order involving the giving or withholding of serious medical treatment;

(iii)   any application for an order that an incapacitated or vulnerable adult be moved into or out of a residential establishment or other institution;

(iv)   any application for a declaration as to capacity to marry or to consent to sexual relations;

(v)   any application for an order involving a restraint on publication of information relating to the proceedings.

18 In all other cases, the starting point is that permission may be given for the judgment to be published whenever a party or an accredited member of the media applies for an order permitting publication, and the judge concludes that permission for the judgment to be published should be given.

19 In deciding whether and if so when to publish a judgment, the judge shall have regard to all the circumstances, the rights arising under any relevant provision of the European Convention on Human Rights, including Articles 6 (right to a fair hearing), 8 (respect for private and family life) and 10 (freedom of expression), and the effect of publication upon any current or potential criminal proceedings.

20 In all cases where a judge gives permission for a judgment to be published:

(i)   public authorities and expert witnesses should be named in the judgment approved for publication, unless there are compelling reasons why they should not be so named;

(ii)   the children who are the subject of the proceedings in the family courts, and other members of their family, and the person who is the subject of proceedings under the inherent jurisdiction of the High Court relating to incapacitated or vulnerable adults, and other members of their family, should not normally be named in the judgment approved for publication unless the judge otherwise orders;

(iii)   anonymity in the judgment as published should not normally extend beyond protecting the privacy of the children and adults who are the subject of the proceedings and other members of their families, unless there are compelling reasons to do so.

21 Unless the judgment is already in anonymised form or the judge otherwise orders, any necessary anonymisation of the judgment shall be carried out, in the case of judgments being published pursuant to paragraphs 16 and 17 above, by the solicitor for the applicant in the proceedings and, in the case of a judgment being published pursuant to paragraph 18 above, by the solicitor for the party or person applying for publication of the judgment. The anonymised version of the judgment must be submitted to the judge within a period specified by the judge for approval. The version approved for publication will contain such rubric as the judge specifies. Unless the rubric specified by the judge provides expressly to the contrary every published judgment shall be deemed to contain the following rubric:

'This judgment was delivered in private. The judge has given leave for this version of the judgment to be published on condition that (irrespective of what is contained in the judgment) in any published version of the judgment the anonymity of the children and members of their family must be strictly preserved. All persons, including representatives of the media, must ensure that this condition is strictly complied with. Failure to do so will be a contempt of court.'

22 The judge will need to consider who should be ordered to bear the cost of transcribing the judgment. Unless the judge otherwise orders:

(i)   in cases falling under paragraph 16 the cost of transcribing the judgment is to be at public expense;

(ii)   subject to (i), in cases falling under paragraph 17 the cost of transcribing the judgment shall be borne equally by the parties to the proceedings;

(iii)   in cases falling under paragraph 18, the cost of transcribing the judgment shall be borne by the party or person applying for publication of the judgment.

23 In all cases where permission is given for a judgment to be published, the version of the judgment approved for publication shall be made available, upon payment of any appropriate charge that may be required, to any person who requests a copy. Where a judgment to which paragraph 16 or 17 applies is approved for publication, it shall as soon as reasonably practicable be placed by the court on the BAILII website. Where a judgment to which paragraph 18 applies is approved for publication, the judge shall consider whether it should be placed on the BAILII website and, if so, it shall as soon as reasonably practicable be placed by the court on the BAILII website.

TRANSPARENCY IN THE COURT OF PROTECTION

PUBLICATION OF JUDGMENTS

**Practice Guidance issued on 16 January 2014 by
Sir James Munby, President of the Court of Protection**

Effective from 3 February 2014

Essential provisions:

7 I propose to adopt an incremental approach. Initially I am issuing this Guidance. This will be followed by further Guidance and in due course more formal Practice Directions and changes to the Rules (the Court of Protection Rules 2007 and the Family Procedure Rules 2010). Changes to primary legislation are unlikely in the near future.

8 As provided in paragraph 14 below, this Guidance applies only to judgments delivered by certain judges. In due course consideration will be given to extending it to judgments delivered by other judges.

The legal framework

9 The effect of section 12 of the Administration of Justice Act 1960 is that it is a contempt of court to publish a judgment in a Court of Protection case unless either the judgment has been delivered in public or, where delivered in private, the judge has authorised publication. In the latter case, the judge normally gives permission for the judgment to be published on condition that the published version protects the anonymity of the person who is subject of the proceedings and members of their family.

10 In every case the terms on which publication is permitted are a matter for the judge and will be set out by the judge in a rubric at the start of the judgment.

11 The normal terms as described in paragraph 9 may be appropriate in a case where no-one wishes to discuss the proceedings otherwise than anonymously. But they may be inappropriate, for example, where family members wish to discuss their experiences in public, identifying themselves and making use of the judgment. Equally, they may be inappropriate in cases where findings have been made against a person and someone else contends and/or the court concludes that it is in the public interest for that person to be identified in any published version of the judgment.

12 If any party wishes to identify himself or herself, or any other party or person, as being a person referred to in any published version of the judgment, their remedy is to seek an order of the court and a suitable modification of the rubric: Media Access

& Reporting, para 82; *Re RB (Adult) (No 4)* [2011] EWHC 3017 (Fam), [2012] 1 FLR 466, paras [17], [19].

13 Nothing in this Guidance affects the exercise by the judge in any particular case of whatever powers would otherwise be available to regulate the publication of material relating to the proceedings. For example, where a judgment is likely to be used in a way that would defeat the purpose of any anonymisation, it is open to the judge to refuse to publish the judgment or to make an order restricting its use.

Guidance

14 This Guidance takes effect from 3 February 2014. It applies to all judgments in the Court of Protection delivered by the Senior Judge, nominated Circuit Judges and High Court Judges.

15 The following paragraphs of this Guidance distinguish between two classes of judgment:

(i)   those that the judge must ordinarily allow to be published (paragraphs 16 and 17); and

(ii)   those that may be published (paragraph 18).

16 Permission to publish a judgment should always be given whenever the judge concludes that publication would be in the public interest and whether or not a request has been made by a party or the media.

17 Where a judgment relates to matters set out in the Schedule below and a written judgment already exists in a publishable form or the judge has already ordered that the judgment be transcribed, the starting point is that permission should be given for the judgment to be published unless there are compelling reasons why the judgment should not be published.

SCHEDULE

Judgments arising from:

(i)   any application for an order involving the giving or withholding of serious medical treatment and any other hearing held in public;

(ii)   any application for a declaration or order involving a deprivation or possible deprivation of liberty;

(iii)   any case where there is a dispute as to who should act as an attorney or a deputy;

(iv)   any case where the issues include whether a person should be restrained from acting as an attorney or a deputy or that an appointment should be revoked or his or her powers should be reduced;

(v)   any application for an order that an incapacitated adult (P) be moved into or out of a residential establishment or other institution;

(vi)   any case where the sale of P's home is in issue
(vii)   any case where a property and affairs application relates to assets (including P's home) of £1 million or more or to damages awarded by a court sitting in public;
(viii)   any application for a declaration as to capacity to marry or to consent to sexual relations;
(ix)   any application for an order involving a restraint on publication of information relating to the proceedings.

18 In all other cases, the starting point is that permission may be given for the judgment to be published whenever a party or an accredited member of the media applies for an order permitting publication, and the judge concludes that permission for the judgment to be published should be given.

19 In deciding whether and if so when to publish a judgment, the judge shall have regard to all the circumstances, the rights arising under any relevant provision of the European Convention on Human Rights, including Articles 6 (right to a fair hearing), 8 (respect for private and family life) and 10 (freedom of expression), and the effect of publication upon any current or potential criminal proceedings.

20 In all cases where a judge gives permission for a judgment to be published:

(i)   public authorities and expert witnesses should be named in the judgment approved for publication, unless there are compelling reasons why they should not be so named;
(ii)   the person who is the subject of proceedings in the Court of Protection and other members of their family should not normally be named in the judgment approved for publication unless the judge otherwise orders;
(iii)   anonymity in the judgment as published should not normally extend beyond protecting the privacy of the adults who are the subject of the proceedings and other members of their families, unless there are compelling reasons to do so.

21 Unless the judgment is already in anonymised form, any necessary anonymisation of the judgment shall be carried out as the judge orders. The version approved for publication will contain such rubric as the judge specifies. Unless the rubric specified by the judge provides expressly to the contrary every published judgment shall be deemed to contain the following rubric:

> 'This judgment was delivered in private. The judge has given leave for this version of the judgment to be published on condition that (irrespective of what is contained in the judgment) in any published version of the judgment the anonymity of the incapacitated person and members of their family must be strictly preserved. All persons, including representatives of the media, must ensure that this condition is strictly complied with. Failure to do so will be a contempt of court.'

22 The judge will need to consider who should be ordered to bear the cost of transcribing the judgment. Unless the judge otherwise orders:

(i)   in cases falling under paragraph 18, the cost of transcribing the judgment shall be borne by the party or person applying for publication of the judgment;

(ii)   in other cases, the cost of transcribing the judgment shall be at public expense.

23 In all cases where permission is given for a judgment to be published, the version of the judgment approved for publication shall be made available, upon payment of any appropriate charge that may be required, to any person who requests a copy. Where a judgment to which paragraph 16 or 17 applies is approved for publication, it shall as soon as reasonably practicable be placed by the court on the BAILII website. Where a judgment to which paragraph 18 applies is approved for publication, the judge shall consider whether it should be placed on the BAILII website and, if so, it shall as soon as reasonably practicable be placed by the court on the BAILII website.

RESOLUTION GUIDANCE NOTE: DISCLOSURE IN FINANCIAL ORDER CASES[1]

Disclosure is required prior to the making of a court order for financial remedy or other financial orders, whether the process leading to the order being made is a contested application to court, arbitration, mediation, the collaborative process or negotiation between solicitors. Increasingly, one or more parties will be litigants in person.

There is a fundamental principle that full and frank financial disclosure is needed for a binding agreement, arbitral award or court order, irrespective of the process used to get there. This principle has been established for many years, although it is tested from time to time in the courts, sometimes with unexpected results. The law continues to develop.

This Good Practice Guide is aimed at assisting members to address these issues in compliance with the Resolution Code of Practice, in the best interests of the clients and families that we serve. It is not a legal textbook – for a full exposition of the current legal and procedural position see Resolution's Privacy and Disclosure for Family Lawyers. Whilst this area of law and practice evolves, and the competing rights to privacy and to a fair trial teeter in the balance, the issues facing families remain the same: how to disentangle the family finances when a relationship breaks down.

The Guide considers the following topics:

- The legal framework – including relevant statutory provisions generally and in the context of self-help, relevant case law and regulatory issues.
- The meaning of disclosure, and the duty to disclose, in this context.
- Privilege.
- Confidentiality and privacy.
- How to explain the issues around potential or actual non-disclosure to clients, and other steps to take where there may be non-disclosure.
- Transparency.
- Good practice.

It does not consider a lawyer's duty to disclose to the appropriate authorities in the context of safeguarding, child protection, anti-money laundering or counter-terrorism.

The legal framework

This area of law is complex, involving competing human rights (the right to respect for one's private and family life and the right to a fair trial); common law

---

[1] This Guidance was revised in December 2014. The law or procedure may have changed since that time.

jurisprudence (e.g. the law of confidence and the evolving tort of misuse of private information); statutory obligations – for example under the Data Protection Act 1998 (DPA 1998), Computer Misuse Act 1990 (CMA 1990), the Regulation of Investigatory Powers Act 2000 (RIPA 2000) and the Copyright, Designs and Patents Act 1988 (CPDA 1988). Also, of course, there are the obligations arising under the Matrimonial Causes Act 1973 (MCA 1973), Schedule I to the Children Act 1989 (CA 1989) and the Family Procedure Rules 2010 (FPR 2010). Statutes may impose civil or criminal sanctions for breach, and may also result in possible actions in tort for breach of statutory duty. Other actions in tort or for breach of contract may also be possible.

Family Procedure Rules 2010

The "overriding objective" of the procedure must always be borne in mind: of "enabling the court to deal with cases justly, having regard to any welfare issues involved" (r1.1 FPR 2010). Rule 1.2 explains that dealing with a case justly includes, as far as is practicable:

- ensuring that it is dealt with expeditiously and fairly, dealing with the case in ways which are proportionate to the nature, importance and complexity of the issues;
- ensuring that the parties are on an equal footing;
- saving expense; and
- allotting to it an appropriate share of the court's resources, while taking into account the need to allot resources to other cases.

Rule 1.3 requires the parties "to help the court to further the overriding objective", and r1.4 sets out the court's duty to manage cases, with examples of how that is to be done.

Practice Direction 9A, on part 9 of the FPR, addresses the issue of financial disclosure in the context of all financial order applications, with specific reference to various rules, and has annexed to it a pre-application protocol, which refers to this guide. The protocol underlines the obligation of parties to make full and frank disclosure of all material facts, documents and other information relevant to the issues, and reminds practitioners that they must tell clients in clear terms of this duty and of the possible consequences of breach of the duty, which may include criminal sanctions under the Fraud Act 2006. The duty of disclosure is an ongoing obligation and includes the duty to disclose any material changes after initial disclosure has been given.

The pre-application protocol annexed to PD9A governs the steps parties should take to seek and provide information from and to each other prior to the commencement of an application for financial orders. Paragraph 12 states:

> "If parties carry out voluntary disclosure before the issue of proceedings, the parties should exchange schedules of assets, income, liabilities and other material facts, using

the financial statement as a guide to the format of the disclosure. Documents should only be disclosed to the extent that they are required by the financial statement. Excessive or disproportionate costs should not be incurred."

The emphasis in the FPR is very much on promoting non-court dispute resolution. It is now necessary for most applicants for financial orders to attend a Mediation Information and Assessment Meeting (MIAM) prior to the issue of an application in accordance with PD3A. Then, when the court process is engaged, the rules are aimed at cases proceeding expeditiously, assisted by active case management, although the possibility of adjourning for further attempts at non-court dispute resolution is also encouraged (see r3.3 FPR 2010). This recognises that for non-court dispute resolution to be effective, the time when it is undertaken is an important factor. For those who are doubtful about the likelihood of success of mediation, particularly in difficult cases, consider *Al-Khatib v Masry & ors* [2004] EWCA Civ 1353, [2004] 3 FCR 573. At first instance, adverse inferences were drawn following inadequate disclosure. There was then an appeal to the Court of Appeal which was compromised with a subsequent successful mediation.

There would appear to be a shift from a position where pre-application disclosure was actively encouraged by the previous pre-application protocol, to a situation where it is specifically discouraged in some situations. The guidance notes to the pre-application protocol annexed to PD 9A at paragraph 2 remind practitioners that:

> "In considering the options of pre-application disclosure and negotiation, solicitors should bear in mind the advantage of having a court timetable and court-managed process. There is sometimes an advantage in preparing disclosure before proceedings are commenced. However, solicitors should bear in mind the objective of controlling costs and in particular the costs of discovery and that the option of pre-application disclosure and negotiation has risks of excessive and uncontrolled expenditure and delay. This option should only be encouraged where both parties agree to follow this route and disclosure is not likely to be an issue or has been adequately dealt with in mediation or otherwise".

Para 3.4 of PD9A states that "any breach of this practice direction or the pre-application protocol annexed to it will be taken into account by the court when deciding whether to depart from the general rule as to costs", and so should be borne in mind. Time will tell whether any more costs orders are made in this context.

Since the Family Proceedings (Amendment) Rules 2006 (SI 2006/352) came into force, the general rule on costs in applications for financial orders has been that the court will not make an order requiring one party to pay the costs of another party, but may do so if appropriate because of the conduct of the party in relation to the proceedings (whether before or during them). This rule is encapsulated in r28 FPR 2010, which contains the general rule that the court will not make an order for costs against a party in proceedings for a financial order except an order for maintenance pending suit/an order pending outcome of proceedings, an interim periodical payments order, or any interim order related to financial order applications (variation applications are covered by PD28A). The court may make a costs order at any stage of the proceedings where it considers it appropriate as a result of the conduct of a party in relation to the proceedings, whether before or during them (r28.3(6)) – i.e. litigation misconduct. The considerations which r28.3(7) requires the court to take into account when deciding whether to make a costs order in this context include any failure by a party to comply with the rules, any order of the court or any PD which the court considers relevant; the manner in which a party has pursued or responded to the application or a particular allegation or issue; and any other aspect of a party's conduct in relation to proceedings which the court considers relevant.

Once proceedings for financial orders have been issued, the timing and extent of disclosure is regulated by the court. The procedure prior to first appointment is set out in r9.14 FPR. Disclosure is initially restricted to completing the financial statement on form E five weeks prior to the first appointment. Rule 9.14(2) provides for the exchange of financial statements. These must be:

a)   verified by a statement of truth; and
b)   accompanied by the following documents only:

- any documents required by the financial statement;
- any other documents necessary to explain or clarify any of the information contained in the financial statement;
- any documents provided to the party producing the financial statement by a person responsible for a pension arrangement, either following a request under r9.30 or as part of a relevant valuation; and
- any notification or other document referred to in r9.37(2), (4) or (5) which has been received by the party producing the financial statement."

Rule 5.2 states that "subject to any rule or practice direction, unless the court directs otherwise, a form must have attached to it any documents which, in the form, are (a) stated to be required; or (b) referred to."

Two weeks before the first appointment the documents specified in r9.14 must be filed with the court and served on the other party, including a statement of concise issues and a questionnaire/request for information and documents that must be referable to the statement of issues. Statements of truth are now required on replies to questionnaires.

Proceedings for contempt of court may be brought against a person who makes, or causes to be made, a false statement in a document verified by a statement of truth without having an honest belief in its truth (r17.6 FPR, and para 6 of PD17A).

Rule 9.14(3) deals with the situation where documents are not yet available and r9.14(4) deals with restrictions on disclosure prior to first appointment.

The duties of the court at the first appointment are set out in r9.15. The district judge must determine the extent of the questions to be answered and decide what further documents are to be produced. After the first appointment neither party is entitled to the production of further documents except by permission of the court (r9.16). At any stage either party may apply for further directions (r9.16(2)). It may be appropriate to seek a direction for the filing of narrative affidavits (see *W v W (Ancillary relief: Practice)* [2000] Fam Law 473), or for other interim remedies such as an order for inspection or preservation of property. Interim remedies are set out in Part 20 of the FPR. Oral evidence may also be given at an interlocutory appointment (see *OS v DS (Oral disclosure: Preliminary hearing* [2004]).

Statutory provisions in the context of "self-help"

Intercepting mail addressed to another may be a criminal offence under s84 of the Postal Services Act 2000 (see also s1 of RIPA 2000).

Tapping of a public telephone may be a criminal offence (s1 RIPA), and is likely also to be an actionable breach of confidence and/or breach of privacy under the Human Rights Act. Although it is not a criminal offence under RIPA for someone to record their private telephone line (if they have the right to control the operation or use of the system – s1(6)), there may be issues arising under the HRA. Before taping telephone conversations between lawyers, the other lawyer should be warned that the conversation is going to be recorded. In a family law case, secretly taping a telephone conversation with another lawyer is not recommended.

Misuse of electronic and other data

The relevant legislation here is the Computer Misuse Act 1980, the Data Protection Act 1998 and the Copyright Designs and Patents Act 1988). The CMA 1980 makes it an offence to have unauthorised access to computer material and to modify computer material without authority. The consequences may be both criminal and tortious, and the sanctions include potential imprisonment/fines. The Act predates the technology it now has to deal with, and it seems that the term "computer" now has a meaning that is wider than could possibly have been anticipated when the legislation was enacted. It is safest to assume that computer material may include any information held on any electronic device with capacity for memory storage/access – including, for example, home or business computers/servers/networks, laptops, external hard drives, memory sticks/disks/CDs, tablets, mobile phones, and information contained within any private email account or private social network.

The DPA 1998 requires those who hold personal data to deal with it in accordance with principles and rules, and applies to private individuals and businesses. Higher standards apply to sensitive personal data. Sanctions for breach may include fines, criminal sanctions, and possible civil claims, e.g. for breach of statutory duty.

The CDPA 1988 protects works (which may include text, pictures, data and software) created by individuals. If, for example, another individual copies the work of another, then damages may be awarded for any economic loss suffered as a result.

Case law

If there is a failure to provide full disclosure, the practical effect of that has been referred to in developing case law for decades. *Livesey v Jenkins* [1985] AC 425 established the two-stage test of (i) was there material non-disclosure, and (ii) was it so important that the original order should be set aside. The House of Lords decided that there was an obligation on the wife to disclose her engagement immediately.

In *E v E* [1990] 2 FLR 233 a husband had failed to disclose information about Swiss bank accounts and land, which necessitated an expensive and rigorous investigation into his affairs. He was ordered to pay the costs of both sides for the investigation. Ewbank J also held that the husband's failure to disclose justified any inferences which were proper to be drawn against him.

Wilson J (as he then was) then considered this in *T v T* [1994] 2 FLR 1083 where he said:

> "I appreciate that it has been held that a spouse's behaviour in the ancillary litigation, specifically a dishonest failure to make full disclosure amounts to [relevant s25(2)] conduct: *Desai v Desai* (1983) 13 Fam Law 46 [[1994] 1 FCR 293] and *B v B* [1988] 2 FLR 490. But I agree with Thorpe J in *P v P* [1994] 1 FLR 293 at p 306A–C that a dishonest disclosure will more appropriately be reflected in the inference that the resources are larger than have been disclosed, in which case it will fall within s25(2)(a) and/or in the order for costs."

See also the current costs rules (above).

In *F v F (Ancillary relief: Substantial assets)* [1995] 2 FLR 45 at 70A Thorpe J (as he then was) said that:

> "ancillary relief applications in the Family Division are not purely adversarial proceedings. The court has an independent duty to discharge the function imposed by statute. The court has from that duty the power to investigate and the power to ensure compliance with the duty of full and frank disclosure owed by litigants."

In *Al Khatib v Masry* [2002] 2 FCR 539 and *TL v ML & ors (Ancillary relief: Claim against assets of extended family)* [2006] 1 FCR 465 adverse inferences were drawn following a failure to provide full and frank disclosure.

The judgment in *GW v RW* [2003] 2 FLR 108 (and that in *W v W (Ancillary relief: Non-disclosure)* [2003] EWHC 2254 (Fam)) sets out the requirement for "an honest and conscientious estimation of the true net worth of the party" and the duty to "give a presentation that is immediately understandable by a solicitor of average financial sophistication" in form E. *GW v RW* has since been over-ruled *Jones v Jones* [2011] EWCA Civ 41 in respect of the approach to be taken to quantifying a spouse's earning capacity, but these comments were not discredited on appeal.

In *OS v DS (Oral disclosure: Preliminary hearing)* [2004] EWHC 2376 Coleridge J gave directions for a preliminary/oral discovery hearing to enable the husband to give evidence on oath about a number of central financial issues before requiring the disclosure or production of further documents. The hearing resulted in the case settling after the husband had been cross-examined.

Solicitors must not mislead the court, for example by only putting 50% of a client's assets on the form E, as in *W v W* [2004] 1 FLR 494. In that case the husband had since remarried and 50% of his assets were not included on his form E on the basis that they should be attributed to his second wife.

In *K v K (Financial relief: Management of difficult cases)* [2005] 2 FLR 1137 at para 22 Baron J said "in my view, this type of case should be managed by an allocated High Court judge from the outset. These cases are demanding and obtaining disclosure is often pivotal". This has been extended since by the financial orders process, which promises "active case management" by the court, and which is given even more focus by r1.4 and Part 4 of the FPR 2010.

Seeking disclosure from a third party should be considered (see *Charman v Charman* [2005] 2 FLR 422).

In respect of whether there is an ongoing duty to provide disclosure after a final order has been made, see *Den Heyer v Newby* [2005] EWCA Civ 1311. There may be an obligation to provide sufficient information to enable a potential claim to be evaluated, for example where there is a substantial joint lives periodical payments order.

In respect of the impact of non-disclosure on the final orders made by the court, on appeal in *M v M* [2006] EWCA Civ 1852 (second appeal following Peter Hughes QC's judgment referred to above) Wall LJ (as he then was) said:

> "In my judgement, the wife is entitled to choose the option [for sale of a property] in which she has the greater confidence. It is at this point that the husband's litigation conduct returns to haunt him. Had he behaved properly during the proceedings, had he given full frank and clear disclosure, had he not breached his undertakings and dissipated funds, I do not think we would be where we are or that we would be having the current argument."

In *L v L and H* [2007] EWHC 140 (QBD) the husband applied successfully for delivery up of copies of the hard drive of his laptop obtained by a computer expert instructed by his wife. Tugendhat J found that the husband had established an arguable case that the laptop contained confidential information, including documents protected by legal professional privilege.

In *R v Waters* [2007] EWCA Crim 222 the applicant (for leave to appeal against sentence) had been convicted of conspiracy to cause unauthorised modification of computer material, and sentenced to four months' imprisonment and ordered to pay £6,500 towards the prosecution's costs. He employed a private detective agency to install spying software on his wife's computer at their business premises. Leave to appeal was refused.

In *I v I* [2008] EWHC 1167 (Fam) Charles J found that negotiations relating to the sale of a property or shares whose value is relevant, or to existing or new employment that would have an impact on income, should generally be disclosed (paras 114 and 115). It would also be prudent for estimates of discretionary bonuses or awards to be given (para 126). If there is any doubt about the effect of the information, disclosure should be given (para 116). Charles J did not allow the wife's application to set aside the consent order where the husband had failed to disclose advanced negotiations in respect of new employment at a significantly higher income in that case. This decision was overturned by consent on appeal, and unusually the Court of Appeal gave a brief judgment anyway so as to make clear its preliminary conclusion that it would have allowed the appeal (see *Bokar-Ingram v Bokar-Ingram* [2009] EWCA Civ 412). Charles J's comments may still though be useful – since the Court of Appeal actually went further in its decision than Charles J did.

Where there has been a long period of time between the date of separation and the application for financial orders, it would seem that the duty to disclose financial developments may not be quite as vigorous (see *Gordon (formerly Stefanou) v Stefanou* [2010] EWCA Civ 1601).

Where an order is vitiated by non-disclosure, the court may, where appropriate, make additional or different provision without setting aside the whole order and there being a new hearing (*Kingdon v Kingdon* [2010] EWCA Civ 1251). See also *Ben Hashem v Al Shayif* [2008] EWHC 2380 (Fam) and *Mahon v Mahon* [2008] EWCA Civ 901.

The Court of Appeal considered the impact of self-help in a pre-emptive application for strike out in *White v Withers LLP and Dearle* [2009] EWCA Civ 1122 (at first instance reported as *Re Z (Restraining solicitors from acting)* [2009] EWHC 3621 Fam). The husband's appeal against the striking out of his claim for damages against his wife's divorce lawyers was allowed, and the Court of Appeal held there was a case to answer relating to trespass to goods and/or conversion, and the claim could not be struck out as an abuse of process. The case arose from the actions of the wife in intercepting the husband's post and taking and passing to her solicitors original and copy documents, including private family letters and correspondence. The action ended in May 2011 with an out of court settlement, and a public apology by Withers to the effect that they had applied the law as they reasonably understood it to be at the time.

The Court of Appeal case *R v K* [2010] 1 FLR 807 related to a criminal prosecution in the context of tax evasion. The court drew a clear distinction between disclosure that is legally required as a matter of law and in relation to which (1) a client is not entitled to invoke the privilege against self-incrimination (which includes disclosure compellable in proceedings for financial orders), and (2) information that is volunteered without compulsion (in that case, in a without prejudice round table meeting), to which the privilege against self-incrimination did not attach. The court held that the FPR, which had the approval of Parliament, must have been intended to abrogate the privilege, since the court could not discharge the duty imposed on it by s25 Matrimonial Causes Act 1973 unless the parties were required to disclose all relevant information, even if tending to incriminate them. The purpose of the legislation would be frustrated if the parties could withhold from the court relevant information, whether relating to their financial affairs or other matters, on the grounds that to disclose it would tend to incriminate. The court went on to say that the public interest in prosecuting crime outweighed the public interest in the settlement of disputes. Admissions made in the course of 'without prejudice' negotiations were not inadmissible in criminal proceedings simply by virtue of the circumstances in which they were made, but could in the exercise of discretion be excluded if their admission would make that criminal trial unfair.

In relation to admissions at the FDR, reference should be made to PD9A, which makes clear that such admissions may not be admissible in evidence except in the trial of a person committing an offence at the appointment or in the very exceptional circumstances indicated in *Re D (Minors) (Conciliation: Disclosure of Information)* [1993] Fam 231.

Imerman v Tchenguiz [2010] EWHC Civ 908 provides a comprehensive review of the law in relation to confidence and privacy and family lawyers are encouraged to read the judgment itself – see further below. See also the subsequent judgment in this case reported as *Tchenguiz-Imerman v Imerman* [2013] EWHC 3627 (Fam) in respect of orders for disclosure against third-party beneficiaries, joined as parties to the proceedings.

Adverse inferences must be properly drawn and reasonable, and the court may attempt to quantify the non-disclosed assets using direct evidence, and evidence of business activities and lifestyle, with the aim of ensuring that the non-discloser is not better off by failing to disclose and not producing an unfair result – see Mostyn J in *NG v SG (Appeal: Non-disclosure)* [2011] EWHC 3270.

See also *UL v BK (Freezing Orders: Safeguards: Standard Examples)* [2013] EWHC 1735 for detailed judicial guidance about freezing and search orders. The wife had illicitly obtained documents from H's safe and briefcase, and her application for the continuation of a freezing order she had obtained preventing her husband from dealing with various assets was dismissed. Her self-help approach and her lack of "duty of candour" did not assist her. The husband had separately (and successfully) brought an action for breach of confidence and misuse of private information in the Queen's

Bench Division where an order had been granted requiring her to hand back the documents to her husband's solicitors.

The appeals to the Supreme Court in *Sharland v Sharland* [2014] EWCA Civ 95 is awaited, and is due to be heard in July 2015. Sir Hugh Bennett QC at first instance, upheld by the majority of the Court of Appeal, found that there had been material and dishonest non-disclosure, but that it would not have made any difference to the outcome. Briggs LJ gave the dissenting view that the *Livesey v Jenkins* two-stage test does not apply to cases of fraud and that the consent order should have been set aside so that the wife could have a fair trial.

N v N [2014] EWCA 314 Civ involved a successful appeal by the husband against an order obtained by the wife setting aside an order varying her maintenance. The Court of Appeal found insufficient evidence for a finding of material non-disclosure, and also suggested that there was no duty of disclosure of changes in financial circumstances during the appeal process in family proceedings, since the appellate court does not look at the case afresh but whether the trial judge was plainly wrong or not. This appears to be different to civil proceedings – see rule 31.11 of the Civil Procedure Rules 2010 (CPR) which specifies that the duty to disclose continues until proceedings are concluded. The CPR continue to be the default rules if the position is not covered by the FPR, and the case law preceding r31.11 CPR suggests a common law duty of this nature. There seems to be some uncertainty about this.

Failure to provide disclosure resulted in the committal of Mr Young to prison for six months and the confiscation of his passport in *Young v Young* [2013] EWHC 34 (see also *Young v Young* [2013] EWHC 3637 for the final financial remedy order).

The court in *BE v DE (Evidence: Without prejudice privilege)* [2014] EWHC 2318 (Fam) revisited the principle that written or oral communications made in a genuine attempt to settle a dispute will not normally be admissible in evidence; that the use of the words "without prejudice" is not essential (although clearly advisable); and the content of such negotiations may not be relied upon subsequently in an open context. The test of whether the parties were trying to compromise the issue in dispute is an objective one.

Regulatory issues

As an officer of the court, a solicitor has a duty not to knowingly allow a client to mislead the court by providing incorrect or inaccurate information (see *W v W* [2004] above). Imputed knowledge of facts could be attributed to a lawyer, for example if information about a client's financial circumstances is known by the firm even if within a different department and in a different capacity. Conflict of interest searches must always be carried out within the firm and proper consideration given to whether the firm can continue to represent that client in relation to their family situation.

The SRA's Solicitors' Code of Conduct at chapter 4 covers confidentiality and disclosure. Outcome 4.4 sets out when you may act, even when material confidential information is held by another member of the firm, and outcome 4.5 requires effective systems and controls to be in place. The duty of confidentiality must be reconciled with the duty of disclosure, and where that is not possible, the protection of confidential information is paramount.

In respect of the duty to disclose all relevant information to the client, outcome 4.2 of the SRA's Solicitors' Code of Conduct requires that "any individual who is advising a client makes that client aware of all information material to that retainer of which the individual has personal knowledge". "Material information" is not defined, but previous guidance has made clear that it must be information which is relevant to the specific retainer with the client and not just information which might be of general interest to the client, and that would seem still to be the case. For more information, consult the Code of Conduct.

See also Bar Council professional conduct guidance on illegally obtained evidence in civil and family proceedings.

When should the lawyer decline to act?

In certain circumstances of non- or misleading disclosure, the lawyer should not continue to act.

If your client refuses to disclose anything at all, you (as their lawyer) must advise them of the costs sanctions and the risk of inferences being made by the court. However, you can continue to act provided you are not privy to any information that is not disclosed or is misleadingly disclosed.

If the client says they have an asset, but gives instructions for the lawyer not to disclose, the lawyer cannot continue to act. The solicitor would be in breach of their duty to the court not to mislead it, and could also commit the offence of conspiracy to defraud, which survives the Fraud Act 2006, or fraud by failing to disclose information under s3 of that Act (see above).

If, after initial disclosure, the client admits to the existence of additional assets and disclosure is then given, the lawyer can continue to act. If the client refuses to disclose, the lawyer cannot continue to act.

A solicitor must never compromise their professional integrity or their duty as an officer of the court. See further the Solicitors' Code of Conduct.

What is disclosure and what is the duty to disclose?

Disclosure relates to both facts and documents. A party discloses a document by stating that the document exists or has existed, and inspection of a document occurs

when a party is permitted to inspect a document disclosed by another person (see r21.1 FPR). For the purposes of disclosure and inspection, "document" means anything in which information of any description is recorded; and "copy", in relation to a document, means anything onto which information recorded in the document has been copied, by whatever means and whether directly or indirectly.

The duty to disclose is, as Charles J sets out in *I v I* [2008]:

> "a duty to provide information that would set the other side on a line of enquiry, or a thought process, on matters to which the court must have regard under s25 MCA 1973... it includes a duty to inform the other side of information that may (a) result in the removal of uncertainty as to the value of assets, or the amount of a party's future income, or (b) inform the assessment of the income or earning capacity of a party to the marriage or the value of his or her assets".

See also *F v F* [1995], *GW v RW* [2003] and *W v W (Ancillary relief: Non-disclosure)* [2003] above.

The duty extends to any fact within a party's knowledge and documents and information which add materially to the overall picture, or alter disclosure already given, or are such as might reasonably affect the negotiating position or the exercise of the statutory discretion. The parties must disclose "facts, information and documents, which are material and sufficiently accurate to enable proper negotiations to take place to settle their differences" (para 11, PD9A).

A failure to disclose in mediation or in the collaborative process may bring an end to that process if discovered during it, and if discovered later may mean that any agreement or consensus reached could be set aside.

A failure to disclose in negotiations between solicitors, in court proceedings or in arbitration may be regarded as "conduct" and may give rise to adverse inferences being drawn – for example, an inference that there are substantially more assets than those disclosed. It may also result in costs orders against a party, possibly against a legal representative, and sometimes on an indemnity basis. Alternatively, costs orders may be limited to the additional costs incurred as a result of the failure to provide full disclosure, and on a standard basis, since costs orders are not intended to be "used as a means of punishment" (Peter Hughes QC in *M v M* [2006] WL 2049700). See also *E v E* [1990], *T v T* [1994], *Al-Khatib v Masry & ors* [2002] and *TL v ML* [2006] above.

Failure to disclose will almost certainly result in a loss of credibility for the non-disclosing party, and very often results in a case progressing through the court process and settling part way through the final hearing in a way beneficial to the other party, albeit with often huge and wasteful expenditure on legal fees. It may also impact on the type of order that the court makes, as it did on appeal in *M v M* [2006] EWCA Civ

1852 (second appeal following Peter Hughes QC's judgment referred to above; see also *Kingdon v Kingdon* [2010] above).

The criminal offence of fraud by failing to disclose information (s3 Fraud Act 2006) may be committed where there is a failure to comply with a legal duty to disclose, with the intention of making a gain or causing a loss, and the defendant realises that the failure is dishonest by the ordinary standards of reasonable and honest people. The privilege against self-incrimination is excluded by s13(1), but s13(2) makes any statement or admission by a person inadmissible in proceedings under the Fraud Act against them or their spouse or civil partner.

It may be appropriate to consider a preliminary hearing to address the issue of non-disclosure, as in *OS v DS (Oral disclosure: Preliminary hearing* (see above). For authority in respect of which court should be asked to deal with the issue and how case management powers should be exercised see *K v K* [2005] above, although that case was pre-FPR 2010, and the rules now require "active case management" by the court – see r1.4 and Part 4).

Privilege

Privileged communications are generally protected from disclosure in evidence in any civil proceedings. The law of privilege is complex. Quite different legal principles can apply to different forms of privilege. This guide provides a summary, but further consideration of this complex issue is beyond the scope of the guide. Privilege belongs to the clients (not the lawyers) and may be waived by them.

Types of privilege

Legal professional privilege (sometimes referred to as solicitor/own client privilege) covers:

a)   communications between the client and their legal advisers (legal advice privilege); and

b)   any communications with a party and with third parties in the preparation and conduct of the case in the context of actual or contemplated litigation (litigation privilege).

The concept of "joint privilege" between various related parties with a joint interest means that privilege can be asserted by those parties against a third party but not each other (e.g. trustee and beneficiary). "Common interest privilege" between parties with a common interest at the time permits sharing of information between those parties without loss of privilege (e.g. between a parent company and subsidiary).

"Without prejudice" privilege attaches in specifically defined instances to correspondence and discussions between the parties and their advisers regarding the compromise of any dispute.

The basic rule of evidence is that communications between parties to a dispute that are written or made with the aim of genuinely attempting to settle that dispute cannot usually be admitted in evidence, whether in the same or subsequent litigation connected with the subject-matter, and irrespective of whether a settlement is reached or not (see *Instance v Denny Bros. Printing Ltd, The Times*, 28 February 2000, Ch D and *Rush & Tompkins v Greater London Council* [1989] 1 AC 1280).

However, any admission or statement of existing facts, or a statement of the strength of a party's case, is not privileged and can be referred to at any hearing, even if marked 'without prejudice' (see *Buckinghamshire County Council v Moran* [1990] Ch 623 CA). So, simply marking a letter as "without prejudice" or "without prejudice save as to costs" does not protect factual disclosure from being treated as open; it is not possible to prevent the disclosure of documents that would otherwise be disclosable as a matter of law simply by marking them "without prejudice" or referring to them in any negotiations (whether in mediation, at FDR, or as part of any other confidential dispute resolution process).

There exists in some circumstances privilege against self-incrimination, as touched on above.

It may be that a form of mediation privilege will develop as a separate category of privilege or confidentiality. Part 35 of the FPR and amendments to the Civil Procedure Rules 1998 came into force on 6 April 2011 to implement the EU Mediation Directive 2008/52/EC in respect of EU cross-border disputes in proceedings to which the rules apply. This area of law is likely to evolve and should be kept under review, particularly by those involved in EU cross-border disputes. See the Guide to Good Practice on Mediation for more detail.

Misdirection of privileged communications and other privileged documents

This can result in two different situations arising.

First, the client may obtain privileged communications. Where a client tells a lawyer that they have obtained lawyer/client privileged communications belonging to their spouse/the other client, the lawyer should tell the client that they do not want to know about the document or its contents and, further, tell the client not to read it, and to replace it, destroy it if it was only a copy, or send it to the lawyer to forward on unread. Acting in this way prevents the lawyer coming into conflict with the client.

Where a lawyer receives information or documents from their client and realises that what they have received is privileged, the lawyer should not read the information/document. The lawyer must tell the client that they must forward the information/document directly to the other lawyer. The client should be advised to disclose that they have obtained, and have read, privileged documents.

A conflict between lawyer and client only arises if the lawyer reads privileged documents and the client does not read them, or does not know about their contents. It does not arise if the client reads privileged documents and the lawyer does not know the contents of those documents.

Secondly, privileged communications may be wrongly sent to the other lawyer. In this situation, the lawyer should not read the communications and is not required to disclose the existence of them to the client (see indicative behaviour 4.4(d) of the Solicitors' Code of Conduct). If a lawyer knows immediately that it was sent by mistake, they should stop reading.

If you, the lawyer, read a material part of the document/communication, realise that it was not meant for you but have to concede that the information already read could be very useful to your client, you are under a duty to discuss the implications with your client. You must tell the client that you have a duty to immediately notify the other side that you have received this document by mistake and explain to your client the likelihood of the other side obtaining an injunction concerning the document, the costs implications, and/or the case being more likely to go to court.

In *Ablitt v Mills & Reeve, The Times*, 25 October 1995, Blackburne J made an injunction restraining solicitors from continuing to act for a party in civil litigation where they mistakenly received privileged documents sent to them by the other side's counsel's clerk and which on direct client instructions they had read. The judge said it offended elementary notions of justice if one party, having knowingly taken advantage of such a mistake, could nevertheless continue to have the services of advisers who now had an accurate view of the other side's adviser's views on the merits.

Confidentiality and privacy

Here we can only provide a summary of the main issues – see Privacy and Disclosure for Family Lawyers, published by Resolution, for more detail and practical guidance. Confidentiality and privacy are terms that are often used interchangeably. There are, though, specific legal meanings that may be relevant – for example in the context of the human right to privacy, or an action for breach of confidence. In *Imerman v Tchenguiz* [2010] the court regarded the question of whether the claimant had a "reasonable expectation of privacy" in respect of information as a good test to apply when considering whether a claim for breach of confidence should be successful. Privacy claims in the courts have doubled in the last five years with 56 cases in the High Court or above reported in the year to April 2014 (*The Times*, 30 August 2014).

What is a confidential (or private) document?

The Court of Appeal in *White v Withers LLP and Dearle* [2009] defined 'confidential documents' very widely:

"Communications which are concerned with an individual's private life, including his personal finances, personal business dealings, and (possibly) his other business dealings are the stuff of personal confidentiality."

It includes all documents connected with family or private life, personal and family assets or business dealings. This will include bank statements, correspondence relating to business or personal finances, and also personal documentation such as diaries. It does not however extend to documents regarding joint assets. It is advisable that clients are reassured that they are able to access and look for documents relating to joint assets – for example statements of joint accounts or a joint mortgage. Many clients will be overly cautious and it is important that they understand that they have the right to locate these documents and forward copies to their solicitor.

The location of the documentation will also have a bearing on its status as confidential and private. *Imerman v Tchenguiz* stated that "confidentiality is not dependent upon locks and keys or their electronic equivalent", and therefore it does not automatically mean that, because a document is not contained within a locked filing cabinet or a password-protected computer, the document can be assessed and copied.

It may be important how the parties conducted their affairs. If it is common practice that documents were and are left on the kitchen table then it may be arguable that any such document is not private or confidential, and that both parties should be able to access them. However, if one party knows that their spouse would not consent to a document being accessed then it is safest to assume that it is confidential. Confidentiality cannot easily be lost – a document does not, for example, lose confidentiality simply by reason of the fact that it has been left lying around the house and is discovered unintentionally by your client.

Imerman v Tchenguiz [2010] provides a comprehensive review of the law in relation to confidence and privacy and family lawyers are encouraged to read the judgment itself. Most divorcing or separating couples agree to exchange financial information openly and honestly, as promoted by the Resolution Code of Practice, but there are always exceptions.

Most importantly, following *Imerman*, married couples are not excepted from the rule that each person has the right to privacy. Confidentiality exists between husband and wife whether prior to or after a breakdown in their relationship, and whether divorce or other legal proceedings have been issued or not.

Imerman has confirmed that *Hildebrand v Hildebrand* [1992] 1 FLR 244 is only good law in relation to the rule that if you have a confidential (and relevant) document, it must be disclosed, at the latest, when you serve a questionnaire. The "*Hildebrand* Rules" do not provide authority for a spouse, in circumstances that would otherwise be unlawful, to take, copy and retain copies of confidential documents – even if there is a suspicion that the other spouse is seeking to obscure assets from view. It is not a defence to appropriating documents from the other party to tell their solicitors that you have them and provide copies prior to the questionnaire stage of proceedings.

The key question now, when assessing whether or not a document could and should be accessed is: "would the other spouse consent to these documents being accessed and copied?". If the answer is no, it is likely that the document is confidential and accessing it could lead to an actionable breach of confidence, action in trespass to goods, or criminal prosecution under the Data Protection Act 1998 and the Computer Misuse Act 1990. The court may also decide that the documents cannot be admitted as evidence in the financial proceedings and conduct may also be penalised in costs either in any injunction and/or ancillary relief proceedings.

The Court of Appeal in *Imerman* also stated that where confidential information has been passed on to solicitors, the court might think it right, and in appropriate circumstances necessary, to go so far as to prevent the client from continuing to instruct those solicitors in the proceedings. This obviously has implications for both the family lawyer and the client.

On the other hand, you and your client may also be concerned that without accessing particular documents, it will be impossible to establish that the other person has the undisclosed assets that your client believes that they have, and it may be that a court will admit any such evidence if it is relevant, irrespective of the source of it. It may be a question of finely balanced judgement in a relevant case.

Explaining issues around disclosure and non-disclosure to clients

Clients should be advised about the current uncertainties in this area – both those who may be inclined not to disclose, and those who are concerned that their former partner may not – and the up-to-date position in the area of confidentiality/privacy law. There is no substitute for reading the judgments in *Imerman v Tchenguiz* [2010] and *UL v BK (Freezing Orders: Safeguards: Standard Examples)* [2013].

Anecdotally, different courts are approaching this issue in very different ways, ranging from "business as usual; this doesn't really apply to us" to the strict application of the Court of Appeal's decision and approach in *Imerman*.

As a minimum, family lawyers should consider explaining what 'confidential documents' are, and that they do not include documentation regarding joint assets. There are very limited circumstances where a party can go looking for information concerning their spouse's financial circumstances, and if they do search and find confidential documents then they may be criticised by the courts and they may be subject to civil or criminal proceedings. As Mostyn J said in *UL v BK*:

> "It is simply and categorically unlawful for a wife… to breach her husband's privacy by furtively copying his documents, whether they exist in hard copy or electronically. There may be factual issues about whether the documents are actually in the husband's

private domain; but if they are (and they almost always are) then it is wholly impermissible for the wife to access and copy them."

One should also explain to clients that, in relation to hard copy documents:

- If information is contained within a locked filing cabinet or equivalent they should not break into it or ask anyone else to do so on their behalf.
- If documents are in open files or in communal office areas, they should not look for, or copy, documents belonging to their spouse unless it is known that they would consent to those documents being viewed/copied.
- If information has been left out openly (i.e. not locked in a drawer or study) but it is known that the spouse would not consent to the information being copied, it should not be taken or copied. A client should be advised that it may be acceptable to make a mental note of what the documents say or contain, or take a written note of the key points, but that this cannot be guaranteed.
- If copies of private documents are taken then *UL v BK* makes clear that if the solicitor acting for the person who has taken copies knows about it, they "must immediately seek to obtain all of them from the wife and must return them, and all copies, to the husband's solicitor (if he has one)". It is a moot point whether any written notes made from memory following sight of private documents could be required to be delivered up to the spouse.
- Any information that is sent to the solicitor has to be disclosed to the owner and their solicitor.
- Original documents should not in any circumstances be taken without agreement.

As mentioned above, information on a computer may include any information held on an electronic device with capacity for memory storage/access, or on cloud software, and any private email or private social network. Confidentiality would not apply to information that is posted on a public "wall".

If the information is password protected and the password is unknown to your client, then they must not obtain access to this information or ask anyone else to do so.

If the information is unprotected, or available with a password which is known (or it was a joint password) then access to this information can be obtained if it is known that the spouse would agree.

It should be explained to the client that if information is sent to the solicitor, then it has to be disclosed to the owner or their solicitor, even if the spouse consented to the client accessing that information.

It is also recommended that in an appropriate case a letter should be sent to the other spouse/their lawyer asking whether they hold any originals or copies of documents in relation to your client's financial situation. This would also include documents such as solicitors' attendance notes (obviously redacted to remove privileged matters), counsel's notes, the spouse's own notes and any correspondence passing between solicitors or any third party relating to the confidential/*Hildebrand* material.

If your client provides you with "*Imerman*" documents, then prior to returning the documentation (without reading it), you may ask for an undertaking that the spouse's solicitor will preserve the documents until the conclusion of the proceedings. However, there is no duty on the spouse's solicitor to retain the confidential information and they may refuse to give the undertaking, although:

> "The husband's solicitor, who owes a high duty to the court, will read them and disclose those of them that are both admissible and relevant to the wife's claim, pursuant to the husband's duty of full and frank disclosure" (*UL v BK*).

If this is the case, consider whether there should be an application to the court for the confidential documentation to be admitted as evidence in the proceedings if they show dishonesty (or likely dishonesty) on the part of the spouse or are in contradiction of existing disclosure in the proceedings. If the spouse does not have a solicitor, then *UL v BK* suggests that you should retain the documents unread and apply to the court for directions.

If you are dealing with a spouse who is being secretive then the alternative options should be discussed with the client (in the context of balancing risk, benefit and cost):

- Issue a court application to ensure that any failure to disclose may be a contempt of court
- Production/disclosure appointments to require third parties such as accountants or business partners to bring documents to court.
- Search and seize orders (previously known as *Anton Piller* orders). These can be for documents and/or electronic data whether at home or in the office. Data may also be stored on hand held devices etc.
- Freezing orders (previously known as *Mareva* injunctions), which can be used to freeze assets pending the resolution of a settlement (see *UL v BK* above).
- If they find information or documentation that shows clearly an intention to hide/move assets to prejudice/defeat claims, then it may be advisable to take copies and give them to you, provided they are fully informed about the risks. This is not something that should be done without very careful consideration.
- If they do see any document or information suggesting the presence of undisclosed assets, they should probably make a mental note of what the document/information says or contains, again provided they are fully informed about the risks.
- Any application for a freezing order based on information obtained from illegitimately obtained documents will require the applicant to "candidly reveal that her knowledge drives from [those documents and she] must explain how she got them" (*UL v BK*), even if this may lead to civil or criminal proceedings.

Transparency

The issue of transparency has been the subject of much debate. Part 27 of the FPR, and PD 27B and 27C now permit duly accredited representatives of news gathering and reporting organisations (i.e. those who have UK Press Card authorisation) into 'private' proceedings from 27 April 2009, although not into hearings such as FDRs.

The fact that the media is allowed to attend a hearing does not currently mean they have the right to see documents that would otherwise be private and does not override the provisions of the statutes that are relevant to the publication of family proceedings (e.g. s12 Administration of Justice Act 1960 (AJA 1960) and s97 Children Act 1989 (CA 1989), as amended). A media representative may apply to the court for sight of documents referred to during proceedings, and the court will balance the competing human rights (Arts 8 and 10) in reaching a decision about whether to grant the application. If permission is granted, that does not of itself permit the publication of the contents of those documents, although the contents of the documents may be published if that is not prohibited by the AJA 1960 or the CA 1989, the general law relating to misuse of private information, rules of court (e.g. r12.73FPR), or any other legal prohibition in force from time to time. Otherwise, reporting is expected to be general in nature, commenting on "the processes involved and the principles by which decisions are made" (foreword of "*Family Justice in View*" CM 7502) and specifically must not substantially prejudice the administration of justice or publish information that is protected by the implied undertaking of confidentiality, being information before a court sitting in private, not in the public domain, and produced as a result of compulsory disclosure.

Family proceedings are held "in private" (Part 27, r27.10 unless the rules or other legislation provide otherwise, or the court directs otherwise), so the implied undertaking of confidentiality prevents either party from using information or documents that come to light in financial remedy proceedings elsewhere, where that information has been disclosed under the compulsion of court proceedings 'before, during and after proceedings' (per Butler-Sloss LJ in *Clibbery v Allan* [2002] EWCA Civ 45; albeit obiter). See *DE v AB* [2014] EWCA Civ 1064 for recent judicial consideration of open justice and privacy.

There has been a suggestion that it may be possible to restrict publication of information in financial remedy applications by application of the Judicial Proceedings (Restrictions of Reports) Act 1926. This topic is the subject of ongoing consultation with further reform expected. For more information see the Resolution publication *Privacy and Disclosure for Family Lawyers*. See also: http://www.medialawyer.press.net/courtapplications/mediaorganisations.jsp and http://www.medialawyer.press.net/courtapplications/standardorder.jsp

Non-court dispute resolution & MIAMs

All methods of non-court dispute resolution should be considered with the client/s at the outset and kept under review subsequently throughout the process of resolution. The client should be informed and reminded regularly about the options and if appropriate encouraged to attend a MIAM to find out more, and also should be informed of the need to attend a MIAM before issuing a contested application to court for financial orders.

The client/s should be assisted with identifying the most appropriate way of providing and receiving disclosure depending on the dispute resolution process being used and the resources available. For example:

- if in mediation, then with or without lawyers assisting the clients and the mediator with the disclosure process;
- using the collaborative process with provision of disclosure on a voluntary basis;
- with the clients' lawyers providing voluntary disclosure in accordance with the pre-application protocol; or
- within the timetable of court proceedings.

The importance of giving disclosure

Disclosure is of vital and fundamental importance to ensuring a just outcome. The lawyers and all those involved in court and non-court dispute resolution should encourage the separating couple at an early stage to give full, frank and clear disclosure of information and to be open in all dealings. The potential consequences of not doing or being so should be explained, at the outset in the terms of engagement letter, and at each relevant stage during the retainer; with specific reference to potential civil and criminal liability. Follow the guidance above in respect of how to explain the issues around disclosure and potential or actual non-disclosure to clients. Whichever dispute resolution process is used, at an early stage the lawyer or mediator should also consider whether, as a matter of good practice, to provide the client/s with a blank form E financial statement or equivalent so that they may see exactly what is required. Consideration also may need to be given in mediation as to who is best placed to assist the clients in providing disclosure – i.e. whether their respective solicitors (if applicable) should do so, or the mediator, depending upon the circumstances of the case, as referred to above.

Where the circumstances are particularly complicated, more disclosure than that required by the form E will be appropriate. However, if there are contested court proceedings, then documents should only be disclosed to the extent that they are required by the financial statement or may otherwise be justified as necessary. Excessive or disproportionate costs should not be incurred either in seeking or providing disclosure (see the pre-application protocol annexed to PD9A, para 11), and regard must be had to proportionality and saving expense (r1.1 FPR). Judicial assistance may be advisable to manage the process, and Part 4 of the FPR contains a non-exhaustive list of possible general case management techniques that may be employed.

If a non-court dispute resolution process is being used, then all schedules of assets, income, liabilities and other material facts produced and/or exchanged should take account of the contents of the form E financial statement as a guide to the format and extent of the disclosure. The disclosure process should be just as rigorous in non-court dispute resolution as in court proceedings, but may be streamlined and targeted to minimise expense, provided that all material information is disclosed. The evidence produced in support of the disclosure process may be limited provided the potential risks of so doing are fully understood and freely agreed to by the separating couple.

In cases in which the client, following advice, decides to issue proceedings immediately, rather than pursue voluntary disclosure or engage in non-court dispute resolution (for example where there may be a forum dispute), attendance at a MIAM may not be necessary, or alternatively part 4 on form FM1 may be completed by the solicitor acting for the applicant explaining why the applicant has not attended a MIAM. Part 4 should be used sparingly.

Privilege, and open and without prejudice communications

Everyone involved in assisting clients to resolve financial matters between them, and the clients themselves, need to understand the open nature of the disclosure process and the distinction between that and privileged without prejudice negotiations about the outcome of the issues in dispute. It is good practice to label documents appropriately and to ensure that all those involved understand the basis on which information is being shared when there may be some doubt (for example, schedules of future income needs). Facts should be disclosed in "open" correspondence or documentation, whichever dispute resolution process is used, and separate correspondence or documentation should set out any privileged proposals or any provisional consensus reached in mediation pending legal advice (e.g. in a memorandum of understanding).

Where factual information is given in another lawyer's privileged letter that lawyer should be invited to repeat it in an open letter or be informed that otherwise the letter will be redacted (i.e. edited) to delete the privileged information so that it may be used in evidence. If necessary the issue will need to be adjudicated on at an interlocutory hearing or as a preliminary issue.

Where there is the suggestion that a client may have committed a criminal offence, they should be advised about the implications of divulging that information in different contexts in light of *R v K* [2010] above.

Clients should be encouraged to make proposals aimed at achieving a negotiated agreement as soon as possible. How this is done will differ according to the process involved; but it is generally good practice to conduct negotiations and put forward proposals focussed on and referring to the clients' "interests" (as opposed to their "positions"), and to emphasise the need for clients to be willing to compromise. Practice Direction 9A para 6.3 states that the court expects parties to make offers and proposals and to give them proper consideration at the FDR appointment. There is a duty to negotiate, but it is necessary for there to have been proper disclosure before offers can be made (see Butler-Sloss LJ as she then was in *Gojkovic v Gojkovic (No 2)* [1991] 2 FLR 233).

In court proceedings, evidence of anything said or of any admission made in the course of an FDR appointment will not be admissible in evidence, except in the very exceptional circumstances indicated in *Re D (Minors) (Conciliation: Disclosure of information)* [1993] Fam 231, sub nom *Re D (Minors) (Conciliation: Privilege)* [1993] 1 FLR 932 (see para 3.2 of the President's Direction of 25 May 2000). See also *Myerson v Myerson* [2008] EWCA Civ 1376, on the issue of whether the FDR judge can hear a subsequent variation application.

Privacy and confidentiality of documents

Consideration should be given with clients to issues of privacy and security in respect of their documents and communications, and in particular advice from their lawyers, especially if the separating couple continue to share a property. Caution should be exercised when communicating with clients and others by email, and it is good practice to consider whether separate correspondence addresses, password-protected email addresses, or possibly if there is no other alternative post office boxes should be used, to ensure private documentation and communications are kept securely.

It is good practice to remind clients of the need for confidentiality at all times – before, during and after proceedings.

The implied duty of confidentiality probably extends to information obtained prior to the issue of financial order proceedings and, as a matter of good practice, lawyers should advise their clients that the same principles do apply, particularly given the developing privacy laws and in light of *Imerman*.

If specific confidential information is requested, particularly affecting third parties or of a market-sensitive nature, it is good practice to ask the requesting party to sign an agreement/undertaking confirming that the information sought will remain confidential and will not be disclosed.

"Self-help" and financial disclosure

Irrespective of the potential legal consequences, clients should be advised to consider the practical and procedural consequences of self-help, including that it may:

- consequently have an adverse effect on their children, if they have any;
- raise tension and hostility between the parties;
- encourage vindictive and/or corresponding action by the other party;
- increase costs;
- result in an order for costs; and
- make settlement much less likely.

Pragmatism and common sense in this area are commended, but practitioners should be aware, and make their clients aware, that civil or criminal proceedings may follow as a result of self-help.

In appropriate cases clients should be advised of the court's powers to make search, preservation and freezing orders (and other interim orders) under Part 20 of the FPR (see *UL v BK* above). It is recognised though that, in practice, cases where such action is appropriate are likely to be far fewer than those in which there are real concerns about non-disclosure. The potential cost, and the risk of bringing such actions when the required evidence to justify it may not be readily available, or where the location and production of such evidence may bring with it the risk of criminal/civil proceedings, is undoubtedly a problem with no clear solution.

Be clear about your position, both personally and professionally, so that you do not potentially become liable for a criminal or civil action. Retain your objectivity, professional judgement and a sense of proportionality. Self-help situations can be dramatic and can result in lawyers overlooking the complex issues of professional conduct and potential illegality that arise in this area. Keep up to date with developments in this area since there is a great deal of uncertainty about how the decision in *Imerman v Tchenguiz* [2010] will be interpreted/developed in the future.

The issue of whether illegally or improperly obtained evidence will be admissible also needs to be considered. Such evidence is not automatically inadmissible (see *Jones v University of Warwick* [2003] 1 WLR 954), and in family proceedings involves a discretionary exercise guided by the balance of the parties' human rights and the overriding objective.

The use of private detective agencies cannot be recommended save in exceptional circumstances and with appropriate instructions being clearly given that information must be obtained lawfully, and that no unlawful action is to be taken (see *R v Waters* [2007] EWCA Crim 222 above).

Communications between lawyers

It is undesirable and unwise for a lawyer to pass on to another lawyer information that they do not want to be disclosed to the other lawyer's client. It is likely to be a breach of the Solicitors' Code of Conduct to accept/receive confidential information from the other lawyer and not disclose it to the client unless such behaviour falls within the indicative behaviours at IB 4.4 of the Code (for example, that there is evidence that serious physical or mental injury will be caused to a person if that information is disclosed to the client, or because the provisions in the money laundering legislation prohibit the disclosure). Some lawyers adopt the practice of having "off the record" conversations with their counterparts. It is good practice to refuse to have such a conversation, in order to comply with the above rule.

Costs consequences in the event of non-disclosure

Litigation misconduct is now the only basis on which an adverse costs order may be made in court proceedings for financial orders, which undoubtedly may include a failure to provide adequate disclosure. The costs implications of non-compliance with the duty to disclose should be considered by the court at the first court appointment and throughout the proceedings. Clients should be advised that producing information at the last moment, including updating or varying disclosure may lead to an adjournment and/or a penalty of costs. Sanctions may also be imposed on their legal advisers in some circumstances. Clients must be advised of the risks, both of the possibility of an order being made, and also the reality that it is often very difficult to secure a costs order.

There is a great deal of jurisprudence in respect of costs in family and civil proceedings. It is difficult to predict the outcome of costs issues, even in cases where there has been a lack of, or late disclosure, and the issue of the proportionality of pursuing the issue must always be borne in mind.

Note

1. This good practice guidance does not and cannot affect any obligations in law, specific court orders or rules of professional conduct.
2. Good practice guidance can inevitably only deal with the generality of situations. It cannot be an absolute rule. The special facts of any particular case may justify and/or require a lawyer to depart from these guidelines.
3. Resolution's view is that this guidance applies to all family law cases for the better conduct and approach to resolution of family breakdown issues, and not just to cases between Resolution members.

(Reproduced by permission of Resolution)

STATEMENT ON THE EFFICIENT CONDUCT OF FINANCIAL REMEDY HEARINGS ALLOCATED TO A HIGH COURT JUDGE WHETHER SITTING AT THE ROYAL COURTS OF JUSTICE OR ELSEWHERE

Revised 1 July 2015

1. I am authorised by the President to release this statement.

2. In order to enhance efficiency in the disposal of financial remedy cases allocated to be heard by a High Court Judge, and to ensure that such cases are allotted an appropriate share of the court's resources, the following standards and procedures must be observed.

3. **Principles of allocation.**

The governing principle is that a case should only be allocated for hearing by a High Court judge if it is exceptionally complex or there is another substantial ground for the case being heard at that level <u>and that</u> allocation to that level is proportionate. Such allocation is rarely likely to be proportionate unless the net assets exceed £7.5m.

In determining whether the governing principle is satisfied the following are relevant considerations:

(1)   The overall net assets exceed £15m; and/or
(2)   The overall net earned annual income exceeds £1m.

In a case falling within (1) or (2) the governing principle will likely, but not necessarily, be satisfied. There will be some relatively straightforward cases falling within (1) or (2) where a transfer to High Court judge level will nevertheless not be proportionate.

In a case not falling within (1) or (2) above but where the net assets are said to exceed £7.5m:

(3)   There is a serious case advanced of non-disclosure of assets.
(4)   Substantial assets are held offshore either directly or through the medium of trust or corporate entities and there may be issues as to the enforceability of any award.
(5)   Substantial assets are held in trusts which are said to be variable nuptial settlements.
(6)   Substantial assets are held through the medium of unquoted corporate entities and detailed expert valuation evidence will be required.

(7)   A serious, carefully considered and potentially influential argument is being advanced of

    a.   compensation,
    b.   non-matrimonial property, or
    c.   conduct.

(8)   There are serious, substantial third party claims to the assets otherwise subject to the dispositive powers of the court.

(9)   There is a serious, carefully considered and potentially influential issue as to the effect of a nuptial agreement.

(10)   The application involves a novel and important point of law.

Where, on any view, the net assets do not exceed £7.5m allocation to a High Court Judge is only likely to be proportionate where the application involves a novel and important point of law.

4. Every case will be allocated to an individual High Court Judge at the earliest opportunity. He or she will, unless this is completely impracticable, conduct all future hearings, including the final hearing, apart from the FDR. Early allocation is essential to achieve judicial continuity which is to be regarded as a critically important objective.

5. Allocation will be undertaken as follows:

a.   If the case is at High Court Judge level by virtue of the self-certification procedure (see para 20 below) then the allocated judge will be determined by the judge in charge of the money list (presently Mostyn J) when granting the certificate. For this purpose it is vital that the available dates of counsel for the First Appointment are stated on the certificate.

b.   If the case has been transferred to High Court Judge level by a district or circuit judge sitting in the Family Court in London or elsewhere on the South-Eastern Circuit the order for transfer, together with available dates of counsel for the next hearing, must be emailed to the judge in charge of the money list (c/o his clerk) who will determine the allocated judge.

c.   If the case has been transferred to High Court Judge level by a district or circuit judge sitting in the Family Court on circuit (other than the South-Eastern Circuit) the order for transfer, together with available dates of counsel for the next hearing, must be emailed to the relevant FDLJ (c/o his or her clerk) who will determine the allocated judge.

d.   If the case has been transferred to High Court Judge level by a High Court Judge (for example on or following an early application for a freezing injunction) that judge will normally allocate the case to himself or herself. If he or she does not do so the procedure in (b) or (c) should apply depending on whether the case was heard in London or on circuit.

6. If the allocated Judge deems it appropriate, the date for the final hearing may be fixed at the First Appointment.

7. The FDR will be listed with a time estimate of 1 day unless (i) the parties certify, giving written reasons, that a lesser period is sufficient and (ii) obtain the written permission of the FDR Judge (before whom the case is listed for hearing) for the reduced time estimate.

8. Any interlocutory application in the course of the proceedings must be made to the allocated Judge, unless to do so would be impracticable or would cause undue delay.

9. Every case allocated to a High Court Judge must be the subject of a Pre-Trial Review before that judge held approximately 4 weeks before the final hearing.
If the case is to be heard on circuit the Pre-Trial Review may be heard before the allocated judge sitting in London by video-link.

10. At the Pre-Trial Review a final hearing template must be prepared. This should:

a.   allow a reasonable and realistic time for judicial reading and judgment writing;
b.   not normally allow longer than one hour for opening; and
c.   not allow for any evidence-in-chief unless the court has expressly authorised this at the Pre-Trial Review within the terms of FPR rules 22.6(2)-(4). Pursuant to rule 22.6(2) the parties' section 25 statements will almost invariably stand as their evidence-in-chief.

11. The parties' section 25 statements must only contain evidence. By virtue of FPR PD22A para 4.3(b) the statement must indicate the source for any matters of information and belief. On no account should a section 25 statement contain argument or other rhetoric.

12. If a direction for a discussion between experts has not previously been made pursuant to FPR rule 25.16 and PD 25E then that matter must be raised at the Pre-Trial Review. There would have to be very good reasons why such a direction should not be made at the Pre-Trial Review.

13. At the Pre-Trial Review a direction should be made which ensures compliance with the indispensable requirement in FPR PD27A para 4.3(b) of provision of an agreed statement of the issues to be determined at the final hearing. To the statement of issues must be attached:

a.   an agreed schedule of assets on which any un-agreed items must be clearly denoted; and
b.   an agreed chronology on which any un-agreed events must be clearly denoted.

It is absolutely unacceptable for the court to be presented at the final hearing with competing asset schedules and chronologies.

14. The court bundle for the final hearing must scrupulously comply with FPR PD27A. This limits the size of the bundle to a single file containing no more than 350 pages: a specific prior direction from the court must be obtained at the Pre-Trial Review if the bundle is to exceed that limit (PD27A para 5.1). The limit of 350 pages includes the skeleton arguments (see para 15 below) and the agreed documents under para 13 above. Only those documents which are relevant to the hearing and which it is necessary for the court to read, or which will actually be referred to during the hearing, may be included: correspondence (including with experts), bank or credit card statements and other financial records must not be included unless a specific prior direction of the court at the Pre-Trial Review has been obtained (PD27A para 4.1). A separate bundle of all authorities relied on must be prepared and this must be agreed between the advocates (PD27A para 4.3). That bundle should not contain more than an absolute maximum of 10 authorities. Practitioners are specifically referred to the decision of the President in *Re L (A Child)* [2015] EWFC 15, paras 9 – 25, and to the earlier pronouncements referred to there, all of which apply fully to financial hearings.

15. Skeleton argument should conform to the prescriptions applicable in the Court of Appeal as laid down in CPR PD52A para 5.1 and PD52C para 31(1). Thus a skeleton argument must:

a. be concise and not exceed 25 pages (excluding agreed documents under para 13 above, but including any other appended schedules);
b. be printed on A4 paper in not less than 12 point font and 1.5 line spacing;
c. both define and confine the areas of controversy;
d. be set out in numbered paragraphs;
e. be cross-referenced to any relevant documents in the bundle;
f. be self-contained and not incorporate by reference material from previous skeleton arguments; and
g. not include extensive quotations from documents.

Where it is necessary to refer to an authority, a skeleton argument must first state the proposition of law the authority demonstrates; and then identify the parts of the authority that support the proposition, but without extensive quotation from it.

16. If a skeleton argument is intended to exceed the limit of 25 pages a direction to that effect should be sought at the Pre-Trial Review. Very good reasons would have to be shown for such a direction to be made. A skeleton argument which breaches the limit will be returned unread for abridgement.

17. At the final hearing the parties' advocates will be expected to adhere to the hearing template. Slippage will not be tolerated unless there are very good reasons. When conducting cross-examination advocates must have in mind the strictures of Lord Judge LCJ in *R v Farooqi & Ors* [2013] EWCA Crim 1649 at para 113, where he stated 'what ought to be avoided is the increasing modern habit of assertion, (often in tendentious terms or incorporating comment), which is not true cross-examination'.

18. If advocates unreasonably fail to comply with paras 13 (provision of agreed statement of issues, schedule of assets and chronology), 15 (length and content of skeleton argument) or 17 (adherence to hearing template) they will risk an order being made disallowing a proportion of their fees pursuant to CPR 44.11(1)(b) and/or section 51(6) Senior Courts Act 1981. In this regard attention is drawn to the comparable warning in CPR PD 52C para 31(4).

19. If, following receipt of a draft written judgment either party wishes to seek permission to appeal, grounds of appeal must be filed at court and served on the other party at least one clear business day before the hearing of the application for permission.

20. The self-certification procedure concerning the allocation of financial remedy cases to a High Court Judge is set out below.

Guidance: Financial Proceedings: cases to be allocated to a judge of the High Court by self-certification

1. This Guidance takes effect from 1 July 2015 and applies, as far as practicable, to cases commenced before, as well as those commenced on or after, that date. It applies to financial remedy applications pending in the Family Court where the parties seek allocation to a judge of the High Court. It is no longer confined to cases proceeding in the CFC.

2. An application for a financial remedy will normally only be considered suitable for hearing by a High Court judge if it is exceptionally complex or there is another substantial ground for the case being heard by a High Court judge.

3. Where the parties seek the allocation of the proceedings to a High Court judge before an allocation direction has been made both counsel or, if counsel are not instructed, solicitor(s) for the parties must complete and file a certificate in the form annexed to this Guidance, stating concisely the reasons for certifying that the application is suitable for determination by a Judge of the Family Division. The completed certificate must be filed with the Clerk of the Rules not less than 21 days before the date fixed for the First Appointment in the Family Court.

[4.] The completed certificate will be referred to and considered by the Judge of the Family Division in charge of the money list who will determine whether the certificate indicates that the case is suitable for hearing by a High Court judge. If so determined, the case will be allocated to a Judge of the Family Division. A date will be fixed for the First Appointment before the allocated Judge and the merits of the certification will be further considered at that appointment.

[5.] If, at the First Appointment, the allocated Judge considers that the certification was not appropriate, the proceedings will be re-allocated within the Family Court and the allocated Judge may give directions as to case management, including the level of judiciary before whom the case should be listed. The allocated Judge may make such orders as to costs as considered appropriate.

[6.] Where proceedings are allocated to a High Court judge under paragraph 3, it is the responsibility of the solicitor for the applicant to ensure that the First Appointment fixed in the Family Court is vacated.

Certificate
IN THE FAMILY COURT **No.**

The marriage of **[Name of applicant]**
and
[Name of Respondent]

Outline facts:
a. The parties married on **[Date]**
b. The parties separated on **[Date]**
c. There are **[Number]** children of the family
d. The **[Petition/Answer]** was issued on **[Date]**
e. The Decree Nisi was pronounced on **[Date]**
f. The Decree Absolute was granted on **[Date]**
g. There is **[not]** a dispute about the jurisdiction of the High Court of England and Wales. The reason for the dispute is **[Give short reasons]**

[Name] being **[Counsel/solicitor]** for the Applicant
[Wife/Husband]

[Name] being **[Counsel/solicitor]** for the Respondent
[Wife/Husband]

We certify that this application should be allocated to a judge of the High Court because:-
Delete/complete as appropriate

(1) The net assets in this case are currently estimated to be in the order of:-
   (a) £10 – £15 million
   (b) £15 – £25 million
   (c) £25 – £50 million
   (d) £50 million plus **[State the figure]**
   (e) Other **[State the figure]**
      If the assets are less than the figures set out in (a) – (d) above state the reasons why the case is fit for allocation to a judge of the High Court.
      [State reasons]

Potential allegations/issues may arise which include:

(2)	Non disclosure of assets	**[Yes/No]**
(3)	Assets are/were held through the medium of offshore trusts/settlements.	**[Yes/No]**
(4)	Assets are/were held through the medium of family/unquoted corporate entities.	**[Yes/No]**
(5)	The value of family assets, trust and/or corporate entities.	**[Yes/No]**
(6)	A nuptial agreement is relied on	**[Yes/No]**
(7)	Assets are held offshore.	**[Yes/No]**
(8)	The parties' respective contributions.	**[Yes/No]**

Give brief details of the potential dispute
[Details of potential dispute]

(9)   There are/may be disputed allegations of 'obvious and gross' conduct. Give a brief outline of the potential matters that may be in dispute.
[Details of conduct allegations]

(10)   There are substantial arguments concerning the illiquidity of assets. Give brief details of the potential matters that may be in dispute.
[Details of illiquidity of assets disputes]

(11)   There may be substantial arguments about:-

(a)	which assets are 'matrimonial assets' or 'non matrimonial assets'	**[Yes/No]**
(b)	assets that were owned prior to the marriage	**[Yes/No]**
(c)	assets that were acquired after the parties' separated	**[Yes/No]**
(d)	other – give brief details of matters that may be in dispute.	**[Yes/No]**

[Details of dispute]

(12) The application involves a novel point of law. Specifically ... (set out in outline the proposition of law that may be involved)

We certify that this case is suitable for transfer to be heard by a High Court Judge

The dates mutually convenient to the advocates for the first appointment are ......

Signed

...... counsel/solicitor for the applicant

...... counsel/solicitor for the respondent

Dated ......

For completion by the Court

Approved/Rejected
First appointment fixed for ......
Allocated to Mr/Mrs Justice ......

Signed

......

Mr/Mrs Justice ...... in private
Sitting at the Royal Courts of Justice

Dated ......

RESOLUTION GUIDANCE NOTE: INSTRUCTING EXPERTS IN APPLICATIONS FOR A FINANCIAL ORDER

This guidance note covers the instruction of financial experts for court proceedings. Those looking to instruct an interdisciplinary team for DR purposes are referred to the 'Assembling the Dispute Resolution Team' chapter of the Resolution Family Disputes Handbook.

1.   Introduction

Applications for financial orders in matrimonial or civil partnership proceedings should be conducted cost effectively and costs not incurred without justification, but in some cases it will be necessary for expert evidence to be obtained to enable the parties to reach an agreement or the court to determine the case. This is usually in relation to the value of particular assets, but an expert can be instructed to give evidence on other matters relevant to the case.

The instruction of experts in family proceedings is governed by Part 25 of the Family Procedure Rules 2010 (FPR) and the associated Practice Directions, which came into force on 6 April 2011 and were amended with effect from 31 January 2013. The Practice Direction in force prior to 31 January 2013 (PD 25A) has been replaced by a series of shorter Practice Directions (PDs 25A, B, C, D, E and F).

The content of the new Practice Directions is as follows:

25A: Experts – Emergencies and Pre-Proceedings Instructions
25B: The Duties of an Expert, the Expert's Report and Arrangements for an Expert to Attend Court
25C: Children Proceedings – The Use of Single Joint Experts and the Process Leading to an Expert Being Instructed or Expert Evidence Being put Before the Court
25D: Financial Remedy Proceedings and Other Family Proceedings (Except Children Proceedings) – The Use of Single Joint Experts and the Process Leading to an Expert Being Instructed or Expert Evidence Being Put Before the Court
25E: Discussions between Experts in Family Proceedings
25F: Assessors in Family Proceedings

The FPR and Practice Directions together provide a detailed procedural framework, and largely replicate Part 35 of the Civil Procedure Rules 1998 (as amended in July 2009). The amendments to Part 25 and the Practice Directions are intended to encourage the court to control and restrict the use of expert evidence.

'The President's Ancillary Relief Advisory Group Best Practice Guide for Instructing a Single Joint Expert' produced in November 2002 (Appendix 14 of The Family Law Protocol) ('The Best Practice Guide') also provided detailed recommendations regarding the procedure for instructing experts specifically in financial proceedings.

While the Best Practice Guide has been superseded by Part 25 and PD 25A FPR 2010, it does contain some helpful practical guidance beyond the scope of PD 25A. Where applicable, that additional guidance has been included within this guide.

Where the instruction of an expert is a consideration, it is important that it is proportionate to the case and how they are instructed is key to this. The court has a duty, under Part 25.1, to restrict expert evidence to that which is necessary to resolve the proceedings. The general approach is that single joint experts should be instructed, rather than each party instructing their own expert, and in the event that the parties cannot agree on a single joint expert, an application to the court should be made to resolve this issue, rather than each party instructing their own experts. Baron J said in *K v K* [2005] 2 FLR 1137 (para 39) that 'the general practice in the Family Division should be that only joint approaches are acceptable and if there is non-cooperation from one side, then this cannot be circumvented by unilateral action and should be dealt with by an application'. However, this case predates the FPR 2010.

It is worth noting that there are aspects of this position which conflicted with the then procedural rules, being Part 35 of the CPR (and now Part 25 FPR), such as in relation to raising questions of an expert.

Part 25.2(2) (Interpretation) includes definitions for 'expert' and 'single joint expert', and the court has power under Part 25.11 to direct that evidence should be given by a single joint expert.

The instruction of a different expert for each party can have the effect of polarising the parties' positions, rather than bringing them closer to agreement, and can have a significant effect on the parties' costs.

Practitioners have a duty to consider, at an early stage, what expert evidence may be required. While it is common for experts to be instructed by both clients jointly, there are circumstances where one party will require an expert's advice themselves. This may be to assist in completing the disclosure process, in preparing a questionnaire following the other party's disclosure, or in advising on the way in which funds might be raised. There will therefore be certain situations where, in acting in the best interests of a client, the instruction of an expert solely for one party may be vital.

This guide is intended to assist practitioners in advising clients on when expert evidence is required, and instructing the expert in such a way as will be of maximum benefit to the client in assisting them, or the court, in reaching a resolution of the financial matters between the parties. It deals with the following issues:

- When is an expert required?
- What is the role of an expert?
- When to instruct an expert – timing.
- How to select an expert.
- Information to obtain about possible experts prior to first appointment.

- The joint letter of instruction
- Providing information to the expert.
- Attendance at meetings with the expert or inspections of property.
- Communications with an expert and supplementary instructions.
- The expert's report.
- Questions following the expert's report.
- An expert's attendance at court.
- Best practice if two experts are to be instructed.
- The instruction of 'shadow experts' – when it is appropriate and their role.

2.   When is an expert required?

The instruction of experts in financial remedy proceedings is most commonly to value land or property, shares or an interest in a company or a business, or to advise on taxation issues and pensions, but expert evidence may be required in relation to a number of other issues, for example medical evidence.

Part 25.1 of the FPR states that: 'Expert evidence will be restricted to that which in the opinion of the court is necessary to assist the court to resolve the proceedings.' In every case where the instruction of an expert is potentially necessary, the first consideration should be whether the instruction and cost are proportionate to the case. Where the instruction of more than one expert is considered, this should be applied to each possible instruction.

Before deciding whether the instruction of an expert is necessary, it is important that the lawyer discusses with the client the advantages and disadvantages of doing so and whether there are any appropriate alternatives to a formal valuation in that particular case, for example market appraisals, or drive-by valuations. The client should be made aware of the likely cost of instructing an expert, and the lawyer should carry out, with the client, a cost-benefit analysis of obtaining a valuation.

In the event that the client does not agree to the instruction of an expert, it is important that they are advised about the court's power, under Part 4.3 of the FPR, to make an order of its own initiative, which could include an order for the instruction of an expert.

If two or more parties wish to instruct an expert, the court has the power, under Part 25.11, to direct that the evidence is to be given by a single joint expert. Under 25.11(2), where the parties cannot agree on who should be instructed, the court may either select the expert from a list prepared by the relevant parties, or make a selection in such other manner as it sees fit.

The client should be advised that they may be ordered to pay all, or a proportion, of the expert's fees, if it is considered appropriate (Part 25.12(4)). If the court does not make specific direction, the parties shall be jointly and severally liable for the expert's fees (Part 25.12(6)).

However, where possible, it is preferable that the instruction of experts is discussed and agreed between the parties at an early stage, usually (but not always) after the exchange of financial disclosure has taken place, whether voluntarily, or within the court process (when permission should be sought at the first appointment, in accordance with Part 9.15 of the FPR).

3.   What is the role of an expert?

In practice, the role of the expert in financial remedy proceedings will be to provide information to enable the parties' lawyers to advise them, or to resolve a particular issue of dispute between the parties to enable settlement discussions or the court process to progress.

However, under Part 25.3 of the FPR, an expert, although instructed and paid for by the parties, has a duty to help the court on matters which are within their expertise. This duty overrides any obligation to the person (or persons) from whom they have received the instructions and by whom they will be paid.

No party may put expert evidence before the court (in any form) without the court's permission.

A party may be concerned that instructing a single joint expert may not produce the best result for them and that instructing their own expert would be to their advantage. It is the role of the lawyer to explain the benefits of a single joint expert, including that their role is an impartial one. The impartiality of a single joint expert is the most important aspect of their role in assisting to resolve matters between parties, rather than increasing the issues in dispute, which can easily happen if each party instructs their own expert. In any event, even where the parties want to submit evidence from separate experts, the court may direct that the evidence be given by a single joint expert (Part 25.11).

Expert evidence is often subjective and it is not uncommon for different experts to come to different conclusions on the same instructions, which is why finding the right single joint expert can be beneficial in resolving issues. Differing opinions between two experts can make an agreement more difficult to reach and can lead to a case reaching a final hearing, with all of the costs that involves, when the matter may have been resolved without the need for a final hearing if a single joint expert had been instructed at an early stage.

However, practitioners are under an obligation to consider whether the evidence of a single joint expert is in the best interest of their client. In more substantial asset cases, there may be a justifiable need for each party to have their own expert as the scope for a wide variation in valuations or opinion is greater. The importance of the need for supportive evidence in such cases should not be ignored. In this respect it is possible for the parties to agree to instruct separate experts (PD25D, 2.5).

In acting in a client's best interest, it is therefore very important to consider at an early stage what evidence may be needed and approach the other party's solicitor to try to agree how this should be undertaken as soon as is practicable.

4.   When to instruct an expert – timing

The possible need for expert evidence should be considered with the client at the first meeting, if appropriate, and the client should be made aware of the court's approach to the instruction of single joint experts and the cost implications of such evidence.

If expert evidence is required, it is usual to raise this with the other party at an early stage. If financial remedy proceedings have been commenced, then it may be appropriate to raise the need for such evidence in form E. If the need for expert evidence will prevent one or both parties entering into an FDR hearing at the first appointment, it should be raised in the statement of issues filed with the court prior to the first appointment.

Part 25.6 of the FPR deals with when the parties should seek permission to instruct an expert. In financial proceedings this should be no later than the first appointment, in private law proceedings it should be no later than the directions appointment, and in public law proceedings it should be no later than the case management conference.

If financial remedy proceedings have not been commenced and the parties have agreed to exchange financial information, it may be appropriate to consider what expert evidence is required with the client and then the other party soon after disclosure has been exchanged. This is to ensure that all of the information required to enable the lawyers to advise their respective clients and to enable the parties to make informed decisions about settlement has been obtained at an early stage.

If these issues have not been considered in the early stages of the proceedings, a settlement meeting or FDR hearing may have to be abandoned without a resolution being reached, causing wasted costs, further delay and more stress to the parties.

It will also be important to take into account what further information may need to be provided to an expert and the time it will take to obtain this. This will also be relevant to the proposed timescale for the provision of a report. The proposed timescale set out in the letter of instruction needs to be realistic to take into account that information will be requested by the expert and may take the client some time to produce.

5.   How to select a particular expert

A party wishing to instruct an expert should give the other party a list of names of one or more experts whom they consider suitable. The other party should respond within 10 business days, indicating any objections to a proposed expert, and, if there are objections, supplying the name of one or more experts whom they consider suitable.

A single joint expert should not generally be someone that either party has instructed previously, unless otherwise agreed or if there are good reasons to the contrary. Each party should disclose whether they have already consulted any of the proposed experts about the issue in question (PD 25D 2.3).

The specialism of the expert required will clearly depend on the evidence that is required in a particular case. Research should be carried out as to an expert's suitability in a particular case, including requesting a copy of their CV and anonymised details of previous instructions they have received in financial remedy cases. Costs are bound to be a significant consideration, but should not be the only one, as it is important to ensure the expert has the right qualifications and skills to produce a report.

Authority should be sought from the client to give a potential expert sufficient details of the case to enable them to confirm that no conflict of interest exists prior to their name being put forward as a possible single joint expert. Care should be taken to ensure that the implied duty of confidentiality is not breached.

An application to the court for permission to put expert evidence before it should comply with the provisions of Part 25.7. This sets out the information that must be included with such an application and helps to ensure that the purpose of the instruction (and, where possible, the identity of the expert) are clear, and that all the relevant preliminary enquiries have been made.

If the parties cannot agree on the identity of a single joint expert, and there are not already proceedings in place, then an application to the court should be considered to enable the court to resolve this disagreement and order which expert, if any, should be instructed, so that the case can move forward productively. As noted above, under Part 25.11(2), where the parties cannot agree the identity of a single joint expert, the court may select the expert from a list prepared by the parties or direct that the expert be selected in another manner.

It should be noted that not every expert is prepared to accept instructions as a single joint expert given the additional pressures that this can bring. It is important to establish an expert's willingness to be instructed on this basis, if that is to be the case.

6. Information to obtain about potential experts prior to first appointment

(This section applies equally to cases where financial remedy proceedings have not been issued but the parties have agreed that a single joint expert should be instructed.)

In cases where financial remedy proceedings have been issued, PD 25D must be complied with. Before instructions are given the parties should, so far as appropriate, comply with the guidance at paragraphs 3.3 and 3.4 to make preliminary enquiries of a potential expert and to obtain the following information (paragraph PD 25B 8.1):

- that there is no conflict of interest;
- that the matter is within their range of expertise;
- that the expert can provide the report within the timescale required;
- whether the expert would be available for any dates that are known to be relevant;
- whether there are any periods when the expert will not be available;
- what the expert's likely fees will be, including their basis of charging and other terms of business;
- if applicable, whether the expert will accept instructions on a publicly funded basis; and
- whether the expert wishes to make any representations to the court about being named or otherwise identified in any public judgment given by the court.

The parties should also have agreed, if possible, in what proportion the single joint expert's fee is to be shared between them (at least in the first instance) and when it is to be paid. It is important that this point is clarified, as the default position under Part 25.8(6) is for the court to order joint and several liability.

If the parties intend to seek the court's direction for use of a single joint expert, they should also comply, so far as appropriate, with PD 25D 3.11 and 3.12. These paragraphs set out in detail what information should be included in an application for the court's permission and what should be set out in the draft order to be attached to the application.

If provision of this level of detail is not possible it is good practice to at least bring to the first appointment the names of specific proposed experts, including confirmation of their willingness to accept joint instructions, if that is the case. This enables the court to make specific directions. The time and costs risks associated with unspecific directions, or directions that cannot be implemented should be avoided.

It can also be helpful to ask a potential expert, particularly in relation to the valuation of shares or an interest in a company or business, whether they have standard details of the information they will need to be produced in every case, which will enable them to then ask for more case-specific information.

It is, however, important that in obtaining this information, one party or their solicitor does not use this as an opportunity to undertake informal discussions with the potential expert, as this may prejudice their impartiality or at least create suspicions in the mind of the other party's advisor.

It is often dangerous to accept valuation evidence regarding a company from the company's own auditors, and caution is therefore advised.

7. The joint letter of instruction

Where a single joint expert is instructed, the instruction should be by jointly agreed letter unless the court directs otherwise (Part 25.12(1)). Paragraph 4.1 of Practice

Direction 25D deals with the contents of the letter in detail. The joint letter of instruction therefore should be agreed between the parties, or their solicitors, in advance of the letter being sent to the expert, and both parties or their solicitors should sign the letter.

The joint letter of instruction is the key document that sets out the basis of the evidence that is being sought from the expert and forms the basis of their report.

The information provided to an expert with a joint letter of instruction will depend on the case itself and the level of disclosure that has taken place at the time of the instruction. It may be that the expert is to produce a list of the information that they require, but it is helpful to provide at least basic information and documents to enable the expert to request more detailed information.

If the expert is instructed but proceedings have not been issued, the joint letter of instruction should make it clear to the expert that they may in due course be reporting to the court (PD 25A 3.1).

If proceedings have been issued, PD 25D 4.1 specifies that the joint letter of instruction shall be prepared, filed and served on the expert within five working days of the permission hearing.

If the instruction of an expert has not been, or cannot be, agreed between the parties, then a draft joint letter of instruction should be prepared in advance of the first appointment (or other hearing of an application to instruct a single joint expert if not the first appointment) for the court's consideration. The court can approve the letter of instruction, with or without amendment as it sees fit, in the event that the parties cannot agree on the terms of the joint letter. If the disagreement occurs after the relevant hearing, the court (or, by prior arrangement, the judge dealing with the proceedings) can be called upon to settle the letter of instruction by email (copied to all parties), and will usually do so without a hearing to avoid delay (Part 25.12(2) and PD 25D 6.1).

It is crucial to allow in the timetable for any delay that may be caused by agreement still needing to be reached on the terms of the letter of instruction, costs or the information to be provided, to ensure that the expert then has sufficient time to obtain further instruction, review this and prepare their report.

Paragraph 4.1 of PD 25D states that the joint letter of instruction should include:

- The context in which the expert's opinion is sought.
- The specific questions to be answered, ensuring that they:
  - (i)   are within the ambit of the expert's area of expertise;
  - (ii)   do not contain unnecessary or irrelevant detail;
  - (iii)   are kept to a manageable number and are clear, focused and direct; and
  - (iv)   reflect what the expert has been requested to do by the court.

- A list of the documentation provided, or indexed and paginated bundle, including:
  - (i) a copy of the order (if applicable) giving permission to instruct the expert;
  - (ii) an agreed list of essential reading; and
  - (iii) copies of PD 25B, 25D and 25E, and, where appropriate, PD 15B.
- Confirmation of the contractual basis upon which the expert is retained and in particular by whom, how much and when the expert will be paid.

It is good practice and therefore recommended that the joint letter should also include:

- basic relevant information;
- any assumptions to be made;
- the principal known issues;
- arrangements for attendance at a property, business or accountant's office or other place; and
- documents necessary for the expert's consideration of the case, sufficient for the purpose, clearly legible, properly sorted, paginated and indexed.

The issue of timing of the report should also be dealt with specifically in the joint letter of instruction.

Appendices A to C contain three example letters:

- a joint letter of instruction to value a property;
- a joint letter of instruction to value shares in a company/interest in a business; and
- a joint letter of instruction to report on pension sharing (or attachment).

The letters are intended to be a guide to practitioners only – they are not exhaustive of the issues that may need addressing in individual cases. It is important that careful consideration is given to the joint letter of instruction and the key issues on which the expert is being asked to report on a specific case-by-case basis.

8.   Providing information to the expert

It is common for the expert, having received the joint letter of instruction, to request further information from one or both of the parties. Any further information should be provided promptly according to the agreed timescale and copies of all information provided to the expert should again be clearly legible, properly sorted, paginated and indexed (where it is proportionate to do so) and copies should be provided to both parties' solicitors.

The court can direct one party to produce information to the expert where it is not reasonably available to the other party under Part 25.13. Under Part 25.17 the expert may file written requests to the court for directions for the purpose of assisting them in carrying out their functions.

A copy of any order or other document affecting the expert which is filed at court after the expert has been instructed must be served on the expert by the instructing party within two days of that party receiving the order or document (Part 25.18).

9. Attendance at meetings with the expert or inspections of property

Any meetings with an expert should be proportionate to the case.

In the event that a meeting with the expert, or an inspection of a property or premises for example, is required, it is recommended that either both or neither party attend. A single joint expert should not attend a meeting with only one of the parties unless the court has directed or the parties have agreed in writing and it is agreed or directed who is to pay the expert's fees for the meeting (PD 25E 4.1). If it is only possible or practical for one party to attend, practitioners should consider whether it would be appropriate for a contemporaneous attendance note to be requested from the expert of the discussions with one party at the meeting or inspection. The proportionality, particularly in respect of costs, should be considered before such a request is made.

10. Communications with an expert and supplementary instructions

Part 25.12(3) of the FPR provides that any instructions to the expert by one party should be simultaneously copied to the other party.

It is good practice for all communications with a single joint expert, including communications both to and from the expert, to be addressed to both parties, or their lawyers, and any communication with one party should be copied to the other.

All communications to the expert by the parties should similarly be sent jointly, unless it is in providing information requested by the expert, for example, in which case it should be copied to the other party simultaneously. This can be done easily with letters and email correspondence, but care should be taken with telephone discussions with an expert. It is recommended that they are avoided, unless it has been agreed in writing between the parties in advance that a discussion can take place. In the event that telephone discussions take place between one party, or their solicitor, and an expert, it is advised that a contemporaneous attendance note is prepared and a copy sent to the other party or their solicitor immediately.

FPR Part 25.8(3) further provides that separate instructions to a single joint expert should only be given with the court's permission. It is likely the court will consider issues of proportionality and whether or not the other party agrees.

11.   The expert's report

This should be provided in writing (Part 25.9) and served on both parties simultaneously. It is recommended that an additional copy is requested and filed with the court.

The report must comply with the requirements of PD 25B, including that at the end of the report there must be a statement that the expert understands and has complied with their duty to the court (Part 25.14(2)). The report must be verified by a statement of truth. PD 25B 9.1 sets out in detail what should be included.

12.   Questions following the expert's report

Part 25.10 provides that either party may put written questions to the expert within 10 days beginning with the date on which the report was served. The questions may only be put to the expert once, and must be for the purpose of clarification of the report only. In the event the questions go further than that, agreement must be obtained from the other party, or permission from the court.

As with all communications with an expert, they should be copied to the other party, or their solicitor, simultaneously.

13.   An expert's attendance at court

The courts are generally reluctant to hear oral evidence from experts at hearings as it increases the costs for the parties and the judicial time required for the hearing. The instruction of single joint experts means that the attendance of experts at hearings is no longer common place and is now the exception rather than the rule. Part 25.9(2) provides that the court will not direct an expert to attend a hearing unless necessary to do so in the interests of justice.

If it is necessary for an expert to attend court to give oral evidence (usually at the final hearing), this must be with permission from the court. This is usually sought at the FDR hearing when directions for the final hearing are set down.

If there is a possibility that an expert may be required to attend and give evidence to the court, it is important that the listing of a final hearing is carried out subject to the expert's availability.

The party responsible for the instruction of the expert, or the 'lead' solicitor in the case of a single joint expert, must comply with PD 25B 10.1 and 10.2 and Part 25.19 prior to, during and after the hearing.

If an expert is required to attend court and the hearing is listed for more than one day, it is usual for them to attend on the first day, to enable them to give evidence first, so that the costs of their attendance are kept to a minimum.

It can often be useful for an expert to attend court to hear the evidence of the parties, especially if one or both parties have instructed their own experts, to enable them to hear the other party's evidence or to support counsel in cross-examination. However, the potential costs do need to be taken into account and the need considered in light of proportionality to the case.

When enquiring as to the costs of an expert preparing a report, this should include the costs of the expert attending court if required to do so, not just of preparing the written report itself.

14.   Best practice if two experts are to be instructed

It is worth noting that, following the case of *Daniels v Walker* [2000] 1 WLR 1382, in some instances there may be a possibility of obtaining the court's permission to obtain a report from an expert acting for only one party.

In these cases, practitioners should consider what directions are going to be necessary following the instruction of separate experts for each party, such as whether the experts should meet to discuss areas of agreement and disagreement between them and whether this should be recorded in an agreed schedule. The court can order discussions between experts under Part 25.16 and that, following a discussion, the experts prepare a statement for the court setting out the issues on which they agree and disagree, including their reasons for disagreeing (Part 25.16(3)). This can often be a cost-effective way of identifying the areas to be resolved between the parties or by the court. If separate experts are to be instructed, it is important that meetings, discussions and documentation of what can and cannot be agreed are timetabled at an early stage.

Further guidance on the subject of experts' discussions and meetings are given in paragraphs 2.1 and 3.1 of PD 25E.

15.   The instruction of 'shadow experts': when it is appropriate and their role

In some cases, it may be necessary to instruct a 'shadow expert' to assist in advising the client on matters that are outside the lawyer's expertise, for example an accountant or tax advisor.

Shadow experts should not be instructed in place of a single joint expert. Where an issue requires expert evidence, a single joint expert should be instructed wherever possible. However, shadow experts can assist in deciding whether expert evidence is required, or in advising the clients on aspects of the expert's evidence once their report has been provided. They can also assist in reviewing the single joint expert's report and identifying any further questions that may need to be put to the expert, jointly by the parties where possible.

The instruction of shadow experts should only be considered in cases where it is proportionate, and would be in the client's best interest to do so. The advice of a shadow expert cannot be put to the court without permission, which is unlikely to be granted in most cases where a single joint expert has been, or could be, instructed.

The instructions of a shadow expert will increase the instructing party's costs and therefore it is important that the costs implications are considered and discussed with the client before the instruction is carried out. It may be more appropriate for another lawyer in the same firm to advise in place of a shadow expert, if that expertise is available. However, this will not always be the case and therefore shadow experts can be important members of a client's advisory team, in the right circumstances.

It should also be noted that it will not usually be appropriate for a shadow expert to then be appointed as a single joint expert in the case.

Appendix A

Example: joint letter of instruction to value a property

Mr J Smith
Smith Surveyors & Co
123 Main Street
Uptown
UP1 2HA

Dear Sir

Valuation Report for the Purposes of Family Proceedings

Mr and Mrs Jones: Uptown House, Main Street, Uptown, UP5 2DR
This letter is written on the joint instruction of Mr and Mrs Jones, who are involved in divorce and associated financial proceedings in the Uptown County Court.

Mr Jones is represented by Mr White of A Firm LLP and Mrs Jones is represented by Ms Green of Law & Co Solicitors of 65 New Street, Uptown, UP1 3KT (Ref: SG).

[It has been agreed] or [An order has been made by District Judge Smith in the Uptown County Court on   [   ]] that a report should be prepared by a Single Joint Expert about the above named property. [A copy of the order is enclosed]

The purpose of this letter is to set out your formal instructions to act as the Single Joint Expert in this matter.

Background

Uptown House is registered under title number [   ] with HM Land Registry. The [freehold][leasehold] title is owned by Mr and Mrs Jones. Mrs Jones is currently living at the property with the parties' three children.

[*Include a description of the property including:*

- *who owns the property*
- *title number or whether unregistered*
- *whether detached, semi-detached or terraced*
- *number of bedrooms and reception rooms*
- *whether there is any land with the property*
- *whether the property, or any part of it is let, and*
- *what the property is used for, i.e. residential, commercial etc.*]

Preliminary information supplied

With this letter we are attaching the following preliminary information:

[This list is not exhaustive. The expert may have their own list of information that needs to be provided at the outset, but provision of the following information should be considered:

1.   *court order containing direction for valuation*
2.   *office copy entries/Index Map search for the property*
3.   *copies of any lease or tenancy agreement(s) relating to the property*
4.   *plans (if relevant)*

You should, at your discretion, ask Mr and Mrs Jones for any additional information that you require, but all requests should be made in writing and copied to both parties' solicitors.

Nature of instructions
Your instructions are to prepare a report as the single joint expert on the following issues:

a)   The [fair][market] value of Uptown House;
b)   [Consider any other issues particular to the property being valued]

When preparing your report, you should assume the following:

- a willing seller;
- sale with vacant possession and unencumbered; and
- the best price which a willing buyer could reasonably be expected to pay a willing seller for the purchase of the property.
- *[any other assumptions the single joint expert is to make in preparing report]*

As you will be aware, the instruction of experts in family proceedings is set out in Part 25 of the Family Procedure Rules 2010 ('FPR'). Please note in particular Part 25.14 of the FPR, which sets out details of the contents of an expert's report and the statement required at the end of your report under Part 25.14(2).

We are attaching a copy of FPR Part 25 and of the relevant Practice Directions to FPR Part 25, known as PD 25A, B, D and E.

As a jointly instructed expert you should not enter into correspondence or engage in conversations with one party or their advisers without copying it to the other party or their solicitor, as your role in the proceedings is an impartial one.

If there is any aspect of this letter which is unclear, please write to both A Firm LLP and Law & Co Solicitors to raise any issues or questions which may arise, including proportionality, lack of clarity or completeness in the instructions and/or the possible effect on fees of complying with the instructions.

[Although this instruction is not following a court order, it is possible that you] [You should be aware that you] may be required to give evidence in person to the Court following your report, by attending a hearing in the case. [Please confirm that you would be willing to do so and if you are aware of any dates that you are unavailable in the next [   ] months, please notify us of these.]

Inspecting the Property

You will need to carry out an inspection of the property and both parties or their representatives [or neither party – consider a third party] should be present at the inspection. We suggest you should arrange a time which is mutually convenient to both by contacting [Mr and Mrs Jones directly] [both parties' solicitors].

Contact details

Mr Jones can be contacted on [Telephone number and email]. Mrs Jones can be contacted on [Telephone number and email].

[Consider whether it is appropriate in each case to include the parties' contact details in the letter as one party may not want the other party to have their contact details in some circumstances. It may be more appropriate for the expert to contact the solicitors for their respective clients' contact details].

Timing

[The court has ordered] or [it has been agreed] that this report should be produced by no later than   [   ].

If you believe that you cannot prepare your report within that timescale please let us know as soon as possible and provide an indication of the timescale that you would consider realistic to complete your report.

Your fees

Mr and Mrs Jones accept that they will each be responsible for 50% of your charges and each solicitor should be invoiced for one half of your fees [or alternative details as agreed or ordered]. Separate invoices should be addressed to [each firm of solicitors] [each client].

[NB Consider what the appropriate costs position should be for the costs associated with raising questions after the report. These costs will usually be in addition to the costs of the main report and therefore how they are to be paid should be dealt with at the outset. A request for this to be included in the directions made by the court is suggested, eg:

In the event that either party raises questions about your report, the party who raises those questions will be responsible for your costs of answering the questions and a separate invoice should be raised for that purpose [or alternative details as agreed or ordered].]

You have indicated that you envisage your fee will be [£   ] plus VAT for the production of your report [inclusive or exclusive of expenses/disbursements]. [Please do not start work on your report until you have provided us with your costs estimate and that estimate has been accepted by both parties.]

Please also indicate what you fees will be for attendance at a hearing, in the unlikely event that this is required.

Law & Co Solicitors have confirmed their agreement to these instructions by countersigning this letter/writing to you direct.

Could you please send one copy of your report to each solicitor and one additional copy to us for filing at court.

We look forward to hearing from you.

Yours faithfully

A FIRM LLP

LAW & CO SOLICITORS
Dated:

Appendix B

Example joint letter of instruction to value shares in a company/interest in a business

Mrs A Brown
Brown Accountants LLP
35 River Street
Uptown
UP1 2GE

Dear Madam

Valuation Report for the Purposes of Family Proceedings
Mr A and Mrs S Jones: ABC Limited

This letter is written on the joint instruction of Mr and Mrs Jones, who are involved in divorce and associated financial proceedings in the Uptown County Court.

Mr Jones is represented by Mr White of A Firm LLP and Mrs Jones is represented by Ms Green of Law & Co Solicitors of 65 New Street, Uptown, UP1 3KT (Ref: SG).

[It has been agreed] or [An order has been made by District Judge Smith in the Uptown County Court on [   ] that a report should be prepared by a Single Joint Expert about the above named company. [A copy of the order is enclosed]

The purpose of this letter is to set out your formal instructions to act as the Single Joint Expert in this matter.

Background of company
[Briefly describe nature of business and party or parties' role in it, family connections, role of third parties.]

Preliminary information supplied
With this letter we are attaching the following preliminary information:

[*This list is not exhaustive. The expert may have their own list of information that needs to be provided at the outset, but provision of the following information should be considered.*

Also see Charles J's comments on the likely information to be required by an expert valuing a company, the likely questions to raise of the expert, and other issues arising following the information produced and the questions raise in D v D [2007] EWHC 278 (Fam) at paragraph 106.]

- the court order containing direction for valuation.
- pages [x to y] of Mr and/or Mrs Jones' Form E (relevant to company/business);
- the memorandum and articles of association of the company/partnership deed;
- the shareholders' agreement dated [   ] (if a company);
- the accounts for the last three years;
- the management accounts since the last year end;
- the shareholders' register (if a company);
- the register of directors (if a company).

You should, at your discretion, ask Mr and Mrs Jones for any additional information that you require, but all requests should be made in writing and copied to both parties' solicitors.

Nature of instructions

Your instructions are to prepare a report as the Single Joint Expert on the following issues:

[*Consider carefully what the expert is being asked to report on. This list is intended to cover a number of the questions that may be raised, but is not exhaustive, and not all of the issues will be relevant in every case.*]

- the value of Mr and/or Mrs Jones' shares in ABC Limited;
- the ways in which that value could be realised whether by a sale, a purchase by the company of its own shares. or otherwise by [Mr and/or Mrs Jones];
- the tax consequences of:
  (i)   a sale of shares; or
  (ii)   a transfer of shares between Mr and Mrs Jones;
- the income which Mr and/or Mrs Jones is and will be able to draw if ABC Limited is retained;
- [any assumptions the single joint expert is to make in preparing their report].

As you will be aware, the instruction of experts in family proceedings is set out in Part 25 of the Family Procedure Rules ('FPR'). Please note in particular Part 25.14 of the FPR which sets out details of the contents of an expert's report and the statement required at the end of your report under Part 25.14(2).

We are attaching a copy of Part 25 FPR and of the relevant Practice Directions to Part 25 FPR, known as PD 25A, B, D and E.

As a jointly instructed expert you should not enter into correspondence or engage in conversations with one party or their advisers without copying it to the other party or their solicitor, as your role in the proceedings is an impartial one.

If there is any aspect of this letter which is unclear, please write to both A Firm LLP and Law & Co Solicitors to raise any issues or questions which may arise, including proportionality, lack of clarity or completeness in the instructions and/or the possible effect on fees of complying with the instructions.

[Although this instruction is not following a court order, it is possible that you] [You should be aware that you] may be required to give evidence in person to the court following your report, by attending a hearing in the case. [Please confirm that you would be willing to do so and if you are aware of any dates that you are unavailable in the next [   ] months, please notify us of these.]

Meeting the parties/visiting the company
[*Consider whether a meeting is necessary and proportionate to the case.*]

In the event that you feel it is necessary to visit ABC Limited and/or meet Mr and/or Mrs Jones, then both parties or their representatives should be present at all meetings. We suggest you should arrange a time which is mutually convenient to both by contacting [both parties directly][both parties' solicitors].

Contact details
Mr Jones can be contacted on [telephone number and email]. Mrs Jones can be contacted on [telephone number and email].

[*Consider whether it is appropriate in each case to include the parties' contact details in the letter as one party may not want the other party to have their contact details in some circumstances. It may be more appropriate for the expert to contact the solicitors for their respective clients' contact details*]

You may also wish to speak with the company/business accountants, who have authority to disclose information to you. If you do, their contact details are as follows:

[   ]
Tel:
E-mail:

Timing
[The court has ordered] or [it has been agreed] that this report should be produced by no later than [   ].

If you believe that you cannot prepare your report within that timescale please let us know as soon as possible and provide an indication of the timescale that you would consider realistic to complete your report.

Your fees
Mr and Mrs Jones accept that they will each be responsible for 50% of your charges and each solicitor should be invoiced for one half of your fees [or alternative details

as agreed or ordered]. Separate invoices should be addressed to [each firm of solicitors] [each client].

[NB Consider what the appropriate costs position should be for the costs associated with raising questions after the report. These costs will usually be in addition to the costs of the main report and therefore how they are to be paid should be dealt with at the outset. A request for this to be included in the directions made by the court is suggested, eg:

In the event that either party raises questions about your report, the party who raises those questions will be responsible for your costs of answering the questions and a separate invoice should be raised for that purpose [or alternative details as agreed or ordered].]

You have indicated that you envisage your fee will be [£   ]   plus VAT for the production of your report [inclusive or exclusive of expenses/disbursements]. [Please do not start work on your report until you have provided us with your costs estimate and that estimate has been accepted by both parties.]

Please also indicate what your fees will be for attendance at a hearing, in the unlikely event that this is required.

Law & Co Solicitors have confirmed their agreement to these instructions by countersigning this letter/writing to you direct.

Could you please send one copy of your report to each solicitor and one additional copy to us for filing at court.

We look forward to hearing from you.
Yours faithfully

A FIRM LLP

                              LAW & CO SOLICITORS
                              Dated:

Appendix C

Example: Joint letter of Instruction to report on pension sharing or earmarking

Mr D Jones
Jones Pension Consultants
1 High Street
Uptown
UP1 3YH

Dear Sir

Pension Report for the Purposes of Family Proceedings
Mr and Mrs Jones

This letter is written on the joint instruction of Mr and Mrs Jones, who are involved in divorce and associated financial proceedings in the Uptown County Court.

Mr Jones is represented by Mr White of A Firm LLP and Mrs Jones is represented by Ms Green of Law & Co Solicitors of 65 New Street, Uptown, UP1 3KT (Ref: SG).

[It has been agreed]/[An order has been made by District Judge Smith in the Uptown County Court on [   ] that a report should be prepared by a single joint expert about [Mr Jones'][Mrs Jones'][the parties'] pension provision and pension sharing [or attachment orders]. [A copy of the order is enclosed.]

The purpose of this letter is to set out your formal instructions to act as the Single Joint Expert in this matter.

Background
Mr Jones' date of birth is [   ] and he is a [occupation]. Mrs Jones' date of birth is [ ] and she works as a [occupation].

Both parties are in good health and neither party is a smoker.

The parties' respective pension assets are summarised in the table below:

Pensions [Details of Scheme/Policy]	Mr Jones (CEV)	Mrs Jones (CEV)
XYZ Insurance Plc	£156,345	
DEF Limited	£78,639	
ABC Retirement Benefit Scheme		£32,987
Total Pension CEVs	**£234,984**	**£32,987**

We enclose the following documentary evidence:

[This list is not exhaustive. The expert may have their own list of information that needs to be provided at the outset, but provision of the following information should be considered.]

- Paragraph 2.13 from each parties' Form E and supporting documents, including evidence of CEVs;
- Form P for each policy and the response from the pension provider/trustee
- State Pension forecasts for each party

We anticipate that you will need to obtain additional information and letters of authority from both parties to enable you to obtain that information directly from the pension providers are also enclosed.

Nature of instructions
[Consider carefully what the expert is being asked to report on. This list is intended to cover common requests, but is not exhaustive.]

You are therefore instructed, as a single joint expert, to provide a report advising on:

- the pension sharing order or orders that would achieve equalisation of pension benefits in retirement, both in respect of income and lump sum, based on the current CEVs of the parties' pensions; and/or
- the pension sharing order or orders that would be required to achieve equalisation of CEVs, based on the current CEVs of the parties' respective pensions; and/or
- *[consider whether the report should include evidence on attachment orders or offsetting]*

It should be assumed for the purposes of your report that:

[These are just examples of assumptions that may be relevant. Again, it is important that the purpose of the report, and therefore the basis on which it is being requested, is considered carefully in each case. These may or may not be relevant and are not exhaustive or in any way standard assumptions]

- Mr Jones will retire at age [   ] and Mrs Jones will retire at age [   ].
- State Pension will be taken into account (for the purposes of 2(a) above);
- Pensions should increase in payment at equivalent rates.
- There will be no income from other sources (so that income tax treatment will be equal).

As you will be aware, the instruction of experts in family proceedings is set out in Part 25 of the Family Procedure Rules ('FPR'). Please note in particular Part 25.14, which sets out details of the contents of an expert's report and the statement required at the end of your report under Part 25.14 (2).

We are attaching a copy of Part 25 FPR and of the relevant Practice Directions to FPR Part 25, known as PD 25A, B, D and E.

As a jointly instructed expert you should not enter into correspondence or engage in conversations with one party or their advisers without copying it to the other party or their solicitor, as your role in the proceedings is an impartial one.

If there is any aspect of this letter which is unclear, please write to both A Firm LLP and Law & Co Solicitors to raise any issues or questions which may arise, including proportionality, lack of clarity or completeness in the instructions and/or the possible effect on fees of complying with the instructions.

[Although this instruction is not following a court order, it is possible that you] [You should be aware that you] may be required to give evidence in person to the Court following your report, by attending a hearing in the case. [Please confirm that you would be willing to do so and if you are aware of any dates that you are unavailable in the next [   ] months, please notify us of these.]

Timing
[The court has ordered] or [it has been agreed] that this report should be produced by no later than [   ].

If you believe that you cannot prepare your report within that timescale please let us know as soon as possible and provide an indication of the timescale that you would consider realistic to complete your report.

Your fees
Mr and Mrs Jones accept that they will each be responsible for 50% of your charges and each solicitor should be invoiced for one half of your fees [or alternative details as agreed or ordered]. Separate invoices should be addressed to [each firm of solicitors] [each client].

[NB Consider what the appropriate costs position should be for the costs associated with raising questions after the report. These costs will usually be in addition to the costs of the main report and therefore how they are to be paid should be dealt with at the outset. A request for this to be included in the directions made by the court is suggested, e.g.:

In the event that either party raises questions about your report, the party who raises those questions will be responsible for your costs of answering the questions and a separate invoice should be raised for that purpose [or alternative details as agreed or ordered].]

You have indicated that you envisage your fee will be [£   ] plus VAT for the production of your report [inclusive or exclusive of expenses/ disbursements]. [Please do not start work on your report until you have provided us with your costs estimate and that estimate has been accepted by both parties.]

Please also indicate what your fees will be for attendance at a hearing, in the unlikely event that this is required.

Law & Co Solicitors have confirmed their agreement to these instructions by countersigning this letter/writing to you direct.

Could you please send one copy of your report to each solicitor and one additional copy to us for filing at court.

We look forward to hearing from you.

Yours faithfully

A FIRM LLP

LAW & CO SOLICITORS
Dated:

(Reproduced by permission of Resolution)

Chapter 5

Essential Protocols

2013 PROTOCOL AND GOOD PRACTICE MODEL

Disclosure of information in cases of alleged child abuse and linked criminal and care directions hearings

October 2013

[For brevity, Contents list, Sections 1–3 (Parties, Scope, Aims and Objectives), Annexes A–G, and list of signatories of Protocol omitted. The full Protocol can be accessed at http://flba.co.uk/wp-content/uploads/2013/06/2013-protocol-and-good-practice-model-final.pdf]

Part A: Disclosure into the Family Justice System

4. Local authority request to the police for disclosure

4.1. As soon as reasonably practicable and in any event on issue of proceedings, the Local Authority will provide notice to the police of the contemplation or existence of Family Proceedings using the form at Annex D to this agreement. The form at Annex D also acts as a request for disclosure from the police (to include a reasonable timescale not exceeding 14 days for the disclosure of the material). The form at Annex D will be sent to the police single point of contact (SPOC) attached at Annex A; (see paragraph 19.2 below).

4.2. Where criminal proceedings have been commenced (or are contemplated), the police will immediately forward a copy of the form at Annex D to the CPS. The CPS will give due priority to making charging decisions in cases involving Family Court Proceedings.

4.3. Where the information or documents sought does not relate to a child abuse investigation, the police SPOC will forward the form at Annex D to the unit or units holding the information or documents and will take responsibility for liaison with those units and to ensure the provision of information to the Local Authority.

4.4. It is to be understood by all Parties that the 2013 protocol should be used proportionately and is designed to facilitate only requests for material held by the police relevant to the central issues in the case. Requests for disclosure should not be drawn any wider than is absolutely necessary and only relevant material should be disclosed. The disclosure request to the police must be focussed identifying the documents which are really needed (*Re H-L (A child)* [2013] EWCA Civ 655).

5. Notification by the police to the local authority of the existence and status of criminal investigation

5.1. Within 5 working days of the commencement of the investigation, the police will provide to the Local Authority SPOC details of the criminal investigation using the form at Annex C to this Protocol (contact details for Local Authority SPOCs are listed at Annex B, see paragraph 19.3 below).

5.2. The police will contact the Local Authority SPOC at the point of charge, providing details of offences, custody status of defendants, bail conditions and court timescales. The police will also provide to the Local Authority contact details for the CPS.

5.3. In the event that the suspect(s) is/are not charged, the police in consultation with the CPS will provide the Local Authority with reasons why there will be no prosecution.

5.4. Within 5 working days of each Case Management Hearing in the Crown Court, the CPS will provide to the Local Authority SPOC (or Local Authority lawyer if known) details of the future timetable of the criminal proceedings and details of any directions relevant to the Local Authority or to concurrent Family Proceedings.

5.5. Within 2 working days of receipt, the Local Authority will forward the details at paragraphs 5.1 to 5.4 above to the Family Court.

6. Voluntary disclosure by police/CPS to local authority and into the family justice system

6.1. Where criminal proceedings have been commenced (or are contemplated), the police should consult with the CPS before a decision is made on whether to disclose police material to the Local Authority. The timing of such consultation must take into account any reasonable timescale specified by the Local Authority at paragraph 4.1 above.

6.2. Within the timescale specified by the Local Authority in Annex D (paragraph 4.1 above), the police will provide (via secure means, e.g. secure email) the requested material to the Local Authority. The police will complete and return the second part of the form at Annex D. The Local Authority agrees that the police material will only be disclosed to the professionals and Parties in the Family Proceedings (unless the permission of the court is obtained to disclose material to others).

6.3. Visually recorded interviews (Achieving Best Evidence interviews) will not be released to the Local Authority except against a written undertaking from the Local Authority in order to prevent the unauthorised use of the evidence. The form of undertaking at Annex G should be used for this purpose.

6.4. Unless disclosure is required to ensure the immediate safety of a child, the police will not disclose material where to do so might prejudice the investigation and/or prosecution (or where on the grounds of confidentiality it is necessary to obtain the consent of persons providing statements). However, redacted disclosure should be made wherever possible. The police will indicate on the form at Annex D the approximate date on which disclosure can be made. The police (in consultation with the CPS) must provide detailed reasons on Annex D as to why any material is being withheld.

6.5. Alternatively, the police can indicate that disclosure will be made in the event that the Local Authority obtains a Family Court order stating that the material is not to be disclosed to named individual(s) (typically, suspects and/or witnesses in the criminal proceedings). Such a court order should also be obtained where possible in the event that disclosure is made (as at paragraph 6.4 above) to ensure the immediate safety of a child.

6.6. The Family Court may request disclosure from the Local Authority of material held by them and relating to the criminal case. Again, the Local Authority will notify the CPS (or the police if criminal proceedings have not commenced) as soon as reasonably practicable. Where the police and/or the CPS object to disclosure, they will make appropriate **and timely** representations to the Family Court explaining why such disclosure might be capable of prejudicing the criminal proceedings.

7. Family court proceedings: orders for disclosure against the police and/or the CPS

7.1. The Local Authority shall notify (within 2 working days of the application being made) the police and the CPS of any application to the Family Court (whether by the Local Authority or any other party) for disclosure of prosecution material. The Local Authority shall notify the police and/or the CPS of the date and time of the Family Court hearing at which disclosure will be determined. Any order by the Family Court for disclosure will be in the form at Annex H to this protocol (use of which by the Family Court is mandatory). Where appropriate, the police and/or the CPS will assist the Local Authority in drafting Directions.

7.2. Where directed, the police and/or the CPS shall attend the Family Court hearing to explain the implications for a criminal trial when

7.3. The Local Authority will ensure that any Order against the police and/or the CPS is served as soon as reasonably practicable (and in any event within 2 working days of the date of the order) on the police and/or the CPS.

7.4. The police and the CPS will comply with any court order.

Part B: Disclosure from the Local Authority/Family Justice System into the Criminal Justice System

8. Notification by local authority to the police of the existence and status of family proceedings

8.1. As soon as reasonably practicable and in any event on issue of proceedings, the Local Authority will provide notice to the police of the contemplation or existence of Family Proceedings using the form at Annex D to this 2013 protocol. Where Family Proceedings have commenced, details of all parties (and legal representatives) will be provided. Details of the allocated Local Authority lawyer will be provided. The form at Annex D will be sent to the police single point of contact (SPOC) attached at Annex A.

8.2. Where the form at Annex D is sent to the police at a stage before details of all parties to the Family Proceedings are known, the Local Authority will notify the police recipient of Annex D of the details of all parties (and legal representatives) to the Family Proceedings. The Local Authority will also provide details of the future timetable of the Family Proceedings. The police will forward the information to the CPS.

8.3. Where criminal proceedings have been commenced (or are contemplated), the police will forward a copy of the form at Annex D to the CPS. The CPS will give due priority to making charging decisions in cases involving Family Court Proceedings.

9. Police request to local authority for disclosure

9.1. Following the commencement of the investigation, the police will provide to the Local Authority SPOC the form at Annex C to this 2013 protocol. Details of the SPOC for each Local Authority are set out at Annex B (see paragraph 19.3 below).

9.2. The Annex C form will include details of the investigation and prosecution if commenced (see paragraph 5.1 above). Requests for material **must** be as prescriptive and detailed as possible and necessary for the pursuit of reasonable lines of enquiry. The form at Annex C will include reasonable timescales for the police to be given access to relevant material, but the presumption will be that the Local Authority will deal with any request from the police as expeditiously as possible so as to not to jeopardise the criminal investigation. Timescales will be case specific taking account of the stage/nature of the investigation and/or prosecution.

10. Disclosure by the local authority to the police

10.1. Upon receipt of the form at Annex C from the police, the Local Authority SPOC (or delegated officer) will identify and collate relevant material from the Children's Services or other files as appropriate, the SPOC (or delegated officer) will liaise with relevant departments within the Local Authority in the collation of such material for the police to assist the criminal investigation.

10.2. The Local Authority will identify for the police the school(s) attended by the child/children subject to the investigation. This will enable the police to approach the school directly. Alternatively, if it is practicable to do so, the Local Authority will obtain and collate relevant educational files for police examination.

10.3. Subject to paragraphs 10.4 and 10.5 below, the Local Authority will ensure that documents relating to Family Court proceedings are not included in the files to be examined by the police. Where there are documents relating to Family Court proceedings, the Local Authority will provide a list (e.g. by providing a copy of redacted court index) of that material without describing what it is, in order for the police and/or the CPS, if appropriate, to apply to the Family Court for disclosure.

10.4. Importantly, the Local Authority can disclose to the police documents which are lodged at court, or used in the proceedings, which already existed (*Re Ward (A Child)* [2010] EWHC 16 (Fam); [2010] 1 FLR 1497) (e.g. pre-existing medical reports). Similarly, the text or summary of a judgment given in the Family Court proceedings can be included in the files to be examined by the police (Rule 12.73(1)(c) Family Procedure Rules 2010 and Practice Direction 12G).

10.5. Paragraph 10.3 above does not prevent the Local Authority providing to the police documents or information relating to Family Court proceedings where (a) the police officer to whom disclosure is made is carrying out duties under section 46 Children Act 1989 or serving in a child protection or paedophile unit and (b) disclosure is for the purposes of child protection and not for the purposes of the criminal investigation (Rule 12.73(1)(a)(viii) Family Procedure Rules 2010).

10.6. Where material is disclosed in accordance with paragraph 10.5 above, the police cannot make onward disclosure of any documentation **or information** contained therein for the purpose of the investigation or prosecution without the express permission of the Family Court (for the avoidance of doubt, this will include disclosure to the CPS).

10.7. Where, in exceptional circumstances, the Local Authority is not able to include other material (not relating to Family Court proceedings) in the files to be examined by the police, the Local Authority will notify the police in writing of the existence of this material; indicating the reason why the material is not being made available to the police. Such a course should be exceptional because the Local Authority recognises that the material will be regarded as sensitive by the police and the CPS. It will not be disclosed to the defence without further consultation with the Local Authority or order of the court (see paragraph 13.9 to 14.3 below).

10.8. Within the timescales set out in the Annex C request (or otherwise agreed between the Local Authority and the police), the police will examine and review the material collated by the Local Authority. The review will usually take place on Local Authority premises but may be elsewhere by agreement. The police may make notes and/or take copies of the material. The material will not be disclosed to the defence without further consultation with the Local Authority or order of the court (see paragraph 13.9 to 14.3 below).

10.9. Where further relevant Local Authority material comes to light after the police examination of the material at paragraph 10.8 above, the Local Authority will contact the police and/or the CPS to arrange an examination of the new material by the police.

10.10. Similarly, where new issues arise in the criminal case (e.g. following the receipt of the defence case statement), the police will submit a further Annex C form requesting access to material not previously examined.

11. Applications by police and the CPS to the family court for disclosure of material relating to family proceedings

11.1. At the stage prior to service of prosecution papers pursuant to section 51 of the Crime and Disorder Act 1998, applications will be generally made by the police. After this stage, applications will generally be made by the CPS.

11.2. Applications by the police for disclosure must contain details of the named officer to whom release is sought (*Re H (Children)* [2009] EWCA Civ. 704; [2009] 1 FLR 1531) and must specify the purpose and use to which the material is intended to be put. Applications should seek leave (where appropriate) to disclose the material to the CPS, to disclose the material to the criminal defence solicitors and (subject to section 98(2) of the Children Act 1989) to use the material in evidence at the criminal proceedings.

11.3. Applications by the CPS must specify the purpose and use to which the material is intended to be put and should seek leave to share the material with the police and with the defence and (subject to section 98(2) Children Act 1989) to use the material in evidence at the criminal proceedings.

11.4. Applications shall be made on Form C2. The application must be served by police or the CPS on all Parties to the Family Proceedings (The Local Authority having informed the police of details of all parties to Family Proceedings as per paragraphs 8.1 and 8.2 of this protocol).

11.5. The application will be determined at a hearing at the Family Court. Police and the CPS will not attend the hearing unless directed to do so by the Family Court.

11.6. Where it is practicable to seek prior written consent to disclosure from **all Parties** to the Family Proceedings, the police or the CPS should do so. Application should then be made in writing to the Family Court seeking a consent order.

11.7. Alternatively (**and whenever this is possible**), the police and/or the CPS will ask the Local Authority allocated lawyer (or SPOC if details of allocated lawyer are not known) to request that the Family Court considers the issue of disclosure to the police and/or the CPS at the next hearing. In this way, the Family Court will be in a position to make any orders as appear appropriate without the need for police and/or the CPS to make application to the Family Court. When requesting the Family Court to make an order in accordance with this paragraph, the Local Authority will put the other parties to the proceedings on notice; and will provide the court with details of the officer to whom disclosure is to be made and the purpose for which it is to be made.

11.8. In rare cases, where it considers it appropriate to do so, the Family Court should make orders for disclosure to the police and/or the CPS without application having been made by the police or the CPS.

12. Text or summary of judgment in family proceedings (Rule 12.73(1)(c) Family Procedure Rules 2010 and Practice Direction 12G)

12.1. The Local Authority will forward to the CPS copies of relevant Family Court judgments (and summaries thereof) in the possession of the Local Authority. The judgments may be appropriately redacted.

12.2. Where the Local Authority is not in possession of a judgment which appears to be relevant to the concurrent criminal proceedings (e.g. fact-finding judgment), it will notify the CPS in order that the CPS can obtain the judgment directly from the Family Court. In these circumstances it will not be necessary to make formal application for disclosure on Form C2; the CPS will request release of the judgment under Practice Direction 12G above.

12.3. Where it appears to the Local Authority that the judgment will be relevant to the criminal proceedings, the Local Authority will request that the Family Court expedites the preparation of the judgment for release to the CPS (and if possible at public expense). Alternatively, the issue of disclosure of the judgment to the CPS under Practice Direction 12G can be considered at a linked directions hearing.

13. Disclosure by the CPS to the criminal defence

13.1. The Criminal Procedure and Investigations Act 1996 requires the prosecution to disclose to the defence any material (including sensitive material) that could reasonably be considered capable of undermining the prosecution case against the accused or of assisting the case for the accused (the 'disclosure test'). Where appropriate, application can be made to the criminal court to withhold sensitive material which satisfies the disclosure test on the grounds of public interest immunity (PII application).

13.2. PII applications to the criminal court for the withholding of sensitive material should be rare. Fairness ordinarily requires that all material which weakens the prosecution case or strengthens that of the defence should be disclosed. There is no basis for making a PII application except where the prosecutor has identified material that fulfils the disclosure test, disclosure of which would create a real risk of serious prejudice to an important public interest (*R v H and C* [2004] 2 AC 134).

13.3. All material obtained from the Local Authority will be listed by the police on the sensitive disclosure schedule MG6D. The lists of material not disclosed by the

Local Authority to the police will also be included on the MG6D (see paragraph 10.3 above: material relating to Family Proceedings; and paragraph 10.7 above: material withheld on the ground of confidentiality).

13.4. Material obtained by the police in accordance with Rule 12.73(1)(a)(viii) Family Procedure Rules 2010 (see paragraphs 10.5 and 10.6 above) must not be disclosed to the CPS. The police will reveal the existence of the material on the MG6D (without describing it). As appropriate, the CPS will seek the permission of the Family Court to access the material.

13.5. Where the material has been obtained following an application by the police to the Family Court, the police must indicate to the CPS whether the Family Court has given permission for the material to be shared with the CPS and with the defence. Further application to the Family Court may be required by the police and/or the CPS as appropriate.

13.6. The CPS will review the material in accordance with its statutory duties and under the Attorney General's Guidelines on Disclosure. Only material which might undermine the prosecution case or might reasonably assist the defence case will fall to be disclosed. There will in no circumstances be 'blanket' disclosure to the defence.

13.7. Where in accordance with paragraph 10.7 above a Local Authority document is not made available to the police on the basis of confidentiality (e.g. consent has not been obtained from the person to whom the document relates), the CPS will consider whether it is appropriate to seek access to such material by means of a witness summons in the criminal court.

13.8. Where in these circumstances application is made by the CPS for a witness summons, the CPS will serve the application on the criminal court and the Local Authority, identifying the Local Authority SPOC as the person who is required to produce the document(s). In addition, where the Crown Court so directs, the CPS will, in accordance with the Criminal Procedure Rules, serve the application on the person to whom the confidential document relates.

13.9. Where any Local Authority material reviewed by the CPS falls within the statutory disclosure test under the CPIA, the CPS will write to the Local Authority SPOC, within 2 working days of review whenever possible, setting out the reasons why the material falls to be disclosed and informing them of that decision. The form at Annex E to this 2013 protocol will be used by the CPS. The CPS will provide to the Local Authority proposals for the editing or summarising of the material for the purposes of disclosure to the defence. Where no material falls for disclosure, the CPS will inform the Local Authority that this is the case.

13.10. Within 5 working days of receipt of that notification, the Local Authority shall be given an opportunity to make any representations in writing to the CPS on the issues of disclosure. This will include objections to disclosure on the basis that the person to whom the material relates has not consented. Note that disclosure of documentation which has been created under the auspices, and for the purposes, of the LSCB, can only be made with the prior consent of the LSCB Chair.

13.11. The form at Annex F to this 2013 protocol will be used for this purpose. Where, exceptionally, the Local Authority is unable to meet the 5 working day timescale, the Local Authority will contact the CPS to discuss whether the timescale can be extended in the particular circumstances of the case.

14. Public Interest Immunity (PII) Application

14.1. If the Local Authority does not agree to disclosure of Local Authority material to the defence, the CPS must negotiate with the Local Authority to explore whether disclosure can be made in edited form or by summarising in another document the issues arising in the material (*R v H and C* [2004] 2 AC 134). Whilst recognising that the prosecution must always comply with its statutory duty of disclosure, the sensitivity can often be removed in this way. PII applications in the criminal court will be rare. Local Authority material relating to a child is no longer a 'class' of material to which PII applies. Depending on the sensitivity of the material, the Local Authority may itself agree that the public interest in the prosecution of crime overrides the interests of confidentiality (*R v Chief Constable of West Midlands ex parte Wiley* [1995] 1 AC 274). In highly exceptional cases, the CPS may need to make disclosure to the defence of the edited/summarised document without the consent of the Local Authority.

14.2. If a PII application is appropriate, the CPS will make a PII application to the criminal court as soon as reasonably practicable. The CPS will notify the Local Authority of the date and venue of the PII application and inform the Local Authority of their right to make representations to the criminal court.

14.3. Where PII is sought on the basis of lack of consent from the person to whom the confidential document relates, CPS must in accordance with the Criminal Procedure Rules notify the person to whom the document relates (as above, notification of date and venue of PII application and the interested person's right to make representations to the court).

Part C: Linked Directions Hearings

15. Linked criminal and care directions hearings – criteria

15.1. This 2013 protocol will apply where a person connected with the child who is the subject of the care proceedings or the child himself is to be tried at the Crown Court for any violent or sexual offence or for an offence of child cruelty against the child, or any other child or any person connected with the child; and either:

(i)   The Local Authority, CPS, or any party to the care proceedings (including the child's guardian) considers that the care and criminal proceedings do, or may, impinge on one another; or

(ii)   In any public law proceedings in the High Court or County Court or in any proceedings in the Crown Court, a judge is satisfied that the protocol does, or may, apply.

16. Arrangements for linked directions hearings

16.1. The allocated case management judge in the Family Court (ACMJ) will consider whether or not there is likely to be a need for a linked directions hearing in respect of the criminal and family cases. If the ACMJ considers that a linked directions hearing is likely to be appropriate he/she shall liaise with the relevant Resident Judge to invite him to nominate a judge to be responsible for the management of the criminal case.

16.2. In the care proceedings it is expected that the ACMJ will issue directions for the linked hearing which will spell out the respective parties' obligations, and which may include, but will not be limited to, recordings and, orders in the form at Annex I to this protocol (use of which by the Family Court is mandatory). At the same time, the ACMJ will consider giving permission to the Local Authority to serve its case summary on the CPS and the Crown Court (in accordance with paragraph 16.6 below).

16.3. Once a judge has been identified to manage the criminal proceedings, the Resident Judge shall direct the listing officers to liaise with family listing to agree the listing of the criminal and care cases for a linked directions hearing before the nominated criminal judge and the ACMJ. In an appropriate case the Resident Judge may agree to the ACMJ undertaking the responsibility for the management of the criminal case if he/she is authorised to try criminal cases, and, where appropriate, serious sexual offence cases.

16.4. If on receipt of criminal proceedings sent from the Magistrates' Courts and consideration of that case by the Resident Judge, or if during a Case Management hearing or other pre-trial hearing listed before the Crown Court, the Resident Judge or judge (as the case may be) is satisfied that this Protocol does or may apply but that no reference has yet been made to the ACMJ for consideration in accordance with paragraph 16.1 above, the judge shall notify the Designated Family Judge accordingly who shall consider with the relevant Resident Judge and the ACMJ, whether a linked directions hearing is required. If there is agreement on the need for a linked directions hearing, the Resident Judge shall nominate a judge to be responsible for the management of the criminal case and arrangements shall then be made for the criminal and care cases to be listed for a linked directions hearing in accordance with paragraph 16.3 above.

16.5. The criminal case shall be listed before the judge at the Crown Court in public with the linked directions appointment in the care proceedings listed for hearing in private immediately thereafter. Subject to any specific objections raised by the parties, the advocates appearing in the criminal case may be invited to remain during the directions appointment in the care proceedings.

16.6. In every case involving a linked directions hearing the Local Authority's legal representative, **by no later than 4.00pm not less than 5 working days prior to the**

linked directions hearing, shall with the permission of the family court prepare and serve on the CPS and the Crown Court a case summary setting out the basis of the Local Authority's application, its contentions in respect of findings sought in relation to the 'threshold criteria' (Local Authority's 'threshold document'), the current position in respect of the child, details of the proposed assessments and/or expert(s) assessments being undertaken and the timescales for the same and the timetable (if any) set for the proceedings within the Family Court.

16.7. The Local Authority's legal representative and the CPS shall agree a schedule of issues identifying those matters which are likely to be considered at the linked directions hearing. The Local Authority shall circulate the Schedule to the solicitors for the other parties in the criminal and care proceedings **by no later than 4.00pm not less than 2 working days prior to the linked directions hearing**.

16.8. On the day of the linked directions hearing the advocates in the criminal and care proceedings shall meet **no later than one hour prior to the time fixed for the hearing** to discuss the schedule of issues with a view to identifying what directions may be required with particular reference to the trial timetable, disclosure and expert evidence and such other matters as may be identified by this Protocol.

16.9. The respective court files in the criminal and care proceedings shall be cross referenced and shall be clearly marked as 'linked' cases.

16.10. The directions hearing will be linked but not wholly combined because of the different parties and different procedural rules (such as with regard to privacy and rights of audience) which apply. The judge shall determine whether it is appropriate for some or all of the directions to be issued at a joint hearing or separately and the order of any directions to be issued.

16.11. At the conclusion of the hearing in the criminal case, counsel for the Crown will be invited to draw the minute of order, to be agreed with the defence, which will be submitted to the judge on the day of the hearing, for his/her approval.

16.12. The approved minute of order made in the criminal proceedings will be copied to the parties in the care proceedings by the CPS.

16.13. With the permission of the family court, the order made in the care proceedings will be copied by the Local Authority to the CPS and defence lawyers in the criminal proceedings.

16.14. The timing of the proceedings in a linked care and criminal case should appear in the Timetable for the Child.

16.15. **Judicial continuity**: Any adjourned linked directions hearing shall be listed before the same judge (unless the judge otherwise directs) but the judge who is the

ACMJ shall not preside over the trial in the criminal proceedings, or pass sentence if there is a guilty plea, nor shall the judge give a 'Goodyear indication'. The judge in the criminal trial or who passes sentence if there is a guilty plea shall notify the ACMJ of the outcome.

17. Matters to be considered at the linked directions hearing

17.1. The timetabling of both the criminal and care proceedings (with a view to such timetabling being coordinated to ensure the most appropriate order of trial and that each case is heard as expeditiously as possible).

17.2. Disclosure of evidence with particular reference to disclosure of evidence from one set of proceedings into the other with such permission as may be required by the relevant procedural rules.

17.3. Expert evidence with particular reference to the identification of expert witnesses, their willingness to act within the court timetable and the requirements of the Practice Direction concerning the instruction of Experts, their availability and role in the criminal and care hearings.

17.4. Any directions to be given in relation to issues of public interest immunity and for any witness summonses required for third party disclosure (Rule 28 Criminal Procedure Rules 2013).

17.5. Arrangements for the interviewing of children in care for the purpose of the criminal proceedings and any arrangements for the child to give evidence at any criminal or family hearing.

17.6. To ensure where appropriate that a transcript of relevant evidence or judgment in the trial heard first in time is available in the subsequent proceedings.

17.7. Issues relating to any question of assessment or therapeutic input required by any child involved in the proceedings.

17.8. Issues in relation to restrictions on publicity which it is considered may be required.

17.9. Issues in relation to any relevant material which may be pertinent to the issue of bad character (in respect of previous convictions or other alleged 'reprehensible behaviour'), whether of defendants or non-defendants.

17.10. Other legal or social work related steps in the Family Court proceedings.

18. Review

18.1. The parties to this 2013 protocol and Good Practice Model and the organisations at paragraphs 1.1 and 1.2 above supporting the 2013 protocol will continuously review and monitor the operation of the provisions. The protocol will be subject to a formal review 12 months after the date of implementation.

19. Local Protocols

19.1. Local agencies should agree and adopt a local protocol to give effect to this 2013 protocol signed by the Crown Court Resident Judges, Designated Family Judges, Police Forces, CPS and Local Authorities in each CPS Area. A local protocol must not depart from the requirements of the PLO and must require that orders used are in the form of Annex H and Annex I.

19.2. Each Police Force signatory to the local protocol will provide on the form at Annex A details of a suitable single point of contact (SPOC) for the receipt by secure email of the Annex D disclosure request from the Local Authority.

19.3. Each Local Authority signatory to the local protocol will provide on the form at Annex B details of a suitable single point of contact (SPOC) for the receipt by secure email of the Annex C disclosure request from the police.

…

[For Annex H and Annex I template directions orders, see Chapter 6, Precedents]

PROTOCOL ON COMMUNICATIONS BETWEEN JUDGES OF THE FAMILY COURT AND IMMIGRATION AND ASYLUM CHAMBERS OF THE FIRST-TIER TRIBUNAL AND UPPER TRIBUNAL

[Footnotes and Annexes 2–4 omitted. Refer to www.judiciary.gov.uk/wp-content/uploads/2013/03/protocol-communications-between-family-court-and-immigration-asylum-tribunals.pdf]

Introduction

1. This protocol has been issued by the Senior President of Tribunals and the President of the Family Division and Head of Family Justice

2. This protocol applies where an immigration appeal is pending before the Tribunal and the welfare of a child in the United Kingdom is likely to be affected by the decision in those proceedings and there are family proceedings in existence relating to that child. It applies to all family proceedings in the High Court, a County Court or a Family Proceedings Court and (once the Family Court has been established) in the High Court or the Family Court. For ease of reference, these courts are all referred to hereafter as the Family Court.

3. It is anticipated that judges in the Tribunal and the Family Court will be assisted by knowing of the existence of the proceedings in the other jurisdiction, the issues arising, the procedure and time scale for determining them and any information disclosed in the other jurisdiction that may be of relevance to the respective immigration or family court decision.

4. This protocol is designed to enable judges in each jurisdiction to communicate in order to obtain information about proceedings in their respective jurisdictions which may affect the outcome of the proceedings before them and to make better informed decisions.

5. The timeline of the respective proceedings is likely to be of assistance to each jurisdiction. Regard should be had to the guidance in *Re M and N (Parallel Family and Immigration Proceedings)* [2008] EWHC Fam 2281, [2008] 2 FLR 2030.

6. It is not the role of the judges in either jurisdiction to predict the outcome of the proceedings in the other jurisdiction. Where the decision in the Family Court is likely to be a weighty consideration in the immigration decision, it is anticipated that it will normally be necessary for the Tribunal to wait until the Family Court judge has reached a decision on the issue relevant to the immigration appeal. If so, either the appeal will be allowed by the Tribunal in anticipation of a short period of leave being granted or the hearing will be adjourned, depending on the anticipated timescale of the family proceedings.

Disclosure of documents and directions

A. Directions

7. Documents in family proceedings cannot be disclosed to third parties including judges in the Tribunal without an order of the Family Court Judge. There are no formal constraints on disclosure of material supplied for the purpose of an appeal in the Tribunal; a direction is sufficient to respond to a request from the Family Court. The First-tier Tribunal's powers to give directions do not include the power to direct disclosure from the parties or third parties although it may issue a witness summons but the Upper Tribunal has such a power where necessary for the fair hearing of the appeal.

8. Where it appears to a judge that there are or may be relevant proceedings pending in another court or Tribunal directions may be issued at case management stage requiring disclosure by the relevant party of the court reference numbers of any past or current immigration proceedings or any past or current family proceedings that have involved any of the parties.

9. The kind of information likely to be relevant that may be held by either jurisdiction is indicated at Annex 1 to this Protocol.

B. Communication

10. A request for disclosure of documents in the immigration proceedings may be sought at the instigation of the family judge using the form of order set out in Annex 2 part 1.

11. An application for disclosure of documents in family proceedings should be directed to the Designated Family Judge and should state clearly the date by which such information is to be needed which should ideally be no longer than four weeks.

12. A request for disclosure of information or documents in the family proceedings may be sought either by one of the parties direct or at the instigation of the Tribunal judge using the form set out in Annex 2 part 3.

13. A request for the supply of information or documents from the Tribunal should be directed to the Resident Judge of the relevant Tribunal Chamber.

C. Supply of information

14. A draft direction of the Tribunal judge responding to the application of the Family judge is set out in Annex 2 part 2.

15. Where a judge of the family court decides that information can be supplied to a judge in the Tribunal, the judge shall inform the Resident Judge of this fact and at the same time indicate any conditions on the use of the material that are necessary in the circumstances. A draft order is set out in Annex 2 part 4.

16. Directions providing for the anonymity of children and where necessary other parties in both family and immigration proceedings will be considered by the judge in accordance with the joint guidance issued by the President of the Family Division, the Judicial College and the Society of Editors in July 2011 (see 17) and Anonymity Directions in the First-tier Tribunal (IAC) Presidential Guidance Note No2 of February 2011 (see 18).

17. http://www.judiciary.gov.uk/publications-and-reports/guidance/2011/family-courts -media-access-reporting

18. http://www.justice.gov.uk/downloads/tribunals/immigration-and-asylum/lower/ guidance-2-2011-.pdf

Date: 19 July 2013

Annex 1

Part One
Suggested case management by the Tribunal judge where there are or may be family proceedings

1. Direct the appellant disclose court reference numbers of any family court proceedings in which s/he was a party or involved.

2. Give consideration to seeking an order for disclosure from the family court judge of;

a)   any interim or final fact finding judgment
b)   care plan
c)   guardian/CAFCASS report
d)   directions
e)   timetable of hearings
f)   other documentation as specified.

Part Two
Suggested case management by the family court judge where there are or may be immigration proceedings.

1. Grant permission for disclosure by the Family Court judge to the Tribunal judge of specific documents, with any specific directions as regards disclosure to third parties attached.

2. Consider giving instructions in the production of the guardian/CAFCASS report to include that the report consider the implications for, and effect, on the child(ren) of the removal/deportation of the adult in question and the effects of restricted contact eg during school holidays only or through Skype etc.

3. Consider requesting disclosure from the relevant Tribunal of:

a)   determinations by the Tribunal of immigration appeals in which any of the parties have been an appellant/respondent;

b)   decision letter of the Home Office;

c)   witness statements, grounds of appeal or skeleton arguments filed in pending immigration proceedings;

d)   any case management directions in pending immigration proceedings;

e)   date of substantive hearing;

f)   other documentation as specified.

4. Consider requesting disclosure direct from the Home Office in accordance with the Guidance reissued in March 2013 by the President of the Family Division (see below: 'Communicating with the Home Office in Family Proceedings' [2013] Fam Law 762).

…

[For Annex 2, Parts 2 and 3, template orders, see Chapter 6, Precedents]

COMMUNICATING WITH THE HOME OFFICE IN FAMILY PROCEEDINGS

Originally issued December 2002
Re-issued March 2013

1) The 'Communicating with the Home Office in Family Proceedings' protocol enables the family courts to communicate with the Home Office (UK Borders Agency and Identity and Passport Service) to obtain immigration, visa and passport information for family court proceedings.

2) This guidance has been reissued to replace & amalgamate previous guidance issued in 2002, 2004, 2006, 2010 and 2012 (including the Communicating with the Passport Service 2004) to reflect the new contact details for the Home Office Liaison Officer who has responsibility for administering requests made under the Protocol. It does not alter the nature or purpose of the Protocol.

3) Where an order is made against the Home Office in Family Proceedings, the court shall draw up the relevant order. The HMCTS form EX660 should be fully completed (including specifying the details of the relevant family members and their relationship to the child). Parties should provide details of both mother and father if known, whether or not they are involved in the proceedings.

4) The sealed order and the completed EX660 should be sent immediately to:

> Home Office Liaison Team
> Her Majesty's Courts and Tribunal Service
> Arnhem House
> PO Box 6987
> Leicester
> LE1 6ZX

> Email: homeofficeliaison@hmcts.gsi.gov.uk
> Telephone: 0116 249 4309
> Fax: 0116 249 4302

5) Please note that all information provided in the EX660 will be forwarded to the Home Office. Parties should ensure that any additional information, such as a case synopsis, which it wishes the Home Office to view, has the required leave of the court, set out in the order, to be disclosed to the Home Office. (Note that it is a contempt of court to disclose this information otherwise).

6) Where the query relates to the proposed adoption of a foreign national minor, the Home Office Liaison Officer can advise as to the additional information which will be required.

7) The order and EX660 should clearly state the time by which the information is required. In order to comply with the agreed four (4) week period for the Home Office to provide a response to the court, parties and court staff should ensure that the Home Office Liaison Officer receives the court order on the day the order is made.

8) Where it will not be possible for court to send the sealed order to the Home Office Liaison Officer on the day it is made, the court when stating the required date of receipt by the court of the information should allow any additional time necessary for the preparation and sending of the order. This is in order to ensure that Home Office has 4 weeks to provide a response from the time it receives the order from the Home Office Liaison Officer. Any reduction in this period may result in a request by the Home Office for further time in which to reply.

9) The request or order should identify the questions it wishes to be answered by the Home Office.

10) Parties should provide the name and contact details of someone who has agreed and is able to provide further information should it be needed.

11) The order and EX660 should be forwarded to the Home Office Liaison Officer together with such information as is sufficient to enable the Home Office to understand the nature of the case, to identify whether the case involves an adoption, and to identify whether the immigration issues raised might relate to an asylum or non-asylum application.

12) The Home Office Liaison Officer will then send to an appropriate officer in the Home Office the enquiry, together with a copy of any order made. The Home Office official will be personally responsible for either:

(a)   answering the query themselves, by retrieving the file and preparing a statement for the court; or

(b)   forwarding the request to a caseworker or relevant official with carriage of that particular file.

13) The Home Office Liaison Officer will follow up as required in order to ensure that the information is received by the court in time, and will receive the information before forwarding it on as instructed by the judge or court making the request.

14) Attached is a sample court order and completed EX660 which should provide further useful guidance [for EX660 – refer to http://www.judiciary.gov.uk/wp-content/uploads/JCO/Documents/Guidance/Communicating-with-the-HO-in-family+proceedings-+Revised-amalgamated+guidance-March-2013+.pdf]. **Please note the change in contact details in the form EX660.**

[Suggested template order:]

IT IS ORDERED THAT:-

1.   In accordance with the President's Protocol of December 2002 the Home Office is requested to provide the following information (also detailed in the attached form EX660) to the court by 4pm on [*date*]:

    a.   What is the current immigration status of the father, *adult* Y?
    b.   Does *adult* Y have any outstanding applications pending before the Home Office?

2.   There be leave to disclose the case synopsis/summary/background to the Home Office.

3.   There be permission granted for any information received from the Home Office to be disclosed to the parties.

Ordered by [*Judge*] on [*date*]

REVISED PROTOCOL FOR REFERRALS OF FAMILIES TO SUPPORTED CHILD CONTACT CENTRES BY JUDGES AND MAGISTRATES

The protocol for referrals of families to Child Contact Centres, designed to assist judges and magistrates who are proposing to make orders for contact involving the use of a Child Contact Centre, was originally introduced in 2000 following widespread consultation and had the endorsement of the President of the Family Division, Division, Dame Elizabeth Butler-Sloss and subsequently that of the former President, Sir Mark Potter.

Following recent changes in arrangements regarding referrals to supervised contact centres this protocol now governs only referrals to Supported Child Contact Centres. Consultation on practical matters affecting Supported Child Contact centres has shown the need to address some matters in more detail and has led to this revised Protocol, which has the support of Sir Nicholas Wall President of the Family Division and Patron of The National Association of Child Contact Centres (NACCC) who said:

> *'Supported Child Contact Centres are integral to the better working of the wider family justice system, offering a most valuable resource to courts dealing with difficult and often acrimonious family disputes over contact. They also provide safe, comfortable and pleasant surroundings for children meeting the non-resident parents.*

> *It is crucial that Supported Child Contact Centres are used appropriately. This means that the safety of the children being referred, the other families using the centre as well as the staff and volunteers must be considered before an order is made. Supported Child Contact Centres offer a voluntary service and must be able to decide whether to accept or refuse a referral.*

> *Furthermore Courts recognise that Supported Contact Centres are charities and nearly all the staff are volunteers. They can only undertake their work if free of any risk of being drawn into individual cases or disputes. Accordingly courts and parties will not require or seek their involvement in resolving disputes, writing reports, noting events or attending, in any capacity, any family court hearing.*

> *This admirable protocol will be of the greatest help to judges and magistrates to ensure that Supported Child Contact Centres are used to their best advantage for children needing this valuable and scarce resource.'*

Sir Nicholas Wall, President of the Family Division
2nd July 2010

Referrals to Supported Contact Centres

Supported Child Contact Centres do not offer Supervised Contact. The provision offered by Supported Child Contact Centres is described in the Manual of Guidance produced by the National Association of Child Contact Centres as follows:

> 'Supported contact takes place in a variety of neutral community venues where there are safe facilities to enable children to develop and maintain positive relationships with non-resident parents and other family members. Supported Child Contact Centres are suitable for families when no risk to the child or those around the child, unmanageable by the centre, has been identified during an intake procedure.'

It is a requirement that the parents and children attend a pre-contact meeting or equivalent (for example a telephone discussion) Parents are seen or spoken to separately so that the Centres can follow their own risk assessment procedure. A number of children's story books about visiting a Child Contact Centre are available via the NACCC website www.naccc.org.uk

The basic elements of supported contact are as follows:

- Impartiality.
- Staff and volunteers are available for practical assistance (for example calming a tearful child) and keeping a watchful eye. They do not monitor or evaluate individual contact/conversations.
- Several families are usually together in one or a number of rooms.
- Families are encouraged to develop mutual trust and consider more satisfactory family venues.
- Apart from confirmation of attendance dates and times, no report will be made to a referrer, CAFCASS, a party's solicitor or court.
- Supported Child Contact Centre staff and volunteers are not available to be called as witnesses unless it is a criminal matter.
- It is acknowledged that the Supported Child Contact Centre is a temporary arrangement, to be reviewed after an agreed period of time.

Things to check

Before making an Order for Contact at a Supported Child Contact Centre (whether interim or final) please check that the matters set out below have been addressed.

1. If you are considering making an Order for contact at a Supported Child Contact Centre, please ensure that you have addressed whether referral to a Supported as opposed to a Supervised Contact Centre is appropriate where any one or a combination of the following are present

a)   Domestic Violence
b)   Drug or substance misuse
c)   Alcohol misuse
d)   Mental illness

2. That the Child Contact Centre Co-ordinator has been contacted and has confirmed that:

a)   The centre is an accredited member of NACCC.
b)   The referral appears to be suitable for that particular Centre, subject to a satisfactory pre-visit or equivalent. (In line with its Safeguarding Policy a Supported Child Contact Centre can refuse to accept families if the circumstances appear to them to be inappropriate for the Centre).
c)   The intended day and times are available at the particular Centre concerned.
d)   A vacancy is available or a place on a waiting list has been allocated.

3. That you have directed that a copy of the Order is provided to the Centre by one or other of the parties within a specified time together with any other injunctive or relevant Orders on the court file.

4. That it has been agreed who will have responsibility for completing and returning the Centre's referral form. Solicitors for both parties should agree the contents and it should be forwarded to the Child Contact Centre within 24 hours of the court hearing.

5. That the parties understand that the Child Contact Centre offers supported contact only; and that parties and their solicitors are aware that apart from attendance dates and times, no report will be made to a referrer, CAFCASS, a party's solicitor or court; and that the parties understand that the centre staff and volunteers are not available to be called as witnesses unless it is a criminal matter.

6. That if contact is to be observed at the Child Contact Centre by a CAFCASS officer or other third party that this is a facility offered by that Centre and that the Centre has agreed to this course of action. Many do not permit such attendance.

7. That where there may be a communication problem related to language, arrangements have been made for the provision of an independent interpreter. This is not the responsibility of the Supported Child Contact Centre

8. That the Order clearly defines whether or not any other family members are to be a part of the Contact visit.

9. That it is agreed who is going to tell the children where and when they will see their non-Resident parent.

10. That it has been agreed who will be responsible for informing the Centre when the place is no longer required.

11. That a date has been set for a review of contact, including the use of the Supported Child Contact Centre and of any other steps parties have been ordered or undertaken to take which are relevant to contact and for further directions if necessary. Only in

exceptional circumstances should an order be made allowing for the open-ended use of a Supported Child Contact Centre.

Please also note

1. The order should be worded 'Subject to the parties' attendance at a pre-contact meeting or equivalent, the availability of a place and the parties abiding by the rules of the centre ...... '

2. The Centre or Centres at which you direct contact should take place will very much welcome a visit from you and your colleagues. Volunteer staff greatly appreciate the Judiciary taking a positive interest in their local Centres. Such visits will also help you to understand the facilities available locally and thus the type of case that is most suited to contact at the Supported Child Contact Centre.

UK-PAKISTAN JUDICIAL PROTOCOL ON CHILDREN MATTERS

The President of the Family Division and the Hon. Chief Justice of Pakistan in consultation with senior members of the family judiciary of the United Kingdom ('the UK') and the Islamic Republic of Pakistan ('Pakistan'), having met on 15th to 17th January 2003 in the Royal Courts of Justice in London, reach the following consensus:

Whereas:

a.   Desiring to protect the children of the UK and Pakistan from the harmful effects of wrongful removal or retention from one country to the other;

b.   Mindful that the UK and Pakistan share a common heritage of law and a commitment to the welfare of children;

c.   Desirous of promoting judicial cooperation, enhanced relations and the free flow of information between the judiciaries of the UK and Pakistan; and

d.   Recognising the importance of negotiation, mediation and conciliation in the resolution of family disputes;

It is agreed that:

1. In normal circumstances the welfare of a child is best determined by the courts of the country of the child's habitual/ordinary residence.

2. If a child is removed from the UK to Pakistan, or from Pakistan to the UK, without the consent of the parent with a custody/residence order or a restraint/interdict order from the court of the child's habitual/ordinary residence, the judge of the court of the country to which the child has been removed shall not ordinarily exercise jurisdiction over the child, save in so far as it is necessary for the court to order the return of the child to the country of the child's habitual/ordinary residence.

3. If a child is taken from the UK to Pakistan, or from Pakistan to the UK, by a parent with visitation/access/contact rights with the consent of the parent with a custody/residence order or a restraint/interdict order from the court of the child's habitual/ordinary residence or in consequence of an order from that court permitting the visit, and the child is retained in that country after the end of the visit without the consent or in breach of the court order, the judge of the court of the country in which the child has been retained shall not ordinarily exercise jurisdiction over the child, save in so far as it is necessary for the court to order the return of the child to the country of the child's habitual/ordinary residence.

4. The above principles shall apply without regard to the nationality, culture or religion of the parents or either parent and shall apply to children of mixed marriages.

5. In cases where the habitual/ordinary residence of the child is in dispute the court to which an application is made should decide the issue of habitual/ordinary residence

before making any decision on the return or the general welfare of the child, and upon determination of the preliminary issue as to habitual/ordinary residence should then apply the general principles set out above.

6. These applications should be lodged by the applicant, listed by the court and decided expeditiously.

7. It is recommended that the respective governments of the UK and Pakistan give urgent consideration to identifying or establishing an administrative service to facilitate or oversee the resolution of child abduction cases (not covered by the 1980 Hague Convention on the Civil Aspects of International Child Abduction).

8. It is further recommended that the judiciaries, the legal practitioners and the nongovernmental organisations in the UK and Pakistan use their best endeavours to advance the objects of this protocol.

9. It is agreed that the UK and Pakistan shall each nominate a judge of the superior court to work in liaison with each other to advance the objects of this protocol.

Dame Elizabeth Butler-Sloss, DBE
President of the Family Division of the High Court of England and Wales

The Hon. Mr. Justice Sh. Riaz Ahmad
Chief Justice of the Supreme Court of Pakistan

Supplemental Judicial Guidelines on UK-Pakistan Protocol

UK-Pakistan Second Judicial Conference – Held at Islamabad on 22nd and 23rd September 2003

Agreed Guidelines
1. Raising public awareness of protocol, maintaining awareness and providing continuing education to judiciary and practitioners involved in family-child cases.

2. Securing access to justice to 'left behind' parents including knowledge of their rights and the opportunity to assert them.

3. To that end, instituting a system whereby the Judge in each Province of Pakistan is tasked with over-seeing the formation of a Committee to provide legal assistance to such parents.

4. Recognition of the importance of mediation within the extended family.

5. Recognition of the importance of liaison between Pakistan and the United Kingdom and, in particular, the importance of using the liaison Judges who need to know about

all relevant cases which are pending or determined. The role of liaison Judge is to exchange orders by the Courts of respective countries in relation to the cases covered by the protocol for information. In case of breach of any such orders, further information is to be exchanged about those cases for appropriate steps to be taken by them in their respective functions. This role of the liaison Judge shall be given proper publicity.

6. Recognition of the importance of retaining judicial links between Pakistan and the United Kingdom, suggesting that Judges of both the countries should meet from time to time to discuss the working/implementation of the protocol, possibly through at least two Judges from each country meeting every two years. Also keeping in regular contact using, if appropriate, video link.

7. Recognition of the need to address the problems that arise upon relocation after the return of a child to the country of his habitual residence. In particular, recognition of the need to afford respect to any undertakings given to the Judge who ordered return or retention of a child.

8. Recommending the establishment of a Body in each country open to approach by an aggrieved person in United Kingdom – Pakistan seeking legal assistance in cases relating to wrongful and illegal removal of children.

Dame Elizabeth Butler-Sloss, DBE
President of the Family Division of the High Court of England and Wales

The Hon. Mr. Justice Sh. Riaz Ahmad
Chief Justice of Pakistan Supreme Court of Pakistan

The Hon. Lady Anne Smith
Supreme Court of Scotland

The Hon. Mr. Justice Gillen
Family Division of the High Court of Northern Ireland

Chapter 6

Precedents

PLO – CASE MANAGEMENT ORDER

IN THE FAMILY COURT AT [place]   Case No. [   ]
[specify if Family Drug and Alcohol Court]

The Children Act 1989
The Adoption and Children Act 2002
The Family Law Act 1996
[delete as appropriate]

THE CHILDREN
Please add a separate sheet if more than 4 children

Child [*name*]; gender [*male/female*]; d.o.b [*DD/MM/YYYY*]
Child [*name*]; gender [*male/female*]; d.o.b [*DD/MM/YYYY*]
Child [*name*]; gender [*male/female*]; d.o.b [*DD/MM/YYYY*]
Child [*name*]; gender [*male/female*]; d.o.b [*DD/MM/YYYY*]

[DRAFT] Case Management Order no [*sequential number in these
proceedings*][*insert date*]

1. THE PARTIES
The applicant local authority is [*name*]
The first respondent (mother) is [*name*]
The second respondent (father/father of ... ...) is [*name*]
The third respondent(s) is/are (the children) by the children's guardian [*name*]
[The first intervenor is[*state relationship to child(ren) or other party*] is [*name*]]

2. THE CHILD(REN) ARE LIVING WITH
[*Name(s)*] [**Placement]
[*use appropriate code for each placement*]
[*list children separately if different placements*]

3. THE REPRESENTATIVES AT THIS HEARING

The parties are represented as follows

a)   The applicant is represented by [*name of counsel/solicitor/advocate*], their contact details being [*telephone and email address*].

b)   The first respondent is represented by [*name of counsel/solicitor/advocate*], their contact details being [*telephone and email address*].

c)   The second respondent is represented by [*name of counsel/solicitor/advocate*], their contact details being [*telephone and email address*].

d)   The third respondent is represented by [*name of counsel/solicitor/advocate*], their contact details being [*telephone and email address*].

e)   Other [*specify*] is represented by [*name of counsel/solicitor/advocate*], their contact details being [*telephone and email address*].

And the following parties are in person
[*name*], their contact details being [*contact details*].

The identity of the children and those named in paragraphs 1 and 2 are not to be disclosed in public without the permission of the court.

4. ALLOCATION

The proceedings were heard today by **/and/but continue to be allocated to Mr(s) Justice [*name*]/His/Her Honour Judge [*sitting as a s.9 judge*][*name*]/District Judge [*name*]/AJC [*name*]

5. THE APPLICATION(S)

a)   The local authority has applied for a care order/supervision order/other Part 4 order [*specify*] [*today/on date*]

b)   [*other applications*]

c)   The [*state party*] has applied for [   ] [*today/on date*]

6. JURISDICTION

a)   The court is satisfied that it has jurisdiction in relation to the child/ren [*give reasons, eg. based on habitual residence*] [*and/or*]

b)   There is an issue as to jurisdiction in respect of the children and consideration needs to be given to this issue [*and the application of Council Regulation (EC) No 2201/2003 (Brussels 2 Revised)*] to these proceedings by the parties as a matter of urgency; and

c)   The local authority shall liaise with the [*identify country*] consular authority in England and Wales or other competent authority in [*name of foreign state*] in relation to the proceedings or make a request to the Central Authority of [*identify country*] for such information as may be relevant to determine issues of jurisdiction.

7. TODAY'S HEARING

a)   Today's case was listed for: [**]

b) Today's hearing has been [EFFECTIVE][CANCELLED – NOT TO BE RELISTED][RE-LISTED AND DELAYED] [ADJOURNED] The main reason why the hearing has been adjourned/re-listed is: [**]

8. THE TIMETABLE FOR THE PROCEEDINGS

[*see in the matter of Re S (a Child) 16th April 2014*]

The timetable for the proceedings is 26 weeks [*or*]

a) The proceedings cannot be completed within 26 weeks, but are to be completed within [   ] weeks or by [*date*]] for the following reason – [*complete (i) or (ii) or (iii) and delete the others*]

   (i) It is necessary to extend the timetable for the proceedings beyond 26 weeks in order to resolve the proceedings justly because: [*specify reason, eg. very heavy cases involving the most complex medical evidence where a separate fact-finding hearing is directed, FDAC type case, cases with an international element where investigations or assessments have to be carried out abroad, cases where the parent's disabilities require recourse to special assessments or measures.*]

   (ii) Despite robust and vigorous case management, the nature of the proceedings has changed and it is necessary to extend the timetable for the proceedings for one or more of the children in order to resolve the proceedings justly because: [*specify reason, eg.   cases proceeding on allegations of neglect or emotional harm where allegations of sexual abuse subsequently surface, cases which are unexpectedly 'derailed' because of the death, serious illness or imprisonment of the proposed carer, cases where a realistic alternative family carer emerges late in the day*]

   (iii) The progress of the case has been delayed because of the litigation failure on behalf of one or more of the parties and it is necessary to extend the timetable for the proceedings in order to resolve the proceedings justly because:[*specify reason:*]

b) AND in each of the above cases, the impact on the welfare of the children of extending the proceedings is [*state impact*   ]

The next hearing is a [**] on [*date and time*   ] at [*place*   ] with a time estimate of [   ]

9. TIMETABLE FOR THE CHILD(REN)

The key dates and events in the Timetable for the Child(ren) are:

Child [*name*]; Event/Permanent placement [*specify*]; Date [*specify*]

Child [*name*]; Event/Permanent placement [*specify*]; Date [*specify*]

Child [*name*]; Event/Permanent placement [*specify*]; Date [*specify*]

10. THRESHOLD

The s.31 threshold for the making of orders is agreed/in dispute/in dispute subject to concessions which have been made. [*the threshold agreement/the threshold concessions is/are annexed to this order*].

11. THE KEY ISSUES IN THE CASE ARE:

a)   [e.g. What significant harm has the child suffered or been at risk of suffering?]
b)   [e.g. What are the identified welfare needs of the child?]
c)   [e.g. Does either the mother or the father have the capability to meet the child's needs?]
d)   [Other   ]

12. THE PARTIES' POSITIONS:

a)   [e.g. The local authority has concluded ... ...]
b)   [e.g. The mother disputes ... ...]
c)   [e.g. The father has now ... ...]
d)   [e.g. The children's guardian supports the ... .]

13. IDENTIFICATION OF PERSON(S) TO BE ASSESSED AS POTENTIAL ALTERNATIVE CARER(S)

a)   The parents have identified all family members they wish to be assessed and the court has explained to them that any persons identified by them in the future may not be assessed due to the delay not being consistent with the timetable for the child.
b)   The person(s) identified by the mother are [*name(s)*]
c)   The person(s) identified by the father are [*name(s)*]
d)   [*Other*]   [*name(s)*]

14. EVIDENCE

After reading the materials filed, which are described in an index/record of hearing

THE COURT ORDERS

15. INTERIM CARE/SUPERVISION ORDER(S)

In the interim, [*Name of child/ren*] is/are placed in the care of/under the supervision of [*name of local authority*] until the finalisation of the proceedings or further order.

16. EXPERTS

a)   An application [*was*][*was not*] today made for the instruction of an expert and the application [*was*][*was not*] granted.
b)   The type of expert whose instruction was [*allowed*][*refused*] by the court [*is***]
c)   The date by which the report is due is:
d)   The report of an expert is necessary to assist the court to resolve the proceedings because [*specify reason*] and the impact on the welfare of the child is [*describe impact*]   ]
[*Repeat if more than one expert*]

17. OTHER ORDERS

[for example:]
Reallocation
Joinder of additional party/ies
Assessment of others
Consideration of how the child(ren)'s views should be communicated to the court
Special measures/interpreters/intermediaries
Disclosure
Paternity/drug/alcohol testing
Timetable for evidence to be filed including the care plan
Further case analysis
Directions for proposed concurrent placement order proceedings
Disclosure to the Independent Reviewing Officer
Making Interim Care Orders and their duration
Contact
Advocates' meetings and preparation for the next hearing
Bundles
[use standard clauses where available locally and put directions in chronological order]

18. COMPLIANCE

No document other than a document specified in this order or filed in accordance with the Rules or any Practice Direction shall be filed by any party without the court's permission.

19. Any application to vary this order or for any other order is to be made to the allocated judge on notice to all parties.

20. All parties must immediately inform the Case Progression Officer on eastlondonnoncomp@hmcts.gsi.gov.uk if any party or person fails to comply with any part of this order.

Please ensure you quote the case name and number, the case manager and clearly explain the non-compliance issue.

21. CASE OUTCOME *[to be completed only if proceedings are finally disposed of at a Case Management/Issues Resolution Hearing]*
A *[set out type of order]* was made today in respect of *[name of child   ]*

Court address: for filing/communication

1. Type of Placement [*for paragraph 2*]

Type of Placement for children
1.   Not removed – At home
2.   Not removed – In RPaCA placement (a residential assessment with parent)
3.   Not removed – In community placement
4.   Removed – To kinship placement
5.   Removed – To foster care
6.   Removed – To potential adoptive placement
7.   Reunification – Assessment placement with parent
8.   Reunification – Assessment placement with kinship placement
9.   Complex needs – In a specialist placement including hospital

2. Type of Hearing [*for paragraph 7 and paragraph 8*]

PLO Stage
Urgent Case Management Hearing
Case Management Hearing (CMH)   Other – Fact Finding
Further Case Management Hearing
 (FCMH)   Other – Directions not part of PLO
Issues Resolution Hearing (IRH)   Other – Contested Interim Care Hearing
Final Hearing (FH)   Other – s38(6))

3. Reasons for Adjournment [*for paragraph 7*]
Please list the **ONE** reason which best explains why the hearing has been adjourned.

Reason for Adjourned Hearing
Local Authority   LA1 – No/poor pre-proceedings preparation by LA, other than
                  social work assessment of the family
                  LA2 – No friends/family identified before the hearing by LA
                  LA3 – No/poor kinship assessments by LA
                  LA4 – No expert instructed by LA
                  LA5 – No/poor/late social work assessment of the family by LA
                  LA6 – New social work report/assessment required following a
                  change in circumstances
                  LA7 – No timetable for the child
                  LA8 – No/poor/late/new/care plan
                  LA9 – Placement order proceedings delay
                  LA10 – No/poor placement evidence by LA
                  LA11 – No threshold set out in the application form

CAFCASS   CA1 – CAFCASS not allocated/present
                  CA2 – No/poor CAFCASS analysis

Other Parties	LW1 – Lawyers not instructed, present or ready, party or witness fails to attend LW2 – No key issue analysis LW3 – No/poor parental evidence or parental non-compliance
HMCTS	HM1 – No courtroom available HM2 – No special measures HM3 – Interpreter or intermediary not available
Judiciary	JU1 – Lack of judicial continuity JU2 – Insufficient time listed to complete hearing
LAA	LS1 – Prior authority from LAA not available LS2 – Other legal aid problem
Official Solicitor	OS1 – Official Solicitor not instructed/ready
Experts	EX1 – Late expert report/assessment/Poor expert report/assessment EX2 – New expert report/assessment required following a change in circumstances
Health	HE1 – No/poor medical records etc from other agency
Crime	CR1 – Police/CPS disclosure/documents incomplete/not available
Other	OT1 – Case reallocated or moved to a different judge at a different location OT2 – Need for an interim contested hearing OT3 – Other non compliance with directions OT4 – Consolidation with other family proceedings OT5 – Parallel proceedings OT6 – New baby/pregnancy OT7 – New Party joined OT8 – Immigration and international difficulties OT9 – Severe weather OT10 – Industrial action

4. Instruction of Expert [*for paragraph 16*]
Please list all that apply.

Expert Code

A – Paediatrician
B – Paediatric Radiologist
C – Other Medical Report
Family Centre Assessment (Parenting Skills):
    D1 – Residential
    D2 –Non-Residential
E – Multi-Disciplinary Assessment
F – Independent Social Worker
G – Paediatrician (now removed)
Psychiatric Report:
    H1 – Parent(s) alone
    H2 – Child(ren) and Parent(s)/carer(s)
    H3 – Psychiatric Report – Child(ren) alone
Psychological Report
    J1 – Clinical – Child(ren) only
    J2 – Educational – Child(ren) only
    J3 – Parent(s) only
    J4 – Parent(s) and Child(ren)
K – Other Expert Report

CAP02 LITE FINAL

In the Family Court
sitting at [place]

Case No

The Children Act 1989

THE CHILDREN

Names	Girl/Boy	Dob.

FHDRA/Directions Hearing Order Number [*Sequential number in these proceedings*]

1.   **THE PARTIES AND REPRESENTATION AT THIS HEARING**
The applicant (mother/father/as appropriate) is [name] and is a litigant in person/represented by [*name of advocate and contact details*]

The [first] respondent (father/mother/as appropriate) is [name] and is a litigant in person/represented by [*name of advocate and contact details*]

[*Other – provide full details as above*]

2.   The child/ren is/are living with ... .

3.   **NOTICE**
Today's hearing is on notice/not on notice/on short notice...[*give details*]

The names of the children set out in the heading to this Order and the names of the persons set out in paragraph 1 are not to be disclosed in public without the permission of the court.

4.   **ALLOCATION/TRANSFER**
The proceedings are today/continue to be allocated to [lay justices/District Judge/Circuit Judge/High Court Judge (*insert name*)] for case management and hearing

This application is transferred to the [Family Court sitting at   ]

5.   **THE APPLICATION(S)**
(a)   The applicant has applied for a Child Arrangements Order/Specific Issue Order/Prohibited Steps Order other Part II order [*delete as appropriate or specify*] [*today/on date*]

(b)   [*If there are other applications add as follows or delete*]

(c)   The [mother/father/as appropriate] has applied for [ ] [*today/on date*]

6.   SAFEGUARDING CHECKS

(a)   The safeguarding checks by Cafcass/CAFCASS Cymru are/are not complete

(b)   The safeguarding checks show no safety issues/that the safety issues are............/that the safety issues are not yet known [*delete as appropriate or specify*]

7.   TIMETABLE FOR THE CHILD(REN)

The key dates and events in the timetable for the child(ren) are

(a)   ... ...

(b)   ... ...

8.   KEY ISSUES

A. The issues which have been agreed &/or are to be determined are:- [specify]

(a)   ... .

(b)   ... .

B. The steps planned to resolve the issues are:-

[*include if the parties intend to refer themselves to mediation or other form of non-court dispute resolution if appropriate*]

(a)   ... .

(b)   ... .

9.   AGREED [INTERIM] ARRANGEMENTS FOR THE CHILDREN

(a)   [*If determined at this hearing, specify, such as:*] Between now and [*date/the final hearing*] the agreed arrangements for the child[ren] will be [as set out in the schedule to this order (*if extensive*)/as follows ...]

(b)   [Between now and [date/the final hearing]] the child[ren] will live with the [mother/father].

(c)   [Between now and [date/the final hearing]], the child[ren] will spend time or otherwise have contact with the [mother/father] as follows/as set out in the schedule to this order (*if extensive*).

10.   OTHER RECITALS AS TO POSITIONS/ISSUES

(a)   ... ...

(b)   ... ...

THE COURT ORDERS:

11.   JOINDER OF CHILD[REN]

(a)   The child[ren] [*name*] are joined as [a party/parties] to the proceedings and pursuant to rule 16.4 and PD16A, Part 4 FPR 2010 an officer of

Cafcass/CAFCASS Cymru shall be appointed to act as [his/her/their] children's guardian.

(b) A copy of this order shall be faxed/e-mailed to the Cafcass/CAFCASS Cymru office and a hard copy of this order shall be sent within two working days of this order.

(c) The service manager [is requested/has agreed to] allocate an officer as children's guardian as promptly as possible following receipt of this order, and to notify the court within 7 days of such allocation.

(d) It is recorded that there are [no] reasons why the Cafcass officer/WFPO dealing with the case should not continue to deal with it as guardian.

(e) In the event that Cafcass/CAFCASS Cymru is unable to provide a children's guardian to act within [28 days] they shall notify the court forthwith, to enable the court to consider the appointment of another person.

12. CHILD ARRANGEMENTS

The following child arrangements order is made

(a) Until [   ] the children shall live with

(b) Until [   ] the children shall spend time or otherwise have contact with [   ] as follows:-

Warning notice

Where a child arrangements order is in force: if you do not comply with this contact order –

(a) **you may be held in contempt of court and be committed to prison or fined: and/or**

(b) **the court may make an order requiring you to undertake unpaid work ('an enforcement order') and/or an order that you pay financial compensation.**

13. OTHER CHILDREN ORDERS

(a) **Prohibited Steps Orders**

Until further order [*Identify name*] is forbidden to

(a) remove the child[ren] from the care of [   ] otherwise than for the purpose of agreed or ordered contact

(b) remove the child[ren] from the United Kingdom without the written consent of the other parent or permission of the court

(c) change the child[ren]'s school[s]

(d) change the child[ren]'s name

(e) other:

(b) **Specific Issue Orders**

(a) The child[ren] shall attend [   ] School

(b) The child[ren] shall be known by the name[s]

(c) Other:

14.   PENAL NOTICE

(a)   **To [   ]: You must obey the instructions contained in this order. If you do not, you will be guilty of contempt of court and you may be sent to prison, fined or your assets may be seized.**

(b)   **This penal notice is attached to the following paragraphs of this order: paragraph**

15.   PARENTAL RESPONSIBILITY

The court grants parental responsibility to ... ..

16.   ACTIVITY DIRECTIONS

The court makes an activity direction and the parties are directed to take part in the following programme on dates and at times as are specified by the activity provider

(a)   a Mediation Information and Assessment Meeting

(b)   a Separated Parents' Information Programme

(c)   a Domestic Violence Perpetrators' Programme

The Court shall forthwith send this order to the provider with the parties' contact details.

The provider shall notify the Court whether the parties attended at the conclusion of the activity directed.

17.   CASE MANAGEMENT AND OTHER ORDERS/DIRECTIONS

(a)   **Safeguarding incomplete:**

    (a)   Cafcass must write to the court by [   ] with the outcome of safeguarding checks;

    (b)   the case is adjourned to [   ] (when the parties' attendance is excused) when the court will either make an order in the terms agreed by the parties or list the case for further consideration.

(b)   **Sending and delivering of evidence**

    (a)   The parties must by 4:00 pm on [*insert date*] send to each other, to the court and to Cafcass written statements of the evidence on which they intend to rely. This includes the statements of the parties themselves and of any witness they intend to rely on.

    (b)   When preparing their statements the parties shall use the witness statement template which shall be provided to them by the court.

(c)   **Fact finding Schedules**

The court considers that a fact finding hearing should take place in this case to determine the following issue(s) [*in summary*] [alleged domestic abuse/alleged harm to the child ... ...]. In the circumstances, the parties must send to each other and to the court a schedule setting out the allegations on which they rely and (using the same document) their responses to such allegations as follows:

- (a) by [*insert time & date*] a schedule of any allegations made by either party
- (b) by [*insert time & date*] the other party's response

(d) **Disclosure from Police/Medical records**

- (a) Cafcass are requested to initiate enhanced checks of the relevant local police force, in particular in respect of their investigation into [ ] and shall deliver any relevant information that is received to the parties and the court.
- (b) The Chief Constable of [*insert area*] is directed to disclose to [the court/the parties directly ...] [*insert number*] copies of all reports, incident logs, statements and interview notes relating to any incidents involving the parties between [*insert dates*]. This order shall be served on the Chief Constable by [*insert time and date*]. The Chief Constable may apply within 7 days of service of this order for it to be varied or discharged.
- (c) [*Identify party*] must by 4:00 pm on [*insert date*] obtain and disclose to [*identify party*] his/her GP and any hospital medical records. A copy of this order shall be sent with the request to the record holder. Any fee charged by the record holder shall be paid by [*identify party*]

(e) **Cafcass/Local Authority s.7 Reports/s.37 investigation and report.**

- (a) The court directs a section 7 report by Cafcass/[Local Authority] dealing with the following matters:
  - (1) The ascertainable wishes and feelings of the children.
  - (2) The home conditions and suitability of the accommodation of the [mother/father]
  - (3) The concerns of the [mother/father] with regard to [*specify*]
  - (4) Whether or not the children's physical/emotional/ educational needs are being met by the [mother/father]
  - (5) How the children will be affected by the proposed change of [*specify*]
  - (6) Whether or not it appears that the children have suffered or at risk of suffering the harm alleged by the [mother/father/]
  - (7) The parenting capacity of the [mother/father] having regard to the allegations that [*specify*]
  - (8) Whether [*specify*] local authority should be requested to report under section 37 Children Act 1989.

(b)   [*named local authority*] is directed to prepare a section 37 report in respect of the child(ren), the Court being of the view that it may be appropriate for a care or supervision order to be made with respect to the child(ren). The authority shall, when advising the court, consider whether they should apply for a care or supervision order, or provide services or assistance to the child(ren), and/or take any further action. The court shall send to the local authority preparing the report the application, any C1A and the Cafcass safeguarding letter [together with]

(c)   The report shall be sent to the court [and to the parties] by no later than 4:00 pm on [*insert time & date*]

(f)   Experts

The Court gives permission for the parties to rely on the following expert evidence. The parties shall take such steps as are necessary to ensure that the expert evidence is obtained and made available to the court in accordance with the directions below, and shall provide any samples that are required for the purpose of testing

(a)   Type of expert:

(b)   The issues on which the expert is to report are:

(c)   The expert is to be instructed by the parties together as a single expert.

(d)   The expert is to be instructed by [   ]

(e)   A copy of this order must be sent to the expert with the expert's instructions.

(f)   Date for delivery of instructions/provision of necessary samples:

(g)   Date for delivery of the expert's report:

(h)   Any expert's fees shall be paid by [   ]

(i)   The expert may [not] see the child[ren] for the purpose of any assessment:

The court gives the following further directions in relation to the obtaining of expert evidence:

18.   CONTACT CENTRE DIRECTION

The order for supported contact at the contact centre is subject to the following conditions for its operation and effect:-

(a)   [   ] shall inform the centre co-ordinator of the contents of this order as soon as practicable.

(b)   The parties shall jointly be responsible for – (i) completing a referral form for the centre co-ordinator; and (ii) providing a copy of this order and any subsisting injunction orders involving the parties to the co-ordinator as soon as practicable and in any event within 2 days of today.

(c)   The parties and any person permitted to accompany them to the centre shall abide by the rules of the centre.

(d)   The following arrangements for the contact sessions shall apply:-

   (1)   The child(ren) shall be taken to the centre by [   ]

   (2)   The child(ren) shall be collected at the conclusion of contact by [   ]

   (3)   [   ] may [not] be accompanied during the contact session [by]

   (4)   [   ] may [not] remain in the same room as the child(ren) during the contact session

   (5)   [Other agreements about contact at the centre]

(e)   The parties shall jointly be responsible for informing the centre co-ordinator when the place is no longer required.

19.   FURTHER HEARINGS

(a)   The next hearing will be a [fact-finding hearing/Dispute Resolution Appointment/other directions hearing/final hearing] before [... [Name]] which will take place at [*identify place*] at 10.30 am on [*identify date*]

(b)   The author of the [section 7] report shall [not] be required to attend the Dispute Resolution Appointment;

(c)   The parties **MUST** arrive at court at least 60 minutes before any future hearings

20.   COSTS

No order as to costs *or*

Costs in the application or

Costs reserved *or*

21.   COMPLIANCE

(a)   No document other than a document specified in this order or delivered in accordance with the Rules or any Practice Direction shall be delivered by any party without the court's permission.

(b)   Any application to vary this order or for any other order is to be made to the allocated judge on notice to [   ]/all parties.

(c)   In the event of non-compliance by any person with any order or direction made today, each party shall be responsible for notifying the court of the same, in order to avoid delay.

Ordered by [*Names*]Lay Justices/District Judge [*Name*]/His Honour Judge/[*Name*]

Dated:

Court address: for filing/communication:

CAP – FINAL ORDER

In the Family Court   **Case No**
Sitting at [place]

The Children Act 1989 – Child Arrangements Programme

Names	Girl/Boy	Dob.

1. THE PARTIES
The applicant (mother/father/as appropriate) is [*name*]
The first respondent (father/mother/as appropriate) is [*name*]
The second respondent (child/father of/as appropriate) is [*name*]
[The third respondent(s) is/are (the children) by their children's guardian [*name*]] [The first intervener [*state relationship to child(ren) or other party*] is [*name*]]

2. The child/ren is/are living with ... .

3. REPRESENTATION AT THIS HEARING
The parties appeared before the court as follows:

Party/Name	In Person	Counsel/Solicitor/ Advocate	Contact telephone and email address
Applicant			
Respondent(s)			
(1)			
(2)			
Other (specify)			

The names set out in paragraph 2 are not to be disclosed in public without the permission of the court.

4. Cafcass/CAFCASS Cymru/Local Authority [*if appointed*]
Name
Professional address
Date of appointment (if children's guardian):
Date of order of [section 7] [section 37] report

5. THE APPLICATIONS
The applicant has applied for a Child Arrangements Order/Specific Issue Order/Prohibited Steps Order/other Part 2 order [*delete as appropriate or specify*] [*today/on date*]
[*If there are other applications add as follows or delete*]
The [*specify party*] has applied for [   ] [*today/on date*]

6. THE HEARING
a. Today's case was listed for: [*]
b. Today's hearing has been [EFFECTIVE AS THE FINAL HEARING] [EFFECTIVE] [CANCELLED] [ADJOURNED]
c. The reason why the hearing has been adjourned is: [*]
The next hearing is a [*] on [*date and time*] at [*court*] with a time estimate of [   ] [this matter is part heard]

7. AGREEMENTS/AGREED ARRANGEMENTS FOR THE CHILDREN
Such as:-
  ▪ The child[ren] will live with the [mother/father/mother and father] as set out in the schedule to this order (*if extensive*)/as follows ...]
  ▪ The [mother/father] agrees to make the child[ren] available to visit/stay with/have indirect contact with the [mother/father] [as set out in the schedule to this order (*if extensive*)/as follows ...]
The [mother/father] may remove the child[ren] from England and Wales [for the purposes of a holiday to [*specify*]][to live in]. The details of the arrangements for the [holiday/removal from the jurisdiction] are to be [as follows .../as set out in the schedule to this order (*if extensive*).

8. UNDERTAKINGS
The [mother/father] gave undertakings to the court [as set out on the [undertaking form] signed by [her/him] on [date] a copy of which is annexed to this order *or* the [mother/father] gave the following undertakings to the court [*specify*]

9. KEY ISSUES [*only if adjourned*]
The issues which remain to be determined are as follows:-
a)
b)
c)
d)

10. After reading the materials provided to the court.
The court heard no oral evidence
or
After hearing the evidence of the following witnesses:-

Name of witness	Called by

THE COURT ORDERS:

11. CHILD ARRANGEMENTS
Such as
- [By consent,] that the arrangements for the children shall be [as set out in the schedule to this order (*if extensive*)/as follows...[*specify*]]
- [a contact warning notice will be endorsed][by consent] that the [father/mother] shall make the child[ren] available to spend time with/have [indirect] contact with] the [father/mother] as set out in the schedule to this order (*if extensive*)/as follows...[*specify*]

12. PARENTAL RESPONSIBILITY
Further to the Child Arrangements Order made [*today/date*], which provides that the child is to live with [the father, who does not currently have parental responsibility]/ [*woman* who is a parent of the child by virtue of section 43 of the Human Fertilisation and Embryology Act 2008, without parental responsibility], the court grants parental responsibility to [the father]/[*the woman*].

Further to the Child Arrangements Order made [*today/date*], which provides that the child is to spend time or otherwise have contact (but not live) with [the father, who does not currently have parental responsibility]/[*woman* who is a parent of the child by virtue of section 43 of the Human Fertilisation and Embryology Act 2008, without parental responsibility], the court grants parental responsibility to [the father]/[*the woman*].

Further to the Child Arrangements Order made [*today/date*], which provides that the child is to spend time or otherwise have contact (but not live) with [*a person who is not the parent or guardian of the child concerned is named in the order as a person with whom the child is to spend time or otherwise have contact but not live*] the court grants parental responsibility for the child for as long as the order is in place.

13. ACTIVITY CONDITIONS
[*if made at this hearing, specify as appropriate*]

Such as:-
The [father/mother] [other party] is directed to take part in:
Set out any order for Activity Direction/Condition [*e.g. Separated Parents Information Programme*] such dates and times as are specified by.......[the provider]

The court shall forthwith send this order to the provider.

14. PROHIBITED STEPS
Specify as appropriate, such as:-
- The [mother/father] shall not cause or permit [name child[ren] to [cease to attend ... *name school*] [live at an address other than [*specify*]] [come into

contact with [*specify*]] without the prior written agreement of the [father/mother] or an order of the court.

- The [mother/father] shall not remove [name child/ren] from England and Wales without the prior written agreement of [father/mother] or an order of the court [except ... [*specify*]]

15. SPECIFIC ISSUE – REMOVAL FROM THE JURISDICTION

(a) The [mother/father] is permitted to remove [name of child(ren)] from England and Wales on or after [date] to live permanently in [as appropriate]

(b) [*for example*] Before the removal of the [name child[ren] from the jurisdiction, the [mother/father] shall obtain, and then deliver and send to the court and to the other parties, an order from [court] an order reflecting the terms of this order insofar as they relate to the child arrangements [or as appropriate].

16. SPECIFIC ISSUE – SCHOOLING

From [date/the start of the ... term ...] [name child[ren]] shall attend [name and address of school]

[*set out any ancillary provisions re schooling e.g. provision of information, fees etc.*]

17. SPECIFIC ISSUE – OTHER STEPS

Specify as appropriate

18. CONTACT CENTRE DIRECTION

The order for supported contact at the [   ] contact centre is subject to the following conditions for its operation and effect:-

a. The [parties/solicitors for the [Mother/Father][   ] shall inform the centre co-ordinator of the contents of this order as soon as practicable.

b. The [parties/solicitors for the parties] shall jointly be responsible for
   i. completing a referral form for the centre co-ordinator and
   ii. providing a copy of this order and any subsisting injunction orders involving the parties to the co-ordinator as soon as practicable and in any event within 2 days of today.

c. Confirmation from the centre co-ordinator that:
   i. the centre is an accredited member of NACCC;
   ii. the referral has been accepted following completion of a preparation for contact interview (which interview is a compulsory requirement of all NACCC centres);
   iii. a vacancy is available or the parties have been allocated a place upon a waiting list (the order for supported contact is suspended during any waiting period until a place is available).

d. The parties and any person permitted to accompany them to the centre shall abide by the rules of the centre.

e. The parties must attend a preparation for contact meeting with the centre co-ordinator (the parties' solicitors, if acting, must take responsibility for ensuring that information about the meeting is passed to the parties).

f. The [Mother/Father] [   ] agrees to take the child(ren) for a pre-contact introductory visit to the centre.

g. The child(ren) will be informed of the contact arrangements by [Mother/Father] [   ]

h. The following arrangements for the contact sessions shall apply:-

    i.   The child(ren) shall be taken to the centre by

    ii. The child(ren) shall be collected at the conclusion of contact by

    iii. The [Father/Mother] [   ] may [not] be accompanied during the contact session [by]

    iv. The [Father/Mother] [   ] may [not] remain in the same room as the child(ren) during the contact session

    v.   After [   ] sessions of contact, the [Father/Mother] [   ] shall not remain in the same room as the child(ren) but may remain in the confines of the centre.

    vi. [Other agreements about contact at the centre]

i. The [parties/the parties' solicitors] shall jointly be responsible for informing the centre co-ordinator when the place is no longer required.

19. MONITORING CONTACT ORDER

(a) Cafcass/CAFCASS Cymru shall, pursuant to s11H Children Act 1989, make an officer available to monitor whether the person required to allow the contact, or the person having contact with the child[ren] complies with the contact order

(b) The contact monitoring order shall remain in force until [ ][up to 12 mths]

(c) The [mother/father/person having contact] shall co-operate with the Cafcass officer/WFPO [in particular by ... .] so that the officer can comply with the order to monitor the contact;

(d) The Cafcass officer/WFPO is directed to prepare a report for the Court (and provide a copy to the parties) if he/she considers that the order is not being complied with; the report shall include any information which the Cafcass officer/WFPO considers relevant to the issue of compliance and shall specifically advise on the question of whether the order should be varied or discharged.

20. FAMILY ASSISTANCE ORDER

(a) Cafcass/CAFCASS Cymru/[ ] Local Authority shall, pursuant to s16 Children Act 1989, make an Officer available to advise assist and (where appropriate) befriend the following persons who have (save for a named child) today consented to the making of this Order:

    a.

(b) The Family Assistance Order shall remain in force until [   ][up to 12 mths]

(c) The Officer is directed to give advice and assistance as regards establishing, improving and maintaining contact to those identified above

(d) The Officer is directed to report to the Court by 16:00hs on [   ] on the following matters (including but limited to the question of whether the s8 order should be varied or discharged):

  a.

(e) It is recorded for the purpose of this Order that

  a. the opinion of the appropriate officer has been obtained and

  b. all relevant persons have been given the opportunity to comment on that opinion prior to the making of this order pursuant to PD12M FPR 2010

(f) The Local Authority/Cafcass/CAFCASS Cymru may send representations to the Court and the other parties on or before [14 days from service] as to the making of the Family Assistance Order pursuant to PD12M FPR 2010. Any party wishing to respond to those representations must do so within 7 days of receipt.

21. COSTS

No order as to costs *or*

Costs in the application *or*

Costs reserved *or*

Funded services assessment of the costs of [*specify*] *or*

Other [*specify*]

Dated

COLLECTION ORDER

SERVICE OF THIS ORDER UPON THE RESPONDENT(S) AND ANY OTHER PERSON IS TO BE EFFECTED ONLY BY THE TIPSTAFF OR BY A POLICE OFFICER ACTING ON HIS DIRECTION OR ON HIS BEHALF. THE COPY PROVIDED TO THE APPLICANT MUST NOT BE USED FOR SERVICE UPON ANY PERSON

In the High Court of Justice   **No:**
Family Division
Sitting at [place]

THE CHILD ABDUCTION AND CUSTODY ACT 1985
COUNCIL REGULATION (EC) No. 2201/2003
THE SENIOR COURTS ACT 1981
THE CHILDREN ACT 1989

(Delete or Adapt as appropriate)

The Child[ren]   **AA (a boy/girl born on dd/mm/yyyy)**
                             [BB (a boy/girl born on dd/mm/yyyy)
                             CC (a boy/girl born on dd/mm/yyyy)]

After hearing [*name the advocate(s) who appeared*] ... .
After consideration of the documents lodged by the applicant
After reading the statements and hearing the witnesses specified in paragraph 6 of the recitals below

COLLECTION ORDER MADE BY [NAME OF JUDGE] ON [DATE] SITTING IN PRIVATE

IMPORTANT WARNING TO [YY] OF [ADDRESS], [ZZ] OF [ADDRESS], AND ANY OTHER PERSON SERVED WITH THIS ORDER

If you YY, or ZZ, or any other person served with this order, disobey this order, you may be held to be in contempt of court and may be imprisoned, fined or have your assets seized.

If any other person who knows of this order and does anything which helps or permits you YY, or ZZ, or any other person served with this order, to breach the terms of this order they may be held to be in contempt of court and may be imprisoned, fined or have their assets seized.

Note: every person intended or expected to be served with the order who is named in para 1 below MUST be named in the warning above and the notice below.

Important Notice to YY, ZZ, or any other person served with this order
At the time of making this order the court has directed the Tipstaff to arrest any person whom he has reasonable cause to believe has been served with this order and has disobeyed any of the obligations imposed by paragraphs 11–14 of it. If he arrests you, the Tipstaff must explain to you the ground for your arrest, must bring you before the court as soon as practicable and in any event no later than the working day immediately following your arrest and must detain you until then.

You have the following legal rights:

(a)   To seek legal advice and, if arrested, to be given the opportunity as soon as practicable to seek legal advice. This right does not entitle you to disobey any part of this order until you have sought legal advice.

(b)   [Subject to the order made at para 21 below,] to require the applicant's solicitors, namely Messrs KKK, (ref: [   ], tel: [   ], email [   ]) at their own expense to supply you with a copy of any affidavit and their note of any oral evidence referred to in para 6 below.

(c)   To apply, whether by counsel or solicitor or in person, to the judge of the High Court, Family Division, assigned to hear urgent applications at the Royal Courts of Justice, Strand, London WC2A 2LL, if practicable after giving notice to the applicant's solicitors, for an order discharging or varying any part of this order or for a direction that information provided by you to the Tipstaff (or his officers) pursuant to this order is not disclosed to any person (other than the court). This right does not entitle you to disobey any part of this order until your application has been heard. If you notify the tipstaff that you propose to make an application to the court that he should not disclose any information or document provided by you to him pursuant to this order he will not do so other than with your consent or pursuant to a further direction of the court given on your application or an application by him, the applicant or an interested person.

(d)   If you do not speak or understand English adequately, to have an interpreter present in court at public expense in order to assist you at the hearing of any application relating to this order.

The Parties
1.   The applicant is XX
        The respondent is YY
        ZZ is … *(for example) the brother of YY*
        Specify any additional respondents or other persons, if known at this stage, on whom it is intended or expected to serve the order
        Specify if any adult party acts by a litigation friend
        Specify if any child acts by a children's guardian

2.   Unless otherwise stated, a reference in this order to 'the respondent' means all of the respondents.

3.   This order is effective against any respondent on whom it is served or who is given notice of it.

Definitions

4.   The Tipstaff is the enforcement officer of the High Court at the Royal Courts of Justice. He has a deputy and assistants and can authorise police officers to act on his behalf. Any obligation to give information to the Tipstaff or to hand over a document to him includes an obligation to do so to his deputy or assistant or a police officer acting on his behalf.

Recitals

5.   This order was made at a hearing without notice to the respondent or ZZ.

6.   The Judge read the following affidavits/witness statements [*set out*] and heard oral testimony from [*name*].

7.   At the time of making this order, the court gave directions to the Tipstaff of the High Court of Justice to locate the child[ren] AA [BB and CC] and then to place them in accordance with the terms of this order.

IT IS ORDERED THAT:

8.   The child[ren] AA [BB and CC] must be [placed into the care of the applicant]/ [provided with accommodation by the appropriate local authority] on a temporary basis, namely until a further hearing of the court which must take place within three clear working days after [the applicant's care of the child[ren]]/[the provision of such accommodation] begins. That hearing will be fixed by the Tipstaff in consultation with the Clerk of the Rules.

9.   Once the child[ren] have/has been [placed into the applicant's care]/[provided with accommodation by the appropriate local authority], the applicant must not remove the child[ren] from England and Wales nor cause or permit the child[ren] to stay overnight at an address other than [an address disclosed to the Tipstaff]/ [an address chosen by that local authority] until the conclusion of the further hearing directed above.

10.   The applicant's solicitors, Messrs KKK, must immediately inform the Tipstaff in writing in the event that the applicant should independently of the Tipstaff [receive the child[ren] into their care]/[place the child[ren]/in accommodation provided by the appropriate local authority] or that for any other reason there is no further need for the Tipstaff's services in this matter.

11.   If the respondent or ZZ or any other person served with this order is in a position to do so, he or she must each deliver immediately the child[ren] into the charge of the Tipstaff.

12. If the respondent or ZZ or any other person served with this order is not in a position to deliver the child[ren] into the charge of the Tipstaff, they must each immediately:

    (a) inform the Tipstaff of the whereabouts of the child[ren], and of the place at which the child[ren] reside[s] within England and Wales if such are known to them; and

    (b) also in any event inform the Tipstaff of all matters within their knowledge or understanding which might reasonably assist him in locating the child[ren], and

    (c) if it is requested by the Tipstaff, the address at which that person will be living in England and Wales and (if practicable) a telephone number and email address at which that person can be contacted.

13. The respondent, ZZ and any other person served with this order must not (i) remove or (ii) knowingly cause or permit the removal of the child[ren] from the jurisdiction of England and Wales.

14. The respondent, ZZ and any other person served with this order must each hand over to the Tipstaff (for safe-keeping until the court makes a further order) as many of the following documents as are in his or her possession or control:

    (a) every passport relating to the child[ren], including an adult's passport by which the child[ren] may travel, and every identity card, ticket, travel warrant or other document which would enable the child[ren] to leave England and Wales; and

    (b) every passport relating to the respondent and every identity card, ticket, travel warrant or other document which would enable the respondent to leave England and Wales.

15. The respondent, ZZ and any person served with this order must not (a) make any application for, (b) obtain, seek to obtain, or (c) knowingly cause, permit, encourage or support any steps being taken to apply for, or obtain any passport, identity card, ticket, travel warrant or other document which would enable either (a) the child[ren], or (b) the respondent to leave England and Wales.

16. The respondent, ZZ and any other person served with this order must, as soon as is practicable after it comes to his or her knowledge inform the Tipstaff of any information referred to in paragraph 12(a) and (b) above, including any change in such information.

17. This order or a faxed or scanned copy of it must be personally served by the Tiptaff or a police officer acting at his direction or on his behalf upon the respondent, ZZ, and upon any other person whom it is proposed to make liable

under it, but if the respondent or any other person refuses or evades or seeks to evade personal service, the court will consider that he or she has been validly served if the effect of the order has been brought to his or her attention.

18.   The obligations under paragraphs 8, 11 and 12 above will continue until the Tipstaff locates the child[ren] and the obligations under paragraphs 9, 10 and 13–17 inclusive will continue until the court by further order provides otherwise, but if the Tipstaff has not located the child[ren] by [*the date six months after the making of the order*] this order shall expire in its entirety.

19.   Anyone served with or notified of this order may apply to the court at any time to vary or discharge this order (or so much of it as affects that person), but they must first inform the applicant's solicitors. If any evidence is to be relied upon in support of the application, the substance of it must be communicated in writing to the applicant's solicitors in advance.

20.   Save with the prior permission of the court the applicant's solicitors, Messrs KKK, must:

(a)   not disclose any information or document obtained by the Tipstaff pursuant to this order to the applicant,

(b)   not use such information and documents for any purpose other than assisting the Tipstaff to enforce this order and in the conduct of these proceedings,

(c)   keep any record of information received by them as a consequence of this order in a separate file marked confidential and with a note that its contents are subject to the orders of the court and will not copy or provide that information to others save for the purposes set out in (b) above, and

(d)   obtain a written undertaking in terms of (a), (b) and (c) above from any person provided with information received by them as a consequence of this order for the purposes set out in (b) above.

[21.   In the event that any person served with this order exercises the right to require the applicant's solicitors, Messrs KKK, at their own expense to supply them with a copy of any affidavit and their note of any oral evidence referred to in para 6 above, such copy or note may be redacted in accordance with the versions approved by the court and placed on the court file.]

Dated:

LOCATION ORDER

SERVICE OF THIS ORDER UPON THE RESPONDENT(S) AND ANY OTHER PERSON IS TO BE EFFECTED ONLY BY THE TIPSTAFF OR BY A POLICE OFFICER ACTING ON HIS DIRECTION OR ON HIS BEHALF. THE COPY PROVIDED TO THE APPLICANT MUST NOT BE USED FOR SERVICE UPON ANY PERSON

In the High Court of Justice   **No:**
Family Division
Sitting at [place]

THE CHILD ABDUCTION AND CUSTODY ACT 1985
COUNCIL REGULATION (EC) No. 2201/2003
THE SENIOR COURTS ACT 1981
THE CHILDREN ACT 1989

(Delete or Adapt as appropriate)

The Child[ren]   **AA (a boy/girl born on dd/mm/yyyy)**
                        [BB (a boy/girl born on dd/mm/yyyy)
                        CC (a boy/girl born on dd/mm/yyyy)]

After hearing [*name the advocate(s) who appeared*] ... .
After consideration of the documents lodged by the applicant
After reading the statements and hearing the witnesses specified in paragraph 6 of the recitals below

LOCATION ORDER MADE BY [NAME OF JUDGE] ON [DATE] SITTING IN PRIVATE

IMPORTANT WARNING TO [YY] OF [ADDRESS], [ZZ] OF [ADDRESS], AND ANY OTHER PERSON SERVED WITH THIS ORDER

If you YY, or ZZ, or any other person served with this order, disobey this order you may be held to be in contempt of court and may be imprisoned, fined or have your assets seized.

If any other person who knows of this order and does anything which helps or permits you YY, or ZZ, or any other person served with this order, to breach the terms of this order they may be held to be in contempt of court and may be imprisoned, fined or have their assets seized.

Note: every person intended or expected to be served with the order who is named in para 1 below MUST be named in the warning above and the notice below.

Important Notice to YY, ZZ or any other person served with this order

At the time of making this order the court has directed the Tipstaff to arrest any person whom he has reasonable cause to believe has been served with this order and has disobeyed any of the obligations imposed by paragraphs 8, 10 or 11 of it. If he arrests you, the Tipstaff must explain to you the ground for your arrest, must bring you before the court as soon as practicable and in any event no later than the working day immediately following your arrest and must detain you until then.

You have the following legal rights:

(a)   To seek legal advice and, if arrested, to be given the opportunity as soon as practicable to seek legal advice. This right does not entitle you to disobey any part of this order until you have sought legal advice.

(b)   [Subject to the order made at para 18 below,] to require the applicant's solicitors, namely Messrs KKK, (ref: [   ], tel: [   ], email [   ]) at their own expense to supply you with a copy of any affidavit and their note of any oral evidence referred to in para 6 below.

(c)   To apply, whether by counsel or solicitor or in person, to the judge of the High Court, Family Division, assigned to hear urgent applications at the Royal Courts of Justice, Strand, London WC2A 2LL, if practicable after giving notice to the applicant's solicitors, for an order discharging or varying any part of this order or for a direction that information provided by you to the Tipstaff (or his officers) pursuant to this order is not disclosed to any person (other than the court). This right does not entitle you to disobey any part of this order until your application has been heard. If you notify the tipstaff that you propose to make an application to the court that he should not disclose any information or document provided by you to him pursuant to this order he will not do so other than with your consent or pursuant to a further direction of the court given on your application or an application by him, the applicant or an interested person.

(d)   If you do not speak or understand English adequately, to have an interpreter present in court at public expense in order to assist you at the hearing of any application relating to this order.

The Parties

1.   The applicant is XX
The respondent is YY
ZZ is …*(for example) the brother of YY*
Specify any additional respondents or other persons, if known at this stage, on whom it is intended or expected to serve the order
Specify if any adult party acts by a litigation friend
Specify if the child acts by a children's guardian

2.   Unless otherwise stated, a reference in this order to 'the respondent' means all of the respondents.

3.   This order is effective against any respondent on whom it is served or who is given notice of it.

Definitions

4.   The Tipstaff is the enforcement officer of the High Court at the Royal Courts of Justice. He has a deputy and assistants and can authorise police officers to act on his behalf. Any obligation to give information to the Tipstaff or to hand over a document to him includes an obligation to do so to his deputy or assistant or a police officer acting on his behalf.

Recitals

5.   This order was made at a hearing without notice to the respondent or ZZ.

6.   The Judge read the following affidavits/witness statements [*set out*] and heard oral testimony from [*name*].

7.   At the time of making this order, the court gave directions to the Tipstaff of the High Court of Justice to locate the child[ren] AA [BB and CC] and as soon as he has done so, unless he has been notified of a proposed application for a direction that he should not do so, to inform the applicant [through solicitors] of the whereabouts of the child[ren].

IT IS ORDERED THAT:

8.   The respondent or ZZ or any other person served with this order must each immediately:

(a)   inform the Tipstaff of the whereabouts of the child[ren], and of the place at which the child[ren] reside[s] within England and Wales if such are known to them; and

(b)   also in any event inform the Tipstaff of all matters within their knowledge or understanding which might reasonably assist him in locating the child[ren], and

(c)   if it is requested by the Tipstaff, the address at which that person will be living in England and Wales and (if practicable) a telephone number and email address at which that person can be contacted.

9.   The applicant's solicitors, Messrs KKK, must forthwith inform the Tipstaff in writing in the event that the applicant should independently of the Tipstaff locate the children or if there is no further need for the Tipstaff's services.

10.   The respondent, ZZ and any other person served with this order must each hand over to the Tipstaff (for safe-keeping until the court makes a further order) as many of the following documents as are in his or her possession or control:

  (a) every passport relating to the child[ren], including an adult's passport by which the child[ren] may travel, and every identity card, ticket, travel warrant or other document which would enable the child[ren] to leave England and Wales; and

  (b) every passport relating to the respondent and every identity card, ticket, travel warrant or other document which would enable the respondent to leave England and Wales.

11. The respondent, ZZ and any other person served with this order must not (i) remove or (ii) knowingly cause or permit the removal of the child[ren] from the jurisdiction of England and Wales.

12. The respondent, ZZ and any person served with this order must not (a) make any application for, (b) obtain, seek to obtain, or (c) knowingly cause, permit, encourage or support any steps being taken to apply for, or obtain any passport, identity card, ticket, travel warrant or other document which would enable either (a) the child[ren], or (b) the respondent to leave England and Wales.

13. The respondent, ZZ and any other person served with this order must, as soon as is practicable after it comes to his or her knowledge inform the Tipstaff of any information referred to in paragraph 10(a) and (b) above, including any change in such information.

14. This order or a faxed or scanned copy of it must be personally served by the Tiptaff or a police officer acting at his direction or on his behalf upon the respondent, ZZ, and upon any other person whom it is proposed to make liable under it, but if the respondent or any other person refuses or evades or seeks to evade personal service, the court will consider that he or she has been validly served if the effect of the order has been brought to his or her attention.

15. The obligations under paragraph 8 above will continue until the Tipstaff locates the child[ren] and the obligations under paragraphs 9–15 inclusive will continue until the court by further order provides otherwise, but if the Tipstaff has not located the child[ren] by [*the date six months after the making of the order*] this order shall expire in its entirety.

16. Anyone served with or notified of this order may apply to the court at any time to vary or discharge this order (or so much of it as affects that person), but they must first inform the applicant's solicitors. If any evidence is to be relied upon in support of the application, the substance of it must be communicated in writing to the applicant's solicitors in advance.

17. Save with the prior permission of the court the applicant's solicitors, Messrs KKK, must:

(a)   not disclose any information or document obtained by the Tipstaff pursuant to this order to the applicant,

(b)   not use such information and documents for any purpose other than assisting the Tipstaff to enforce this order and in the conduct of these proceedings,

(c)   keep any record of information received by them as a consequence of this order in a separate file marked confidential and with a note that its contents are subject to the orders of the court and will not copy or provide that information to others save for the purposes set out in (b) above, and

(d)   obtain a written undertaking in terms of (a), (b) and (c) above from any person provided with information received by them as a consequence of this order for the purposes set out in (b) above.

[18.   In the event that any person served with this order exercises the right to require the applicant's solicitors, Messrs KKK, at their own expense to supply them with a copy of any affidavit and their note of any oral evidence referred to in para 6 above, such copy or note may be redacted in accordance with the versions approved by the court and placed on the court file.]

Dated:

PASSPORT ORDER

SERVICE OF THIS ORDER UPON THE RESPONDENT(S) AND ANY OTHER PERSON IS TO BE EFFECTED ONLY BY THE TIPSTAFF OR BY A POLICE OFFICER ACTING ON HIS DIRECTION OR ON HIS BEHALF. THE COPY PROVIDED TO THE APPLICANT MUST NOT BE USED FOR SERVICE UPON ANY PERSON

In the High Court of Justice   No:
Family Division
Sitting at [place]

THE CHILD ABDUCTION AND CUSTODY ACT 1985
COUNCIL REGULATION (EC) No. 2201/2003
THE SENIOR COURTS ACT 1981
THE CHILDREN ACT 1989
THE FAMILY LAW ACT 1986, PART 4A
THE FEMALE GENITAL MUTILATION ACT 2003, SCHEDULE 2

(Delete or Adapt as appropriate)

The Child(ren)   **AA (a boy/girl born on dd/mm/yyyy)**
                            [BB (a boy/girl born on dd/mm/yyyy)
                            CC (a boy/girl born on dd/mm/yyyy)]
Or

The Vulnerable Adult[s] **AA (a male/female born on dd/mm/yyyy)**
                            [BB (a male/female born on dd/mm/yyyy)
                            CC (a male/female born on dd/mm/yyyy)]

After hearing [*name the advocate(s) who appeared*] ... .
After consideration of the documents lodged by the applicant
After reading the statements and hearing the witnesses specified in paragraph 6 of the recitals below

PASSPORT ORDER MADE BY [NAME OF JUDGE] ON [DATE] SITTING IN PRIVATE

IMPORTANT WARNING TO [YY] OF [ADDRESS], AND ANY OTHER PERSON SERVED WITH THIS ORDER

If you YY, or ZZ, or any other person served with this order, disobey this order you may be held to be in contempt of court and may be imprisoned, fined or have your assets seized.

If any other person who knows of this order and does anything which helps or permits you YY, or ZZ, or any other person served with this order, to breach the terms of this order they may be held to be in contempt of court and may be imprisoned, fined or have their assets seized.

Note: every person intended or expected to be served with the order who is named in para 1 below MUST be named in the warning above and the notice below

Important Notice to YY, ZZ or any other person served with this order

At the time of making this order the court has directed the Tipstaff to arrest any person whom he has reasonable cause to believe has been served with this order and has disobeyed any of the obligations imposed by paragraphs 8 and 10–13 of it. If he arrests you, the Tipstaff must explain to you the ground for your arrest, must bring you before the court as soon as practicable and in any event no later than the working day immediately following your arrest and must detain you until then.

You have the following legal rights:

(a) To seek legal advice and, if arrested, to be given the opportunity as soon as practicable to seek legal advice. This right does not entitle you to disobey any part of this order until you have sought legal advice.

(b) [Subject to the order made at para 18 below,] to require the applicant's solicitors, namely Messrs KKK, (ref: [ ], tel: [ ], email [ ]) at their own expense to supply you with a copy of any affidavit and their note of any oral evidence referred to in para 6 below.

(c) To apply, whether by counsel or solicitor or in person, to the judge of the High Court, Family Division, assigned to hear urgent applications at the Royal Courts of Justice, Strand, London WC2A 2LL, if practicable after giving notice to the applicant's solicitors, for an order discharging or varying any part of this order or for a direction that information provided by you to the Tipstaff (or his officers) pursuant to this order is not disclosed to any person (other than the court). This right does not entitle you to disobey any part of this order until your application has been heard. If you notify the tipstaff that you propose to make an application to the court that he should not disclose any information or document provided by you to him pursuant to this order he will not do so other than with your consent or pursuant to a further direction of the court given on your application or an application by him, the applicant or an interested person.

(d) If you do not speak or understand English adequately, to have an interpreter present in court at public expense in order to assist you at the hearing of any application relating to this order.

The Parties

1. The applicant is XX
   The respondent is YY
   ZZ is … *(for example) the brother of YY*

> *Specify any additional respondents or other persons, if known at this stage, on whom it is intended or expected to serve the order*
> *Specify if any adult party acts by a litigation friend*
> *Specify if any child acts by a children's guardian*

2. Unless otherwise stated, a reference in this order to 'the respondent' means all of the respondents.

3. This order is effective against any respondent on whom it is served or who is given notice of it.

Definitions

4. The Tipstaff is the enforcement officer of the High Court at the Royal Courts of Justice. He has a deputy and assistants and can authorise police officers to act on his behalf. Any obligation to give information to the Tipstaff or to hand over a document to him includes an obligation to do so to his deputy or assistant or a police officer acting on his behalf.

Recitals

5. This order was made at a hearing without notice to the respondent or ZZ.

6. The Judge read the following affidavits/witness statements [*set out*] and heard oral testimony from [*name*].

7. At the time of making this order, the court gave directions to the Tipstaff of the High Court of Justice to obtain and, until further direction of the court, to seize and keep safely the documents referred to in paragraph 10 of this order.

IT IS ORDERED THAT:

8. The respondent, ZZ and any other person served with this order must each hand over to the Tipstaff (for safe-keeping until the court makes a further order) as many of the following documents as are in his or her possession or control:

    (a) every passport relating to the child[ren]/vulnerable adult[s] (including an adult's passport by which the child[ren] may travel) and every identity card, ticket, travel warrant or other document which would enable the child[ren] /vulnerable adult[s] to leave England and Wales; and

    (b) every passport relating to the respondent and every identity card, ticket, travel warrant or other document which would enable the respondent to leave England and Wales.

9. The applicant's solicitors, Messrs KKK, must immediately inform the Tipstaff in writing in the event that there is no further need for the Tipstaff's services in this matter.

10. The respondent, ZZ and any other person served with this order must not (i) remove or (ii) knowingly cause or permit the removal of the child[ren]/vulnerable adult[s] from the jurisdiction of England and Wales.

11. The respondent, ZZ and any person served with this order must not (a) make any application for, (b) obtain, seek to obtain, or (c) knowingly cause, permit, encourage or support any steps being taken to apply for, or obtain any passport, identity card, ticket, travel warrant or other document which would enable either (a) the child[ren]/vulnerable adult[s], or (b) the respondent to leave England and Wales.

12. The respondent and/or any other person served with this order must inform the Tipstaff of the address of the place at which the children/vulnerable adult[s] reside within England and Wales, if such is known to him or her, and of any change in that information as soon as it is known to him or her.

13. The respondent, ZZ and any other person served with this order must not (a) change, or (b) knowingly cause permit or encourage any change of, the place at which the children/vulnerable adult[s]presently reside within England and Wales.

14. This order or a faxed or scanned copy of it must be personally served by the Tiptaff or a police officer acting at his direction or on his behalf upon the respondent, ZZ, and upon any other person whom it is proposed to make liable under it, but if the respondent or any other person refuses or evades or seeks to evade personal service, the court will consider that he or she has been validly served if the effect of the order has been brought to his or her attention.

15. The obligations under paragraphs 8–13 will continue until the court by further order provides otherwise, but if the Tipstaff has not recovered the documents referred to in paragraph 8 by [*the date six months after the making of the order*] this order shall expire in its entirety.

16. Anyone served with or notified of this order may apply to the court at any time to vary or discharge this order (or so much of it as affects that person), but they must first inform the applicant's solicitors. If any evidence is to be relied upon in support of the application, the substance of it must be communicated in writing to the applicant's solicitors in advance.

17. Save with the prior permission of the court the applicant's solicitors, Messrs KKK, must:

     (a) not disclose any information or document obtained by the Tipstaff pursuant to this order to the applicant,

(b)   not use such information and documents for any purpose other than assisting the Tipstaff to enforce this order and in the conduct of these proceedings,

(c)   keep any record of information received by them as a consequence of this order in a separate file marked confidential and with a note that its contents are subject to the orders of the court and will not copy or provide that information to others save for the purposes set out in (b) above, and

(d)   obtain a written undertaking in terms of (a), (b) and (c) above from any person provided with information received by them as a consequence of this order for the purposes set out in (b) above.

[18.   In the event that any person served with this order exercises the right to require the applicant's solicitors, Messrs KKK, at their own expense to supply them with a copy of any affidavit and their note of any oral evidence referred to in para 6 above, such copy or note may be redacted in accordance with the versions approved by the court and placed on the court file.]

Dated:

PRODUCTION ORDER (OF PRISONER)

IN THE FAMILY COURT AT [place]   **Case No. [   ]**

The Children Act 1989
The Adoption and Children Act 2002
The Family Law Act 1996
[*delete as appropriate*]

[DRAFT] Case Management Order No/FHDRA/Directions Hearing Order No
[*Sequential number in these proceedings*]
(ADAPT TEMPLATE FOR PLO OR CAP, AS APPROPRIATE)

1. THE PARTIES
The applicant is [*name*]
The first respondent is [*name*]
The second respondent is [*name*]
The third respondent(s) is/are [*name(s)*]
[The first intervenor is [*state relationship to child(ren) or other party*] is [*name*]]

UPON HEARING counsel/solicitor for [*name*] ... .
AND UPON reading ... .

ORDER:

1.   The Governor of HMP [*name*] is requested to produce [*name*] (who is a party to the proceedings) at the Family Court sitting at [*location of court*] for the purpose of a hearing on [*date*] at [*time*], Time Estimate – [   ].

2.   The court confirms that the personal attendance of [*name*] at the hearing is desirable in the interests of justice, if he/she wishes to attend.

3.   This order may be disclosed to the relevant Prison Governor.

Ordered by [*Names*] Lay Justices/District Judge [*Name*]/His/Her Honour Judge/[*Name*]

Dated:

Court address: for filing/communication:

2013 PROTOCOL AND GOOD PRACTICE MODEL

DISCLOSURE OF INFORMATION IN CASES OF ALLEGED CHILD ABUSE AND LINKED CRIMINAL AND CARE DIRECTIONS HEARINGS

Disclosure direction to police

In the Court   **No**
Sitting at [Place]

The Children Act 1989

The Protocol concerning the disclosure of information in cases of alleged child abuse and linked criminal and care directions hearings dated [dd/mm] 2013 ('The Protocol')

The Marriage/Civil Partnership/Relationship/Family of XX and YY
The Children   **AA (a boy/girl born on dd/mm/yyyy)**
                                BB (a boy/girl born on dd/mm/yyyy)
                                CC (a boy/girl born on dd/mm/yyyy)

(Adapt as appropriate)

After hearing [*name the advocate(s) who appeared*] ... .
After consideration of the documents lodged by the Parties

ORDER MADE BY [NAME OF JUDGE] ON [DATE] SITTING IN OPEN COURT/PRIVATE

The Parties
1.   The applicant is XX ('The Local Authority')
         The respondent is YY
         The second respondent is ZZ
         Specify if any party acts by a litigation friend
         The third respondent is AA (acting by his/her guardian FF)
         The third respondent is BB (acting by his/her guardian FF)
         The fourth respondent is CC (acting by his/her guardian FF)
         Delete or Adapt as appropriate

Recitals
2.   This is an order for information to be provided to this court by the [*name of police force*].
3.   The reason that this request for information is made is [*specify*].
4.   This order was made at a hearing [without notice]/[on short informal notice] to the [*name of police force*]. The reason why the order was made [without notice]/[on short informal notice] to the [*name of police force*] was [set out].

The [*name of police force*] has the right to apply to the court to vary or discharge the order – see **'The right to seek variation or discharge of this order'** below

IT IS ORDERED (BY CONSENT):

5. The [Commissioner of the Metropolitan Police]/[Chief Constable of [*name*] Police] shall by 16:00 on [*date no sooner than 28 days from the date of the order*] disclose to the Local Authority the following information:

    The following are examples:

    (a) Copies of police call out records and logs relating to [   ], date of birth [   ], and [   ], date of birth [   ], at [*address(es)*] between the dates of [   ] and [   ].

    (b) Evidence relating to the allegations made by [   ] against [   ], date of birth [   ], of [*address*] including all statements made and photographs taken in connection with the allegations.

    (c) A copy of any video-taped interview of [   ], date of birth [   ], on [*date*] together with a copy of any transcript available of that interview when completed.

    (d) A copy of any audio-taped interview of [   ], date of birth [   ], on [*date*] together with a copy of any transcript available of that interview when completed.

6. The Local Authority [*or other named party*] shall serve a copy of this order on [*specify the relevant police officer*] together with a letter setting out in respect of the solicitors representing each party the full name of the firm, the full postal address, and the reference at that firm dealing with the matter giving his/her email address and direct telephone number.

7. The Local Authority [*or other named party*] shall file with this court and serve on the other parties the above evidence by 16:00 on [*date*].

8. The information when supplied may be used only for the purposes of these proceedings and must not be disclosed to any third party without the express permission of this court.

The right to seek variation or discharge of this order

9. *(Where the order was made on no, or short, notice)* The [Commissioner of the Metropolitan Police]/[Chief Constable of [*name*] Police] may apply for discharge or variation of this order, upon giving two clear business days' notice of the hearing to the parties, by 16:00 on [*date no later than 14 days from date of the order*].

DATED

2013 PROTOCOL AND GOOD PRACTICE MODEL

DISCLOSURE OF INFORMATION IN CASES OF ALLEGED CHILD ABUSE AND LINKED CRIMINAL AND CARE DIRECTIONS HEARINGS

Linked criminal and care directions

In the Court   **No:**
Sitting at [Place]

The Children Act 1989
The Protocol concerning the disclosure of information in cases of alleged child abuse and linked criminal and care directions hearings dated [dd/mm] 2013 ('The Protocol')

The Marriage/Civil Partnership/Relationship/Family of XX and YY
The Children   AA (a boy/girl born on dd/mm/yyyy)
**   BB (a boy/girl born on dd/mm/yyyy)**
**   CC (a boy/girl born on dd/mm/yyyy)**

Adapt as appropriate

After hearing [*name the advocate(s) who appeared*] ... .
After consideration of the documents lodged by the Parties

ORDER MADE BY [NAME OF JUDGE] ON [DATE] SITTING IN OPEN COURT/PRIVATE

The Parties
1.   The applicant is XX ('The Local Authority')
        The respondent is YY
        The second respondent is ZZ
        Specify if any party acts by a litigation friend
        The third respondent is AA (acting by his/her guardian FF)
        The third respondent is BB (acting by his/her guardian FF)
        The fourth respondent is CC (acting by his/her guardian FF)
        Delete or Adapt as appropriate

Recitals
2.   [*name*] has been charged with offences of [*specify the alleged offences and against whom they were committed*] to which (s)he pleaded not guilty on [date] and the proceedings under case number [xxx] are listed for [trial]/[plea and case management] on [*date*] at the [*name*] Crown Court.

3.   This court on [*date*] made a police disclosure direction order. The order [was complied with on]/[is expected to be complied with by] [*date*].

4. *(for example)* ZZ is [to be]/[being] assessed by Dr [*name*], Consultant Psychiatrist, in readiness for the Plea and Case Management Hearing on [*date*].

5. It is recognised that the CPS will seek disclosure of the papers from these proceedings [and from the previous proceedings] regarding [*names of children*] the children of [*name*] and [*name*] [deceased] as well as documents held by the Local Authority on its Social Services files.

6. The Local Authority is expected to ensure that a copy of the Protocol is made available to the CPS solicitor with conduct of the criminal proceedings and the defence solicitor(s) (who will supply it to instructed counsel).

Request
7. Pursuant to Part C of the Protocol this court considers that a linked directions hearing is appropriate. This court by this order requests that the Resident Judge should nominate a judge to be responsible for the management of the criminal case with a view to listing a linked directions hearing at the [*name*] Crown Court before the nominated judge and the Allocated Case Management Judge in this case namely [*name*].

IT IS ORDERED (BY CONSENT):

8. These proceedings and the criminal proceedings are listed for a linked directions hearing at 10.00am on [*date*] before His/Her Honour Judge [*name*] and His/Her Honour Judge [*name*] sitting at the [*name*] Crown Court, [*address*] (estimate 1 hour).

9. The Local Authority shall by 14:00 on [*date*] serve on the Crown Court, the CPS and the defence solicitors a case summary as set out in para 17.6 of the Protocol, and shall file and serve a copy of it in these proceedings.

10. In accordance with para 17.7 of the Protocol the Local Authority and the CPS shall agree a schedule of issues, setting out those matters which are likely to be considered at the linked directions hearing and the Local Authority shall circulate the schedule to the solicitors for the other parties in the criminal and care proceedings by no later than 16:00 on [*date*].

11. The Local Authority shall by 12:00 on [*date*] file with the Court an agreed bundle prepared in accordance with the Family Procedure Rules 2010 PD 27A to include the case summary, the schedule of issues (agreed if possible), and the proposed directions to be sought. The Local Authority shall by the same time file and serve on each of the respondents an index to the bundle. If any respondent is unrepresented the Local Authority shall supply him/her with a full copy of the bundle.

12. The Governor of HM Prison [*name*] is directed to ensure that the respondent (father) ZZ is produced at 09:30 for the hearing on [*date*].

13.   The Local Authority shall serve a copy of this order on the CPS prosecutor with conduct of the criminal proceedings and on the defence solicitor(s) (who shall provide copies to instructed counsel).

Dated

CASE MANAGEMENT ORDERS FOR FAMILY COURTS AND IMMIGRATION AND ASYLUM CHAMBERS OF THE FIRST-TIER TRIBUNAL AND UPPER TRIBUNAL

[Footnote omitted]

Part 1

In the Court   **No:**
Sitting at [Place]

The [name of statute] Act [year]

The Immigration and Asylum Acts

The Marriage/Civil Partnership/Relationship/Family of XX and YY
The Children   **AA (a boy/girl born on dd/mm/yyyy)**
                              BB (a boy/girl born on dd/mm/yyyy)
                              CC (a boy/girl born on dd/mm/yyyy)
Adapt as appropriate

After hearing ... .

After consideration of the documents lodged by the Parties

ORDER MADE BY [NAME OF JUDGE] ON [DATE] SITTING IN OPEN COURT/PRIVATE

The Parties
1.   The applicant is XX
      The respondent is YY
      The second respondent is ZZ
      Specify if any party acts by a litigation friend
      The third respondent is AA (acting by his/her guardian FF)
      The third respondent is BB (acting by his/her guardian FF)
      The fourth respondent is CC (acting by his/her guardian FF)
      Delete or Adapt as appropriate

Recitals
2.   This is a request made to Resident Judge [name of Judge see Annex 3 below] of the FtT/Upper Tribunal Immigration and Asylum Chamber sitting at [name of centre see Annex 3 below] for information to be provided to this court by the [First Tier Tribunal (IAC)]/[Upper Tribunal (IAC)] in accordance with the Protocol made between President of the Family Division and the Senior President of Tribunals dated 19 July 2013.

3.   The name of the appellant in the immigration proceedings is ... .. and the file number of the appeal is ... ...

4.   The reason that this request for information is made is [*specify.*]

Request

5.   This court requests that the following information be provided by the [First Tier Tribunal (IAC)]/[Upper Tribunal (IAC)]:

The following are examples

(a)   What immigration decision has been made and in respect of who?

(b)   What nationality is the child concerned with the immigration proceedings and his/her parents or carers?

(c)   What possible outcomes are there as a result of the appeal and what immigration rules are in point?

(d)   What stage has the hearing reached?

(e)   When is the next hearing?

6.   The information should be supplied to [*specify*] by [*date and time – allow a minimum of 2 weeks*].

7.   If the [First Tier Tribunal (IAC)]/[Upper Tribunal (IAC)] requires any further information it should contact [*specify with telephone number and email address*].

IT IS ORDERED (BY CONSENT):

8.   For the purposes of enabling the [First Tier Tribunal (IAC)]/[Upper Tribunal (IAC)] to consider this request fully the following documents shall be disclosed to it [*specify the documents and any redactions which are considered necessary*].

9.   The documents listed in para 8 shall be disclosed by [*name person or body*] by [*date and time*]. They shall be returned by the [First Tier Tribunal (IAC)]/[Upper Tribunal (IAC)] when the requested information is supplied.

10.   The requested information when supplied may be used only for the purposes of these proceedings and must not be disclosed to any third party without the express permission of this court.

Dated

Part 4

In the Court   **No:**
Sitting at [Place]

The [name of statute] Act [year]

The Immigration and Asylum Acts

The Marriage/Civil Partnership/Relationship/Family of XX and YY
The Children   **AA (a boy/girl born on dd/mm/yyyy)**
                          BB (a boy/girl born on dd/mm/yyyy)
                          CC (a boy/girl born on dd/mm/yyyy)
Adapt as appropriate

After hearing ... .
After consideration of the documents lodged by the Parties

ORDER MADE BY [NAME OF JUDGE] ON [DATE] SITTING IN OPEN COURT/PRIVATE

The Parties
1.	The applicant is XX
	The respondent is YY
	The second respondent is ZZ
	Specify if any party acts by a litigation friend
	The third respondent is AA (acting by his/her guardian FF)
	The third respondent is BB (acting by his/her guardian FF)
	The fourth respondent is CC (acting by his/her guardian FF)
	Delete or Adapt as appropriate

Recitals
2.	This court has received a request for disclosure by the [First Tier Tribunal (IAC)]/[Upper Tribunal (IAC)].

3.	The reason that this request has been made is [*specify*].

4.	This court has decided to grant the request, subject to the conditions set out at paras 6–8 below, for the following reasons [*specify*].

5.	If the [First Tier Tribunal (IAC)]/[Upper Tribunal (IAC)] requires any further information it should contact [*specify with telephone number and email address*].

IT IS ORDERED (BY CONSENT):

6. The following information and documents shall be disclosed to the [First Tier Tribunal (IAC)]/[Upper Tribunal (IAC)] [*specify the documents and any redactions which are considered necessary*].

7. The information and documents listed in para 6 shall be disclosed to [*name person or body*] by [*name person or body*] by [*date and time*]. They shall be returned by the [First Tier Tribunal (IAC)]/[Upper Tribunal (IAC)] when the proceedings in that tribunal have been concluded.

8. The information and documents listed in para 6 may be used only for the purposes of those proceedings and must not be disclosed to any third party without the express permission of [this court]/[the [First Tier Tribunal (IAC)]/[Upper Tribunal (IAC)]].

Dated

FINANCIAL REMEDY DIRECTIONS ORDERS OMNIBUS – LONGER VERSION

[The Orders Project]

Table of Contents

[The page numbers below are for the purposes of this book and are not as in the original version.]

In the Family Court　　　　　　　　　　　　　　**No:**
Sitting at [Place]

The Matrimonial Causes Act 1973
The Civil Partnership Act 2004
The Child Support Act 1991
Schedule 1 to the Children Act 1989
The Inheritance (Provision for Family and Dependants) Act 1975
The Matrimonial and Family Proceedings Act 1984 and Schedule 7 to the Civil
Partnership Act 2004
The Trusts of Land and Appointment of Trustees Act 1996
The Married Women's Property Act 1882 and ss 67, 68 and 74 of the Civil
Partnership Act 2004
Delete as appropriate

The Marriage of XX and YY, or
The Civil Partnership of XX and YY, or
The Relationship of XX and YY, or
The Family of XX and YY
Adapt as necessary

After hearing [*name the advocate(s) who appeared*] ... .
After consideration of the documents lodged by the parties
(*In the case of an order made without notice*) After reading the statements and hearing
the witnesses specified in para [*insert*] of the Recitals below

ORDER MADE BY [NAME OF JUDGE] ON [DATE] SITTING IN OPEN
COURT/PRIVATE AT A FIRST DIRECTIONS APPOINTMENT/ FINANCIAL
DISPUTE RESOLUTION APPOINTMENT/CASE MANAGEMENT HEARING
[*Delete as appropriate*]

WARNING: IF YOU DO NOT COMPLY WITH THIS ORDER, YOU MAY
BE HELD TO BE IN CONTEMPT OF COURT AND YOU MAY BE SENT
TO PRISON, BE FINED, OR HAVE YOUR ASSETS SEIZED.

The parties
1.　　The applicant is XX
　　　The [first] respondent is YY
　　　The [intervener]/[second respondent] is ZZ
　　　Specify if any party acts by a litigation friend

Definitions
2.　　*For example*: The 'family home' shall mean [*insert address including*
　　　postcode] registered at HM Land Registry with title number [*insert*].

Recitals
Recital for without notice hearings
3. (*In the case of an order made without notice*)
    a. This order was made at a hearing without notice to the respondent. The reason why the order was made without notice to the respondent was [*set out*].
    b. The Judge read the following affidavits/witness statements [*set out*] and heard oral testimony from [*name*].

Recital for short informal notice hearings
4. (*In the case of an order made following the giving of short informal notice*)
    This order was made at a hearing without full notice having been given to the respondent. The reason why the order was made without full notice having been given to the respondent was [*set out*].

Recital as to a MIAM
5. [It is recorded that the [applicant]/[respondent]/[parties] have attended a MIAM and have sent to the court a completed Form FM1 dated [*insert*]]/[It is recorded that the [applicant has not]/[respondent has not]/[neither of the parties have] attended a MIAM; and it is further recorded that [it appears to the court that a MIAM would not be appropriate within these proceedings]/[it appears to the court that neither party has provided any reason that in the view of the court would render mediation unlikely to be effective]]

Agreements
6. (*Record any agreements reached between the parties – for example*: The parties have agreed the value of the family home at [*insert address including postcode*] at [*insert value*] for FDR purposes).

Undertakings to the court
7. (*Record any undertakings given*).

Undertaking for without notice hearings
8. By [*insert time and date*] the applicant shall [use [his]/[her] best endeavours personally to serve upon the respondent]/[serve upon the respondent, by [*insert method of service – for example posting to the respondent's usual address*]], together with this order:
    a. a copy of the application;
    b. copies of the witness statement(s) and exhibits containing the evidence relied upon by the applicant, and any other documents provided to the court on the making of the application; and
    c. a note [prepared by [his]/[her] solicitor] recording the substance of the dialogue with the court at the hearing and the reasons given by the court for making the order, which note shall include (but not be limited to) any allegation of fact made orally to the court where such allegation is

not contained in the witness statement(s) or draft witness statement(s) read by the judge.

Undertaking to pay mortgage and outgoings on property

9.   The [applicant]/[respondent] shall make the following payments pending [the financial dispute resolution appointment]/[the final determination of these proceedings]:- [*insert – for example* all interest and capital repayments due in respect of the mortgage secured against the family home; and all [reasonable] sums due in respect of service charge, council tax, utilities (including but not limited to gas, electricity, water and telephone accounts), and buildings and contents insurance premiums in respect of the family home].

Undertaking where a legal services order is made

10.   The [applicant]/[respondent] shall repay to the [respondent]/[applicant] such part of the amounts paid under the legal services order below if, and to the extent that, the court is of the opinion, when considering costs at the conclusion of the proceedings, that (s)he ought to do so.

You may be held to be in contempt of court and imprisoned or fined, or your assets may be seized, if you break the promises that you have given to the court.

If you fail to pay any sum of money which you have promised the court that you will pay, a person entitled to enforce the undertaking may apply to the court for an order. You may be sent to prison if it is proved that you-

(a)   have, or have had since the date of your undertaking, the means to pay the sum; and

(b)   have refused or neglected, or are refusing or neglecting, to pay that sum.

I understand the undertakings that I have given, and that if I break any of my promises to the court I may be sent to prison for contempt of court.

....

Orders

IT IS ORDERED (BY CONSENT) THAT:

Maintenance Pending Suit

11.   The [applicant]/[respondent] shall pay to the [respondent]/[applicant] maintenance pending suit until the date of decree absolute and afterwards interim periodical payments at the rate of £[*insert*] per annum, payable

[weekly]/[monthly] [in advance]/[in arrears] by standing order from [*insert date, including a date earlier than the date of the order if backdating*] until further order. [The [applicant]/[respondent] shall be given credit for the payment(s) of £[*insert*] made on [*insert dates*]].

OR

The [applicant]/[respondent] shall pay to the [respondent]/[applicant] maintenance pending suit until the date of decree absolute and afterwards interim periodical payments. Payments shall be at the rate of £[*insert*] per annum, payable [weekly]/[monthly] [in advance]/[in arrears] by standing order.

Payments shall start on [*insert date, including a date earlier than the date of the order if backdating*], and shall end on the first to occur of:
a. the death of either the applicant or the respondent;
b. the [respondent's]/[applicant's] remarriage;
c. the determination of the applicant's application for a financial order; or
d. a further order.
[The [applicant]/[respondent] shall be given credit for the payment(s) of £[*insert*] made on [*insert date*]].

Legal Services Order
12.
a. This is a legal services order made pursuant to s 22ZA of the Matrimonial Causes Act 1973/para 38A of Schedule 5 to the Civil Partnership Act 2004.
b. The court was satisfied that without the amount specified below, the [applicant]/[respondent] would not reasonably be able to obtain appropriate legal services for the purposes of the proceedings.
c. The [respondent/applicant] shall pay the amount of £[*insert amount*] [by *insert time and date*]/[per calendar month commencing on *insert time and date* until *insert time and date*] to [*insert name*], the legal representatives of the [applicant/respondent].

Order to attend a MIAM and to send form FM1 to the Court
13. The [applicant]/[respondent] shall attend a Mediation Information and Assessment Meeting and shall send a completed Form FM1 to the court by [*insert time and date*].

Form E/Form E1
14.
a. The [applicant]/[respondent] shall send to the court and serve on the [respondent]/[applicant] a signed copy of [his]/[her] [Form E]/[Form E1] together with all relevant attachments and accompanying documents by [*insert time and date*].

b. If the [applicant]/[respondent] has not been personally served with this order by [*insert date*], and the [applicant]/[respondent] has thus not completed the steps by [*insert time and date*], then [he]/[she] shall send to the court and serve on the [respondent]/[applicant] a complete signed copy of [his]/[her] [Form E]/[Form E1] together with all relevant attachments and accompanying documents by no later than 4pm on the date [*insert*] days after the date on which [he]/[she] is personally served with this order. If that date falls on a date on which the courts are closed, then [he]/[she] shall send to the court and serve on the [respondent]/[applicant] [his]/[her] [Form E]/[Form E1] by 4pm on the next day that they are open.

First appointment documents

15. The [applicant]/[respondent] shall send to the court and serve on the [respondent]/[applicant]:
    a. a chronology;
    b. a statement of issues; and
    c. a questionnaire and request for further documents [if so advised] by [*insert time and date*].

Replies to questionnaire

16. The [applicant]/[respondent]/[both parties] shall send to the court and serve on the [respondent]/[applicant]/[other party] [his]/[her]/[their respective] replies to the other's questionnaire and request for further documents [as amended by the judge]/[save for just exceptions] by [*insert time and date*].

Schedule of deficiencies and supplemental questionnaire

17. The [applicant]/[respondent] shall send to the court and serve on the [respondent]/[applicant] a schedule of deficiencies and supplemental questionnaire and request for further documents [if so advised] by [*insert time and date*].

Replies to schedule of deficiencies and supplemental questionnaire

18. The [applicant]/[respondent]/[both parties] shall send to the court and serve on the [respondent]/[applicant]/[other party] [his]/[her]/[their] respective replies to the other's schedule of deficiencies and supplemental questionnaire and request for further documents [as amended by the judge]/[save for just exceptions] by [*insert time and date*].

Statements

19.

a. The [applicant]/[respondent]/[both parties] shall send to the court and serve on [the respondent]/[the applicant]/[the other party] a concise narrative statement [dealing with all of the relevant factors listed in [*insert the relevant section of the statute(s) or the statute(s)*]]/[dealing with [*insert*]]/[limited to dealing with [*insert*]] by [*insert time and date*].

b.   The [respondent]/[applicant] [shall]/[has permission, if so advised, to] send to the court and serve on the [applicant]/[respondent] a concise narrative statement in answer to that sent by the [applicant]/[respondent] [dealing with]/[limited to] the same issues by [*insert time and date*].

Statements dealing with conduct

20.

a.   In the event that the [applicant]/[respondent] continues to seek to advance a conduct case, [he]/[she] shall send to the court and serve on the [respondent]/[applicant] a concise statement [(limited to [*insert*] pages)] by [*insert time and date*], restricted to addressing the following issues:

    i.   what conduct exactly [he]/[she] is seeking to rely upon;

    ii.   the basis for [his]/[her] conduct allegations; and

    iii.   what effect this alleged conduct should have on the current [financial remedy] application.

b.   The [respondent]/[applicant] has permission to send to the court and serve on the [applicant]/[respondent] a statement in answer, if so advised, by [*insert time and date*].

Permission regarding other evidence

21.   The [applicant]/[respondent] has permission to send to the court and serve on the [respondent]/[applicant] [evidence]/[a letter]/[a statement] from [*insert*] if so advised [dealing with [*insert*]/limited to dealing with [*insert*]] by [*insert time and date*].

Evidence regarding mortgage raising capacity and housing needs

22.

a.   Each party shall serve on the other party copy particulars of properties they consider to be suitable to meet [their own] and/or [the child[ren] of the family's] housing needs, and the housing needs of [the other] and/or [the child[ren] of the family's], (limited to 5 of each) [by [*insert time and date*]]/[by [*insert time*] on the date [*insert*] weeks prior to the [financial dispute resolution appointment]/[final hearing]].

b.   Each party shall serve on the other party evidence of their mortgage raising capacity by [*insert time and date*]/by [*insert time*] on the date [*insert*] weeks prior to the [financial dispute resolution appointment]/[final hearing], [such evidence to be in the form of a certificate from a mortgage broker, indicating (i) the maximum mortgage that the broker believes [he]/[she] will be able to secure and (ii) the repayments that would be required on that mortgage on a repayment basis and on an interest only basis].

c.   Each party shall have permission to serve on the other party such evidence upon which they seek to rely in relation to the other's mortgage capacity within [*insert*] days of receipt of the other's evidence as to their own mortgage capacity.

Updating disclosure

23.   Each party shall serve on the other party their updating disclosure by [*insert time and date*]/by [*insert time*] on the date [*insert*] weeks prior to the [financial dispute resolution appointment]/[final hearing]. Updating disclosure means the disclosure of the following documents:-

a.   copies of all bank and building society statements relating to accounts in the category required by paragraph 2.3 of Form E, covering the period from the last statement which has been disclosed to the date of updating disclosure, or covering the period from the opening of the account to the date of updating disclosure for any such accounts which have come into existence since Form E;

b.   a copy of the most up to date statement or dividend counterfoil relating to investments in the category required by paragraph 2.4 of Form E, including in respect of any investments which have come into existence since Form E;

c.   a copy of an up to date surrender value for policies in the category required by paragraph 2.5 of Form E, including in respect of any policies which have come into existence since Form E;

d.   copies of documents evidencing the up to date amount due on liabilities in the category required by paragraph 2.9 or 2.10 of Form E, including in respect of any liabilities which have come into existence since Form E;

e.   copies of any business accounts which have become available since Form E for businesses in the category required by paragraph 2.11 of Form E, including in respect of any businesses which have come into existence since Form E, identifying the expected share of business profits from these accounts;

f.   copies of an up to date statement showing the Cash Equivalent of any pension rights (or value of any PPF rights) in the category required by paragraph 2.13 of Form E, including in respect of any pension rights or PPF rights which have come into existence since Form E;

g.   copies of all P60s and P11Ds received since Form E, and all pay slips received since the last P60;

h.   copies of all tax returns sent to HMRC and tax assessments since Form E; and

i.   copies of all documents evidencing all income received since Form E in the nature of dividends, interest, rental income, state benefits or otherwise.

[Important note: paras 24 – 51 cover all possible directions concerning expert evidence. The rules differ between children and non-children cases. In financial remedy proceedings any application which relates 'wholly or mainly to the maintenance of a minor' will be classified as children proceedings – see FPR 2010 rule 25.2(1). For convenience these are referred to here as Schedule 1 proceedings. Paras 22 – 27 and 34 – 44 relate to non-Schedule 1 proceedings and paras 28 – 33 and 45 – 49 relate to Schedule 1 proceedings]

Valuation of land and real property [for non-Schedule 1 cases]

Order for one party to instruct an expert **[where valuer has been identified]**
24.

a. The [applicant]/[respondent] shall instruct [*insert expert*] as an expert to provide a [valuation report]/[market appraisal] in respect of the property at [*insert address and postcode*].

b. The letter of instruction shall be drafted by the [applicant]/[respondent] by [*insert time and date*].

c. The letter of instruction [and [*insert any other documents*]] shall be sent to the expert by [*insert time and date*].

d. The report shall be sent to the court (in both hardcopy and electronic form) and served on the [applicant]/[respondent] by [*insert time and date*].

e. The [applicant]/[respondent] shall disclose the report to the [respondent]/[applicant] by [*insert time and date*].

f. The costs charged by the expert for preparing the report shall be met by the [applicant]/[respondent]/[parties equally] in the first instance.

g. [Any questions shall be put to the expert by no later than 10 days after receipt of the report (in accordance with FPR 2010, rule 25.10)].

h. [The expert shall respond to those questions by [*insert time and date*]].

i. [The costs charged by the expert for answering those questions shall be met by the [applicant]/[respondent]/[parties equally]/[party raising them] in the first instance].

j. [Save as is expressly ordered by the court, the [applicant's]/ [respondent's] expert's]/[both experts'] written report(s) shall be admissible without the attendance at court of the expert(s). However, [the applicant's expert]/[the respondent's expert]/[both experts] shall attend the final hearing to give oral evidence, unless agreement about the opinions given by the expert(s) is reached by [*insert time and date*]].

Order for one party to instruct an expert **[where valuer has not been identified]**
25.

a. The [applicant]/[respondent] shall instruct an [estate agent]/[chartered surveyor]/[appropriate expert] to provide a [valuation report]/[market appraisal] in respect of the property at [*insert address and postcode*].

b. The letter of instruction shall be drafted by the [applicant]/[respondent] by [*insert time and date*].

c. The letter of instruction [and [*insert any other documents*]] shall be sent to the expert by [*insert time and date*].

d. The report shall be sent to the court (in both hardcopy and electronic form) and served on the [applicant]/[respondent] by [*insert time and date*].

e. The [applicant]/[respondent] shall disclose the report to the [respondent]/[applicant] by [*insert time and date*].

f. The costs charged by the expert for preparing the report shall be met by the [applicant]/[respondent]/[parties equally] in the first instance.

g. [Any questions shall be put to the expert by no later than 10 days after receipt of the report (in accordance with FPR 2010, rule 25.10)].

h. [The expert shall respond to those questions by [*insert time and date*]].

i. [The costs charged by the expert for answering those questions shall be met by the [applicant]/[respondent]/[parties equally]/[party raising them] in the first instance].

j. [Save as is expressly ordered by the court, the [applicant's]/ [respondent's] expert's]/[both experts'] written report(s) shall be admissible without the attendance at court of the expert. However, [the applicant's expert]/[the respondent's expert]/[both experts] shall attend the final hearing to give oral evidence, unless agreement about the opinions given by the expert(s) is reached by [*insert time and date*]].

Order for individually instructed experts to exchange reports/meet
26.

a. The [applicant]/[the respondent]/[the parties] shall [each] disclose [his]/[her]/[their] expert's [valuation report]/[market appraisal to [the respondent's]/[the applicant's]/[the other's] expert by [*insert time and date*].

b. There shall be a meeting between the [applicant's]/[respondent's] expert and [respondent's]/[applicant's] expert by [*insert time and date*] to discuss:

   i.   the reasons for disagreement on any expert question and what, if any, action needs to be taken to resolve any outstanding disagreement or question;

   ii. what existing evidence or additional evidence needs to be obtained to assist the Court to determine the issues;

   iii. etc.

At least five business days prior to this meeting, [*insert nominated professional in accordance with FPR PD 25E, para 3.1*] shall formulate an agenda including a list of questions for consideration at the meeting, and at least two business days prior to this meeting, [*insert nominated professional in accordance with FPR PD 25E, para 3.1]* shall send the agenda to both experts].

c. A statement of agreement and disagreement shall be prepared by the experts following their meeting and shall be served on both parties not later than 5 business days after the meeting has taken place.

d. [Save is as expressly ordered by the court, the [applicant's]/ [respondent's] expert's]/[both experts'] written report(s) shall be admissible without the attendance at court of the expert(s). However, [the applicant's expert]/[the respondent's expert]/[both experts] shall attend the final hearing to give oral evidence, unless agreement about the opinions given by the expert(s) is reached by [*insert time and date*]].

Order to instruct a single joint expert [where valuer has been identified]

27.

The parties shall jointly instruct [*insert expert*] as a single joint expert to provide a [valuation report]/[market appraisal] in respect of the property at [*insert address and postcode*], in accordance with the attached letter of instruction, and the following consequential provisions shall apply:

a. The letter of instruction [and [*insert any other documents*]] shall be sent to the expert by [*insert time and date*].

b. The report shall be sent to the court (in both hardcopy and electronic format) and served on the parties simultaneously by [*insert time and date*].

c. The costs charged by the expert for preparing the report shall be met by the [applicant]/[respondent]/[parties equally] in the first instance.

d. [Any questions shall be put to the expert by no later than 10 days after receipt of the report (in accordance with FPR 2010, rule 25.10)].

e. [The expert shall respond to those questions by [*insert time and date*]].

f. [The costs charged by the expert for answering those questions shall be met by the [applicant]/[respondent]/[parties equally]/[party raising them] in the first instance].

g. [Save as is expressly ordered by the court, the expert's written report shall be admissible without the attendance at court of the expert. However, the expert shall attend the final hearing to give oral evidence, unless agreement about the opinions given by the expert is reached by [*insert time and date*]].

OR

The parties [shall] jointly instruct [*insert expert*] as a single joint expert to provide a [valuation report]/[market appraisal] in respect of the property at [*insert address and postcode*], and the following consequential provisions shall apply:

[a.   The letter of instruction shall be drafted by the [applicant]/[respondent] and agreed with the [respondent]/[applicant] by [*insert time and date*], or determined by the court in default of agreement.

b.   The letter of instruction [and [*insert any other documents*]] shall be sent to the expert by [*insert time and date*];

c.   The report shall be sent to the court (in both hardcopy and electronic format) and served on the parties simultaneously by [*insert time and date*].

d.   The costs charged by the expert for preparing the report shall be met by the [applicant]/[respondent]/[parties equally] in the first instance.

e.   [Any questions shall be put to the expert by no later than 10 days after receipt of the report (in accordance with FPR 2010, rule 25.10)].

f.   [The expert shall respond to those questions by [*insert time and date*]].

g.   [The costs charged by the expert for answering those questions shall be met by the [applicant]/[respondent]/[parties equally]/[party raising them] in the first instance].

h.   [Save as is expressly ordered by the court, the expert's written report shall be admissible without the attendance at court of the expert. However, the expert shall attend the final hearing to give oral evidence, unless agreement about the opinions given by the expert is reached by [*insert time and date*]].

Order to instruct a single joint expert [where valuer has not been identified]

28.   The value of the property at [*insert address and postcode*] shall be agreed if possible. In default of agreement by [*insert time and date*], the parties shall jointly instruct an [estate agent]/[chartered surveyor]/[appropriate expert] to act as a single joint expert and to provide a [valuation report]/[market appraisal] in respect of the property at [*insert address and postcode*] and the following consequential provisions shall apply:

a.   [The parties shall agree the identity of the single joint expert by [*insert time and date*]. If the parties cannot agree the identity of the single joint expert, [the President of the Royal Institution of Chartered Surveyors shall nominate an [estate agent]/[surveyor]]/[the [applicant]/[respondent] shall provide the [respondent]/[applicant] with a list of three appropriate experts by [*insert date and time*], and the [respondent]/[applicant] shall select one of the experts from the list by [*insert time and date*].

b.   The letter of instruction shall be drafted by the [applicant]/[respondent] and agreed with the [respondent]/[applicant] by [*insert time and date*], or determined by the court in default of agreement.

c.   The letter of instruction [and [*insert any other documents*]] shall be sent to the expert by [*insert time and date*].

d.   The report shall be sent to the court (in both hardcopy and electronic format) and served on the parties simultaneously by [*insert time and date*].

e. The costs charged by the expert for preparing the report shall be met by the [applicant]/[respondent]/[parties equally] in the first instance.

f. [Any questions shall be put to the expert by no later than 10 days after receipt of the report (in accordance with FPR 2010, rule 25.10)].

g. [The expert shall respond to those questions by [*insert time and date*]].

h. [The costs charged by the expert for answering those questions shall be met by the [applicant]/[respondent]/[parties equally]/[party raising them] in the first instance].

i. [Save as is expressly ordered by the court, the expert's written report shall be admissible without the attendance at court of the expert. However, the expert shall attend the final hearing to give oral evidence, unless agreement about the opinions given by the expert is reached by [*insert time and date*]].

Other

29. [The valuation of the property at [*insert address and postcode*] prepared by [*insert name*] and dated [*insert date*] shall be the valuation to be used for the purposes of the [financial dispute resolution appointment]/[final hearing]/[as appropriate.]

OR

[The parties have]/[The applicant has]/[The respondent has] permission to rely on the valuation of the property at [*insert address and postcode*] prepared by [*insert name*] and dated [*insert date*], and this shall be the valuation to be used, for the purposes of the [financial dispute resolution appointment]/[final hearing]/[as appropriate.]

Valuation of land and real property [for Schedule 1 cases]

Permission to one party to instruct an expert [where valuer has been identified]

30.

a. The [applicant]/[respondent] has permission to instruct [*insert expert*] as an expert to provide a [valuation report]/[market appraisal] in respect of the property at [*insert address and postcode*].

b. The question(s) which the [applicant]/[respondent] shall ask of [*insert expert*] shall be as follows:

  i. set out the estimated amount which a willing buyer could be expected to pay a willing seller for the property in an arms-length transaction after proper marketing of the property on the open market, where both the buyer and the seller have acted knowledgably, prudently and without compulsion;

  ii. etc

c. The letter of instruction shall be drafted by the [applicant]/[respondent] by [*insert time and date*].

d.   The letter of instruction [and [*insert any other documents*]] shall be sent to the expert by [*insert time and date*].

e.   The report shall be sent to the court (in both hardcopy and electronic form) and served on the [applicant]/[respondent] by [*insert time and date*].

f.   The [applicant]/[respondent] shall disclose the report to the [respondent]/[applicant] by [*insert time and date*].

g.   The costs charged by the expert for preparing the report shall be met by the [applicant]/[respondent]/[parties equally] in the first instance.

h.   [Any questions shall be put to the expert by no later than 10 days after receipt of the report (in accordance with FPR 2010, rule 25.10)].

i.   [The expert shall respond to those questions by [*insert time and date*]].

j.   [The costs charged by the expert for answering those questions shall be met by the [applicant]/[respondent]/[parties equally]/[party raising them] in the first instance].

k.   [Save as is expressly ordered by the court, the [applicant's]/ [respondent's] expert's]/[both experts'] written report(s) shall be admissible without the attendance at court of the expert(s). However, [the applicant's expert]/[the respondent's expert]/[both experts] shall attend the final hearing to give oral evidence, unless agreement about the opinions given by the expert(s) is reached by [*insert time and date*]].

Permission to one party to instruct an expert [where valuer has not been identified]
31.

a.   The [applicant]/[respondent] has permission to instruct an [estate agent]/[chartered surveyor]/[appropriate expert] to provide a [valuation report]/[market appraisal] in respect of the property at [insert address and postcode]

b.   The question(s) which the [applicant]/[respondent] shall ask of the expert shall be as follows:

   i.   set out the estimated amount which a willing buyer could be expected to pay a willing seller for the property in an arms-length transaction after proper marketing of the property on the open market, where both the buyer and the seller have acted knowledgably, prudently and without compulsion;

   ii.   etc

c.   The letter of instruction shall be drafted by the [applicant]/[respondent] by [*insert time and date*].

d.   The letter of instruction [and [*insert any other documents*]] shall be sent to the expert by [*insert time and date*].

e.   The report shall be sent to the court (in both hardcopy and electronic form) and served on the [applicant]/[respondent] by [*insert time and date*].

f. The [applicant]/[respondent] shall disclose the report to the [respondent]/[applicant] by [*insert time and date*].

g. The costs charged by the expert for preparing the report shall be met by the [applicant]/[respondent]/[parties equally] in the first instance.

h. [Any questions shall be put to the expert by no later than 10 days after receipt of the report (in accordance with FPR 2010, rule 25.10)].

i. [The expert shall respond to those questions by [*insert time and date*]].

j. [The costs charged by the expert for answering those questions shall be met by the [applicant]/[respondent]/[parties equally]/[party raising them] in the first instance].

k. [Save as is expressly ordered by the court, the [applicant's]/ [respondent's] expert's]/[both experts'] written report(s) shall be admissible without the attendance at court of the expert(s). However, [the applicant's expert]/[the respondent's expert]/[both experts] shall attend the final hearing to give oral evidence, unless agreement about the opinions given by the expert(s) is reached by [*insert time and date*]].

Order for individually instructed experts to exchange reports/meet

32.

a. [The applicant]/[the respondent]/[the parties] shall [each] disclose [his]/[her]/[their] expert's [valuation report]/[market appraisal to [the respondent's]/[the applicant's]/[the other's] expert by [*insert time and date*].

b. There shall be a meeting between the [applicant's]/[respondent's] expert and [respondent's]/[applicant's] expert by [*insert time and date*] to discuss:

　　i. the reasons for disagreement on any expert question and what, if any, action needs to be taken to resolve any outstanding disagreement or question;

　　ii. what existing evidence or additional evidence needs to be obtained to assist the Court to determine the issues;

　　iii. etc.

At least five business days prior to this meeting, [*insert nominated professional in accordance with FPR PD 25E, para 3.1*] shall formulate an agenda including a list of questions for consideration at the meeting, and at least two business days prior to this meeting, [*insert nominated professional in accordance with FPR PD 25E, para 3.1*] shall send the agenda to both experts].

c. A statement of agreement and disagreement shall be prepared by the experts following their meeting and shall be served on both parties not later than 5 business days after the meeting has taken place.

d. [Save as is expressly ordered by the court, the [applicant's]/ [respondent's] expert's]/[both experts'] written report(s) shall be admissible without the attendance at court of the expert(s). However, [the applicant's expert]/[the respondent's expert]/[both experts] shall attend the final hearing to give oral evidence, unless agreement about the opinions given by the expert(s) is reached by [*insert time and date*]].

Permission to instruct a single joint expert [where valuer has been identified]

33.   The parties have permission to jointly instruct [*insert expert*] as a single joint expert to provide a [valuation report]/[market appraisal] in respect of the property at [insert address and postcode], in accordance with the attached letter of instruction, and the following consequential provisions shall apply:

    a.   The question(s) which the parties shall ask of the expert shall be as follows:

       i.   set out the estimated amount which a willing buyer could be expected to pay a willing seller for the property in an arms-length transaction after proper marketing of the property on the open market, where both the buyer and the seller have acted knowledgably, prudently and without compulsion; and

       ii.   etc

    b.   The letter of instruction [and [*insert any other documents*]] shall be sent to the expert by [*insert time and date*].

    c.   The report shall be sent to the court (in both hardcopy and electronic format) and served on the parties simultaneously by [*insert time and date*].

    d.   The costs charged by the expert for preparing the report shall be met by the [applicant]/[respondent]/[parties equally] in the first instance.

    e.   [Any questions shall be put to the expert by no later than 10 days after receipt of the report (in accordance with FPR 2010, rule 25.10)].

    f.   [The expert shall respond to those questions by [*insert time and date*]].

    g.   [The costs charged by the expert for answering those questions shall be met by the [applicant]/[respondent]/[parties equally]/[party raising them] in the first instance].

    h.   [Save as is expressly ordered by the court, the expert's written report shall be admissible without the attendance at court of the expert. However, the expert shall attend the final hearing to give oral evidence, unless agreement about the opinions given by the expert is reached by [*insert time and date*]].

OR

The parties have permission to jointly instruct [*insert expert*] as a single joint expert to provide a [valuation report]/[market appraisal] in respect of the property at [*insert address and postcode*], and the following consequential provisions shall apply:

    a.   The question(s) which the parties shall ask of the expert shall be as follows:

    i.   set out the estimated amount which a willing buyer could be expected to pay a willing seller for the property in an arms-length transaction after proper marketing of the property on the open market, where both the buyer and the seller have acted knowledgably, prudently and without compulsion; and

    ii.   etc.

b.   The letter of instruction shall be drafted by the [applicant]/[respondent] and agreed with the [respondent]/[applicant] by [*insert time and date*], or determined by the court in default of agreement.

c.   The letter of instruction [and [*insert any other documents*]] shall be sent to the expert by [*insert time and date*];

d.   The report shall be sent to the court (in both hardcopy and electronic format) and served on the parties simultaneously by [*insert time and date*].

e.   The costs charged by the expert for preparing the report shall be met by the [applicant]/[respondent]/[parties equally] in the first instance.

f.   [Any questions shall be put to the expert by no later than 10 days after receipt of the report (in accordance with FPR 2010, rule 25.10)].

g.   [The expert shall respond to those questions by [*insert time and date*]].

h.   [The costs charged by the expert for answering those questions shall be met by the [applicant]/[respondent]/[parties equally]/[party raising them] in the first instance].

i.   [Save as is expressly ordered by the court, the expert's written report shall be admissible without the attendance at court of the expert. However, the expert shall attend the final hearing to give oral evidence, unless agreement about the opinions given by the expert is reached by [*insert time and date*]].

Permission to instruct a single joint expert [where valuer has not been identified]

34.   The value of the property at [*insert address and postcode*] shall be agreed if possible. In default of agreement by [*insert time and date*], the parties have permission to jointly instruct an [estate agent]/[chartered surveyor]/[appropriate expert] to act as a single joint expert and to provide a [valuation report]/[market appraisal] in respect of the property at [*insert address and postcode*] the following consequential provisions shall apply:

a.   The question(s) which the parties shall ask of the expert shall be as follows:

    i.   set out the estimated amount which a willing buyer could be expected to pay a willing seller for the property in an arms-length transaction after proper marketing of the property on the open market, where both the buyer and the seller have acted knowledgably, prudently and without compulsion;

    ii.   etc

b.   [The parties shall agree the identity of the single joint expert by [*insert time and date*]. If the parties cannot agree the identity of the single joint expert, [the President of the Royal Institution of Chartered Surveyors shall nominate an [estate agent]/[surveyor]/[the [applicant]/ [respondent] shall provide the [respondent]/[applicant] with a list of three appropriate experts by [*insert date and time*], and the [respondent]/[applicant] shall select one of the experts from the list by [*insert time and date*]].

c.   The letter of instruction shall be drafted by the [applicant]/[respondent] and agreed with the [respondent]/[applicant] by [*insert time and date*], or determined by the court in default of agreement.

d.   The letter of instruction [and [*insert any other documents*]] shall be sent to the expert by [*insert time and date*].

e.   The report shall be sent to the court (in both hardcopy and electronic format) and served on the parties simultaneously by [*insert time and date*].

f.   The costs charged by the expert for preparing the report shall be met by the [applicant]/[respondent]/[parties equally] in the first instance.

g.   [Any questions shall be put to the expert by no later than 10 days after receipt of the report (in accordance with FPR 2010, rule 25.10)].

h.   [The expert shall respond to those questions by [*insert time and date*]].

i.   [The costs charged by the expert for answering those questions shall be met by the [applicant]/[respondent]/[parties equally]/[party raising them] in the first instance].

j.   [Save as is expressly ordered by the court, the expert's written report shall be admissible without the attendance at court of the expert. However, the expert shall attend the final hearing to give oral evidence, unless agreement about the opinions given by the expert is reached by [*insert time and date*]].

Other

35.   [The valuation of the property at [*insert address and postcode*] prepared by [*insert name*] and dated [*insert date*] shall be the valuation to be used for the purposes of the [financial dispute resolution appointment]/[final hearing]/[as appropriate.]]/[The parties have]/[The applicant has]/[The respondent has] permission to rely on the valuation of the property at [insert address and postcode] prepared by [*insert name*] and dated [*insert date*], and this shall be the valuation to be used, for the purposes of the [financial dispute resolution appointment]/[final hearing]/[as appropriate.]]

Updating property valuations for final hearing

36.   In relation to any real property valued prior to the financial dispute resolution appointment and in relation to which either party wishes to assert that the value has significantly changed since that valuation was undertaken, the parties shall instruct (by way of an agreed joint letter of instruction) the single joint expert to express a view on whether there has been any change in value since the initial report and, if so, what is the current value. The costs of this exercise shall be met by the parties equally in the first instance.

Other expert reports – pensions report [for non-Schedule 1 cases]

Pensions information

37. The [pension provider]/[pension scheme] shall [complete, send to the court and serve on the parties a copy of the Form P1 (pension inquiry form)]/ [provide the information required by Regulations 2, 3 and 4 of the Pensions on Divorce etc (Provision of Information Regulations) 2000] by [*insert date and time*].

Order for one party to instruct an expert [*where expert has been identified*]

38.

    a.   The [applicant]/[respondent] shall instruct [insert actuary/pensions expert] as an expert to provide a report, addressing:

        i.   the most cost-effective way to divide the pension provision available to [the applicant]/[the respondent]/[both parties] between the parties so as to provide equality of pension income [now]/[when the [applicant]/[respondent] reaches the age of 60, 65 or as appropriate];

        ii.   an estimate of the pension income that would be receivable by the [applicant]/[respondent] in each of the scenarios in paragraph (ii) above;

        iii.   the most cost-effective way to divide the pension provision available to [the applicant]/[the respondent]/[both parties] between the parties so as to achieve equality of [capital value]/[CE] of those pensions;

        iv.   etc

    b.   The letter of instruction shall be drafted by the [applicant]/[respondent] by [*insert time and date*].

    c.   The letter of instruction [and [*insert any other documents*]] shall be sent to the expert by [*insert time and date*].

    d.   The report shall be sent to the court (in both hardcopy and electronic form) and served on the [applicant]/[respondent] by [*insert time and date*].

    e.   The [applicant]/[respondent] shall disclose the report to the [respondent]/[applicant] by [*insert time and date*].

    f.   The costs charged by the expert for preparing the report shall be met by the [applicant]/[respondent]/[parties equally] in the first instance.

    g.   [Any questions shall be put to the expert by no later than 10 days after receipt of the report (in accordance with FPR 2010, rule 25.10)].

    h.   [The expert shall respond to those questions by [*insert time and date*]].

    i.   [The costs charged by the expert for answering those questions shall be met by the [applicant]/[respondent]/[parties equally]/[party raising them] in the first instance].

    j.   [Save as is expressly ordered by the court, the [applicant's]/ [respondent's] expert's]/[both experts'] written report(s) shall be admissible without the attendance at court of the expert(s). However, [the applicant's expert]/[the respondent's expert]/[both experts] shall attend the final hearing to give oral evidence, unless agreement about the opinions given by the expert(s) is reached by [*insert time and date*]].

Order for one party to instruct an expert [where expert has not been identified]
39.

a. The [applicant]/[respondent] shall instruct an [actuary]/[pensions expert]/[appropriate expert] to provide a report, addressing:

    i. the most cost-effective way to divide the pension provision available to [the applicant]/[the respondent]/[both parties] between the parties so as to provide equality of pension income [now]/[when the [applicant]/[respondent] reaches the age of 60, 65 or as appropriate];

    ii. an estimate of the pension income that would be receivable by the [applicant]/[respondent] in each of the scenarios in paragraph (ii) above;

    iii. the most cost-effective way to divide the pension provision available to [the applicant]/[the respondent]/[both parties] between the parties so as to achieve equality of [capital value]/[CE] of those pensions;

    iv. etc

b. The letter of instruction shall be drafted by the [applicant]/[respondent] by [*insert time and date*].

c. The letter of instruction [and [*insert any other documents*]] shall be sent to the expert by [*insert time and date*].

d. The report shall be sent to the court (in both hardcopy and electronic form) and served on the [applicant]/[respondent] by [*insert time and date*].

e. The [applicant]/[respondent] shall disclose the report to the [respondent]/[applicant] by [*insert time and date*].

f. The costs charged by the expert for preparing the report shall be met by the [applicant]/[respondent]/[parties equally] in the first instance.

g. [Any questions shall be put to the expert by no later than 10 days after receipt of the report (in accordance with FPR 2010, rule 25.10)].

h. [The expert shall respond to those questions by [*insert time and date*]].

i. [The costs charged by the expert for answering those questions shall be met by the [applicant]/[respondent]/[parties equally]/[party raising them] in the first instance].

j. [Save as is expressly ordered by the court, the [applicant's]/ [respondent's] expert's]/[both experts'] written report(s) shall be admissible without the attendance at court of the expert(s). However, [the applicant's expert]/[the respondent's expert]/[both experts] shall attend the final hearing to give oral evidence, unless agreement about the opinions given by the expert(s) is reached by [*insert time and date*]].

Order for individually instructed experts to exchange reports/meet

40.

    a.   [The applicant]/[the respondent]/[the parties] shall [each] disclose [his]/[her]/[their] expert's report to [the respondent's]/[the applicant's]/[the other's] expert by [*insert time and date*].

    b.   There shall be a meeting between the [applicant's]/[respondent's] expert and [respondent's]/[applicant's] expert by [*insert time and date*] to discuss:

        i.   the reasons for disagreement on any expert question and what, if any, action needs to be taken to resolve any outstanding disagreement or question;

        ii.   what existing evidence or additional evidence needs to be obtained to assist the Court to determine the issues;

        iii.   etc.

    At least five business days prior to this meeting, [*insert nominated professional in accordance with FPR PD 25E, para 3.1*] shall formulate an agenda including a list of questions for consideration at the meeting, and at least two business days prior to this meeting, [*insert nominated professional in accordance with FPR PD 25E, para 3.1*] shall send the agenda to both experts].

    c.   A statement of agreement and disagreement shall be prepared by the experts following their meeting and shall be served on both parties not later than 5 business days after the meeting has taken place.

    d.   [Save as is expressly ordered by the court, the [applicant's]/[respondent's] expert's]/[both experts'] written report(s) shall be admissible without the attendance at court of the expert(s). However, [the applicant's expert]/[the respondent's expert]/[both experts] shall attend the final hearing to give oral evidence, unless agreement about the opinions given by the expert(s) is reached by [*insert time and date*]].

Order to instruct a single joint expert [where expert has been identified]

41.

    a.   The parties shall jointly instruct [*insert actuary/pensions expert*] as a single joint expert to provide a report in accordance with the attached letter of instruction, addressing

        i.   the most cost-effective way to divide the pension provision available to [the applicant]/[the respondent]/[both parties] between the parties so as to provide equality of pension income [now]/[when the [applicant]/[respondent] reaches the age of 60, 65 or as appropriate];

        ii.   an estimate of the pension income that would be receivable by the [applicant]/[respondent] in each of the scenarios in paragraph (ii) above;

  iii. the most cost-effective way to divide the pension provision available to [the applicant]/[the respondent]/[both parties] between the parties so as to achieve equality of [capital value]/[CE] of those pensions;

  iv. etc

b. The letter of instruction [and [*insert any other documents*]] shall be sent to the expert by [*insert time and date*].

c. The report shall be sent to the court (in both hardcopy and electronic format) and served on the parties simultaneously by [*insert time and date*].

d. The costs charged by the expert for preparing the report shall be met by the [applicant]/[respondent]/[parties equally] in the first instance.

e. [Any questions shall be put to the expert by no later than 10 days after receipt of the report (in accordance with FPR 2010, rule 25.10)].

f. [The expert shall respond to those questions by [*insert time and date*]].

g. [The costs charged by the expert for answering those questions shall be met by the [applicant]/[respondent]/[parties equally]/[party raising them] in the first instance].

h. [Save as is expressly ordered by the court, the expert's written report shall be admissible without the attendance at court of the expert. However, the expert shall attend the final hearing to give oral evidence, unless agreement about the opinions given by the expert is reached by [*insert time and date*]].

OR

The parties shall jointly instruct [*insert actuary/pensions expert*] as a single joint expert to provide a report, addressing the following matters:

a. the most cost-effective way to divide the pension provision available to [the applicant]/[the respondent]/[both parties] between the parties so as to provide equality of pension income [now]/[when the [applicant]/ [respondent] reaches the age of 60, 65 or as appropriate];

b. an estimate of the pension income that would be receivable by the [applicant]/[respondent] in each of the scenarios in paragraph (a) above;

c. the most cost-effective way to divide the pension provision available to [the applicant]/[the respondent]/[both parties] between the parties so as to achieve equality of [capital value]/[CETV] of those pensions;

d. ...

and the following consequential provisions shall apply:

e. The letter of instruction shall be drafted by the [applicant]/[respondent] and agreed with the [respondent]/[applicant] by [*insert time and date*], or determined by the court in default of agreement.

f. The letter of instruction [and [*insert any other documents*]] shall be sent to the expert by [*insert time and date*].

g.   The report shall be sent to the court (in both hardcopy and electronic format) and served on the parties simultaneously by [*insert time and date*].

h.   The costs charged by the expert for preparing the report shall be met by the [applicant]/[respondent]/[parties equally] in the first instance.

i.   [Any questions shall be put to the expert by no later than 10 days after receipt of the report (in accordance with FPR 2010, rule 25.10)].

j.   [The expert shall respond to those questions by [*insert time and date*]].

k.   [The costs charged by the expert for answering those questions shall be met by the [applicant]/[respondent]/[parties equally]/[party raising them] in the first instance].

l.   [Save as is expressly ordered by the court, the expert's written report shall be admissible without the attendance at court of the expert. However, the expert shall attend the final hearing to give oral evidence, unless agreement about the opinions given by the expert is reached by [*insert time and date*]].

Order to instruct a single joint expert [where expert has not been identified]

42.   The parties shall jointly instruct an [actuary]/[pensions expert]/[appropriate expert] to act as a single joint expert and to provide a report, addressing the following matters:

a.   the most cost-effective way to divide the pension provision available to [the applicant]/[the respondent]/[both parties] between the parties so as to provide equality of pension income [now]/[when the [applicant]/[respondent] reaches the age of 60, 65 or as appropriate];

b.   an estimate of the pension income that would be receivable by the [applicant]/[respondent] in each of the scenarios in paragraph (a) above;

c.   the most cost-effective way to divide the pension provision available to [the applicant]/[the respondent]/[both parties] between the parties so as to achieve equality of [capital value]/[CE] of those pensions;

d.   ...

and the following consequential provisions shall apply:

e.   The [applicant]/[respondent] shall provide the [respondent]/[applicant] with a list of three appropriate experts by [*insert date and time*].

f.   The [respondent]/[applicant] shall select one of the experts from the list by [*insert time and date*].

g.   The letter of instruction shall be drafted by the [applicant]/[respondent] and agreed with the [respondent]/[applicant] by [*insert time and date*], or determined by the court in default of agreement.

h.   The letter of instruction [and [*insert any other documents*]] shall be sent to the expert by [*insert time and date*].

i.   The report shall be sent to the court (in both hardcopy and electronic form) and served on the parties simultaneously by [*insert time and date*].

j.   The costs charged by the expert for preparing the report shall be met by the [applicant]/[respondent]/[parties equally] in the first instance.

k.   [Any questions shall be put to the expert by no later than 10 days after receipt of the report (in accordance with FPR 2010, rule 25.10)].

l.   [The expert shall respond to those questions by [*insert time and date*]].

m.   [The costs charged by the expert for answering those questions shall be met by the [applicant]/[respondent]/[parties equally]/[party raising them] in the first instance].

n.   [Save as is expressly ordered by the court, the expert's written report shall be admissible without the attendance at court of the expert. However, the expert shall attend the final hearing to give oral evidence, unless agreement about the opinions given by the expert is reached by [*insert time and date*]].

Other expert reports – tax report [for non-Schedule 1 cases]

Order to one party to instruct an expert [where expert has been identified]

43.

a.   The [applicant]/[respondent] shall instruct [*insert expert*] as an expert to provide a report, addressing the tax liabilities, if any, and date(s) for payment, which would arise whether in the UK or elsewhere in each of the following scenarios:

    i.   the disposal by [the applicant]/[the respondent] of [his]/[her] interest in [*insert property*];

    ii.   the transfer by [the applicant]/[the respondent] of [his]/[her] interest in [*insert property*] to [the respondent]/[the applicant];

    iii.   the settling by [the applicant]/[the respondent] of [his]/[her] interest in [*insert property*] on [the respondent]/[the applicant];

    iv.   the disposal by either party of any of their other assets, including the [applicant's]/[respondent's] offshore assets;

    v.   the transfer by either party of any of their other assets to the other, including the [applicant's]/[respondent's] offshore assets;

    vi.   the repatriation of any of the [applicant's]/[respondent's] offshore assets;

    vii.   the possible methods of mitigating the amount of tax due in any of the above scenarios, and the likely effects of such mitigation on the amounts of tax due;

    viii.   etc

b.   The letter of instruction shall be drafted by the [applicant]/[respondent] by [*insert time and date*].

c.   The letter of instruction [and [*insert any other documents*]] shall be sent to the expert by [*insert time and date*].

d.   The report shall be sent to the court (in both hardcopy and electronic form) and served on the [applicant]/[respondent] by [*insert time and date*].

e.   The [applicant]/[respondent] shall disclose the report to the [respondent]/[applicant] by [*insert time and date*].

f.   The costs charged by the expert for preparing the report shall be met by the [applicant]/[respondent]/[parties equally] in the first instance.

g.   The [applicant]/[respondent]/[both parties] shall provide the expert with any reasonable assistance requested in compiling the report, including providing any necessary information and documentation within a reasonable timeframe of the request.

h.   [Any questions shall be put to the expert by no later than 10 days after receipt of the report (in accordance with FPR 2010, rule 25.10)].

i.   [The expert shall respond to those questions by [*insert time and date*]].

j.   [The costs charged by the expert for answering those questions shall be met by the [applicant]/[respondent]/[parties equally]/[party raising them] in the first instance].

k.   [Save as is expressly ordered by the court, the [applicant's]/[respondent's] expert's]/[both experts'] written report(s) shall be admissible without the attendance at court of the expert(s). However, [the applicant's expert]/[the respondent's expert]/[both experts] shall attend the final hearing to give oral evidence, unless agreement about the opinions given by the expert(s) is reached by [*insert time and date*]].

Order to one party to instruct an expert **[where expert has not been identified]**

44.

a.   The [applicant]/[respondent] shall instruct an [accountant]/[appropriate expert] to provide a report, addressing the tax liabilities, if any, and date(s) for payment, which would arise whether in the UK or elsewhere in each of the following scenarios:

    i.   the disposal by [the applicant]/[the respondent] of [his]/[her] interest in [*insert property*];

    ii.   the transfer by [the applicant]/[the respondent] of [his]/[her] interest in [*insert property*] to [the respondent]/[the applicant];

    iii.   the settling by [the applicant]/[the respondent] of [his]/[her] interest in [*insert property*] on [the respondent]/[the applicant];

    iv.   the disposal by either party of any of their other assets, including the [applicant's]/[respondent's] offshore assets;

    v.   the transfer by either party of any of their other assets to the other, including the [applicant's]/[respondent's] offshore assets;

    vi.   the repatriation of any of the [applicant's]/[respondent's] offshore assets;

vii.   the possible methods of mitigating the amount of tax due in any of the above scenarios, and the likely effects of such mitigation on the amounts of tax due;

viii.   etc

b.   The letter of instruction shall be drafted by the [applicant]/[respondent] by [*insert time and date*].

c.   The letter of instruction [and [*insert any other documents*]] shall be sent to the expert by [*insert time and date*].

d.   The report shall be sent to the court (in both hardcopy and electronic form) and served on the [applicant]/[respondent] by [*insert time and date*].

e.   The [applicant]/[respondent] shall disclose the report to the [respondent]/[applicant] by [insert time and date].

f.   The costs charged by the expert for preparing the report shall be met by the [applicant]/[respondent]/[parties equally] in the first instance.

g.   The [applicant]/[respondent]/[both parties] shall provide the expert with any reasonable assistance requested in compiling the report, including providing any necessary information and documentation within a reasonable timeframe of the request.

h.   [Any questions shall be put to the expert by no later than 10 days after receipt of the report (in accordance with FPR 2010, rule 25.10)].

i.   [The expert shall respond to those questions by [*insert time and date*]].

j.   [The costs charged by the expert for answering those questions shall be met by the [applicant]/[respondent]/[parties equally]/[party raising them] in the first instance].

k.   [Save as is expressly ordered by the court, the [applicant's]/ [respondent's] expert's]/[both experts'] written report(s) shall be admissible without the attendance at court of the expert(s). However, [the applicant's expert]/[the respondent's expert]/[both experts] shall attend the final hearing to give oral evidence, unless agreement about the opinions given by the expert(s) is reached by [*insert time and date*]].

Order for individually instructed experts to exchange reports/meet

45.

a.   [The applicant]/[the respondent]/[the parties] shall [each] disclose [his]/[her]/[their] expert's [valuation report]/[market appraisal to [the respondent's]/[the applicant's]/[the other's] expert by [*insert time and date*].

b.   There shall be a meeting between the [applicant's]/[respondent's] expert and [respondent's]/[applicant's] expert by [*insert time and date*] to discuss:

i.   the reasons for disagreement on any expert question and what, if any, action needs to be taken to resolve any outstanding disagreement or question;

ii. what existing evidence or additional evidence needs to be obtained to assist the Court to determine the issues;

iii. etc.

At least five business days prior to this meeting, [*insert nominated professional in accordance with FPR PD 25E, para 3.1*] shall formulate an agenda including a list of questions for consideration at the meeting, and at least two business days prior to this meeting, [*insert nominated professional in accordance with FPR PD 25E, para 3.1*] shall send the agenda to both experts].

c. A statement of agreement and disagreement shall be prepared by the experts following their meeting and shall be served on both parties not later than 5 business days after the meeting has taken place.

d. [Save as is expressly ordered by the court, the [applicant's]/ [respondent's] expert's]/[both experts'] written report(s) shall be admissible without the attendance at court of the expert(s). However, [the applicant's expert]/[the respondent's expert]/[both experts] shall attend the final hearing to give oral evidence, unless agreement about the opinions given by the expert(s) is reached by [*insert time and date*]].

Order to instruct a single joint expert [where expert has been identified]

46.

a. The parties shall jointly instruct [*insert accountant*] as a single joint expert to provide a report, in accordance with the attached letter of instruction, addressing the tax liabilities, if any, and date(s) for payment, which would arise whether in the UK or elsewhere in each of the following scenarios:

i. the disposal by [either party]/[the applicant]/[the respondent] of [any of their interests in their real property]/[[his]/[her] interest in [*insert property*];

ii. the transfer by [either party]/[the applicant]/[the respondent] of [any of their interests in their real property to the other]/[of [his]/[her] interest in [insert property] to [the respondent]/[the applicant]];

iii. the settling by [the applicant]/[the respondent] of [his]/[her] interest in [*insert property*] on [the respondent]/[the applicant];

iv. the disposal by either party of any of their other assets, including the [applicant's]/[respondent's] offshore assets;

v. the transfer by either party of any of their other assets to the other, including the [applicant's]/[respondent's] offshore assets;

vi. the repatriation of any of the [applicant's]/[respondent's] offshore assets;

vii.   the possible methods of mitigating the amount of tax due in any of the above scenarios, and the likely effects of such mitigation on the amounts of tax due;

viii.   etc

b.   The letter of instruction [and [*insert any other documents*]] shall be sent to the expert by [*insert time and date*].

c.   The report shall be sent to the court (in both hardcopy and electronic format) and served on the parties simultaneously by [*insert time and date*].

d.   The costs charged by the expert for preparing the report shall be met by the [applicant]/[respondent]/[parties equally] in the first instance.

e.   The [applicant]/[respondent]/[both parties] shall provide the expert with any reasonable assistance requested in compiling the report, including providing any necessary information and documentation within a reasonable timeframe of the request.

f.   [Any questions shall be put to the expert by no later than 10 days after receipt of the report (in accordance with FPR 2010, rule 25.10)].

g.   [The expert shall respond to those questions by [*insert time and date*]].

h.   [The costs charged by the expert for answering those questions shall be met by the [applicant]/[respondent]/[parties equally]/[party raising them] in the first instance].

i.   [Save as is expressly ordered by the court, the expert's written report shall be admissible without the attendance at court of the expert. However, the expert shall attend the final hearing to give oral evidence, unless agreement about the opinions given by the expert is reached by [*insert time and date*]].

OR

a.   The parties shall jointly instruct [*insert accountant*] as a single joint expert to provide a report, addressing the tax liabilities, if any, and date(s) for payment, which would arise whether in the UK or elsewhere in each of the following scenarios:

i.   the disposal by [either party]/[the applicant]/[the respondent] of [any of their interests in their real property]/[[his]/[her] interest in [*insert property*]];

ii.   the transfer by [either party]/[the applicant]/[the respondent] of [any of their interests in their real property to the other]/[of [his]/[her] interest in [insert property] to [the respondent]/[the applicant]];

iii.   the settling by [the applicant]/[the respondent] of [his]/[her] interest in [*insert property*] on [the respondent]/[the applicant];

iv.   the disposal by either party of any of their other assets, including the [applicant's]/[respondent's] offshore assets;

v. the transfer by either party of any of their other assets to the other, including the [applicant's]/[respondent's] offshore assets;

vi. the repatriation of any of the [applicant's]/[respondent's] offshore assets; and

vii. the possible methods of mitigating the amount of tax due in any of the above scenarios, and the likely effects of such mitigation on the amounts of tax due.

b. The letter of instruction shall be drafted by the [applicant]/[respondent] and agreed with the [respondent]/[applicant] by [*insert time and date*], or determined by the court in default of agreement.

c. The letter of instruction [and [*insert any other documents*]] shall be sent to the expert by [*insert time and date*].

d. The report shall be sent to the court (in both hardcopy and electronic format) and served on the parties simultaneously by [*insert time and date*].

e. The costs charged by the expert for preparing the report shall be met by the [applicant]/[respondent]/[parties equally] in the first instance.

f. The [applicant]/[respondent]/[both parties] shall provide the expert with any reasonable assistance requested in compiling the report, including providing any necessary information and documentation within a reasonable timeframe of the request.

g. [Any questions shall be put to the expert by no later than 10 days after receipt of the report (in accordance with FPR 2010, rule 25.10)].

h. [The expert shall respond to those questions by [*insert time and date*]].

i. [The costs charged by the expert for answering those questions shall be met by the [applicant]/[respondent]/[parties equally]/[party raising them] in the first instance].

j. [Save as is expressly ordered by the court, the expert's written report shall be admissible without the attendance at court of the expert. However, the expert shall attend the final hearing to give oral evidence, unless agreement about the opinions given by the expert is reached by [*insert time and date*]].

Order to instruct a single joint expert [where expert has not been identified]

47.

a. The parties shall jointly instruct an [accountant]/[appropriate expert] to act as a single joint expert and to provide a report, addressing the tax liabilities, if any, and date(s) for payment, which would arise whether in the UK or elsewhere in each of the following scenarios:

i. the disposal by [either party]/[the applicant]/[the respondent] of [any of their interests in their real property]/[[his]/[her] interest in [*insert property*];

ii. the transfer by [either party]/[the applicant]/[the respondent] of [any of their interests in their real property to the other]/[of

      [his]/[her] interest in [insert property] to [the respondent]/[the applicant]];

iii.   the settling by [the applicant]/[the respondent] of [his]/[her] interest in [*insert property*] on [the respondent]/[the applicant];

iv.   the disposal by either party of any of their other assets, including the [applicant's]/[respondent's] offshore assets;

v.   the transfer by either party of any of their other assets to the other, including the [applicant's]/[respondent's] offshore assets;

vi.   the repatriation of any of the [applicant's]/[respondent's] offshore assets; and

vii.   the possible methods of mitigating the amount of tax due in any of the above scenarios, and the likely effects of such mitigation on the amounts of tax due;

b.   The [applicant]/[respondent] shall provide the [respondent]/[applicant] with a list of three appropriate experts by [*insert date and time*].

c.   The [respondent]/[applicant] shall select one of the experts from the list by [*insert time and date*].

d.   The letter of instruction shall be drafted by the [applicant]/[respondent] and agreed with the [respondent]/[applicant] by [*insert time and date*], or determined by the court in default of agreement.

e.   The letter of instruction [and [*insert any other documents*]] shall be sent to the expert by [*insert time and date*].

f.   The report shall be sent to the court (in both hardcopy and electronic form) and served on the parties simultaneously by [*insert time and date*].

g.   The costs charged by the expert for preparing the report shall be met by the [applicant]/[respondent]/[parties equally] in the first instance.

h.   [Any questions shall be put to the expert by no later than 10 days after receipt of the report (in accordance with FPR 2010, rule 25.10)].

i.   [The expert shall respond to those questions by [*insert time and date*]].

j.   [The costs charged by the expert for answering those questions shall be met by the [applicant]/[respondent]/[parties equally]/[party raising them] in the first instance].

k.   [Save as is expressly ordered by the court, the expert's written report shall be admissible without the attendance at court of the expert. However, the expert shall attend the final hearing to give oral evidence, unless agreement about the opinions given by the expert is reached by [*insert time and date*]].

Other expert reports – tax report [for Schedule 1 cases]

Permission to one party to instruct an expert **[where expert has been identified]**

48.

a.   The [applicant]/[respondent] has permission to instruct [*insert expert*] as an expert to provide a report, going to the following issue in these proceedings: [*insert*].

b.   The question(s) which the report shall address shall be the tax liabilities, if any, and date(s) for payment, which would arise whether in the UK or elsewhere in each of the following scenarios:

    i.   the disposal by [the applicant]/[the respondent] of [his]/[her] interest in [*insert property*];

    ii.   the transfer by [the applicant]/[the respondent] of [his]/[her] interest in [*insert property*] to [the respondent]/[the applicant];

    iii.   the settling by [the applicant]/[the respondent] of [his]/[her] interest in [*insert property*] on [the respondent]/[the applicant];

    iv.   the possible methods of mitigating the amount of tax due in any of the above scenarios, and the likely effects of such mitigation on the amounts of tax due;

    v.   etc

c.   The letter of instruction shall be drafted by the [applicant]/[respondent] by [*insert time and date*].

d.   The letter of instruction [and [*insert any other documents*]] shall be sent to the expert by [*insert time and date*].

e.   The report shall be sent to the court (in both hardcopy and electronic form) and served on the [applicant]/[respondent] by [*insert time and date*].

f.   The [applicant]/[respondent] shall disclose the report to the [respondent]/[applicant] by [*insert time and date*].

g.   The costs charged by the expert for preparing the report shall be met by the [applicant]/[respondent]/[parties equally] in the first instance.

h.   The [applicant]/[respondent]/[both parties] shall provide the expert with any reasonable assistance requested in compiling the report, including providing any necessary information and documentation within a reasonable timeframe of the request.

i.   [Any questions shall be put to the expert by no later than 10 days after receipt of the report (in accordance with FPR 2010, rule 25.10)].

j.   [The expert shall respond to those questions by [*insert time and date*]].

k.   [The costs charged by the expert for answering those questions shall be met by the [applicant]/[respondent]/[parties equally]/[party raising them] in the first instance].

l.   [Save as is expressly ordered by the court, the [applicant's]/ [respondent's] expert's]/[both experts'] written report(s) shall be admissible without the attendance at court of the expert(s). However, [the applicant's expert]/[the respondent's expert]/[both experts] shall attend the final hearing to give oral evidence, unless agreement about the opinions given by the expert(s) is reached by [*insert time and date*]].

Permission to one party to instruct an expert [where expert has not been identified]
49.

a.   The [applicant]/[respondent] has permission to instruct an [accountant]/[appropriate expert] to provide a report, going to the following issue in these proceedings: [*insert*].

b.   The question(s) which the report shall address shall be the tax liabilities, if any, and date(s) for payment, which would arise whether in the UK or elsewhere in each of the following scenarios:

   i.   the disposal by [the applicant]/[the respondent] of [his]/[her] interest in [*insert property*];

   ii.   the transfer by [the applicant]/[the respondent] of [his]/[her] interest in [*insert property*] to [the respondent]/[the applicant];

   iii.   the settling by [the applicant]/[the respondent] of [his]/[her] interest in [*insert property*] on [the respondent]/[the applicant];

   iv.   the possible methods of mitigating the amount of tax due in any of the above scenarios, and the likely effects of such mitigation on the amounts of tax due;

   v.   etc

c.   The letter of instruction shall be drafted by the [applicant]/[respondent] by [*insert time and date*].

d.   The letter of instruction [and [*insert any other documents*]] shall be sent to the expert by [*insert time and date*].

e.   The report shall be sent to the court (in both hardcopy and electronic form) and served on the [applicant]/[respondent] by [*insert time and date*].

f.   The [applicant]/[respondent] shall disclose the report to the [respondent]/[applicant] by [*insert time and date*].

g.   The costs charged by the expert for preparing the report shall be met by the [applicant]/[respondent]/[parties equally] in the first instance.

h.   The [applicant]/[respondent]/[both parties] shall provide the expert with any reasonable assistance requested in compiling the report, including providing any necessary information and documentation within a reasonable timeframe of the request.

i.   [Any questions shall be put to the expert by no later than 10 days after receipt of the report (in accordance with FPR 2010, rule 25.10)].

j.   [The expert shall respond to those questions by [*insert time and date*]].

k.   [The costs charged by the expert for answering those questions shall be met by the [applicant]/[respondent]/[parties equally]/[party raising them] in the first instance].

l.   [Save as is expressly ordered by the court, the [applicant's]/[respondent's] expert's]/[both experts'] written report(s) shall be admissible without the attendance at court of the expert(s). However, [the applicant's expert]/[the respondent's expert]/[both experts] shall attend the final hearing to give oral evidence, unless agreement about the opinions given by the expert(s) is reached by [*insert time and date*]].

Order for individually instructed experts to exchange reports/meet

50.

    a.   [The applicant]/[the respondent]/[the parties] shall [each] disclose [his]/[her]/[their] expert's [valuation report]/[market appraisal to [the respondent's]/[the applicant's]/[the other's] expert by [*insert time and date*].

    b.   There shall be a meeting between the [applicant's]/[respondent's] expert and [respondent's]/[applicant's] expert by [insert time and date] to discuss:

        i.   the reasons for disagreement on any expert question and what, if any, action needs to be taken to resolve any outstanding disagreement or question;

        ii.   what existing evidence or additional evidence needs to be obtained to assist the Court to determine the issues;

        iii.   etc.

At least five business days prior to this meeting, [*insert nominated professional in accordance with FPR PD 25E, para 3.1*] shall formulate an agenda including a list of questions for consideration at the meeting, and at least two business days prior to this meeting, [*insert nominated professional in accordance with FPR PD 25E, para 3.1*] shall send the agenda to both experts].

    c.   A statement of agreement and disagreement shall be prepared by the experts following their meeting and shall be served on both parties not than 5 business days after the meeting has taken place.

    d.   [Save as is expressly ordered by the court, the [applicant's]/[respondent's] expert's]/[both experts'] written report(s) shall be admissible without the attendance at court of the expert(s). However, [the applicant's expert]/[the respondent's expert]/[both experts] shall attend the final hearing to give oral evidence, unless agreement about the opinions given by the expert(s) is reached by [*insert time and date*]].

Permission to instruct a single joint expert [where expert has been identified]

51.

    a.   The parties have permission to jointly instruct [*insert accountant*] as a single joint expert to provide a report, in accordance with the attached letter of instruction, going to the following issue in these proceedings: [*insert*].

b. The question(s) which the report shall address shall be the tax liabilities, if any, and date(s) for payment, which would arise whether in the UK or elsewhere in each of the following scenarios:

  i. the disposal by [either party]/[the applicant]/[the respondent] of [any of their interests in their real property]/[[his]/[her] interest in [*insert property*];

  ii. the transfer by [either party]/[the applicant]/[the respondent] of [any of their interests in their real property to the other]/[of [his]/[her] interest in [*insert property*] to [the respondent]/[the applicant]];

  iii. the settling by [the applicant]/[the respondent] of [his]/[her] interest in [*insert property*] on [the respondent]/[the applicant];

  iv. the possible methods of mitigating the amount of tax due in any of the above scenarios, and the likely effects of such mitigation on the amounts of tax due;

  v. etc

c. The letter of instruction [and [*insert any other documents*]] shall be sent to the expert by [*insert time and date*].

d. The report shall be sent to the court (in both hardcopy and electronic format) and served on the parties simultaneously by [*insert time and date*].

e. The costs charged by the expert for preparing the report shall be met by the [applicant]/[respondent]/[parties equally] in the first instance.

f. The [applicant]/[respondent]/[both parties] shall provide the expert with any reasonable assistance requested in compiling the report, including providing any necessary information and documentation within a reasonable timeframe of the request.

g. [Any questions shall be put to the expert by no later than 10 days after receipt of the report (in accordance with FPR 2010, rule 25.10)].

h. [The expert shall respond to those questions by [*insert time and date*]].

i. [The costs charged by the expert for answering those questions shall be met by the [applicant]/[respondent]/[parties equally]/[party raising them] in the first instance].

j. [Save as is expressly ordered by the court, the expert's written report shall be admissible without the attendance at court of the expert. However, the expert shall attend the final hearing to give oral evidence, unless agreement about the opinions given by the expert is reached by [*insert time and date*]].

OR

a. The parties have permission to jointly instruct [*insert accountant*] as a single joint expert to provide a report, going to the following issue in these proceedings: [*insert*].

b. The question(s) which the report shall address shall be the tax liabilities, if any, and date(s) for payment, which would arise whether in the UK or elsewhere in each of the following scenarios:

    i.   the disposal by [either party]/[the applicant]/[the respondent] of [any of their interests in their real property]/[[his]/[her] interest in [*insert property*];

    ii.   the transfer by [either party]/[the applicant]/[the respondent] of [any of their interests in their real property to the other]/[of [his]/[her] interest in [insert property] to [the respondent]/[the applicant]];

    iii.   the settling by [the applicant]/[the respondent] of [his]/[her] interest in [*insert property*] on [the respondent]/[the applicant];

    iv.   the possible methods of mitigating the amount of tax due in any of the above scenarios, and the likely effects of such mitigation on the amounts of tax due;

    v.   etc

c.   The letter of instruction shall be drafted by the [applicant]/[respondent] and agreed with the [respondent]/[applicant] by [*insert time and date*], or determined by the court in default of agreement.

d.   The letter of instruction [and [*insert any other documents*]] shall be sent to the expert by [*insert time and date*].

e.   The report shall be sent to the court (in both hardcopy and electronic format) and served on the parties simultaneously by [*insert time and date*].

f.   The costs charged by the expert for preparing the report shall be met by the [applicant]/[respondent]/[parties equally] in the first instance.

g.   The [applicant]/[respondent]/[both parties] shall provide the expert with any reasonable assistance requested in compiling the report, including providing any necessary information and documentation within a reasonable timeframe of the request.

h.   [Any questions shall be put to the expert by no later than 10 days after receipt of the report (in accordance with FPR 2010, rule 25.10)].

i.   [The expert shall respond to those questions by [*insert time and date*]].

j.   [The costs charged by the expert for answering those questions shall be met by the [applicant]/[respondent]/[parties equally]/[party raising them] in the first instance].

k.   [Save as is expressly ordered by the court, the expert's written report shall be admissible without the attendance at court of the expert. However, the expert shall attend the final hearing to give oral evidence, unless agreement about the opinions given by the expert is reached by [*insert time and date*]].

Permission to instruct a single joint expert **[where expert has not been identified]**

52.

a.   The parties have permission to jointly instruct an [accountant]/[appropriate expert] to act as a single joint expert and to provide a report, going to the following issue in these proceedings: [*insert*].

b.   The question(s) which the report shall address shall be the tax liabilities, if any, and date(s) for payment, which would arise whether in the UK or elsewhere in each of the following scenarios:

     i.   the disposal by [either party]/[the applicant]/[the respondent] of [any of their interests in their real property]/[[his]/[her] interest in [*insert property*];

     ii.   the transfer by [either party]/[the applicant]/[the respondent] of [any of their interests in their real property to the other]/[of [his]/[her] interest in [*insert property*] to [the respondent]/[the applicant]];

     iii.   the settling by [the applicant]/[the respondent] of [his]/[her] interest in [*insert property*] on [the respondent]/[the applicant];

     iv.   the possible methods of mitigating the amount of tax due in any of the above scenarios, and the likely effects of such mitigation on the amounts of tax due;

     v.   etc

c.   The [applicant]/[respondent] shall provide the [respondent]/[applicant] with a list of three appropriate experts by [*insert date and time*].

d.   The [respondent]/[applicant] shall select one of the experts from the list by [*insert time and date*].

e.   The letter of instruction shall be drafted by the [applicant]/[respondent] and agreed with the [respondent]/[applicant] by [*insert time and date*], or determined by the court in default of agreement.

f.   The letter of instruction [and [*insert any other documents*]] shall be sent to the expert by [*insert time and date*].

g.   The report shall be sent to the court (in both hardcopy and electronic form) and served on the parties simultaneously by [*insert time and date*].

h.   The costs charged by the expert for preparing the report shall be met by the [applicant]/[respondent]/[parties equally] in the first instance.

i.   The [applicant]/[respondent]/[both parties] shall provide the expert with any reasonable assistance requested in compiling the report, including providing any necessary information and documentation within a reasonable timeframe of the request.

j.   [Any questions shall be put to the expert by no later than 10 days after receipt of the report (in accordance with FPR 2010, rule 25.10)].

k.   [The expert shall respond to those questions by [*insert time and date*]].

l.   [The costs charged by the expert for answering those questions shall be met by the [applicant]/[respondent]/[parties equally]/[party raising them] in the first instance].

m.   [Save as is expressly ordered by the court, the expert's written report shall be admissible without the attendance at court of the expert. However, the expert shall attend the final hearing to give oral evidence, unless agreement about the opinions given by the expert is reached by [*insert time and date*]].

No other expert evidence without the court's permission
53. Save as is expressly ordered by the court, no further expert evidence shall be admissible before the court.

Variation of settlement
54.
   a. A copy of the applicant's application for variation of the [*insert*] marriage settlement [and a copy of [*insert other documents to be served*]] shall be served on the following beneficiaries under the settlement [*insert beneficiaries*] by [*insert time and date*].
   b. The beneficiaries have permission leave to send to the court and serve signed statements in answer or otherwise in response to the application [by [*insert time and date*]]/[within [*insert*] days after service on them].

Consolidation of proceedings
55.
   a. The [applicant's] [and]/[or] [first respondent's]/[second respondent's] [respective] applications under [*insert statutes* – e.g. the Matrimonial Causes Act 1973, Schedule 1 to the Children Act 1989, Trust of Land and Appointment of Trustee Act 1996] are consolidated.
   b. The applicant's application under [*insert statute*] shall become the lead application, and the consolidated applications shall proceed under case number [*insert*].
   c. The [applicant]/[first respondent]/[second respondent] shall serve on the [first respondent]/[second respondent] etc copies of the following documents in relation to the [applicant's]/[first respondent's]/[second respondent's] application(s) under [*insert statutes* – e.g. the Matrimonial Causes Act 1973, Schedule 1 to the Children Act 1989, Trust of Land and Appointment of Trustee Act 1996]: [*insert documents*]

Intervener(s)
56. [*Insert name*] is given permission to intervene in these proceedings.

Joinder of parties
57. [*Insert name*] and [*insert name*] are joined as [second]/[third] [etc as appropriate] respondents to these proceedings.

Evidence to be served on intervener(s)/additional parties
58. The [applicant's]/[respondent's] [solicitors] shall by [*insert time and date*] serve upon the [intervenor]/[second]/[third etc respondent] copies of the following documents:
   a. [*Insert*]

Evidence of intervener(s)/additional parties
59. The parties shall identify the basis of the dispute between them by complying with the following directions:

a.   The [applicant]/[respondent]/[intervener]/[second respondent] shall by [*Insert time and date*] send to the court and serve on the other parties points of claim, [setting out [his]/[her]/[their] case as to [insert] fully]/[dealing with [*insert*]/limited to dealing with [*insert*]] by [*insert date and time*]].

b.   The [applicant]/[respondent]/[intervener]/[second respondent] shall by [*insert time and date*] send to the court and serve on the other parties [points of dispute]/[a defence], [setting out [his]/[her]/[their] case in reply by [*insert time and date*]].

c.   The [applicant]/[respondent]/[intervener]/[second respondent] shall by [*insert time and date*] send to the court and serve on the other parties any witness statements upon which [he]/[she]/[they] intend to rely.

d.   There be the following additional directions for disclosure: [*insert*].

Documents to be produced by trustees

60.   The [second] [third etc] respondent shall by [*insert time and date*] send to the court and serve on the applicant and the respondent the following information and documents in respect of the [*insert*] settlement:

a.   copies of the deed of trust and all subsequent deeds of variation and appointment;

b.   copies of the completed and approved trust accounts for the last [*insert*] years;

c.   copies of any letter of wishes;

d.   confirmation as to the identity of the present trustees [and protector] of the trust;

e.   confirmation as to the identity of the present beneficiaries of the trust;

f.   a schedule authenticated by the trustees setting out all distributions and appointments made to or on behalf of the [applicant]/[respondent]/ [*insert*] since [*insert date*];

g.   a short narrative statement setting out the trustees anticipated position in respect of any further distributions to or on behalf of the [applicant]/[respondent]/[*insert as appropriate*];

h.   ...

Preliminary issue hearing

61.   The issue of the [*insert*] interest in [*insert*] be listed for determination by way of a preliminary issue before a District Judge sitting at [*insert*] court at [*insert*] on [*insert*] with a time estimate of [*insert*].

Scott schedule

62.   The [applicant]/[respondent][parties] shall [each] prepare a Scott Schedule, stating in relation to each item of property in dispute [their]/[each party's] case as to:

a.   the party by whom it was acquired;

b.   how and from whom it was acquired [purchase/inheritance/gift etc] with documentary evidence in support;

    c.   its current value with documentary evidence in support;

    d.   what order is sought and the justification for seeking it;

    e.   ...

by [*insert time and date*].

63.   [The parties shall send to the court and serve their schedules on each other by [*insert time and date*]]/[The [applicant]/[respondent] shall send to the court and serve on the [respondent]/[applicant] [his]/[her] schedule by [*insert time and date*], and the [respondent]/[applicant] shall send to the court and serve on the [applicant]/[respondent] [his]/[her] response to the schedule by [*insert time and date*]].

Permission to disclose order to CMS

64.

    a.   There be permission to the [applicant]/[respondent] under FPR 2010, rule 12.73(1)(b) to produce to the CMS a copy of the [respondent's]/[applicant's] [Form E]/[Form E1] and Replies to Questionnaire if so advised.

    b.   The [applicant]/[respondent] shall send the [respondent]/[applicant] a copy of any letter and supporting documentation sent to the CMS forthwith after sending it.

Further hearing(s)

65.   The application shall be listed for a [mention hearing]/[further directions appointment]/[financial dispute resolution appointment]/[case management appointment]/[pre-trial review]/[final hearing] before [*insert name or level of judge*] at the [*insert court*] on [*insert date and time*]/[on the first open day after [*insert date*] [suitable to counsel for both parties]/[on a date to be fixed in consultation with counsel's clerks] with a time estimate of [*insert*]. [The parties and their legal advisors shall send to court their dates to avoid by [*insert time and date*]. [The parties and their legal advisers shall attend the court building at least one hour prior to the listing time of the financial dispute resolution appointment to negotiate and attempt to narrow the issues].

Adjournment

66.   This hearing is adjourned until [*insert time and date*] on the following terms [*set out directions to prevail*].

Adjournment for settlement negotiations/mediation/arbitration/private financial dispute resolution appointment

67.   This application is adjourned until [*insert time and date*] to enable the parties to attempt to resolve the matters in dispute by means of [negotiation]/[mediation (*details of mediator and start date could be inserted here if useful and available*)]/[arbitration (*insert details if available*)]/[a private financial

dispute resolution appointment [arranged in front of [*insert*]]/[to be arranged in front of [*insert*]]/[other]

Note: if an adjournment for arbitration is made then give consideration to the available orders in the arbitration section.

Evidence at the financial dispute resolution appointment

68.

    a.   The [applicant]/[respondent] shall prepare a bundle containing:

        i.   an [agreed] chronology;

        ii.   an [agreed] summary of the history of the case;

        iii.   an [agreed] summary of the issues to be determined;

        iv.   an [agreed] schedule of assets. Where the schedule cannot be agreed then the bundle should include the schedule of assets contended for by each party which should identify which items are not agreed between the parties;

        v.   [*list other documents to be included* – for example [all applications and orders made in these proceedings], [the parties' narrative Forms E], [the parties' narrative replies to questionnaire], [the parties' etc narrative witness statements], [the expert reports].

    b.   The bundle shall be agreed [if possible] by both parties. The [applicant]/[respondent] shall send the [respondent]/[applicant] a draft index for the bundle by [[*insert time and date*]/[not later than [*insert*] days before the financial dispute resolution appointment]], and the [respondent]/[applicant] shall send the [applicant]/[respondent] any comments on the index by [[*insert time and date*]/[not later than [*insert*] days before the financial dispute resolution appointment]].

    c.   The bundle must be paginated and the documents shall be in chronological order within each section.

    d.   The [applicant]/[respondent] shall send the bundle to the court by [[*insert time and date*]/[not later than [*insert*] days before the financial dispute resolution appointment]], and shall provide a copy of the bundle to the [respondent]/[applicant] by [[*insert time and date*]/[not later than [*insert*] days before the financial dispute resolution appointment]] provided that the [respondent]/[applicant] agrees to discharge [his]/[her] reasonable costs of photocopying the bundle. If [he]/[she] does not do so, the [applicant]/[respondent] shall provide an index for the bundle to the [respondent]/[applicant] by [[*insert time and date*]/[not later than [*insert*] days before the financial dispute resolution appointment]].

Evidence at final hearing

69.

    a.   Both parties shall attend the final hearing to give oral evidence.

    b.   Any witness [swearing an affidavit]/[sending to the court and serving on the parties a witness statement] shall attend the final hearing to give oral evidence [unless their evidence is not disputed].

    c.   The hearing shall not be before [District/Circuit/High Court] Judge [*insert*].

    d.   The [applicant]/[respondent] shall prepare a bundle containing:

        i.   an [agreed] chronology;

        ii.   an [agreed] summary of the history of the case;

        iii.   an [agreed] summary of the issues to be determined;

        iv.   an [agreed] schedule of assets. Where the schedule cannot be agreed then the bundle should include the schedule of assets contended for by each party which should identify which items are not agreed between the parties;

        v.   [*list other documents to be included* – for example [all applications and orders made in these proceedings], [the parties' Forms E], [the parties' Replies to Questionnaire], [the parties' etc witness statements], [the expert reports].

    e.   The bundle shall be agreed [if possible] by both parties. The [applicant]/[respondent] shall send the [respondent]/[applicant] a draft index for the bundle by [[*insert time and date*]/[not later than [*insert*] days before the final hearing]], and the [respondent]/[applicant] shall send the [applicant]/[respondent] any comments on the index by [[*insert time and date*]/[not later than [*insert*] days before the final hearing]].

    f.   The bundle must be paginated and the documents shall be in chronological order within each section.

    g.   The [applicant]/[respondent] shall send the bundle to court by [[*insert time and date*]/[not later than [*insert*] days before the final hearing]], and shall provide a copy of the bundle to the [respondent]/[applicant] by [[*insert time and date*]/[not later than [*insert*] days before the final hearing]] provided that the [respondent]/[applicant] agrees to discharge [his]/[her] reasonable costs of photocopying the bundle. If [he]/[she] does not do so, the [applicant]/[respondent] shall provide an index for the bundle to the [respondent]/[applicant] by [[*insert time and date*]/[not later than [*insert*] days before the final hearing]].

Costs Estimates

70.

    a.   [The [applicant]/[respondent]/[second respondent]/[third respondent] etc shall send to the court and serve on the other parties costs estimates in Form H not later than [*insert*] days before the [adjourned directions appointment]/[financial dispute resolution appointment]/ [case management hearing]].

b.   [The [applicant]/[respondent]/[second respondent]/[third respondent] etc shall send to the court and serve on the other parties costs estimates in Form H1 not later than [*insert*] days before the final hearing].

Offers for financial dispute resolution appointment
71.

a.   [The parties shall exchange without prejudice proposals for the resolution of the matters in dispute [by [*insert date and time*]]/[not later than [*insert*] days before the financial dispute resolution appointment].]

b.   [The [applicant]/[respondent] shall serve [his]/[her] without prejudice proposals for the resolution of the matters in dispute on the [respondent]/[applicant] by [*insert date and time*]/[not later than [*insert*] days before the financial dispute resolution appointment], and the [respondent]/[applicant] shall serve [his]/[her] without prejudice proposals on the [applicant]/[respondent] for the resolution of the matters in dispute in reply by [*insert date and time*]/[not later than [*insert*] days before the financial dispute resolution appointment].]

c.   The [applicant]/[respondent] shall send to the court a schedule of the without prejudice and open proposals made by each party for the resolution of the matters in dispute by [*insert date and time*]/[not later than [*insert*] days before the financial dispute resolution appointment].

d.   The [applicant]/[respondent]/[both parties] may, if so advised, decline to send to the court and serve on the [respondent]/[applicant]/[other party] without prejudice proposals for the resolution of the matters in dispute. If [he]/[she] decides not to send to the court such proposals [he]/[she] shall notify the [respondent]/[applicant] by [*insert time and date*]/[not later than [*insert*] days before the financial dispute resolution appointment].

Offers for other hearings
72.

a.   [The parties shall exchange open proposals for the resolution of the matters in dispute [by [*insert date and time*]]/[not later than [*insert*] days before the [adjourned directions appointment]/[case management hearing]/[final hearing]].]

b.   [The [applicant]/[respondent] shall serve [his]/[her] open proposals for the resolution of the matters in dispute on the [respondent]/[applicant] [by [*insert date and time*]]/[not later than [*insert*] days before the [adjourned directions appointment]/[case management hearing]/[final hearing]], and the [respondent]/[applicant] shall serve [his]/[her] open proposals for the resolution of the matters in dispute in reply on the [applicant]/[respondent] [by [*insert date and time*]]/[not later than [*insert*] days before the [adjourned directions appointment]/[case management hearing]/[final hearing]].]

c. The [applicant]/[respondent] shall send to the court a schedule of the open proposals made by each party for the resolution of the matters in dispute [by [*insert date and time*]]/[not later than [*insert*] days before the [adjourned directions appointment]/[case management hearing]/[final hearing]].

d. The [applicant]/[respondent]/[both parties] may, if so advised, decline to send to the court and serve on the [respondent]/[applicant]/[other party] open proposals for the resolution of the matters in dispute. If [he]/[she] decides not to send to the court such proposals [he]/[she] shall notify the [respondent]/[applicant]/[other party] [by [*insert time and date*]]/[not later than [*insert*] days before the [adjourned directions appointment]/[case management hearing]/[final hearing]].

Costs

73. [Costs in the application]/[No order as to costs]/[The [applicant]/[respondent] shall pay £[*insert*] towards the [respondent's]/[applicant's] costs of and relating to this hearing by [*insert date*], [summarily assessed at [£*insert amount*]]/[subject to detailed assessment if not agreed]]/[The [applicant]/[respondent] shall pay the [respondent's]/[applicant's] costs of and relating to this hearing by [*insert date*] [including the costs reserved by the order(s) made on [*insert date(s)*], [summarily assessed at [£*insert amount*]]/[subject to detailed assessment if not agreed].]

Costs – order against a publicly funded party

74. The [applicant]/[respondent] shall pay [the [respondent's]/[applicant's] costs]/[[*insert* %] of the [respondent's]/[applicant's] costs], [summarily assessed at £[*insert*]]/[to be subject to detailed assessment in default of agreement between the parties], by [*insert time*] on [*insert date*], subject to there being a determination pursuant to section 11 of the Access to Justice Act 1999 that it is reasonable for the [applicant]/[respondent] to do so. [This order for costs shall not be enforced without the court's permission].

Delayed costs order

75. The time for commencement of proceedings for the assessment of the costs under the Community Legal Services (Financial) Regulations 2000 shall not start until the date of completion of the [transfer]/[sale] of the [family home]/[property] referred to in paragraph [*insert*] of this order.

Dated

(*Source*: Financial Remedies Working Group, www.judiciary.gov.uk/wp-content/uploads/2014/08/report-of-the-financial-remedies-working-grp-annex7.pdf.)

Chapter 7

Family Procedure Rules and Practice Directions (essential selections only from Parts and PDs below)

PART 1 – OVERRIDING OBJECTIVE

The overriding objective

1.1

(1)   These rules are a new procedural code with the overriding objective of enabling the court to deal with cases justly, having regard to any welfare issues involved.

(2)   Dealing with a case justly includes, so far as is practicable –

    (a)   ensuring that it is dealt with expeditiously and fairly;

    (b)   dealing with the case in ways which are proportionate to the nature, importance and complexity of the issues;

    (c)   ensuring that the parties are on an equal footing;

    (d)   saving expense; and

    (e)   allotting to it an appropriate share of the court's resources, while taking into account the need to allot resources to other cases.

Application by the court of the overriding objective

1.2

(1)   The court must seek to give effect to the overriding objective when it –

    (a)   exercises any power given to it by these rules; or

    (b)   interprets any rule.

Duty of the parties

1.3

The parties are required to help the court to further the overriding objective.

Court's duty to manage cases

1.4

(1)   The court must further the overriding objective by actively managing cases.

PART 2 – APPLICATION AND INTERPRETATION OF THE RULES

Interpretation

2.3

(1)   In these rules –

'the 1958 Act' means the Maintenance Orders Act 1958;

'the 1973 Act' means the Matrimonial Causes Act 1973;

'the 1978 Act' means the Domestic Proceedings and Magistrates' Courts Act 1978;

'the 1980 Hague Convention' means the Convention on the Civil Aspects of International Child Abduction which was signed at The Hague on 25 October 1980;

'the 1984 Act' means the Matrimonial and Family Proceedings Act 1984;

'the 1986 Act' means the Family Law Act 1986;

'the 1989 Act' means the Children Act 1989;

'the 1990 Act' means the Human Fertilisation and Embryology Act 1990;

'the 1991 Act' means the Child Support Act 1991;

'the 1996 Act' means the Family Law Act 1996;

'the 1996 Hague Convention' means the Convention on Jurisdiction, Applicable Law, Recognition, Enforcement and Co-Operation in Respect of Parental Responsibility and Measures for the Protection of Children;

'the 2002 Act' means the Adoption and Children Act 2002;

'the 2004 Act' means the Civil Partnership Act 2004;

'the 2005 Act' means the Mental Capacity Act 2005;

'the 2007 Hague Convention' means the Convention on the International Recovery of Child Support and other forms of Family Maintenance done at The Hague on 23 November 2007;

'the 2008 Act' means the Human Fertilisation and Embryology Act 2008;

'the 2014 Act' means the Children and Families Act 2014;

'adoption proceedings' means proceedings for an adoption order under the 2002 Act;

'application form' means a document in which the applicant states his intention to seek a court order other than in accordance with the Part 18 procedure;

'application notice' means a document in which the applicant states his intention to seek a court order in accordance with the Part 18 procedure;

'Article 11 form' means a form published by the Permanent Bureau of the Hague Conference under Article 11(4) of the 2007 Hague Convention for use in relation to an application under Article 10 of that Convention, and includes a Financial Circumstances Form as defined in rule 9.3(1) which accompanies such an application;

'Assembly' means the National Assembly for Wales;

'bank holiday' means a bank holiday under the Banking and Financial Dealings Act 1971 –

  (a)   for the purpose of service of a document within the United Kingdom, in the part of the United Kingdom where service is to take place; and

  (b)   for all other purposes, in England and Wales.

'business day' means any day other than –

  (a)   a Saturday, Sunday, Christmas Day or Good Friday; or

  (b)   a bank holiday;

'care order' has the meaning assigned to it by section 31(11) of the 1989 Act;

'CCR' means the County Court Rules 1981, as they appear in Schedule 2 to the CPR;

'child' means a person under the age of 18 years who is the subject of the proceedings; except that –

(a)   in adoption proceedings, it also includes a person who has attained the age of 18 years before the proceedings are concluded; and

(b)   in proceedings brought under the Council Regulation, the 1980 Hague Convention or the European Convention, it means a person under the age of 16 years who is the subject of the proceedings;

'child arrangements order' has the meaning given to it by section 8(1) of the 1989 Act;

'child of the family' has the meaning given to it by section 105(1) of the 1989 Act;

'children and family reporter' means an officer of the Service or a Welsh family proceedings officer who has been asked to prepare a welfare report under section 7(1)(a) of the 1989 Act or section 102(3)(b) of the 2002 Act;

'children's guardian' means –

(a)   in relation to a child who is the subject of and a party to specified proceedings or proceedings to which Part 14 applies, the person appointed in accordance with rule 16.3(1); and

(b)   in any other case, the person appointed in accordance with rule 16.4;

'civil partnership order' means one of the orders mentioned in section 37 of the 2004 Act;

'civil partnership proceedings' means proceedings for a civil partnership order;

'civil restraint order' means an order restraining a party –

(a)   from making any further applications in current proceedings (a limited civil restraint order);

(b)   from making certain applications in specified courts (an extended civil restraint order); or

(c)   from making any application in specified courts (a general civil restraint order);

'consent order' means an order in the terms applied for to which the respondent agrees;

'the Council Regulation' means Council Regulation (EC) No 2201/2003 of 27 November 2003 on jurisdiction and the recognition and enforcement of judgments in matrimonial matters and in matters of parental responsibility;

'court' means, subject to any rule or other enactment which provides otherwise, the High Court, or the family court;

(rule 2.5 relates to the power to perform functions of the court.)

'court officer' means a member of court staff;

'CPR' means the Civil Procedure Rules 1998;

'deputy' has the meaning given in section 16(2)(b) of the 2005 Act;

'detailed assessment proceedings' means the procedure by which the amount of costs is decided in accordance with Part 47 of the CPR;

'directions appointment' means a hearing for directions;

'the European Convention' means the European Convention on Recognition and Enforcement of Decisions concerning Custody of Children and on the Restoration of Custody of Children which was signed in Luxembourg on 20 May 1980;

'filing', in relation to a document, means delivering it, by post or otherwise, to the court office;

'financial order' means–

(a)   an avoidance of disposition order;

(b)   an order for maintenance pending suit;

(c)   an order for maintenance pending outcome of proceedings;

(d)   an order for periodic payments or lump sum provision as mentioned in section 21(1) of the 1973 Act, except an order under section 27(6) of that Act;

(e)   an order for periodical payments or lump sum provision as mentioned in paragraph 2(1) of Schedule 5 to the 2004 Act, made under Part 1 of Schedule 5 to that Act;

(f)   a property adjustment order;

(g)   a variation order;

(h)   a pension sharing order;

(i)   a pension compensation sharing order; or

(j)   an order for payment in respect of legal services

('variation order', 'pension compensation sharing order' and 'pension sharing order' are defined in rule 9.3.)

'financial remedy' means –

(a)   a financial order;

(b)   an order under Schedule 1 to the 1989 Act;

(c)   an order under Part 3 of the 1984 Act except an application under section 13 of the 1984 Act for permission to apply for a financial remedy;

(d)   an order under Schedule 7 to the 2004 Act except an application under paragraph 4 of Schedule 7 to the 2004 Act for permission to apply for an order under paragraph 9 or 13 of that Schedule;

(e)   an order under section 27 of the 1973 Act;

(f)   an order under Part 9 of Schedule 5 to the 2004 Act;

(g)   an order under section 35 of the 1973 Act;

(h)   an order under paragraph 69 of Schedule 5 to the 2004 Act;

(i)   an order under Part 1 of the 1978 Act;

(j)   an order under Schedule 6 to the 2004 Act;

(k)   an order under section 10(2) of the 1973 Act; or

(l)   an order under section 48(2) of the 2004 Act;

'hearing' includes a directions appointment;

'hearsay' means a statement made, otherwise than by a person while giving oral evidence in proceedings, which is tendered as evidence of the matters stated, and references to hearsay include hearsay of whatever degree;

'incoming protection measure' means a protection measure that has been ordered in a Member State of the European Union other than the United Kingdom or Denmark;

'inherent jurisdiction' means the High Court's power to make any order or determine any issue in respect of a child, including in wardship proceedings, where it would be just and equitable to do so unless restricted by legislation or case law;

(Practice Direction 12D (Inherent Jurisdiction (including Wardship Proceedings)) provides examples of inherent jurisdiction proceedings.)

'judge' means –

- (a) in the High Court, a judge or a district judge of that court (including a district judge of the principal registry) or a person authorised to act as such; and

- (b) in the family court, a person who is –
    - (i) the Lord Chief Justice;
    - (ii) the Master of the Rolls;
    - (iii) the President of the Queen's Bench Division;
    - (iv) the President of the Family Division;
    - (v) the Chancellor of the High Court;
    - (vi) an ordinary judge of the Court of Appeal (including the vice-president, if any, of either division of that court);
    - (vii) the Senior President of Tribunals;
    - (viii) a puisne judge of the High Court;
    - (ix) a deputy judge of the High Court;
    - (x) a person who has been a judge of the Court of Appeal or a puisne judge of the High Court who may act as a judge of the family court by virtue of section 9 of the Senior Courts Act 1981;
    - (xi) the Chief Taxing Master;
    - (xii) a taxing master of the Senior Courts;
    - (xiii) a person appointed to act as a deputy for the person holding office referred to in sub-paragraph (xiii) or to act as a temporary additional officer for any such office;
    - (xiv) a circuit judge;
    - (xv) a Recorder;
    - (xvi) the Senior District Judge of the Family Division;
    - (xvii) a district judge of the principal registry;
    - (xviii) a person appointed to act as a deputy for the person holding office referred to in sub-paragraph (xvii) or to act as a temporary additional office holder for any such office;
    - (xix) a district judge;
    - (xx) a deputy district judge appointed under section 102 of the Senior Courts Act 1981 or section 8 of the County Courts Act 1984;

(xxi)   a District Judge (Magistrates' Courts);

(xxii)   a lay Justice;

(xxiii)   any other judge referred to in section 31C(1) of the 1984 Act who is authorised by the President of the Family Division to conduct particular business in the family court;

'jurisdiction' means, unless the context requires otherwise, England and Wales and any part of the territorial waters of the United Kingdom adjoining England and Wales;

'justices' clerk' has the meaning assigned to it by section 27(1) of the Courts Act 2003;

'lay justice' means a justice of the peace who is not a District Judge (Magistrates' Courts);

'legal representative' means a –

(a)   barrister;

(b)   solicitor;

(c)   solicitor's employee;

(d)   manager of a body recognised under section 9 of the Administration of Justice Act 1985; or

(e)   person who, for the purposes of the Legal Services Act 2007, is an authorised person in relation to an activity which constitutes the conduct of litigation (within the meaning of the Act),

who has been instructed to act for a party in relation to proceedings;

'litigation friend' has the meaning given –

(a)   in relation to a protected party, by Part 15; and

(b)   in relation to a child, by Part 16;

'the Maintenance Regulation' means Council Regulation (EC) No 4/2009 of 18th December 2008 on jurisdiction, applicable law, recognition and enforcement of decisions and co-operation in matters relating to maintenance obligations, including as applied in relation to Denmark by virtue of the Agreement made on 19th October 2005 between the European Community and the Kingdom of Denmark;

'matrimonial cause' means proceedings for a matrimonial order;

'matrimonial order' means –

(a)   a decree of divorce made under section 1 of the 1973 Act;

(b)   a decree of nullity made on one of the grounds set out in section 11, 12 or 12A of the 1973 Act;

(c)   a decree of judicial separation made under section 17 of the 1973 Act;

non-court dispute resolution' means methods of resolving a dispute, including mediation, other than through the normal court process;

'note' includes a record made by mechanical means;

'officer of the Service' has the meaning given by section 11(3) of the Criminal Justice and Court Services Act 2000;

'order' includes directions of the court;

'order for maintenance pending outcome of proceedings' means an order under paragraph 38 of Schedule 5 to the 2004 Act;

'order for maintenance pending suit' means an order under section 22 of the 1973 Act;

'order for payment for legal services' means an order under section 22ZA of the 1973 Act or an order under paragraph 38A of Part 8 of Schedule 5 to the 2004 Act;

'parental order proceedings' has the meaning assigned to it by rule 13.1;

'parental responsibility' has the meaning assigned to it by section 3 of the 1989 Act;

'placement proceedings' means proceedings for the making, varying or revoking of a placement order under the 2002 Act;

'principal registry' means the principal registry of the Family Division of the High Court;

'proceedings' means, unless the context requires otherwise, family proceedings as defined in section 75(3) of the Courts Act 2003;

'professional acting in furtherance of the protection of children' includes –

    (a)   an officer of a local authority exercising child protection functions;

    (b)   a police officer who is–

        (i)   exercising powers under section 46 of the Act of 1989; or

        (ii)   serving in a child protection unit or a paedophile unit of a police force;

    (c)   any professional person attending a child protection conference or review in relation to a child who is the subject of the proceedings to which the information regarding the proceedings held in private relates;

    (d)   an officer of the National Society for the Prevention of Cruelty to Children; or

    (e)   a member or employee of the Disclosure and Barring Service, being the body established under section 87(1) of the Protection of Freedoms Act 2012;

'professional legal adviser' means a –

    (a)   barrister;

    (b)   solicitor;

    (c)   solicitor's employee;

    (d)   manager of a body recognised under section 9 of the Administration of Justice Act 1985; or

    (e)   person who, for the purposes of the Legal Services Act 2007, is an authorised person in relation to an activity which constitutes the conduct of litigation (within the meaning of that Act),

who is providing advice to a party but is not instructed to represent that party in the proceedings;

'property adjustment order' means –

- (a)   in proceedings under the 1973 Act, any of the orders mentioned in section 21(2) of that Act;
- (b)   in proceedings under the 1984 Act, an order under section 17(1)(a)(ii) of that Act;
- (c)   in proceedings under Schedule 5 to the 2004 Act, any of the orders mentioned in paragraph 7(1);or
- (d)   in proceedings under Schedule 7 to the 2004 Act, an order for property adjustment under paragraph 9(2) or(3);

'protected party' means a party, or an intended party, who lacks capacity (within the meaning of the 2005 Act) to conduct proceedings;

'protection measure' has the meaning given to it in the Protection Measures Regulation;

'Protection Measures Regulation' means the Regulation (EU) No 606/2013 of the European Parliament and of the Council of 12th June 2013 on mutual recognition of protection measures in civil matters;

'reporting officer' means an officer of the Service or a Welsh family proceedings officer appointed to witness the documents which signify a parent's or guardian's consent to the placing of the child for adoption or to the making of an adoption order or a section 84 order;

'risk assessment' has the meaning assigned to it by section 16A(3) of the 1989 Act;

'RSC' means the Rules of the Supreme Court 1965 as they appear in Schedule 1 to the CPR;

'section 8 order' has the meaning assigned to it by section 8(2) of the 1989 Act;

'section 84 order' means an order made by the High Court under section 84 of the 2002 Act giving parental responsibility prior to adoption abroad;

'section 89 order' means an order made by the High Court under section 89 of the 2002 Act –

- (a)   annulling a Convention adoption or Convention adoption order;
- (b)   providing for an overseas adoption or determination under section 91 of the 2002 Act to cease to be valid; or
- (c)   deciding the extent, if any, to which a determination under section 91 of the 2002 Act has been affected by a subsequent determination under that section;

'Service' has the meaning given by section 11 of the Criminal Justice and Court Services Act 2000;

'the Service Regulation' means Regulation (EC) No. 1393/2007 of the European Parliament and of the Council of 13 November2007 on the service in the Member States of judicial and extra judicial documents in civil or commercial matters (service of documents), and repealing Council Regulation (EC) No. 1348/2000, as amended from time to time and as applied by the Agreement made on 19 October 2005 between the European Community and the Kingdom of Denmark on the service of judicial and extra judicial documents in civil and commercial matters;

'specified proceedings' has the meaning assigned to it by section 41(6) of the 1989 Act and rule 12.27;

'welfare officer' means a person who has been asked to prepare a report under section 7(1)(b) of the 1989 Act;

'Welsh family proceedings officer' has the meaning given by section 35(4) of the Children Act 2004.

(2) In these rules a reference to –

    (a) an application for a matrimonial order or a civil partnership order is to be read as a reference to a petition for –

        (i) a matrimonial order; or

        (ii) omitted

        (iii) a civil partnership order,

    and includes a petition by a respondent asking for such an order;

    (b) 'financial order' in matrimonial proceedings is to be read as a reference to 'ancillary relief';

    (c) 'matrimonial proceedings' is to be read as a reference to a matrimonial cause.

(3) Where these rules apply the CPR, they apply the CPR as amended from time to time.

(4) Where these Rules apply RSC Order 52 and CCR Order 29, they apply those rules as they appeared in Schedule 1 and Schedule 2 to the CPR on 30 September 2012.

Computation of time

2.9

(1) This rule shows how to calculate any period of time for doing any act which is specified –

    (a) by these rules;

    (b) by a practice direction; or

    (c) by a direction or order of the court.

(2) A period of time expressed as a number of days must be computed as clear days.

(3) In this rule 'clear days' means that in computing the numbers of days –

    (a) the day on which the period begins; and

    (b) if the end of the period is defined by reference to an event, the day on which that event occurs,

are not included.

(4) Where the specified period is 7 days or less and includes a day which is not a business day, that day does not count.

(5) When the period specified –

    (a) by these rules or a practice direction; or

    (b) by any direction or order of the court,

for doing any act at the court office ends on a day on which the office is closed, that act will be in time if done on the next day on which the court office is open.

Dates for compliance to be calendar dates and to include time of day
2.10

(1)   Where the court makes an order or gives a direction which imposes a time limit for doing any act, the last date for compliance must, wherever practicable –

    (a)   be expressed as a calendar date; and

    (b)   include the time of day by which the act must be done.

(2)   Where the date by which an act must be done is inserted in any document, the date must, wherever practicable, be expressed as a calendar date.

(3)   Where 'month' occurs in any order, direction or other document, it means a calendar month.

PART 3 – NON-COURT DISPUTE RESOLUTION

The court's duty to consider non-court dispute resolution
3.3

(1)   The court must consider, at every stage in proceedings, whether non-court dispute resolution is appropriate.

(2)   In considering whether non-court dispute resolution is appropriate in proceedings which were commenced by a relevant family application, the court must take into account –

    (a)   whether a MIAM took place;

    (b)   whether a valid MIAM exemption was claimed or mediator's exemption was confirmed; and

    (c)   whether the parties attempted mediation or another form of non-court dispute resolution and the outcome of that process.

PART 4 – GENERAL CASE MANAGEMENT POWERS

The court's general powers of management
4.1

(1)   In this Part, 'statement of case' means the whole or part of, an application form or answer.

(2)   The list of powers in this rule is in addition to any powers given to the court by any other rule or practice direction or by any other enactment or any powers it may otherwise have.

(3)   Except where these rules provide otherwise, the court may –

    (a)   extend or shorten the time for compliance with any rule, practice direction or court order (even if an application for extension is made after the time for compliance has expired);

    (b)   make such order for disclosure and inspection, including specific disclosure of documents, as it thinks fit;

    (c)   adjourn or bring forward a hearing;

    (d)   require a party or a party's legal representative to attend the court;

    (e)   hold a hearing and receive evidence by telephone or by using any other method of direct oral communication;

(f)   direct that part of any proceedings be dealt with as separate proceedings;

(g)   stay the whole or part of any proceedings or judgment either generally or until a specified date or event;

(h)   consolidate proceedings;

(i)   hear two or more applications on the same occasion;

(j)   direct a separate hearing of any issue;

(k)   decide the order in which issues are to be heard;

(l)   exclude an issue from consideration;

(m)   dismiss or give a decision on an application after a decision on a preliminary issue;

(n)   direct any party to file and serve an estimate of costs; and

(o)   take any other step or make any other order for the purpose of managing the case and furthering the overriding objective.

(Rule 21.1 explains what is meant by disclosure and inspection.)

(4)   When the court makes an order, it may –

(a)   make it subject to conditions, including a condition to pay a sum of money into court; and

(b)   specify the consequence of failure to comply with the order or a condition.

(5)   Where the court gives directions it will take into account whether or not a party has complied with any relevant pre-action protocol.

(6)   A power of the court under these rules to make an order includes a power to vary or revoke the order.

(7)   Any provision in these rules –

(a)   requiring or permitting directions to be given by the court is to be taken as including provision for such directions to be varied or revoked; and

(b)   requiring or permitting a date to be set is to be taken as including provision for that date to be changed or cancelled.

(8)   The court may not extend the period within which an application for a section 89 order must be made.

PART 9 – APPLICATIONS FOR A FINANCIAL REMEDY

I APPLICATION AND INTERPRETATION

Application
9.1
The rules in this Part apply to an application for a financial remedy.
('Financial remedy' and 'financial order' are defined in rule 2.3)

Omitted
9.2

Interpretation

9.3

(1)   In this Part –

'avoidance of disposition order' means –

    (a)   in proceedings under the 1973 Act, an order under section 37(2)(b) or (c) of that Act;

    (b)   in proceedings under the 1984 Act, an order under section 23 (2)(b) or 23(3) of that Act;

    (c)   in proceedings under Schedule 5 to the 2004 Act, an order under paragraph 74(3) or (4); or

    (d)   in proceedings under Schedule 7 to the 2004 Act, an order under paragraph 15(3) or (4);

'the Board' means the Board of the Pension Protection Fund;

'FDR appointment' means a Financial Dispute Resolution appointment in accordance with rule 9.17;

'Financial Circumstances Form' means the Financial Circumstances Form published by the Permanent Bureau of the Hague Conference under Article 11(4) of the 2007 Hague Convention for use in relation to applications under Article 10 of that Convention;

'order preventing a disposition' means –

    (a)   in proceedings under the 1973 Act, an order under section 37(2)(a) of that Act;

    (b)   in proceedings under the 1984 Act, an order under section 23(2)(a) of that Act;

    (c)   in proceedings under Schedule 5 to the 2004 Act, an order under paragraph 74(2); or

    (d)   in proceedings under Schedule 7 to the 2004 Act, an order under paragraph 15(2);

'pension arrangement' means –

    (a)   an occupational pension scheme;

    (b)   a personal pension scheme;

    (c)   shareable state scheme rights;

    (d)   a retirement annuity contract;

    (e)   an annuity or insurance policy purchased, or transferred, for the purpose of giving effect to rights under an occupational pension scheme or a personal pension scheme; and

    (f)   an annuity purchased, or entered into, for the purpose of discharging liability in respect of a pension credit under section 29(1)(b) of the Welfare Reform and Pensions Act 1999 or under corresponding Northern Ireland legislation;

'pension attachment order' means –

    (a)   in proceedings under the 1973 Act, an order making provision under section 25B or 25C of that Act;

    (b)   in proceedings under the 1984 Act, an order under section 17(1)(a)(i) of that Act making provision equivalent to an order referred to in paragraph (a);

(c)   in proceedings under Schedule 5 to the 2004 Act, an order making provision under paragraph 25 or paragraph 26; or

(d)   in proceedings under Schedule 7 to the 2004 Act, an order under paragraph 9(2) or (3) making provision equivalent to an order referred to in paragraph (c);

'pension compensation attachment order' means –

(a)   in proceedings under the 1973 Act, an order making provision under section 25F of that Act;

(b)   in proceedings under the 1984 Act, an order under section 17(1)(a)(i) of that Act making provision equivalent to an order referred in to paragraph (a);

(c)   in proceedings under Schedule 5 to the 2004 Act, an order under paragraph 34A; and

(d)   in proceedings under Schedule 7 to the 2004 Act, an order under paragraph 9(2) or (3) making provision equivalent to an order referred to in paragraph (c);

'pension compensation sharing order' means –

(a)   in proceedings under the 1973 Act, an order under section 24E of that Act;

(b)   in proceedings under the 1984 Act, an order under section 17(1)(c) of that Act;

(c)   in proceedings under Schedule 5 to the 2004 Act, an order under paragraph 19A ; and

(d)   in proceedings under Schedule 7 to the 2004 Act, an order under paragraph 9(2) or (3) making provision equivalent to an order referred to in paragraph (c);

'pension sharing order' means –

(a)   in proceedings under the 1973 Act, an order making provision under section 24B of that Act;

(b)   in proceedings under the 1984 Act, an order under section 17(1)(b) of that Act;

(c)   in proceedings under Schedule 5 to the 2004 Act, an order under paragraph 15; or

(d)   in proceedings under Schedule 7 to the 2004 Act, an order under paragraph 9(2) or (3) making provision equivalent to an order referred to in paragraph (c);

'pension scheme' means, unless the context otherwise requires, a scheme for which the Board has assumed responsibility in accordance with Chapter 3 of Part 2 of the Pensions Act 2004 (pension protection) or any provision in force in Northern Ireland corresponding to that Chapter;

'PPF compensation' has the meaning given to it –

(a)   in proceedings under the 1973 Act, by section 21C of the 1973 Act;

(b)   in proceedings under the 1984 Act, by section 18(7) of the 1984 Act; and

(c)   in proceedings under the 2004 Act, by paragraph 19F of Schedule 5 to the 2004 Act;

'relevant valuation' means a valuation of pension rights or benefits as at a date not more than 12 months earlier than the date fixed for the first appointment which has been furnished or requested for the purposes of any of the following provisions –

(a)   the Pensions on Divorce etc (Provision of Information) Regulations 2000;

(b)   regulation 5 of and Schedule 2 to the Occupational Pension Schemes (Disclosure of Information) Regulations 1996 and regulation 11 of and Schedule 1 to the Occupational Pension Schemes (Transfer Value) Regulations 1996;

(c)   section 93A or 94(1)(a) or (aa) of the Pension Schemes Act 1993;

(d)   section 94(1)(b) of the Pension Schemes Act 1993 or paragraph 2(a) (or, where applicable, 2(b)) of Schedule 2 to the Personal Pension Schemes (Disclosure of Information) Regulations 1987;

(e)   the Dissolution etc. (Pensions) Regulations 2005;

'variation order' means –

(a)   in proceedings under the 1973 Act, an order under section 31 of that Act; or

(b)   in proceedings under the 2004 Act, an order under Part 11 of Schedule 5 to that Act.

(2)   Omitted

(3)

(a)   Where an application is made under Article 56 of, and using the form in Annex VII to, the Maintenance Regulation, references in this Part to 'financial statement' apply to the applicant as if for the words 'financial statement' were substituted 'the form in Annex VII to the Maintenance Regulation';

(aa)   where an application for establishment or modification of maintenance is made under Article 10 of the2007 Hague Convention, references in this Part to 'financial statement' apply to the applicant as if for 'financial statement' there were substituted 'Financial Circumstances Form';

(b)   Sub-paragraphs (a) and (aa) do not apply where the relief sought includes relief which is of a type to which the Maintenance Regulation or the 2007 Hague Convention, as the case may be, does not apply.

II PROCEDURE FOR APPLICATIONS

When an Application for a financial order may be made
9.4

An application for a financial order may be made –

(a)   in an application for a matrimonial or civil partnership order; or

(b)   at any time after an application for a matrimonial or civil partnership order has been made.

Where to start proceedings

9.5

(1)   An application for a financial remedy must be filed –

    (a)   if there are proceedings for a matrimonial order or a civil partnership order which are proceeding in the family court, in that court; or

    (b)   if there are proceedings for a matrimonial order or a civil partnership order which are proceeding in the High Court, in the registry in which those proceedings are taking place.

(2)   Omitted

(3)   An application for a financial remedy under Part 3 of the 1984 Act or Schedule 7 to the 2004 Act which is proceeding in the High Court must be heard by a judge, but not a district judge, of that court unless a direction has been made that the application may be heard by a district judge of the principal registry.

(Rule 8.28 enables a judge to direct that an application for a financial remedy under Part 3 of the 1984 Act or Schedule 7 to the 2004 Act which is proceeding in the High Court may be heard by a district judge of the principal registry.)

Application for an order preventing a disposition

9.6

(1)   The Part 18 procedure applies to an application for an order preventing a disposition.

(2)   An application for an order preventing a disposition may be made without notice to the respondent.

('Order preventing a disposition' is defined in rule 9.3.)

Application for interim orders

9.7

(1)   A party may apply at any stage of the proceedings for –

    (a)   an order for maintenance pending suit;

    (b)   an order for maintenance pending outcome of proceedings;

    (c)   an order for interim periodical payments;

    (d)   an interim variation order (da) an order for payment in respect of legal services; or

    (e)   any other form of interim order.

(2)   An application for an order mentioned in paragraph (1) shall be made using the Part 18 procedure.

(3)   Where a party makes an application before filing a financial statement, the written evidence in support must –

    (a)   explain why the order is necessary; and

    (b)   give up to date information about that party's financial circumstances.

(4)   Unless the respondent has filed a financial statement, the respondent must, at least 7 days before the court is to deal with the application, file a statement of his means and serve a copy on the applicant.

(5)   An application for an order mentioned in paragraph (1)(e) may be made without notice.

Application for periodical payments order at same rate as an order for maintenance pending suit
9.8
(1)   This rule applies where there are matrimonial proceedings and –
- (a)   a decree nisi of divorce or nullity of marriage has been made;
- (b)   at or after the date of the decree nisi an order for maintenance pending suit is in force; and
- (c)   the spouse in whose favour the decree nisi was made has made an application for an order for periodical payments.

(2)   The spouse in whose favour the decree nisi was made may apply, using the Part 18 procedure, for an order providing for payments at the same rate as those provided for by the order for maintenance pending suit.

Application for periodical payments order at same rate as an order for maintenance pending outcome of proceedings
9.9
(1)   This rule applies where there are civil partnership proceedings and –
- (a)   a conditional order of dissolution or nullity of civil partnership has been made;
- (b)   at or after the date of the conditional order an order for maintenance pending outcome of proceedings is in force;
- (c)   the civil partner in whose favour the conditional order was made has made an application for an order for periodical payments.

(2)   The civil partner in whose favour the conditional order was made may apply, using the Part 18 procedure, for an order providing for payments at the same rate as those provided for by, the order for maintenance pending the outcome of proceedings.

III APPLICATIONS FOR FINANCIAL REMEDIES FOR CHILDREN

Application by parent, guardian etc for financial remedy in respect of children
9.10
(1)   The following people may apply for a financial remedy in respect of a child –
- (a)   a parent, guardian or special guardian of any child of the family;
- (b)   any person who is named in a child arrangements order as a person with whom a child of the family is to live, and any applicant for such an order;
- (c)   any other person who is entitled to apply for a child arrangements order which names that person as a person with whom a child is to live;
- (d)   a local authority, where an order has been made under section 31(1)(a) of the 1989 Act placing a child in its care;
- (e)   the Official Solicitor, if appointed the children's guardian of a child of the family under rule 16.24; and

(f)   subject to paragraph (1A), a child of the family who has been given permission to apply for a financial remedy.

(1A)   Where the application is –

(a)   for the variation of an order under section 2(1)(c), 6 or 7 of the 1978 Act or paragraph 2(1)(c) of, or Part 2 or 3 of, Schedule 6 to the 2004 Act for periodical payments in respect of a child;

(b)   the application is made by the child in question; and

(c)   the child in question is aged 16 or over,

the child does not require permission to make the application.

Children to be separately represented on certain applications

9.11

(1)   Where an application for a financial remedy includes an application for an order for a variation of settlement, the court must, unless it is satisfied that the proposed variation does not adversely affect the rights or interests of any child concerned, direct that the child be separately represented on the application.

(2)   On any other application for a financial remedy the court may direct that the child be separately represented on the application.

(3)   Where a direction is made under paragraph (1) or (2), the court may if the person to be appointed so consents, appoint –

(a)   a person other than the Official Solicitor; or

(b)   the Official Solicitor,

to be a children's guardian and rule16.24(5) and (6) and rules 16.25 to 16.28 apply as appropriate to such an appointment.

IV PROCEDURE AFTER FILING AN APPLICATION

Duties of the court and the applicant upon issuing an application

9.12

(1)   When an application under this Part is issued, except where Chapter 5 of this Part applies –

(a)   the court will fix a first appointment not less than 12 weeks and not more than 16 weeks after the date of the filing of the application; and

(b)   subject to paragraph (2),within 4 days beginning with the date on which the application was filed, a court officer will –

(i)   serve a copy of the application on the respondent; and

(ii)   give notice of the date of the first appointment to the applicant and the respondent.

(2)   Where the applicant wishes to serve a copy of the application on the respondent and on filing the application so notifies the court

(a)   paragraph (1)(b) does not apply;

(b)   a court officer will return to the applicant the copy of the application and the notice of the date of the first appointment; and

(c)   the applicant must, –

(i)   within 4 days beginning with the date on which the copy of the application is received from the court, serve the copy of the application and notice of the date of the first appointment on the respondent; and

(ii) file a certificate of service at or before the first appointment.

(Rule 6.37 sets out what must be included in a certificate of service.)

(3) The date fixed under paragraph (1), or for any subsequent appointment, must not be cancelled except with the court's permission and, if cancelled, the court must immediately fix a new date.

(4) In relation to an application to which the Maintenance Regulation or the 2007 Hague Convention applies, where the applicant does not already know the address of the respondent at the time the application is issued, paragraph (2) does not apply and the court will serve the application in accordance with paragraph (1).

Service of application on mortgagees, trustees etc
9.13

(1) Where an application for a financial remedy includes an application for an order for a variation of settlement, the applicant must serve copies of the application on –

(a) the trustees of the settlement;

(b) the settlor if living; and

(c) such other persons as the court directs.

(2) In the case of an application for an avoidance of disposition order, the applicant must serve copies of the application on the person in whose favour the disposition is alleged to have been made.

(3) Where an application for a financial remedy includes an application relating to land, the applicant must serve a copy of the application on any mortgagee of whom particulars are given in the application.

(4) Any person served under paragraphs (1), (2) or (3) may make a request to the court in writing, within 14 days beginning with the date of service of the application, for a copy of the applicant's financial statement or any relevant part of that statement.

(5) Any person who –

(a) is served with copies of the application in accordance with paragraphs (1), (2) or (3); or

(b) receives a copy of a financial statement, or a relevant part of that statement, following an application made under paragraph (4),

may within 14 days beginning with the date of service or receipt file a statement in answer.

(6) Where a copy of an application is served under paragraphs (1), (2) or (3), the applicant must file a certificate of service at or before the first appointment.

(7) A statement in answer filed under paragraph (5) must be verified by a statement of truth.

Procedure before the first appointment

9.14

(1) Not less than 35 days before the first appointment both parties must simultaneously exchange with each other and file with the court a financial statement in the form referred to in Practice Direction 5A.

(2) The financial statement must–

    (a) be verified by a statement of truth; and

    (b) accompanied by the following documents only –

        (i) any documents required by the financial statement;

        (ii) any other documents necessary to explain or clarify any of the information contained in the financial statement; and

        (iii) any documents provided to the party producing the financial statement by a person responsible for a pension arrangement, either following a request under rule 9.30 or as part of a relevant valuation; and

        (iv) any notification or other document referred to in rule 9.37(2), (4) or (5) which has been received by the party producing the financial statement.

(2ZA) Paragraph (2A) applies where the court has determined that the procedure in this Chapter should apply to an application under Article 56 of the Maintenance Regulation or Article 10 of the 2007 Hague Convention.

(2A) The requirement of paragraph (2)(a)relating to verification by a statement of truth does not apply to the financial statement of either party where the application has been made under–

    (a) Article 56 of the Maintenance Regulation, using the form in Annex VII to that Regulation; or

    (b) Article 10 of the 2007 Hague Convention, using the Financial Circumstances Form,

and the relief sought is limited to a type to which that Regulation or that Convention, as appropriate, applies, but the court may at any time direct that the financial statement of either party shall be verified by a statement of truth.

(3) Where a party was unavoidably prevented from sending any document required by the financial statement, that party must at the earliest opportunity –

    (a) serve a copy of that document on the other party; and

    (b) file a copy of that document with the court, together with a written explanation of the failure to send it with the financial statement.

(4) No disclosure or inspection of documents may be requested or given between the filing of the application for a financial remedy and the first appointment, except –

    (a) copies sent with the financial statement, or in accordance with paragraph (3); or

    (b) in accordance with paragraphs (5) and (6).

(Rule 21.1 explains what is meant by disclosure and inspection.)

(5)   Not less than 14 days before the hearing of the first appointment, each party must file with the court and serve on the other party –

    (a)   a concise statement of the issues between the parties;

    (b)   a chronology;

    (c)   a questionnaire setting out by reference to the concise statement of issues any further information and documents requested from the other party or a statement that no information and documents are required; and

    (d)   a notice stating whether that party will be in a position at the first appointment to proceed on that occasion to a FDR appointment.

(6)   Not less than 14 days before the hearing of the first appointment, the applicant must file with the court and serve on the respondent confirmation –

    (a)   of the names of all persons served in accordance with rule 9.13(1) to (3); and

    (b)   that there are no other persons who must be served in accordance with those paragraphs.

Duties of the court at the first appointment

9.15

(1)   The first appointment must be conducted with the objective of defining the issues and saving costs.

(2)   At the first appointment the court must determine –

    (a)   the extent to which any questions seeking information under rule 9.14(5)(c) must be answered; and

    (b)   what documents requested under rule 9.14(5)(c) must be produced,

and give directions for the production of such further documents as may be necessary.

(3)   The court must give directions where appropriate about –

    (a)   the valuation of assets (including the joint instruction of joint experts);

    (b)   obtaining and exchanging expert evidence, if required;

    (c)   the evidence to be adduced by each party; and

    (d)   further chronologies or schedules to be filed by each party.

(4)   If the court decides that a referral to a FDR appointment is appropriate it must direct that the case be referred to a FDR appointment.

(5)   If the court decides that a referral to a FDR appointment is not appropriate it must direct one or more of the following –

    (a)   that a further directions appointment be fixed;

    (b)   that an appointment be fixed for the making of an interim order;

    (c)   that the case be fixed for a final hearing and, where that direction is given, the court must determine the judicial level at which the case should be heard.

(Under Part 3 the court may also direct that the case be adjourned if it considers that non-court dispute resolution is appropriate.)

(6)   In considering whether to make a costs order under rule 28.3(5), the court must have particular regard to the extent to which each party has complied with the requirement to send documents with the financial statement and the explanation given for any failure to comply.

(7)   The court may –

(a)   where an application for an interim order has been listed for consideration at the first appointment, make an interim order;

(b)   having regard to the contents of the notice filed by the parties under rule 9.14(5)(d), treat the appointment (or part of it) as a FDR appointment to which rule 9.17 applies;

(c)   in a case where a pension sharing order or a pension attachment order is requested, direct any party with pension rights to file and serve a Pension Inquiry Form, completed in full or in part as the court may direct; and

(d)   in a case where a pension compensation sharing order or a pension compensation attachment order is requested, direct any party with PPF compensation rights to file and serve a Pension Protection Fund Inquiry Form, completed in full or in part as the court may direct.

(8)   Both parties must personally attend the first appointment unless the court directs otherwise.

After the first appointment
9.16

(1)   Between the first appointment and the FDR appointment, a party is not entitled to the production of any further documents except –

(a)   in accordance with directions given under rule 9.15(2); or

(b)   with the permission of the court.

(2)   At any stage –

(a)   a party may apply for further directions or a FDR appointment;

(b)   the court may give further directions or direct that parties attend a FDR appointment.

The FDR appointment
9.17

(1)   The FDR appointment must be treated as a meeting held for the purposes of discussion and negotiation.

(2)   The judge hearing the FDR appointment must have no further involvement with the application, other than to conduct any further FDR appointment or to make a consent order or a further directions order.

(3)   Not less than 7 days before the FDR appointment, the applicant must file with the court details of all offers and proposals, and responses to them.

(4)   Paragraph (3) includes any offers, proposals or responses made wholly or partly without prejudice, but paragraph (3) does not make any material admissible as evidence if, but for that paragraph, it would not be admissible.

(5)   At the conclusion of the FDR appointment, any documents filed under paragraph (3), and any filed documents referring to them, must, at the request of the party who filed them, be returned to that party and not retained on the court file.

(6)   Parties attending the FDR appointment must use their best endeavours to reach agreement on matters in issue between them.

(7)   The FDR appointment may be adjourned from time to time.

(8)   At the conclusion of the FDR appointment, the court may make an appropriate consent order.

(9)   If the court does not make an appropriate consent order as mentioned in paragraph (8), the court must give directions for the future course of the proceedings including, where appropriate –

    (a)   the filing of evidence, including up to date information; and

    (b)   fixing a final hearing date.

(10)   Both parties must personally attend the FDR appointment unless the court directs otherwise.

V PROCEDURE AFTER FILING PARTICULAR APPLICATIONS

Duties of the court and the applicant upon filing an application
9.18

(A1)   This Chapter applies where an application is made –

    (a)   under –

        (i)   the 1978 Act;

        (ii)   Schedule 6 to the 2004 Act;

        (iii)   Schedule 1 to the 1989 Act; or

        (iv)   Article 56 of the Maintenance Regulation; or

        (v)   Article 10 of the 2007 Hague Convention.

    (b)   for the variation of an order for a financial remedy.

(1)   Where an application is issued –

    (a)   the court will fix a first hearing date not less than 4 weeks and not more than 8 weeks after the date of the filing of the application; and

    (b)   subject to paragraph (2), within 4 days beginning with the date on which the application was filed, a court officer will –

        (i)   serve a copy of the application on the respondent;

        (ii)   give notice of the date of the first hearing to the applicant and the respondent; and

        (iii)   send a blank financial statement to both the applicant and the respondent.

(2)   Where the applicant wishes to serve a copy of the application on the respondent and, on filing the application, so notifies the court –

    (a)   paragraph (1)(b) does not apply;

    (b)   a court officer will return to the applicant the copy of the application and the notice of the date of the first hearing; and

    (c)   the applicant must –

(i)   within 4 days beginning with the date on which the copy of the application is received from the court, serve the copy of the application and notice of the date of the first hearing on the respondent;

(ii)   send a blank financial statement to the respondent; and

(iii)   file a certificate of service at or before the first hearing.

(3)   The date fixed under paragraph (1), or for any other subsequent hearing or appointment must not be cancelled except with the court's permission and, if cancelled, the court must immediately fix a new date.

(4)   The requirement in paragraph (1)(b)(iii) for the court officer to send a blank financial statement to the applicant does not apply where the application has been made under –

(a)   Article 56 of the Maintenance Regulation, using the form in Annex VII to that Regulation; or

(b)   Article 10 of the 2007 Hague Convention, using the Financial Circumstances Form.

(5)   In relation to an application to which the Maintenance Regulation or the 2007 Hague Convention applies, where the applicant does not already know the address of the respondent at the time the application is issued, paragraph (2) does not apply and the court will serve the application in accordance with paragraph (1).

Request for change of procedure

9.18A

(1)   This rule applies if the applicant wishes to seek a direction from the court that the procedure in Chapter 4 of this Part should apply to an application for an order in proceedings referred to in rule 9.18(A1).

(2)   The application for the order must state –

(a)   that the applicant seeks a direction that the procedure in Chapter 4 of this Part should apply; and

(b)   the applicant's reasons for seeking such a direction.

(3)   The court will –

(a)   determine without notice to the parties and before the first hearing whether the procedure in Chapter 4 or Chapter 5 of this Part should apply to the application; and

(b)   notify the parties of its determination and any directions made in consequence of that determination.

Procedure before the first hearing

9.19

(1)   Not more than 14 days after the date of the issue of the application both parties must simultaneously exchange with each other and file with the court a financial statement referred to in Practice Direction 5A.

(2)   The financial statement must –

(a)   be verified by a statement of truth; and

(b)   contain the following documents only –

       (i)   any documents required by the financial statement; and

       (ii)   any other documents necessary to explain or clarify any of the information contained in the financial statement.

(2A)   The requirement of paragraph (2)(a)relating to verification by statement of truth does not apply to the financial statement of either party where the application has been made under –

     (a)   Article 56 of the Maintenance Regulation, using the form in Annex VII to that Regulation; or

     (b)   Article 10 of the 2007 Hague Convention, using the Financial Circumstances Form,

but the court may at any time direct that the financial statement of either party shall be verified by a statement of truth.

(3)   Where a party was unavoidably prevented from sending any document required by the financial statement, that party must at the earliest opportunity –

     (a)   serve a copy of that document on the other party; and

     (b)   file a copy of that document with the court, together with a statement explaining the failure to send it with the financial statement.

(4)   No disclosure or inspection of documents may be requested or given between the filing of the application for a financial remedy and the first hearing except copies sent with the financial statement or in accordance with paragraph (3).

(Rule 21.1 explains what is meant by disclosure and inspection.)

Power of the court to direct filing of evidence and set dates for further hearings
9.20

Unless the court is able to determine the application at the first hearing the court may direct that further evidence be filed and set a date for a directions hearing or appointment or final hearing.

Who the respondent is on an application under section 20 or section 20A of the 1978 Act or Part 6 of Schedule 6 to the 2004 Act
9.21

In relation to proceedings set out in column 1 of the following table, column 2 sets out who the respondents to those proceedings will be.

Proceedings	Respondent
Application under section 20 of the 1978 Act	The other party to the marriage; and where the order to which the application relates requires periodical payments to be made to, or in respect of, a child who is 16 years of age or over, that child.

Proceedings	Respondent
Application under paragraphs 30 to 34 of Schedule 6 to the 2004 Act	The other party to the civil partnership; and where the order to which the application relates requires periodical payments to be made to, or in respect of, a child who is 16 years of age or over, that child.
Application for the revival of an order under section 20A of the 1978 Act or paragraph 40 of Schedule 6 to the 2004 Act	The parties to the proceedings leading to the order which it is sought to have revived

Duty to make entries in the court's register
9.21A

Where a court officer receives notice of any direction made in the High Court or family court under section 28 of the 1978 Act by virtue of which an order made under that Act or the 2004 Act ceases to have effect, particulars of the direction must be noted in the court's records.

VA CERTAIN APPLICATIONS

Application for a maintenance order, or revocation of a maintenance order to which the 1982 Act, the Lugano Convention, the 1988 Convention or the Maintenance Regulation applies
9.22

(1)   This rule applies where a person makes an application for a maintenance order, or for the variation or the revocation of a maintenance order, in relation to which the court has jurisdiction by virtue of the 1982 Act, the Lugano Convention, the 1988 Convention or the Maintenance Regulation, and the respondent is outside the United Kingdom.

(2)   Where the respondent does not enter an appearance and is not represented at the hearing –

    (a)   the court will apply the provisions of Article 20 of the 1968 Convention, Article 20 of the 1988 Convention, Article 26 of the Lugano Convention, or Article 11 of the Maintenance Regulation as appropriate;

    (b)   where the court proceeds to hear the application having applied the appropriate provision referred to in sub-paragraph (a), the court will take into account any written representations made and any evidence given by the respondent under these rules.

(3)   Omitted

(4)   In this rule –

    (a)   'the 1982 Act', 'the Lugano Convention' and 'the 1988 Convention' have the meanings given to them in rule 34.1(2);

    (b)   'the 1968 Convention' has the meaning given to it in the Civil Jurisdiction and Judgments Act 1982.

Omitted
9.23

VI GENERAL PROCEDURE

Power to order delivery up of possession etc.
9.24
(1)   This rule applies where the court has made an order under –
   (a)   section 24A of the 1973 Act;
   (b)   section 17(2) of the 1984 Act;
   (c)   Part 3 of Schedule 5 to the 2004 Act; or
   (d)   paragraph 9(4) of Schedule 7 to the 2004 Act.
(2)   When the court makes an order mentioned in paragraph (1), it may order any party to deliver up to the purchaser or any other person –
   (a)   possession of the land, including any interest in, or right over, land;
   (b)   receipt of rents or profits relating to it; or
   (c)   both.

Where proceedings may be heard
9.25
(1)   Paragraph (2) applies to an application –
   (a)   for a financial order;
   (b)   under Part 3 of the 1984 Act; or
   (c)   under Schedule 7 to the 2004 Act.
(2)   An application mentioned in paragraph (1) must be heard –
   (a)   Omitted
   (b)   where the case is proceeding in the High Court –
      (i)   at the Royal Courts of Justice; or
      (ii)   in matrimonial or civil partnership proceedings, any court at which sittings of the High Court are authorised.

Applications for consent orders for financial remedy
9.26
(1)   Subject to paragraph (5) and to rule 35.2, in relation to an application for a consent order –
   (a)   the applicant must file two copies of a draft of the order in the terms sought, one of which must be endorsed with a statement signed by the respondent to the application signifying agreement; and
   (b)   each party must file with the court and serve on the other party, a statement of information in the form referred to in Practice Direction 5A.
(2)   Where each party's statement of information is contained in one form, it must be signed by both the applicant and respondent to certify that they have read the contents of the other party's statement.
(3)   Where each party's statement of information is in a separate form, the form of each party must be signed by the other party to certify that they have read the contents of the statement contained in that form.

(4)   Unless the court directs otherwise, the applicant and the respondent need not attend the hearing of an application for a consent order.

(5)   Where all or any of the parties attend the hearing of an application for a financial remedy the court may –

    (a)   dispense with the filing of a statement of information; and

    (b)   give directions for the information which would otherwise be required to be given in such a statement in such a manner as it thinks fit.

(6)   In relation to an application for a consent order under Part 3 of the 1984 Act or Schedule 7 to the 2004 Act, the application for permission to make the application may be heard at the same time as the application for a financial remedy if evidence of the respondent's consent to the order is filed with the application.

(The following rules contain provision in relation to applications for consent orders – rule 9.32 (pension sharing order), rule 9.34 (pension attachment order), rule 9.41 (pension compensation sharing orders) and rule 9.43 (pension compensation attachment orders.)

Questions as to the court's jurisdiction or whether the proceedings should be stayed

9.26A

(1)   This rule applies to applications for maintenance where a question as to jurisdiction arises under –

    (a)   the 1968 Convention;

    (b)   the 1988 Convention;

    (c)   the Lugano Convention;

    (d)   the Maintenance Regulation; or

    (e)   Article 18 of the 2007 Hague Convention.

(2)   If at any time after the issue of the application it appears to the court that it does not or may not have jurisdiction to hear an application, or that under the instruments referred to in paragraph (1) it is or may be required to stay the proceedings or to decline jurisdiction, the court must –

    (a)   stay the proceedings, and

    (b)   fix a date for a hearing to determine jurisdiction or whether there should be a stay or other order.

(3)   The court officer will serve notice of the hearing referred to at paragraph (2)(b) on the parties to the proceedings.

(4)   The court must, in writing –

    (a)   give reasons for its decision under paragraph (2), and

    (b)   where it makes a finding of fact, state such finding.

(5)   The court may with the consent of all the parties deal with any question as to the jurisdiction of the court, or as to whether the proceedings should be stayed, without a hearing.

(6)   In this rule –

    (a)   'the 1968 Convention' has the meaning given to it in the Civil Jurisdiction and Judgments Act 1982;

(b)   'the 1988 Convention' and 'the Lugano Convention' have the meanings given to them in rule 34.1(2).

International Maintenance Obligations: Communication with the Central Authority for England and Wales
9.26AA

(1)   Where the Lord Chancellor requests information or a document from the court officer for the relevant court for the purposes of Article 58 of the Maintenance Regulation or Articles 12 or 25(2) of the 2007 Hague Convention, the court officer shall provide the requested information or document to the Lord Chancellor forthwith.

(2)   In this rule, 'relevant court' means the court at which an application under Article 56 of the Maintenance Regulation or Article 10 of the 2007 Hague Convention has been filed.

[The Lord Chancellor is the Central Authority for England and Wales in relation to the 2007 Hague Convention and the Maintenance Regulation]

Adding or removing parties
9.26B

(1)   The court may direct that a person or body be added as a party to proceedings for a financial remedy if –

(a)   it is desirable to add the new party so that the court can resolve all the matters in dispute in the proceedings; or

(b)   there is an issue involving the new party and an existing party which is connected to the matters in dispute in the proceedings, and it is desirable to add the new party so that the court can resolve that issue.

(2)   The court may direct that any person or body be removed as a party if it is not desirable for that person or body to be a party to the proceedings.

(3)   If the court makes a direction for the addition or removal of a party under this rule, it may give consequential directions about –

(a)   the service of a copy of the application form or other relevant documents on the new party; and

(b)   the management of the proceedings.

(4)   The power of the court under this rule to direct that a party be added or removed may be exercised either on the court's own initiative or on the application of an existing party or a person or body who wishes to become a party.

(5)   An application for an order under this rule must be made in accordance with the Part 18 procedure and, unless the court directs otherwise, must be supported by evidence setting out the proposed new party's interest in or connection with the proceedings or, in the case of removal of a party, the reasons for removal.

Method of making periodical payments
9.26C
(1)   This rule applies where under section 1(4) or (4A) of the Maintenance Enforcement Act 1991 the court orders that payments under a qualifying periodical maintenance order are to be made by a particular means.

(2)   The court officer will record on a copy of the order the means of payment that the court has ordered.

(3)   The court officer will notify in writing the person liable to make payments under the order how the payments are to be made.

(4)   Where under section 1(4A) of the Maintenance Enforcement Act 1991 the court orders payment to the court by a method of payment under section 1(5) of that Act, the court officer will notify the person liable to make payments under the order of sufficient details of the account into which payments should be made to enable payments to be made into that account.

(5)   Where payments are made to the court, the court officer will give or send a receipt to any person who makes such a payment and who asks for a receipt.

(6)   Where payments are made to the court, the court officer will make arrangements to make the payments to –
   (a)   the person entitled to them; or
   (b)   if the person entitled to them is a child, to the child or to the person with whom the child has his or her home.

(7)   The Part 18 procedure applies to an application under section 1(7) of the Maintenance Enforcement Act 1991 (application from an interested party to revoke, suspend, revive or vary the method of payment).

(8)   Where the court makes an order under section 1(7) of the Maintenance Enforcement Act 1991 or dismisses an application for such an order, the court officer will, as far as practicable, notify in writing all interested parties of the effect of the order and will take the steps set out in paragraphs (2), (3) and (4), as appropriate.

(9)   In this rule, 'interested party' and 'qualifying periodical maintenance order' have the meanings given in section 1(10) of the Maintenance Enforcement Act 1991.

Court officer to notify subsequent marriage or formation of civil partnership of a person entitled to payments under a maintenance order
9.26D
(1)   This rule applies where –
   (a)   there is an order of a type referred to in paragraph (4) which requires payments to be made to the court or to an officer of the court; and
   (b)   the court is notified in writing by –
      (i)   the person entitled to receive payments under the order;
      (ii)   the person required to make payments under the order; or
      (iii)   the personal representative of such a person,
      that the person entitled to receive payments under the order has subsequently married or formed a civil partnership.

(2)   The court officer will, where practicable, notify in writing the courts referred to in paragraph (3) of the notification of the subsequent marriage or formation of a civil partnership.

(3)   The courts to be notified are –

(a)   any other court which has made an order of a type referred to in paragraph (4);

(b)   in the case of a provisional order made under section 3 of the 1920 Act or section 3 of the 1972 Act, the court which confirmed the order;

(c)   if an order of a type referred to in paragraph (4) has been transmitted abroad for registration under section 2 of the 1920 Act or section 2 of the 1972 Act, the court in which the order is registered; and

(d)   any other court in which an application to enforce the order has been made.

(4)   The orders are –

(a)   those to which the following provisions apply—

(i)   section 38 of the 1973 Act;

(ii)   section 4(2) of the 1978 Act;

(iii)   paragraph 65 of Schedule 5 to the 2004 Act; and

(iv)   paragraph 26(2) of Schedule 6 to the 2004 Act; and

(b)   an attachment of earnings order made to secure payments under an order referred to in sub-paragraph (a).

(5)   In this rule –

'the 1920 Act' means the Maintenance Orders (Facilities for Enforcement) Act 1920; and

'the 1972 Act' means the Maintenance Orders (Reciprocal Enforcement) Act 1972.

Enforcement and apportionment where periodical payments are made under more than one order

9.26E

(1)   This rule applies where periodical payments are required to be made by a payer to a payee under more than one periodical payments order.

(2)   Proceedings for the recovery of payments under more than one order may be made in one application by the payee, which must indicate the payments due under each order.

(3)   Paragraphs (4) and (5) apply where any sum paid to the court on any date by a payer who is liable to make payments to the court under two or more periodical payments orders is less than the total sum that the payer is required to pay to the court on that date in respect of those orders.

(4)   The payment made will be apportioned between the orders in proportion to the amounts due under each order over a period of one year.

(5)   If, as a result of the apportionment referred to in paragraph (4), the payments under any periodical payments order are no longer in arrears, the residue shall be applied to the amount due under the other order or, if there is more than one other order, shall be apportioned between the other orders in accordance with paragraph (4).

(6) In this rule –

'payee' means a person entitled to receive payments under a periodical payments order; and

'payer' means a person required to make payments under a periodical payments order."

VII ESTIMATES OF COSTS

Estimates of Costs
9.27

(1) Subject to paragraph (2), at every hearing or appointment each party must produce to the court an estimate of the costs incurred by that party up to the date of that hearing or appointment.

(2) Not less than 14 days before the date fixed for the final hearing of an application for a financial remedy, each party ('the filing party') must (unless the court directs otherwise) file with the court and serve on each other party a statement giving full particulars of all costs in respect of the proceedings which the filing party has incurred or expects to incur, to enable the court to take account of the parties' liabilities for costs when deciding what order (if any) to make for a financial remedy.

(Rule 28.3 makes provision for orders for costs in financial remedy proceedings.)

Duty to make open proposals
9.28

(1) Not less than 14 days before the date fixed for the final hearing of an application for a financial remedy, the applicant must (unless the court directs otherwise) file with the court and serve on the respondent an open statement which sets out concise details, including the amounts involved, of the orders which the applicant proposes to ask the court to make.

(2) Not more than 7 days after service of a statement under paragraph (1), the respondent must file with the court and serve on the applicant an open statement which sets out concise details, including the amounts involved, of the orders which the respondent proposes to ask the court to make.

VIII PENSIONS

Application and interpretation of this Chapter
9.29

(1) This Chapter applies –

    (a) where an application for a financial remedy has been made; and

    (b) the applicant or respondent is the party with pension rights.

(2) In this Chapter –

    (a) in proceedings under the 1973 Act and the 1984 Act, all words and phrases defined in sections 25D(3) and (4) of the 1973 Act have the meaning assigned by those subsections;

(b)   in proceedings under the 2004 Act –
   (i)   all words and phrases defined in paragraphs 16(4) to (5) and 29 of Schedule 5 to that Act have the meanings assigned by those paragraphs; and
   (ii)   'the party with pension rights' has the meaning given to 'civil partner with pension rights' by paragraph 29 of Schedule 5 to the 2004 Act;

(c)   all words and phrases defined in section 46 of the Welfare Reform and Pensions Act 1999 have the meanings assigned by that section.

What the party with pension rights must do when the court fixes a first appointment
9.30

(1)   Where the court fixes a first appointment as required by rule 9.12(1)(a) the party with pension rights must request the person responsible for each pension arrangement under which the party has or is likely to have benefits to provide the information referred to in regulation 2(2) of the Pensions on Divorce etc (Provision of Information) Regulations 2000.

(The information referred to in regulation 2 of the Pensions on Divorce etc (Provision of Information) Regulations 2000 relates to the valuation of pension rights or benefits.)

(2)   The party with pension rights must comply with paragraph (1) within 7 days beginning with the date on which that party receives notification of the date of the first appointment.

(3)   Within 7 days beginning with the date on which the party with pension rights receives the information under paragraph (1) that party must send a copy of it to the other party, together with the name and address of the person responsible for each pension arrangement.

(4)   A request under paragraph (1) need not be made where the party with pension rights is in possession of, or has requested, a relevant valuation of the pension rights or benefits accrued under the pension arrangement in question.

Applications for pension sharing orders
9.31

Where an application for a financial remedy includes an application for a pension sharing order, or where a request for such an order is added to an existing application for a financial remedy, the applicant must serve a copy of the application on the person responsible for the pension arrangement concerned.

Applications for consent orders for pension sharing
9.32

(1)   This rule applies where –
   (a)   the parties have agreed on the terms of an order and the agreement includes a pension sharing order;

    (b)   service has not been effected under rule 9.31; and

    (c)   the information referred to in paragraph (2) has not otherwise been provided.

(2)   The party with pension rights must –

    (a)   request the person responsible for the pension arrangement concerned to provide the information set out in Section C of the Pension Inquiry Form; and

    (b)   on receipt, send a copy of the information referred to in sub-paragraph (a) to the other party.

Applications for pension attachment orders

9.33

(1)   Where an application for a financial remedy includes an application for a pension attachment order, or where a request for such an order is added to an existing application for a financial remedy, the applicant must serve a copy of the application on the person responsible for the pension arrangement concerned and must at the same time send –

    (a)   an address to which any notice which the person responsible is required to serve on the applicant is to be sent;

    (b)   an address to which any payment which the person responsible is required to make to the applicant is to be sent; and

    (c)   where the address in sub-paragraph (b) is that of a bank, a building society or the Department of National Savings, sufficient details to enable the payment to be made into the account of the applicant.

(2)   A person responsible for a pension arrangement who receives a copy of the application under paragraph (1) may, within 21 days beginning with the date of service of the application, request the party with the pension rights to provide that person with the information disclosed in the financial statement relating to the party's pension rights or benefits under that arrangement.

(3)   If the person responsible for a pension arrangement makes a request under paragraph (2), the party with the pension rights must provide that person with a copy of the section of that party's financial statement that relates to that party's pension rights or benefits under that arrangement.

(4)   The party with the pension rights must comply with paragraph (3) –

    (a)   within the time limited for filing the financial statement by rule 9.14(1); or

    (b)   within 21 days beginning with the date on which the person responsible for the pension arrangement makes the request,

    whichever is the later.

(5)   A person responsible for a pension arrangement who receives a copy of the section of a financial statement as required pursuant to paragraph (4) may, within 21 days beginning with the date on which that person receives it, send to the court, the applicant and the respondent a statement in answer.

(6)   A person responsible for a pension arrangement who files a statement in answer pursuant to paragraph (5) will be entitled to be represented at the first appointment, or such other hearing as the court may direct, and the court must

within 4 days, beginning with the date on which that person files the statement in answer, give the person notice of the date of the first appointment or other hearing as the case maybe.

Applications for consent orders for pension attachment
9.34
(1)   This rule applies where service has not been effected under rule 9.33(1).
(2)   Where the parties have agreed on the terms of an order and the agreement includes a pension attachment order, then they must serve on the person responsible for the pension arrangement concerned –
    (a)   a copy of the application for a consent order;
    (b)   a draft of the proposed order, complying with rule 9.35; and
    (c)   the particulars set out in rule 9.33(1).
(3)   No consent order that includes a pension attachment order must be made unless either –
    (a)   the person responsible for the pension arrangement has not made any objection within 21 days beginning with the date on which the application for a consent order was served on that person; or
    (b)   the court has considered any such objection, and for the purpose of considering any objection the court may make such direction as it sees fit for the person responsible to attend before it or to furnish written details of the objection.

Pension sharing orders or pension attachment orders
9.35
An order for a financial remedy, whether by consent or not, which includes a pension sharing order or a pension attachment order, must –
(a)   in the body of the order, state that there is to be provision by way of pension sharing or pension attachment in accordance with the annex or annexes to the order; and
(b)   be accompanied by a pension sharing annex or a pension attachment annex as the case may require, and if provision is made in relation to more than one pension arrangement there must be one annex for each pension arrangement.

Duty of the court upon making a pension sharing order or a pension attachment order
9.36
(1)   A court which varies or discharges a pension sharing order or a pension attachment order, must send, or direct one of the parties to send –
    (a)   to the person responsible for the pension arrangement concerned; or
    (b)   where the Board has assumed responsibility for the pension scheme or part of it, the Board;
the documents referred to in paragraph (4).
(2)   A court which makes a pension sharing order or pension attachment order, must send, or direct one of the parties to send to the person responsible for the pension arrangement concerned, the documents referred to in paragraph (4).

(3)   Where the Board has assumed responsibility for the pension scheme or part of it after the making of a pension sharing order or attachment order but before the documents have been sent to the person responsible for the pension arrangement in accordance with paragraph (2), the court which makes the pension sharing order or the pension attachment order, must send, or direct one of the parties to send to the Board the documents referred to in paragraph (4).

(4)   The documents to be sent in accordance with paragraph (1) to (3) are –
   (a)   in the case of –
      (i)   proceedings under the 1973 Act, a copy of the decree of judicial separation;
      (ii)   proceedings under Schedule 5 to the 2004 Act, a copy of the separation order;
      (iii) proceedings under Part 3 of the 1984 Act, a copy of the document of divorce, annulment or legal separation;
      (iv)   proceedings under Schedule 7 to the 2004 Act, a copy of the document of dissolution, annulment or legal separation;
   (b)   in the case of divorce or nullity of marriage, a copy of the decree absolute under rule 7.31or 7.32; or
   (c)   in the case of dissolution or nullity of civil partnership, a copy of the order making the conditional order final under rule 7.31 or 7.32; and
   (d)   a copy of the pension sharing order or the pension attachment order, or as the case may be of the order varying or discharging that order, including any annex to that order relating to that pension arrangement but no other annex to that order.

(5)   The documents referred to in paragraph (4) must be sent –
   (a)   in proceedings under the 1973 Act and the 1984 Act, within 7 days beginning with the date on which –
      (i)   the relevant pension sharing or pension attachment order, or any order varying or discharging such an order, is made; or
      (ii)   the decree absolute of divorce or nullity or decree of judicial separation is made,
      whichever is the later; and
   (b)   in proceedings under the 2004 Act, within 7 days beginning with the date on which –
      (i)   the relevant pension sharing or pension attachment order, or any order varying or discharging such an order, is made; or
      (ii)   the final order of dissolution or nullity or separation order is made,
      whichever is the later.

Procedure where Pension Protection Fund becomes involved with the pension scheme
9.37
(1)   This rule applies where –
   (a)   rules 9.30 to 9.34 or 9.36 apply; and

(b)   the party with the pension rights ("the member") receives or has received notification in compliance with the Pension Protection Fund (Provision of Information) Regulations 2005 ('the 2005 Regulations') –

  (i)   from the trustees or managers of a pension scheme, that there is an assessment period in relation to that scheme; or

  (ii)   from the Board that it has assumed responsibility for the pension scheme or part of it.

(2)   If the trustees or managers of the pension scheme notify or have notified the member that there is an assessment period in relation to that scheme, the member must send to the other party, all the information which the Board is required from time to time to provide to the member under the 2005 Regulations including –

  (a)   a copy of the notification; and

  (b)   a copy of the valuation summary,

in accordance with paragraph (3).

(3)   The member must send the information or any part of it referred to in paragraph (2) –

  (a)   if available, when the member sends the information received under rule 9.30(1); or

  (b)   otherwise, within 7 days of receipt.

(4)   If the Board notifies the member that it has assumed responsibility for the pension scheme, or part of it, the member must –

  (a)   send a copy of the notification to the other party within 7 days of receipt; and

  (b)   comply with paragraph (5).

(5)   Where paragraph (4) applies, the member must –

  (a)   within 7 days of receipt of the notification, request the Board in writing to provide a forecast of the member's compensation entitlement as described in the 2005 Regulations; and

  (b)   send a copy of the forecast of the member's compensation entitlement to the other party within 7 days of receipt.

(6)   In this rule –

  (a)   'assessment period' means an assessment period within the meaning of Part 2 of the Pensions Act 2004; and

  (b)   'valuation summary' has the meaning assigned to it by the 2005 Regulations.

IX PENSION PROTECTION FUND COMPENSATION

Application and interpretation of this Chapter
9.38

(1)   This Chapter applies –

  (a)   where an application for a financial remedy has been made; and

  (b)   the applicant or respondent is, the party with compensation rights.

(2)   In this Chapter 'party with compensation rights' –

(a)   in proceedings under the 1973 Act and the 1984 Act, has the meaning given to it by section 25G(5) of the 1973 Act;

(b)   in proceedings under the 2004 Act, has the meaning given to 'civil partner with compensation rights' by paragraph 37(1) of Schedule 5 to the 2004 Act.

What the party with compensation rights must do when the court fixes a first appointment
9.39

(1)   Where the court fixes a first appointment as required by rule 9.12(1)(a) the party with compensation rights must request the Board to provide the information about the valuation of entitlement to PPF compensation referred to in regulations made by the Secretary of State under section 118 of the Pensions Act 2008.

(2)   The party with compensation rights must comply with paragraph (1) within 7 days beginning with the date on which that party receives notification of the date of the first appointment.

(3)   Within 7 days beginning with the date on which the party with compensation rights receives the information under paragraph (1) that party must send a copy of it to the other party, together with the name and address of the trustees or managers responsible for each pension scheme.

(4)   Where the rights to PPF Compensation are derived from rights under more than one pension scheme, the party with compensation rights must comply with this rule in relation to each entitlement.

Applications for pension compensation sharing orders
9.40
Where an application for a financial remedy includes an application for a pension compensation sharing order or where a request for such an order is added to an existing application for a financial remedy, the applicant must serve a copy of the application on the Board.

Applications for consent orders for pension compensation sharing
9.41

(1)   This rule applies where –

(a)   the parties have agreed on the terms of an order and the agreement includes a pension compensation sharing order;

(b)   service has not been effected under rule 9.40; and

(c)   the information referred to in paragraph (2) has not otherwise been provided.

(2)   The party with compensation rights must –

(a)   request the Board to provide the information set out in Section C of the Pension Protection Fund Inquiry Form; and

(b)   on receipt, send a copy of the information referred to in sub-paragraph (a) to the other party.

Applications for pension compensation attachment orders
9.42

Where an application for a financial remedy includes an application for a pension compensation attachment order or where a request for such an order is added to an existing application for a financial remedy, the applicant must serve a copy of the application on the Board and must at the same time send –

(a)   an address to which any notice which the Board is required to serve on the applicant is to be sent;

(b)   an address to which any payment which the Board is required to make to the applicant is to be sent; and

(c)   where the address in sub-paragraph (b) is that of a bank, a building society or the Department of National Savings, sufficient details to enable the payment to be made into the account of the applicant.

Applications for consent orders for pension compensation attachment
9.43

(1)   This rule applies where service has not been effected under rule 9.42.

(2)   Where the parties have agreed on the terms of an order and the agreement includes a pension compensation attachment order, then they must serve on the Board –

(a)   a copy of the application for a consent order;

(b)   a draft of the proposed order, complying with rule 9.44; and

(c)   the particulars set out in rule 9.42.

Pension compensation sharing orders or pension compensation attachment orders
9.44

An order for a financial remedy, whether by consent or not, which includes a pension compensation sharing order or a pension compensation attachment order, must –

(a)   in the body of the order, state that there is to be provision by way of pension compensation sharing or pension compensation attachment in accordance with the annex or annexes to the order; and

(b)   be accompanied by a pension compensation sharing annex or a pension compensation attachment annex as the case may require, and if provision is made in relation to entitlement to PPF compensation that derives from rights under more than one pension scheme there must be one annex for each such entitlement.

Duty of the court upon making a pension compensation sharing order or a pension compensation attachment order
9.45

(1)   court which makes, varies or discharges a pension compensation sharing order or a pension compensation attachment order, must send, or direct one of the parties to send, to the Board –

(a)   in the case of –

(i)   proceedings under Part 3 of the 1984 Act, a copy of the document of divorce, annulment or legal separation;

     (ii)   proceedings under Schedule 7 to the 2004 Act, a copy of the document of dissolution, annulment or legal separation;

(b)   in the case of –

     (i)   divorce or nullity of marriage, a copy of the decree absolute under rule 7.32 or 7.33;

     (ii)   dissolution or nullity of civil partnership, a copy of the order making the conditional order final under rule 7.32 or 7.33;

(c)   in the case of separation –

     (i)   in the matrimonial proceedings, a copy of the decree of judicial separation;

     (ii)   in civil partnership proceedings, a copy of the separation order; and

(d)   a copy of the pension compensation sharing order or the pension compensation attachment order, or as the case may be of the order varying or discharging that order, including any annex to that order relating to that PPF compensation but no other annex to that order.

(2)   The documents referred to in paragraph (1) must be sent –

(a)   in proceedings under the 1973 Act and the 1984 Act, within 7 days beginning with the date on which –

     (i)   the relevant pension compensation sharing or pension compensation attachment order is made; or

     (ii)   the decree absolute of divorce or nullity or the decree of judicial separation is made,

     whichever is the later; and

(b)   in proceedings under the 2004 Act, within 7 days beginning with the date on which –

     (i)   the relevant pension compensation sharing or pension compensation attachment order is made; or

     (ii)   the final order of dissolution or nullity or separation order is made,

     whichever is the later.

PART 12 – PROCEEDINGS RELATING TO CHILDREN EXCEPT PARENTAL ORDER PROCEEDINGS AND PROCEEDINGS FOR APPLICATIONS IN ADOPTION, PLACEMENT AND RELATED PROCEEDINGS

I INTERPRETATION AND APPLICATION OF THIS PART

Application of this Part

12.1

(1)   The rules in this Part apply to–

(a)   emergency proceedings;

(b)   private law proceedings;

(c)   public law proceedings;

(d)   proceedings relating to the exercise of the court's inherent jurisdiction (other than applications for the court's permission to start such proceedings);

(e)   proceedings relating to child abduction and the recognition and enforcement of decisions relating to custody under the European Convention;

(f)   proceedings relating to the Council Regulation or the 1996 Hague Convention in respect of children; and

(g)   any other proceedings which may be referred to in a practice direction.

(Part 18 sets out the procedure for making an application for permission to bring proceedings.)

(Part 31 sets out the procedure for making applications for recognition and enforcement of judgments under the Council Regulation or the 1996 Hague Convention.)

(2)   The rules in Chapter 7 of this Part also apply to family proceedings which are not within paragraph (1) but which otherwise relate wholly or mainly to the maintenance or upbringing of a minor.

Interpretation
12.2   In this Part–
'the 2006 Act' means the Childcare Act 2006;
'activity condition' has the meaning given to it by section 11C(2) of the 1989 Act;
'activity direction' has the meaning given to it by section 11A(3) of the 1989 Act;
'advocate' means a person exercising a right of audience as a representative of, or on behalf of, a party;
'care proceedings' means proceedings for a care order under section 31(1)(a) of the 1989 Act;
'Case Management Order' means an order in the form referred to in Practice Direction 12A;
'child assessment order' has the meaning assigned to it by section 43(2) of the 1989 Act;
'contribution order' has the meaning assigned to it by paragraph 23(2) of Schedule 2 to the 1989 Act;
'education supervision order' has the meaning assigned to it by section 36(2) of the 1989 Act;
'emergency proceedings' means proceedings for –
(a)   the disclosure of information as to the whereabouts of a child under section 33 of the 1986 Act;
(b)   an order authorising the taking charge of and delivery of a child under section 34 of the 1986 Act;
(c)   an emergency protection order;
(d)   an order under section 44(9)(b) of the 1989 Act varying a direction in an emergency protection order given under section 44(6) of that Act;

(e) an order under section 45(5) of the 1989 Act extending the period during which an emergency protection order is to have effect;

(f) an order under section 45(8)of the 1989 Act discharging an emergency protection order;

(g) an order under section 45(8A)of the 1989 Act varying or discharging an emergency protection order in so far as it imposes an exclusion requirement on a person who is not entitled to apply for the order to be discharged;

(h) an order under section 45(8B)of the 1989 Act varying or discharging an emergency protection order in so far as it confers a power of arrest attached to an exclusion requirement;

(i) warrants under sections 48(9)and 102(1) of the 1989 Act and under section 79 of the 2006 Act; or

(j) a recovery order under section50 of the 1989 Act;

'emergency protection order' means an order under section 44 of the 1989 Act;

'enforcement order' has the meaning assigned to it by section 11J(2) of the 1989 Act;

'financial compensation order' means an order made under section 11O(2) of the 1989 Act;

'interim order' means an interim care order or an interim supervision order referred to in section 38(1) of the 1989 Act;

'Part 4 proceedings' means proceedings for –

(a) a care order, or the discharge of such an order, under section 39(1) of the 1989 Act;

(b) an order giving permission to change a child's surname or remove a child from the United Kingdom under section 33(7) of the 1989 Act;

(c) a supervision order, the discharge or variation of such an order under section 39(2) of the 1989 Act, or the extension of such an order under paragraph 6(3) of Schedule 3 to that Act;

(d) an order making provision regarding contact under section 34(2) to (4) of the 1989 Act or an order varying or discharging such an order under section 34(9) of that Act;

(e) an education supervision order, the extension of an education supervision order under paragraph 15(2) of Schedule 3 to the 1989 Act, or the discharge of such an order under paragraph 17(1) of Schedule 3 to that Act;

(f) an order varying directions made with an interim care order or interim supervision order under section 38(8)(b) of the 1989 Act;

(g) an order under section 39(3) of the 1989 Act varying a supervision order in so far as it affects a person with whom the child is living but who is not entitled to apply for the order to be discharged;

(h)   an order under section 39(3A) of the 1989 Act varying or discharging an interim care order in so far as it imposes an exclusion requirement on a person who is not entitled to apply for the order to be discharged;

(i)   an order under section 39(3B) of the 1989 Act varying or discharging an interim care order in so far as it confers a power of arrest attached to an exclusion requirement; or

(j)   the substitution of a supervision order for a care order under section 39(4) of the 1989 Act;

'private law proceedings' means proceedings for –

(a)   a section 8 order except a child arrangements order to which section 9(6B) of the 1989 Act applies with respect to a child who is in the care of a local authority;

(b)   a parental responsibility order under sections 4(1)(c),4ZA(1)(c) or 4A(1)(b) of the 1989 Act or an order terminating parental responsibility under sections 4(2A), 4ZA(5) or 4A(3) of that Act;

(c)   an order appointing a child's guardian under section 5(1) of the 1989 Act or an order terminating the appointment under section 6(7) of that Act;

(d)   an order giving permission to change a child's surname or remove a child from the United Kingdom under sections 13(1) or 14C(3) of the 1989 Act;

(e)   a special guardianship order except where that order relates to a child who is subject of a care order;

(f)   an order varying or discharging such an order under section 14D of the 1989 Act;

(g)   an enforcement order;

(h)   a financial compensation order;

(i)   an order under paragraph 9 of Schedule A1 to the 1989 Act following a breach of an enforcement order;

(j)   an order under Part 2 of Schedule A1 to the 1989 Act revoking or amending an enforcement order; or

(k)   an order that a warning notice be attached to a child arrangements order;

'public law proceedings' means Part 4 proceedings and proceedings for –

(a)   a child arrangements order to which section 9(6B) of the 1989 Act applies with respect to a child who is in the care of a local authority;

(b)   a special guardianship order relating to a child who is the subject of a care order;

(c)   a secure accommodation order under section 25 of the 1989 Act;

(d)   omitted

(e)   omitted

(f) omitted

(g) omitted

(h) omitted

(i) omitted

(j) omitted

(k) omitted

(l) omitted

(m) omitted

(n) a child assessment order, or the variation or discharge of such an order under section 43(12) of the 1989 Act;

(o) an order permitting the local authority to arrange for any child in its care to live outside England and Wales under paragraph 19(1) of Schedule 2 to the 1989 Act;

(p) a contribution order, or revocation of such an order under paragraph 23(8) of Schedule 2 to the 1989 Act;

(q) an appeal under paragraph 8(1)of Schedule 8 to the 1989 Act;

'special guardianship order' has the meaning assigned to it by section 14A(1) of the 1989 Act;

'supervision order' has the meaning assigned to it by section 31(11) of the 1989 Act;

'supervision proceedings' means proceedings for a supervision order under section 31(1)(b) of the 1989 Act;

'warning notice' means a notice attached to an order pursuant to section 8(2) of the Children and Adoption Act 2006.

(The 1980 Hague Convention, the 1996 Hague Convention, the Council Regulation, and the European Convention are defined in rule 2.3.)

II GENERAL RULES

Who the parties are

12.3

(1) In relation to the proceedings set out in column 1 of the following table, column 2 sets out who may make the application and column 3 sets out who the respondents to those proceedings will be.

Proceedings for	Applicants	Respondents
A parental responsibility order (section 4(1)(c), 4ZA(1)(c), or section 4A(1)(b) of the 1989 Act)	• The child's father; the step parent; or the child's parent (being a woman who is a parent by virtue of section 43 of the Human Fertilisation and Embryology Act 2008 and who is not a person to whom section 1(3) of the Family Law Reform Act	• Every person whom the applicant believes to have parental responsibility for the child; where the child is the subject of a care order, every person whom the

Proceedings for	Applicants	Respondents
	1987 applies) (sections4(1)(c), 4ZA(1)(c) and 4A(1)(b) of the 1989 Act)	applicant believes to have had parental responsibility immediately prior to the making of the care order; in the case of an application to extend, vary or discharge an order, the parties to the proceedings leading to the order which it is sought to have extended, varied or discharged; in the case of specified proceedings, the child
An order terminating a parental responsibility order or agreement (section 4(2A), 4ZA(5) or section 4A(3) of the 1989 Act	• Any person who has parental responsibility for the child; or with the court's permission, the child (section 4(3), 4ZA(6) and section 4A(3) of the 1989 Act)	As above
An order appointing a guardian(section 5(1) of the 1989 Act)	• An individual who wishes to be appointed as guardian (section 5(1) of the 1989 Act)	As above
An order terminating the appointment of a guardian (section 6(7) of the 1989 Act)	• Any person who has parental responsibility for the child; or with the court's permission, the child (section 6(7) of the 1989 Act)	As above
A section 8 order	• Any person who is entitled to apply for a section 8 order with respect to the child (section 10(4) to (7)of the 1989 Act); or with the court's permission, any person (section10(2)(b) of the 1989 Act)	As above
An enforcement order (section 11J of the 1989 Act)	• A person who is, for the purposes of the child arrangements order, a person with whom the child concerned lives or is to live; any person whose contact with the child concerned is provided for in the child arrangements order; any individual subject to a condition under section 11(7)(b) of	• The person the applicant alleges has failed to comply with the child arrangements order

Proceedings for	Applicants	Respondents
	the 1989 Act or a an activity condition imposed by a child arrangements order; or with the court's permission, the child (section 11J(5) of the 1989 Act)	
A financial compensation order (section 11O of the 1989 Act)	• Any person who is, for the purposes of the child arrangements order, a person with whom the child concerned lives or is to live; any person whose contact with the child concerned is provided for in the child arrangements order; any individual subject to a condition under section 11(7)(b) of the 1989 Act or a an activity condition imposed by a child arrangements order; or with the court's permission, the child (section 11O(6) of the 1989 Act)	• The person the applicant alleges has failed to comply with the child arrangements order
An order permitting the child's name to be changed or the removal of the child from the United Kingdom (section13(1), 14C(3) or 33(7) of the 1989 Act)	• Any person (section 13(1),14C(3), 33(7) of the 1989 Act)	• As for a parental responsibility order
A special guardianship order (section14A of the 1989 Act)	• Any guardian of the child; any individual who is named in a child arrangements order as a person with whom the child is to live; any individual listed in subsection (5)(b) or (c) of section 10 (as read with subsection (10) of that section) of the 1989 Act; a local authority foster parent with whom the child has lived for a period of at least one year immediately preceding the application; or any person with the court's permission (section 14A(3) of the 1989 Act) (more than one such individual can apply jointly	• As above, and if a care order is in force with respect to the child, the child

Proceedings for	Applicants	Respondents
	(section 14A(3) and (5) of that Act))	
Variation or discharge of a special guardianship order (section 14D of the 1989 Act)	• The special guardian (or any of them, if there is more than one); any individual who is named in a child arrangements order as a person with whom the child is to live; the local authority designated in a care order with respect to the child; any individual within section 14D(1)(d) of the 1989 Act who has parental responsibility for the child; the child, any parent or guardian of the child and any step-parent of the child who has acquired, and has not lost, parental responsibility by virtue of section 4A of that Act with the court's permission; or any individual within section 14D(1)(d) of that Act who immediately before the making of the special guardianship order had, but no longer has, parental responsibility for the child with the court's permission	As above
A secure accommodation order (section 25 section of the 1989 Act)	• The local authority which is looking after the child; or the Health Authority, Secretary of State, National Health Service Commissioning Board, clinical commissioning group, National Health Service Trust established under section 25 of the National Health Service Act 2006 or section 18(1) of the National Health Service (Wales) Act 2006, National Health Service Foundation Trust or any local authority providing or arranging accommodation for the child (unless the child is looked after by a local authority)	As above
A care or supervision order (section 31 of the 1989 Act)	• Any local authority; the National Society for the Prevention of Cruelty to Children	As above

Proceedings for	Applicants	Respondents
	and any of its officers (section 31(1) of the1989 Act); or any authorised person	
An order varying directions made with an interim care or interim supervision order (section 38(8)(b) of the 1989 Act)	• The parties to proceedings in which directions are given under section 38(6) of the 1989 Act; or any person named in such a direction	As above
An order discharging a care order (section 39(1) of the 1989 Act)	• Any person who has parental responsibility for the child; the child; or the local authority designated by the order (section 39(1) of the 1989 Act)	As above
An order varying or discharging an interim care order in so far as it imposes an exclusion requirement (section 39(3A) of the 1989 Act)	• A person to whom the exclusion requirement in the interim care order applies who is not entitled to apply for the order to be discharged (section 39(3A) of the 1989 Act)	As above
An order varying or discharging an interim care order in so far as it confers a power of arrest attached to an exclusion requirement (section 39(3B) of the 1989 Act)	• Any person entitled to apply for the discharge of the interim care order in so far as it imposes the exclusion requirement (section 39(3B) of the 1989 Act)	As above
An order substituting a supervision order for a care order (section 39(4) of the 1989 Act)	• Any person entitled to apply for a care order to be discharged under section 39(1) (section 39(4) of the 1989 Act)	As above
A child assessment order (section 43(1) of the 1989 Act)	• Any local authority; the National Society for the Prevention of Cruelty to Children and any of its officers; or any person authorised by order of the Secretary of State to bring the proceedings and any officer of a body who is so authorised (section 43(1) and (13) of the 1989 Act)	As above
An order varying or discharging a child	• The applicant for an order that has been made under section 43(1) of	As above

Proceedings for	Applicants	Respondents
assessment order (section 43(12) of the 1989 Act)	the 1989 Act; or the persons referred to in section 43(11) of the 1989 Act (section 43(12) of that Act)	
An emergency protection order (section 44(1) of the 1989 Act)	• Any person (section 44(1) of the 1989 Act)	As for a parental responsibility order
An order extending the period during which an emergency protection order is to have effect (section 45(4) of the 1989 Act)	• Any person who– has parental responsibility for a child as the result of an emergency protection order; and is entitled to apply for a care order with respect to the child (section 45(4) of the 1989 Act)	As above
An order discharging an emergency protection order (section 45(8) of the 1989 Act)	• The child; a parent of the child; any person who is not a parent of the child but who has parental responsibility for the child; or any person with whom the child was living before the making of the emergency protection order (section 45(8) of the 1989 Act)	As above
An order varying or discharging an emergency protection order in so far as it imposes the exclusion requirement (section 45(8A) of the 1989 Act)	• A person to whom the exclusion requirement in the emergency protection order applies who is not entitled to apply for the emergency protection order to be discharged (section 45(8A) of the 1989 Act)	As above
An order varying or discharging an emergency protection order in so far as it confers a power of arrest attached to an exclusion requirement (section 45(8B) of the 1989 Act)	• Any person entitled to apply for the discharge of the emergency protection order in so far as it imposes the exclusion requirement (section 45(8B) of the 1989 Act)	As above
An emergency protection order by the police (section 46(7) of the 1989 Act)	• The officer designated for the purposes of section 46(3)(e) of the 1989 Act (section 46(7) of the 1989 Act)	As above

Proceedings for	Applicants	Respondents
A warrant authorising a constable to assist in exercise of certain powers to search for children and inspect premises (section 48 of the 1989 Act)	▪ Any person attempting to exercise powers under an emergency protection order who has been or is likely to be prevented from doing so by being refused entry to the premises concerned or refused access to the child concerned (section 48(9) of the 1989 Act)	As above
A warrant authorising a constable to assist in exercise of certain powers to search for children and inspect premises (section 102 of the 1989 Act)	▪ Any person attempting to exercise powers under the enactments mentioned in section 102(6) of the 1989Act who has been or is likely to be prevented from doing so by being refused entry to the premises concerned or refused access to the child concerned (section 102(1) of that Act)	As above
An order revoking an enforcement order (paragraph 4 of Schedule A1 to the 1989 Act) .	▪ The person subject to the enforcement order	▪ The person who was the applicant for the enforcement order; and, where the child was a party to the proceedings in which the enforcement order was made, the child
An order amending an enforcement order (paragraphs 5 to 7 of Schedule A1 to the 1989 Act)	▪ The person subject to the enforcement order	▪ The person who was the applicant for the enforcement order. (Rule 12.33 makes provision about applications under paragraph 5 of Schedule A1 to the 1989 Act.)
An order following breach of an enforcement order (paragraph 9 of Schedule A1 to the 1989 Act)	▪ Any person who is, for the purposes of the child arrangements order, the person with whom the child lives or is to live; any person whose contact with the child concerned is provided for in the child arrangements order; any individual subject to a condition under section 11(7)(b) of the 1989 Act or an activity condition imposed by a child arrangements order; or	▪ The person the applicant alleges has failed to comply with the unpaid work requirement imposed by an enforcement order; and where the child was a party to the proceedings in which the enforcement order was made, the child

Proceedings for	Applicants	Respondents
	with the court's permission, the child (paragraph 9 of Schedule A1 to the 1989 Act)	
An order permitting the local authority to arrange for any child in its care to live outside England and Wales (Schedule 2, paragraph 19(1), to the 1989 Act)	• The local authority (Schedule 2, paragraph 19(1), to the 1989 Act)	As for a parental responsibility order
A contribution order (Schedule 2, paragraph 23(1), to the 1989 Act).	• The local authority (Schedule 2, paragraph 23(1), to the 1989 Act)	As above and the contributor
An order revoking a contribution order (Schedule 2, paragraph 23(8), to the 1989 Act)	• The contributor; or the local authority	As above
An order relating to contact with the child in care and any named person (section 34(2) of the 1989 Act) or permitting the local authority to refuse contact (section 34(4) of that Act)	• The local authority; or the child (section 34(2) or 34(4) of the 1989 Act)	• As above; and the person whose contact with the child is the subject of the application
An order relating to contact with the child in care (section 34(3) of the 1989 Act)	• The child's parents; any guardian or special guardian of the child; any person who by virtue of section 4A of the 1989 Act has parental responsibility for the child; where there was a child arrangements order in force with respect to the child immediately before the care order was made, any person named in that order as a person with whom the child was to live; a person who by virtue of an order made in the exercise of the High Court's inherent jurisdiction with respect to children had care of the child immediately before the care	• As above; and the person whose contact with the child is the subject of the application

Proceedings for	Applicants	Respondents
	order was made (section 34(3)(a) of the 1989 Act); or with the court's permission, any person (section 34(3) (b) of that Act)	
An order varying or discharging an order for contact with a child in care under section 34 (section 34((9) of the1989 Act)	• The local authority; the child; or any person named in the order (section 34(9) of the 1989 Act)	• As above; and the person whose contact with the child is the subject of the application
An education supervision order (section 36 of the 1989 Act)	• Any local authority (section 36(1) of the 1989 Act)	• As above; and the child
An order varying or discharging a supervision order (section 39(2) of the 1989 Act)	• Any person who has parental responsibility for the child; the child; or the supervisor (section 39(2) of the 1989 Act)	• As above; and the supervisor
An order varying a supervision order in so far as it affects the person with whom the child is living (section 39(3) of the 1989 Act)	• The person with whom the child is living who is not entitled to apply for the order to be discharged (section 39(3) of the 1989 Act)	• As above; and the supervisor
An order varying a direction under section 44(6) of the 1989 Act in an emergency protection order (section 44(9)(b) of that Act)	• The parties to the application for the emergency protection order in respect of which it is sought to vary the directions; the children's guardian; the local authority in whose area the child is ordinarily resident; or any person who is named in the directions	• As above, and the parties to the application for the order in respect of which it is sought to vary the directions; any person who was caring for the child prior to the making of the order; and any person named in a child arrangements order as a person with whom the child is to spend time or otherwise have contact and who is affected by the direction which it is sought to have varied

Proceedings for	Applicants	Respondents
A recovery order (section 50 of the 1989 Act)	• Any person who has parental responsibility for the child by virtue of a care order or an emergency protection order; or where the child is in police protection the officer designated for the purposes of section 46(3)(e) of the 1989 Act (section 50(4) of the 1989 Act)	• As above; and the person whom the applicant alleges to have effected or to have been or to be responsible for the taking or keeping of the child
An order discharging an education supervision order (Schedule 3, paragraph 17(1), to the 1989 Act)	• The child concerned; a parent of the child; or the local authority concerned (Schedule 3, paragraph 17(1), to the 1989 Act)	• As above; and the local authority concerned; and the child
An order extending an education supervision order (Schedule 3, paragraph 15(2), to the 1989 Act)	• The local authority in whose favour the education supervision order was made (Schedule 3, paragraph 15(2), to the 1989 Act)	• As above; and the child
An appeal under paragraph (8) of Schedule 8 to the 1989 Act	• A person aggrieved by the matters listed in paragraph 8(1) of Schedule 8 to the 1989 Act	• The appropriate local authority
An order for the disclosure of information as to the whereabouts of a child under section 33 of the 1986 Act	• Any person with a legitimate interest in proceedings for an order under Part 1 of the 1986 Act; or a person who has registered an order made elsewhere in the United Kingdom or a specified dependent territory	• Any person alleged to have information as to the whereabouts of the child
An order authorising the taking charge of and delivery of a child under section 34 of the 1986 Act	• The person to whom the child is to be given up under section 34(1) of the 1986 Act	• As above; and the person who is required to give up the child in accordance with section 34(1) of the 1986 Act
An order relating to the exercise of the court's inherent jurisdiction (including wardship proceedings)	• A local authority (with the court's permission); any person with a genuine interest in or relation to the child; or the child (wardship proceedings only)	• The parent or guardian of the child; any other person who has an interest in or relationship to the child; and the child (wardship

Proceedings for	Applicants	Respondents
		proceedings only and with the court's permission as described at rule 12.37)
A warrant under section 79 of the 2006 Act authorising any constable to assist Her Majesty's Chief Inspector for Education, Children's Services and Skills in the exercise of powers conferred on him by section 77 of the 2006 Act	• Her Majesty's Chief Inspector for Education, Children's Services and Skills	• Any person preventing or likely to prevent Her Majesty's Chief Inspector for Education, Children's Services and Skills from exercising powers conferred on him by section 77 of the 2006 Act
An order in respect of a child under the 1980 Hague Convention	• Any person, institution or body who claims that a child has been removed or retained in breach of rights of custody or claims that there has been a breach of rights of access in relation to the child	• The person alleged to have brought the child into the United Kingdom; the person with whom the child is alleged to be; any parent or guardian of the child who is within the United Kingdom and is not otherwise a party; any person in whose favour a decision relating to custody has been made if that person is not otherwise a party; and any other person who appears to the court to have sufficient interest in the welfare of the child
An order concerning the recognition and enforcement of decisions relating to custody under the European Convention	• Any person who has a court order giving that person rights of custody in relation to the child	As above
An application for the High Court to request transfer of jurisdiction under Article 15 of the	• Any person with sufficient interest in the welfare of the child and who would be entitled to make a proposed application in relation to	• As directed by the court in accordance with rule 12.65

Proceedings for	Applicants	Respondents
Council Regulation or Article 9 of the 1996 Hague Convention (rule 12.65)	that child, or who intends to seek the permission of the court to make such application if the transfer is agreed	
An application under rule 12.71 for a declaration as to the existence, or extent, of parental responsibility under Article 16 of the 1996 Convention	• Any interested person including a person who holds, or claims to hold, parental responsibility for the child under the law of another State which subsists in accordance with Article 16 of the 1996 Hague Convention following the child becoming habitually resident in a territorial unit of the United Kingdom	• Every person whom the applicant believes to have parental responsibility for the child; any person whom the applicant believes to hold parental responsibility for the child under the law of another State which subsists in accordance with Article 16 of the 1996 Hague Convention following the child becoming habitually resident in a territorial unit of the United Kingdom; and where the child is the subject of a care order, every person whom the applicant believes to have had parental responsibility immediately prior to the making of the care order
A warning notice	• The person who is, for the purposes of the child arrangements order, the person with whom the child concerned lives or is to live; the person whose contact with the child concerned is provided for in the child arrangements order; any individual subject to a condition under section 11(7)(b) of the 1989 Act or an activity condition imposed by the child arrangements order; or with the court's permission, the child	• Any person who was a party to the proceedings in which the child arrangements order was made. (Rule 12.33 makes provision about applications for warning notices)

(2)   The court will direct that a person with parental responsibility be made a party to proceedings where that person requests to be one.

(3)   Subject to rule 16.2, the court may at any time direct that –

(a)   any person or body be made a party to proceedings; or

(b)   a party be removed.

(4)   If the court makes a direction for the addition or removal of a party under this rule, it may give consequential directions about –

    (a)   the service of a copy of the application form or other relevant documents on the new party;

    (b)   the management of the proceedings.

(5)   In this rule –

    'a local authority foster parent' has the meaning assigned to it by section 23(3) of the 1989 Act; and

    'care home', 'independent hospital', 'local authority' and 'clinical commissioning group' have the meanings assigned to them by section 105 of the 1989 Act.

(Part 16 contains the rules relating to the representation of children.)

Notice of proceedings to person with foreign parental responsibility

12.4

(1)   This rule applies where a child is subject to proceedings to which this Part applies and –

    (a)   a person holds or is believed to hold parental responsibility for the child under the law of another State which subsists in accordance with Article 16 of the 1996 Hague Convention following the child becoming habitually resident in a territorial unit of the United Kingdom; and

    (b)   that person is not otherwise required to be joined as a respondent under rule 12.3.

(2)   The applicant shall give notice of the proceedings to any person to whom the applicant believes paragraph (1) applies in any case in which a person whom the applicant believed to have parental responsibility under the 1989 Act would be a respondent to those proceedings in accordance with rule 12.3.

(3)   The applicant and every respondent to the proceedings shall provide such details as they possess as to the identity and whereabouts of any person they believe to hold parental responsibility for the child in accordance with paragraph (1) to the court officer, upon making, or responding to the application as appropriate.

(4)   Where the existence of a person who is believed to have parental responsibility for the child in accordance with paragraph (1) only becomes apparent to a party at a later date during the proceedings, that party must notify the court officer of those details at the earliest opportunity.

(5)   Where a person to whom paragraph (1) applies receives notice of proceedings, that person may apply to the court to be joined as a party using the Part 18 procedure.

Directions

12.12

(1)   This rule does not apply to proceedings under Chapter 6 of this Part.

(2)   At any stage in the proceedings, the court may give directions about the conduct of the proceedings including –

    (a)   the management of the case;

    (b)   the timetable for steps to be taken between the giving of directions and the final hearing;

    (c)   the joining of a child or other person as a party to the proceedings in accordance with rules 12.3(2) and (3);

    (d)   the attendance of the child;

    (e)   the appointment of a children's guardian or of a solicitor under section 41(3) of the 1989 Act;

    (f)   the appointment of a litigation friend;

    (g)   the service of documents;

    (h)   the filing of evidence including experts' reports; and

    (i)   the exercise by an officer of the Service, Welsh family proceedings officer or local authority officer of any duty referred to in rule 16.38(1)

(3)   Paragraph (4) applies where –

    (a)   an officer of the Service or a Welsh family proceedings officer has filed a report or a risk assessment as a result of exercising a duty referred to in rule 16.38(1)(a); or

    (b)   a local authority officer has filed a report as a result of exercising a duty referred to in rule 16.38(1)(b).

(4)   The court may –

    (a)   give directions setting a date for a hearing at which that report or risk assessment will be considered; and

    (b)   direct that the officer who prepared the report or risk assessment attend any such hearing.

(5)   The court may exercise the powers in paragraphs (2) and (4) on an application or of its own initiative.

(6)   Where the court proposes to exercise its powers of its own initiative the procedure set out in rule 4.3(2) to (6) applies.

(7)   Directions of a court which are still in force immediately prior to the transfer of proceedings to another court will continue to apply following the transfer subject to –

    (a)   any changes of terminology which are required to apply those directions to the court to which the proceedings are transferred; and

    (b)   any variation or revocation of the direction.

(8)   The court or court officer will –

    (a)   take a note of the giving, variation or revocation of a direction under this rule; and

    (b)   as soon as practicable serve a copy of the note on every party.

(Rule 12.48 provides for directions in proceedings under the 1980 Hague Convention and the European Convention.)

Setting dates for hearings and setting or confirming the timetable and date for the final hearing

12.13

(1)　At the –

　　(a)　transfer to a court of proceedings;

　　(b)　postponement or adjournment of any hearing; or

　　(c)　conclusion of any hearing at which the proceedings are not finally determined,

　　the court will set a date for the proceedings to come before the court again for the purposes of giving directions or for such other purposes as the court directs.

(2)　At any hearing the court may –

　　(a)　confirm a date for the final hearing or the week within which the final hearing is to begin (where a date or period for the final hearing has already been set);

　　(b)　set a timetable for the final hearing unless a timetable has already been fixed, or the court considers that it would be inappropriate to do so; or

　　(c)　set a date for the final hearing or a period within which the final hearing of the application is to take place.

(3)　The court officer will notify the parties of –

　　(a)　the date of a hearing fixed in accordance with paragraph (1);

　　(b)　the timetable for the final hearing; and

　　(c)　the date of the final hearing or the period in which it will take place.

(4)　Where the date referred to in paragraph (1) is set at the transfer of proceedings, the date will be as soon as possible after the transfer.

(5)　The requirement in paragraph (1) to set a date for the proceedings to come before the court again is satisfied by the court setting or confirming a date for the final hearing.

Attendance at hearings

12.14

(1)　This rule does not apply to proceedings under Chapter 6 of this Part except for proceedings for a declaration under rule 12.71.

(2)　Unless the court directs otherwise and subject to paragraph (3), the persons who must attend a hearing are –

　　(a)　any party to the proceedings;

　　(b)　any litigation friend for any party or legal representative instructed to act on that party's behalf; and

　　(c)　any other person directed by the court or required by Practice Directions 12A or 12B or any other practice direction to attend.

(3)　Proceedings or any part of them will take place in the absence of a child who is a party to the proceedings if –

　　(a)　the court considers it in the interests of the child, having regard to the matters to be discussed or the evidence likely to be given; and

　　(b)　the child is represented by a children's guardian or solicitor.

(4)　When considering the interests of the child under paragraph (3) the court will give –

    (a)   the children's guardian;

    (b)   the solicitor for the child; and

    (c)   the child, if of sufficient understanding,

an opportunity to make representations.

(5)   Subject to paragraph (6), where at the time and place appointed for a hearing, the applicant appears but one or more of the respondents do not, the court may proceed with the hearing.

(6)   The court will not begin to hear an application in the absence of a respondent unless the court is satisfied that –

    (a)   the respondent received reasonable notice of the date of the hearing; or

    (b)   the circumstances of the case justify proceeding with the hearing.

(7)   Where, at the time and place appointed for a hearing one or more of the respondents appear but the applicant does not, the court may –

    (a)   refuse the application; or

    (b)   if sufficient evidence has previously been received, proceed in the absence of the applicant.

(8)   Where at the time and place appointed for a hearing neither the applicant nor any respondent appears, the court may refuse the application.

(9)   Paragraphs (5) to (8) do not apply to a hearing where the court –

    (a)   is considering –

        (i)   whether to make a an activity direction or to attach a an activity condition to a child arrangements order; or

        (ii)   an application for a financial compensation order, an enforcement order or an order under paragraph 9 of Schedule A1 to the 1989 Act following a breach of an enforcement order; and

    (b)   has yet to obtain sufficient evidence from, or in relation to, the person who may be the subject of the direction, condition or order to enable it to determine the matter.

(10)   Nothing in this rule affects the provisions of Article 18 of the Council Regulation in cases to which that provision applies.

(The Council Regulation makes provision in Article 18 for the court to stay proceedings where the respondent is habitually resident in another Member State of the European Union and has not been adequately served with the proceedings as required by that provision.)

Steps taken by the parties

12.15   If –

    (a)   the parties or any children's guardian agree proposals for the management of the proceedings (including a proposed date for the final hearing or a period within which the final hearing is to take place); and

    (b)   the court considers that the proposals are suitable,

it may approve them without a hearing and give directions in the terms proposed.

(Practice Direction 12A gives guidance as to the application of this rule to Part 4 proceedings in the light of the period that is for the time being allowed under section 32(1)(a)(ii) of the 1989 Act)

Applications without notice
12.16
(1) This rule applies to –
    (a) proceedings for a section 8 order;
    (b) emergency proceedings; and
    (c) proceedings relating to the exercise of the court's inherent jurisdiction (other than an application for the court's permission to start such proceedings and proceedings for collection, location and passport orders where Chapter 6 applies).

(2) An application in proceedings referred to in paragraph (1) may, be made without notice in which case the applicant must file the application –
    (a) where the application is made by telephone, the next business day after the making of the application; or
    (b) in any other case, at the time when the application is made.

(3) Omitted

(4) Where –
    (a) a section 8 order;
    (b) an emergency protection order;
    (c) an order for the disclosure of information as to the whereabouts of a child under section 33 of the 1986 Act; or
    (d) an order authorising the taking charge of and delivery of a child under section 34 of the 1986 Act,
is made without notice, the applicant must serve a copy of the application on each respondent within 48 hours after the order is made.

(5) Within 48 hours after the making of an order without notice, the applicant must serve a copy of the order on–
    (a) the parties, unless the court directs otherwise;
    (b) any person who has actual care of the child or who had such care immediately prior to the making of the order; and
    (c) in the case of an emergency protection order and a recovery order, the local authority in whose area the child lives or is found.

(6) Where the court refuses to make an order on an application without notice it may direct that the application is made on notice in which case the application will proceed in accordance with rules 12.3 to 12.15.

(7) Where the hearing takes place outside the hours during which the court office is normally open, the court or court officer will take a note of the proceedings.

(Practice Direction 12E (Urgent Business) provides further details of the procedure for out of hours applications. See also Practice Direction 12D (Inherent Jurisdiction (including Wardship Proceedings).)

(Rule 12.47 provides for without-notice applications in proceedings under Chapter 6, section 1 of this Part, (proceedings under the 1980 Hague Convention and the European Convention).)

Investigation under section 37 of the 1989 Act
12.17

(1)   This rule applies where a direction is given to an appropriate authority by the court under section 37(1) of the 1989 Act.

(2)   On giving the direction the court may adjourn the proceedings.

(3)   As soon as practicable after the direction is given the court will record the direction.

(4)   As soon as practicable after the direction is given the court officer will –
   (a)   serve the direction on –
      (i)   the parties to the proceedings in which the direction is given; and
      (ii)   the appropriate authority where it is not a party;
   (b)   serve any documentary evidence directed by the court on the appropriate authority.

(5)   Where a local authority informs the court of any of the matters set out in section 37(3)(a) to (c) of the 1989 Act it will do so in writing.

(6)   Unless the court directs otherwise, the court officer will serve a copy of any report to the court under section 37 of the 1989 Act on the parties.

(Section 37 of the 1989 Act refers to the appropriate authority and section 37(5) of that Act sets out which authority should be named in a particular case.)

Disclosure of a report under section 14A(8) or (9) of the 1989 Act
12.18

(1)   In proceedings for a special guardianship order, the local authority must file the report under section 14A(8) or (9) of the 1989 Act within the timetable fixed by the court.

(2)   The court will consider whether to give a direction that the report under section 14A(8) or (9) of the 1989 Act be disclosed to each party to the proceedings.

(3)   Before giving a direction for the report to be disclosed, the court must consider whether any information should be deleted from the report.

(4)   The court may direct that the report must not be disclosed to a party.

(5)   The court officer must serve a copy of the report in accordance with any direction under paragraph (2).

(6)   In paragraph (3), information includes information which a party has declined to reveal under rule 29.1(1).

Additional evidence
12.19

(1)   This rule applies to proceedings for a section 8 order or a special guardianship order.

(2) Unless the court directs otherwise, a party must not –

  (a) file or serve any document other than in accordance with these rules or any practice direction;

  (b) in completing a form prescribed by these rules or any practice direction, give information or make a statement which is not required or authorised by that form; or

  (c) file or serve at a hearing –

    (i) any witness statement of the substance of the oral evidence which the party intends to adduce; or

    (ii) any copy of any document (including any experts' report) which the party intends to rely on.

(3) Where a party fails to comply with the requirements of this rule in relation to any witness statement or other document, the party cannot seek to rely on that statement or other document unless the court directs otherwise.

Hearings

12.21

(1) The court may give directions about the order of speeches and the evidence at a hearing.

(2) Subject to any directions given under paragraph (1), the parties and the children's guardian must adduce their evidence at a hearing in the following order –

  (a) the applicant;

  (b) any party with parental responsibility for the child;

  (c) other respondents;

  (d) the children's guardian;

  (e) the child, if the child is a party to proceedings and there is no children's guardian.

III SPECIAL PROVISIONS ABOUT PUBLIC LAW PROCEEDINGS

Timetable for the proceedings

12.22 In public law proceedings other than Part 4 proceedings, in so far as practicable the court will draw up the timetable for the proceedings or revise that timetable with a view to disposing of the application without delay and in any event within 26 weeks beginning with the date on which the application is issued.

(In relation to Part 4 proceedings, section 32(1)(a) of the 1989 Act requires the court to draw up a timetable with a view to disposing of the application without delay and in any event within 26 weeks beginning with the day on which the application is issued.)

Directions

12.24

(1) The court will direct the parties to –

  (a) monitor compliance with the court's directions; and

  (b) tell the court or court officer about –

(i)   any failure to comply with a direction of the court; and

(ii)   any other delay in the proceedings.

The Case Management Hearing and the Issues Resolution Hearing

12.25

(1)   The court will conduct the Case Management Hearing with the objective of –

    (a)   confirming the level of judge to which the proceedings have been allocated;

    (b)   drawing up a timetable for the proceedings including the time within which the proceedings are to be resolved;

    (c)   identifying the issues; and

    (d)   giving directions in accordance with rule 12.12 and Practice Direction 12A to manage the proceedings.

(2)   The court may hold a further Case Management Hearing only where this hearing is necessary to fulfil the objectives of the Case Management Hearing set out in paragraph (1).

(3)   The court will conduct the Issues Resolution Hearing with the objective of –

    (a)   identifying the remaining issues in the proceedings;

    (b)   as far as possible resolving or narrowing those issues; and

    (c)   giving directions to manage the proceedings to the final hearing in accordance with rule 12.12 and Practice Direction 12A.

(4)   Where it is possible for all the issues in the proceedings to be resolved at the Issues Resolution Hearing, the court may treat the Issues Resolution Hearing as a final hearing and make orders disposing of the proceedings.

(5)   The court may set a date for the Case Management Hearing, a further Case Management Hearing and the Issues Resolution Hearing at the times referred to in Practice Direction 12A.

(6)   The matters which the court will consider at the hearings referred to in this rule are set out in Practice Direction 12A.

(Rule 25.6 (experts: when to apply for the court's permission) provides that unless the court directs otherwise, parties must apply for the court's permission as mentioned in section 13(1), (3) and (5) of the 2014 Act as soon as possible and in Part 4 proceedings and in so far as practicable other public law proceedings no later than the Case Management Hearing.)

Discussion between advocates

12.26

(1)   When setting a date for the Case Management Hearing or the Issues Resolution Hearing the court will direct a discussion between the parties' advocates to –

    (a)   discuss the provisions of a draft of the Case Management Order; and

    (b)   consider any other matter set out in Practice Direction 12A.

(2)   Where there is a litigant in person the court will give directions about how that person may take part in the discussions between the parties' advocates.

(3)   Unless the court directs otherwise –

(a)   any discussion between advocates must take place no later than 2 days before the Case Management Hearing; and

(b)   a draft of the Case Management Order must be filed with the court no later than 11a.m. on the day before the Case Management Hearing.

(4)   Unless the court directs otherwise –

(a)   any discussion between advocates must take place no later than 7 days before the Issues Resolution Hearing; and

(b)   a draft of the Case Management Order must be filed with the court no later than 11a.m. on the day before the Issues Resolution Hearing.

(5)   For the purposes of this rule 'advocate' includes a litigant in person.

Application for extension of the time limit for disposing of the application

12.26A

(1)   An application requesting the court to grant an extension must state –

(a)   the reasons for the request;

(b)   the period of extension being requested; and

(c)   a short explanation of –

(i)   why it is necessary for the request to be granted to enable the court to resolve the proceedings justly;

(ii)   the impact which any ensuing timetable revision would have on the welfare of the child to whom the application relates;

(iii)   the impact which any ensuing timetable revision would have on the duration and conduct of the proceedings; and

(iv)   the reasons for the grant or refusal of any previous request for extension.

(2)   Part 18 applies to an application requesting the grant of an extension.

(3)   In this rule –

'ensuing timetable revision' has the meaning given to it by section 32(6) of the 1989 Act;

'extension' means an extension of the period for the time being allowed under section 32(1)(a)(ii) of the 1989 Act which is to end no more than 8 weeks after the later of the times referred to in section 32(8) of that Act.

Exclusion requirements: interim care orders and emergency protection orders

12.28

(1)   This rule applies where the court includes an exclusion requirement in an interim care order or an emergency protection order.

(2)   The applicant for an interim care order or emergency protection order must –

(a)   prepare a separate statement of the evidence in support of the application for an exclusion requirement;

(b)   serve the statement personally on the relevant person with a copy of the order containing the exclusion requirement (and of any power of arrest which is attached to it);

(c)   inform the relevant person of that person's right to apply to vary or discharge the exclusion requirement.

(3)   Where a power of arrest is attached to an exclusion requirement in an interim care order or an emergency protection order, the applicant will deliver –

       (a)   a copy of the order; and

       (b)   a statement showing that the relevant person has been served with the order or informed of its terms (whether by being present when the order was made or by telephone or otherwise),

    to the officer for the time being in charge of the police station for the area in which the dwelling-house in which the child lives is situated (or such other police station as the court may specify).

(4)   Rules 10.6(2) and 10.10 to 10.17 will apply, with the necessary modifications, for the service, variation, discharge and enforcement of any exclusion requirement to which a power of arrest is attached as they apply to an order made on an application under Part 4 of the 1996 Act.

(5)   The relevant person must serve the parties to the proceedings with any application which that person makes for the variation or discharge of the exclusion requirement.

(6)   Where an exclusion requirement ceases to have effect whether –

       (a)   as a result of the removal of a child under section 38A(10) or 44A(10) of the 1989 Act;

       (b)   because of the discharge of the interim care order or emergency protection order; or

       (c)   otherwise,

    the applicant must inform –

       (i)   the relevant person;

       (ii)   the parties to the proceedings;

       (iii)   any officer to whom a copy of the order was delivered under paragraph (3); and

       (iv)   (where necessary) the court.

(7)   Where the court includes an exclusion requirement in an interim care order or an emergency protection order of its own motion, paragraph (2) will apply with the omission of any reference to the statement of the evidence.

(8)   In this rule, 'the relevant person' has the meaning assigned to it by sections 38A(2) and 44A(2) of the 1989 Act.

Notification of consent
12.29

(1)   Consent for the purposes of the following provisions of the 1989 Act –

       (a)   section 16(3);

       (b)   section 38A(2)(b)(ii) or44A(2)(b)(ii); or

       (c)   paragraph 19(3)(c) or (d) of Schedule 2,

    must be given either –

       (i)   orally to the court; or

       (ii)   in writing to the court signed by the person giving consent.

(2)   Any written consent for the purposes of section 38A(2) or 44A(2) of the 1989 Act must include a statement that the person giving consent –

(a)   is able and willing to give to the child the care which it would be reasonable to expect a parent to give; and

(b)   understands that the giving of consent could lead to the exclusion of the relevant person from the dwelling-house in which the child lives.

Proceedings for secure accommodation orders: copies of reports

12.30 In proceedings under section 25 of the 1989 Act, the court will, if practicable, arrange for copies of all written reports filed in the case to be made available before the hearing to –

(a)   the applicant;

(b)   the parent or guardian of the child to whom the application relates;

(c)   any legal representative of the child;

(d)   the children's guardian; and

(e)   the child, unless the court directs otherwise,

and copies of the reports may, if the court considers it desirable, be shown to any person who is entitled to notice of any hearing in accordance with Practice Direction 12C.

IV SPECIAL PROVISIONS ABOUT PRIVATE LAW PROCEEDINGS

The First Hearing Dispute Resolution Appointment

12.31

(1)   The court may set a date for the First Hearing Dispute Resolution Appointment after the proceedings have been issued.

(2)   The court officer will give notice of any of the dates so fixed to the parties.

(Provisions relating to the timing of and issues to be considered at the First Hearing Dispute Resolution Appointment are contained in Practice Direction 12B.)

Answer

12.32 A respondent must file and serve on the parties an answer to the application for an order in private law proceedings within 14 days beginning with the date on which the application is served.

Applications for warning notices or applications to amend enforcement orders by reason of change of residence

12.33

(1)   his rule applies in relation to an application for –

    (a)   a warning notice to be attached to a child arrangements; or

    (b)   an order under paragraph 5 of Schedule A1 to the 1989 Act to amend an enforcement order by reason of change of residence.

(2)   The application must be made without notice.

(3)   The court may deal with the application without a hearing.

(4)   If the court decides to deal with the application at a hearing, rules 12.5, 12.7 and 12.8 will apply.

Service of a risk assessment
12.34

(1)   Where an officer of the Service or a Welsh family proceedings officer has filed a risk assessment with the court, subject to paragraph (2), the court officer will as soon as practicable serve copies of the risk assessment on each party.

(2)   Before serving the risk assessment, the court must consider whether, in order to prevent a risk of harm to the child, it is necessary for –

    (a)   information to be deleted from a copy of the risk assessment before that copy is served on a party; or

    (b)   service of a copy of the risk assessment (whether with information deleted from it or not) on a party to be delayed for a specified period,

and may make directions accordingly.

Service of enforcement orders or orders amending or revoking enforcement orders
12.35

(1)   Paragraphs (2) and (3) apply where the court makes –

    (a)   an enforcement order; or

    (b)   an order under paragraph 9(2) of Schedule A1 to the 1989 Act (enforcement order made following a breach of an enforcement order).

(2)   As soon as practicable after an order has been made, a copy of it must be served by the court officer on–

    (a)   the parties, except the person against whom the order is made;

    (b)   the officer of the Service or the Welsh family proceedings officer who is to comply with a request under section 11M of the 1989 Act to monitor compliance with the order; and

    (c)   the responsible officer.

(3)   Unless the court directs otherwise, the applicant must serve a copy of the order personally on the person against whom the order is made.

(4)   The court officer must send a copy of an order made under paragraph 4, 5, 6 or 7 of Schedule A1 to the 1989 Act (revocation or amendment of an enforcement order) to –

    (a)   the parties;

    (b)   the officer of the Service or the Welsh family proceedings officer who is to comply with a request under section 11M of the 1989 Act to monitor compliance with the order;

    (c)   the responsible officer; and

    (d)   in the case of an order under paragraph 5 of Schedule A1 to the 1989 Act (amendment of enforcement order by reason of change of residence), the responsible officer in the former local justice area.

(5)   In this rule, 'responsible officer' has the meaning given in paragraph 8(8) of Schedule A1 to the 1989 Act.

V SPECIAL PROVISIONS ABOUT INHERENT JURISDICTION PROCEEDINGS

Where to start proceedings
12.36
(1)   An application for proceedings under the Inherent Jurisdiction of the court must be started in the High Court.
(2)   Wardship proceedings, except applications for an order that a child be made or cease to be a ward of court, may be transferred to the family court unless the issues of fact or law make them more suitable for hearing in the High Court.

(The question of suitability for hearing in the High Court is explained in Practice Direction 12D (Inherent Jurisdiction (including Wardship Proceedings)).)

Child as respondent to wardship proceedings
12.37
(1)   A child who is the subject of wardship proceedings must not be made a respondent to those proceedings unless the court gives permission following an application under paragraph (2).
(2)   Where nobody other than the child would be a suitable respondent to wardship proceedings, the applicant may apply without notice for permission to make the wardship application –
      (a)   without notice; or
      (b)   with the child as the respondent.

Registration requirements
12.38 The court officer will send a copy of every application for a child to be made a ward of court to the principal registry for recording in the register of wards

Notice of child's whereabouts
12.39
(1)   Every respondent, other than a child, must file with the acknowledgment of service a notice stating –
      (a)   the respondent's address; and
      (b)   either –
            (i)   the whereabouts of the child; or
            (ii)   that the respondent is unaware of the child's whereabouts if that is the case.
(2)   Unless the court directs otherwise, the respondent must serve a copy of that notice on the applicant.
(3)   Every respondent other than a child must immediately notify the court in writing of –
      (a)   any subsequent changes of address; or
      (b)   any change in the child's whereabouts,

and, unless the court directs otherwise, serve a copy of that notice on the applicant.

(4)   In this rule a reference to the whereabouts of a child is a reference to –
   (a)   the address at which the child is living;
   (b)   the person with whom the child is living; and
   (c)   any other information relevant to where the child may be found.

Enforcement of orders in wardship proceedings

12.40 The High Court may secure compliance with any direction relating to a ward of court by an order addressed to the tipstaff.

(The role of the tipstaff is explained in Practice Direction 12D (Inherent Jurisdiction (including Wardship Proceedings)).)

Child ceasing to be ward of court
12.41
(1)   A child who, by virtue of section 41(2) of the Senior Courts Act 1981, automatically becomes a ward of court on the making of a wardship application will cease to be a ward on the determination of the application unless the court orders that the child be made a ward of court.
(2)   Nothing in paragraph (1) affects the power of the court under section 41(3) of the Senior Courts Act 1981 to order that any child cease to be a ward of court

Adoption of a child who is a ward of court
12.42 An application for permission –
(a)   to start proceedings to adopt a child who is a ward of court;
(b)   to place such a child for adoption with parental consent; or
(c)   to start proceedings for a placement order in relation to such a child,
may be made without notice in accordance with Part 18.

VII COMMUNICATION OF INFORMATION: CHILDREN PROCEEDINGS

Communication of information: general
12.73
(1)   For the purposes of the law relating to contempt of court, information relating to proceedings held in private (whether or not contained in a document filed with the court) may be communicated –
   (a)   where the communication is to–
      (i)   a party;
      (ii)   the legal representative of a party;
      (iii)   a professional legal adviser;
      (iv)   an officer of the service or a Welsh family proceedings officer;
      (v)   the welfare officer;
      (vi)   the Director of Legal Aid Casework (within the meaning of section 4 of the Legal Aid, Sentencing and Punishment of Offenders Act 2012);

      (vii)   an expert whose instruction by a party has been authorised by the court for the purposes of the proceedings;

      (viii)   a professional acting in furtherance of the protection of children;

      (ix)   an independent reviewing officer appointed in respect of a child who is, or has been, subject to proceedings to which this rule applies;

  (b)   where the court gives permission; or

  (c)   subject to any direction of the court, in accordance with rule 12.75 and Practice Direction 12G.

(2)   Nothing in this Chapter permits the communication to the public at large, or any section of the public, of any information relating to the proceedings.

(3)   Nothing in rule 12.75 and Practice Direction 12G permits the disclosure of an unapproved draft judgment handed down by any court.

Communication of information for purposes connected with the proceedings
12.75

(1)   A party or the legal representative of a party, on behalf of and upon the instructions of that party, may communicate information relating to the proceedings to any person where necessary to enable that party –

  (a)   by confidential discussion, to obtain support, advice or assistance in the conduct of the proceedings;

  (b)   to attend a mediation information and assessment meeting, or to engage in mediation or other forms of non-court dispute resolution;

  (c)   to make and pursue a complaint against a person or body concerned in the proceedings; or

  (d)   to make and pursue a complaint regarding the law, policy or procedure relating to a category of proceedings to which this Part applies.

(2)   Where information is communicated to any person in accordance with paragraph (1)(a) of this rule, no further communication by that person is permitted.

(3)   When information relating to the proceedings is communicated to any person in accordance with paragraphs (1)(b),(c) or (d) of this rule –

  (a)   the recipient may communicate that information to a further recipient, provided that –

      (i)   the party who initially communicated the information consents to that further communication; and

      (ii)   the further communication is made only for the purpose or purposes for which the party made the initial communication; and

  (b)   the information may be successively communicated to and by further recipients on as many occasions as may be necessary to fulfil the purpose for which the information was initially communicated, provided that on each such occasion the conditions in sub-paragraph (a) are met.

PART 14 – PROCEDURE FOR APPLICATIONS IN ADOPTION, PLACEMENT AND RELATED PROCEEDINGS

Application of this Part and interpretation

14.1

(1)   The rules in this Part apply to the following proceedings –

    (a)   adoption proceedings;

    (b)   placement proceedings; and

    (c)   proceedings for –

        (i)   the making of an order under section 26 or an order under section 51A(2)(a) of the 2002 Act;

        (i)(aa)   the making of an order under section 51A(2)(b) of the 2002 Act;

        (ii)   the variation or revocation of;

            (aa)   an order under section 27 of the 2002 Act; or

            (bb)   an order under section 51A(2) of the 2002 Act in accordance with section 51B(1)(c);

        (iii)   an order giving permission to change a child's surname or remove a child from the United Kingdom under section 28(2) and (3) of the 2002 Act;

        (iv)   a section 84 order;

        (v)   a section 88 direction;

        (vi)   a section 89 order; or

        (vii)   any other order that may be referred to in a practice direction.

(2)   In this Part –

'Central Authority' means –

    (a)   in relation to England, the Secretary of State; and

    (b)   in relation to Wales, the Welsh Ministers;

'Convention adoption order' means an adoption order under the 2002 Act which, by virtue of regulations under section 1 of the Adoption (Intercountry Aspects) Act 1999 (regulations giving effect to the Convention on Protection of Children and Co-operation in Respect of Intercountry Adoption, concluded at the Hague on 29th May 1993), is made as a Convention adoption order;

'guardian' means –

    (a)   a guardian (other than the guardian of the estate of a child) appointed in accordance with section 5 of the 1989 Act; and

    (b)   a special guardian within the meaning of section 14A of the 1989 Act;

'provision for contact' has the meaning given to it in rule 13.1(2);

'section 88 direction'' means a direction given by the High Court under section 88 of the 2002 Act that section 67(3) of that Act (status conferred by adoption) does not apply or does not apply to any extent specified in the direction.

Date for first directions hearing

14.7

Unless the court directs otherwise, the first directions hearing must be within 4 weeks beginning with the date on which the application is issued.

The first directions hearing

14.8

(1)   At the first directions hearing in the proceedings the court will –

    (a)   fix a timetable for the proceedings including a timetable for the filing of –

        (i)   any report relating to the suitability of the applicants to adopt a child;

        (ii)   any report from the local authority;

        (iii)   any report from a children's guardian, reporting officer or children and family reporter;

        (iv)   if a statement of facts has been filed, any amended statement of facts;

        (v)   any other evidence, and

        (vi)   give directions relating to the reports and other evidence;

    (b)   consider whether the child or any other person should be a party to the proceedings and, if so, give directions in accordance with rule 14.3(2) or (3) joining that child or person as a party;

    (c)   give directions relating to the appointment of a litigation friend for any protected party or child who is a party to, but not the subject of, proceedings unless a litigation friend has already been appointed;

    (d)   consider in accordance with rule 29.17 whether the case needs to be transferred to another court and, if so, give directions to transfer the proceedings to another court;

    (e)   give directions about –

        (i)   tracing parents or any other person the court considers to be relevant to the proceedings;

        (ii)   service of documents;

        (iii)   subject to paragraph (2), disclosure as soon as possible of information and evidence to the parties; and

        (iv)   the final hearing.

(Under Part 3 the court may also direct that the case be adjourned if it considers that non-court dispute resolution is appropriate.)

(2)   Rule 14.13(2) applies to any direction given under paragraph (1)(e)(iii) as it applies to a direction given under rule 14.13(1).

(3)   In addition to the matters referred to in paragraph (1), the court will give any of the directions listed in Practice Direction 14B in proceedings for –

    (a)   a Convention adoption order;

    (b)   a section 84 order;

    (c)   a section 88 direction;

(d)   a section 89 order; or

(e)   an adoption order where section 83(1) of the 2002 Act applies (restriction on bringing children in).

(4)   The parties or their legal representatives must attend the first directions hearing unless the court directs otherwise.

(5)   Directions may also be given at any stage in the proceedings –

    (a)   of the court's own initiative; or

    (b)   on the application of a party or any children's guardian or, where the direction concerns a report by a reporting officer or children and family reporter, the reporting officer or children and family reporter.

(6)   For the purposes of giving directions or for such purposes as the court directs –

    (a)   the court may set a date for a further directions hearing or other hearing; and

    (b)   the court officer will give notice of any date so fixed to the parties and to any children's guardian, reporting officer or children and family reporter.

(7)   After the first directions hearing the court will monitor compliance by the parties with the court's timetable and directions.

Requesting the court to dispense with the consent of any parent or guardian
14.9

(1)   This rule applies where the applicant wants to ask the court to dispense with the consent of any parent or guardian of a child to –

    (a)   the child being placed for adoption;

    (b)   the making of an adoption order except a Convention adoption order; or

    (c)   the making of a section 84 order.

(2)   The applicant requesting the court to dispense with the consent must –

    (a)   give notice of the request in the application form or at any later stage by filing a written request setting out the reasons for the request; and

    (b)   file a statement of facts setting out a summary of the history of the case and any other facts to satisfy the court that –

        (i)   the parent or guardian cannot be found or is incapable of giving consent; or

        (ii)   the welfare of the child requires the consent to be dispensed with.

(3)   If a serial number has been assigned to the applicant under rule 14.2, the statement of facts supplied under paragraph (2)(b) must be framed so that it does not disclose the identity of the applicant.

(4)   On receipt of the notice of the request –

    (a)   a court officer will –

        (i)   inform the parent or guardian of the request unless the parent or guardian cannot be found; and

        (ii)   send a copy of the statement of facts filed in accordance with paragraph (2)(b) to –

(aa) the parent or guardian unless the parent or guardian cannot be found;

(bb) any children's guardian, reporting officer or children and family reporter;

(cc) any local authority to whom notice under section 44 of the 2002 Act (notice of intention to adopt or apply for a section 84 order) has been given; and

(dd) any adoption agency which has placed the child for adoption; and

(b) if the applicant considers that the parent or guardian is incapable of giving consent, the court will consider whether to –

(i) appoint a litigation friend for the parent or guardian under rule 15.6(1); or

(ii) give directions for an application to be made under rule 15.6(3),

(iii) unless a litigation friend is already appointed for that parent or guardian.

Communication of information relating to proceedings
14.14

For the purposes of the law relating to contempt of court, information (whether or not it is recorded in any form) relating to proceedings held in private may be communicated –

(a) where the court gives permission;

(b) unless the court directs otherwise, in accordance with Practice Direction 14E; or

(c) where the communication is to –

(i) a party;

(ii) the legal representative of a party;

(iii) a professional legal adviser;

(iv) an officer of the service or a Welsh family proceedings officer;

(v) a welfare officer;

(vi) the Director of Legal Aid Casework (within the meaning of section 4 of the Legal Aid, Sentencing and Punishment of Offenders Act 2012);

(vii) an expert whose instruction by a party has been authorised by the court for the purposes of the proceedings; or

(viii) a professional acting in furtherance of the protection of children.

Notice of final hearing
14.15

A court officer will give notice to the parties, any children's guardian, reporting officer or children and family reporter and to any other person to whom a practice direction may require such notice to be given –

(a) of the date and place where the application will be heard; and

(b) of the fact that, unless the person wishes or the court requires, the person need not attend.

The final hearing

14.16

(1)　Any person who has been given notice in accordance with rule 14.15 may attend the final hearing and, subject to paragraph (2), be heard on the question of whether an order should be made.

(2)　A person whose application for the permission of the court to oppose the making of an adoption order under section 47(3) or (5) of the 2002 Act has been refused is not entitled to be heard on the question of whether an order should be made.

(3)　Any member or employee of a party which is a local authority, adoption agency or other body may address the court at the final hearing if authorised to do so.

(4)　The court may direct that any person must attend a final hearing.

(5)　Paragraphs (6) and (7) apply to –
　　(a)　an adoption order;
　　(b)　a section 84 order; or
　　(c)　a section 89 order.

(6)　Subject to paragraphs (7) and (8), the court cannot make an order unless the applicant and the child personally attend the final hearing.

(7)　The court may direct that the applicant or the child need not attend the final hearing.

(8)　In a case of adoption by a couple under section 50 of the 2002 Act, the court may make an adoption order after personal attendance of one only of the applicants if there are special circumstances.

(9)　The court cannot make a placement order unless a legal representative of the applicant attends the final hearing.

Proof of identity of the child

14.17

(1)　Unless the contrary is shown, the child referred to in the application will be deemed to be the child referred to in the form of consent –
　　(a)　to the child being placed for adoption;
　　(b)　to the making of an adoption order; or
　　(c)　to the making of a section 84 order,
where the conditions in paragraph (2) apply.

(2)　The conditions are –
　　(a)　the application identifies the child by reference to a full certified copy of an entry in the registers of live-births;
　　(b)　the form of consent identifies the child by reference to a full certified copy of an entry in the registers of live-births attached to the form; and
　　(c)　the copy of the entry in the registers of live-births referred to in sub-paragraph (a) is the same or relates to the same entry in the registers of live-births as the copy of the entry in the registers of live-births attached to the form of consent.

(3)　Where the child is already an adopted child paragraph (2) will have effect as if for the references to the registers of live-births there were substituted references to the Adopted Children Register.

(4) Subject to paragraph (7), where the precise date of the child's birth is not proved to the satisfaction of the court, the court will determine the probable date of birth.

(5) The probable date of the child's birth may be specified in the placement order, adoption order or section 84 order as the date of the child's birth.

(6) Subject to paragraph (7), where the child's place of birth cannot be proved to the satisfaction of the court –

    (a) the child may be treated as having been born in the registration district and sub-district in which the court sits where it is probable that the child may have been born in –

        (i) the United Kingdom;

        (ii) the Channel Islands; or

        (iii) the Isle of Man; or

    (b) in any other case, the particulars of the country of birth may be omitted from the placement order, adoption order or section 84 order.

(7) A placement order identifying the probable date and place of birth of the child will be sufficient proof of the date and place of birth of the child in adoption proceedings and proceedings for a section 84 order.

Disclosing information to an adopted adult

14.18

(1) The adopted person has the right, on request, to receive from the court which made the adoption order a copy of the following –

    (a) the application form for an adoption order (but not the documents attached to that form);

    (b) the adoption order and any other orders relating to the adoption proceedings;

    (c) orders containing any provision for contact with the child after the adoption order was made; and

    (d) any other document or order referred to in Practice Direction 14F.

(2) The court will remove any protected information from any copy of a document or order referred to in paragraph (1) before the copies are given to the adopted person.

(3) This rule does not apply to an adopted person under the age of 18 years.

(4) In this rule 'protected information' means information which would be protected information under section 57(3) of the 2002 Act if the adoption agency gave the information and not the court.

Translation of documents

14.19

(1) Where a translation of any document is required for the purposes of proceedings for a Convention adoption order the translation must –

    (a) unless the court directs otherwise, be provided by the applicant; and

    (b) be signed by the translator to certify that the translation is accurate.

(2) This rule does not apply where the document is to be served in accordance with the Service Regulation.

Application for recovery orders
14.20

(1)   An application for any of the orders referred to in section 41(2) of the 2002 Act (recovery orders) may be made without notice, in which case the applicant must file the application –

    (a)   where the application is made by telephone, the next business day after the making of the application; or

    (b)   in any other case, at the time when the application is made.

(2)   Where the court refuses to make an order on an application without notice it may direct that the application is made on notice in which case the application will proceed in accordance with rules 14.1 to 14.17.

(3)   The respondents to an application under this rule are –

    (a)   in a case where –

        (i)   placement proceedings;

        (ii)   adoption proceedings; or

        (iii)   proceedings for a section 84 order,

    are pending, all parties to those proceedings;

    (b)   any adoption agency authorised to place the child for adoption or which has placed the child for adoption;

    (c)   any local authority to whom notice under section 44 of the 2002 Act (notice of intention to adopt or apply for a section 84 order) has been given;

    (d)   any person having parental responsibility for the child;

    (e)   any person in whose favour there is provision for contact;

    (f)   any person who was caring for the child immediately prior to the making of the application; and

    (g)   any person whom the applicant alleges to have effected, or to have been or to be responsible for, the taking or keeping of the child.

Inherent jurisdiction and fathers without parental responsibility
14.21

Where no proceedings have started an adoption agency or local authority may ask the High Court for directions on the need to give a father without parental responsibility notice of the intention to place a child for adoption.

PART 15 – REPRESENTATION OF PROTECTED PARTIES

Application of this Part
15.1

This Part contains special provisions which apply in proceedings involving protected parties.

Requirement for litigation friend in proceedings
15.2

A protected party must have a litigation friend to conduct proceedings on that party's behalf.

Stage of proceedings at which a litigation friend becomes necessary

15.3

(1)   person may not without the permission of the court take any step in proceedings except –

(a)   filing an application form; or

(b)   applying for the appointment of a litigation friend under rule 15.6,

until the protected party has a litigation friend.

(2)   If during proceedings a party lacks capacity (within the meaning of the 2005 Act) to continue to conduct proceedings, no party may take any step in proceedings without the permission of the court until the protected party has a litigation friend.

(3)   Any step taken before a protected party has a litigation friend has no effect unless the court orders otherwise.

Who may be a litigation friend for a protected party without a court order

15.4

(1)   This rule does not apply if the court has appointed a person to be a litigation friend.

(2)   A person with authority as a deputy to conduct the proceedings in the name of a protected party or on that party's behalf is entitled to be the litigation friend of the protected party in any proceedings to which that person's authority extends.

(3)   If there is no person with authority as a deputy to conduct the proceedings in the name of a protected party or on that party's behalf, a person may act as a litigation friend if that person –

(a)   can fairly and competently conduct proceedings on behalf of the protected party;

(b)   has no interest adverse to that of the protected party; and

(c)   subject to paragraph (4), undertakes to pay any costs which the protected party may be ordered to pay in relation to the proceedings, subject to any right that person may have to be repaid from the assets of the protected party.

(4)   Paragraph (3)(c) does not apply to the Official Solicitor.

('deputy' is defined in rule 2.3.)

How a person becomes a litigation friend without a court order

15.5

(1)   If the court has not appointed a litigation friend, a person who wishes to act as a litigation friend must follow the procedure set out in this rule.

(2)   A person with authority as a deputy to conduct the proceedings in the name of a protected party or on that party's behalf must file an official copy of the order, declaration or other document which confers that person's authority to act.

(3)   Any other person must file a certificate of suitability stating that that person satisfies the conditions specified in rule 15.4(3).

(4)   A person who is to act as a litigation friend must file –
    (a)   the document conferring that person's authority to act; or
    (b)   the certificate of suitability,
at the time when that person first takes a step in the proceedings on behalf of the protected party.

(5)   A court officer will send the certificate of suitability to every person on whom, in accordance with rule 6.28, the application form should be served.

(6)   This rule does not apply to the Official Solicitor.

How a person becomes a litigation friend by court order
15.6

(1)   The court may, if the person to be appointed so consents, make an order appointing –
    (a)   a person other than the Official Solicitor; or
    (b)   the Official Solicitor,
as a litigation friend.

(2)   An order appointing a litigation friend may be made by the court of its own initiative or on the application of –
    (a)   a person who wishes to be a litigation friend; or
    (b)   a party to the proceedings.

(3)   The court may at any time direct that a party make an application for an order under paragraph (2).

(4)   An application for an order appointing a litigation friend must be supported by evidence.

(5)   Unless the court directs otherwise, a person appointed under this rule to be a litigation friend for a protected party will be treated as a party for the purpose of any provision in these rules requiring a document to be served on, or sent to, or notice to be given to, a party to the proceedings.

(6)   Subject to rule 15.4(4), the court may not appoint a litigation friend under this rule unless it is satisfied that the person to be appointed complies with the conditions specified in rule 15.4(3).

Court's power to change litigation friend and to prevent person acting as litigation friend
15.7

(1)   The court may –
    (a)   direct that a person may not act as a litigation friend;
    (b)   terminate a litigation friend's appointment; or
    (c)   appoint a new litigation friend in substitution for an existing one.

(2)   An application for an order or direction under paragraph (1) must be supported by evidence.

(3)   Subject to rule 15.4(4), the court may not appoint a litigation friend under this rule unless it is satisfied that the person to be appointed complies with the conditions specified in rule 15.4(3).

Appointment of litigation friend by court order – supplementary

15.8

(1)   A copy of the application for an order under rule 15.6 or 15.7 must be sent by a court officer to –

(a)   every person on whom, in accordance with rule 6.28, the application form should be served; and

(b)   unless the court directs otherwise, the protected party.

(2)   A copy of an application for an order under rule 15.7 must also be sent to –

(a)   the person who is the litigation friend, or who is purporting to act as the litigation friend when the application is made; and

(b)   the person, if not the applicant, who it is proposed should be the litigation friend.

Procedure where appointment of litigation friend comes to an end

15.9

(1)   When a party ceases to be a protected party, the litigation friend's appointment continues until it is brought to an end by a court order.

(2)   An application for an order under paragraph (1) may be made by –

(a)   the former protected party;

(b)   the litigation friend; or

(c)   a party.

(3)   On the making of an order under paragraph (1), the court officer will send a notice to the other parties stating that the appointment of the protected party's litigation friend to act has ended.

PART 16 – REPRESENTATION OF CHILDREN AND REPORTS IN PROCEEDINGS INVOLVING CHILDREN

I APPLICATION OF THIS PART

Application of this Part

16.1

This Part –

(a)   sets out when the court will make a child a party in family proceedings; and

(b)   contains special provisions which apply in proceedings involving children.

II CHILD AS PARTY IN FAMILY PROCEEDINGS

When the court may make a child a party to proceedings

16.2

(1)   The court may make a child a party to proceedings if it considers it is in the best interests of the child to do so.

(2)   This rule does not apply to a child who is the subject of proceedings –

(a)   which are specified proceedings; or

(b)   to which Part 14 applies.

(The Practice Direction 16A sets out the matters which the court will take into consideration before making a child a party under this rule.)

III WHEN A CHILDREN'S GUARDIAN OR LITIGATION FRIEND WILL BE APPOINTED

Appointment of a children's guardian in specified proceedings or proceedings to which Part 14 applies

16.3

(1)   Unless it is satisfied that it is not necessary to do so to safeguard the interests of the child, the court must appoint a children's guardian for a child who is –

(a)   the subject of; and

(b)   a party to,

proceedings –

(i)   which are specified proceedings; or

(ii)   to which Part 14 applies.

(Rules 12.6 and 14.6 set out the point in the proceedings when the court will appoint a children's guardian in specified proceedings and proceedings to which Part 14 applies respectively.)

(2)   At any stage in the proceedings –

(a)   a party may apply, without notice to the other parties unless the court directs otherwise, for the appointment of a children's guardian; or

(b)   the court may of its own initiative appoint a children's guardian.

(3)   Where the court refuses an application under paragraph (2)(a) it will give reasons for the refusal and the court or a court officer will –

(a)   record the refusal and the reasons for it; and

(b)   as soon as practicable, notify the parties and either the Service or the Assembly of a decision not to appoint a children's guardian.

(4)   When appointing a children's guardian the court will consider the appointment of anyone who has previously acted as a children's guardian of the same child.

(5)   Where the court appoints a children's guardian in accordance with this rule, the provisions of Chapter 6 of this Part apply.

Appointment of a children's guardian in proceedings not being specified proceedings or proceedings to which Part 14 applies

16.4

(1)   Without prejudice to rule 8.42 or 16.6, the court must appoint a children's guardian for a child who is the subject of proceedings, which are not proceedings of a type referred to in rule 16.3(1), if –

(a)   the child is an applicant in the proceedings;

(b)   a provision in these rules provides for the child to be a party to the proceedings; or

(c)   the court has made the child a party in accordance with rule 16.2.

(2)   The provisions of Chapter 7 of this Part apply where the appointment of a children's guardian is required in accordance with paragraph (1).

('children's guardian' is defined in rule 2.3.)

Requirement for a litigation friend
16.5
(1)   Without prejudice to rule 16.6, where a child is –
(a)   a party to proceedings; but
(b)   not the subject of those proceedings,
the child must have a litigation friend to conduct proceedings on the child's behalf.
(2)   The provisions of Chapter 5 of this Part apply where a litigation friend is required in accordance with paragraph (1).

VI CHILDREN'S GUARDIAN APPOINTED UNDER RULE 16.3

Where the child instructs a solicitor or conducts proceedings on the child's own behalf
16.21
(1)   Where it appears to the children's guardian that the child –
(a)   is instructing a solicitor direct; or
(b)   intends to conduct and is capable of conducting the proceedings on that child's own behalf,
the children's guardian must inform the court of that fact.
(2)   Where paragraph (1) applies the children's guardian –
(a)   must perform such additional duties as the court may direct;
(b)   must take such part in the proceedings as the court may direct; and
(c)   may, with the permission of the court, have legal representation in the conduct of those duties.

PART 17 – STATEMENTS OF TRUTH

Interpretation
17.1
(1)   In this Part 'statement of case' has the meaning given to it in Part 4 except that a statement of case does not include –
(a)   an application for a matrimonial or a civil partnership order or an answer to such an application;
(b)   an application under Article 56 of the Maintenance Regulation made on the form in Annex VI or VII to that Regulation;
(c)   an application under Article 10 of the 2007 Hague Convention using the Financial Circumstances Form.

(Rule 4.1 defines 'statement of case' for the purposes of Part 4.)

(2)   In this rule, 'Financial Circumstances Form' has the meaning given to it in rule 9.3(1).

Documents to be verified by a statement of truth

17.2

(1)   Subject to paragraph (9), the following documents must be verified by a statement of truth –

    (a)   a statement of case;

    (b)   a witness statement;

    (c)   an acknowledgement of service in a claim begun by the Part 19 procedure;

    (d)   a certificate of service;

    (e)   omitted

    (f)   a statement of information filed under rule 9.26(1)(b); and

    (g)   any other document where a court order, rule or practice direction requires it.

(2)   Where a statement of case is amended, the amendments must be verified by a statement of truth unless the court orders otherwise.

(3)   Subject to paragraph (10), if an applicant wishes to rely on matters set out in the application form or application notice as evidence, the application form or notice must be verified by a statement of truth.

(4)   Subject to paragraph (5), a statement of truth is a statement that –

    (a)   the party putting forward the document;

    (b)   in the case of a witness statement, the maker of the witness statement; or

    (c)   in the case of a certificate of service, the person who signs the certificate,

believes the facts stated in the document are true.

(5)   If a party is conducting proceedings with a litigation friend, the statement of truth in –

    (a)   a statement of case; or

    (b)   an application notice,

is a statement that the litigation friend believes the facts stated in the document being verified are true.

(6)   The statement of truth must be signed by –

    (a)   in the case of a statement of case –

        (i)   the party or litigation friend; or

        (ii)   the legal representative on behalf of the party or litigation friend; and

    (b)   in the case of a witness statement the maker of the statement.

(7)   A statement of truth, which is not contained in the document which it verifies, must clearly identify that document.

(8)   A statement of truth in a statement of case may be made by –

    (a)   a person who is not a party; or

    (b)   by two parties jointly,

where this is permitted by a practice direction.

(9) An application that does not contain a statement of facts need not be verified by a statement of truth.

(10) Notwithstanding paragraph (3), and subject to any direction given under rule 9.14(2A) or rule 9.19(2A), the court may permit a party to rely upon matters set out in an application form which has not been verified by a statement of truth as evidence where the application has been made under –

    (a) Article 56 of the Maintenance Regulation on the form in Annex VI or VII to that Regulation; or

    (b) Article 10 of the 2007 Hague Convention on an Article 11 form.

(Practice Direction 17A sets out the form of statement of truth.)

Failure to verify a statement of case
17.3

(1) If a party fails to verify that party's statement of case by a statement of truth –

    (a) the statement of case shall remain effective unless struck out; but

    (b) the party may not rely on the statement of case as evidence of any of the matters set out in it.

(2) The court may strikeout a statement of case which is not verified by a statement of truth.

(3) Any party may apply for an order under paragraph (2).

Failure to verify a witness statement
17.4

If the maker of a witness statement fails to verify the witness statement by a statement of truth, the court may direct that it shall not be admissible as evidence.

Power of the court to require a document to be verified
17.5

(1) The court may order a person who has failed to verify a document in accordance with rule 17.2 to verify the document.

(2) Any party may apply for an order under paragraph (1).

False statements
17.6

(1) Proceedings for contempt of court may be brought against a person who makes, or causes to be made, a false statement in a document verified by a statement of truth without an honest belief in its truth.

(2) Proceedings under this rule may be brought only –

    (a) by the Attorney General; or

    (b) with the permission of the court.

PART 20 – INTERIM REMEDIES AND SECURITY FOR COSTS

II SECURITY FOR COSTS

Security for costs
20.6
(1)   A respondent to any application may apply under this Chapter of this Part for security for costs of the proceedings.

(Part 4 provides for the court to order payment of sums into court in other circumstances.)

(2)   An application for security for costs must be supported by written evidence.
(3)   Where the court makes an order for security for costs, it will –
    (a)   determine the amount of security; and
    (b)   direct –
        (i)   the manner in which; and
        (ii)   the time within which,
the security must be given.

Conditions to be satisfied
20.7
(1)   The court may make an order for security for costs under rule 20.6 if –
    (a)   it is satisfied, having regard to all the circumstances of the case, that it is just to make such an order; and
    (b)   either –
        (i)   one or more of the conditions in paragraph (2) applies; or
        (ii)   an enactment permits the court to require security for costs.
(2)   The conditions are –
    (a)   the applicant is –
        (i)   resident out of the jurisdiction; but
        (ii)   not resident in a Brussels Contracting State, a State bound by the Lugano Convention, a State bound by the 2007 Hague Convention which is an EEA State, a Regulation State or a Maintenance Regulation State, as defined in section 1(3) of the Civil Jurisdiction and Judgments Act 1982, or a Member State bound by the Council Regulation;
    (b)   the applicant has changed address since the application was started with a view to evading the consequences of the litigation;
    (c)   the applicant failed to give an address in the application form, or gave an incorrect address in that form;
    (d)   the applicant has taken steps in relation to the applicant's assets that would make it difficult to enforce an order for costs against the applicant.

(3)   The court may not make an order for security for costs under rule 20.6 in relation to the costs of proceedings under the 1980 Hague Convention.

(Rule 4.4 allows the court to strike out a statement of case.)

('EEA State' is defined in Schedule 1 to the Interpretation Act 1978.)

Security for costs of an appeal
20.8
The court may order security for costs of an appeal against –
(a)   an appellant;
(b)   a respondent who also appeals,
on the same grounds as it may order security for costs against an applicant under this Part.

PART 21 – MISCELLANEOUS RULES ABOUT DISCLOSURE AND INSPECTION OF DOCUMENTS

Interpretation
21.1
(1)   A party discloses a document by stating that the document exists or has existed.
(2)   Inspection of a document occurs when a party is permitted to inspect a document disclosed by another person.
(3)   For the purposes of disclosure and inspection –
        (a)   'document' means anything in which information of any description is recorded; and
        (b)   'copy' in relation to a document, means anything onto which information recorded in the document has been copied, by whatever means and whether directly or indirectly.

Orders for disclosure against a person not a party
21.2
(1)   This rule applies where an application is made to the court under any Act for disclosure by a person who is not a party to the proceedings.
(2)   The application –
        (a)   may be made without notice; and
        (b)   must be supported by evidence.
(3)   The court may make an order under this rule only where disclosure is necessary in order to dispose fairly of the proceedings or to save costs.
(4)   An order under this rule must –
        (a)   specify the documents or the classes of documents which the respondent must disclose; and
        (b)   require the respondent, when making disclosure, to specify any of those documents –
                (i)   which are no longer in the respondent's control; or

       (ii)   in respect of which the respondent claims a right or duty to withhold inspection.

(5)   Such an order may –
     (a)   require the respondent to indicate what has happened to any documents which are no longer in the respondent's control; and
     (b)   specify the time and place for disclosure and inspection.

(6)   An order under this rule must not compel a person to produce any document which that person could not be compelled to produce at the final hearing.

(7)   This rule does not limit any other power which the court may have to order disclosure against a person who is not a party to proceedings.

(Rule 35.3 contains provisions in relation to the disclosure and inspection of evidence arising out of mediation of cross-border disputes.)

Claim to withhold inspection or disclosure of a document
21.3

(1)   A person may apply, without notice, for an order permitting that person to withhold disclosure of a document on the ground that disclosure would damage the public interest.

(2)   Unless the court otherwise orders, an order of the court under paragraph (1) –
     (a)   must not be served on any other person; and
     (b)   must not be open to inspection by any other person.

(3)   A person who wishes to claim a right or a duty to withhold inspection of a document, or part of a document, must state in writing –
     (a)   the right or duty claimed; and
     (b)   the grounds on which that right or duty is claimed.

(4)   The statement referred to in paragraph (3) must be made to the person wishing to inspect the document.

(5)   A party may apply to the court to decide whether a claim made under paragraph (3) should be upheld.

(6)   Where the court is deciding an application under paragraph (1) or (5) it may –
     (a)   require the person seeking to withhold disclosure or inspection of a document to produce that document to the court; and
     (b)   invite any person, whether or not a party, to make representations.

(7)   An application under paragraph (1) or (5) must be supported by evidence.

(8)   This Part does not affect any rule of law which permits or requires a document to be withheld from disclosure or inspection on the ground that its disclosure or inspection would damage the public interest.

PART 22 – EVIDENCE

I GENERAL RULES

Power of court to control evidence
22.1

(1)   The court may control the evidence by giving directions as to –
     (a)   the issues on which it requires evidence;

    (b)   the nature of the evidence which it requires to decide those issues; and

    (c)   the way in which the evidence is to be placed before the court.

(2)   The court may use its power under this rule to exclude evidence that would otherwise be admissible.

(3)   The court may permit a party to adduce evidence, or to seek to rely on a document, in respect of which that party has failed to comply with the requirements of this Part.

(4)   The court may limit cross-examination.

Evidence of witnesses – general rule

22.2

(1)   The general rule is that any fact which needs to be proved by the evidence of witnesses is to be proved –

    (a)   at the final hearing, by their oral evidence; and

    (b)   at any other hearing, by their evidence in writing.

(2)   The general rule does not apply –

    (a)   to proceedings under Part 12 for secure accommodation orders, interim care orders or interim supervision orders; or

    (b)   where an enactment, any of these rules, a practice direction or a court order provides to the contrary.

(Section 45(7) of the Children Act 1989 (emergency protection orders) is an example of an enactment which makes provision relating to the evidence that a court may take into account when hearing an application.)

PART 30 – APPEALS

Scope and interpretation

30.1

(1)   The rules in this Part apply to appeals to –

    (a)   the High Court; and

    (b)   the family court.

(2)   This Part does not apply to an appeal in detailed assessment proceedings against a decision of an authorised court officer.

(Rules 47.21 to 47.24 of the CPR deal with appeals against a decision of an authorised court officer in detailed assessment proceedings.)

(3)   In this Part –

    'appeal court' means the court to which an appeal is made;

    'appeal notice' means an appellant's or respondent's notice;

    'appellant' means a person who brings or seeks to bring an appeal;

    'costs judge' means –

        (a)   the Chief Taxing Master;

        (b)   a taxing master of the Senior Courts; or

(c)   a person appointed to act as deputy for the person holding office referred to in paragraph (b) or to act as temporary additional officer for any such office;

'district judge' means –

(a)   the Senior District Judge of the Family Division

(b)   a district judge of the Principal Registry of the Family Division;

(c)   a person appointed to act as deputy for the person holding office referred to in paragraph (b) or to act as temporary additional officer for any such office;

(d)   a district judge;

(e)   a deputy district judge appointed under section 102 of the Senior Courts Act 1981 or section 8 of the County Courts Act 1984; or

(f)   a District Judge (Magistrates' Courts);

'lower court' means the court from which, or the person from whom, the appeal lies; and

'respondent' means –

(a)   a person other than the appellant who was a party to the proceedings in the lower court and who is affected by the appeal; and

(b)   a person who is permitted by the appeal court to be a party to the appeal.

(4)   This Part is subject to any rule, enactment or practice direction which sets out special provisions with regard to any particular category of appeal.

Parties to comply with the practice direction

30.2   All parties to an appeal must comply with Practice Direction 30A.

Permission

30.3

(1)   An appellant or respondent requires permission to appeal –

(a)   against a decision in proceedings where the decision appealed against was made by a district judge or a costs judge, unless paragraph (2) applies; or

(b)   as provided by Practice Direction 30A.

(2)   Permission to appeal is not required where the appeal is against –

(a)   a committal order;

(b)   a secure accommodation order under section 25 of the 1989 Act; or

(c)   a refusal to grant habeas corpus for release in relation to a minor.

(3)   An application for permission to appeal may be made –

(a)   to the lower court at the hearing at which the decision to be appealed was made; or

(b)   to the appeal court in an appeal notice.

(Rule 30.4 sets out the time limits for filing an appellant's notice at the appeal court. Rule 30.5 sets out the time limits for filing a respondent's notice at the appeal court. Any application for permission to appeal to the appeal court must be made in the appeal notice (see rules 30.4(1) and 30.5(3).)

(4) Where the lower court refuses an application for permission to appeal, a further application for permission to appeal may be made to the appeal court.

(5) Subject to paragraph (5A), where the appeal court, without a hearing, refuses permission to appeal, the person seeking permission may request the decision to be reconsidered at a hearing.

(5A) Where a judge of the High Court or in the family court, a judge of the High Court or a Designated Family Judge refuses permission to appeal without a hearing and considers that the application is totally without merit, the judge may make an order that the person seeking permission may not request the decision to be reconsidered at a hearing.

(5B) Rule 4.3(5) will not apply to an order that the person seeking permission may not request the decision to be reconsidered at a hearing made under paragraph (5A).

(6) A request under paragraph (5) must be filed within 7 days beginning with the date on which the notice that permission has been refused was served.

(7) Permission to appeal may be given only where –
   (a) the court considers that the appeal would have a real prospect of success; or
   (b) there is some other compelling reason why the appeal should be heard.

(8) An order giving permission may –
   (a) limit the issues to be heard; and
   (b) be made subject to conditions.

Appellant's notice
30.4

(1) Where the appellant seeks permission from the appeal court it must be requested in the appellant's notice.

(2) Subject to paragraph (3), the appellant must file the appellant's notice at the appeal court within –
   (a) such period as may be directed by the lower court (which may be longer or shorter than the period referred to in sub-paragraph (b)); or
   (b) where the court makes no such direction, 21 days after the date of the decision of the lower court against which the appellant wishes to appeal.

(3) Where the appeal is against –
   (a) a case management decision; or
   (b) an order under section 38(1) of the 1989 Act,
   the appellant must file the appellant's notice within 7 days beginning with the date of the decision of the lower court.

(4)   Unless the appeal court orders otherwise, an appellant's notice must be served on each respondent and the persons referred to in paragraph (5) –
    (a)   as soon as practicable; and
    (b)   in any event not later than 7 days,
    after it is filed.

(5)   The persons referred to in paragraph (4) are –
    (a)   any children's guardian, welfare officer, or children and family reporter;
    (b)   a local authority who has prepared a report under section 14A(8) or (9) of the 1989 Act;
    (c)   an adoption agency or local authority which has prepared a report on the suitability of the applicant to adopt a child;
    (d)   a local authority which has prepared a report on the placement of the child for adoption; and

Respondent's notice
30.5

(1)   A respondent may file and serve a respondent's notice.

(2)   A respondent who –
    (a)   is seeking permission to appeal from the appeal court; or
    (b)   wishes to ask the appeal court to uphold the order of the lower court for reasons different from or additional to those given by the lower court,
    must file a respondent's notice.

(3)   Where the respondent seeks permission from the appeal court it must be requested in the respondent's notice.

(4)   Subject to paragraph (4A), a respondent's notice must be filed within –
    (a)   such period as may be directed by the lower court; or
    (b)   where the court makes no such direction, 14 days beginning with the date referred to in paragraph (5).

(4A)   Where the appeal is against a case management decision, a respondent's notice must be filed within –
    (a)   such period as may be directed by the lower court; or
    (b)   where the court makes no such direction, 7 days beginning with the date referred to in paragraph (5).

(5)   The date referred to in paragraph (4) is –
    (a)   the date on which the respondent is served with the appellant's notice where –
        (i)   permission to appeal was given by the lower court; or
        (ii)   permission to appeal is not required;
    (b)   the date on which the respondent is served with notification that the appeal court has given the appellant permission to appeal; or
    (c)   the date on which the respondent is served with notification that the application for permission to appeal and the appeal itself are to be heard together.

(6)   Unless the appeal court orders otherwise, a respondent's notice must be served on the appellant, any other respondent and the persons referred to in rule 30.4(5) –

(a)   as soon as practicable; and

(b)   in any event not later than 7 days,

after it is filed.

(7)   Where there is an appeal against an order under section 38(1) of the 1989 Act –

(a)   a respondent may not, in that appeal, bring an appeal from the order or ask the appeal court to uphold the order of the lower court for reasons different from or additional to those given by the lower court; and

(b)   paragraphs (2) and (3) do not apply.

Grounds of appeal

30.6   The appeal notice must state the grounds of appeal.

Variation of time

30.7

(1)   An application to vary the time limit for filing an appeal notice must be made to the appeal court.

(2)   The parties may not agree to extend any date or time limit set by –

(a)   these rules;

(b)   Practice Direction 30A; or

(c)   an order of the appeal court or the lower court.

(Rule 4.1(3)(a) provides that the court may extend or shorten the time for compliance with a rule, practice direction or court order (even if an application for extension is made after the time for compliance has expired).)

(Rule 4.1(3)(c) provides that the court may adjourn or bring forward a hearing.)

Stay

30.8   Unless the appeal court or the lower court orders otherwise, an appeal does not operate as a stay of any order or decision of the lower court.

Amendment of appeal notice

30.9   An appeal notice may not be amended without the permission of the appeal court.

Striking out appeal notices and setting aside or imposing conditions on permission to appeal

30.10

(1)   The appeal court may –

(a)   strike out the whole or part of an appeal notice;

(b)   set aside permission to appeal in whole or in part;

(c)   impose or vary conditions upon which an appeal may be brought.

(2)   The court will only exercise its powers under paragraph (1) where there is a compelling reason for doing so.

(3)   Where a party was present at the hearing at which permission was given that party may not subsequently apply for an order that the court exercise its powers under paragraphs (1)(b) or (1)(c).

Appeal court's powers
30.11
(1)   In relation to an appeal the appeal court has all the powers of the lower court.

(Rule 30.1(4) provides that this Part is subject to any enactment that sets out special provisions with regard to any particular category of appeal.)

(2)   The appeal court has power to –
    (a)   affirm, set aside or vary any order or judgment made or given by the lower court;
    (b)   refer any application or issue for determination by the lower court;
    (c)   order a new hearing;
    (d)   make orders for the payment of interest;
    (e)   make a costs order.

(3)   The appeal court may exercise its powers in relation to the whole or part of an order of the lower court.

(Rule 4.1 contains general rules about the court's case management powers.)

(4)   If the appeal court –
    (a)   refuses an application for permission to appeal;
    (b)   strikes out an appellant's notice; or
    (c)   dismisses an appeal,
and it considers that the application, the appellant's notice or the appeal is totally without merit, the provisions of paragraph (5) must be complied with.

(5)   Where paragraph (4) applies –
    (a)   the court's order must record the fact that it considers the application, the appellant's notice or the appeal to be totally without merit; and
    (b)   the court must at the same time consider whether it is appropriate to make a civil restraint order.

Hearing of appeals
30.12
(1)   Every appeal will be limited to a review of the decision of the lower court unless –
    (a)   an enactment or practice direction makes different provision for a particular category of appeal; or
    (b)   the court considers that in the circumstances of an individual appeal it would be in the interests of justice to hold a re-hearing.

(2)   Unless it orders otherwise, the appeal court will not receive –

(a)   oral evidence; or

(b)   evidence which was not before the lower court.

(3)   The appeal court will allow an appeal where the decision of the lower court was –

(a)   wrong; or

(b)   unjust because of a serious procedural or other irregularity in the proceedings in the lower court.

(4)   The appeal court may draw any inference of fact which it considers justified on the evidence.

(5)   At the hearing of the appeal a party may not rely on a matter not contained in that party's appeal notice unless the appeal court gives permission.

Assignment of appeals to the Court of Appeal

30.13

(1)   Where the court from or to which an appeal is made or from which permission to appeal is sought ('the relevant court') considers that –

(a)   an appeal which is to be heard by a county court or the High Court would raise an important point of principle or practice; or

(b)   there is some other compelling reason for the Court of Appeal to hear it,

the relevant court may order the appeal to be transferred to the Court of Appeal.

(2)   Paragraph (1) does not allow an application for permission to appeal to be transferred to the Court of Appeal.

Reopening of final appeals

30.14

(1)   The High Court will not reopen a final determination of any appeal unless –

(a)   it is necessary to do so in order to avoid real injustice;

(b)   the circumstances are exceptional and make it appropriate to reopen the appeal; and

(c)   there is no alternative effective remedy.

(2)   In paragraphs (1), (3), (4) and (6), 'appeal' includes an application for permission to appeal.

(3)   This rule does not apply to appeals to the family court.

(4)   Permission is needed to make an application under this rule to reopen a final determination of an appeal.

(5)   There is no right to an oral hearing of an application for permission unless, exceptionally, the judge so directs.

(6)   The judge will not grant permission without directing the application to be served on the other party to the original appeal and giving that party an opportunity to make representations.

(7)   There is no right of appeal or review from the decision of the judge on the application for permission, which is final.

(8)   The procedure for making an application for permission is set out in Practice Direction 30A.

PART 34 – RECIPROCAL ENFORCEMENT OF MAINTENANCE ORDERS

Scope and interpretation of this Part
34.1
(1)   This Part contains rules about the reciprocal enforcement of maintenance orders.
(2)   In this Part –

'the 1920 Act' means the Maintenance Orders (Facilities for Enforcement) Act 1920;

'the1972 Act' means the Maintenance Orders (Reciprocal Enforcement) Act 1972;

'the 1982 Act' means the Civil Jurisdiction and Judgments Act 1982;

'the 1988 Convention' means the Convention on jurisdiction and the enforcement of judgments in civil and commercial matters done at Lugano on 16th September 1988;

'the Judgments Regulation' means Council Regulation (EC) No. 44/2001 of 22nd December 2000 on jurisdiction and the recognition and enforcement of judgments in civil and commercial matters; and

'the Lugano Convention' means the Convention on jurisdiction and the recognition and enforcement of judgments in civil and commercial matters, between the European Community and the Republic of Iceland, the Kingdom of Norway, the Swiss Confederation and the Kingdom of Denmark signed on behalf of the European Community on 30th October 2007.

(3)   Chapter 1 of this Part relates to the enforcement of maintenance orders in accordance with the 1920 Act.
(4)   Chapter 2 of this Part relates to the enforcement of maintenance orders in accordance with Parts 1 and 2 of the 1972 Act.
(5)   Chapter 3 of this Part relates to the enforcement of maintenance orders in accordance with –
(a)   the 1982 Act;
(b)   the Judgments Regulation;
(c)   the Lugano Convention;
(d)   the Maintenance Regulation; and
(e)   the 2007 Hague Convention.

Meaning of prescribed officer in the family court
34.2
(1)   For the purposes of the 1920 Act, the prescribed officer in relation to the family court is the court officer.
(2)   For the purposes of Part 1 of the 1972 Act and section 5(2) of the 1982 Act, the prescribed officer in relation to the family court is the court officer.
(3)   For the purposes of an application under Article 30 of the Maintenance Regulation for a declaration of enforceability of a maintenance order or under Article 23(2) or (3) of the 2007 Hague Convention for registration of a maintenance order, the prescribed officer in relation to the family court is the court officer.

Registration of maintenance orders in the family court
34.3
Where the family court is required by any of the enactments referred to in rule 34.1(2) or by virtue of the Maintenance Regulation or the 2007 Hague Convention to register a foreign order the court officer must –
(a)   enter a memorandum of the order in the register; and
(b)   state on the memorandum the statutory provision or international instrument under which the order is registered.

I ENFORCEMENT OF MAINTENANCE ORDERS UNDER THE MAINTENANCE ORDERS (FACILITIES FOR ENFORCEMENT) ACT 1920

Interpretation
34.4
(1)   In this Chapter–
'payer', in relation to a maintenance order, means the person liable to make the payments for which the order provides; and
'reciprocating country' means a country or territory to which the 1920 Act extends.
(2)   In this Chapter, an expression defined in the 1920 Act has the meaning given to it in that Act.

Confirmation of provisional orders made in a reciprocating country
34.5
(1)   This rule applies where, in accordance with section 4(1) of the 1920 Act, the court officer receives a provisional maintenance order.
(2)   The court must fix the date, time and place for a hearing.
(3)   The court officer must register the order in accordance with rule 34.3.
(4)   The court officer must serve on the payer –
(a)   certified copies of the provisional order and accompanying documents; and
(b)   a notice –
(i)   specifying the time and date fixed for the hearing; and
(ii)   stating that the payer may attend to show cause why the order should not be confirmed.
(5)   The court officer must inform –
(a)   the court which made the provisional order; and
(b)   the Lord Chancellor,
whether the court confirms, with or without modification, or decides not to confirm, the order.

Payment of sums due under registered orders
34.6
Where an order made by a reciprocating country is registered in the family court under section 1 of the 1920 Act, the court must order payments due to be made to the court.

(Practice Direction 34A contains further provisions relating to the payment of sums due under registered orders.)

Collection and enforcement of sums due under registered orders
34.7
(1)　This rule applies to –
　　(a)　an order made in a reciprocating county which is registered in the family court; and
　　(b)　a provisional order made in a reciprocating country which has been confirmed by the family court,
　　where the court has ordered that payments due under the order be made to the court.
(2)　The court officer must –
　　(a)　collect the monies due under the order; and
　　(b)　send the monies collected to –
　　　　(i)　the court in the reciprocating country which made the order; or
　　　　(ii)　such other person or authority as that court or the Lord Chancellor may from time to time direct.
(3)　The court officer may take proceedings in that officer's own name for enforcing payment of monies due under the order.

(Rule 32.33 makes provision in relation to a court officer taking such proceedings.)

Prescribed notice for the taking of further evidence
34.8
(1)　This rule applies where a court in a reciprocating country has sent a provisional order to the family court for the purpose of taking further evidence.
(2)　The court officer must send a notice to the person who applied for the provisional order specifying –
　　(a)　the further evidence required; and
　　(b)　the time and place fixed for taking the evidence.

Transmission of maintenance orders made in a reciprocating country to the High Court
34.9
A maintenance order to be sent by the Lord Chancellor to the High Court in accordance with section 1(1) of the 1920 Act will be –
(a)　sent to the senior district judge who will register it in the register kept for the purpose of the 1920 Act; and
(b)　filed in the principal registry.

Transmission of maintenance orders made in the High Court to a reciprocating country
34.10
(1)　This rule applies to maintenance orders made in the High Court.

(2)   An application for a maintenance order to be sent to a reciprocating country under section 2 of the 1920Act must be made in accordance with this rule.

(3)   The application must be made to a district judge in the principal registry unless paragraph (4) applies.

(4)   If the order was made in the course of proceedings in a district registry, the application may be made to a district judge in that district registry.

(5)   The application must be –
   (a)   accompanied by a certified copy of the order; and
   (b)   supported by a record of the sworn written evidence.

(6)   The written evidence must give –
   (a)   the applicant's reason for believing that the payer resides in the reciprocating country;
   (b)   such information as the applicant has as to the whereabouts of the payer; and
   (c)   such other information as maybe set out in Practice Direction 34A.

Inspection of the register in the High Court
34.11

(1)   A person may inspect the register and request copies of a registered order and any document filed with it if the district judge is satisfied that that person is entitled to, or liable to make, payments under a maintenance order made in –
   (a)   the High Court; or
   (b)   a court in a reciprocating country.

(2)   The right to inspect the register referred to in paragraph (1) may be exercised by –
   (a)   a solicitor acting on behalf of the person entitled to, or liable to make, the payments referred to in that paragraph; or
   (b)   with the permission of the district judge, any other person.

II ENFORCEMENT OF MAINTENANCE ORDERS UNDER PART 1 OF THE 1972 ACT

Interpretation
34.12

(1)   In this Chapter –
   (a)   'reciprocating country' means a country to which Part 1 of the 1972 Act extends; and
   (b)   'relevant court in the reciprocating country' means, as the case may be –
      (i)   the court which made the order which has been sent to England and Wales for confirmation;
      (ii)   the court which made the order which has been registered in a court in England and Wales;
      (iii)   the court to which an order made in England and Wales has been sent for registration; or

(iv) the court to which a provisional order made in England and Wales has been sent for confirmation.

(2) In this Chapter, an expression defined in the 1972 Act has the meaning given to it in that Act.

(3) In this Chapter, 'Hague Convention Countries' means the countries listed in Schedule 1 to the Reciprocal Enforcement of Maintenance Orders (Hague Convention Countries) Order 1993.

Scope
34.13

(1) Section 1 of this Chapter contains rules relating to the reciprocal enforcement of maintenance orders under Part 1of the 1972 Act.

(2) Section 2 of this Chapter modifies the rules contained in Section 1 of this Chapter in their application to –
(a) omitted
(b) the Hague Convention Countries; and
(c) the United States of America.

(3) Section 3 of this Chapter contains a rule in relation to notification of proceedings in a Hague Convention Country or the United States of America.

(4) Section 4 of this Chapter contains rules in relation to proceedings under Part 2 of the 1972 Act (reciprocal enforcement of claims for the recovery of maintenance).

(Practice Direction 34A sets out in full the rules for the Hague Convention Countries and the United States of America as modified by Section 2 of this Chapter.)

SECTION 1
Reciprocal enforcement of maintenance orders under Part 1 of the 1972 Act

Application for transmission of maintenance order to reciprocating country
34.14

An application for a maintenance order to be sent to a reciprocating country under section 2 of the 1972 Act must be made in accordance with Practice Direction 34A.

Certification of evidence given on provisional orders
34.15

A document setting out or summarising evidence is authenticated by a court in England and Wales by a certificate signed, by the judge before whom that evidence was given.

(Section 3(5)(b), 5(4) and 9(5) of the 1972 Act require a document to be authenticated by the court.)

Confirmation of a provisional order made in a reciprocating country
34.16

(1) This rule applies to proceedings for the confirmation of a provisional order made in a reciprocating country, including proceedings in the family court for the

confirmation of a provisional order made in a reciprocating country varying a maintenance order to which section 5(5) or 9(6) of the 1972 Act applies.

(2)   Paragraph (3) applies on receipt by the court of –

(a)   a certified copy of the order; and

(b)   the documents required by the1972 Act to accompany the order.

(3)   On receipt of the documents referred to in paragraph (2) –

(a)   the court must fix the date, time and place for a hearing or a directions appointment; and

(b)   the court officer must send to the payer notice of the date, time and place fixed together with a copy of the order and accompanying documents.

(4)   The date fixed for the hearing must be not less than 21 days beginning with the date on which the court officer sent the documents to the payer in accordance with paragraph (2).

(5)   The court officer will send to the relevant court in the reciprocating country a certified copy of any order confirming or refusing to confirm the provisional order.

(Section 5(5) and 7 of the 1972 Act provide for proceedings for the confirmation of a provisional order.)

(Rule 34.22 provides for the transmission of documents to a court in a reciprocating country.)

Consideration of revocation of a provisional order made by the family court

34.17

(1)   This rule applies where –

(a)   the family court has made a provisional order by virtue of section 3 of the 1972 Act;

(b)   before the order is confirmed, evidence is taken by the court or received by it as set out in section 5(9) of the 1972 Act; and

(c)   on consideration of the evidence the court considers that the order ought not to have been made.

(Section 5(9) of the1972 Act provides that the family court may revoke a provisional order made by it, before the order has been confirmed in a reciprocating country, if it receives new evidence.)

(2)   The court officer must serve on the person who applied for the provisional order ('the applicant') a notice which must –

(a)   set out the evidence taken or received by the court;

(b)   inform the applicant that the court considers that the order ought not to have been made; and

(c)   inform the applicant that the applicant may –

(i)   make representations in relation to that evidence either orally or in writing; and

(ii)   adduce further evidence.

(3)   If an applicant wishes to adduce further evidence –
    (a)   the applicant must notify the court officer at the court which made the order;
    (b)   the court will fix a date for the hearing of the evidence; and
    (c)   the court officer will notify the applicant in writing of the date fixed.

Notification of variation or revocation of a maintenance order by the High Court or the family court
34.18
(1)   This rule applies where –
    (a)   a maintenance order has been sent to a reciprocating country in pursuance of section 2 of the 1972 Act; and
    (b)   the court makes an order, not being a provisional order, varying or revoking that order.
(2)   The court officer must send a certified copy of the order of variation or revocation to the relevant court in the reciprocating country.

(Rule 34.22 provides for the transmission of documents to a court in a reciprocating country.)

Notification of confirmation, variation or revocation of a maintenance order by the family court
34.19
(1)   This rule applies where the family court makes an order –
    (a)   not being a provisional order, revoking or varying a maintenance order to which section 5 of the 1972 Act applies;
    (b)   under section 9 of the 1972Act, revoking or varying a registered order; or
    (c)   under section 7(2) of the 1972Act, confirming an order to which section 7 of that Act applies.
(2)   The court officer must send written notice of the making, variation, revocation or confirmation of the order, as appropriate, to the relevant court in the reciprocating country.

(Section 5 of the 1972 Act applies to a provisional order made by the family court in accordance with section 3 of that Act which has been confirmed by a court in a reciprocating country.)

(Rule 34.22 provides for the transmission of documents to a court in a reciprocating country.)

Taking of evidence for court in reciprocating country
34.20
(1)   This rule applies where a request is made by or on behalf of a court in a reciprocating country for the taking of evidence for the purpose of proceedings relating to a maintenance order to which Part 1 of the 1972 Act applies.

(Section 14 of the1972 Act makes provision for the taking of evidence needed for the purpose of certain proceedings.)

(2) The High Court has power to take the evidence where –
  (a) the request for evidence relates to a maintenance order made by a superior court in the United Kingdom; and
  (b) the witness resides in England and Wales.
(3) The family court has power to take evidence where –
  (a) the request for evidence relates to a maintenance order –
    (i) made by the family court; or
    (ii) registered in the family court; or
  (b) the Lord Chancellor sends to the family court a request to take evidence.

(Practice Direction 34E makes further provision on this matter)

(4) Omitted
(5) Omitted
(6) The evidence is to be taken in accordance with Part 22.

Request for the taking of evidence by a court in a reciprocating country

34.21

(1) This rule applies where a request is made by the family court for the taking of evidence in a reciprocating country in accordance with section 14(5) of the 1972 Act.
(2) The request must be made in writing to the court in the reciprocating country.

(Rule 34.22 provides for the transmission of documents to a court in a reciprocating country.)

Transmission of documents

34.22

(1) This rule applies to any document, including a notice or request, which is required to be sent to a court in a reciprocating country by –
  (a) Part 1 of the 1972 Act; or
  (b) Section 1 of Chapter 2 of this Part of these rules.
(2) The document must be sent to the Lord Chancellor for transmission to the court in the reciprocating country.

Method of payment under registered orders

34.23

(1) Where an order is registered in the family court in accordance with section 6(3) of the 1972 Act, the court must order that the payment of sums due under the order be made –
  (a) to the registering court; and
  (b) at such time and place as the court officer directs.

(Section 6(3) of the 1972 Act makes provision for the registration of maintenance orders made in a reciprocating country.)

(2)   Where the court orders payments to be made to the court, whether in accordance with paragraph (1) or otherwise, the court officer must send the payments –

     (a)   by post to either –

         (i)   the court which made the order; or

         (ii)   such other person or authority as that court, or the Lord Chancellor, directs; or

     (b)   if the court which made the order is a country or territory specified in the Practice Direction 34A–

         (i)   to the Crown Agents for Overseas Governments and Administrations for transmission to the person to whom they are due; or

         (ii)   as the Lord Chancellor directs.

(Practice Direction 34A contains further provisions relating to the payment of sums due under registered orders.)

Enforcement of payments under registered orders
34.24

(1)   This rule applies where a court has ordered periodical payments under a registered maintenance order to be made to the court.

(2)   The court officer must take reasonable steps to notify the payee of the means of enforcement available.

(3)   Paragraph (4) applies where periodical payments due under a registered order are in arrears.

(4)   The court officer, on that officer's own initiative –

     (a)   may; or

     (b)   if the sums due are more than 4 weeks in arrears, must, proceed in that officer's own name for the recovery of the sums due unless of the view that it is unreasonable to do so.

Notification of registration and cancellation
34.25

(1)   The court officer must send written notice to the Lord Chancellor of the due registration of orders registered in accordance with section 6(3), 7(5), or 10(4) of the 1972 Act.

(2)   The court officer must, when registering an order in accordance with section 6(3), 7(5), 9(10), 10(4) or (5)or 23(3) of the 1972 Act, send written notice to the payer stating –

     (a)   that the order has been registered;

     (b)   that payments under the order should be made to the court officer; and

     (c)   the hours during which and the place at which the payments should be made.

(3)   The court officer must, when cancelling the registration of an order in accordance with section 10(1) of the 1972 Act, send written notice of the cancellation to the payer.

SECTION 2
Modification of rules in Section 1 of this Chapter

SUB-SECTION 1 Omitted

Omitted
34.26

SUB-SECTION 2 Hague Convention Countries

Application of Section 1 of this Chapter to the Hague Convention Countries
34.27

(1)   In relation to the Hague Convention Countries, Section 1 of this Chapter has effect as modified by this rule.

(2)   A reference in this rule, and in any rule which has effect in relation to the Hague Convention Countries by virtue of this rule to –

     (a)   the 1972 Act is a reference to the 1972 Act as modified by Schedule 2 to the Reciprocal Enforcement of Maintenance Orders (Hague Convention Countries) Order 1993; and

     (b)   a section under the 1972 Act is a reference to the section so numbered in the 1972 Act as so modified.

(3)   A reference to a reciprocating country in rule 34.12(1) and Section 1 of this Chapter is a reference to a Hague Convention Country.

(4)   Rules 34.15 (certification of evidence given on provisional orders), 34.16 (confirmation of provisional orders), 34.19 (notification of confirmation, variation or revocation of a maintenance order by the family court) and 34.21 (request for the taking of evidence by a court in a reciprocating country) do not apply.

(5)   For rule 34.17 (consideration of revocation of a provisional order made by the family court) substitute –

> **'Consideration of variation or revocation of a maintenance order made by the family court**
> **34.17**
> (1) This rule applies where –
> (a) an application has been made to a the family court by a payee for the variation or revocation of an order to which section 5 of the 1972 Act applies; and
> (b) the payer resides in a Hague Convention Country.
> (2) The court officer must serve on the payee, by post, a copy of any representations or evidence adduced by or on behalf of the payer.'.

(6)   For rule 34.18 (notification of variation or revocation of a maintenance order by the High Court or the family court) substitute –

'**Notification of variation or revocation of a maintenance order by the High Court or a county court**
34.18
(1) This rule applies if the High Court or a county court makes an order varying or revoking a maintenance order to which section 5 of the 1972 Act applies.
(2) If the time for appealing has expired without an appeal having been entered, the court officer will send to the Lord Chancellor –
(a) the documents required by section 5(8) of the 1972 Act; and
(b) a certificate signed by a judge stating that the order of variation or revocation is enforceable and no longer subject to the ordinary forms of review.
(3) A party who enters an appeal against the order of variation or revocation must, at the same time, give written notice to the court officer.'.

(7)   For rule 34.23(2) (method of payment under registered orders) substitute –
'(2) Where the court orders payment to be made to the court, the court officer must send the payments by post to the payee under the order.'.

(8)   For rule 34.25 (notification of registration and cancellation) substitute –
'**Notification of registration and cancellation**
34.25 The court officer must send written notice to –
(a) the Lord Chancellor, on the due registration of an order under section 10(4) of the 1972 Act; and
(b) the payer under the order, on –
(i) the registration of an order under section 10(4) of the 1972 Act; or
(ii) the cancellation of the registration of an order under section 10(1) of the 1972 Act.'.

(9)   After rule 34.25 insert –
'**General provisions as to notices**
34.25A
(1) A notice to a payer of the registration of an order in the family court in accordance with section 6(3) of the 1972 Act must be in the form referred to in a practice direction.
(Section 6(8) of the 1972 Act requires notice of registration to be given to the payer.)
(2) If the court sets aside the registration of a maintenance order following an appeal under section 6(9) of the 1972 Act, the court officer must send written notice of the decision to the Lord Chancellor.
(3) A notice to a payee that the court officer has refused to register an order must be in the form referred to in a practice direction.
(Section 6(11) of the 1972 Act requires notice of refusal of registration to be given to the payee.)
(4) Where, under any provision of Part 1 of the 1972 Act, a court officer serves a notice on a payer who resides in a Hague Convention Country, the court officer must send to the Lord Chancellor a certificate of service.'.

SUB-SECTION 3 United States of America

Application of Section 1 of this Chapter to the United States of America
34.28

(1)   In relation to the United States of America, Section 1 of this Chapter has effect as modified by this rule.

(2)   A reference in this rule and in any rule which has effect in relation to the United States of America by virtue of this rule to –

   (a)   the 1972 Act is a reference to the 1972 Act as modified by Schedule 1 to the Reciprocal Enforcement of Maintenance Orders (United States of America) Order 2007; and

   (b)   a section under the 1972 Act is a reference to the section so numbered in the 1972 Act as so modified.

(3)   A reference to a reciprocating country in rule 34.12(1) and Section 1 of this Chapter is a reference to the United States of America.

(4)   Rules 34.15 (certification of evidence given on provisional orders), 34.16 (confirmation of provisional orders), 34.19 (notification of confirmation, variation or revocation of a maintenance order made by the family court) and 34.21 (request for the taking of evidence in a reciprocating country) do not apply.

(5)   For rule 34.17 (consideration of revocation of a provisional order made by the family court) substitute –

   'Consideration of variation or revocation of a maintenance order made by the family court

   34.17

   (1) This rule applies where –

   (a) an application has been made to the family court by a payee for the variation or revocation of an order to which section 5 of the 1972 Act applies; and

   (b) the payer resides in the United States of America.

   (2) The court officer must serve on the payee by post a copy of any representations or evidence adduced by or on behalf of the payer.'.

(6)   For rule 34.18 (notification of variation or revocation), substitute –

   'Notification of variation or revocation

   34.18 If the High Court or the family court makes an order varying or revoking a maintenance order to which section 5 of the 1972 Act applies, the court officer will send to the Lord Chancellor the documents required by section 5(7) of that Act.'.

(7)   For rule 34.23(2) (method of payment under registered orders) substitute –

   '(2) Where the court orders payment to be made to the court, the court officer must send the payments by post to the payee under the order.'.

(8)   For rule 34.25 (notification of registration and cancellation) substitute –

   'Notification of registration and cancellation

   34.25 The court officer must send written notice to –

   (a) the Lord Chancellor, on the due registration of an order under section 10(4) of the 1972 Act; or

(b) the payer under the order, on –

(i) the registration of an order under section 10(4) of the 1972 Act; or

(ii) the cancellation of the registration of an order under section 10(1) of that Act.'

SECTION 3
Proceedings in a Hague Convention Country or in the United States of America

Notification of proceedings in a Hague Convention Country or in the United States of America
34.28ZA

Practice Direction 34E applies where the court officer receives from the Lord Chancellor notice of the institution of proceedings, including notice of the substance of a claim, in a Hague Convention Country or in the United States of America in relation to the making, variation or revocation of a maintenance order.

SECTION 4
Reciprocal enforcement of claims for the recovery of maintenance

Interpretation
34.28ZB

In this Section –

'convention country' means a country or territory specified in an Order in Council made under section 25 of the 1972 Act; and

an expression defined in the 1972 Act has the meaning given to it in that Act.

Dismissal of an application under section 27A of the 1972 Act or application for variation
34.28ZC

(1) Where the family court dismisses an application under –

(a) section 27A of the 1972 Act (application for recovery of maintenance); or

(b) an application by a person in a convention country for the variation of a registered order,

the court officer will send a written notice of the court's decision to the Lord Chancellor.

(2) The notice will include a statement of the court's reasons for its decision.

Application for recovery of maintenance in England and Wales: section 27B of the 1972 Act
34.28ZD

(1) Where the family court receives an application for the recovery of maintenance sent from the Lord Chancellor under section 27B of the 1972 Act, the court will –

(a) fix the date, time and place for a hearing or directions appointment, allowing sufficient time for service under this rule to be effected at least 21 days before the date fixed; and

(b)   serve copies of the application and any accompanying documents, together with a notice stating the date, time and place so fixed, on the respondent.

(2)   Within 14 days of service under this rule, the respondent must file an answer to the application in the form referred to in Practice Direction 5A.

Application under section 26(1) or (2) of the 1972 Act and certificate under section 26(3A) of the 1972 Act: registration
34.28ZE

Where –

(a)   an application under section 26(1) or (2) of the 1972 Act; or

(b)   a certificate under section 26(3A) of the 1972 Act,

is required to be registered in the family court by virtue of the Recovery of Maintenance (United States of America) Order 2007, the court officer will enter a minute or memorandum of the application or certificate in the register.

Registration of an order: sections 27C(7) and 32(3) and (6) of the 1972 Act
34.28ZF

(1)   Where the family court makes an order which is required under section 27C(7) of the 1972 Act to be registered, the court officer will enter a minute or memorandum of the order in the register.

(2)   Where a court officer receives under section 32(3) of the 1972 Act a certified copy of an order, the court officer will register the order by means of a minute or memorandum in the register.

(3)   Every minute or memorandum entered under paragraph (1) or (2) will specify the section and subsection of the 1972 Act under which the order in question is registered.

(4)   Where a court officer registers an order as required by section 27C(7) or 32(3) of the 1972 Act, the court officer will send written notice to the Lord Chancellor that the order has been registered.

(5)   Where a court officer is required by section 32(6) of the 1972 Act to give notice of the registration of an order, the court officer will do this by sending written notice to the officer specified in that subsection that the order has been registered.

Payments made to the family court
34.28ZG

(1)   Where payments are made to the family court by virtue of section 27C or 34A of the 1972 Act, the court officer will send those payments by post to such person or authority as the Lord Chancellor may from time to time direct.

(2)   Subject to paragraph (3), if it appears to a court officer that any sums payable under a registered order are in arrears, the officer may proceed in the officer's own name for the recovery of those sums.

(3)   Where it appears to the officer that sums payable under the order are in arrears to an amount equal –

(a)   in the case of payments to be made monthly or less frequently, to twice the sum payable periodically; or

(b)   in any other case, to four times the sum payable periodically,

the officer will proceed in the officer's own name for the recovery of those sums, unless it appears to the officer that it is unreasonable in the circumstances to do so.

Method of payment
34.28ZH

(1)   This rule applies where the family court exercises its duties or power sunder section 27C or 34A of the 1972 Act.

(2)   Where the court orders that payments under the order are to be made by a particular means –

    (a)   the court will record on the copy of the order the means of payment that the court has ordered; and

    (b)   the court officer will, as soon as practicable, notify, in writing, the person liable to make the payments under the order how payments are to be made.

(3)   Paragraph (4) applies where the court orders that payments be made to the court by a method of payment falling within section 1(5) of the Maintenance Enforcement Act 1991.

(4)   The court officer will notify the person liable to make the payments under the order of sufficient details of the account into which the payments should be made to enable payments to be made into that account.

Application under section 34 of the 1972 Act: variation or revocation
34.28ZI

(1)   This rule applies in relation to an application under section 34 of the 1972 Act for the variation or revocation of a registered order.

(2)   An application which is made directly to the registering court must be filed in the form referred to in Practice Direction 5A.

(3)   Where the court receives an application, either filed in accordance with paragraph (2) or sent from the Lord Chancellor under section 34(3) of the 1972 Act –

    (a)   the court will set the date, time and place for a hearing or directions appointment; and

    (b)   the court officer will notify the applicant of the date, time and place.

Application under section 35 of the 1972 Act: variation or revocation
34.28ZJ

(1)   This rule applies in relation to an application under section 35 of the 1972 Act for the variation or revocation of a registered order.

(2)   Notice under section 35(3)(b) of the 1972 Act of the time and place appointed for the hearing of the application will be in the form specified in Practice Direction 34D.

(3)   The court officer will send the notice by post to the Lord Chancellor for onward transmission to the appropriate authority in the convention country in which the respondent is residing.

(4)   The time appointed for the hearing of the application will not be less than six weeks later than the date on which the notice is sent to the Lord Chancellor.

Request under section 38(1) of the 1972 Act to the family court
34.28ZK

(1)   This rule applies where the family court receives from the Lord Chancellor a request under section 38(1) of the 1972 Act (taking evidence at the request of a court in a convention country) to take the evidence of any person.

(2)   Subject to paragraph (3) –

      (a)   the evidence will be taken in the same manner as if the person concerned were a witness in family proceedings;

      (b)   any oral evidence so taken will be put into writing and read to the person who gave it, who must sign the document; and

      (c)   the judge who takes any such evidence of any person will certify at the foot of the document setting out the evidence of, or produced in evidence by, that person that such evidence was taken, or document received in evidence, as the case may be, by that judge.

(3)   Where the request referred to in section 38(2) of the 1972 Act includes a request that the evidence be taken in a particular manner, the court by which the evidence is taken will, so far as circumstances permit, comply with that request.

Request under section 38(1) of the 1972 Act to the officer of the court
34.28ZL

(1)   This rule applies where an officer of the court receives from the Lord Chancellor a request under section 38(1) of the 1972 Act to take the evidence of any person.

(2)   Subject to paragraph (3) –

      (a)   the person whose evidence is to be taken will be examined on oath by or before a justices' clerk or any other court officer determined by the Lord Chancellor;

      (b)   any oral evidence will be put into writing and read to the person who gave it, who must sign the document; and

      (c)   the justices' clerk or other officer will certify at the foot of the document setting out the evidence of, or produced by, that person, that such evidence was taken, or document received in evidence, as the case may be, by that justices' clerk or other officer.

(3)   Where the request referred to in section 38(1) of the 1972 Act includes a request that the evidence be taken in a particular manner, the justices' clerk or other officer by whom the evidence is taken will, so far as circumstances permit, comply with that request.

(4)   For the purposes of this rule, the justices' clerk or other officer has the same power to administer oaths as a single justice of the peace.

Onward transmission of documents
34.28ZM

Any document mentioned in rule 34.28ZK(2)(c) or rule 34.28ZL(2)(c) will be sent to the Lord Chancellor for onward transmission to the appropriate authority in the convention country in which the request referred to in section 38(1) of the 1972 Act originated.

III ENFORCEMENT OF MAINTENANCE ORDERS UNDER THE CIVIL JURISDICTION AND JUDGMENTS ACT 1982, THE JUDGMENTS REGULATION, THE MAINTENANCE REGULATION, THE 2007 HAGUE CONVENTION AND THE LUGANO CONVENTION

Application of this Chapter
34.28A

(1)   In this Chapter –

    (a)   references to a maintenance order include –

        (I)   a decision, a court settlement or an authentic instrument within the meaning of Article 2 of the Maintenance Regulation where that Regulation applies;

        (II)   a maintenance decision to which Chapter V of the 2007 Hague Convention applies by virtue of Article 19(1) of that Convention;

        (III)   a maintenance arrangement (as defined in Article 3(e) of the 2007 Hague Convention) which is to be recognised and enforceable in the same way as a maintenance decision by virtue of Article 30 of that Convention;

    (b)   references to the Hague Protocol are to the Protocol on the Law Applicable to Maintenance Obligations done at The Hague on 23 November 2007;

    (c)   'the 1968 Convention' has the meaning given in the 1982 Act.

(2)   In relation to the Maintenance Regulation –

    (a)   Section 1 applies to maintenance orders to which Sections 2 and 3 of Chapter IV of the Maintenance Regulation apply (decisions given in a Member State which does not apply the rules of the Hague Protocol, that is, Denmark, and decisions to which Sections 2 and 3 of Chapter IV of that Regulation apply by virtue of Article 75(2)(a) or (b));

    (2)   Section 2 applies to all maintenance orders made in a magistrates' court in England and Wales for which reciprocal enforcement is sought in any Member State of the European Union, including Denmark.

SECTION 1

Registration and Enforcement in a Magistrates' Court of Maintenance Orders made in a Contracting State to the 1968 Convention, a Contracting State to the 1988 Convention, a Regulation State, a State bound by the 2007 Hague Convention other than a Member State of the European Union or a State bound by the Lugano Convention

Interpretation
34.29
In this Section –
(a)   an expression defined in the1982 Act has the meaning given to it in that Act, subject to paragraph (b); and
(b)   'Regulation State' means a Member State of the European Union which does not apply the rules of the Hague Protocol, or, where registration is sought for a maintenance order to which Article 75(2)(a) or (b) of the Maintenance Regulation applies, the Member State of the European Union from which the order originated.

Registration of maintenance orders
34.30
(1)   Omitted
(2)   This rule and Practice Direction 34E apply where the family court receives –
    (a)   an application under Article 31 of the 1968 Convention for the enforcement of a maintenance order made in a Contracting State other than the United Kingdom;
    (b)   an application under Article 31 of the 1988 Convention for the enforcement of a maintenance order made in a State bound by the 1988 Convention other than a Member State of the European Union;
    (c)   an application under Article 26 of the Maintenance Regulation for a declaration of enforceability of a maintenance order made in a Regulation State other than the United Kingdom;
    (d)   an application under Article 38 of the Lugano Convention for the enforcement of a maintenance order made in a State bound by the Lugano Convention other than a Member State of the European Union; or
    (e)   an application under Article 23 of the 2007 Hague Convention for registration of a maintenance order made in a State bound by that Convention other than a Member State of the European Union.
(3)   Omitted
(4)   Omitted
(5)   Omitted
(6)   Except where Practice Direction 34E provides otherwise, the court must register the order unless –
    (a)   in the case of an application under Article 31 of the 1968 Convention, Articles 27 or 28 of that Convention apply;
    (b)   in the case of an application under Article 31 of the 1988 Convention, Articles 27 or 28 of that Convention apply; and
    (c)   in the case of an application under Article 23(2) or (3) of the 2007 Hague Convention, Article 22(a) of that Convention applies.
(7)   If the court refuses to register an order to which this rule relates the court officer must notify the applicant.
(8)   If the court registers an order the court officer must send written notice of that fact to –

(a)   the Lord Chancellor;
(b)   the payer; and
(c)   the applicant.

Appeal from a decision relating to registration
34.31
(1)   This rule applies to an appeal under –
    (a)   Article 36 or Article 40 of the 1968 Convention;
    (b)   Article 36 or Article 40 of the 1988 Convention;
    (c)   Article 32 of the Maintenance Regulation;
    (d)   Article 43 of the Lugano Convention; or
    (e)   Article 23(5) of the 2007 Hague Convention.
(2)   The appeal must be to the family court.

(Practice Direction 34E makes provision in relation to such cases.)

Payment of sums due under a registered order
34.32
(1)   An order is registered in accordance with section 5(3) of the 1982 Act, Article 38 of the Judgments Regulation, Article 38 of the Lugano Convention or Article 23 of the 2007 Hague Convention or declared enforceable under Article 26 of the Maintenance Regulation by virtue of registration, the court may order that payment of sums due under the order be made to the court, at such time and place as directed.
(2)   Where the court orders payments to be made to the court, whether in accordance with paragraph (1) or otherwise, the court officer must send the payments by post either –
    (a)   to the court which made the order; or
    (b)   to such other person or authority as that court, or the Lord Chancellor, directs.

(Practice Direction 34A contains further provisions relating to the payment of sums due under registered orders.)

Enforcement of payments under registered orders
34.33
(1)   This rule applies where a court has ordered periodical payments under a registered maintenance order to be made to the family court.
(2)   The court officer must take reasonable steps to notify the payee of the means of enforcement available.
(3)   Paragraph (4) applies where periodical payments due under a registered order are in arrears.
(4)   The court officer, on that officer's own initiative –
    (a)   may; or
    (b)   if the sums due are more than 4 weeks in arrears, must,
proceed in that officer's own name for the recovery of the sums due unless of the view that it is unreasonable to do so.

Variation and revocation of registered orders

34.34

(1)   This rule applies where the court officer for a registering court receives notice that a registered maintenance order has been varied or revoked by a competent court in a Contracting State to the 1968 Convention, a Contracting State to the 1988 Convention (other than a Member State of the European Union), a Regulation State or a State bound by the Lugano Convention or by the 2007 Hague Convention, other than a Member State of the European Union.

(2)   The court officer for the registering court must –

    (a)   register the order of variation or revocation; and

    (b)   send notice of the registration by post to the payer and payee under the order.

(3)   Where the court officer for a registering court receives notice that a maintenance order registered in that court by virtue of the provisions of the Judgments Regulation has been varied or revoked by a competent court in another Member State of the European Union, the court officer must –

    (a)   note against the entry in the register that the original order so registered has been varied or revoked, as the case may be; and

    (b)   send notice of the noting of the variation or revocation, as the case may be, by post to the payer and payee under the order.

Registered order: payer residing in an area covered by a different Maintenance Enforcement Business Centre

34.35

Practice Direction 34E makes provision for cases where a court officer in the Maintenance Enforcement Business Centre for the Designated Family Judge area where an order is registered considers that the payer is residing in a Designated Family Judge area covered by a different Maintenance Enforcement Business Centre.

(For the way in which information will be provided to enable Maintenance Enforcement Business Centres to be identified, see Practice Direction 34E.)

Cancellation of registered orders

34.36

(1)   Where the court officer for the registering court—

    (a)   has no reason to send papers to another Maintenance Enforcement Business Centre under Practice Direction 34E; and

    (b)   considers that the payer under the registered order is not residing within the area covered by the Maintenance Enforcement Business Centre for the Designated Family Judge area where the order is registered and has no assets in England and Wales,

the court officer must cancel the registration.

(2)   The court officer must –

    (a)   give notice of cancellation to the payee; and

    (b)   send to the Lord Chancellor—

        (i)   the information and documents relating to the registration;

(ii)   a certificate of arrears, if applicable, signed by the court officer;

(iii)   a statement giving such information as the court officer possesses as to the whereabouts of the payer and the nature and location of the payer's assets; and

(iv)   any other relevant documents which the court officer has relating to the case.

(Practice Direction 34E makes further provision on this matter.)

Directions as to stays, documents and translations
34.36A

At any stage in proceedings for registration of a maintenance order under this Section of this Chapter, the court may give directions about the conduct of the proceedings, including –

(a)   staying of proceedings in accordance with –
   (i)   Article 30 or 38 of the 1968 Convention,
   (ii)   Article 30 or 38 of the 1988 Convention,
   (iii)   Article 37 or 46 of the Lugano Convention,
   (iv)   Article 25 or 35 of the Maintenance Regulation, or
   (v)   Article 30(6) of the 2007 Hague Convention;

(b)   the provision of documents in accordance with –
   (i)   Article 48 of the 1968 Convention,
   (ii)   Article 48 of the 1988 Convention,
   (iii)   Article 55 of the Lugano Convention,
   (iv)   Article 29 of the Maintenance Regulation, or
   (v)   Article 25 or 30 of the 2007 Hague Convention;

(c)   the provision of translations in accordance with –
   (i)   Article 48 of the 1968 Convention,
   (ii)   Article 48 of the 1988 Convention,
   (iii)   Article 55 of the Lugano Convention,
   (iv)   Article 28 of the Maintenance Regulation, or
   (v)   in relation to an application under this Section relating to the 2007 Hague Convention, without prejudice to Article 44 of that Convention.

International Maintenance Obligations; Communication with the Central Authority for England and Wales
34.36B

(1)   Where the Lord Chancellor requests information or a document from the court officer for the relevant court for the purposes of Article 58 of the Maintenance Regulation, or Article 12 or 25(2) of the 2007 Hague Convention, the court officer shall provide the requested information or document to the Lord Chancellor forthwith.

(2)   In this rule, 'relevant court' means the court at which an application under Article 56 of the Maintenance Regulation or Article 10 of the 2007 Hague Convention has been filed.

[The Lord Chancellor is the Central Authority for the 2007 Hague Convention and the Maintenance Regulation]

The Maintenance Regulation: applications for enforcement or for refusal or suspension of enforcement
34.36C
Practice Direction 34E makes provision regarding –
(a)   an application for enforcement of a maintenance decision to which section 1 of Chapter IV of the Maintenance Regulation applies; and
(b)   an application by a debtor under Article 21 of the Maintenance Regulation for refusal or suspension of enforcement.

SECTION 2
Reciprocal enforcement in a Contracting State or a Member State of the European Union of Orders of a court in England and Wales

Omitted
34.37

Admissibility of Documents
34.38
(1)   This rule applies to a document, referred to in paragraph (2) and authenticated in accordance with paragraph (3), which comprises, records or summarises evidence given in, or information relating to, proceedings in a court in another part of the UK, another Contracting State to the 1968 Convention or the 1988 Convention, Member State of the European Union or State bound by the Lugano Convention, or by the 2007 Hague Convention, and any reference in this rule to 'the court', without more, is a reference to that court.
(2)   The documents referred to at paragraph (1) are documents which purport to –
    (a)   set out or summarise evidence given to the court;
    (b)   have been received in evidence to the court;
    (c)   set out or summarise evidence taken in the court for the purpose of proceedings in a court in England and Wales to which the 1982 Act, the Judgments Regulation, the Maintenance Regulation or the 2007 Hague Convention applies; or
    (d)   record information relating to payments made under an order of the court.
(3)   A document to which paragraph (1) applies shall, in any proceedings in the family court relating to a maintenance order to which the 1982 Act, the Judgments Regulation, the Maintenance Regulation or the 2007 Hague Convention applies, be admissible as evidence of any fact stated in it to the same extent as oral evidence of that fact is admissible in those proceedings.
(4)   A document to which paragraph (1) applies shall be deemed to be authenticated –
    (a)   in relation to the documents listed at paragraph 2(a) or (c), if the document purports to be –
        (i)   certified by the judge or official before whom the evidence was given or taken; or
        (ii)   the original document recording or summarising the evidence, or a true copy of that document;

(b)   in relation to a document listed at paragraph (2)(b), if the document purports to be certified by a judge or official of the court to be, or to be a true copy of, the document received in evidence; and

(c)   in relation to the document listed at paragraph (2)(d), if the document purports to be certified by a judge or official of the court as a true record of the payments made under the order.

(5)   It shall not be necessary in any proceedings in which evidence is to be received under this rule to prove the signature or official position of the person appearing to have given the certificate referred to in paragraph (4).

(6)   Nothing in this rule shall prejudice the admission in evidence of any document which is admissible in evidence apart from this rule.

(7)   Any request by the family court for the taking or providing of evidence by a court in a State listed in paragraph (8) for the purposes of proceedings to which an instrument listed in that paragraph applies, or by a court in another part of the United Kingdom, shall be communicated in writing to the court in question.

(8)   The States and instruments referred to in paragraph (7) are –

(a)   a Contracting State to the 1968 Convention;

(b)   a Contracting State to the 1988 Convention;

(c)   a State bound by the Lugano Convention;

(d)   Denmark, in relation to proceedings to which the Maintenance Regulation applies;

(e)   a State bound by the 2007 Hague Convention,

but this paragraph and paragraph (7) do not apply where the State in question is a Member State of the European Union to which the Taking of Evidence Regulation (as defined in rule 24.15) applies.

(Chapter 2 of Part 24 makes provision for taking of evidence by a court in another Member State of the European Union).

Enforcement of orders of the family court
34.39

(1)   A person who wishes to enforce a maintenance order obtained in the family court in a State to which paragraph (2) applies must apply for a certified copy of the order and, where required by Practice Direction 34A, a certificate giving particulars relating to the judgment and proceedings in which it was given.

(2)   The States referred to in paragraph (1) are –

(a)   a Contracting State to the 1968 Convention;

(b)   a Contracting State to the 1988 Convention (other than a Member State of the European Union);

(c)   a Member State of the European Union;

(d)   a State bound by the Lugano Convention (other than a Member State of the European Union); or

(e)   a State bound by the 2007 Hague Convention (other than a Member State of the European Union).

(3) An application under this rule must be made in writing to the court officer and must specify –
    (a) the names of the parties to the proceedings;
    (b) the date, or approximate date, of the proceedings in which the maintenance order was made and the nature of those proceedings;
    (c) the State in which the application for recognition or enforcement has been made or is to be made; and
    (d) the postal address of the applicant.
(4) The court officer must, on receipt of the application, send a copy of the order to the applicant certified in accordance with practice direction 34A, together with a copy of any certificate required by that practice direction applies, a completed extract from the decision in the form of Annex II to that Regulation.
(5) Paragraph (6) applies where –
    (a) a maintenance order is registered in the family court; and
    (b) a person wishes to obtain a certificate giving details of any payments made or arrears accrued under the order while it has been registered, for the purposes of an application made or to be made in connection with that order in –
        (i) another Contracting State to the 1968 Convention;
        (ii) another Contracting State to the 1988 Convention (other than a Member State of the European Union);
        (iii) another Member State of the European Union;
        (iv) another State bound by the Lugano Convention (other than a Member State of the European Union);
        (v) another part of the United Kingdom; or
        (vi) another State bound by the 2007 Hague Convention (other than a Member State of the European Union).
(6) The person wishing to obtain the certificate referred to in paragraph (5) may make a written application to the court officer for the registering court.
(7) On receipt of an application under paragraph (6) the court officer must send to the applicant a certificate giving the information requested.

(Rule 74.12 (application for certified copy of a judgment) and 74.13 (evidence in support) of the CPR apply in relation to the application for a certified copy of a judgment obtained in the High Court or a county court.)

Enforcement of orders of the High Court or the family court
34.40
(1) This rule applies where a person wishes to enforce a maintenance order obtained in the High Court or the family court (including the principal registry when treated as a divorce county court or, where the enforcement application relates to a civil partnership matter and the Maintenance Regulation, a civil partnership proceedings county court) in a Member State of the European Union or a State bound by the 2007 Hague Convention (other than a Member State of the European Union).

(2)　Subject to the requirements of Practice Direction 34A, rules 74.12 (application for a certified copy of a judgment) and 74.13 (evidence in support) of the CPR apply in relation to –

　　　(a)　an application under Article 40(2) of the Maintenance Regulation for a certified copy of a judgment and an extract relating to that judgment in the form of Annex II to that Regulation;

　　　(b)　an application for a certified copy of a judgment and a certificate giving particulars relating to the judgment and the proceedings in which it was given.

PART 37 – APPLICATIONS AND PROCEEDINGS IN RELATION TO CONTEMPT OF COURT

I SCOPE AND INTERPRETATION

Scope
37.1

(1)　This Part sets out the procedure in respect of –

　　　(a)　committal for breach of a judgment, order, undertaking to do or abstain from doing an act or of an incoming protection measure;

　　　(b)　contempt in the face of the court;

　　　(c)　committal for interference with the due administration of justice;

　　　(d)　committal for making a false statement of truth;

　　　(e)　sequestration to enforce a judgment, order or undertaking; and

　　　(f)　the penal, contempt and disciplinary provisions of the County Courts Act 1984.

(2)　So far as applicable, and with the necessary modifications, this Part applies in relation to an order requiring a person –

　　　(a)　guilty of contempt of court; or

　　　(b)　punishable by virtue of any enactment as if that person had been guilty of contempt of the High Court,

　　to pay a fine or to give security for good behaviour, as it applies in relation to an order of committal.

(3)　Unless otherwise stated, this Part applies to procedure in the High Court and family court.

Requirement for a penal notice on judgments and orders
37.9

(1)　Subject to paragraph (2), a judgment or order to do or not do an act may not be enforced under rule 37.4 unless there is prominently displayed, on the front of the copy of the judgment or order served in accordance with this Chapter, a warning to the person required to do or not do the act in question that disobedience to the order would be a contempt of court punishable by imprisonment, a fine or sequestration of assets.

(2)　The following may be enforced under rule 37.4 notwithstanding that the judgment or order does not contain the warning described in paragraph (1) –

(a)   an undertaking to do or not do an act which is contained in a judgment or order; and

(b)   an incoming protection measure.

(3)   In the case of –

    (a)   a section 8 order (within the meaning of section 8(2) of the Children Act 1989);

    (b)   an order under section 14A, 14B(2)(b), 14C(3)(b) or 14D of the Children Act 1989 enforceable by committal order;

    (c)   an order prohibiting contact with a child under section 51A(2)(b) of the 2002 Act,

the court may, on the application of the person entitled to enforce the order, direct that the court officer issue a copy of the order, endorsed with or incorporating a notice as to the consequences of disobedience, for service in accordance with this rule, and no copy of the order shall be issued with any such notice endorsed or incorporated save in accordance with such a direction.

How to make the committal application

37.10

(1)   A committal application is made by an application notice using the Part 18 procedure in the proceedings in which the judgment or order was made or the undertaking was given.

(2)   Where the committal application is made against a person who is not an existing party to the proceedings, it is made against that person by an application notice using the Part 18 procedure.

(3)   The application notice must –

    (a)   set out in full the grounds on which the committal application is made and must identify, separately and numerically, each alleged act of contempt including, if known, the date of each of the alleged acts; and

    (b)   be supported by one or more affidavits containing all the evidence relied upon.

(4)   Subject to paragraph (5), the application notice and the evidence in support must be served personally on the respondent.

(5)   The court may –

    (a)   dispense with service under paragraph (4) if it considers it just to do so; or

    (b)   make an order in respect of service by an alternative method or at an alternative place.

III CONTEMPT IN THE FACE OF THE COURT

Contempt in the face of the court

37.12

Where –

(a)   contempt has occurred in the face of the court; and

(b)   that court has power to commit for contempt,

the court may deal with the matter of its own initiative and give such directions as it thinks fit for the disposal of the matter.

Court to which application for permission under this Chapter is to be made
37.14
(1)   Where the contempt of court is committed in connection with any family proceedings, the application for permission may be made only to a single judge of the Family Division.

(2)   Where the contempt of court is committed otherwise than in connection with any proceedings, Part 81 of the CPR applies.

Application for permission
37.15
(1)   The application for permission to make a committal application must be made using the Part 18 procedure, and the application notice must include or be accompanied by –

     (a)   a detailed statement of the applicant's grounds for making the committal application; and

     (b)   an affidavit setting out the facts and exhibiting all documents relied upon.

(2)   The application notice and the documents referred to in paragraph (1) must be served personally on the respondent unless the court otherwise directs.

(3)   Within 14 days of service on the respondent of the application notice, the respondent –

     (a)   must file and serve an acknowledgment of service; and

     (b)   may file and serve evidence.

(4)   The court will consider the application for permission at an oral hearing, unless it considers that such a hearing is not appropriate.

(5)   If the respondent intends to appear at the permission hearing referred to in paragraph (4), the respondent must give 7 days' notice in writing of such intention to the court and any other party and at the same time provide a written summary of the submissions which the respondent proposes to make.

(6)   Where permission to proceed is given, the court may give such directions as it thinks fit, and may –

     (a)   transfer the proceedings to another court; or

     (b)   direct that the application be listed for hearing before a single judge or a Divisional Court.

VII GENERAL RULES ABOUT COMMITTAL APPLICATIONS, ORDERS FOR COMMITTAL AND WRITS OF SEQUESTRATION

The hearing
37.27
(1)   Unless the court hearing the committal application or application for sequestration otherwise permits, the applicant may not rely on –

     (a)   any grounds other than –

         (i)   those set out in the application notice; or

         (ii)   in relation to committal application under Chapter 4, the statement of grounds required by rule 37.15(1)(a) (where not included in the application notice);

(b)   any evidence unless it has been served in accordance with the relevant Chapter of this Part or the Practice Direction supplementing this Part.

(2)   At the hearing, the respondent is entitled –

(a)   to give oral evidence, whether or not the respondent has filed or served written evidence, and, if doing so, may be cross-examined; and

(b)   with the permission of the court, to call a witness to give evidence whether or not the witness has made an affidavit or witness statement.

(3)   The court may require or permit any party or other person (other than the respondent) to give oral evidence at the hearing.

(4)   The court may give directions requiring the attendance for cross-examination of a witness who has given written evidence.

(5)   The general rule is that a committal application, application for sequestration or application for discharge from custody will be heard, and judgment given, in public, but a hearing, or any part of it, may be in private (but with the matters in paragraph (6) always stated in public) if –

(a)   publicity would defeat the object of the hearing;

(b)   it involves matters relating to national security;

(c)   it involves confidential information (including information relating to personal financial matters) and publication would damage that confidentiality;

(d)   a private hearing is necessary to protect the interests of any child or protected party;

(e)   it is a hearing of an application made without notice and it would be unjust to any respondent for there to be a public hearing; or

(f)   the court considers this to be necessary, in the interests of justice.

(6)   If the court hearing an application in private decides to make a committal order against the respondent, it will in public state –

(a)   the name of the respondent;

(b)   in general terms, the nature of the contempt of court in respect of which the committal order is being made; and

(c)   the length of the period of the committal order.

(7)   Where a committal order is made in the absence of the respondent, the court may on its own initiative fix a date and time when the respondent is to be brought before the court.

Power to suspend execution of a committal order

37.28

(1)   The court making the committal order may also order that execution of the order will be suspended for such period or on such terms and conditions as the court may specify.

(2)   Unless the court otherwise directs, the applicant must serve on the respondent a copy of any order made under paragraph (1).

PRACTICE DIRECTION 9A – APPLICATION FOR A FINANCIAL REMEDY

This Practice Direction supplements FPR Part 9

Introduction
1.1

Part 9 of the Family Procedure Rules sets out the procedure applicable to the financial proceedings that are included in the definition of a 'financial remedy'.

1.2

The shorter procedure set out in Chapter 5 of Part 9 of the Family Procedure Rules applies in respect of –

(a)   proceedings under –
   (i)   the 1978 Act,
   (ii)   Schedule 6 to the 2004 Act,
   (iii)   Schedule 1 to the 1989 Act;
   (iv)   Article 56 of the Maintenance Regulation; and
   (v)   Article 10 of the 2007 Hague Convention
   any application for the variation of an order for a financial remedy.

(b)   The longer procedure set out in Chapter 4 of Part 9 applies in respect of all other applications for a financial remedy. In a case to which the shorter Chapter 5 procedure applies, the initial application can include a request for the court instead to apply the longer Chapter 4 procedure. Examples of cases in which it may be appropriate to make such a request include an application under Schedule 1 to the 1989 Act in which there are contested issues about the settlement of property, or a variation application in which a capital payment or pension sharing order is proposed.

1.3

Where an application for a financial remedy includes an application relating to land, details of any mortgagee must be included in the application.

Pre-application protocol
2.1

The 'pre-application protocol' annexed to this Direction outlines the steps parties should take to seek and provide information from and to each other prior to the commencement of any application for a financial remedy. The court will expect the parties to comply with the terms of the protocol.

Costs
3.1

Rule 9.27 requires each party to produce to the court, at every hearing or appointment, an estimate of the costs incurred by the party up to the date of that hearing or appointment.

3.2

The purpose of this rule is to enable the court to take account of the impact of each party's costs liability on their financial situations. Parties should ensure that the information contained in the estimate is as full and accurate as possible and that any sums already paid in respect of a party's financial remedy costs are clearly set out. Where relevant, any liability arising from the costs of other proceedings between the parties should continue to be referred to in the appropriate section of a party's financial statement; any such costs should not be included in the estimates under rule 9.27.

3.3

Rule 28.3 provides that the general rule in financial remedy proceedings is that the court will not make an order requiring one party to pay the costs of another party. However the court may make such an order at any stage of the proceedings where it considers it appropriate to do so because of the conduct of a party in relation to the proceedings.

3.4

Any breach of this practice direction or the pre-application protocol annexed to it will be taken into account by the court when deciding whether to depart from the general rule as to costs.

Procedure before the first appointment

4.1

In addition to the matters listed at rule 9.14(5), the parties should, if possible, with a view to identifying and narrowing any issues between the parties, exchange and file with the court –

(a)   a summary of the case agreed between the parties;

(b)   a schedule of assets agreed between the parties; and

(c)   details of any directions that they seek, including, where appropriate, the name of any expert they wish to be appointed.

4.2

Where a party is prevented from sending the details referred to in (c) above, the party should make that information available at the first appointment.

Financial Statements and other documents

5.1

Practice Direction 22A (Written Evidence) applies to any financial statement filed in accordance with rules 9.14 or 9.19 and to any exhibits to a financial statement. In preparing a bundle of documents to be exhibited to or attached to a financial statement, regard must be had in particular to paragraphs 11.1 to 11.3 and 13.1 to 13.4 of that Direction. Whereon account of their bulk, it is impracticable for the exhibits to a financial statement to be retained on the court file after the First Appointment, the court may give directions as to their custody pending further hearings.

5.2

Where the court directs a party to provide information or documents by way of reply to a questionnaire or request by another party, the reply must be verified by a statement of truth. Unless otherwise directed, a reply to a questionnaire or request for information and documents shall not be filed with the court.

(Part 17 and Practice Direction 17Amake further provision about statements of truth)

Financial Dispute Resolution (FDR) Appointment
6.1

A key element in the procedure is the Financial Dispute Resolution (FDR) appointment. Rule 9.17 provides that the FDR appointment is to be treated as a meeting held for the purposes of discussion and negotiation. Such meetings have been developed as a means of reducing the tension which inevitably arises in family disputes and facilitating settlement of those disputes.

6.2

In order for the FDR to be effective, parties must approach the occasion openly and without reserve. Non-disclosure of the content of such meetings is vital and is an essential prerequisite for fruitful discussion directed to the settlement of the dispute between the parties. The FDR appointment is an important part of the settlement process. As a consequence of *Re D (Minors) (Conciliation: Disclosure of Information)* [1993] Fam 231, evidence of anything said or of any admission made in the course of an FDR appointment will not be admissible in evidence, except at the trial of a person for an offence committed at the appointment or in the very exceptional circumstances indicated in *Re D*.

6.3

Courts will therefore expect –
(a)   parties to make offers and proposals;
(b)   recipients of offers and proposals to give them proper consideration; and
(c)   (subject to paragraph 6.4), that parties, whether separately or together, will not seek to exclude from consideration at the appointment any such offer or proposal.

6.4

Paragraph 6.3(c) does not apply to an offer or proposal made during non-court dispute resolution.

6.5

In order to make the most effective use of the first appointment and the FDR appointment, the legal representatives attending those appointments will be expected to have full knowledge of the case.

6.6
Omitted

Consent orders
7.1
Rule 9.26 (1)(a) requires an application for a consent order to be accompanied by two copies of the draft order in the terms sought, one of which must be endorsed with a statement signed by the respondent to the application signifying the respondent's agreement. The rule is considered to have been properly complied with if the endorsed statement is signed by solicitors on record as acting for the respondent; but where the consent order applied for contains undertakings, it should be signed by the party giving the undertakings as well as by that party's solicitor.

(Provision relating to the enforcement of undertakings is contained in the Practice Direction 33A supplementing Part 33 of the FPR)

7.2
Rule 9.26(1)(b) requires each party to file with the court and serve on the other party a statement of information. Where this is contained in one form, both parties must sign the statement to certify that each has read the contents of the other's statement.

7.3
Rule 35.2 deals with applications for a consent order in respect of a financial remedy where the parties wish to have the content of a written mediation agreement to which the Mediation Directive applies made the subject of a consent order.

Section 10(2) of the Matrimonial Causes Act 1973 and section 48(2)of the Civil Partnership Act 2004
8.1
Where a respondent who has applied under section 10(2) of the Matrimonial Causes Act 1973, or section 48(2) of the Civil Partnership Act 2004, for the court to consider his or her financial position after a divorce or dissolution elects not to proceed with the application, a notice of withdrawal of the application signed by the respondent or by the respondent's solicitor may be filed without leave of the court. In this event a formal order dismissing or striking out the application is unnecessary. Notice of withdrawal should also be given to the applicant's solicitor.

8.2
An application under section 10(2) or section 48(2) which has been withdrawn is not a bar to making in matrimonial proceedings, the decree absolute and in civil partnership proceedings, the final order.

Maintenance Orders – registration in the family court
9.1
Where periodic payments are required to be made to a child under an order registered in the family court, section 31L(3) and (4) of the1984 Act permits the payments to be made instead to the person with whom the child has his home. That person may proceed in his own name for variation, revival or revocation of the order and may enforce payment in his own name.

9.2

The registration in the family court of an order made direct to a child entails a considerable amount of work. Accordingly, when the High Court is considering the form of an order where there are children, care should be taken not to make orders for payment direct where such orders would be of no benefit to the parties.

Pensions

10.1

The phrase 'party with pension rights' is used in FPR Part 9, Chapter 8. For matrimonial proceedings, this phrase has the meaning given to it by section 25D(3) of the Matrimonial Causes Act 1973 and means 'the party to the marriage who has or is likely to have benefits under a pension arrangement'. There is a definition of 'civil partner with pension rights' in paragraph 29 of Schedule 5 to the Civil Partnership Act 2004 which mirrors the definition of 'party with pension rights' in section 25D(3) of the 1973 Act. The phrase 'is likely to have benefits' in these definitions refers to accrued rights to pension benefits which are not yet in payment.

PPF Compensation

11.1

The phrase 'party with compensation rights' is used in FPR Part 9, Chapter 9. For matrimonial proceedings, the phrase has the meaning given to it by section 25G(5) of the Matrimonial Causes Act 1973 and means the party to the marriage who is or is likely to be entitled to PPF compensation. There is a definition of 'civil partner with compensation rights' in paragraph 37(1) of Schedule 5 to the Civil Partnership Act 2004 which mirrors the definition of 'party with compensation rights' in section 25G(5). The phrase 'is likely to be entitled to PPF Compensation' in those definitions refers to statutory entitlement to PPF Compensation which is not yet in payment.

Orders for payment in respect of legal services

12.1

An application for an order for payment in respect of legal services under section 22ZA of the 1973 Act or paragraph 38A of Part 8 of Schedule 5 to the 2004 Act must be made in accordance with FPR 9.7 using the Part 18 procedure. Where the application is made at the same time as an application for an order for maintenance pending suit or maintenance pending outcome, the applications may be included in one application notice, and evidence in support of or in response to the applications may be contained in one witness statement.

(Where an application is made for an order under FPR 9.7, a copy of the application notice must be served in accordance with the provisions of FPR Part 6 at least 14 days before the court is to deal with the application: FPR 18.8(1)(b).)

12.2

The evidence filed in support of an application for an order for payment in respect of legal services must, in addition to the matters referred to in rule 9.7(3), include a concise statement of the applicant's case on –

(a)   the criteria set out in section 22ZA(3) and (4) of the 1974 Act or paragraph 38A(3) and (4) of Part 8 of Schedule 5 to the 2004 Act as applicable; and

(b)   the matters set out in section 22ZB(1) of the 1973 Act or paragraph 38B(1) of Part 8 of Schedule 5 to the 2004 Act as applicable.

Annex Pre-application protocol

Notes of guidance

Scope of the Protocol

1.

This protocol is intended to apply to all applications for a financial remedy as defined by rule 2.3. It is designed to cover all classes of case, ranging from a simple application for periodical payments to an application for a substantial lump sum and property adjustment order. The protocol is designed to facilitate the operation of the procedure for financial remedy applications.

2.

In considering the options of pre-application disclosure and negotiation, solicitors should bear in mind the advantage of having a court timetable and court managed process. There is sometimes an advantage in preparing disclosure before proceedings are commenced. However, solicitors should bear in mind the objective of controlling costs and in particular the costs of discovery and that the option of pre-application disclosure and negotiation has risks of excessive and uncontrolled expenditure and delay. This option should only be encouraged where both parties agree to follow this route and disclosure is not likely to be an issue or has been adequately dealt with in mediation or otherwise.

3.

Solicitors should consider at an early stage and keep under review whether it would be appropriate to suggest mediation and/or collaborative law to the clients as an alternative to solicitor negotiation or court based litigation.

4.

Making an application to the court should not be regarded as a hostile step or a last resort, rather as a way of starting the court timetable, controlling disclosure and endeavouring to avoid the costly final hearing and the preparation for it.

First letter

5.

The circumstances of parties to an application for a financial remedy are so various that it would be difficult to prepare a specimen first letter. The request for information will be different in every case. However, the tone of the initial letter is important and the guidelines in paragraphs 14 and 15 should be followed. It should be approved in advance by the client. Solicitors writing to an unrepresented party should always recommend that he seeks independent legal advice and enclose a second copy of the letter to be passed to any solicitor instructed. A reasonable time limit for an answer may be 14 days.

Negotiation and Settlement
6.

In the event of pre-application disclosure and negotiation, as envisaged in paragraph 12 an application should not be issued when a settlement is a reasonable prospect.

Disclosure
7.

The protocol underlines the obligation of parties to make full and frank disclosure of all material facts, documents and other information relevant to the issues. Solicitors owe their clients a duty to tell them in clear terms of this duty and of the possible consequences of breach of the duty, which may include criminal sanctions under the Fraud Act 2006. This duty of disclosure is an ongoing obligation and includes the duty to disclose any material changes after initial disclosure has been given. Solicitors are referred to the Good Practice Guides available to Resolution members at www.resolution.org.uk and can also contact the Law Society's Practice Advice Service on 0870 606 2522.

The Protocol

General principles
8.

All parties must always bear in mind the overriding objective set out at rules 1.1 to 1.4 and try to ensure that applications should be resolved and a just outcome achieved as speedily as possible without costs being unreasonably incurred. The needs of any children should be addressed and safeguarded. The procedures which it is appropriate to follow should be conducted with minimum distress to the parties and in a manner designed to promote as good a continuing relationship between the parties and any children affected as is possible in the circumstances.

9.

The principle of proportionality must be borne in mind at all times. It is unacceptable for the costs of any case to be disproportionate to the financial value of the subject matter of the dispute.

10.

Parties should be informed that where a court is considering whether to make an order requiring one party to pay the costs of another party, it will take into account pre-application offers to settle and conduct of disclosure.

Identifying the issues
11.

Parties must seek to clarify their claims and identify the issues between them as soon as possible. So that this can be achieved, they must provide full, frank and clear disclosure of facts, information and documents, which are material and sufficiently accurate to enable proper negotiations to take place to settle their differences. Openness in all dealings is essential.

Disclosure
12.
If parties carry out voluntary disclosure before the issue of proceedings the parties should exchange schedules of assets, income, liabilities and other material facts, using the financial statement as a guide to the format of the disclosure. Documents should only be disclosed to the extent that they are required by the financial statement. Excessive or disproportionate costs should not be incurred.

Correspondence
13.
Any first letter and subsequent correspondence must focus on the clarification of claims and identification of issues and their resolution. Protracted and unnecessary correspondence and 'trial by correspondence' must be avoided.

14.
The impact of any correspondence upon the reader and in particular the parties must always be considered. Any correspondence which raises irrelevant issues or which might cause the other party to adopt an entrenched, polarised or hostile position is to be discouraged.

Summary
15.
The aim of all pre-application proceedings steps must be to assist the parties to resolve their differences speedily and fairly or at least narrow the issues and, should that not be possible, to assist the court to do so.

PRACTICE DIRECTION 12D – INHERENT JURISDICTION (INCLUDING WARDSHIP) PROCEEDINGS

This Practice Direction supplements FPR Part 12, Chapter 5

The nature of inherent jurisdiction proceedings
1.1
It is the duty of the court under its inherent jurisdiction to ensure that a child who is the subject of proceedings is protected and properly taken care of. The court may in exercising its inherent jurisdiction make any order or determine any issue in respect of a child unless limited by case law or statute. Such proceedings should not be commenced unless it is clear that the issues concerning the child cannot be resolved under the Children Act 1989.

1.2
The court may under its inherent jurisdiction, in addition to all of the orders which can be made in family proceedings, make a wide range of injunctions for the child's protection of which the following are the most common –
(a)   orders to restrain publicity;
(b)   orders to prevent an undesirable association;
(c)   orders relating to medical treatment;
(d)   orders to protect abducted children, or children where the case has another substantial foreign element; and
(e)   orders for the return of children to and from another state.

1.3
The court's wardship jurisdiction is part of and not separate from the court's inherent jurisdiction. The distinguishing characteristics of wardship are that –
(a)   custody of a child who is a ward is vested in the court; and
(b)   although day to day care and control of the ward is given to an individual or to a local authority, no important step can be taken in the child's life without the court's consent.

Transfer of proceedings to family court
2.1
Whilst the family court does not have jurisdiction to deal with applications that a child be made or cease to be a ward of court, consideration should be given to transferring the case in whole or in part to the family court where a direction has been given confirming the wardship and directing that the child remain a ward of court during his minority or until further order.

2.2
The family court must transfer the case back to the High Court if a decision is required as to whether the child should remain a ward of court.

2.3

The following proceedings in relation to a ward of court will be dealt with in the High Court unless the nature of the issues of fact or law makes them more suitable for hearing in the family court –

(a)   those in which an officer of the Cafcass High Court Team or the Official Solicitor is or becomes the litigation friend or children's guardian of the ward or a party to the proceedings;

(b)   those in which a local authority is or becomes a party;

(c)   those in which an application for paternity testing is made;

(d)   those in which there is a dispute about medical treatment;

(e)   those in which an application is opposed on the grounds of lack of jurisdiction;

(f)   those in which there is a substantial foreign element;

(g)   those in which there is an opposed application for leave to take the child permanently out of the jurisdiction or where there is an application for temporary removal of a child from the jurisdiction and it is opposed on the ground that the child may not be duly returned.

Parties

3.1

Where the child has formed or is seeking to form an association, considered to be undesirable, with another person, that other person should not be made a party to the application. Such a person should be made a respondent only to an application within the proceedings for an injunction or committal. Such a person should not be added to the title of the proceedings nor allowed to see any documents other than those relating directly to the proceedings for the injunction or committal. He or she should be allowed time to obtain representation and any injunction should in the first instance extend over a few days only.

Removal from jurisdiction

4.1

A child who is a ward of court may not be removed from England and Wales without the court's permission. Practice Direction 12F (International Child Abduction) deals in detail with locating and protecting children at risk of unlawful removal.

Criminal Proceedings

5.1

Where a child has been interviewed by the police in connection with contemplated criminal proceedings and the child subsequently becomes a ward of court, the permission of the court deciding the wardship proceedings ('the wardship court') is not required for the child to be called as a witness in the criminal proceedings.

5.2

Where the police need to interview a child who is already a ward of court, an application must be made for permission for the police to do so. Where permission is given the order should, unless there is some special reason to the contrary, give permission for any number of interviews which may be required by the prosecution or the police. If a need arises to conduct any interview beyond the permission contained in the order, a further application must be made.

5.3
The above applications must be made with notice to all parties.

5.4
Where a person may become the subject of a criminal investigation and it is considered necessary for the child who is a ward of court to be interviewed without that person knowing that the police are making inquiries, the application for permission to interview the child may be made without notice to that party. Notice should, however, where practicable be given to the children's guardian.

5.5
There will be other occasions where the police need to deal with complaints, or alleged offences, concerning children who are wards of court where it is appropriate, if not essential, for action to be taken straight away without the prior permission of the wardship court, for example –
(a)   serious offences against the child such as rape, where a medical examination and the collection of forensic evidence ought to be carried out promptly;
(b)   where the child is suspected by the police of having committed a criminal act and the police wish to interview the child in respect of that matter;
(c)   where the police wish to interview the child as a potential witness.

5.6
In such instances, the police should notify the parent or foster parent with whom the child is living or another 'appropriate adult' (within the Police and Criminal Evidence Act 1984 – Code of Practice C for the Detention, Treatment and Questioning of Persons by Police Officers) so that that adult has the opportunity of being present when the police interview the child. Additionally, if practicable the child's guardian (if one has been appointed) should be notified and invited to attend the police interview or to nominate a third party to attend on the guardian's behalf. A record of the interview or a copy of any statement made by the child should be supplied to the children's guardian. Where the child has been interviewed without the guardian's knowledge, the guardian should be informed at the earliest opportunity of this fact and (if it be the case) that the police wish to conduct further interviews. The wardship court should be informed of the situation at the earliest possible opportunity thereafter by the children's guardian, parent, foster parent (through the local authority) or other responsible adult.

Applications to the Criminal Injuries Compensation Authority
6.1
Where a child who is a ward of court has a right to make a claim for compensation to the Criminal Injuries Compensation Authority ('CICA'), an application must be made

by the child's guardian, or, if no guardian has been appointed, the person with care and control of the child, for permission to apply to CICA and disclose such documents on the wardship proceedings file as are considered necessary to establish whether or not the child is eligible for an award plus, as appropriate, the amount of the award.

6.2

Any order giving permission should state that any award made by CICA should normally be paid into court immediately upon receipt and, once that payment has been made, application should made to the court as to its management and administration. If it is proposed to invest the award in any other way, the court's prior approval must be sought

The role of the tipstaff

7.1

The tipstaff is the enforcement officer for all orders made in the High Court. The tipstaff's jurisdiction extends throughout England and Wales. Every applicable order made in the High Court is addressed to the tipstaff in children and family matters (eg 'The Court hereby directs the Tipstaff of the High Court of Justice, whether acting by himself or his assistants or a police officer as follows…').

7.2

The tipstaff may effect an arrest and then inform the police. Sometimes the local bailiff or police will detain a person in custody until the tipstaff arrives to collect that person or give further directions as to the disposal of the matter. The tipstaff may also make a forced entry although there will generally be a uniformed police officer standing by to make sure there is no breach of the peace.

7.3

There is only one tipstaff (with two assistants) but the tipstaff can also call on any constable or bailiff to assist in carrying out the tipstaff's duties.

7.4

The majority of the tipstaff's work involves locating children and taking them into protective custody, including cases of child abduction abroad.

PRACTICE DIRECTION 12E – URGENT BUSINESS

This Practice Direction supplements FPR Part 12

Introduction
1.1

This Practice Direction describes the procedure to be followed in respect of urgent and out of hours cases in the Family Division of the High Court. For the avoidance of doubt, it does not relate to cases in respect of adults.

1.2

Urgent or out of hours applications, particularly those which have become urgent because they have not been pursued sufficiently promptly, should be avoided. A judge who has concerns that the urgent or out of hours facilities may have been abused may require a representative of the applicant to attend at a subsequent directions hearing to provide an explanation.

1.3

Urgent applications should whenever possible be made within court hours. The earliest possible liaison is required with the Clerk of the Rules who will attempt to accommodate genuinely urgent applications (at least for initial directions) in the Family Division applications court, from which the matter may be referred to another judge.

1.4

When it is not possible to apply within court hours, contact should be made with the security office at the Royal Courts of Justice (020 7947 6000 or 020 7947 6260) who will refer the matter to the urgent business officer. The urgent business officer can contact the duty judge. The judge may agree to hold a hearing, either convened at court or elsewhere, or by telephone.

1.5

When the hearing is to take place by telephone it should, unless not practicable, be by tape-recorded conference call arranged (and paid for in the first instance) by the applicant's solicitors. Solicitors acting for potential applicants should consider having standing arrangements with their telephone service providers under which such conference calls can be arranged. All parties (especially the judge) should be informed that the call is being recorded by the service provider. The applicant's solicitors should order a transcript of the hearing from the service provider. Otherwise the applicant's legal representative should prepare a note for approval by the judge.

General Issues
2.1

Parents, carers or other necessary respondents should whenever possible be given the opportunity to have independent legal advice or at least to have access to support or counselling.

2.2
In suitable cases, application may be made for directions providing for anonymity of the parties and others involved in the matter in any order or subsequent listing of the case. Exceptionally, a reporting restriction order may be sought.

2.3
Either the Official Solicitor or Cafcass, or CAFCASS CYMRU, as the case may be, may be invited by the court to be appointed as advocate to the court.

Medical treatment and press injunction cases
3.1
It may be desirable for a child who is the subject of such proceedings to be made a party and represented through a children's guardian (usually an officer of Cafcass or a Welsh Family Proceedings Officer). Cafcass and CAFCASS CYMRU stand ready to arrange for an officer to accept appointment as a children's guardian. They should be contacted at the earliest opportunity where an urgent application is envisaged. For urgent out of hours applications, the urgent business officer will contact a representative of Cafcass. CAFCASS CYMRU is not able to deal with cases that arise out of office hours and those cases should be referred to Cafcass who will deal with the matter on behalf of CAFCASS CYMRU until the next working day. A child of sufficient understanding to instruct his or her own solicitor should be made a party and given notice of any application.

3.2
Interim declarations/orders under the wardship jurisdiction or Children Act 1989 may be made on application either by an NHS trust, a local authority, an interested adult (where necessary with the leave of the court) or by the child if he or she has sufficient understanding to make the application.

Consultation with Cafcass, CAFCASS CYMRU and Official Solicitor
4.1
Cafcass, CAFCASS CYMRU and members of the Official Solicitor's legal staff are prepared to discuss cases before proceedings are issued. In all cases in which the urgent and out of hours procedures are to be used it would be helpful if the Official Solicitor, Cafcass or CAFCASS CYMRU have had some advance notice of the application and its circumstances.

4.2
Enquiries about children cases should be directed to the High Court Team Duty Manager at Cafcass National Office, 3rd Floor, 21 Bloomsbury Street, London, WC1B 3HF. DX: Cafcass DX 310101 Bloomsbury 11. Telephone 01753 235273 (Cafcass High Court Team) or 01753 235295 (Cafcass Legal Duty Lawyer). e-mail: HighCourtGM@Cafcass.gsi.gov.uk (office hours only). Enquiries should be marked "F.A.O. High Court Team" or "F.A.O. HCT".

4.3

Enquiries about children cases in Wales should be directed to the Social Care Team, Legal Services, Welsh Assembly Government, Cathays Park, Cardiff CF10 3NQ, telephone 02920 370888, fax 0872 437 7306.

4.4

Medical and welfare cases relating to an adult lacking capacity in relation to their medical treatment or welfare are brought in the Court of Protection. Enquiries about adult medical and welfare cases should be addressed to the Court of Protection Healthcare and Welfare Team, Office of the Official Solicitor, Victory House, 30-34 Kingsway, London, WC2B 6EX, telephone 020 3681 2751, fax 020 3681 2762, email enquiries@offsol.gsi.gov.uk. Reference should also be made to Practice Direction E, accompanying Part 9 of the Court of Protection Rules 2007, and to Practice Direction B accompanying Part 10 of those Rules. Information for parties and practitioners is available on the website of the Ministry of Justice www.justice.gov.uk and general information for members of the public is available on www.direct.gov.uk.

PRACTICE DIRECTION 12F – INTERNATIONAL CHILD ABDUCTION

This Practice Direction supplements FPR Part 12, Chapters 5 and 6

PART 1

Introduction
1.1
This Practice Direction explains what to do if a child has been brought to, or kept in, England and Wales without the permission of anyone who has rights of custody in respect of the child in the country where the child was habitually resident immediately before the removal or retention. It also explains what to do if a child has been taken out of, or kept out of, England and Wales[1] without the permission of a parent or someone who has rights of custody in respect of the child. These cases are called 'international child abduction cases' and are dealt with in the High Court. This Practice Direction also explains what to do if you receive legal papers claiming that you have abducted a child. You can find the legal cases which are mentioned in this Practice Direction, and other legal material, on the website http://www.bailii.org/ (British and Irish Legal Information Institute).

1.2
If you have rights of custody in respect of a child and the child has been brought to England or Wales without your permission, or has been brought here with your permission but the person your child is staying with is refusing to return the child, then you can apply to the High Court of Justice, which covers all of England and Wales, for an order for the return of the child.

1.3
How you make an application to the High Court, what evidence you need to provide and what orders you should ask the court to make are all explained in this Practice Direction.

1.4
If your child is under 16 years of age and has been brought to England or Wales from a country which is a party (a 'State party') to the 1980 Hague Convention on the Civil Aspects of International Child Abduction ('the 1980 Hague Convention') then you can make an application to the High Court for an order under that Convention for the return of your child to the State in which he or she was habitually resident immediately before being removed or being kept away. This is explained in Part 2 below.

1.5
If your child is over 16 years of age and under 18, or has been brought to England or Wales from a country which is not a State party to the 1980 Hague Convention, then you can make an application for the return of your child under the inherent jurisdiction

of the High Court with respect to children. In exercising this jurisdiction over children, the High Court will make your child's welfare its paramount consideration. How to make an application under the inherent jurisdiction of the High Court with respect to children is explained in Part 3 below.

1.6

It might be necessary for you to make an urgent application to the court if you are not sure where your child is, or you think that there is a risk that the person who is keeping your child away from you might take the child out of the United Kingdom or hide them away. Part 4 below explains how to make an urgent application to the High Court for orders to protect your child until a final decision can be made about returning the child and also how to ask for help from the police and government agencies if you think your child might be taken out of the country.

Rights of Access

1.7

Rights of access to children (also called contact or visitation) may be enforced in England and Wales. Access orders made in other Member States of the European Union can be enforced under EU law, and the 1980 Hague Convention expects State parties to comply with orders and agreements concerning access as well as rights of custody. If you have an access order and you want to enforce it in England or Wales, you should read Part 5 below.

PART 2

Hague Convention Cases

2.1

States which are party to the 1980 Hague Convention have agreed to return children who have been either wrongfully removed from, or wrongfully retained away from, the State where they were habitually resident immediately before the wrongful removal or retention. There are very limited exceptions to this obligation.

2.2

'Wrongfully removed' or 'wrongfully retained' means removed or retained in breach of rights of custody in respect of the child attributed to a person or a body or an institution. 'Rights of custody' are interpreted very widely (see paragraph 2.16 below).

2.3

The text of the 1980 Hague Convention and a list of Contracting States (that is, State parties) can be found on the website of the Hague Conference on Private International Law at http://www.hcch.net. All Member States of the European Union are State parties to the 1980 Hague Convention, and all but Denmark are bound by an EU Regulation which supplements the operation of the 1980 Hague Convention between the Member States of the EU (Council Regulation (EC) No 2201/2003, see paragraph 2.6).

2.4
In each State party there is a body called the Central Authority whose duty is to help people use the 1980 Hague Convention.

2.5
If you think that your child has been brought to, or kept in, England or Wales, and your State is a State party to the 1980 Hague Convention, then you should get in touch with your own Central Authority who will help you to send an application for the return of your child to the Central Authority for England and Wales. However, you are not obliged to contact your own Central Authority. You may contact the Central Authority for England and Wales directly, or you may simply instruct lawyers in England or Wales to make an application for you. The advantage of making your application through the Central Authority for England and Wales if you are applying from outside the United Kingdom is that you will get public funding ('legal aid') to make your application, regardless of your financial resources.

The Central Authority for England and Wales
2.6
The Child Abduction and Custody Act 1985 brings the 1980 Hague Convention into the law of England and Wales and identifies the Lord Chancellor as the Central Authority. His duties as the Central Authority are carried out by the International Child Abduction and Contact Unit (ICACU). ICACU also carries out the duties of the Central Authority for two other international instruments. These are the European Convention on Recognition and Enforcement of Decisions concerning Custody of Children signed at Luxembourg on 20 May 1980 (called 'the European Convention' in this Practice Direction but sometimes also referred to as 'the Luxembourg Convention') and the European Union Council Regulation (EC) No 2201/2003 of 27 November 2003 on jurisdiction and the recognition and enforcement of judgments in matrimonial matters and in matters of parental responsibility ('the Council Regulation[2]'). The Council Regulation has direct effect in the law of England and Wales.

2.7
ICACU is open Mondays to Fridays from 9.00 a.m. to 5.00 p.m. It is located in the Office of the Official Solicitor and Public Trustee and its contact details are as follows:
International Child Abduction and Contact Unit
Office of the Official Solicitor
Victory House
30–34 Kingsway
London
WC2B 6EX
Email: ICACU@offsol.gsi.gov.uk
Tel: + 44 (20) 3681 2608 (10.00am to 4.00pm)
Fax: +44 (20) 3681 2763

In an emergency (including out of normal working hours) contact should be made with the Royal Courts of Justice on one of the following telephone numbers:
+ 44 (0)20 7947 6000, or
+ 44 (0) 20 7947 6260

In addition, in an emergency or outside normal working hours advice on international child abduction can be sought from reunite International Child Abduction Centre on + 44 (0)1162 556 234. Outside office hours you will be directed to the 24hour emergency service. You can also see information on reunite's website http://www.reunite.org/.

What ICACU Will Do
2.8

When ICACU receives your application for the return of your child, unless you already have a legal representative in England and Wales whom you want to act for you, it will send your application to a solicitor whom it knows to be experienced in international child abduction cases and ask them to take the case for you. You will then be the solicitor's client and the solicitor will make an application for public funding to meet your legal costs. The solicitor will then apply to the High Court for an order for the return of your child.

2.9

You can find out more about ICACU and about the 1980 Hague Convention and the other international instruments mentioned at paragraph 2.6 on two websites: Information for parties and practitioners is available on http://www.justice.gov.uk and general information for members of the public is available on www.gov.uk.
Applying to the High Court – the Form and Content of Application

2.10

An application to the High Court for an order under the 1980 Hague Convention must be made in the Principal Registry of the Family Division in Form C67. If the Council Regulation applies, then the application must be headed both 'in the matter of the Child Abduction and Custody Act 1985' and 'in the matter of Council Regulation (EC) 2201/2003'. This is to ensure that the application is handled quickly (see paragraph. 2.14 below) and to draw the court's attention to its obligations under the Council Regulation.

2.11

The application must include –
(a)   the names and dates of birth of the children;
(b)   the names of the children's parents or guardians;
(c)   the whereabouts or suspected whereabouts of the children;
(d)   the interest of the applicant in the matter (e.g. mother, father, or person with whom the child lives and details of any order placing the child with that person);
(e)   the reasons for the application;

(f)   details of any proceedings (including proceedings not in England or Wales, and including any legal proceedings which have finished) relating to the children;

(g)   where the application is for the return of a child, the identity of the person alleged to have removed or retained the child and, if different, the identity of the person with whom the child is thought to be;

(h)   in an application to which the Council Regulation also applies, any details of measures of which you are aware that have been taken by courts or authorities to ensure the protection of the child after its return to the Member State of habitual residence.

2.12
The application should be accompanied by all relevant documents including (but not limited to) –

(a)   an authenticated copy of any relevant decision or agreement;

(b)   a certificate or an affidavit from a Central Authority, or other competent authority of the State of the child's habitual residence, or from a qualified person, concerning the relevant law of that State.

2.13
As the applicant you may also file a statement in support of the application, although usually your solicitor will make and file a statement for you on your instructions. The statement must contain and be verified by a statement of truth in the following terms:
'I make this statement knowing that it will be placed before the court, and I confirm that to the best of my knowledge and belief its contents are true.'

(Further provisions about statements of truth are contained in Part 17 of these Rules and in Practice Direction 17A.).

The Timetable for the Case
2.14
Proceedings to which the Council Regulation applies must be completed in 6 weeks 'except where exceptional circumstances make this impossible'. The following procedural steps are intended to ensure that applications under the 1980 Hague Convention and the Council Regulation are handled quickly –

(a)   the application must be headed both 'in the matter of the Child Abduction and Custody Act 1985' and 'in the matter of Council Regulation (EC) 2201/2003';

(b)   the court file will be marked to –
    (i)   draw attention to the nature of the application; and
    (ii)   state the date on which the 6 week period will expire (the 'hear-by date');

(c)   listing priority will, where necessary, be given to such applications;

(d)   the trial judge will expedite the transcript of the judgment and its approval and ensure that it is sent to the Central Authority without delay.

[The above is taken from the judgment of the Court of Appeal, Civil Division in *Vigreux v Michel & anor* [2006] EWCA Civ 630, [2006] 2 FLR 1180.]

Applications for Declarations
2.15
If a child has been taken from England and Wales to another State party, the judicial or administrative authorities of that State may ask for a declaration that the removal or retention of the child was wrongful. Or it might be thought that a declaration from the High Court that a child has been wrongfully removed or retained away from the United Kingdom would be helpful in securing his return. The High Court can make such declarations under section 8 of the Child Abduction and Custody Act 1985. An application for a declaration is made in the same way as an application for a return order, the only difference being that the details of relevant legal proceedings in respect of which the declaration is sought (if any), including a copy of any order made relating to the application, should be included in the documentation.

Rights of Custody
2.16
'Rights of custody' includes rights relating to the care of the person of the child and, in particular, the right to determine the child's place of residence. Rights of custody may arise by operation of law (that is, they are conferred on someone automatically by the legal system in which they are living) or by a judicial or administrative decision or as a result of an agreement having legal effect. The rights of a person, an institution or any other body are a matter for the law of the State of the child's habitual residence, but it is for the State which is being asked to return the child to decide: if those rights amount to rights of custody for the purposes of the 1980 Hague Convention; whether at the time of the removal or retention those rights were actually being exercised; and whether there has been a breach of those rights.

2.17
In England and Wales a father who is not married to the mother of their child does not necessarily have 'rights of custody' in respect of the child. An unmarried father in England and Wales who has parental responsibility for a child has rights of custody in respect of that child. In the case of an unmarried father without parental responsibility, the concept of rights of custody may include more than strictly legal rights and where immediately before the removal or retention of the child he was exercising parental functions over a substantial period of time as the only or main carer for the child he may have rights of custody. An unmarried father can ask ICACU or his legal representative for advice on this. It is important to remember that it will be for the State which is being asked to return the child to decide if the father's circumstances meet that State's requirements for the establishment of rights of custody.

2.18
Sometimes, court orders impose restrictions on the removal of children from the country in which they are living. These can be orders under the Children Act 1989 ('section 8' orders) or orders under the inherent jurisdiction of the High Court (sometimes called 'injunctions'). Any removal of a child in breach of an order imposing such a restriction would be wrongful under the 1980 Hague Convention.

2.19

The fact that court proceedings are in progress about a child does not of itself give rise to a prohibition on the removal of the child by a mother with sole parental responsibility from the country in which the proceedings are taking place unless:

(a)   the proceedings are Wardship proceedings in England and Wales (in which case removal would breach the rights of custody attributed to the High Court and fathers with no custody rights could rely on that breach); or

(b)   the court is actually considering the custody of the child, because then the court itself would have rights of custody.

Particular provisions for European Convention applications

2.20

The European Convention provides for the mutual recognition and enforcement of decisions relating to custody and access, so if a child has been brought here or retained here in breach of a custody order, then that order can be enforced. The European Convention has now been superseded to a very great extent by the Council Regulation. If however you want to make an application under the European Convention, then you make it in the same way as is described in paragraphs 2.10 and 2.11 above, but in addition you must include a copy of the decision relating to custody (or rights of access – see paragraph 5.1 below) which you are seeking to register or enforce, or about which you are seeking a declaration by the court.

Defending Abduction Proceedings

2.21

If you are served with an application – whether it is under the 1980 Hague or the European Convention or the inherent jurisdiction of the High Court – you must not delay. You must obey any directions given in any order with which you have been served, and you should seek legal advice at the earliest possible opportunity, although neither you nor the child concerned will automatically be entitled to legal aid.

2.22

It is particularly important that you tell the court where the child is, because the child will not be permitted to live anywhere else without the permission of the court, or to leave England and Wales, until the proceedings are finished.

2.23

It is also particularly important that you present to the court any defence to the application which you or the child might want to make at the earliest possible opportunity, although the orders with which you will have been served are likely to tell you the time by which you will have to do this.

2.24

If the child concerned objects to any order sought in relation to them, and if the child is of an age and understanding at which the court will take account of their views, the court is likely to direct that the child is seen by an officer of the Children and Family Court Advisory and Support Service (Cafcass) or in Wales CAFCASS CYMRU. You should cooperate in this process. Children are not usually made parties to abduction cases, but in certain exceptional circumstances the court can make them parties so that they have their own separate legal representation. These are all matters about which you should seek legal advice.

(Provisions about the power of the court to join parties are contained in rule 12.3 and provisions about the joining and representation of children are contained in Part 16 of these Rules and the Practice Direction 16A (Representation of Children.).

PART 3

Non-Convention Cases
3.1

Applications for the return of children wrongfully removed or retained away from States which are not parties to the 1980 Hague Convention or in respect of children to whom that Convention does not apply, can be made to the High Court under its inherent jurisdiction with respect to children. Such proceedings are referred to as 'non-Convention' cases. In proceedings under the inherent jurisdiction of the High Court with respect to children, the child's welfare is the court's paramount consideration. The extent of the court's enquiry into the child's welfare will depend on the circumstances of the case; in some cases the child's welfare will be best served by a summary hearing and, if necessary, a prompt return to the State from which the child has been removed or retained. In other cases a more detailed enquiry may be necessary (see *Re J (Child Returned Abroad: Convention Rights)* [2005] UKHL 40; [2005] 2 FLR 802).

3.2

Every application for the return of a child under the inherent jurisdiction must be made in the Principal Registry of the Family Division and heard in the High Court.

Provision about the inherent jurisdiction is made at Chapter 5 of Part 12 of the Rules and in Practice Direction 12D (Inherent Jurisdiction (including Wardship) Proceedings).

The Form and content of the application
3.3

An application for the return of a child under the inherent jurisdiction must be made in Form C66 and must include the information in paragraph 2.11 above.

3.4

You must file a statement in support of your application, which must exhibit all the relevant documents. The statement must contain and be verified by a statement of truth in the following terms:

'I make this statement knowing that it will be placed before the court, and I confirm that to the best of my knowledge and belief its contents are true.'

(Further provisions about statements of truth are contained in Part 17 of these Rules and Practice Direction 17A.).

Timetable for Non-Convention Cases
3.5
While the 6 week deadline referred to in paragraph 2.14 is set out in the 1980 Hague Convention and in the Council Regulation, non-Convention child abduction cases must similarly be completed in 6 weeks except where exceptional circumstances make this impossible. Paragraph 2.14 applies to these cases as appropriate for a non-Convention case.

PART 4

General Provisions

Urgent applications, or applications out of business hours
4.1
Guidance about urgent and out of hours applications is in Practice Direction 12E (Urgent Business).

Police assistance to prevent removal from England and Wales
4.2
The Child Abduction Act 1984 sets out the circumstances in which the removal of a child from this jurisdiction is a criminal offence. The police provide the following 24 hour service to prevent the unlawful removal of a child –
(a)   they inform ports directly when there is a real and imminent threat that a child is about to be removed unlawfully from the country; and
(b)   they liaise with Immigration Officers at the ports in an attempt to identify children at risk of removal.

4.3
Where the child is under 16, it is not necessary to obtain a court order before seeking police assistance. The police do not need an order to act to protect the child. If an order has already been obtained it should however be produced to the police. Where the child is between 16 and 18, an order must be obtained restricting or restraining removal before seeking police assistance.

4.4
Where the child is a ward of court (see Practice Direction 12D (Inherent Jurisdiction (including Wardship) Proceedings) the court's permission is needed to remove that child from the jurisdiction. When the court has not given that permission and police assistance is sought to prevent the removal of the ward, the applicant must produce evidence that the child is a ward such as –
(a)   an order confirming wardship;
(b)   an injunction; or

(c)   where the matter is urgent and no order has been made, a certified copy of the wardship application.

4.5

The application for police assistance must be made by the applicant or his legal representative to the applicant's local police station except that applications may be made to any police station –
(a)   in urgent cases;
(b)   where the wardship application has just been issued; or
(c)   where the court has just made the order relied on.

4.6

The police will, if they consider it appropriate, institute the 'port alert' system (otherwise known as 'an all ports warning') to try to prevent removal from the jurisdiction where the danger of removal is –
(a)   real (i.e., not being sought merely by way of insurance); and
(b)   imminent (i.e. within 24 to 48 hours).

4.7

The request for police assistance must be accompanied by as much of the following information as possible –
(a)   *the child*: the name, sex, date of birth, physical description, nationality and passport number; if the child has more than one nationality or passport, provide details;
(b)   *the person likely to remove*: the name, age, physical description, nationality, passport number, relationship to the child, and whether the child is likely to assist him or her; if the person has more than one nationality or passport, provide details;
(c)   *person applying for a port alert*: the name, relationship to the child, nationality, telephone number and (if appropriate) solicitor's or other legal representative's name and contact details; if the person has more than one nationality, provide details;
(d)   likely destination;
(e)   likely time of travel and port of embarkation and, if known, details of travel arrangements;
(f)   grounds for port alert (as appropriate) –
        (i)   suspected offence under section 1 or section 2 of the Child Abduction Act 1984;
        (ii)   the child is subject to a court order.
(g)   details of person to whom the child should be returned if intercepted.

4.8

If the police decide that the case is one in which the port-alert system should be used, the child's name will remain on the stop list for four weeks. *After that time it will be removed automatically unless a further application is made.*

HM Passport Office

4.9

Where the court makes an order prohibiting or otherwise restricting the removal of a child from the United Kingdom, or from any specified part of it, or from a specified dependent territory, the court may make an order under section 37 of the Family Law Act 1986 requiring any person to surrender any UK passport which has been issued to, or contains particulars of, the child.

4.10

HM Passport Office ('HMPO') will take action to prevent a United Kingdom passport or replacement passport being issued only where HMPO has been served with a court order expressly requiring a United Kingdom passport to be surrendered, or expressly prohibiting the issue of any further United Kingdom passport facilities to the child without the consent of the court, or the holder of such an order. Accordingly, in every case in which such an order has been made, HMPO must be served the same day if possible, or at the latest the following day, with a copy of the order. It is the responsibility of the applicant to do this. The specimen form of letter set out below should be used and a copy of the court order must be attached to the letter. Delay in sending the letter to HMPO must be kept to an absolute minimum.

"Intelligence Hub
Her Majesty's Passport Office
3 Northgate
96 Milton Street
Glasgow
G4 0BT

Dear Sir/Madam
..............v...........
Case no: ....

This is to inform you that the court has today made an order

*prohibiting the issue of a passport/passports to [name(s)] [date of birth (if known)] of [address] without the consent of the holder of the order.
*requiring [name(s)] [date of birth (if known)] of [address] to surrender the passport(s) issued to him/her/them/the following child[ren] / or which contain(s) particulars of the following child[ren]:

Name Date of Birth

*and has granted an injunction/*made an order restraining the removal of the child[ren] from the jurisdiction.
(*Delete as appropriate)

Please add these names to your records to prevent the issue of further passport facilities for the child[ren]. I enclose a copy of the court order.

Yours faithfully

Applicant's name / Applicant's Solicitor's name"

4.11

Following service on HMPO of an order either expressly requiring a United Kingdom passport to be surrendered by, or expressly prohibiting the issue of any further United Kingdom passport facilities to the child, HMPO will maintain a prohibition on issuing a passport, or further passport facilities until the child's 16th birthday. The order should state that a passport must not be granted/applied for without the consent of the court or the holder of the order.

Note: These requests may also be sent to any of the regional Passport Offices.

4.12

Further information on communicating with HMPO where the court has made a request of, or an order against, HMPO, may be found in: The President's Guidance reissued in October 2014: Communicating with the Home Office in Family Proceedings. Annex 1 to this Practice Direction contains that Guidance and Annex 2 contains the current version (as at June 2015) of the relevant court form.

4.13

Information about other circumstances, in which HMPO will agree not to issue a passport to a child if HMPO receives an application, or an order in more general terms than set out at 4.11 above, from a person who claims to have parental responsibility for the child, is available from HMPO or at www.gov.uk.

The Home Office
4.14

Information about communicating with the Home Office, where a question of the immigration status of a party arises in family proceedings, may be found in the Protocol: *Communicating with the Home Office in Family Proceedings* (revised and re-issued October 2010).

Press Reporting
4.15

When a child has been abducted and a judge considers that publicity may help in tracing the child, the judge may adjourn the case for a short period to enable representatives of the Press to attend to give the case the widest possible publicity.

4.16

If a Child Rescue Alert has been used concerning a child, within the UK or abroad, it will give rise to media publicity. The court should be informed that this has happened. If there are already court proceedings concerning a child, it is advisable to obtain the agreement of the court before there is publicity to trace a missing child. If the court has not given its permission for a child who is the subject of children proceedings to be identified as the subject of proceedings, to do so would be contempt of court.

Other Assistance
4.17
The Missing Persons Bureau will be participating for the UK in the European Union wide 116 000 hotline for missing children. Parents and children can ring this number for assistance. (It is primarily intended to deal with criminal matters, for example stranger kidnapping.)

4.18
It may also be possible to trace a child by obtaining a court order under the inherent jurisdiction or the wardship jurisdiction of the High Court addressed to certain government departments, as set out in Practice Direction 6C.

PART 5

Applications about rights of access
5.1
Access orders made in another Member State of the European Union (except Denmark) can be enforced in England or Wales under the Council Regulation.

5.2
Chapter III of the Council Regulation sets out provision for recognition and enforcement of parental responsibility orders, which include orders for custody and access (child arrangements) between Member States. Under Article 41 of the Council Regulation you can enforce an access order in your favour from another Member State directly, provided you produce the certificate given under Article 41(2) by the court which made the order. This is a quick procedure. The unsuccessful party is not allowed to oppose recognition of the order.

5.3
The rules on recognition and enforcement of parental responsibility orders are in Part 31. You should apply to the High Court using Form C69. Rule 31.8 covers applications for Article 41 of the Council Regulation. You can make the application without notice.

5.4
If the Council Regulation does not apply, and the access order was made by a State party to the European Convention, an application can be made to enforce the order under Article 11 of the European Convention. Paragraph 2.20 above gives further information about how to make the application.

5.5
Article 21 of the 1980 Hague Convention requires the States parties to respect rights of access. However, in the case of *Re G (A Minor) (Hague Convention: Access)* [1993] 1 FLR 669, the Court of Appeal took the view that Article 21 conferred no jurisdiction

to determine matters relating to access, or to recognise or enforce foreign access orders (see *Practice Note* of 5 March 1993: *Child Abduction Unit: Lord Chancellor's Department* set out in Annex 3 to this Practice Direction). (The Child Abduction Unit is now called ICACU see paragraph 2.6.) An access order which does not fall within the Council Regulation or the (very limited) application of the European Convention may only be enforced by applying for a child arrangements order under section 8 of the Children Act 1989.

5.6

This means that if, during the course of proceedings under the 1980 Hague Convention for a return order, the applicant decides to ask for access (contact) instead of the return of the child, but no agreement can be reached, a separate application for a child arrangements order will have to be made, or the court invited to make a child arrangements order without an application being made (Children Act 1989, s10(1)(b)).

PART 6

Child abduction cases between the United Kingdom and Pakistan
6.1
A consensus was reached in January 2003 between the President of the Family Division and the Hon. Chief Justice of Pakistan as to the principles to be applied in resolving child abduction cases between the UK and Pakistan.

The Protocol setting out that consensus can be accessed at: http://www.fco.gov.uk/resources/en/pdf/2855621/3069133. (See also Chapter 5.)

Annex 1

Communicating with the Home Office in Family Proceedings

[See Chapter 5. Accessible at www.judiciary.gov.uk/_/guidance-communicating-with-home-office-revised-march2012/.]

Annex 2

Court request for information to the Home Office

[See Chapter 5. Accessible at www.familylaw.co.uk/system/uploads/attachments/0000/2114/Court_rrequest_for_info_to_HO.]

Annex 3

See paragraph 5.5
Practice Note
5 March 1993
Citations: [1993] 1 FLR 804

Child Abduction Unit: Lord Chancellor's Department

Duties of the Central Authority for England and Wales under Article 21 of the Hague Convention on the Civil Aspects of International Child Abduction

Child Abduction and Custody Act 1985

In the case of *Re G (A Minor) (Hague Convention: Access)* [1993] 1 FLR 669 the Court of Appeal considered the duties of the Central Authority for England and Wales on receiving an application in respect of rights of access under Art 21 of the Hague Convention.

The Court of Appeal took the view that Art 21 conferred no jurisdiction to determine matters relating to access, or to recognise or enforce foreign access orders. It provides, however, for executive co-operation in the enforcement of such recognition as national law allows.

Accordingly, the duty of the Central Authority is to make appropriate arrangements for the applicant by providing solicitors to act on his behalf in applying for legal aid and instituting proceedings in the High Court under s 8 of the Children Act 1989.

If, during the course of proceedings under Art 21 of the Convention, the applicant decides to seek access instead of the return of the child, but no agreement can be reached and the provisions of the European Convention on the Recognition and Enforcement of Decisions Concerning Custody of Children and on Restoration of Custody of Children are not available, a separate application under s 8 of the Children Act 1989 will have to be made.

Central Authority for England and Wales

NOTE: The Child Abduction Unit is now called ICACU, see paragraph 2.6.

Footnotes

1. The child must be taken or kept out of the United Kingdom without the permission of a parent or someone who has rights of custody for it to be an international child abduction. This practice direction relates to the law as it applies in England and Wales. If the child has been taken or kept out of the United Kingdom when the child was habitually resident in Scotland, you should contact the Central Authority for Scotland, Scottish Government Justice Directorate, Civil Law Division, St Andrew's House, Regent Road, Edinburgh EH1 3DG Tel: +44 (0) 131 244 4827/4832 Fax: +44 (0) 131

244 4848 Website: http://www.gov.scot/Topics/Justice/law/17867/fm-children-root/18533. If the child has been taken or kept out of the United Kingdom when the child was habitually resident in Northern Ireland, you should contact the Central Authority for Northern Ireland, Northern Ireland Courts and Tribunals Service, Civil Policy and Tribunal Reform Division, 3rd Floor Laganside House, 23–27 Oxford Street, Belfast BT1 3LA Tel: + 44 (0)28 9072 8808 or + 44 (0) 28 9072 8819; fax +44 (0) 28 9072 8945. Website: http://www.nics.gov.uk/ or http://www.courtsni.gov.uk/en-GB/Services/ChildAbduction/

2. The Council Regulation (EC) No 2201/2003 of 27 November 2003 concerning jurisdiction and the recognition and enforcement of judgments in matrimonial matters and the matters of parental responsibility, repealing Regulation (EC) No 1347/2000 is also known as Brussels IIa, or Brussels II Revised, or Brussels II bis.

PRACTICE DIRECTION 12G – COMMUNICATION OF INFORMATION

This Practice Direction supplements FPR Part 12, Chapter 7

1.1
Chapter 7 deals with the communication of information (whether or not contained in a document filed with the court) relating to proceedings which relate to children.

1.2
Subject to any direction of the court, information may be communicated for the purposes of the law relating to contempt in accordance with paragraphs 2.1, 3.1 or 4.1.

Communication of information by a party etc. for other purposes
2.1
A person specified in the first column of the following table may communicate to a person listed in the second column such information as is specified in the third column for the purpose or purposes specified in the fourth column –

A party	A lay adviser, a McKenzie Friend, or a person arranging or providing pro bono legal services	Any information relating to the proceedings	To enable the party to obtain advice or assistance in relation to the proceedings
A party	A health care professional or a person or body providing counselling services for children or families		To enable the party or any child of the party to obtain health care or counselling
A party	The Secretary of State, a McKenzie Friend, a lay adviser or the First-tier Tribunal dealing with an appeal made under section 20 of the Child Support Act 1991		For the purposes of making or responding to an appeal under section 20 of the Child Support Act 1991 or the determination of such an appeal
A party	An adoption panel		To enable the adoption panel to discharge its functions as appropriate
A party	A local authority's medical adviser appointed under the Adoption Agencies Regulations 2005 or the Adoption Agencies (Wales) Regulations 2005		To enable the medical adviser to discharge his or her functions as appropriate.

A party	The European Court of Human Rights		For the purpose of making an application to the European Court of Human Rights
A party or any person lawfully in receipt of information	The Children's Commissioner or the Children's Commissioner for Wales		To refer an issue affecting the interests of children to the Children's Commissioner or the Children's Commissioner for Wales
A party, any person lawfully in receipt of information or a proper officer	A person or body conducting an approved research project		For the purpose of an approved research project
A legal representative or a professional legal adviser	A person or body responsible for investigating or determining complaints in relation to legal representatives or professional legal advisers		For the purposes of the investigation or determination of a complaint in relation to a legal representative or a professional legal adviser
A legal representative or a professional legal adviser	A person or body assessing quality assurance systems		To enable the legal representative or professional legal adviser to obtain a quality assurance assessment
A legal representative or a professional legal adviser	An accreditation body	Any information relating to the proceedings providing that it does not, or is not likely to, identify any person involved in the proceedings	To enable the legal representative or professional legal adviser to obtain accreditation
A party	A police officer	The text or summary of the whole or part of a judgment given in the proceedings	For the purpose of a criminal investigation
A party or any person lawfully in receipt of information	A member of the Crown Prosecution Service		To enable the Crown Prosecution Service to discharge its functions under any enactment

Communication for the effective functioning of Cafcass and CAFCASS CYMRU

3.1

An officer of the Service or a Welsh family proceedings officer, as appropriate, may communicate to a person listed in the second column such information as is specified in the third column for the purpose or purposes specified in the fourth column –

A Welsh family proceedings officer	A person or body exercising statutory functions relating to inspection of CAFCASS CYMRU	Any information relating to the proceedings which is required by the person or body responsible for the inspection	For the purpose of an inspection of CAFCASS CYMRU by a body or person appointed by the Welsh Ministers
An officer of the Service or a Welsh family proceedings officer	The Health and Care Professions Council or the Care Council for Wales	Any information relating to the proceedings providing that it does not, or is not likely to, identify any person involved in the proceedings	For the purpose of initial and continuing accreditation as a social worker of a person providing services to Cafcass or CAFCASS CYMRU in accordance with section 13(2) of the Criminal Justice and Courts Services Act 2000 or section 36 of the Children Act 2004 as the case may be
An officer of the Service or a Welsh family proceedings officer	A person or body providing services relating to professional development or training to Cafcass or CAFCASS CYMRU	Any information relating to the proceedings providing that it does not, or is not likely to, identify any person involved in the proceedings without that person's consent	To enable the person or body to provide the services, where the services cannot be effectively provided without such disclosure
An officer of the Service or a Welsh family proceedings officer	A person employed by or contracted to Cafcass or CAFCASS CYMRU for the purposes of carrying out the functions referred to in column 4 of this row	Any information relating to the proceedings	Engagement in processes internal to Cafcass or CAFCASS CYMRU which relate to the maintenance of necessary records concerning the proceedings, or to ensuring that Cafcass or CAFCASS CYMRU functions are carried out to a satisfactory standard

Communication to and by Ministers of the Crown and Welsh Ministers
4.1

A person specified in the first column of the following table may communicate to a person listed in the second column such information as is specified in the third column for the purpose or purposes specified in the fourth column –

A party or any person lawfully in receipt of information relating to the proceedings	A Minister of the Crown with responsibility for a government department engaged, or potentially engaged, in an application before the European Court of Human Rights relating to the proceedings	Any information relating to the proceedings of which he or she is in lawful possession	To provide the department with information relevant, or potentially relevant, to the proceedings before the European Court of Human Rights
A Minister of the Crown	The European Court of Human Rights		For the purpose of engagement in an application before the European Court of Human Rights relating to the proceedings
A Minister of the Crown	Lawyers advising or representing the United Kingdom in an application before the European Court of Human Rights relating to the proceedings		For the purpose of receiving advice or for effective representation in relation to the application before the European Court of Human Rights
A Minister of the crown or a Welsh Minister	Another Minister, or Ministers, of the Crown or a Welsh Minister		For the purpose of notification, discussion and the giving or receiving of advice regarding issues raised by the information in which the relevant departments have, or may have, an interest

5.1

This paragraph applies to communications made in accordance with paragraphs 2.1, 3.1 and 4.1 and the reference in this paragraph to 'the table' means the table in the relevant paragraph.

5.2

A person in the second column of the table may only communicate information relating to the proceedings received from a person in the first column for the purpose or purposes –

(a)   for which he or she received that information; or

(b)   of professional development or training, providing that any communication does not, or is not likely to, identify any person involved in the proceedings without that person's consent.

6.1

In this Practice Direction –

'accreditation body' means –

(a)   The Law Society,

(b)   Resolution, or

(c)   the Lord Chancellor in exercise of the Lord Chancellor's functions in relation to legal aid;

'adoption panel' means a panel established in accordance with regulation 3 of the Adoption Agencies Regulations 2005 or regulation 3 of the Adoption Agencies (Wales) Regulations 2005;

'approved research project' means a project of research-

(a)   approved in writing by a Secretary of State after consultation with the President of the Family Division,

(b)   approved in writing by the President of the Family Division, or

(c)   conducted under section 83 of the Act of 1989 or section 13 of the Criminal Justice and Court Services Act 2000;

'body assessing quality assurance systems' includes –

(a)   The Law Society,

(b)   the Lord Chancellor in exercise of the Lord Chancellor's functions in relation to legal aid, or

(c)   The General Council of the Bar;

'body or person responsible for investigating or determining complaints in relation to legal representatives or professional legal advisers' means –

(a)   The Law Society,

(b)   The General Council of the Bar,

(c)   The Institute of Legal Executives,

(d)   The Legal Services Ombudsman; or

(e)   The Office of Legal Complaints.

'Cafcass' has the meaning assigned to it by section 11 of the Criminal Justice and Courts Services Act 2000;

'CAFCASS CYMRU' means the part of the Welsh Assembly Government exercising the functions of Welsh Ministers under Part 4 of the Children Act 2004;

'criminal investigation' means an investigation conducted by police officers with a view to it being ascertained –

(a)   whether a person should be charged with an offence, or

(b)   whether a person charged with an offence is guilty of it;

'health care professional' means –

(a)   a registered medical practitioner,

    (b)   a registered nurse or midwife,

    (c)   a clinical psychologist, or

    (d)   a child psychotherapist;

'lay adviser' means a non-professional person who gives lay advice on behalf of an organisation in the lay advice sector;

'McKenzie Friend' means any person permitted by the court to sit beside an unrepresented litigant in court to assist that litigant by prompting, taking notes and giving him advice; and

'social worker' has the meaning assigned to it by section 55 of the Care Standards Act 2000.

PRACTICE DIRECTION 12I – APPLICATIONS FOR REPORTING RESTRICTION ORDERS

1.1
This direction applies to any application in the Family Division founded on Convention rights for an order restricting publication of information about children or incapacitated adults.

Applications to be heard in the High Court
2.1
Orders can only be made in the High Court and are normally dealt with by a Judge of the Family Division. If the need for an order arises in existing proceedings in the family court, judges should either transfer the application to the High Court or consult their Family Division Liaison Judge. Where the matter is urgent, it can be heard by the Urgent Applications Judge of the Family Division (out of hours contact number 020 7947 6000).

Service of Application on the National News Media
3.1
Section 12(2) of the Human Rights Act 1998 means that an injunction restricting the exercise of the right to freedom of expression must not be granted where the person against whom the application is made is neither present nor represented unless the court is satisfied –
(a)   that the applicant has taken all practicable steps to notify the respondent, or
(b)   that there are compelling reasons why the respondent should not be notified.

3.2
Service of applications for reporting restriction orders on the national media can now be effected via the Press Association's CopyDirect service, to which national newspapers and broadcasters subscribe as a means of receiving notice of such applications.

3.3
The court will bear in mind that legal advisers to the media –
(i)   are used to participating in hearings at very short notice where necessary; and
(ii)   are able to differentiate between information provided for legal purposes and information for editorial use.
Service of applications via the CopyDirect service should henceforth be the norm.

3.4
The court retains the power to make without notice orders, but such cases will be exceptional, and an order will always give persons affected liberty to apply to vary or discharge it at short notice.

Further Guidance

4.1

The Practice Note 'Applications for Reporting Restriction Orders' dated 18 March 2005 and issued jointly by the Official Solicitor and the Deputy Director of Legal Services, provides valuable guidance and should be followed.

4.2

Issued with the concurrence and approval of the Lord Chancellor.

PRACTICE DIRECTION 12J – CHILD ARRANGEMENTS AND CONTACT ORDERS: DOMESTIC VIOLENCE AND HARM

This Practice Direction supplements FPR Part 12, and incorporates and supersedes the President's Guidance in Relation to Split Hearings (May 2010) as it applies to proceedings for child arrangements orders.

Summary

1

This Practice Direction applies to any family proceedings in the Family Court under the relevant parts of the Children Act 1989 or the relevant parts of the Adoption and Children Act 2002 ('the 2002 Act') in which an application is made for a child arrangements order, or in which any question arises about where a child should live, or about contact between a child and a parent or other family member, where the court considers that an order should be made.

2

The purpose of this Practice Direction is to set out what the Family Court should do in any case in which it is alleged or admitted, or there is other reason to believe, that the child or a party has experienced domestic violence or abuse perpetrated by another party or that there is a risk of such violence or abuse.

3

For the purpose of this Practice Direction –

'Domestic violence' includes any incident or pattern of incidents of controlling, coercive or threatening behaviour, violence or abuse between those aged 16 or over who are or have been intimate partners or family members regardless of gender or sexuality. This can encompass, but is not limited to, psychological, physical, sexual, financial, or emotional abuse.

'Controlling behaviour' means an act or pattern of acts designed to make a person subordinate and/or dependent by isolating them from sources of support, exploiting their resources and capacities for personal gain, depriving them of the means needed for independence, resistance and escape and regulating their everyday behaviour.

'Coercive behaviour' means an act or a pattern of acts of assault, threats, humiliation and intimidation or other abuse that is used to harm, punish, or frighten the victim.

General principles

4

The Family Court presumes that the involvement of a parent in a child's life will further the child's welfare, so long as the parent can be involved in a way that does not put the child or other parent at risk of suffering harm.

5

Domestic violence and abuse is harmful to children, and/or puts children at risk of harm, whether they are subjected to violence or abuse, or witness one of their parents being violent or abusive to the other parent, or live in a home in which violence or abuse is perpetrated (even if the child is too young to be conscious of the behaviour). Children may suffer direct physical, psychological and/or emotional harm from living with violence or abuse, and may also suffer harm indirectly where the violence or abuse impairs the parenting capacity of either or both of their parents.

6

The court must, at all stages of the proceedings, and specifically at the First Hearing Dispute Resolution Appointment ('FHDRA'), consider whether domestic violence is raised as an issue, either by the parties or by Cafcass or CAFCASS Cymru or otherwise, and if so must –

- identify at the earliest opportunity (usually at the FHDRA) the factual and welfare issues involved;
- consider the nature of any allegation, admission or evidence of domestic violence or abuse, and the extent to which it would be likely to be relevant in deciding whether to make a child arrangements order and, if so, in what terms;
- give directions to enable contested relevant factual and welfare issues to be tried as soon as possible and fairly;
- ensure that where violence or abuse is admitted or proven, that any child arrangements order in place protects the safety and wellbeing of the child and the parent with whom the child is living, and does not expose them to the risk of further harm. In particular, the court must be satisfied that any contact ordered with a parent who has perpetrated violence or abuse is safe and in the best interests of the child; and
- ensure that any interim child arrangements order (i.e. considered by the court before determination of the facts, and in the absence of admission) is only made having followed the guidance in paragraphs 25–27 below.

7

In all cases it is for the court to decide whether a child arrangements order accords with Section 1(1) of the Children Act 1989; any proposed child arrangements order, whether to be made by agreement between the parties or otherwise must be scrutinised by the court accordingly. The court shall not make a child arrangements order by consent or give permission for an application for a child arrangements order to be withdrawn, unless the parties are present in court, all initial safeguarding checks have been obtained by the court, and an officer of Cafcass or CAFCASS Cymru has spoken to the parties separately, except where it is satisfied that there is no risk of harm to the child in so doing.

8

In considering, on an application for a child arrangements order by consent, whether there is any risk of harm to the child, the court shall consider all the evidence and information available. The court may direct a report under Section 7 of the Children Act 1989, to be provided either orally or in writing, before it makes its decision; in such a case, the court may ask for information about any advice given by the officer preparing the report to the parties and whether they, or the child, have been referred to any other agency, including local authority children's services. If the report is not in writing, the court shall make a note of its substance on the court file.

Before the FHDRA
9

Where any information provided to the court before the FHDRA or other first hearing (whether as a result of initial safeguarding enquiries by Cafcass or CAFCASS Cymru or on form C1A or otherwise) indicates that there are issues of domestic violence or abuse which may be relevant to the court's determination, the court must ensure that the issues are addressed at the hearing, and that the parties are not expected to engage in conciliation or other forms of dispute resolution which are not suitable.

10

If at any stage the court is advised by the applicant, by Cafcass or CAFCASS Cymru or otherwise that there is a need for special arrangements to secure the safety of any party or child attending any hearing, the court shall ensure that appropriate arrangements are made for the hearing and for all subsequent hearings in the case, unless it considers that these are no longer necessary.

First hearing/FHDRA
11

At the FHDRA, if the parties have not been provided with the safeguarding letter/report by Cafcass/CAFCASS Cymru, the court shall inform the parties of the content of any safeguarding letter or report or other information which has been provided by Cafcass or CAFCASS Cymru, unless it considers that to do so would create a risk of harm to a party or the child.

12

Where the results of Cafcass or CAFCASS Cymru safeguarding checks are not available at the FHDRA, and no other reliable safeguarding information is available, the court shall adjourn the FHDRA until the results of safeguarding checks are available. The court shall not generally make an interim child arrangements order, or orders for contact, in the absence of safeguarding information, unless it is to protect the safety of the child.

13

There is a continuing duty on the Cafcass Officer/Welsh FPO which requires them to provide a risk assessment for the court under section 16A Children Act 1989 if they are given cause to suspect that the child concerned is at risk of harm. Specific provision about service of a risk assessment under section 16A of the 1989 Act is made by rule 12.34 of the FPR 2010.

14

The court must ascertain at the earliest opportunity whether domestic violence or abuse is raised as an issue of risk of harm to the child which is likely to be relevant to any decision of the court relating to the welfare of the child, and specifically on the making of any child arrangements order.

Admissions
15

Where at any hearing an admission of domestic violence or abuse toward another person or the child is made by a party, the admission should be recorded in writing and retained on the court file. A copy of any record of admissions must be made available as soon as possible to any Cafcass officer or officer of CAFCASS Cymru or local authority officer preparing a report under section 7 of the Children Act 1989.

Directions for a fact-finding hearing
16

The court should determine as soon as possible whether it is necessary to conduct a fact-finding hearing in relation to any disputed allegation of domestic violence or abuse –

(a)   in order to provide a factual basis for any welfare report or for assessment of the factors set out in paragraphs 36 and 37 (below);

(b)   in order to provide a basis for an accurate assessment of risk; or

(c)   before it can consider any final welfare-based order(s) in relation to child arrangements; or

(d)   before it considers the need for a domestic violence-related Activity (such as a Domestic Violence Perpetrator Programme (DVPP)).

17

In determining whether it is necessary to conduct a fact-finding hearing, the court should consider –

(a)   the views of the parties and of Cafcass or CAFCASS Cymru;

(b)   whether there are admissions by a party which provide a sufficient factual basis on which to proceed;

(c)   if a party is in receipt of legal aid, whether the evidence required to be provided to obtain legal aid provides a sufficient factual basis on which to proceed;

(d)   whether there is other evidence available to the court that provides a sufficient factual basis on which to proceed;

(e)   whether the factors set out in paragraphs 36 and 37 below can be determined without a fact-finding hearing;

(f)   the nature of the evidence required to resolve disputed allegations;

(g)   whether the nature and extent of the allegations, if proved, would be relevant to the issue before the court; and

(h)   whether a separate fact-finding hearing would be necessary and proportionate in all the circumstances of the case.

18

Where the court determines that a finding of fact hearing is not necessary, the order shall record the reasons for that decision.

19

Where the court considers that a fact-finding hearing is necessary, it must give directions as to how the proceedings are to be conducted to ensure that the matters in issue are determined as soon as possible, fairly and proportionately, and within the capabilities of the parties. In particular it should consider –

(a)　what are the key facts in dispute;

(b)　whether it is necessary for the fact-finding to take place at a separate (and earlier) hearing than the welfare hearing;

(c)　whether the key facts in dispute can be contained in a schedule or a table (known as a Scott Schedule) which sets out what the applicant complains of or alleges, what the respondent says in relation to each individual allegation or complaint; the allegations in the schedule should be focused on the factual issues to be tried; and if so, whether it is practicable for this schedule to be completed at the first hearing, with the assistance of the judge;

(d)　what evidence is required in order to determine the existence of a pattern of coercive, controlling or threatening behaviour, violence or abuse;

(e)　directing the parties to file written statements giving details of such behaviour and of any response;

(f)　whether documents are required from third parties such as the police or health services and giving directions for those documents to be obtained;

(g)　whether oral evidence may be required from third parties and if so, giving directions for the filing of written statements from such third parties;

(h)　whether any other evidence is required to enable the court to decide the key issues and giving directions for that evidence to be provided;

(i)　what evidence the alleged victim of violence is able to give and what support the alleged victim may require at the fact-finding hearing in order to give that evidence;

(j)　what support the alleged perpetrator may need in order to have a reasonable opportunity to challenge the evidence; and

(k)　whether a pre-hearing review would be useful prior to the fact-finding hearing to ensure directions have been complied with and all the required evidence is available.

20

Where the court fixes a fact-finding hearing, it must at the same time fix a Dispute Resolution Appointment to follow. Subject to the exception in paragraph 31 below, the hearings should be arranged in such a way that they are conducted by the same judge or, wherever possible, by the same panel of lay justices; where it is not possible to assemble the same panel of justices, the resumed hearing should be listed before at least the same chairperson of the lay justices. Judicial continuity is important.

Reports under Section 7

21

In any case where a risk of harm to a child resulting from domestic violence or abuse is raised as an issue, the court should consider directing that a report on the question of contact, or any other matters relating to the welfare of the child, be prepared under section 7 of the Children Act 1989 by an Officer of Cafcass or a Welsh family proceedings officer (or local authority officer if appropriate), unless the court is satisfied that it is not necessary to do so in order to safeguard the child's interests.

22

If the court directs that there shall be a fact-finding hearing on the issue of domestic violence or abuse, the court will not usually request a section 7 report until after that hearing. In that event, the court should direct that any judgment is provided to Cafcass/CAFCASS Cymru; if there is no transcribed judgment, an agreed list of findings should be provided.

23

Any request for a section 7 report should set out clearly the matters the court considers need to be addressed.

Representation of the child

24

Subject to the seriousness of the allegations made and the difficulty of the case, the court shall consider whether it is appropriate for the child who is the subject of the application to be made a party to the proceedings and be separately represented. If the court considers that the child should be so represented, it shall review the allocation decision so that it is satisfied that the case proceeds before the correct level of judge in the Family Court.

Interim orders before determination of relevant facts

25

Where the court gives directions for a fact-finding hearing, the court should consider whether an interim child arrangements order is in the interests of the child; and in particular whether the safety of the child and (bearing in mind the impact which domestic violence against a parent can have on the emotional well-being of the child) the parent who has made the allegation and is at any time caring for the child can be secured before, during and after any contact.

26

In deciding any interim child arrangements question pending a full hearing the court should –

(a)   take into account the matters set out in section 1(3) of the Children Act 1989 or section 1(4) of the Adoption and Children Act 2002 ('the welfare check-list'), as appropriate; and

(b)   give particular consideration to the likely effect on the child, and on the care given to the child by the parent who has made the allegation of domestic violence, of any contact and any risk of harm, whether physical, emotional or psychological, which the child and that parent is likely to suffer as a consequence of making or declining to make an order.

27
Where the court is considering whether to make an order for interim contact, it should in addition consider –
(a) the arrangements required to ensure, as far as possible, that any risk of harm to the child and the parent who is at any time caring for the child is minimised and that the safety of the child and the parties is secured; and in particular:
    (i) whether the contact should be supervised or supported, and if so, where and by whom;
    (ii) the availability of appropriate facilities for that purpose
(b) if direct contact is not appropriate, whether it is in the best interests of the child to make an order for indirect contact; and
(c) whether contact will be beneficial for the child.

The fact-finding hearing
28
While ensuring that the allegations are properly put and responded to, the fact-finding hearing can be an inquisitorial (or investigative) process, which at all times must protect the interests of all involved. At the fact-finding hearing –

- Each party can be asked to identify what questions they wish to ask of the other party, and to set out or confirm in sworn evidence their version of the disputed key facts.
- The judge or lay justices should be prepared where necessary and appropriate to conduct the questioning of the witnesses on behalf of the parties, focusing on the key issues in the case.

Victims of violence are likely to find direct cross-examination by their alleged abuser frightening and intimidating, and thus it may be particularly appropriate for the judge or lay justices to conduct the questioning on behalf of the other party in these circumstances, in order to ensure both parties are able to give their best evidence.

29
The court should, wherever practicable, make findings of fact as to the nature and degree of any domestic violence or abuse which is established and its effect on the child, the child's parents and any other relevant person. The court shall record its findings in writing, and shall serve a copy on the parties. A copy of any record of findings of fact or of admissions must be sent to any officer preparing a report under Section 7 of the 1989 Act.

30
At the conclusion of any fact-finding hearing, the court shall consider, notwithstanding any earlier direction for a section 7 report, whether it is in the best interests of the child for the court to give further directions about the preparation or scope of any report under section 7; where necessary, it may adjourn the proceedings

for a brief period to enable the officer to make representations about the preparation or scope of any further enquiries. The court should also consider whether it would be assisted by any social work, psychiatric, psychological or other assessment of any party or the child (such as an expert risk assessment), and if so (subject to any necessary consent) make directions for such assessment to be undertaken and for the filing of any consequent report. Any section 7 or other report should address the factors set out in paragraphs 36 and 37, unless the court directs otherwise.

31

Where the court has made findings of fact on disputed allegations, any subsequent hearing in the proceedings should be conducted by the same judge or by at least the same chairperson of the justices. Exceptions may be made only where observing this requirement would result in delay to the planned timetable and the judge or chairperson is satisfied, for reasons recorded in writing, that the detriment to the welfare of the child would outweigh the detriment to the fair trial of the proceedings.

In all cases where domestic violence or abuse has occurred
32

The court should take steps to obtain (or direct the parties or an Officer of Cafcass or a Welsh family proceedings officer to obtain) information about the facilities available locally to assist any party or the child in cases where domestic violence or abuse has occurred.

33

Following any determination of the nature and extent of domestic violence or abuse, whether or not following a fact-finding hearing, the court should consider whether any party should seek advice, treatment or other intervention as a precondition to any child arrangements order being made or as a means of assisting the court in ascertaining the likely risk of harm to the child and to the parent with whom the child is living from that person, and may (with the consent of that party) give directions for such attendance and the filing of any consequent report.

34

Further or as an alternative to the advice, treatment or other intervention referred to in paragraph 33 above, the court may make an Activity Direction under section 11A and 11B Children Act 1989. Any intervention directed pursuant to this provision should be one commissioned and approved by Cafcass. It is acknowledged that acceptance on a DVPP is subject to a suitability assessment by the service provider, and that completion of a DVPP will take time in order to achieve the aim of risk-reduction for the long-term benefit of the child and the parent with whom the child is living.

Factors to be taken into account when determining whether to make child arrangements orders in all cases where domestic violence or abuse has occurred
35

When deciding the issue of child arrangements the court should ensure that any order for contact will be safe and in the best interests of the child.

36

In the light of any findings of fact the court should apply the individual matters in the welfare checklist with reference to those findings; in particular, where relevant findings of domestic violence or abuse have been made, the court should in every case consider any harm which the child and the parent with whom the child is living has suffered as a consequence of that violence or abuse, and any harm which the child and the parent with whom the child is living, is at risk of suffering if a child arrangements order is made. The court should only make an order for contact if it can be satisfied that the physical and emotional safety of the child and the parent with whom the child is living can, as far as possible, be secured before during and after contact, and that the parent with whom the child is living will not be subjected to further controlling or coercive behaviour by the other parent.

37

In every case where a finding of domestic violence or abuse is made, the court should consider the conduct of both parents towards each other and towards the child; in particular, the court should consider –

(a) the effect of the domestic violence or abuse on the child and on the arrangements for where the child is living;

(b) the effect of the domestic violence or abuse on the child and its effect on the child's relationship with the parents;

(c) whether the applicant parent is motivated by a desire to promote the best interests of the child or is using the process to continue a process of violence, abuse, intimidation or harassment or controlling or coercive behaviour against the other parent;

(d) the likely behaviour during contact of the parent against whom findings are made and its effect on the child; and

(e) the capacity of the parents to appreciate the effect of past violence or abuse and the potential for future violence or abuse.

Directions as to how contact is to proceed

38

Where the court has made findings of domestic violence or abuse but, having applied the welfare checklist, nonetheless considers that direct contact is safe and beneficial for the child, the court should consider what, if any, directions or conditions are required to enable the order to be carried into effect and in particular should consider –

(a) whether or not contact should be supervised, and if so, where and by whom;

(b) whether to impose any conditions to be complied with by the party in whose favour the order for contact has been made and if so, the nature of those conditions, for example by way of seeking intervention (subject to any necessary consent);

(c) whether such contact should be for a specified period or should contain provisions which are to have effect for a specified period; and

(d) whether it will be necessary, in the child's best interests, to review the operation of the order; if so the court should set a date for the review consistent with the timetable for the child, and shall give directions to ensure that at the review the court has full information about the operation of the order.

39

Where the court does not consider direct contact to be appropriate, it shall consider whether it is safe and beneficial for the child to make an order for indirect contact.

The reasons of the court
40

In its judgment or reasons the court should always make clear how its findings on the issue of domestic violence or abuse have influenced its decision on the issue of arrangements for the child. In particular, where the court has found domestic violence or abuse proved but nonetheless makes an order which results in the child having future contact with the perpetrator of domestic violence or abuse, the court should always explain, whether by way of reference to the welfare check-list the factors in paragraphs 36 and 37 or otherwise, why it takes the view that the order which it has made is safe and beneficial for the child.

This Practice Direction is issued by the President of the Family Division, as the nominee of the Lord Chief Justice, with the agreement of the Lord Chancellor.

PRACTICE DIRECTION 12K – CHILDREN ACT 1989: EXCLUSION REQUIREMENT

Under s 38A(5) and s 44A(5) of the Children Act 1989 the court may attach a power of arrest to an exclusion requirement included in an interim care order or an emergency protection order. In cases where an order is made which includes an exclusion requirement, the following shall apply –

1.1

If a power of arrest is attached to the order then unless the person to whom the exclusion requirement refers was given notice of the hearing and attended the hearing, the name of that person and that an order has been made including an exclusion requirement to which a power of arrest has been attached shall be announced in open court at the earliest opportunity. This may be either on the same day when the court proceeds to hear cases in open court or where there is no further business in open court on that day at the next listed sitting of the court.

1.2

When a person arrested under a power of arrest cannot conveniently be brought before the relevant judicial authority sitting in a place normally used as a court room within 24 hours after the arrest, he may be brought before the relevant judicial authority at any convenient place but, as the liberty of the subject is involved, the press and the public should be permitted to be present, unless security needs make this impracticable.

1.3

Any order of committal made otherwise than in public or in a courtroom open to the public, shall be announced in open court at the earliest opportunity. This may be either on the same day when the court proceeds to hear cases in open court or where there is no further business in open court on that day at the next listed sitting of the court. The announcement shall state –

(a)   the name of the person committed,

(b)   in general terms the nature of the contempt of the court in respect of which the order of committal has been made and

(c)   the length of the period of committal.

PRACTICE DIRECTION 12O – CHILD: ARRIVAL BY AIR

1.1

Where a person seeks an order for the return to him of children about to arrive in England by air and desires to have information to enable him to meet the aeroplane, the judge should be asked to include in his order a direction that the airline operating the flight, and, if he has the information, the immigration officer at the appropriate airport, should supply such information to that person.

1.2

To obtain such information in such circumstances in a case where a person already has an order for the return to him of children, that person should apply to a judge ex parte for such a direction.

PRACTICE DIRECTION 12P – REMOVAL FROM JURISDICTION: ISSUE OF PASSPORTS

Removal from jurisdiction

1.1

The President has directed that on application for leave to remove from the jurisdiction for holiday periods a ward of court who has been placed by a local authority with foster-parents whose identity the court considers should remain confidential, for example because they are prospective adopters, it is important that such foster-parents should not be identified in the court's order. In such cases the order should be expressed as giving leave to the local authority to arrange for the child to be removed from England and Wales for the purpose of holidays.

1.2

It is also considered permissible, where care and control has been given to a local authority, or to an individual, for the court to give general leave to make such arrangements in suitable cases, thereby obviating the need to make application for leave each time it is desired to remove the child from the jurisdiction.

Issue of Passports

2.1

It is the practice of the Passport Department of the Home Office to issue passports for wards in accordance with the court's direction. This frequently results in passports being restricted to the holiday period specified in the order giving leave. It is the President's opinion that it is more convenient for wards' passports to be issued without such restriction.

2.2

The Passport Department has agreed to issue passports on this basis unless the court otherwise directs. It will, of course, still be necessary for the leave of the court to be obtained for the child's removal.

PRACTICE DIRECTION 14E – COMMUNICATION OF INFORMATION RELATING TO PROCEEDINGS

This Practice Direction supplements Part 14, rule 14.14(b) of the Family Procedure Rules 2010

Communication of information relating to proceedings

1.1

Rule 14.14 deals with the communication of information (whether or not it is recorded in any form) relating to proceedings.

1.2

Subject to any direction of the court, information may be communicated for the purposes of the law relating to contempt in accordance with paragraphs 1.3 or 1.4.

1.3

A person specified in the first column of the following table may communicate to a person listed in the second column such information as is specified in the third column for the purpose or purposes specified in the fourth column.

Communication of information without permission of the court

Communicated by	To	Information	Purpose
A party	A lay adviser or a McKenzie Friend	Any information relating to the proceedings	To enable the party to obtain advice or assistance in relation to the proceedings.
A party	The party's spouse, civil partner, cohabitant or close family member		For the purpose of confidential discussions enabling the party to receive support from his spouse, civil partner, cohabitant or close family member.
A party	A health care professional or a person or body providing counselling services for children or families		To enable the party or any child of the party to obtain health care or counselling.
A party	The Secretary of State, a McKenzie Friend, a lay adviser or an appeal tribunal dealing with an appeal made under section		For the purposes of making or responding to an appeal under section 20 of the Child Support Act

Communication of information without permission of the court

Communicated by	To	Information	Purpose
	20 of the Child Support Act 1991[1]		1991 or the determination of such an appeal.
A party	An adoption panel		To enable the adoption panel to discharge its functions as appropriate.
A party	A local authority's medical adviser appointed under the Adoption Agencies Regulations 2005 or the Adoption Agencies (Wales) Regulations 2005		To enable the medical adviser to discharge his or her functions as appropriate.
A party or any person lawfully in receipt of information	The Children's Commissioner or the Children's Commissioner for Wales		To refer an issue affecting the interests of children to the Children's Commissioner or the Children's Commissioner for Wales.
A party or a legal representative	A mediator		For the purpose of mediation in relation to the proceedings.
A party, any person lawfully in receipt of information or a proper officer	A person or body conducting an approved research project		For the purpose of an approved research project.
A party, a legal representative or a professional legal adviser	A person or body responsible for investigating or determining complaints in relation to legal representatives or professional legal advisers		For the purposes of making a complaint or the investigation or determination of a complaint in relation to a legal representative or a professional legal adviser.
A legal representative or a professional legal adviser	A person or body assessing quality assurance systems		To enable the legal representative or professional legal adviser to obtain a quality assurance assessment.
A legal representative or a	An accreditation body	Any information relating to the	To enable the legal representative or

Communication of information without permission of the court

Communicated by	To	Information	Purpose
professional legal adviser		proceedings providing that it does not, or is not likely to, identify any person involved in the proceedings	professional legal adviser to obtain accreditation.
A party	An elected representative or peer	The text or summary of the whole or part of a judgment given in the proceedings	To enable the elected representative or peer to give advice, investigate any complaint or raise any question of policy or procedure.
A party	The General Medical Council		For the purpose of making a complaint to the General Medical Council.
A party	A police officer		For the purpose of a criminal investigation.
A party or any person lawfully in receipt of information	A member of the Crown Prosecution Service		To enable the Crown Prosecution Service to discharge its functions under any enactment.

1.4

A person in the second column of the table in paragraph 1.3 may only communicate information relating to the proceedings received from a person in the first column for the purpose or purposes –

(a)   for which he received that information, or

(b)   of professional development or training, providing that any communication does not, or is not likely to, identify any person involved in the proceedings without that person's consent.

1.5

In this Practice Direction –

(1)   'accreditation body' means –

    (a)   The Law Society,

    (b)   Resolution, or

    (c)   the Lord Chancellor in exercise of the Lord Chancellor's functions in relation to legal aid;

(1A)   'adoption panel' means a panel established in accordance with regulation 3 of the Adoption Agencies Regulations 2005[2] or regulation 3 of the Adoption Agencies (Wales) Regulations 2005[3];

(2)   'approved research project' means a project of research –

    (a)   approved in writing by a Secretary of State after consultation with the President of the Family Division,

    (b)   approved in writing by the President of the Family Division, or

    (c)   conducted under section 83 of the Act of 1989 or section 13 of the Criminal Justice and Court Services Act 2000;

(3)   'body assessing quality assurance systems' includes –

    (a)   The Law Society,

    (b)   the Lord Chancellor in exercise of the Lord Chancellor's functions in relation to legal aid, or

    (c)   The General Council of the Bar;

(4)   'body or person responsible for investigating or determining complaints in relation to legal representatives or professional legal advisers' means –

    (a)   The Law Society,

    (b)   The General Council of the Bar,

    (c)   The Institute of Legal Executives, or

    (d)   The Legal Services Ombudsman;

(5)   'cohabitant' means one of two persons who are neither married to each other nor civil partners of each other but are living together as husband and wife or as if they were civil partners;

(6)   'criminal investigation' means an investigation conducted by police officers with a view to it being ascertained –

    (a)   whether a person should be charged with an offence, or

    (b)   whether a person charged with an offence is guilty of it;

(7)   'elected representative' means–

    (a)   a member of the House of Commons,

    (b)   a member of the National Assembly for Wales, or

    (c)   a member of the European Parliament elected in England and Wales;

(8)   'health care professional' means –

    (a)   a registered medical practitioner,

    (b)   a registered nurse or midwife,

    (c)   a clinical psychologist, or

    (d)   a child psychotherapist;

(9)   'lay adviser' means a non-professional person who gives lay advice on behalf of an organisation in the lay advice sector;

(10)   'McKenzie Friend' means any person permitted by the court to sit beside an unrepresented litigant in court to assist that litigant by prompting, taking notes and giving him advice;

(11)   'mediator' means a family mediator who is –

    (a)   undertaking, or has successfully completed, a family mediation training course approved by the United Kingdom College of Family Mediators, or

    (b)   a member of the Law Society's Family Mediation Panel;

(12)   'peer' means a member of the House of Lords as defined by the House of Lords Act 1999.

Footnotes

1. 1991 c.48, section 20 as originally enacted was substituted by the Social Security Act 1998 (c.14); and was further substituted by the Child Support, Pensions and Social Security Act 2000 (c.19); and modified by the Family Proceedings Appeals (Jurisdiction of Courts) Order 1993 S.I. 1993/961.

2. S.I. 2005/389.

3. S.I. 2005/1313.

PRACTICE DIRECTION 14F – DISCLOSING INFORMATION TO AN ADOPTED ADULT

This Practice Direction supplements FPR Part 14, rule 14.18(1)(d)

How to request for information
1.1
Rule 14.18 states that an adopted person who is over the age of 18 has the right to receive from the court which made the adoption order a copy of –

(a)   the application form for an adoption order (but not the documents attached to that form);

(b)   the adoption order and any other orders relating to the adoption proceedings; and

(c)   orders allowing any person contact with the child after the adoption order was made.

1.2
An application under rule 14.18 must be made in form A64 which is contained in the practice direction supplementing Part 5 and must have attached to it a full certified copy of the entry in the Adopted Children Register relating to the applicant.

1.3
The completed application form must be taken to the court which made the adoption order along with evidence of the applicant's identity showing a photograph and signature, such as a passport or driving licence.

Additional documents that the adopted person is also entitled to receive from the court
2.1
The adopted adult is also entitled to receive the following documents –

(a)   any transcript or written reasons of the court's decision; and

(b)   a report made to the court by –

    (i)   a children's guardian, reporting officer or children and family reporter;

    (ii)   a local authority; or

    (iii)   an adoption agency.

Before the documents are sent to the adopted adult
3.1
The court will remove protected information from documents before they are sent to the adopted adult.

PRACTICE DIRECTION 15A – PROTECTED PARTIES

This Practice Direction supplements FPR Part 15

General
1.1
A protected party must have a litigation friend to conduct proceedings on the protected party's behalf.

1.2
In the proceedings the protected party should be referred to in the title as "A.B. (by C.D. his/her litigation friend)".

Duties of the Litigation Friend
2.1
It is the duty of a litigation friend fairly and competently to conduct proceedings on behalf of a protected party. The litigation friend must have no interest in the proceedings adverse to that of the protected party and all steps and decisions the litigation friend takes in the proceedings must be taken for the benefit of the protected party.

Becoming a Litigation Friend without a court order
3.1
In order to become a litigation friend without a court order the person who wishes to act as litigation friend must –

(a)   file an official copy of the order, declaration or other document which confers the litigation friend's authority as a deputy to conduct the proceedings in the name of a protected party or on his/her behalf; or

(b)   file a certificate of suitability –

    (i)   stating that the litigation friend consents to act;

    (ii)   stating that the litigation friend knows or believes that the [applicant]/ [respondent] lacks capacity (within the meaning of the 2005 Act) to conduct proceedings;

    (iii)   stating the grounds of that belief and if the belief is based upon medical opinion attaching any relevant document to the certificate;

    (iv)   stating that the litigation friend can fairly and competently conduct proceedings on behalf of the protected party and has no interest adverse to that of the protected arty;

    (v)   undertaking to pay any costs which the protected party may be ordered to pay in relation to the proceedings, subject to any right the litigation friend may have to be repaid from the assets of the protected party; and

    (vi)   which the litigation friend has verified by a statement of truth.

3.2
Paragraph 3.1 does not apply to the Official Solicitor.

3.3
The court officer will send the certificate of suitability to the person who is the attorney of a registered enduring power of attorney, donee of a lasting power of attorney or deputy or, if there is no such person, to the person with whom the protected party resides or in whose care the protected party is.

3.4
The court officer is not required to send the documents referred to in paragraph 3.1(b)(iii) when sending the certificate of suitability to the person to be served under paragraph 3.3.

3.5
The litigation friend must file either the certificate of suitability or the authority referred to in paragraph 3.1(a) at a time when the litigation friend first takes a step in the proceedings on behalf of the protected party.

Application for a court order appointing a litigation friend
4.1
An application for a court order appointing a litigation friend should be made in accordance with Part 18 and must be supported by evidence.

4.2
The court officer must serve the application notice –
(a)   on the persons referred to in paragraph 3.3; and
(b)   on the protected party unless the court directs otherwise.

4.3
The evidence in support must satisfy the court that the proposed litigation friend –
(a)   consents to act;
(b)   can fairly and competently conduct proceedings on behalf of the protected party;
(c)   has no interest adverse to that of the protected party; and
(d)   undertakes to pay any costs which the protected party may be ordered to pay in relation to the proceedings, subject to any right the litigation friend may have to be repaid from the assets of the protected party.

4.4
Paragraph 4.3(d) does not apply to the Official Solicitor.

4.5
The proposed litigation friend may be one of the persons referred to in paragraph 3.3 where appropriate, or otherwise may be the Official Solicitor. Where it is sought to appoint the Official Solicitor, provision must be made for payment of his charges.

Change of litigation friend and prevention of person acting as litigation friend
5.1
Where an application is made for an order under rule 15.7, the application must set out the reasons for seeking it and must be supported by evidence.

5.2

Subject to paragraph 4.4, if the order sought is substitution of a new litigation friend for an existing one, the evidence must satisfy the court of the matters set out in paragraph 4.3.

5.3

The court officer will serve the application notice on –

(a)   the persons referred to in paragraph 3.3; and

(b)   the litigation friend or person purporting to act as litigation friend.

Procedure where the need for a litigation friend has come to an end

6.1

Where a person who was a protected party regains or acquires capacity (within the meaning of the 2005 Act) to conduct the proceedings, an application under rule 15.9(2) must be made for an order under rule 15.9(1) that the litigation friend's appointment has ceased.

6.2

The application must be supported by the following evidence –

(a)   a medical report or other suitably qualified expert's report indicating that the protected party has regained or acquired capacity (within the meaning of the 2005 Act) to conduct the proceedings; and

(b)   a copy of any relevant order or declaration of the Court of Protection.

PRACTICE DIRECTION 15B – ADULTS WHO MAY BE PROTECTED PARTIES AND CHILDREN WHO MAY BECOME PROTECTED PARTIES IN FAMILY PROCEEDINGS

This Practice Direction supplements FPR Part 15

What the court will do where an adult may be a protected party

Litigation Capacity

1.1

The court will investigate as soon as possible any issue as to whether an adult party or intended party to family proceedings lacks capacity (within the meaning of the Mental Capacity Act 2005) to conduct the proceedings. An adult who lacks capacity to conduct the proceedings is a protected party and must have a litigation friend to conduct the proceedings on his or her behalf. The expectation of the Official Solicitor is that the Official Solicitor will only be invited to act for the protected party as litigation friend if there is no other person suitable or willing to act.

Attention is drawn to the Checklist "Protected Parties in Family Proceedings: Checklist For the Appointment of a Litigation Friend (including the Official Solicitor)" (published in *Family Law* (January 2014)).

1.2

Any issue as to the capacity of an adult to conduct the proceedings must be determined before the court gives any directions relevant to that adult's role in the proceedings. Where a party has a solicitor, it is the solicitor who is likely to first identify that the party may lack litigation capacity. Expert evidence as to whether a party lacks such capacity is likely to be necessary for the court to make a determination relating to the party's capacity to conduct proceedings. However, there are some cases where the court may consider that evidence from a treating clinician such as a treating psychiatrist is all the evidence of lack of litigation capacity which may be necessary. There may also be cases where it will be clear that a party does not have litigation capacity such as where the party is in a coma, minimally conscious or in a persistent vegetative state. In those cases the court may well consider that a letter from a treating doctor confirming the party's condition is sufficient evidence of lack of litigation capacity and not need a report from an expert.

1.3

If at any time during the proceedings there is reason to believe that a party may lack capacity to conduct the proceedings, then the court must be notified and directions sought to ensure that this issue is investigated without delay. The presumption of capacity should not be forgotten. For example, where a person has an identified difficulty such as a learning disability or a mental illness, that difficulty should not automatically lead to an investigation about that party's capacity to litigate. Where a party has a solicitor, the starting point is whether that solicitor has concerns about the party's capacity to litigate.

Ability to give evidence as a witness
1.4

Where the court determines that a party does not have capacity to conduct the proceedings, the court may well also have to determine whether that party is able to give evidence and if so whether 'special measures' are required. Expert evidence is also likely to be necessary for the court to make such determinations. However, as in relation to the question of litigation capacity, the court may consider that evidence from a treating clinician who has a good understanding of the party's difficulties may be sufficient. If the treating clinician is provided with information about the legal framework, the clinician may be able to provide that evidence more readily and more quickly than an expert instructed to give an opinion as to the party's ability to give evidence.

1.5

Where the protected party is able to give evidence, the representative will wish to consider (and ask the expert to consider) the impact on that party of giving evidence. When making a determination as to whether that protected party should give evidence, the court may need to consider whether the impact of giving evidence would be so adverse to their condition that it would not be in that party's best interests to do so. The representative may put forward an argument on behalf of the protected party that the protected party should not give evidence.

Instruction of an expert where an adult is a protected party
2.1

Where there is concern that a party or intended party may lack capacity to conduct the proceedings, that party's representative must take the lead in any instruction of an expert for the purpose of assessment of the party's capacity to conduct the proceedings. In the event that the assessment is that the party does lack capacity to conduct the proceedings, it may be appropriate to ask that the expert advise about a party's ability to give evidence as a witness. Such expert evidence would relate to the party's particular difficulties and vulnerabilities (in particular in the context of cross-examination) including the techniques or measures which could be used to assist the party to give his or her evidence to the best of his or her ability and to ensure that the party's support needs are identified and addressed in advance of any final hearing.

Factors to be considered when the court is deciding whether to give permission as mentioned in FPR 25.4(1) or (2)
3.1

FPR 25.5 lists factors to which the court is to have particular regard when deciding whether to give permission in all family proceedings for expert evidence to be put before the court, and in children proceedings also for an expert to be instructed or for a child to be medically or psychiatrically examined or assessed for the purposes of obtaining expert evidence. In relation to children proceedings, one factor to be considered by the court is whether evidence could be given by another person on matters on which the expert would give evidence. For the avoidance of doubt this factor is not intended to suggest that evidence of another party to the proceedings is a substitute for expert evidence relating to a party's capacity to conduct the proceedings, ability to give evidence or special measures as mentioned in paragraphs 1.2, 1.4 and 2.1 above.

3.2
In addition, in children proceedings, it should be noted that expert evidence or other evidence from a treating clinician about a party's litigation capacity in previous proceedings is no substitute for such evidence in current proceedings. Litigation capacity has to be considered in relation to the proceedings before the court. For example, a parent may have been found to lack litigation capacity in care proceedings about child A three years before the current proceedings. That finding about litigation capacity in previous proceedings is not evidence that the parent lacks litigation capacity in subsequent proceedings about child B. It may be that the subsequent proceedings are simpler in terms of the issues and evidence before the court or that the parent's previous difficulty leading to lack of litigation capacity has improved.

Fluctuation in a party's capacity to conduct litigation
4.1
A party's capacity to conduct the litigation may fluctuate over the course of the proceedings. Litigation capacity may be lost or regained during the proceedings as a result of deterioration or improvement in the impairment of, or disturbance in the functioning of, the party's mind or brain. The necessity for expert evidence or evidence of a treating clinician as to a party's capacity can therefore arise at any time during the proceedings.

4.2
Fluctuation in a party's capacity to conduct litigation means that a litigation friend may not represent that party throughout the proceedings. It is expected that where the litigation friend has been appointed or reappointed, the court will be likely to make a direction in accordance with FPR 25.10(2) permitting such a litigation friend to put written questions to the expert after the 10 day period referred to in FPR 25.10(2)(c) where the 10 days referred to in that rule would be insufficient time for the litigation friend to become familiar with the case or latest developments in the case while assimilating the expert's report and formulating any questions.

Single joint experts
5.1
FPR 25.11 and 25.12 and paragraphs 2.1 to 2.7 of Practice Direction 25C and of Practice Direction 25D make provision for two or more parties to put expert evidence before the court from a single joint expert. 'Single joint expert' ('SJE') is defined by FPR 25.2(1) as a person who provides expert evidence for use in proceedings on behalf of two or more parties (including the applicant) to the proceedings. No provision of the FPR nor the Practice Directions compel the use of an SJE. Paragraph 2.1 of Practice Direction 25C and of Practice Direction 25D provide that a SJE should be used 'wherever possible'. The expectation is that expert evidence as mentioned in paragraphs 1.2, 1.4 and 2.1 above, including on whether a party lacks capacity to

conduct the proceedings, would not be evidence which is likely to be appropriately given by a SJE. However, there may be circumstances where expert evidence is needed by two or more parties relating to, for example, the capacity of a party when he or she gave consent to the making of a consent order made by the court in financial remedy proceedings and such evidence may be considered by the court to be appropriately given by a SJE. But these are circumstances where the expert evidence relates to an issue in the proceedings.

Child aged 16–17 who is the subject of the proceedings likely to lack relevant decision making capacity at age 18
6.1
Where the child who is the subject of the proceedings is aged 16 to 17 consideration should be given as to whether it is necessary to obtain expert evidence on whether that child will lack capacity (within the meaning of the Mental Capacity Act 2005) to make one or more of the decisions relevant to the proceedings (for example, in relation to residence, contact with family or about care arrangements) when that child reaches 18.

6.2
Attention is drawn to the fact that the Mental Capacity Act 2005 provides for a framework for decision making in respect of persons over 16 who lack capacity to makes decisions about their own finances, health and welfare. The Mental Capacity Act 2005 (Transfer of Proceedings) Order 2007 (SI2007/1899) includes provision for the transfer of proceedings from a court having jurisdiction under the Children Act 1989 to the Court of Protection.

Child who is not the subject of proceedings likely to lack capacity to conduct the proceedings when he or she reaches 18
7.1
Where it appears that a child is –
(a) a party to the proceedings and not the subject of them;
(b) nearing age 18; and
(c) considered likely to lack capacity to conduct the proceedings when 18,
the court will consider giving directions for the child's capacity in this respect to be investigated.

Definition of 'expert' and 'children proceedings'
8.1
The definitions of 'expert' and 'children proceedings' in FPR 25.2 (1) apply to this Practice Direction and the explanation of an expert team in paragraph 2.2 of Practice Direction 25B also applies.

PRACTICE DIRECTION 16A – REPRESENTATION OF CHILDREN

This Practice Direction supplements FPR Part 16

...

PART 3
Children's Guardian Appointed under Rule 16.3

How the children's guardian exercises duties – investigations and appointment of solicitor

6.1
The children's guardian must make such investigations as are necessary to carry out the children's guardian's duties and must, in particular –

(a)   contact or seek to interview such persons as the children's guardian thinks appropriate or as the court directs; and

(b)   obtain such professional assistance as is available which the children's guardian thinks appropriate or which the court directs be obtained.

6.2
The children's guardian must –

(a)   appoint a solicitor for the child unless a solicitor has already been appointed;

(b)   give such advice to the child as is appropriate having regard to that child's understanding; and

(c)   where appropriate instruct the solicitor representing the child on all matters relevant to the interests of the child arising in the course of proceedings, including possibilities for appeal.

6.3
Where the children's guardian is authorised in the terms mentioned by and in accordance with section 15(1) of the Criminal Justice and Court Services Act 2000 or section 37(1) of the Children Act 2004 (right of officer of the Service or Welsh family proceedings officer to conduct litigation or exercise a right of audience), paragraph 6.2(a) will not apply if the children's guardian intends to have conduct of the proceedings on behalf of the child unless –

(a)   the child wishes to instruct a solicitor direct; and

(b)   the children's guardian or the court considers that the child is of sufficient understanding to do so.

6.4
Where rule 16.21 (Where the child instructs a solicitor or conducts proceedings on the child's own behalf) applies, the duties set out in paragraph 6.2(a) and (c) do not apply.

How the children's guardian exercises duties – attendance at court, advice to the court and reports

6.5

The children's guardian or the solicitor appointed under section 41(3) of the 1989 Act or in accordance with paragraph 6.2(a) must attend all directions hearings unless the court directs otherwise.

6.6

The children's guardian must advise the court on the following matters –

(a)   whether the child is of sufficient understanding for any purpose including the child's refusal to submit to a medical or psychiatric examination or other assessment that the court has the power to require, direct or order;

(b)   the wishes of the child in respect of any matter relevant to the proceedings including that child's attendance at court;

(c)   the appropriate forum for the proceedings;

(d)   the appropriate timing of the proceedings or any part of them;

(e)   the options available to it in respect of the child and the suitability of each such option including what order should be made in determining the application; and

(f)   any other matter on which the court seeks advice or on which the children's guardian considers that the court should be informed.

6.7

The advice given under paragraph 6.6 may, subject to any direction of the court, be given orally or in writing. If the advice is given orally, a note of it must be taken by the court or the court officer.

6.8

The children's guardian must –

(a)   unless the court directs otherwise, file a written report advising on the interests of the child in accordance with the timetable set by the court; and

(b)   in proceedings to which Part 14 applies, where practicable, notify any person the joining of whom as a party to those proceedings would be likely, in the opinion of the children's guardian, to safeguard the interests of the child, of the court's power to join that person as a party under rule 14.3 and must inform the court –

    (i)   of any notification;

    (ii)   of anyone whom the children's guardian attempted to notify under this paragraph but was unable to contact; and

    (iii)   of anyone whom the children's guardian believes may wish to be joined to the proceedings.

(Part 18 sets out the procedure for making an application to be joined as a party in proceedings.)

How the children's guardian exercises duties – service of documents and inspection of records

6.9

The children's guardian must serve and accept service of documents on behalf of the child in accordance with rule 6.31 and, where the child has not himself been served and has sufficient understanding, advise the child of the contents of any document so served.

6.10

Where the children's guardian inspects records of the kinds referred to in –

(a)   section 42 of the 1989 Act (right to have access to local authority records); or

(b)   section 103 of the 2002 Act (right to have access to adoption agency records)

the children's guardian must bring all records and documents which may, in the opinion of the children's guardian, assist in the proper determination of the proceedings to the attention of –

(i)   the court; and

(ii)   unless the court directs otherwise, the other parties to the proceedings.

How the children's guardian exercises duties – communication of a court's decision to the child

6.11

The children's guardian must ensure that, in relation to a decision made by the court in the proceedings –

(a)   if the children's guardian considers it appropriate to the age and understanding of the child, the child is notified of that decision; and

(b)   if the child is notified of the decision, it is explained to the child in a manner appropriate to that child's age and understanding.

PART 4
Appointment of Children's Guardian under Rule 16.4

Section 1 – When a child should be made a party to proceedings

7.1

Making the child a party to the proceedings is a step that will be taken only in cases which involve an issue of significant difficulty and consequently will occur in only a minority of cases. Before taking the decision to make the child a party, consideration should be given to whether an alternative route might be preferable, such as asking an officer of the Service or a Welsh family proceedings officer to carry out further work or by making a referral to social services or, possibly, by obtaining expert evidence.

7.2

The decision to make the child a party will always be exclusively that of the court, made in the light of the facts and circumstances of the particular case. The following are offered, solely by way of guidance, as circumstances which may justify the making of such an order –

(a)   where an officer of the Service or Welsh family proceedings officer has notified the court that in the opinion of that officer the child should be made a party;

(b)   where the child has a standpoint or interest which is inconsistent with or incapable of being represented by any of the adult parties;

(c)   where there is an intractable dispute over residence or contact, including where all contact has ceased, or where there is irrational but implacable hostility to contact or where the child may be suffering harm associated with the contact dispute;

(d)   where the views and wishes of the child cannot be adequately met by a report to the court;

(e)   where an older child is opposing a proposed course of action;

(f)   where there are complex medical or mental health issues to be determined or there are other unusually complex issues that necessitate separate representation of the child;

(g)   where there are international complications outside child abduction, in particular where it may be necessary for there to be discussions with overseas authorities or a foreign court;

(h)   where there are serious allegations of physical, sexual or other abuse in relation to the child or there are allegations of domestic violence not capable of being resolved with the help of an officer of the Service or Welsh family proceedings officer;

(i)   where the proceedings concern more than one child and the welfare of the children is in conflict or one child is in a particularly disadvantaged position;

(j)   where there is a contested issue about scientific testing.

7.3

It must be recognised that separate representation of the child may result in a delay in the resolution of the proceedings. When deciding whether to direct that a child be made a party, the court will take into account the risk of delay or other facts adverse to the welfare of the child. The court's primary consideration will be the best interests of the child.

7.4

When a child is made a party and a children's guardian is to be appointed –

(a)   Consideration should first be given to appointing an officer of the Service or Welsh family proceedings officer. Before appointing an officer, the court will cause preliminary enquiries to be made of Cafcass or CAFCASS CYMRU. For the relevant procedure, reference should be made to the practice note issued by Cafcass in June 2006 and any modifications of that practice note.

(b)   If Cafcass or CAFCASS CYMRU is unable to provide a children's guardian without delay, or if for some other reason the appointment of an officer of the Service of Welsh family proceedings officer is not appropriate, rule 16.24 makes further provision for the appointment of a children's guardian.

Section 2 – Children's guardian appointed under rule 16.4
Duties of the children's guardian
7.6
It is the duty of a children's guardian fairly and competently to conduct proceedings on behalf of the child. The children's guardian must have no interest in the proceedings adverse to that of the child and all steps and decisions the children's guardian takes in the proceedings must be taken for the benefit of the child.

7.7
A children's guardian who is an officer of the Service or a Welsh family proceedings officer has, in addition, the duties set out in Part 3 of this Practice Direction and must exercise those duties as set out in that Part.

Becoming a children's guardian without a court order
7.8
In order to become a children's guardian without a court order the person who wishes to act as children's guardian must file a certificate of suitability –
(a)   stating that the children's guardian consents to act;
(b)   stating that the children's guardian knows or believes that the [applicant]/ [respondent] is a child to whom rule 16.4 and Chapter 7 of Part 16 apply;
(c)   stating that the children's guardian can fairly and competently conduct proceedings on behalf of the child and has no interest adverse to that of the child;
(d)   undertaking to pay any costs which the child may be ordered to pay in relation to the proceedings, subject to any right the children's guardian may have to be repaid from the assets of the child; and
(e)   which the children's guardian has verified by a statement of truth.

7.9
Paragraph 7.8 does not apply to the Official Solicitor, an officer of the Service or a Welsh family proceedings officer.

7.10
The court officer will send the certificate of suitability to one of the child's parents or guardians or, if there is no parent or guardian, to the person with whom the child resides or in whose care the child is.

7.11
The children's guardian must file either the certificate of suitability at a time when the children's guardian first takes a step in the proceedings on behalf of the child.

Application for a court order appointing a children's guardian
7.12
An application for a court order appointing a children's guardian should be made in accordance with Part 18 and must be supported by evidence.

7.13

The court officer must serve the application notice on the persons referred to in paragraph 7.10.

7.14

The evidence in support must satisfy the court that the proposed children's guardian –

(a)   consents to act;

(b)   can fairly and competently conduct proceedings on behalf of the child;

(c)   has no interest adverse to that of the child; and

(d)   undertakes to pay any costs which the child may be ordered to pay in relation to the proceedings, subject to any right the children's guardian may have to be repaid from the assets of the child.

7.15

Paragraph 7.14 does not apply to the Official Solicitor, an officer of the Service of a Welsh family proceedings officer.

7.16

The proposed children's guardian may be one of the persons referred to in paragraph 7.10 where appropriate, or otherwise may be the Official Solicitor, an officer of the Service or a Welsh family proceedings officer. Where it is sought to appoint the Official Solicitor, an officer of the Service or a Welsh family proceedings officer, provision should be made for payment of that person's charges.

Change of children's guardian and prevention of person acting as children's guardian

7.17

Where an application is made for an order under rule 16.25, the application must set out the reasons for seeking it and must be supported by evidence.

7.18

Subject to paragraph 7.15, if the order sought is substitution of a new children's guardian for an existing one, the evidence must satisfy the court of the matters set out in paragraph 7.14.

7.19

The court officer will serve the application notice on –

(a)   the persons referred to in paragraph 7.10; and

(b)   the children's guardian or person purporting to act as children's guardian.

…

PRACTICE DIRECTION 17A – STATEMENTS OF TRUTH

This Practice Direction supplements FPR Part 17

Documents to be verified by a statement of truth
1.1
Rule 17.2 sets out the documents which must be verified by a statement of truth.

1.2
If an applicant wishes to rely on matters set out in his application notice as evidence, the application notice must be verified by a statement of truth.

1.3
An expert's report should also be verified by a statement of truth. For the form of the statement of truth verifying an expert's report (which differs from that set out below), see paragraph 9.1(j) of Practice Direction 25B (The Duties Of An Expert, The Expert's Report and Arrangements For An Expert To Attend Court).

1.4
In addition, the following documents must be verified by a statement of truth –
(a)   an application notice for –
    (i)   a third party debt order (CPR Part 72 as modified by rule 33.24);
    (ii)   a hardship payment order (CPR Part 72 as modified by rule 33.24); or
    (iii)   a charging order (CPR Part 73 as modified by rule 33.25); and
(b)   a notice of objections to an account being taken by the court, unless verified by an affidavit or witness statement.

1.5
The statement of truth may be contained in the document it verifies or it may be in a separate document served subsequently, in which case it must identify the document to which it relates.

1.6
Where the form to be used includes a jurat for the content to be verified by an affidavit, then a statement of truth is not required in addition.

1.7
In this Practice Direction, 'statement of case' has the meaning given to it by rule 17.1.

Form of the statement of truth
2.1
The form of the statement of truth verifying a statement of case or an application notice should be as follows:
'[I believe] [the *(applicant or as may be)* believes] that the facts stated in this *[name document being verified]* are true.'

2.2

The form of the statement of truth verifying a witness statement should be as follows:
'I believe that the facts stated in this witness statement are true.'

2.3

Where the statement of truth is contained in a separate document, the document containing the statement of truth must be headed with the title of and court reference for the proceedings. The document being verified should be identified in the statement of truth as follows –

(a)   application form: 'the application form issued on [*date*]';

(b)   statement of case: 'the (application or answer as may be) served on [*name of party*] on [*date*]';

(c)   application notice: 'the application notice issued on [*date*] for [*set out the remedy sought*]';

(d)   witness statement: 'the witness statement filed on [*date*] or served on [*party*] on [*date*]'.

Who may sign the statement of truth

3.1

In a statement of case or an application notice, the statement of truth must be signed by –

(a)   the party or his litigation friend; or

(b)   the legal representative of the party or litigation friend.

3.2

A statement of truth verifying a witness statement must be signed by the witness.

3.3

A statement of truth verifying a notice of objections to an account must be signed by the objecting party or his or her legal representative.

3.4

Where a document is to be verified on behalf of a company or corporation, subject to paragraph 3.7 below, the statement of truth must be signed by a person holding a senior position in the company or corporation. That person must state the office or position he or she holds.

3.5

Each of the following persons is a person holding a senior position –

(a)   in respect of a registered company or corporation, a director, the treasurer, secretary, chief executive, manager or other officer of the company or corporation; and

(b)   in respect of a corporation which is not a registered company, in addition to those persons set out in (a), the major, chairman, president, chief executive of a local authority or town clerk or other similar officer of the corporation.

3.6

Where the document is to be verified on behalf of a partnership, those who may sign the statement of truth are –

(a)   any of the partners; or

(b)   a person having the management or control of the partnership business.

3.7

Where a party is legally represented, the legal representative may sign the statement of truth on his or her behalf. The statement signed by the legal representative will refer to the client's belief, not his or her own. In signing he or she must state the capacity in which he or she signs and the name of his or her firm where appropriate.

3.8

Where a legal representative has signed a statement of truth, his or her signature will be taken by the court as his or her statement –

(a)   that the client on whose behalf he or she has signed had authorised him or her to do so;

(b)   that before signing he or she had explained to the client that in signing the statement of truth he or she would be confirming the client's belief that the facts stated in the document were true; and

(c)   that before signing he or she had informed the client of the possible consequences to the client if it should subsequently appear that the client did not have an honest belief in the truth of those facts (see rule 17.6).

3.9

A legal representative who signs a statement of truth must print his or her full name clearly beneath his or her signature.

3.10

The individual who signs a statement of truth must sign in his or her own name and not that of his or her firm or employer.

3.11

The following are examples of the possible application of this practice direction describing who may sign a statement of truth verifying statements in documents other than a witness statement. These are only examples and not an indication of how a court might apply the practice direction to a specific situation.

Managing Agent

An agent who manages property or investments for the party cannot sign a statement of truth. It must be signed by the party or by the legal representative of the party.

Trusts

Where some or all of the trustees comprise a single party one, some or all of the trustees comprising the party may sign a statement of truth. The legal representative of the trustees may sign it.

Companies

Paragraphs 3.4 and 3.5 apply. The word 'manager' will be construed in the context of the phrase 'a person holding a senior position' which it is used to define. The court will consider the size of the company and the importance and nature of the proceedings. It would expect the manager signing the statement of truth to have personal knowledge of the content of the document or to be responsible for those who have that knowledge of the content. A small company may not have a manager, apart from the directors, who holds a senior position. A large company will have many such managers. In a large company with specialist claims, insurance or legal departments the statement may be signed by the manager of such a department if he or she is responsible for handling the claim or managing the staff handling it.

Inability of persons to read or sign documents to be verified by a statement of truth

4.1

Where a document containing a statement of truth is to be signed by a person who is unable to read or sign the document, it must contain a certificate made by an authorised person.

4.2

An authorised person is a person able to administer oaths and take affidavits but need not be independent of the parties or their representatives.

4.3

The authorised person must certify –

(a)   that the document has been read to the person signing it;

(b)   that the person appeared to understand it and approved its content as accurate;

(c)   that the declaration of truth has been read to that person;

(d)   that that person appeared to understand the declaration and the consequences of making a false declaration; and

(e)   that that person signed or made his mark in the presence of the authorised person.

4.4

The form of the certificate is set out at the Annex to this Practice Direction.

Consequences of failure to verify

5.1

If a statement of case is not verified by a statement of truth, the statement of case will remain effective unless it is struck out, but a party may not rely on the contents of a statement of case as evidence until it has been verified by a statement of truth.

5.2

Any party may apply to the court for an order that unless within such period as the court may specify the statement of case is verified by the service of a statement of truth, the statement of case will be struck out.

5.3

The usual order for the costs of an application referred to in paragraph 5.2 will be that the costs be paid by the party who had failed to verify, in any event and immediately.

Penalty

6.

Attention is drawn to rule 17.6 which sets out the consequences of verifying a statement of case containing a false statement without an honest belief in its truth, and to the procedures set out in Chapter 5 of Part 37 and in paragraphs 4.1 to 4.7 of Practice Direction 37A (Applications and proceedings in relation to contempt of court).

Annex

Certificate to be used where a person is unable to read or sign a document to be verified by a statement of truth

I certify that I [name and address of authorised person] have read the contents of this document and the declaration of truth to the person signing the document [if there are exhibits, add 'and explained the nature and effect of the exhibits referred to in it'] who appeared to understand (a) the document and approved its content as accurate and (b) the declaration of truth and the consequences of making a false declaration, and made his or her mark in my presence.

PRACTICE DIRECTION 21A – DISCLOSURE AND INSPECTION

This Practice Direction supplements FPR Part 21

CHAPTER 1
Orders for Disclosure and Inspection of Documents

Interpretation
1.1
A party discloses a document by stating that the document exists or has existed. Inspection occurs when a party is permitted to inspect a document disclosed by another party.

1.2
For the purposes of disclosure and inspection in family proceedings –
> 'document' means anything in which information of any description is recorded and any copy of a document which contains a modification, obliteration or other marking or feature shall be treated as a separate document; and
> 'copy', in relation to a document, means anything on which information recorded in the document has been copied, by whatever means and whether directly or indirectly.

Types of order for disclosure in family proceedings
2.1
In family proceedings other than proceedings for a financial remedy, where the court orders disclosure, the normal order will be for disclosure by each party setting out, in a list or questionnaire, the documents material to the proceedings, of the existence of which that party is aware and which are or have been in that party's control. This process is known as 'standard disclosure'.

2.2
In proceedings for a financial remedy, the process of disclosure is staged. First, Form E (the financial statement referred to in rule 9.14(1)) is served together with the documents which are required to be attached to it. The second stage occurs by the parties requesting (further) disclosure of each other by a questionnaire served before the first appointment; the questionnaire can request both information and documents. With the court's permission, a further questionnaire can be served later in the proceedings.

2.3
In matrimonial and civil partnership proceedings, under rule 7.15, the court – either on its own initiative or on the application of the other party – may order a party to clarify any matter which is in dispute in the proceedings or give additional information

in relation to any such matter, whether or not the matter is contained in or referred to in the application or in the answer.

2.4

In any family proceedings, the court may order 'specific disclosure', which is an order that a party must –

(a)   disclose documents or classes of documents specified in the order;

(b)   carry out a search to the extent stated in the order; or

(c)   disclose any documents located as a result of that search.

PRACTICE DIRECTION 25D – FINANCIAL REMEDY PROCEEDINGS AND OTHER FAMILY PROCEEDINGS (EXCEPT CHILDREN PROCEEDINGS) – THE USE OF SINGLE JOINT EXPERTS AND THE PROCESS LEADING TO EXPERT EVIDENCE BEING PUT BEFORE THE COURT

This Practice Direction supplements FPR Part 25

Scope of this Practice Direction

1.1

This Practice Direction applies to financial remedy proceedings and other family proceedings except children proceedings and contains guidance on –

(a)   the use of single joint experts;

(b)   how to prepare for the hearing at which the court will consider whether to give permission for putting expert evidence (in any form) before the court including –

    (i)   preliminary enquiries of experts;

    (ii)   information to be given to the court before the hearing;

(c)   the letter of instruction to the expert.

Single joint experts

2.1

FPR 25.4 applies to a single joint expert ('SJE') in addition to an expert instructed by one party. This means that the court's permission is required to put expert evidence from an SJE (in any form) before the court. However, in family proceedings (except children proceedings) there is no requirement for the court's permission to be obtained before instructing an expert. Wherever possible, expert evidence should be obtained from a single joint expert instructed by both or all the parties ('SJE'). To that end, a party wishing to instruct an expert should first give the other party or parties a list of the names of one or more experts in the relevant speciality whom they consider suitable to be instructed.

2.2

Within 10 business days after receipt of the list of proposed experts, the other party or parties should indicate any objection to one or more of the named experts and, if so, supply the name(s) of one or more experts whom they consider suitable.

2.3

Each party should disclose whether they have already consulted any of the proposed experts about the issue(s) in question.

2.4

Where the parties cannot agree on the identity of the expert, each party should think carefully before instructing their own expert and seeking the permission of the court to put that expert evidence before it because of the costs implications. Disagreements about the use and identity of an expert may be better managed by the court in the context of an application for the court's permission to put the expert evidence before the court and for directions for the use of an SJE (see paragraph 2.6 below).

Agreement to instruct separate experts
2.5
If the parties agree to instruct separate experts and to seek the permission of the court to put the separate expert evidence before it –
(a)   they should agree in advance that the reports will be disclosed; and
(b)   the instructions to each expert should comply, so far as appropriate, with paragraphs 4.1 and 6.1 below *(Letter of instruction)*.

Agreement to instruct an SJE
2.6
If there is agreement to instruct an SJE, before applying to the court for permission to put the expert evidence before it and directions for the use of an SJE, the parties should –
(a)   so far as appropriate, comply with the guidance in paragraphs 3.3 (Preliminary enquiries of the expert) and paragraphs 3.11 and 3.12 below;
(b)   receive the expert's confirmation in response to preliminary enquiries referred to in paragraph 8.1 of Practice Direction 25B;
(c)   have agreed in what proportion the SJE's fee is to be shared between them (at least in the first instance) and when it is to be paid; and
(d)   if applicable, have obtained agreement for public funding.

2.7
The instructions to the SJE should comply, so far as appropriate, with paragraphs 4.1 and 6.1 below *(Letter of instruction)*.

The test for permission and preparation for the permission hearing
3.1
The test in FPR 25.4(3) which the court is to apply to determine whether permission should be given for expert evidence to be put before the court has been altered from one which refers to expert evidence being restricted by the court to that which is reasonably required to resolve the proceedings to one which refers to the expert evidence being in the opinion of the court necessary to assist the court to resolve the proceedings. The overriding objective of the FPR, which is to enable the court to deal with cases justly, having regard to any welfare issues involved, continues to apply when the court is making the decision whether to give permission. In addition, the rules (FPR 25.5(2)) now tell the court what factors it is to have particular regard to when deciding whether to give permission.

3.2
Paragraphs 3.3 to 3.12 below give guidance on how to prepare for the hearing at which the court will apply the test in FPR 25.4(3) and the factors in FPR 25.5(2) and decide whether to give permission for expert evidence to be put before the court. The purpose

of the preparation is to ensure that the court has the information required to enable it to exercise its powers under FPR 25.4(2) and 25.5(2) in line with FPR 25.4(3).

Preliminary enquiries of the expert
3.3

In good time for the information requested to be available for the hearing at which the court will consider whether to give permission for expert evidence to be put before the court, the party or parties intending to instruct the expert shall approach the expert with the following information –

(a) the nature of the proceedings and the issues likely to require determination by the court;

(b) the issues in the proceedings to which the expert evidence is to relate;

(c) the questions about which the expert is to be asked to give an opinion and which relate to the issues in the case;

(d) whether permission is to be asked of the court for the use of another expert in the same or any related field (that is, to give an opinion on the same or related questions);

(e) the volume of reading which the expert will need to undertake;

(f) whether or not it will be necessary for the expert to conduct interviews and, if so, with whom;

(g) the likely timetable of legal steps;

(h) when the expert's report is likely to be required;

(i) whether and, if so, what date has been fixed by the court for any hearing at which the expert may be required to give evidence (in particular the Final Hearing); and whether it may be possible for the expert to give evidence by telephone conference or video link: see paragraphs 10.1 and 10.2 *(Arrangements for experts to give evidence)* of Practice Direction 25B;

(j) the possibility of making, through their instructing solicitors, representations to the court about being named or otherwise identified in any public judgment given by the court;

(k) whether the instructing party has public funding and the legal aid rates of payment which are applicable.

Expert's response to preliminary enquiries
3.4

In good time for the hearing at which the court will consider whether to give permission for expert evidence to be put before the court, the solicitors or party intending to instruct the expert must obtain the confirmations from the expert referred to in paragraph 8.1 of Practice Direction 25B. These confirmations include that the work is within the expert's expertise, the expert is available to do the work within the relevant timescale and the expert's costs.

3.5

Where parties cannot agree who should be the single joint expert before the hearing at which the court will consider whether to give permission for expert evidence to be put before the court, they should obtain the above confirmations in respect of all experts whom they intend to put to the court for the purposes of rule 25.11(2)(a) as candidates for the appointment.

The application for the court's permission to put expert evidence before the court
Timing and oral applications for the court's permission
3.6
An application for the court's permission to put expert evidence before the court should be made as soon as it becomes apparent that it is necessary to make it. FPR 25.6 makes provision about the time by which applications for the court's permission should be made.

3.7
Applications should, wherever possible, be made so that they are considered at any directions hearing or other hearing for which a date has been fixed or for which a date is about to be fixed. It should be noted that one application notice can be used by a party to make more than one application for an order or direction at a hearing held during the course of proceedings. An application for the court's permission to put expert evidence before the court may therefore be included in an application notice requesting other orders to be made at such a hearing.

3.8
Where a date for a hearing has been fixed, a party who wishes to make an application at that hearing but does not have sufficient time to file an application notice should as soon as possible inform the court (if possible in writing) and, if possible, the other parties of the nature of the application and the reason for it. The party should provide the court and the other party with as much as possible of the information referred to in FPR 25.7 and paragraph 3.11 below. That party should then make the application orally at the hearing. An oral application of this kind should be the exception and reserved for genuine cases where circumstances are such that it has only become apparent shortly before the hearing that an expert opinion is necessary.

3.9
In financial remedy proceedings, unless the court directs otherwise, parties must apply for permission to put expert evidence before the court as soon as possible and no later than the first appointment. The expectation is that the court will give directions extending the time by which permission should be obtained where there is good reason for parties to delay the decision whether to use expert evidence and make an application for the court's permission.

3.10
Examples of situations where the time for requesting permission to put expert evidence before the court is likely to be extended are where –
(a) a decision about the need for expert evidence cannot be made until replies to questionnaires in relation to Forms E have been fully considered; or

(b)   valuations of property are agreed for the purposes of the Financial Dispute Resolution appointment but no agreement is reached to resolve the proceedings at that appointment and the court cannot make a consent order as mentioned in FPR 9.17(8). In these circumstances, it may become clear to a party that he or she will want to use expert valuations of property and an application for the court's permission for such valuation to be put before it may be made orally at the end of the appointment to avoid the need for a separate hearing about this issue. As with other oral applications, the party should provide the court and the other party with as much as possible of the information referred to in FPR 25.7 and paragraph 3.11 below. FPR 9.17(9) requires the court to give directions for the future course of the proceedings where it has not made a consent order including, where appropriate, the filing of evidence.

The application

3.11

In addition to the matters specified in FPR 25.7(2)(a), an application for the court's permission to put expert evidence before the court must state –

(a)   the discipline, qualifications and expertise of the expert (by way of C.V. where possible);

(b)   the expert's availability to undertake the work;

(c)   the timetable for the report;

(d)   the responsibility for instruction;

(e)   whether the expert evidence can properly be obtained by only one party;

(f)   why the expert evidence proposed cannot properly be given by an expert already instructed in the proceedings;

(g)   the likely cost of the report on an hourly or other charging basis:

(h)   the proposed apportionment (at least in the first instance) of any jointly instructed expert's fee; when it is to be paid; and, if applicable, whether public funding has been approved.

The draft order to be attached to the application for the court's permission

3.12

FPR 25.7(2)(b) provides that a draft of the order giving the court's permission to put expert evidence before the court is to be attached to the application for the court's permission. That draft order must set out the following matters –

(a)   the issues in the proceedings to which the expert evidence is to relate;

(b)   the party who is to be responsible for drafting the letter of instruction and providing the documents to the expert;

(c)   the timetable within which the report is to be prepared, filed and served;

(d)   the disclosure of the report to the parties and to any other expert;

(e)   the organisation of, preparation for and conduct of any experts' discussion (see Practice Direction 25E – Discussions between Experts in Family Proceedings);

(f)   the preparation of a statement of agreement and disagreement by the experts following an experts' discussion;

(g)   making available to the court at an early opportunity the expert reports in electronic form;

(h)   the attendance of the expert at court to give oral evidence (alternatively, the expert giving his or her evidence in writing or remotely by video link), whether at or for the Final Hearing or another hearing; unless agreement about the opinions given by the expert is reached by a date specified by the court prior to the hearing at which the expert is to give oral evidence.

Letter of instruction

4.1

The party responsible for instructing the expert shall, within 5 business days after the permission hearing, prepare (in agreement with the other parties where appropriate), file and serve a letter of instruction to the expert which shall –

(a)   set out the context in which the expert's opinion is sought (including any ethnic, cultural, religious or linguistic contexts);

(b)   set out the questions which the expert is required to answer and ensuring that they –

    (i)   are within the ambit of the expert's area of expertise;

    (ii)   do not contain unnecessary or irrelevant detail;

    (iii)   are kept to a manageable number and are clear, focused and direct; and

    (iv)   reflect what the expert has been requested to do by the court;

(c)   list the documentation provided, or provide for the expert an indexed and paginated bundle which shall include –

    (i)   an agreed list of essential reading; and

    (ii)   a copy of this Practice Direction and Practice Directions 25B, 25E and where appropriate Practice Direction 15B;

(d)   identify any materials provided to the expert which have not been produced either as original medical (or other professional) records or in response to an instruction from a party, and state the source of that material (such materials may contain an assumption as to the standard of proof, the admissibility or otherwise of hearsay evidence, and other important procedural and substantive questions relating to the different purposes of other enquiries);

(e)   identify all requests to third parties for disclosure and their responses in order to avoid partial disclosure, which tends only to prove a case rather than give full and frank information;

(f)   identify the relevant people concerned with the proceedings and inform the expert of his or her right to talk to them provided that an accurate record is made of the discussions;

(g)   identify any other expert instructed in the proceedings and advise the expert of their right to talk to the other experts provided that an accurate record is made of the discussions;

(h)   subject to any public funding requirement for prior authority, define the contractual basis upon which the expert is retained and in particular the funding mechanism including how much the expert will be paid (an hourly rate and overall estimate should already have been obtained), when the expert will be paid, and what limitation there might be on the amount the expert can charge for the work which they will have to do. In cases where the parties are publicly funded, there may also be a brief explanation of the costs and expenses excluded from public funding by Funding Code criterion 1.3 and the detailed assessment process.

Adult who is a protected party
5.1

Where the adult is a protected party, that party's representative shall be involved in any instruction of an expert, including the instruction of an expert to assess whether the adult, although a protected party, is competent to give evidence *(see Practice Direction 15B – Adults Who May Be Protected Parties and Children Who May Become Protected Parties in Family Proceedings)*.

Asking the court to settle the letter of instruction to a single joint expert
6.1

Where possible, the written request for the court to consider the letter of instruction referred to in rule 25.12(2) should be set out in an e-mail to the court and copied by e-mail to the other instructing parties. The request should be sent to the relevant court or (by prior arrangement only) directly to the judge dealing with the proceedings. Where a legal adviser has been appointed as the case manager, the request should also be sent to the appointed legal adviser. The court will settle the letter of instruction, usually without a hearing to avoid delay; and will send (where practicable, by e-mail) the settled letter to the party responsible for instructing the expert for transmission forthwith to the expert, and copy it to the other instructing parties for information.

PRACTICE DIRECTION 27A – FAMILY PROCEEDINGS: COURT BUNDLES (UNIVERSAL PRACTICE TO BE APPLIED IN THE HIGH COURT AND FAMILY COURT)

This Practice Direction supplements FPR Part 27

1.1
The President of the Family Division has issued this practice direction to achieve consistency across the country in the Family Court and the Family Division of the High Court in the preparation of court bundles and in respect of other related matters.

Application of the practice direction
2.1
Except as specified in paragraph 2.4, and subject to specific directions given in any particular case, the following practice applies to –
(a)   all hearings before a judge sitting in the Family Division of the High Court wherever the court may be sitting; and
(b)   all hearings in the Family Court.

2.2
'Hearing' includes all appearances before the court, whether with or without notice to other parties and whether for directions or for substantive relief.

2.3
This practice direction applies whether a bundle is being lodged for the first time or is being re-lodged for a further hearing (see paragraph 9.2).

2.4
This practice direction does not apply to the hearing of any urgent application if and to the extent that it is impossible to comply with it.

Responsibility for the preparation of the bundle
3.1
A bundle for the use of the court at the hearing shall be provided by the party in the position of applicant at the hearing (or, if there are cross-applications, by the party whose application was first in time) or, if that person is a litigant in person, by the first listed respondent who is not a litigant in person. Where all the parties are litigants in person none of them shall, unless the court otherwise directs, be obliged to provide a bundle, but any bundle which they choose to lodge must be prepared and lodged so as to comply with this practice direction.

3.2
The party preparing the bundle shall paginate it using Arabic numbering throughout. If possible the contents of the bundle shall be agreed by all parties.

Contents of the bundle

4.1

The bundle shall contain copies of only those documents which are relevant to the hearing and which it is necessary for the court to read or which will actually be referred to during the hearing. In particular, copies of the following classes of documents must not be included in the bundle unless specifically directed by the court –

(a)   correspondence (including letters of instruction to experts);

(b)   medical records (including hospital, GP and health visitor records);

(c)   bank and credit card statements and other financial records;

(d)   notes of contact visits;

(e)   foster carer logs;

(f)   social services files (with the exception of any assessment being relied on by any of the parties);

(g)   police disclosure.

This does not prevent the inclusion in the bundle of specific documents which it is necessary for the court to read or which will actually be referred to during the hearing.

4.2

The documents in the bundle shall be arranged in chronological order from the front of the bundle, paginated individually and consecutively (starting with page 1 and using Arabic numbering throughout), indexed and divided into separate sections (each section being separately paginated) as follows –

(a)   preliminary documents (see paragraph 4.3) and any other case management documents required by any other practice direction;

(b)   applications and orders;

(c)   statements and affidavits (which must be dated in the top right corner of the front page) but without exhibiting or duplicating documents referred to in para 4.1;

(d)   care plans (where appropriate);

(e)   experts' reports and other reports (including those of a guardian, children's guardian or litigation friend); and

(f)   other documents, divided into further sections as may be appropriate.

All statements, affidavits, care plans, experts' reports and other reports included in the bundle must be copies of originals which have been signed and dated.

4.3

At the commencement of the bundle there shall be inserted the following documents (the preliminary documents) –

(a)   an up to date case summary of the background to the hearing confined to those matters which are relevant to the hearing and the management of the case and limited, if practicable, to four A4 pages;

(b)   a statement of the issue or issues to be determined (1) at that hearing and (2) at the final hearing;

(c)   a position statement by each party including a summary of the order or directions sought by that party (1) at that hearing and (2) at the final hearing;

(d)   an up to date chronology, if it is a final hearing or if the summary under (i) is insufficient;

(e)   skeleton arguments, if appropriate;

(f)   a list of essential reading for that hearing; and

(g)   the time estimate (see paragraph 10.1).

Copies of all authorities relied on must be contained in a separate composite bundle agreed between the advocates.

4.4

Each of the preliminary documents shall be as short and succinct as possible and shall state on the front page immediately below the heading the date when it was prepared and the date of the hearing for which it was prepared. Where proceedings relating to a child are being heard by magistrates the summary of the background shall be prepared in anonymised form, omitting the names and identifying information of every person referred to other than the parties' legal representatives, and stating the number of pages contained in the bundle. Identifying information can be contained in all other preliminary documents.

4.5

The summary of the background, statement of issues, chronology, position statement and any skeleton arguments shall be cross-referenced to the relevant pages of the bundle.

4.6

The summary of the background, statement of issues, chronology and reading list shall in the case of a final hearing, and shall so far as practicable in the case of any other hearing, each consist of a single document in a form agreed by all parties. Where the parties disagree as to the content the fact of their disagreement and their differing contentions shall be set out at the appropriate places in the document.

4.7

Where the nature of the hearing is such that a complete bundle of all documents is unnecessary, the bundle (which need not be repaginated) may comprise only those documents necessary for the hearing, but –

(a)   the summary of the background must commence with a statement that the bundle is limited or incomplete; and

(b)   the bundle shall if reasonably practicable be in a form agreed by all parties.

4.8

Where the bundle is re-lodged in accordance with paragraph 9.2, before it is re-lodged –

(a)   the bundle shall be updated as appropriate; and

(b)   all superseded documents (and in particular all outdated summaries, statements of issues, chronologies, skeleton arguments and similar documents) shall be removed from the bundle.

Format of the bundle
5.1
Unless the court has specifically directed otherwise, being satisfied that such direction is necessary to enable the proceedings to be disposed of justly, the bundle shall be contained in one A4 size ring binder or lever arch file limited to no more than 350 sheets of A4 paper and 350 sides of text.

5.2
All documents in the bundle shall (a) be copied on one side of paper only, unless the court has specifically directed otherwise, and (b) be typed or printed in a font no smaller than 12 point and with 1½ or double spacing.

5.3
The ring binder or lever arch file shall have clearly marked on the front and the spine –
(a)   the title and number of the case;
(b)   the place where the case has been listed;
(c)   the hearing date and time;
(d)   if known, the name of the judge hearing the case; and
(e)   where in accordance with a direction of the court there is more than one ring binder or lever arch file, a distinguishing letter (A, B, C etc).

Timetable for preparing and lodging the bundle
6.1
The party preparing the bundle shall, whether or not the bundle has been agreed, provide a paginated index to all other parties not less than 4 working days before the hearing.

6.2
Where counsel is to be instructed at any hearing, a paginated bundle shall (if not already in counsel's possession) be delivered to counsel by the person instructing that counsel not less than 3 working days before the hearing.

6.3
The bundle (with the exception of the preliminary documents if and insofar as they are not then available) shall be lodged with the court not less than 2 working days before the hearing, or at such other time as may be specified by the court.

6.4
The preliminary documents shall be lodged with the court no later than 11 am on the day before the hearing and, where the hearing is before a judge of the High Court and the name of the judge is known, shall (with the exception of the authorities, which are to be lodged in hard copy and not sent by email) at the same time be sent by email to the judge's clerk.

Lodging the bundle

7.1

The bundle shall be lodged at the appropriate office. If the bundle is lodged in the wrong place the court may –

(a)   treat the bundle as having not been lodged; and

(b)   take the steps referred to in paragraph 12.

7.2

Unless the court has given some other direction as to where the bundle in any particular case is to be lodged (for example a direction that the bundle is to be lodged with the judge's clerk) the bundle shall be lodged –

(a)   for hearings at the RCJ, in the office of the Clerk of the Rules, 1st Mezzanine (Rm 1M), Queen's Building, Royal Courts of Justice, Strand, London WC2A 2LL (DX 44450 Strand);

(b)   for hearings at any other place, at such place as may be designated by the designated family judge responsible for that place and in default of any such designation at the court office for the place where the hearing is to take place.

7.3

Any bundle sent to the court by post, DX or courier shall be clearly addressed to the appropriate office and shall show the date and place of the hearing on the outside of any packaging as well as on the bundle itself.

7.4

Unless the court has given some other direction or paragraph 7.5 applies only one copy of the bundle shall be lodged with the court but the party who is responsible for lodging the bundle shall bring to court at each hearing at which oral evidence may be called a copy of the bundle for use by the witnesses.

7.5

In the case of a hearing listed before a bench of magistrates four copies of the bundle shall be lodged with the court.

7.6

In the case of hearings at the RCJ or at any other place where the designated family judge responsible for that place has directed that this paragraph shall apply, parties shall –

(a)   if the bundle or preliminary documents are delivered personally, ensure that they obtain a receipt from the clerk accepting it or them; and

(b)   if the bundle or preliminary documents are sent by post or DX, ensure that they obtain proof of posting or despatch.

The receipt (or proof of posting or despatch, as the case may be) shall be brought to court on the day of the hearing and must be produced to the court if requested. If the receipt (or proof of posting or despatch) cannot be produced to the court the judge may: (a) treat the bundle as having not been lodged; and (b) take the steps referred to in paragraph 12.

Lodging the bundle – additional requirements for Family Division or Family Court cases being heard at the RCJ

8.1

Bundles or preliminary documents delivered after 11 am on the day before the hearing may not be accepted by the Clerk of the Rules and if not shall be delivered

(a)   in a case where the hearing is before a judge of the High Court, directly to the clerk of the judge hearing the case;

(b)   in a case where the hearing is before any other judge, to such place as may be specified by the Clerk of the Rules.

8.2

Upon learning before which judge a hearing is to take place, the clerk to counsel, or other advocate, representing the party in the position of applicant shall no later than 3 pm the day before the hearing –

(a)   in a case where the hearing is before a judge of the High Court, telephone the clerk of the judge hearing the case;

(b)   in a case where the hearing is before any other judge email the Clerk of the Rules at RCJ.familyhighcourt@hmcts.gsi.gov.uk;

to ascertain whether the judge has received the bundle (including the preliminary documents) and, if not, shall organise prompt delivery by the applicant's solicitor.

Removing and re-lodging the bundle

9.1

Unless either the court wishes to retain the bundle or specific alternative arrangements have been agreed with the court, the party responsible for the bundle shall, following completion of the hearing, retrieve the bundle from the court immediately or, if that is not practicable, collect it from the court within 5 working days. Bundles which are not collected in due time are liable to be destroyed without further notice.

9.2

The bundle shall be re-lodged for the next and any further hearings in accordance with the provisions of this practice direction and in a form which complies with para 4.7.

Time estimates

10.1

In every case a time estimate (which shall be inserted at the front of the bundle) shall be prepared which shall so far as practicable be agreed by all parties and shall –

(a)   specify separately: (i) the time estimated to be required for judicial pre-reading; and (ii) the time required for hearing all evidence and submissions; and (iii) the time estimated to be required for preparing and delivering judgment;

(b)   be prepared on the basis that before they give evidence all witnesses will have read all relevant filed statements and reports; and

(c)   take appropriate account of any additional time likely to be incurred by the use of interpreters or intermediaries.

10.2

Once a case has been listed, any change in time estimates shall be notified immediately by telephone (and then immediately confirmed in writing) –

(a)   in the case of hearings in the RCJ, to the Clerk of the Rules; and

(b)   in the case of hearings elsewhere, to the relevant listing officer.

Taking cases out of the list

11.1

As soon as it becomes known that a hearing will no longer be effective, whether as a result of the parties reaching agreement or for any other reason, the parties and their representatives shall immediately notify the court by telephone and email which shall be confirmed by letter. The letter, which shall wherever possible be a joint letter sent on behalf of all parties with their signatures applied or appended, shall include –

(a)   a short background summary of the case;

(b)   the written consent of each party who consents and, where a party does not consent, details of the steps which have been taken to obtain that party's consent and, where known, an explanation of why that consent has not been given;

(c)   a draft of the order being sought; and

(d)   enough information to enable the court to decide (i) whether to take the case out of the list and (ii) whether to make the proposed order.

Penalties for failure to comply with the practice direction

12.1

Failure to comply with any part of this practice direction may result in the judge removing the case from the list or putting the case further back in the list and may also result in a 'wasted costs' order or some other adverse costs order.

Commencement of the practice direction and application of other practice directions

13.1

Subject to paragraph 13.2 this practice direction shall have effect from 22 April 2014.

13.2

Sub-paragraphs (a)–(c) and (e)–(g) of paragraph 4.1 and paragraphs 5.1 and 5.3(e) shall have effect from 31 July 2014. In the meantime paragraphs 5.1 and 5.3(e) shall have effect as if –

(a)   paragraph 5.1 read "The bundle shall be contained in one or more A4 size ring binders or lever arch files (each lever arch file being limited to no more than 350 pages)."; and

(b)   in paragraph 5.3(e) the words "in accordance with a direction of the court" were omitted.

14.1

This practice direction should where appropriate be read in conjunction with the Public Law Outline 2014 (PD12A) and the Child Arrangements Programme 2014

(PD12B). In particular, nothing in this practice direction is to be read as removing or altering any obligation to comply with the requirements of the Public Law Outline 2014 and the Child Arrangements Programme 2014.

This Practice Direction is issued –

(a)   in relation to family proceedings, by the President of the Family Division, as the nominee of the Lord Chief Justice, with the agreement of the Lord Chancellor; and

(b)   to the extent that it applies to proceedings to which section 5 of the Civil Procedure Act 1997 applies, by the Master of the Rolls as the nominee of the Lord Chief Justice, with the agreement of the Lord Chancellor.

PRACTICE DIRECTION 30A – APPEALS, EXTRACTS

This Practice Direction supplements FPR Part 30

Application and interpretation

1.1 This practice direction applies to all appeals to which Part 30 applies.

1.2 In this Practice Direction in relation to the family court –

'the 1984 Act' means the Matrimonial and Family Proceedings Act 1984;

'assistant to a justices' clerk' has the meaning given in section 27(5) of the Courts Act 2003;

'authorised' means authorised by the President of the Family Division or nominated by or on behalf of the Lord Chief Justice to conduct particular business in the family court, in accordance with Part 3 of rules relating to the composition of the court and distribution of business made in accordance with section 31 D of the 1984 Act;

'costs judge means –

    (a)   the Chief Taxing Master;

    (b)   a taxing master of the Senior Courts; or

    (c)   a person appointed to act as deputy for the person holding office referred to in paragraph (b) or to act as a temporary additional officer for any such office;

'judge of circuit judge level means –

    (a)   a circuit judge who, where applicable, is authorised;

    (b)   a Recorder who, where applicable, is authorised;

    (c)   any other judge of the family court authorised to sit as a judge of circuit judge level in the family court;

'judge of district judge level' means –

    (a)   the Senior District Judge of the Family Division;

    (b)   a district judge of the Principal Registry of the Family Division ("PRFD");

    (c)   a person appointed to act as deputy for the person holding office referred to in paragraph (b) or to act as a temporary additional officer for any such office;

    (d)   a district judge who, where applicable, is authorised;

    (e)   a deputy district judge appointed under section 102 of the Senior Courts Act 1981 or section 8 of the County Courts Act 1984 who, where applicable, is authorised;

    (f)   an authorised District Judge (Magistrates' Courts);

    (g)   any other judge of the family court authorised to sit as a judge of district judge level in the family court.

'judge of High Court judge level' means –

    (a)   a deputy judge of the High Court;

    (b)   a puisne judge of the High Court;

    (c)   a person who has been a judge of the Court of Appeal or a puisne judge of the High Court who may act as a judge of the family court by virtue of section 9 of the Senior Courts Act 1981;

(d)   the Senior President of Tribunals;

(e)   the Chancellor of the High Court;

(f)   an ordinary judge of the Court of Appeal (including the vice-president, if any, of either division of that court);

(g)   the President of the Queen's Bench Division;

(h)   the President of the Family Division;

(i)   the Master of the Rolls;

(j)   the Lord Chief Justice;

'justices' clerk' has the meaning given in section 27(1) of the Courts Act 2003; and

'lay justice' means an authorised justice of the peace who is not a District Judge (Magistrates' Courts).

Routes of appeal

2.1   The following table sets out to which court or judge an appeal is to be made (subject to obtaining any necessary permission) from decisions of the family court –

Decision of judge sitting in the family court	Permission generally required (subject to exception in rules of court, for example, no permission required to appeal against a committal order)	Appeal to
1. A bench of – • two or three lay magistrates; • or a lay justice	No	• a judge of circuit judge level sitting in the family court; • a judge of High Court judge level sitting in the family court where a Designated Family Judge or a judge of High Court Judge level considers that the appeal would raise an important point of principle or practice. • (NB a judge of High Court judge level may hear the appeal in interests of effective and efficient use of local judicial resource and the resource of the High Court bench)
2. A judge of district judge level (except the Senior District Judge of the Family Division or a District Judge (PRFD) in	Yes	As above

Decision of judge sitting in the family court	Permission generally required (subject to exception in rules of court, for example, no permission required to appeal against a committal order)	Appeal to
proceedings for a financial remedy)		
3. District Judge (PRFD) in proceedings for financial remedy	Yes	Judge of High Court judge level sitting in the family court
4. Senior District Judge of the Family Division in proceedings for financial remedy	Yes	Judge of High Court judge level sitting in the family court
5. Judge of circuit judge level	Yes	Court of Appeal
6. Costs Judge	Yes	Judge of High Court judge level sitting in the family court
7. Judge of High Court judge level	Yes	Court of Appeal

(Provisions setting out routes of appeal include section 31K(1) of the 1984 Act for appeals against decisions from the family court and section 13(2A) of the Administration of Justice Act 1960 for appeals against decisions or orders from the family court relating to contempt of court.

The Access to Justice Act 1999 (Destination of Appeals) (Family Proceedings) Order 2014 (S. I. 2014/602) routes appeals from certain judges and office holders to the family court instead of to the Court of Appeal and rules relating to the composition of the court and distribution of business made in accordance with section 31 D of the 1984 Act make provision for appeals within the family court.

The leapfrogging provision in section 57 of the Access to Justice Act 1999 applies to appeals where in any proceedings in the family court a person appeals or seeks permission to appeal to a court other than the Court of Appeal or the Supreme Court.)

2.2 The following table sets out to which court or judge an appeal is to be made (subject to obtaining any necessary permission) from decisions of the High Court –

Decision of judge	Permission generally required (subject to exception in rules of court, for example, no permission required to appeal against a committal order)	Appeal to
1. District Judge of the High Court; or • a deputy district judge appointed under section 102 of the Senior Courts Act 1981	Yes	High Court Judge
2. The Senior District Judge of the Family Division; • District Judge of the PRFD; or • a person appointed to act as deputy for a District Judge of the PRFD or to act as a temporary additional officer for such office	Yes	High Court Judge
3. Costs judge; or • a person appointed to act as deputy for a costs judge who is a taxing master of the senior courts or to act as a temporary additional officer for such office	Yes	High Court Judge
4. Judge of the High Court (including a person acting as a judge of the High Court in accordance with section 9(1) or section 9(4) of the Senior Courts Act 1981)	Yes	Court of Appeal

(Provisions setting out routes of appeal include section 16(1) of the Senior Courts Act 1981 (as amended) for appeals against decisions from the High Court and section 13 of the Administration of Justice Act 1960 for appeals against an order or decision of the High Court relating to contempt of court. The Access to Justice Act 1999 (Destination of Appeals) (Family Proceedings) Order 2011 (S. I. 2011/1044) routes appeals against decisions of certain judges to the High Court instead of the Court of Appeal. The leapfrogging provision in section 57 of the Access to Justice Act 1999 referred to above applies.

The general rule is that appeals under section 8(1) of the Gender Recognition Act 2004 must be started in the family court as both the High Court and the family court have jurisdiction to hear the appeal (see section 8 of the 2004 Act and FPR 5.4). The procedure for appeals to the Court of Appeal is governed by the Civil Procedure Rules 1998, in particular CPR Part 52.).

2.3 A justices' clerk and assistant to a justices' clerk are not judges of the family court but they perform functions of the court in accordance with rules made under section 31 O of the 1984 Act (see, for example, the Justices' Clerks and Assistants Rules 2014 (S.I. 2014/603)). Appeals against decisions of a justices' clerk or an assistant to a justices' clerk are to a judge of circuit judge level sitting in the family court. However, it is expected that such appeals will be rare as a justices' clerk and an assistant to a justices' clerk may refer a matter to the court as appropriate before making a decision.

2.4 Where the decision to be appealed is a decision in a Part 19 (Alternative Procedure For Applications) application on a point of law in a case which did not involve any substantial dispute of fact, the court to which the appeal lies, where that court is the High Court or the family court and unless the appeal would lie to the Court of Appeal in any event, must consider whether to order the appeal to be transferred to the Court of Appeal under FPR 30.13 (Assignment of Appeals to the Court of Appeal).

Grounds for appeal
3.1 Rule 30.12 (hearing of appeals) sets out the circumstances in which the appeal court will allow an appeal.

3.2 The grounds of appeal should –
(a) set out clearly the reasons why rule 30.12 (3)(a) or (b) is said to apply; and
(b) specify in respect of each ground, whether the ground raises an appeal on a point of law or is an appeal against a finding of fact.

Permission to appeal
4.1 FPR 30.3 (Permission) sets out the circumstances when permission to appeal is required. At present permission to appeal is required where the decision of the family court appealed against was made by a district judge (including a District Judge (Magistrates' Courts)) or a costs judge. Permission to appeal is required where the decision of the High Court appealed against is a decision of a district judge or a costs judge. However, no permission is required where FPR 30.3(2) applies (appeals against a committal order, a secure accommodation order under section 25 of the Children Act 1989, or a refusal to grant habeas corpus for release in relation to a minor).

Court to which permission to appeal application should be made
4.2 An application for permission should be made orally at the hearing at which the decision to be appealed against is made.

4.3 Where –
(a) no application for permission to appeal is made at the hearing; or
(b) the lower court refuses permission to appeal,
an application for permission to appeal may be made to the appeal court in accordance with rules 30.3(3) and (4) (Permission).

(Rule 30.1(3) defines 'lower court'.)

4.4	Where no application for permission to appeal has been made in accordance with rule 30.3(3)(a) (Permission) but a party requests further time to make such an application the court may adjourn the hearing to give that party an opportunity to do so.

4.5	There is no appeal from a decision of the appeal court to allow or refuse permission to appeal to that court. However, where the appeal court, without a hearing, refuses permission to appeal, the person seeking permission may request that decision to be reconsidered at a hearing, unless an order has been made under rule 30.3(5A) that the person seeking permission may not do so (where the application for permission is considered to be totally without merit) – see section 54(4) of the Access to Justice Act 1999 and rule 30.3(5), (5A) (Permission).

Permission and case management decisions

4.5A	Where the application is for permission to appeal from a case management decision, the factors to which the court is to have particular regard include whether –
(a)	the issue is of sufficient significance to justify an appeal;
(b)	the procedural consequences of an appeal (e.g. the impact upon the timetable) outweigh the significance of the case management decision;
(c)	it would be more convenient to adjourn the determination of the issue.

4.5B	Case management decisions include decisions made under FPR 4.1(3) and decisions about disclosure, filing of witness statements or experts' reports, directions about the timetable of the proceedings and adding a party to the proceedings.
Material omission from a judgment of the lower court

4.6	Where a party's advocate considers that there is a material omission from a judgment of the lower court or, where the decision is made by a lay justice or justices, the written reasons for the decision of the lower court (including inadequate reasons for the lower court's decision), the advocate should before the drawing of the order give the lower court which made the decision the opportunity of considering whether there is an omission and should not immediately use the omission as grounds for an application to appeal.

4.7	Paragraph 4.8 below applies where there is an application to the lower court for permission to appeal on the grounds of a material omission from a judgment or written reasons (where a decision is made in the family court by a lay justice or justices) of the lower court. Paragraph 4.9 below applies where there is an application for permission to appeal to the appeal court on the grounds of a material omission from a judgment or written reasons (where a decision is made in the family court by a lay justice or justices) of the lower court.

4.8	Where the application for permission to appeal is made to the lower court, the court which made the decision must –
(a)	consider whether there is a material omission and adjourn for that purpose if necessary; and

(b) where the conclusion is that there has been such an omission, provide additions to the judgment.

4.9 Where the application for permission to appeal is made to the appeal court, the appeal court –

(a) must consider whether there is a material omission; and

(b) where the conclusion is that there has been such an omission, may adjourn the application and remit the case to the lower court with an invitation to provide additions to the judgment.

Consideration of Permission without a hearing

4.10 An application for permission to appeal may be considered by the appeal court without a hearing.

4.11 If permission is granted without a hearing the parties will be notified of that decision and the procedure in paragraphs 6.1 to 6.8 will then apply.

4.12 If permission is refused without a hearing the parties will be notified of that decision with the reasons for it. The decision is subject to the appellant's right to have it reconsidered at an oral hearing. This may be before the same judge. However the appellant has no right to have the application considered at an oral hearing where a High Court Judge or Designated Family Judge refused permission to appeal without a hearing and made an order under rule 30.3(5A) that the appellant may not request the decision to be reconsidered at a hearing because he or she considered the application for permission to be totally without merit.

4.13 A request for the decision to be reconsidered at an oral hearing must be filed at the appeal court within 7 days after service of the notice that permission has been refused. A copy of the request must be served by the appellant on the respondent at the same time. This does not apply where an order has been made under rule 30.3(5A) that the appellant may not request the decision to be reconsidered at a hearing.

Permission hearing

4.14 Where an appellant, who is represented, makes a request for a decision to be reconsidered at an oral hearing, the appellant's advocate must, at least 4 days before the hearing, in a brief written statement –

(a) inform the court and the respondent of the points which the appellant proposes to raise at the hearing;

(b) set out the reasons why permission should be granted notwithstanding the reasons given for the refusal of permission; and

(c) confirm, where applicable, that the requirements of paragraph 4.17 have been complied with (appellant in receipt of legal aid).

4.15 The respondent will be given notice of a permission hearing, but is not required to attend unless requested by the court to do so.

4.16	If the court requests the respondent's attendance at the permission hearing, the appellant must supply the respondent with a copy of the appeal bundle (see paragraph 5.9) within 7 days of being notified of the request, or such other period as the court may direct. The costs of providing that bundle shall be borne by the appellant initially, but will form part of the costs of the permission application.

Appellants in receipt of services funded by the Legal Services Secretary of State applying for permission to appeal
4.17	Where the appellant is in receipt of legal aid and permission to appeal has been refused by the appeal court without a hearing, the appellant must send a copy of the reasons the appeal court gave for refusing permission to the Director of legal aid casework as soon as it has been received from the court. The court will require confirmation that this has been done if a hearing is requested to re-consider the question of permission.

Limited permission
4.18	Where a court under rule 30.3 (Permission) gives permission to appeal on some issues only, it will –
(a)	refuse permission on any remaining issues; or
(b)	reserve the question of permission to appeal on any remaining issues to the court hearing the appeal.

4.19	If the court reserves the question of permission under paragraph 4.18(b), the appellant must, within 14 days after service of the court's order, inform the appeal court and the respondent in writing whether the appellant intends to pursue the reserved issues. If the appellant does intend to pursue the reserved issues, the parties must include in any time estimate for the appeal hearing, their time estimate for the reserved issues.

4.20	If the appeal court refuses permission to appeal on the remaining issues without a hearing and the applicant wishes to have that decision reconsidered at an oral hearing, the time limit in rule 30.3(6) (Permission) shall apply. Any application for an extension of this time limit should be made promptly. The court hearing the appeal on the issues for which permission has been granted will not normally grant, at the appeal hearing, an application to extend the time limit in rule 30.3 (6) for the remaining issues.

4.21	If the appeal court refuses permission to appeal on remaining issues at or after an oral hearing, the application for permission to appeal on those issues cannot be renewed at the appeal hearing (see section 54(4) of the Access to Justice Act 1999).

Respondents' costs of permission applications
4.22	In most cases, applications for permission to appeal will be determined without the court requesting –
(a)	submissions from; or
(b)	if there is an oral hearing, attendance by,
the respondent.

4.23 Where the court does not request submissions from or attendance by the respondent, costs will not normally be allowed to a respondent who volunteers submissions or attendance.

4.24 Where the court does request –
(a) submissions from; or
(b) attendance by the respondent,
the court will normally allow the costs of the respondent if permission is refused.

Allocation-appropriate procedure
4A.1 Where a party is dissatisfied with allocation that party may appeal or request the court to reconsider allocation at a hearing under FPR 29.19.

4A.2 Where allocation was made at a hearing, the party who is dissatisfied may appeal.

4A.3 Where allocation was made without a hearing, the party who is dissatisfied should request the court to reconsider allocation at a hearing.

Appellant's notice
5.1 An appellant's notice must be filed and served in all cases. Where an application for permission to appeal is made to the appeal court it must be applied for in the appellant's notice.

Human Rights
5.2 Where the appellant seeks –
(a) to rely on any issue under the Human Rights Act 1998; or
(b) a remedy available under that Act,
for the first time in an appeal the appellant must include in the appeal notice the information required by rule 29.5(2).

5.3 Practice Direction 29A (Human Rights, Joining the Crown) will apply as if references to the directions hearing were to the application for permission to appeal.

Extension of time for filing appellant's notice
5.4 If an extension of time is required for filing the appellant's notice the application must be made in that notice. The notice should state the reason for the delay and the steps taken prior to the application being made.

5.5 Where the appellant's notice includes an application for an extension of time and permission to appeal has been given or is not required the respondent has the right to be heard on that application and must be served with a copy of the appeal bundle (see paragraph 5.9). However, a respondent who unreasonably opposes an extension of time runs the risk of being ordered to pay the appellant's costs of that application.

5.6 If an extension of time is given following such an application the procedure at paragraphs 6.1 to 6.8 applies.

Applications

5.7 Notice of an application to be made to the appeal court for a remedy incidental to the appeal (e.g. an interim injunction under rule 20.2 (Orders for interim remedies)) may be included in the appeal notice or in a Part 18 (Procedure For Other Applications in Proceedings) application notice.

(Paragraph 13 of this practice direction contains other provisions relating to applications.).

Documents

5.8 The appellant must file the following documents together with an appeal bundle (see paragraph 5.9) with his or her appellant's notice –
- (a) two additional copies of the appellant's notice for the appeal court;
- (b) one copy of the appellant's notice for each of the respondents;
- (c) one copy of the appellant's skeleton argument for each copy of the appellant's notice that is filed;
- (d) a sealed or stamped copy of the order being appealed or a copy of the notice of the making of an order;
- (e) a copy of any order giving or refusing permission to appeal, together with a copy of the court's reasons for allowing or refusing permission to appeal;
- (f) any witness statements or affidavits in support of any application included in the appellant's notice.

5.9 An appellant must include the following documents in his or her appeal bundle –
- (a) a sealed or stamped copy of the appellant's notice;
- (b) a sealed or stamped copy of the order being appealed, or a copy of the notice of the making of an order;
- (c) a copy of any order giving or refusing permission to appeal, together with a copy of the court's reasons for allowing or refusing permission to appeal;
- (d) any affidavit or witness statement filed in support of any application included in the appellant's notice;
- (e) where the appeal is against a consent order, a statement setting out the change in circumstances since the order was agreed or other circumstances justifying a review or re-hearing;
- (f) a copy of the appellant's skeleton argument;
- (g) a transcript or note of judgment or, in a magistrates' court, written reasons for the court's decision (see paragraph 5.23), and in cases where permission to appeal was given by the lower court or is not required those parts of any transcript of evidence which are directly relevant to any question at issue on the appeal;
- (h) the application form;

(i)   any application notice (or case management documentation) relevant to the subject of the appeal;

(j)   any other documents which the appellant reasonably considers necessary to enable the appeal court to reach its decision on the hearing of the application or appeal; and

(k)   such other documents as the court may direct.

5.10   All documents that are extraneous to the issues to be considered on the application or the appeal must be excluded. The appeal bundle may include affidavits, witness statements, summaries, experts' reports and exhibits but only where these are directly relevant to the subject matter of the appeal.

5.11   Where the appellant is represented, the appeal bundle must contain a certificate signed by the appellant's solicitor, counsel or other representative to the effect that the appellant has read and understood paragraph 5.10 and that the composition of the appeal bundle complies with it.

5.12   Where it is not possible to file all the above documents, the appellant must indicate which documents have not yet been filed and the reasons why they are not currently available. The appellant must then provide a reasonable estimate of when the missing document or documents can be filed and file them as soon as reasonably practicable.

Skeleton arguments

5.13   The appellant's notice must, subject to paragraphs 5.14 and 5.15, be accompanied by a skeleton argument. Alternatively the skeleton argument may be included in the appellant's notice. Where the skeleton argument is so included it will not form part of the notice for the purposes of rule 30.9 (Amendment of appeal notice).

5.14   Subject to paragraph 5.14A, where it is impracticable for the appellant's skeleton argument to accompany the appellant's notice it must be filed and served on all respondents within 14 days of filing the notice.

5.14A   In appeals against case management decisions, where the appellant's skeleton argument cannot accompany the appellant's notice it must be filed as soon as practicable or as directed by the court, but in any event not less than 3 days before the hearing of the appeal.

5.15   An appellant who is not represented need not file a skeleton argument but is encouraged to do so since this will be helpful to the court.

5.16   A skeleton argument must contain a numbered list of the points which the party wishes to make. These should both define and confine the areas of controversy. Each point should be stated as concisely as the nature of the case allows.

5.17   A numbered point must be followed by a reference to any document on which the party wishes to rely.

5.18   A skeleton argument must state, in respect of each authority cited –
(a)   the proposition of law that the authority demonstrates; and
(b)   the parts of the authority (identified by page or paragraph references) that support the proposition.

5.19   If more than one authority is cited in support of a given proposition, the skeleton argument must briefly state the reason for taking that course.

5.20   The statement referred to in paragraph 5.19 should not materially add to the length of the skeleton argument but should be sufficient to demonstrate, in the context of the argument –
(a)   the relevance of the authority or authorities to that argument; and
(b)   that the citation is necessary for a proper presentation of that argument.

5.21   The cost of preparing a skeleton argument which –
(a)   does not comply with the requirements set out in this paragraph; or
(b)   was not filed within the time limits provided by this Practice Direction (or any further time granted by the court),
will not be allowed on assessment except to the extent that the court otherwise directs.

5.22   The appellant should consider what other information the appeal court will need. This may include a list of persons who feature in the case or glossaries of technical terms. A chronology of relevant events will be necessary in most appeals.

Suitable record of the judgment
5.23   Where the judgment to be appealed has been officially recorded by the court, an approved transcript of that record should accompany the appellant's notice. Photocopies will not be accepted for this purpose. However, where there is no officially recorded judgment, the following documents will be acceptable –
Written judgments – where a decision is made by a lay justice or justices in the family court, a copy of the written reasons for the court's decision.
Written reasons – in a magistrates' court, a copy of the written reasons for the court's decision.
Note of judgment – When judgment was not officially recorded or made in writing a note of the judgment (agreed between the appellant's and respondent's advocates) should be submitted for approval to the judge whose decision is being appealed. If the parties cannot agree on a single note of the judgment, both versions should be provided to that judge with an explanatory letter. For the purpose of an application for permission to appeal the note need not be approved by the respondent or the lower court judge.
Advocates' notes of judgments where the appellant is unrepresented – When the appellant was unrepresented in the lower court it is the duty of any advocate

for the respondent to make the advocate's note of judgment promptly available, free of charge to the appellant where there is no officially recorded judgment or if the court so directs. Where the appellant was represented in the lower court it is the duty of the appellant's own former advocate to make that advocate's note available in these circumstances. The appellant should submit the note of judgment to the appeal court.

5.24   An appellant may not be able to obtain an official transcript or other suitable record of the lower court's decision within the time within which the appellant's notice must be filed. In such cases the appellant's notice must still be completed to the best of the appellant's ability on the basis of the documentation available. However it may be amended subsequently with the permission of the appeal court in accordance with rule 30.9 (Amendment of appeal notice).

Advocates' notes of judgments

5.25   Advocates' brief (or, where appropriate, refresher) fee includes –

(a)   remuneration for taking a note of the judgment of the court;

(b)   having the note transcribed accurately;

(c)   attempting to agree the note with the other side if represented;

(d)   submitting the note to the judge for approval where appropriate;

(e)   revising it if so requested by the judge,

(f)   providing any copies required for the appeal court, instructing solicitors and lay client; and

(g)   providing a copy of the note to an unrepresented appellant.

5.26   Omitted

Appeals under section 8(1) of the Gender Recognition Act 2004

5.27   Paragraph 5.28 to 5.30 apply where the appeal is brought under section 8(1) of the Gender Recognition Act 2004 on a point of law against a decision by the Gender Recognition Panel to reject the application under sections 1(1), 5(2), 5(A)(2) or 6(1) of the 2004 Act. The appeal is to the High Court or to the family court. However, FPR 5.4 provides that where the family court has jurisdiction to deal with a matter, the proceedings relating to that matter must be started in the family court except where the court otherwise directs, any rule, other enactment or Practice Direction provides otherwise or proceedings relating to the same parties are already being heard by the High Court. Most appeals under section 8(1) of the Gender Recognition Act 2004 are therefore likely to be to the family court and be heard by a judge of High Court Judge level sitting in that court in accordance with the rules relating to the composition of the court and distribution of business made in accordance with section 31 D of the 1984 Act.

5.28   Where the appeal is to the High Court, the appeal notice must be –

(a)   filed in the PRFD; and

(b)   served on the Secretary of State and the President of the Gender Recognition Panels.

5.28A Where the appeal is to the family court the appeal notice must be served on the Secretary of State and the President of the Gender Recognition Panels.

5.29   The Secretary of State may appear and be heard in the proceedings on the appeal.

5.30   Where the High Court issues a gender recognition certificate under section 8(3)(a) of the Gender Recognition Act 2004, the court officer must send a copy of that certificate to the Secretary of State.

Transcripts or Notes of Evidence
5.31   When the evidence is relevant to the appeal an official transcript of the relevant evidence must be obtained. Transcripts or notes of evidence are generally not needed for the purpose of determining an application for permission to appeal.

Notes of evidence
5.32   If evidence relevant to the appeal was not officially recorded, a typed version of the judge's or justices' clerk's /assistant clerk's notes of evidence must be obtained. Transcripts at public expense

5.33   Where the lower court or the appeal court is satisfied that –
(a)   an unrepresented appellant; or
(b)   an appellant whose legal representation is provided free of charge to the appellant and not funded by the Community Legal Service,
is in such poor financial circumstances that the cost of a transcript would be an excessive burden the court may certify that the cost of obtaining one official transcript should be borne at public expense.

5.34   In the case of a request for an official transcript of evidence or proceedings to be paid for at public expense, the court must also be satisfied that there are reasonable grounds for appeal. Whenever possible a request for a transcript at public expense should be made to the lower court when asking for permission to appeal.

Filing and service of appellant's notice
5.35   Rule 30.4 (Appellant's notice) sets out the procedure and time limits for filing and serving an appellant's notice. Subject to paragraph 5.36, the appellant must file the appellant's notice at the appeal court within such period as may be directed by the lower court, which should not normally exceed 14 days or, where the lower court directs no such period within 21 days of the date of the decision that the appellant wishes to appeal.

5.36   Rule 30.4(3) (Appellant's notice) provides that unless the appeal court orders otherwise, where the appeal is against an order under section 38(1) of the 1989 Act or a case management decision in any proceedings, the appellant must file the appellant's notice within 7 days beginning with the date of the decision of the lower court.

5.37 Where the lower court announces its decision and reserves the reasons for its judgment or order until a later date, it should, in the exercise of powers under rule 30.4 (2)(a))(Appellant's notice), fix a period for filing the appellant's notice at the appeal court that takes this into account.

5.38 Except where the appeal court orders otherwise a sealed or stamped copy of the appellant's notice, including any skeleton arguments must be served on all respondents and other persons referred to in rule 30.4(5) (Appellant's notice) in accordance with the timetable prescribed by rule 30.4(4)) (Appellant's notice) except where this requirement is modified by paragraph 5.14 or 5.14A in which case the skeleton argument should be served as soon as it is filed.

5.39 Where the appellant's notice is to be served on a child, then rule 6.33 (supplementary provision relating to service on children) applies and unless the appeal court orders otherwise a sealed or stamped copy of the appellant's notice, including any skeleton arguments must be served on the persons or bodies mentioned in rule 6.33(2). For example, the appeal notice must be served on any children's guardian, welfare officer or children and family reporter who is appointed in the proceedings.

5.40 Unless the court otherwise directs, a respondent need not take any action when served with an appellant's notice until such time as notification is given to the respondent that permission to appeal has been given.

5.41 The court may dispense with the requirement for service of the notice on a respondent.

5.42 Unless the appeal court directs otherwise, the appellant must serve on the respondent the appellant's notice and skeleton argument (but not the appeal bundle), where the appellant is applying for permission to appeal in the appellant's notice.

5.43 Where permission to appeal –
(a)   has been given by the lower court; or
(b)   is not required,
the appellant must serve the appeal bundle on the respondent and the persons mentioned in paragraph 5.39 with the appellant's notice.

Amendment of Appeal Notice
5.44 An appeal notice may be amended with permission. Such an application to amend and any application in opposition will normally be dealt with at the hearing unless that course would cause unnecessary expense or delay in which case a request should be made for the application to amend to be heard in advance.

Procedure after permission is obtained
6.1   This paragraph sets out the procedure where –
(a)   permission to appeal is given by the appeal court; or
(b)   the appellant's notice is filed in the appeal court and –

(i)   permission was given by the lower court; or

(ii)   permission is not required.

6.2   If the appeal court gives permission to appeal, the appeal bundle must be served on each of the respondents within 7 days of receiving the order giving permission to appeal.

6.3   The appeal court will send the parties –

(a)   notification of the date of the hearing or the period of time (the 'listing window') during which the appeal is likely to be heard;

(b)   where permission is granted by the appeal court a copy of the order giving permission to appeal; and

(c)   any other directions given by the court.

6.4   Where the appeal court grants permission to appeal, the appellant must add the following documents to the appeal bundle –

(a)   the respondent's notice and skeleton argument (if any);

(b)   those parts of the transcripts of evidence which are directly relevant to any question at issue on the appeal;

(c)   the order granting permission to appeal and, where permission to appeal was granted at an oral hearing, the transcript (or note) of any judgment which was given; and

(d)   any document which the appellant and respondent have agreed to add to the appeal bundle in accordance with paragraph 7.16.

6.5   Where permission to appeal has been refused on a particular issue, the appellant must remove from the appeal bundle all documents that are relevant only to that issue.

Time estimates

6.6   If the appellant is legally represented, the appeal court must be notified, in writing, of the advocate's time estimate for the hearing of the appeal.

6.7   The time estimate must be that of the advocate who will argue the appeal. It should exclude the time required by the court to give judgment.

6.8   A court officer will notify the respondent of the appellant's time estimate and if the respondent disagrees with the time estimate the respondent must inform the court within 7 days of the notification. In the absence of such notification the respondent will be deemed to have accepted the estimate proposed on behalf of the appellant.

Respondent

7.1   A respondent who wishes to ask the appeal court to vary the order of the lower court in any way must appeal and permission will be required on the same basis as for an appellant.

(Paragraph 3.2 applies to grounds of appeal by a respondent.).

7.2   A respondent who wishes to appeal or who wishes to ask the appeal court to uphold the order of the lower court for reasons different from or additional to those given by the lower court must file a respondent's notice.

7.3   A respondent who does not file a respondent's notice will not be entitled, except with the permission of the court, to rely on any reason not relied on in the lower court. This paragraph and paragraph 7.2 do not apply where the appeal is against an order under section 38(1) of the 1989 Act (see rule 30.5(7) (Respondent's notice)).

7.4   Paragraphs 5.3 (Human Rights and extension for time for filing appellant's notice) and 5.4 to 5.6 (extension of time for filing appellant's notice) of this practice direction also apply to a respondent and a respondent's notice.

Time limits
7.5   The time limits for filing a respondent's notice are set out in rule 30.5(4) and (5) (Respondent's notice).

7.6   Where an extension of time is required the extension must be requested in the respondent's notice and the reasons why the respondent failed to act within the specified time must be included.

7.7   Except where paragraphs 7.8 7.9A and 7.10 apply, the respondent must file a skeleton argument for the court in all cases where the respondent proposes to address arguments to the court. The respondent's skeleton argument may be included within a respondent's notice. Where a skeleton argument is included within a respondent's notice it will not form part of the notice for the purposes of rule 30.9 (Amendment of appeal notice).

7.8   Subject to paragraph 7.9A, a respondent who –
(a)   files a respondent's notice; but
(b)   does not include a skeleton argument with that notice,
must file the skeleton argument within 14 days of filing the notice.

7.9   Subject to paragraph 7.9A, a respondent who does not file a respondent's notice but who files a skeleton argument must file that skeleton argument at least 7 days before the appeal hearing.

(Rule 30.5(4) (Respondent's notice) sets out the period for filing a respondent's notice.).

7.9A   In appeals against case management decisions, where –
(a)   the respondent's skeleton argument cannot accompany the respondent's notice; or
(b)   a respondent does not file a respondent's notice but files a skeleton argument,
the skeleton argument must be filed as soon as practicable or as directed by the court, but in any event not less than 3 days before the hearing of the appeal.

7.10   A respondent who is not represented need not file a skeleton argument but is encouraged to do so in order to assist the court.

7.11   The respondent must serve the skeleton argument on –
(a)   the appellant; and
(b)   any other respondent;
at the same time as the skeleton argument is filed at court. Where a child is an appellant or respondent the skeleton argument must also be served on the persons listed in rule 6.33(2) unless the court directs otherwise.

7.12   A respondent's skeleton argument must conform to the directions at paragraphs 5.16 to 5.22 with any necessary modifications. It should, where appropriate, answer the arguments set out in the appellant's skeleton argument.

Applications within respondent's notices
7.13   A respondent may include an application within a respondent's notice in accordance with paragraph 5.7.

Filing respondent's notices and skeleton arguments
7.14   The respondent must file the following documents with the respondent's notice in every case –
(a)   two additional copies of the respondent's notice for the appeal court; and
(b)   one copy each for the appellant, any other respondents and any persons referred to in paragraph 5.39.

7.15   The respondent may file a skeleton argument with the respondent's notice and –
(a)   where doing so must file two copies; and
(b)   where not doing so must comply with paragraph 7.8.

7.16   If the respondent considers documents in addition to those filed by the appellant to be necessary to enable the appeal court to reach its decision on the appeal and wishes to rely on those documents, any amendments to the appeal bundle should be agreed with the appellant if possible.

7.17   If the representatives for the parties are unable to reach agreement, the respondent may prepare a supplemental bundle.

7.18   The respondent must file any supplemental bundle so prepared, together with the requisite number of copies for the appeal court, at the appeal court –
(a)   with the respondent's notice; or
(b)   if a respondent's notice is not filed, within 21 days after the respondent is served with the appeal bundle.

7.19   The respondent must serve –
(a)   the respondent's notice;

(b)   the skeleton argument (if any); and
(c)   the supplemental bundle (if any), on –
     (i)   the appellant; and
     (ii)   any other respondent;
at the same time as those documents are filed at the court. Where a child is an appellant or respondent the documents referred to in paragraphs (a) to (c) above must also be served on the persons listed in rule 6.33(2) unless the court directs otherwise.

Appeals to the High Court
Application
8.1   The appellant's notice must be filed in –
(a)   the principal registry of the Family Division; or
(b)   the district registry which is nearest to the designated family court area.

8.2   A respondent's notice must be filed at the court where the appellant's notice was filed.

8.3   In the case of appeals from district judges of the High Court, applications for permission and any other applications in the appeal, appeals may be heard and directions in the appeal may be given by a High Court Judge or by any person authorised under section 9 of the Senior Courts Act 1981 to act as a judge of the High Court.

...

PRACTICE DIRECTION 34A – RECIPROCAL ENFORCEMENT OF MAINTENANCE ORDERS

This Practice Direction supplements FPR Part 34

Noting Record of Means of Payment

1.1

Where the family court orders payments under a maintenance order to which Part 34 applies to be made in a particular way, the court must record that on a copy of the order.

1.2

If the court orders payment to be made to the court by a method referred to in section 1(5) of the Maintenance Enforcement Act 1991, the court may vary the method of payment on the application of an interested party and where it does so the court must record the variation on a copy of the order.

(Section 1(5) refers to payment by standing order or other methods which require transfer between accounts of a specific amount on a specific date during the period for which the authority to make the payment is in force.)

Notification by court officer

2.1

The court officer must, as soon as practicable, notify in writing the person liable to make the payments of the method by which they must be made.

2.2

If the court orders payment to be made to the court by a method referred to in section 1(5) of the Maintenance Enforcement Act 1991 the court officer must inform the person liable to make the payments of the number and location of the account to which the payments must be made.

2.3

If, on application, the court varies the method of payment, the court officer will notify all parties of the result of the application, in writing and as soon as possible.

Applications under section 2 of the 1920 Act

3.1

This paragraph refers to an application for the transmission of a maintenance order to a reciprocating country under section 2 of the 1920 Act in accordance with rule 34.10.

3.2

The applicant's written evidence must include such information as may be required by the law of the reciprocating country for the purpose of enforcement of the order.

3.3

If, in accordance with section 2 of the 1920 Act, the court sends a maintenance order to the Lord Chancellor for transmission to a reciprocating country, it shall record the fact in the court records.

Applications under section 2 of the 1972 Act (rule 34.14)

Introduction
4.1

An application for a maintenance order to be sent to a reciprocating country under section 2 of the 1972 Act is made by lodging specified documents with the court. The documents to be lodged vary according to which country it is intended that the maintenance order is be sent and the requirements are set out in this paragraph.

General provision
4.2

The general requirement is that the following documents should be lodged with the court –

(a)   an affidavit by the applicant stating –

  (i)   the reason that the applicant has for believing that the payer under the maintenance order is residing in the reciprocating country; and

  (ii) the amount of any arrears due to the applicant under the order, the date to which those arrears have been calculated and the date on which the next payment under the order falls due;

(b)   a certified copy of the maintenance order;

(c)   a statement giving such information as the applicant has as to the whereabouts of the payer;

(d)   a statement giving such information as the applicant has for facilitating the identification of the payer, (including, if known to the applicant, the name and address of any employer of the payer, his occupation and the date and place of issue of any passport of the payer); and

(e)   if available to the applicant, a photograph of the payer.

4.3

Omitted

4.4

Omitted

Hague Convention Country
4.5

If the country to which it is intended to send the maintenance order is a Hague Convention country (as defined in rule 34.12), then the following changes to the general requirements apply.

4.6

In addition to the matters stated in that paragraph, the affidavit referred to in paragraph 4.2(a) must also state whether the time for appealing against the maintenance order has expired and whether an appeal is pending.

4.7

The applicant must lodge the following documents with the court in addition to those set out in paragraph 4.2 –

(a)   a statement as to whether or not the payer appeared in the proceedings in which the maintenance order was made;

(b)   if the payer did not so appear –

    (i)   the original of a document which establishes that notice of the institution of proceedings, including notice of the substance of the claim, was served on the payer; or

    (ii)   a copy of such a document certified by the applicant or the applicant's solicitor to be a true copy;

(c)   a document which establishes that notice of the order was sent to the payer;

(d)   a written statement as to whether or not the payee received legal aid in the proceedings in which the order was made, or in connection with the application under section 2 of the 1972 Act; and

(e)   if the payee did receive legal aid, a copy certified by the applicant or the applicant's solicitor to be a true copy of the legal aid certificate.

United States of America
4.8

If the country to which it is intended to send the maintenance order is the United States of America, then the following changes to the general requirements apply.

4.9

There is no requirement to lodge a statement giving information as to the whereabouts of the payer since this information must be contained in the affidavit as mentioned in paragraph 4.10.

4.10

In addition to the matters stated in that paragraph, the affidavit referred to in paragraph 4.2(a) must also state –

(a)   the address of the payee;

(b)   such information as is known as to the whereabouts of the payer; and

(c)   a description, so far as is known, of the nature and location of any assets of the payer available for execution.

4.11

The applicant must lodge three certified copies of the maintenance order.

Transitional Provision in respect of the United States of America
4A.1
Where, by virtue of article 6(2) of the Reciprocal Enforcement of Maintenance Orders (United States of America) Order 2007, the Reciprocal Enforcement of Maintenance Orders (United States of America) Order 1995 continues in full force and effect, the FPR shall apply with such modifications as are necessary.

Notification to the Lord Chancellor
5.1
Where, in accordance with Part 1 of the 1972 Act, the family court registers a maintenance order sent to it from a Hague Convention Country, the court officer must send written notice of the registration to the Lord Chancellor.

Notification of means of enforcement
6.1
The court officer of the family court must take reasonable steps to notify the person to whom payments are due under a registered order of the means of enforcement available in respect of it.

Certified copies of orders issued under rules 34.39 and 34.40
7.1
In an application under rule 34.39 or 34.40 by a person wishing to enforce abroad a maintenance order, the certified copy of the order will be a sealed copy and will be accompanied by a certificate signed by the court officer.

7.2
In an application under the 1982 Act, the certificate signed by the court officer must state that it is a true copy of the order concerned and must give particulars of the proceedings in which it was made.

7.3
In an application under the Judgments Regulation, the certificate will be in the form of Annex V to the Regulation.

7.4
In an application under the Lugano Convention, the certificate will be in the form of Annex V to the Convention.

7.5
In an application under the Maintenance Regulation, the certificate will be in the form of Annex II to that Regulation.

7.6
In an application under the 2007 Hague Convention, the certificate will be comprised of the following Article 11 forms duly completed by the court officer –

(a)   the Abstract of a Decision;
(b)   the Statement of Enforceability; and
(c)   the Statement of Proper Notice.

7.7
In an application under the 2007 Hague Convention, the certificate will additionally state the jurisdictional basis upon which the order was made, with reference to the jurisdictional criteria in Article 20(1) of that Convention to be applied by the State in which recognition and/or enforcement is to be sought.

Countries and Territories in which Sums are Payable through Crown Agents for Overseas Governments and Territories (rule 34.23)
8.1
Gibraltar, Barbados, Bermuda, Ghana, Kenya, Fiji, Hong Kong, Singapore, Turks and Caicos Islands, United Republic of Tanzania (except Zanzibar), Anguilla, Falkland Islands and Dependencies, St Helena.

Part 1 of the 1972 Act – Modified Rules
9.1
The annexes to this Practice Direction set out rules 34.14 to 34.25 as they are modified –
(a)   in relation to the Republic of Ireland, by rule 34.26 (Annex 1) (but see the note in that Annex regarding the ongoing relevance of those rules following revocation of rule 34.26);
(b)   in relation to the Hague Convention Countries, by rule 34.27 (Annex 2); and
(c)   in relation to the United States of America, by rule 34.28 (Annex3).

9.2
The statutory references in the annexes are construed in accordance with rule 34.26(2), 34.27(2) or 34.28(2) as the case may be.

Annex 1 Application of Section 1 of Chapter 2 of Part 34 to the Republic of Ireland

NOTE – rule 34.26 was revoked by S.I.2011/1328. Reciprocal enforcement of maintenance as between the UK and the Irish Republic has been governed by the Maintenance Regulation (Council Regulation (EC) no 4/2009) since 18th June 2011 and the relevant rules for that Regulation are contained in Chapter 3 of Part 34 of the Rules. The provisions of this Annex are therefore of relevance only where either –
(a)   the application for registration of an order relating to an Irish maintenance order was made on or before the 18th June 2011 and was still pending on that date; or
(b)   the order was registered prior to the 18th June 2011.
All other applications are governed by the Maintenance Regulation. Practice Direction 34C provides further information regarding which rules apply to applications relating to other European Union Member States.

Application for transmission of maintenance order to the Republic of Ireland
34.14
An application for a maintenance order to be sent to the Republic of Ireland under section 2 of the 1972 Act must be made in accordance with Practice Direction 34A.

Certification of evidence given on provisional orders
34.15
A document setting out or summarising evidence is authenticated by a court in England and Wales by a certificate signed, as appropriate, by –
(a)   one of the justices; or
(b)   the District Judge (Magistrates' Courts),
before whom that evidence was given.

(Section 3(5)(b) or 5(3) of the1972 Act require a document to be authenticated by the court.)

Confirmation of a provisional order ...
34.16
[This rule does not apply to the Republic of Ireland]

Consideration of confirmation of a provisional order made by a magistrates' court
34.17
(1)   This rule applies where –
    (a)   a magistrates' court has made a provisional order by virtue of section 3 of the 1972 Act;
    (b)   the payer has made representations or adduced evidence to the court; and
    (c)   the court has fixed a date for the hearing at which it will consider confirmation of the order.
(2)   The court officer must serve on the applicant for the provisional order –
    (a)   a copy of the representations or evidence; and
    (b)   written notice of the date fixed for the hearing.

Notification of variation or revocation of a maintenance order by the High Court
34.18
Where the High Court makes an order varying or revoking an order to which section 5 of the 1972 Act applies the court officer must send –
(a)   a certified copy of the order of variation or revocation; and
(b)   a statement as to the service on the payer of the documents mentioned in section 5(3) of the 1972 Act;
to the court in the Republic of Ireland.

(Rule 34.22 provides for the transmission of documents to a court in a reciprocating country.)

Notification of variation or revocation of a maintenance order by the High Court
34.19

Where a magistrates' court makes an order revoking an order to which section 5 of the 1972 Act applies, the court officer must send written notice of the making of the order to the Lord Chancellor.

(Section 5 of the 1972 Act applies to a maintenance order sent to the Republic of Ireland in accordance with section 2 of that Act and a provisional order made by a magistrates' court in accordance with section 3 of that Act which has been confirmed by such a court.)

(Provision in respect of notification of variation of a maintenance order by a magistrates' court under the 1972 Act is made in Rules made under section 144 of the Magistrates' Courts Act 1980.)

Taking of evidence for court in the Republic of Ireland
34.20

(1)   This rule applies where a request is made by or on behalf of a court in the Republic of Ireland for the taking of evidence for the purpose of proceedings relating to a maintenance order to which Part 1 of the 1972 Act applies.

(Section 14 of the 1972 Act makes provision for the taking of evidence needed for the purpose of certain proceedings.)

(2)   The High Court has power to take the evidence where –
    (a)   the request for evidence relates to a maintenance order made by a superior court in the United Kingdom; and
    (b)   the witness resides in England and Wales.

(3)   The county court has power to take the evidence where –
    (a)   the request for evidence relates to a maintenance order made by a county court; and
    (b)   the maintenance order has not been registered in a magistrates' court under the 1958 Act.

(4)   The following magistrates' courts have power to take the evidence, that is –
    (a)   where the proceedings in the Republic of Ireland relate to a maintenance order made by a magistrates' court, the court which made the order;
    (b)   where the proceedings relate to an order which is registered in a magistrates' court, the court in which the order is registered; and
    (c)   a magistrates' court to which the Secretary of State sends the request to take evidence.

(5)   A magistrates' court not mentioned in paragraph (4) has power to take the evidence if the magistrates' court which would otherwise have that power consents because the evidence could be taken more conveniently.

(6)   The evidence is to be taken in accordance with Part 22.

Selected Family Procedure Rules and Practice Directions   563

Request for the taking of evidence by a court ...
34.21
[This rule does not apply to the Republic of Ireland]

Transmission of documents
34.22
(1) This rule applies to any document, including a notice or request, which is required to be sent to a court in the Republic of Ireland by –
   (a) Part 1 of the 1972 Act; or
   (b) Section 1 of Chapter 2 of this Part of these Rules.
(2) The document must be sent to the Lord Chancellor for transmission to the court in the Republic of Ireland.

Method of payment under registered orders
34.23
(1) Where an order is registered in a magistrates' court in accordance with section 6(3) of the 1972 Act, the court must order that the payment of sums due under the order be made–
   (a) to the court officer for the registering court; and
   (b) at such time and place as the court officer directs.

(Section 6(3) of the 1972 Act makes provision for the registration of maintenance orders made in the Republic of Ireland.)

(2) Where the court orders payment to be made to the court officer, the court officer must send the payments by post –
   (a) to the payee under the order; or
   (b) where a public authority has been authorised by the payee to receive the payments, to that public authority.

(Practice Direction 34A contains further provisions relating to the payment of sums due under registered orders.)

Enforcement of payments under registered orders
34.24
(1) This rule applies where periodical payments under a registered order are in arrears.
(2) The court officer must, on the written request of the payee, proceed in that officer's own name for the recovery of the sums due unless of the view that it is unreasonable to do so.
(3) If the sums due are more than 4 weeks in arrears the court officer must give the payee notice in writing of that fact stating the particulars of the arrears.

Notification of registration and cancellation
34.25
The court officer must send written notice to –

(a)   the Lord Chancellor, on the due registration of an order under section 6(3) or 10(4) of the 1972 Act; and

(b)   to the payer under the order, on –

       (i)   the registration of an order under section 10(4) of the 1972 Act; or

       (ii)   the cancellation of the registration of an order under section 10(1) of that Act.

Other notices under section 6 of the 1972 Act
34.25A

(1)   A notice required under section 6(6) or (10) of the 1972 Act must be in the form referred to in a practice direction.

(2)   Where a magistrates' court sets aside the registration of an order following an appeal under section 6(7) of the 1972 Act, the court officer must send written notice of the court's decision to the payee.

(Section 6(6) of the 1972 Act provides for notice of registration in a United Kingdom court of a maintenance order made in the Republic of Ireland, and section 6(10) of that Act for notice that a maintenance order made in the Republic of Ireland has not been registered in a United Kingdom court.)

Annex 2 Application of Section 1 of Chapter 2 of Part 34 to the Hague Convention Countries

Application for transmission of maintenance order to a Hague Convention Country
34.14

An application for a maintenance order to be sent to a Hague Convention Country under section 2 of the 1972 Act must be made in accordance with Practice Direction 34A.

Certification of evidence given on provisional orders
34.15

[This rule does not apply to the Hague Convention Countries]

Confirmation of a provisional order made in a reciprocating country
34.16

[This rule does not apply to the Hague Convention Countries]

Consideration of revocation of a maintenance order made by a magistrates' court
34.17

(1)   This rule applies where –

       (a)   an application has been made to a magistrates' court by a payee for the revocation of an order to which section 5 of the 1972 Act applies; and

       (b)   the payer resides in a Hague Convention Country.

(2)   The court officer must serve on the payee, by post, a copy of any representations or evidence adduced by or on behalf of the payer.

(Provision relating to consideration of variation of a maintenance order made by a magistrates' court to which section 5 of the 1972 Act applies is made in Rules made under section 144 of the Magistrates' Courts Act 1980.)

Notification of variation or revocation of a maintenance order by the High Court or a county court

34.18

(1)   This rule applies if the High Court or a county court makes an order varying or revoking a maintenance order to which section 5 of the 1972 Act applies.

(2)   If the time for appealing has expired without an appeal having been entered, the court officer will send to the Lord Chancellor –

    (a)   the documents required by section 5(8) of the 1972 Act; and

    (b)   a certificate signed by the district judge stating that the order of variation or revocation is enforceable and no longer subject to the ordinary forms of review.

(3)   A party who enters an appeal against the order of variation or revocation must, at the same time, give written notice to the court officer.

Notification of confirmation or revocation of a maintenance order by a magistrates' court

34.19

[This rule does not apply to the Hague Convention Countries]

Taking of evidence for court in a Hague Convention Country

34.20

(1)   This rule applies where a request is made by or on behalf of a court in a Hague Convention Country for the taking of evidence for the purpose of proceedings relating to a maintenance order to which Part 1 of the 1972 Act applies.

(Section 14 of the 1972 Act makes provision for the taking of evidence needed for the purpose of certain proceedings.)

(2)   The High court has power to take the evidence where –

    (a)   the request for evidence relates to a maintenance order made by a superior court in the United Kingdom: and

    (b)   the witness resides in England and Wales.

(3)   The county court has power to take the evidence where –

    (a)   the request for evidence relates to a maintenance order made by a county court; and

    (b)   the maintenance order has not been registered in a magistrates' court under the 1958 Act.

(4)   The following magistrates' courts have power to take the evidence, that is –

(a)   where the proceedings in the Hague Convention Country relate to a maintenance order made by a magistrates' court, the court which made the order;

(b)   where the proceedings relate to an order which is registered in a magistrates' court, the court in which the order is registered; and

(c)   a magistrates' court to which the Secretary of State sends the request to take evidence.

(5)   A magistrates' court not mentioned in paragraph (4) has power to take the evidence if the magistrates' court which would otherwise have that power consents because the evidence could be taken more conveniently.

(6)   The evidence is to be taken in accordance with Part 22.

Request for the taking of evidence by a court in a Hague Convention country
34.21
[This rule does not apply to the Hague Convention countries.]

Transmission of documents
34.22
(1)   This rule applies to any document, including a notice or request, which is required to be sent to a court in a Hague Convention country by –

(a)   Part 1 of the 1972 Act; or

(b)   Section 1 of Chapter 2 of this Part of these Rules.

(2)   The document must be sent to the Lord Chancellor for transmission to the court in the Hague Convention country.

Method of payment under registered orders
34.23
(1)   Where an order is registered in a magistrates' court in accordance with section 6(3) of the 1972 Act, the court must order that the payment of sums due under the order be made –

(a)   to the court officer for the registering court; and

(b)   at such time and place as the court officer directs.

(Section 6(3) of the 1972 Act makes provision for the registration of maintenance orders made in a Hague Convention country.)

(2)   Where the court orders payment to be made to the court officer, the court officer must send the payments by post to the payee under the order.

(Practice Direction 34A contains further provision relating to the payment of sums due under registered orders.)

Enforcement of payments under registered orders
34.24
(1)   This rule applies where a court has ordered periodical payments under a registered maintenance order to be made to the court officer.

(2)   The court officer must take reasonable steps to notify the payee of the means of enforcement available.

(3)   Paragraph (4) applies where periodical payments due under a registered order are in arrears.

(4)   The court officer, on that officer's own initiative –

(a)   may; or

(b)   if the sums due are more than 4 weeks in arrears, must,

proceed in that officer's own name for the recovery of the sums due unless of the view that it is unreasonable to do so.

Notification of registration and cancellation
34.25

The court officer must send written notice to –

(a)   the Lord Chancellor, on the due registration of an order under section 10(4) of the 1972 Act; and

(b)   the payer under the order, on –

(i)   the registration of an order under section 10(4) of the 1972 Act; or

(ii)   the cancellation of the registration of an order under section 10(1) of the 1972 Act.

General provisions as to notices
34.25A

(1)   A notice to a payer of the registration of an order in a magistrates' court in accordance with section 6(3) of the 1972 Act must be in the form referred to in a practice direction.

(Section 6(8) of the 1972 Act requires notice of registration to be given to the payer.)

(2)   If the court sets aside the registration of a maintenance order following an appeal under section 6(9) of the 1972 Act, the court officer must send written notice of the decision to the Lord Chancellor.

(3)   A notice to a payee that the court officer has refused to register an order must be in the form referred to in a practice direction.

(Section 6(11) of the 1972 Act requires notice of refusal of registration to be given to the payee.)

(4)   Where, under any provision of Part 1 of the 1972 Act, a court officer serves a notice on a payer who resides in a Hague Convention Country, the court officer must send to the Lord Chancellor a certificate of service.

Annex 3 Application for Section 1 of Chapter 2 of Part 34 to the United States of America

Application for transmission of maintenance order to the United States of America
34.14
An application for a maintenance order to be sent to the United States of America under section 2 of the 1972 Act must be made in accordance with Practice Direction 34A.

Certification of evidence given on provisional orders
34.15
[This rule does not apply to the United States of America]

Confirmation of a provisional order made in a reciprocating country
34.16
[This rule does not apply to the United States of America]

Consideration of revocation of a maintenance order made by a magistrates' court
34.17
(1)   This rule applies where –
   (a)   an application has been made to a magistrates' court by a payee for the revocation of an order to which section 5 of the 1972 Act applies; and
   (b)   the payer resides in the United States of America.
(2)   The court officer must serve on the payee by post a copy of any representations or evidence adduced by or on behalf of the payer.

(Provision relating to consideration of variation of a maintenance order made by a magistrates' court to which section 5 of the 1972 Act applies is made in rules made under section 144 of the Magistrates' Courts Act 1980.)

Notification of variation or revocation
34.18
If the High Court or a county court makes an order varying or revoking a maintenance order to which section 5 of the 1972 Act applies, the court officer will send to the Lord Chancellor the documents required by section 5(7) of that Act.

Notification of confirmation or revocation of a maintenance order by a magistrates' court
34.19
[This rule does not apply to the United States of America]

Taking of evidence for court in United States of America
34.20
(1)   This rule applies where a request is made by or on behalf of a court in the United States of America for the taking of evidence for the purpose of

proceedings relating to a maintenance order to which Part 1 of the 1972 Act applies.

(Section 14 of the1972 Act makes provision for the taking of evidence needed for the purpose of certain proceedings.)

(2)   The High Court has power to take the evidence where –
- (a)   the request for evidence relates to a maintenance order made by a superior court in the United Kingdom; and
- (b)   the witness resides in England and Wales.

(3)   The county court has power to take the evidence where –
- (a)   the request for evidence relates to a maintenance order made by a county court; and
- (b)   the maintenance order has not been registered in a magistrates' court under the 1958 Act.

(4)   The following magistrates' courts have power to take the evidence, that is –
- (a)   where the proceedings in the United States of America relate to a maintenance order made by a magistrates' court, the court which made the order;
- (b)   where the proceedings relate to an order which is registered in a magistrates' court, the court in which the order is registered; and
- (c)   a magistrates' court to which the Secretary of State sends the request to take evidence.

(5)   A magistrates' court not mentioned in paragraph (4) has power to take the evidence if the magistrates' court which would otherwise have that power consents because the evidence could be taken more conveniently.

(6)   The evidence is to be taken in accordance with Part 22.

Request for the taking of evidence by a court in a reciprocating country
34.21
[This rule does not apply to the United States of America]

Transmission of documents
34.22

(1)   This rule applies to any document, including a notice or request, which is required to be sent to a court in the United States of America by –
- (a)   Part 1 of the 1972 Act; or
- (b)   Section 1 of Chapter 2 of this Part of these Rules.

(2)   The document must be sent to the Lord Chancellor for transmission to the court in the United States of America.

Method of payment under registered orders
34.23

(1)   Where an order is registered in a magistrates' court in accordance with section 6(3) of the 1972 Act, the court must order that the payment of sums due under the order be made –

(a)   to the court officer for the registering court; and

(b)   at such time and place as the court officer directs.

(Section 6(3) of the 1972 Act makes provision for the registration of maintenance orders made in the United States of America.)

(2)   Where the court orders payment to be made to the court officer, the court officer must send the payments by post to the payee under the order.

(Practice Direction 34A contains further provisions relating to the payment of sums due under registered orders.)

Enforcement of payments under registered orders
34.24

(1)   This rule applies where a court has ordered periodical payments under a registered maintenance order to be made to the court officer.

(2)   The court officer must take reasonable steps to notify the payee of the means of enforcement available.

(3)   Paragraph (4) applies where periodical payments due under a registered order are in arrears.

(4)   The court officer, on that officer's own initiative –

(a)   may; or

(b)   if the sums due are more than 4 weeks in arrears, must,

proceed in that officer's own name for the recovery of the sums due unless of the view that it is unreasonable to do so.

Notification of registration and cancellation
34.25

The court officer must send written notice to –

(a)   the Lord Chancellor, on the due registration of an order under section 10(4) of the 1972 Act; or

(b)   the payer under the order, on –

(i)   the registration of an order under section 10(4) of the 1972 Act; or

(ii)   the cancellation of the registration of an order under section 10(1) of that Act.

PRACTICE DIRECTION: COMMITTAL FOR CONTEMPT OF COURT – OPEN COURT

Preamble

1. This Practice Direction applies to all proceedings for committal for contempt of court, including contempt in the face of the court, whether arising under any statutory or inherent jurisdiction and, particularly, supplements the provisions relating to contempt of court in the Civil Procedure Rules 1998, the Family Procedure Rules 2010, the Court of Protection Rules 2007, and the Criminal Procedure Rules 2014 and any related Practice Directions supplementing those various provisions. It applies in all courts in England and Wales, including the Court of Protection, and supersedes the *Practice Guidance: Committal for Contempt* [2013] 1 WLR 1326, dated 3 May 2013; *Practice Guidance (Committal Proceedings: Open Court) (No. 2)* [2013] 1 WLR 1753, dated 4 June 2013; and *President's Circular: Committals* Family Court Practice 2014 at 2976, dated 2 August 2013.

2. Any reference in this Practice Direction to a judgment includes reference to written reasons provided in accordance with rule 27.2 of the Family Procedure Rules 2010.

Open Justice

3. Open justice is a fundamental principle. The general rule is that hearings are carried out in, and judgments and orders are made in, public. This rule applies to all hearings, whether on application or otherwise, for committal for contempt irrespective of the court in which they are heard or of the proceedings in which they arise.

4. Derogations from the general principle can only be justified in exceptional circumstances, when they are strictly necessary as measures to secure the proper administration of justice. Derogations shall, where justified, be no more than strictly necessary to achieve their purpose.

Committal Hearings – in Public

5.
   (1) All committal hearings, whether on application or otherwise and whether for contempt in the face of the court or any other form of contempt, shall be listed and heard in public.

   (2) They shall, except where paragraph 5(3) applies, be listed in the public court list as follows:

   > FOR HEARING IN OPEN COURT
   > Application by (*full name of applicant*) for
   > the Committal to prison of
   > (*full name of the person alleged to be in contempt*)

(3)   In those cases where the person alleged to be in contempt is subject to arrest for an alleged breach of an order, including a location or collection order or an order made under the Family Law Act 1996, the hearing shall be listed in the public court list as follows:

> FOR HEARING IN OPEN COURT [add, where there has been a remand in custody: in accordance with the order of (*name of judge*) dated (*date*)]

> Proceedings for the Committal to prison of
> (*full name of the person alleged to be in contempt*)
> who was arrested on (*date*) in accordance with and for alleged breach of a [location/collection/Family Law Act 1996/other] order made by (*name of judge*) on (*date*).

6.   Where it is not possible to publish the details required by paragraph 5(3) in the public court list in the usual way the day before the hearing i.e., in such circumstances where the alleged contemnor is produced at court by the Tipstaff or a constable on the morning of the hearing, having been arrested over night, the following steps should be taken:

(1)   Where, as in the Royal Courts of Justice, the public court list is prepared and accessible in electronic form, it should be updated with the appropriate entry as soon as the court becomes aware that the matter is coming before it;

(2)   Notice of the hearing should at the same time be placed outside the door of the court in which the matter is being, or is to be heard, and at whatever central location in the building the various court lists are displayed;

(3)   Notice should be given to the national print and broadcast media, via the Press Association's CopyDirect service, of the fact that the hearing is taking or is shortly due to take place.

If an alleged contemnor is produced at court, having been arrested overnight, the person shall immediately be produced before a judge who shall sit in public.

7.   Where the committal hearing is brought by way of application notice, the court may authorise any person who is not a party to proceedings to obtain a copy of the application notice, upon request and subject to payment of any appropriate fee. Authorisation shall be granted in all but exceptional circumstances. Where authorisation is refused, the reasons for that refusal shall be set out in writing by the judge and supplied to the person who made the request.

Committal Hearings – in Private

8. Where the court, either on application or otherwise, is considering derogating from the general rule and holding a committal hearing in private, or imposing any other such derogation from the principle of open justice:

    (1) it shall in all cases before the hearing takes place, notify the national print and broadcast media, via the Press Association's CopyDirect service, of the fact of the committal hearing (whether it is brought on application or otherwise) when and where it is listed for hearing, and the nature of the proposed derogation; and

    (2) at the outset of the committal hearing the court shall hear submissions from the parties and/or the media on the question whether to impose the proposed derogation.

9. In considering the question whether there are exceptional circumstances justifying a derogation from the general rule, and whether that derogation is no more than strictly necessary the fact that the committal hearing is made in the Court of Protection or in any proceedings relating to a child does not of itself justify the matter being heard in private. Moreover the fact that the hearing may involve the disclosure of material which ought not to be published does not of itself justify hearing the application in private if such publication can be restrained by an appropriate order.

10. Where the court decides to exercise its discretion to derogate from the general rule, and particularly where it decides to hold a committal hearing in private, it shall, before it continues to do so, sit in public in order to give a reasoned public judgment setting out why it is doing so.

11. Where, having decided to exercise its discretion to hold a committal hearing in private, the court further decides that the substantive committal application is to be adjourned to a future date, the adjourned hearing shall be listed in the public court list as follows:

    FOR HEARING IN PRIVATE
    In accordance with the order of (name of judge) dated (*date*)
    [On the application of (*full name of applicant*)]
    Proceedings for the Committal to prison of
    (*full name of the person alleged to be in contempt*)

12. Orders directing a committal hearing be heard in private or of other such derogations from the principle of open justice shall not be granted by consent of the parties: see *JIH v News Group Newspapers* [2011] EWCA Civ 42, [2011] WLR 1645 at [21].

Judgments

13.

(1)   In all cases, irrespective of whether the court has conducted the hearing in public or in private, and the court finds that a person has committed a contempt of court, the court shall at the conclusion of that hearing sit in public and state:

  (i)   the name of that person;
  (ii)   in general terms the nature of the contempt of court in respect of which the committal order, which for this purpose includes a suspended committal order, is being made;
  (iii)   the punishment being imposed; and
  (iv)   provide the details required by (i) to (iii) to the national media, via the CopyDirect service, and to the Judicial Office, at judicialwebupdates@judiciary.gsi.gov.uk, for publication on the website of the Judiciary of England and Wales.

(2)   There are no exceptions to these requirements. There are never any circumstances in which any one may be committed to custody or made subject to a suspended committal order without these matters being stated by the court sitting in public.

14.   In addition to the requirements at paragraph 13, the court shall, in respect of all committal decisions, also either produce a written judgment setting out its reasons or ensure that any oral judgment is transcribed, such transcription to be ordered the same day as the judgment is given and prepared on an expedited basis. It shall do so irrespective of its practice prior to this Practice Direction coming into force and irrespective of whether or not anyone has requested this.

15.   Copies of the written judgment or transcript of judgment shall then be provided to the parties and the national media via the CopyDirect service. Copies shall also be supplied to BAILII and to the Judicial Office at judicialwebupdates@judiciary.gsi.gov.uk for publication on their websites as soon as reasonably practicable.

16.   Advocates and the judge (except judges and justices of the peace in the Magistrates' courts) shall be robed for all committal hearings.

This Direction is made by the Lord Chief Justice, following consultation with the Master of the Rolls, President of the Queen's Bench Division, President of the Family Division and of the Court of Protection, and Chancellor of the High Court. It is issued in accordance with the procedure laid down in Part 1 of Schedule 2 to the Constitutional Reform Act 2005.

Lord Thomas LCJ
26 March 2015